Ontario Back Road

DELUXE EDITION

Welcome to our best-selling Ontario road atlas.

We hope you'll find our atlas of Ontario to be a
valued asset - with our detailed, clear, full colour maps you
can continue to find everything the province has to offer.

Legend . . . . .Inside Front Cover
Key Maps 2-3
Detailed Back Road Mapping 4-103
Ontario Distance Chart 70
Northern Ontario Road Maps 104-109
Places Index 110-116
Roads Index 117-145

We are working hard to make excellent products. We would like to extend our sincere thanks for
purchasing this product. For the many readers who supplied comments and criticism from the
previous edition, we appreciate your help and interest in allowing us to improve the maps. Both
positive and negative feedback allows us to provide a better product, and because of the large
amount of information contained in these maps, we encourage you to continue to forward your
comments to us.

We can be reached by telephone at 905-436-2525, fax at 905-723-6677, or e-mail us at
inquiries@mapart.com.

Please supply page number and co-ordinates to help us locate your comment.

TABLE OF CONTENTS

How to Use this Atlas

come see us @ www.mapart.com

MapArt. DIRECTION + DESIGN

PRODUCTION TEAM Lisa Alberga   Brent Carey   Michael Foell
Karen Gillingham   Werner Mantei   David McCarthy   Carl Nanders
Dave Scott   Kyu Shim   Jennifer Thomson
Sam Tung-Ding Ho   Matthew Wadley

© mapmobility 2012 Edition
Published by Peter Heiler Ltd.
Distribution by **MapArt Publishing Corp.**
70 Bloor St. E., Oshawa, Ontario L1H 3M2
☎ 905-436-2525   FAX 905-723-6677
Printed in Canada  Imprimé au Canada

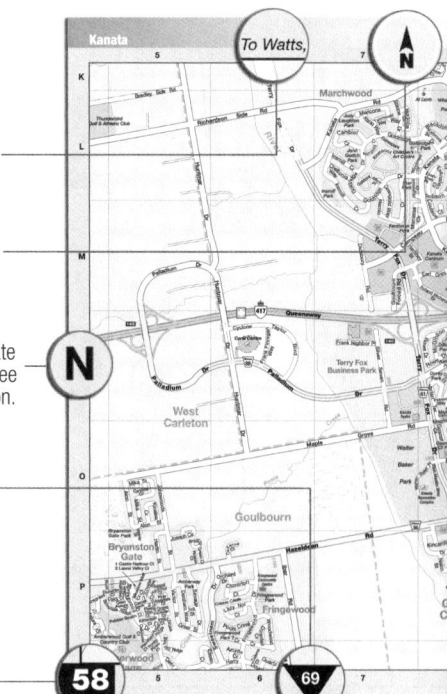

DESTINATIONS - indicate the town or
city the road or highway leads to.

NORTH ARROWS - indicate general
direction pointing north.

GRID REFERENCES - are used to locate
places, streets or roads in the index. See
page 110 or 117 for further explanation.

PAGE ARROWS - indicate continued
coverage of the map and page.

PAGE NUMBERING

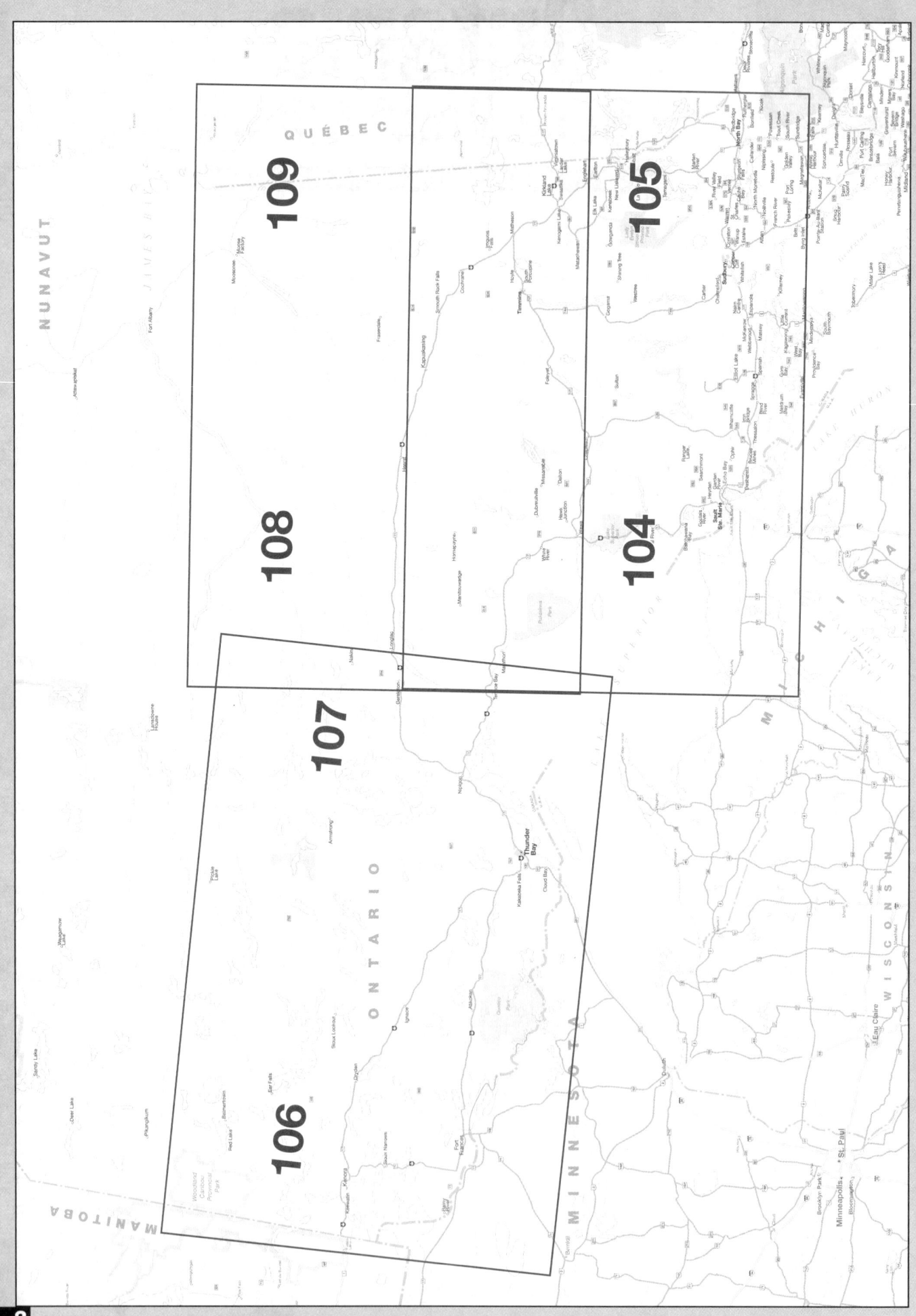

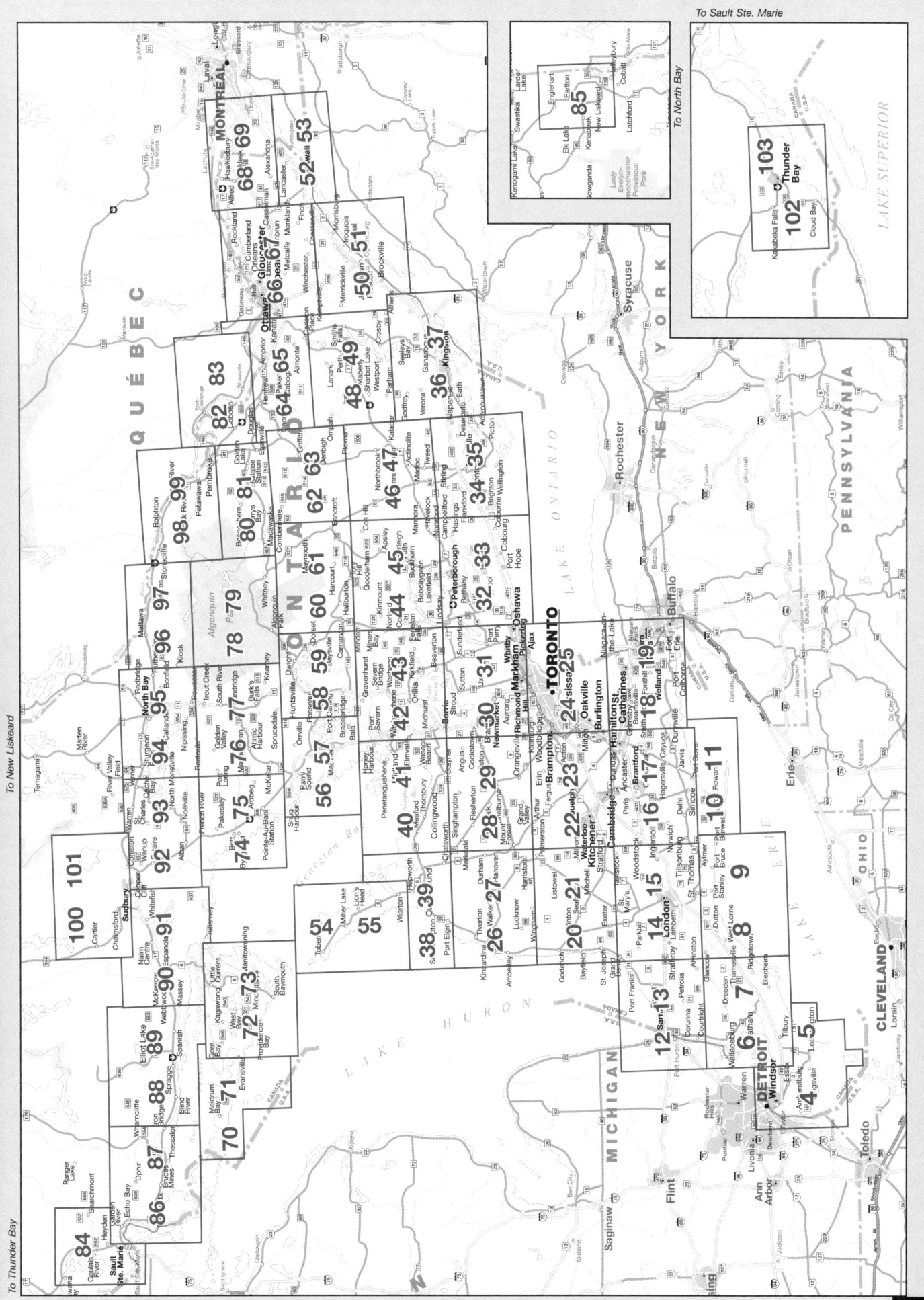

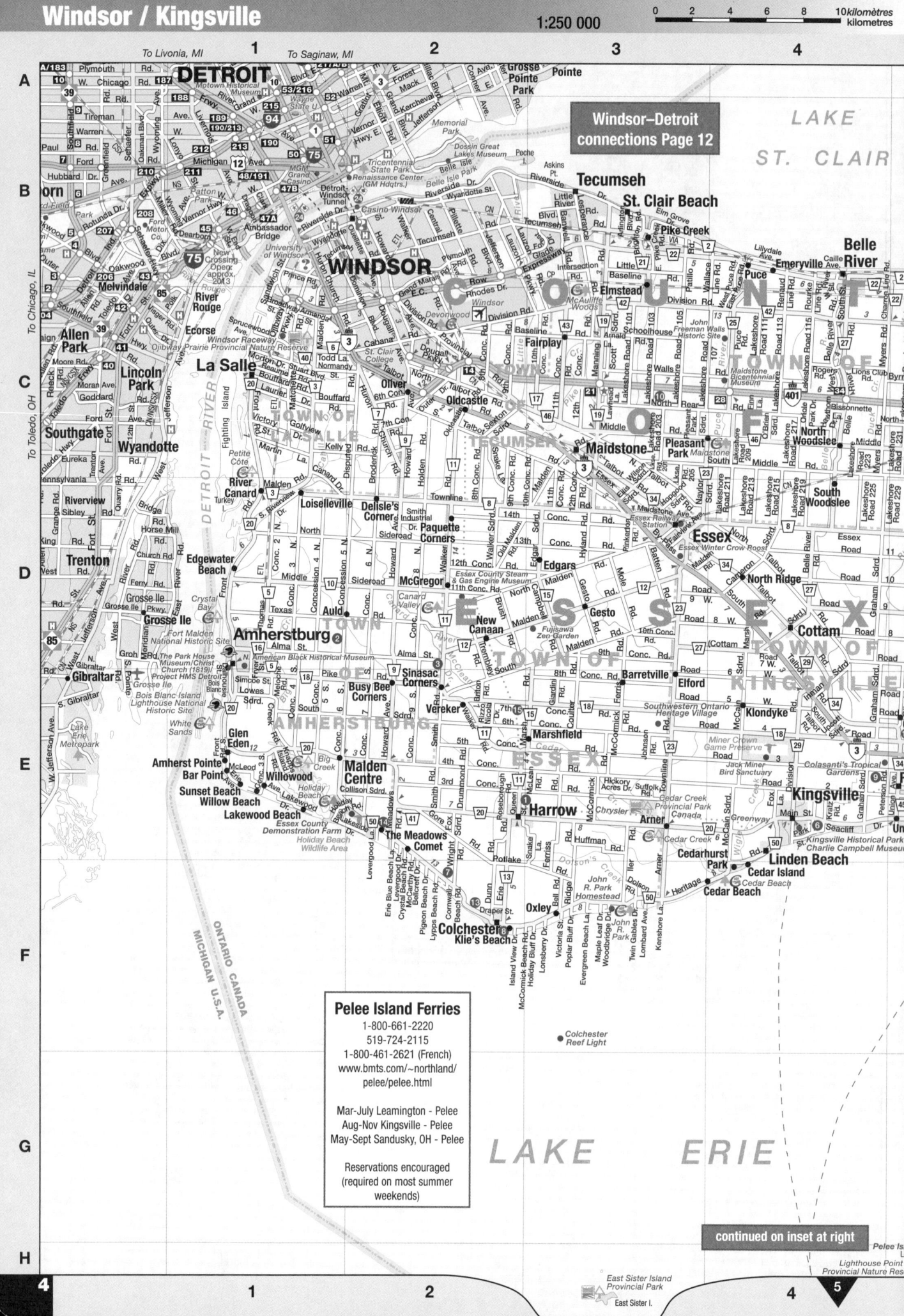

1:250 000

0 2 4 6 8 10 kilomètres
kilometres

1   2   3   4

To Livonia, MI   To Saginaw, MI

DETROIT

Windsor–Detroit
connections Page 12

LAKE
ST. CLAIR

Tecumseh

St. Clair Beach

Pike Creek

Belle
River

Emeryville

WINDSOR

Elmstead

Puce

COUNTY

Fairplay

TOWN OF

John
Freeman Walls
Historic Site

Melvindale

River
Rouge

La Salle

Oldcastle

Oliver

North
Woodslee

Allen
Park

Lincoln
Park

Maidstone

Pleasant
Park

Southgate

Wyandotte

Maidstone
South

Lakeshore Road 203

Lakeshore Road 209

Lakeshore Road 211

Lakeshore Road 213

Lakeshore Road 215

Lakeshore Road 217

Lakeshore Road 219

Lakeshore Road 221

Lakeshore Road 223

Lakeshore Road 225

Lakeshore Road 229

River
Canard

Loiselleville

Delisle's
Corner

Paquette
Corners

Smith
Industrial

Essex

South
Woodslee

Riverview

Trenton

Edgewater
Beach

McGregor

Canard
Valley
Steam
& Gas Engine Museum

Edgars

Edgars

Essex
Road

Grosse Ile

Auld

Canard

Gesto

North Ridge

Cottam

TOWN OF

Amherstburg

New
Canaan

Malden

Barretville

Elford

TOWN OF
KINGSVILLE

Gibraltar

Sinasac
Corners

Busy Bee
Corners

Klondyke

Fort Malden
National Historic Site
The Park House
Museum/Christ
Church (1819)
Project HMS Detroit
Bois Blanc Island
Lighthouse National
Historic Site

Vereker

Southwestern Ontario
Heritage Village

White
Sands

TOWN OF
AMHERSTBURG

Marshfield

ESSEX

Miner Crown
Game Preserve

Lake
Erie
Metropark

Glen Eden

Amherst Pointe
Bar Point

Willowood

Malden
Centre

Jack Miner
Bird Sanctuary

Colasanti's Tropical
Gardens

Kingsville

Sunset Beach
Willow Beach
Lakewood Beach

Holiday
Beach

The Meadows
Comet

Harrow

Cedar Creek
Provincial Park
Canada

Arner

Cedarhurst
Park

Linden Beach

Essex County
Demonstration Farm
Holiday Beach
Wildlife Area

John R. Park
Homestead

Cedar Island
Cedar Beach

Kingsville Historical Park /
Charlie Campbell Museum

Oxley

Colchester
Klie's Beach

John R.
Park
Homestead

ONTARIO CANADA
MICHIGAN U.S.A.

Colchester
Reef Light

Pelee Island Ferries
1-800-661-2220
519-724-2115
1-800-461-2621 (French)
www.bmts.com/~northland/
pelee/pelee.html

Mar-July Leamington - Pelee
Aug-Nov Kingsville - Pelee
May-Sept Sandusky, OH - Pelee

Reservations encouraged
(required on most summer
weekends)

LAKE   ERIE

continued on inset at right

Pelee Isl

Lighthouse Point
Provincial Nature Rese

East Sister Island
Provincial Park
East Sister I.

Transverse Mercator Projection

N

Lake Erie North Shore Wineries - see red bullets on the map

1 Colio 4 E2-3
2 D'Angelo Estates 4 D1
3 Sanson Estate 4 D-E2
4 LeBlanc Estates 4 E3
5 Pelee Island Pavilion 5 H4
6 Pelee Island 4 E4
7 Erie Shore 4 F2
8 Viewpointe Estate 4 F2
9 Mastronardi Estate 5 E4

10 Wagner Estate 4 C3
11 Aleksander Estate 5 E5
12 Smith & Wilson Estate . . .7 C10
13 Colchester Ridge Estate . . .4 F2
14 Sprucewood Shores Estate . .4 E2
15 Muscedere Vineyards 4 E2

Niagara Area Wineries – pg 18
Prince Edward County Area Wineries – pg 34

LAKE ERIE

MUNICIPALITY OF CHATHAM

CHATHAM-KENT

MUNICIPALITY OF LAKESHORE

MUNICIPALITY OF LEAMINGTON

POINT PELEE NATIONAL PARK

Pelee Point

Pelee Passage Light

Pelee Island Light
Lighthouse Pt
Nature Reserve

Pelee Island

POINT PELEE NATIONAL PARK

Pelee Point

continued at bottom on left

Pelee Passage Light

Pelee Island Light
Lighthouse Point
Provincial Nature Reserve

North Bay

Sheridan Pt.
Sheridan Point Rd.
Northshore Rd.
Scudder

Harris-Garno Rd.
Lizard Pt.
Brown's Rd.

Middle Pt.

Pelee Island

Pelee Island Heritage Centre

Pelee Island Wine Pavilion

Pelee Island

Pelee Island Glacial Grooves
Stone Road Alvar

Pelee Island South

Mosquito Pt.

Mosquito Bay

South Bay

Fish Point
Provincial Nature Reserve

Fish Pt.

CANADA ONTARIO
OHIO U.S.A.

Southernmost point in Canada
POINT PELEE NATIONAL PARK
Middle I.

5

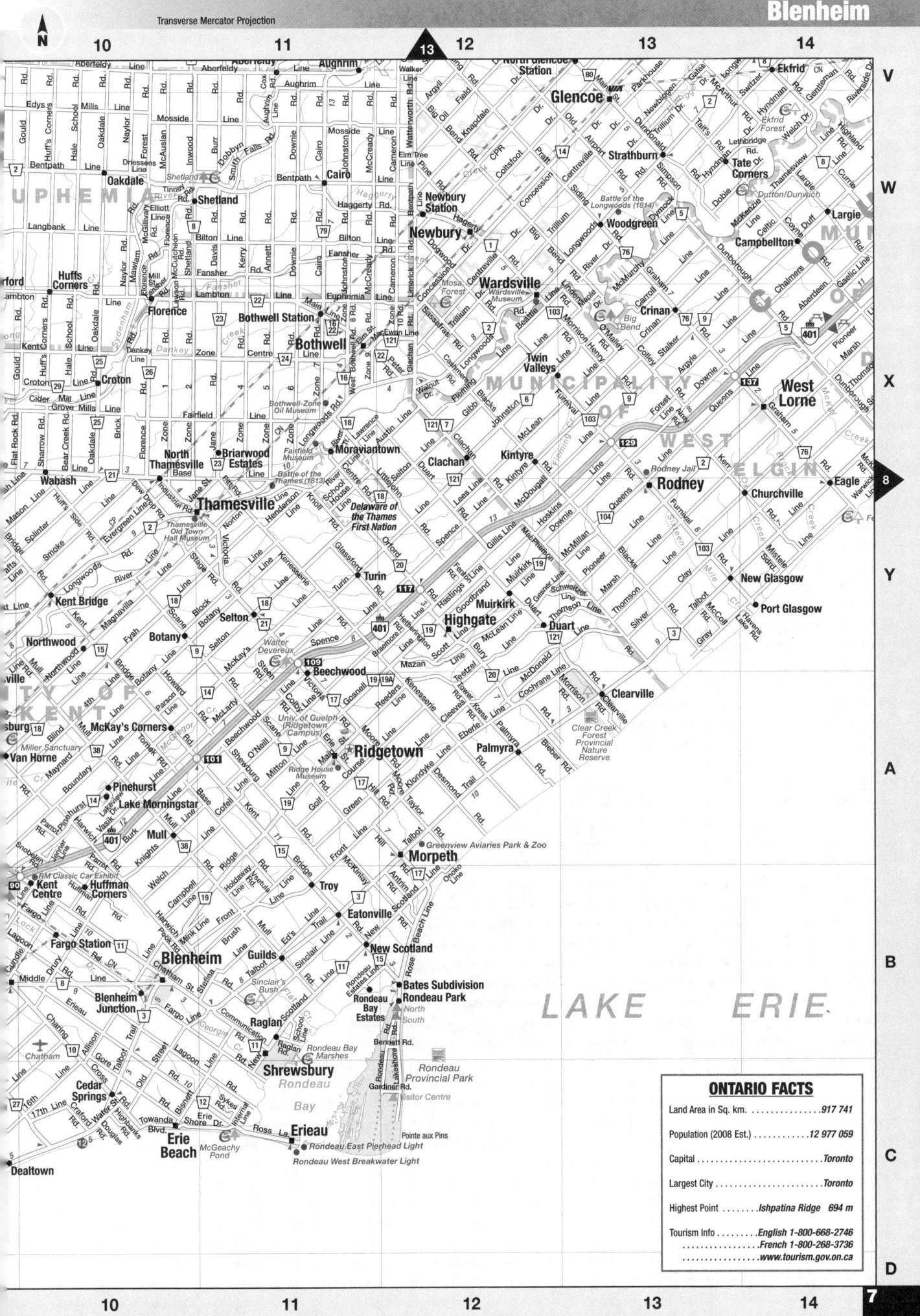

Transverse Mercator Projection

N

ONTARIO FACTS

Land Area in Sq. km. 917 741

Population (2008 Est.) 12 977 059

Capital .... Toronto

Largest City .... Toronto

Highest Point .... Ishpatina Ridge 694 m

Tourism Info .... English 1-800-668-2746
.... French 1-800-268-3736
.... www.tourism.gov.on.ca

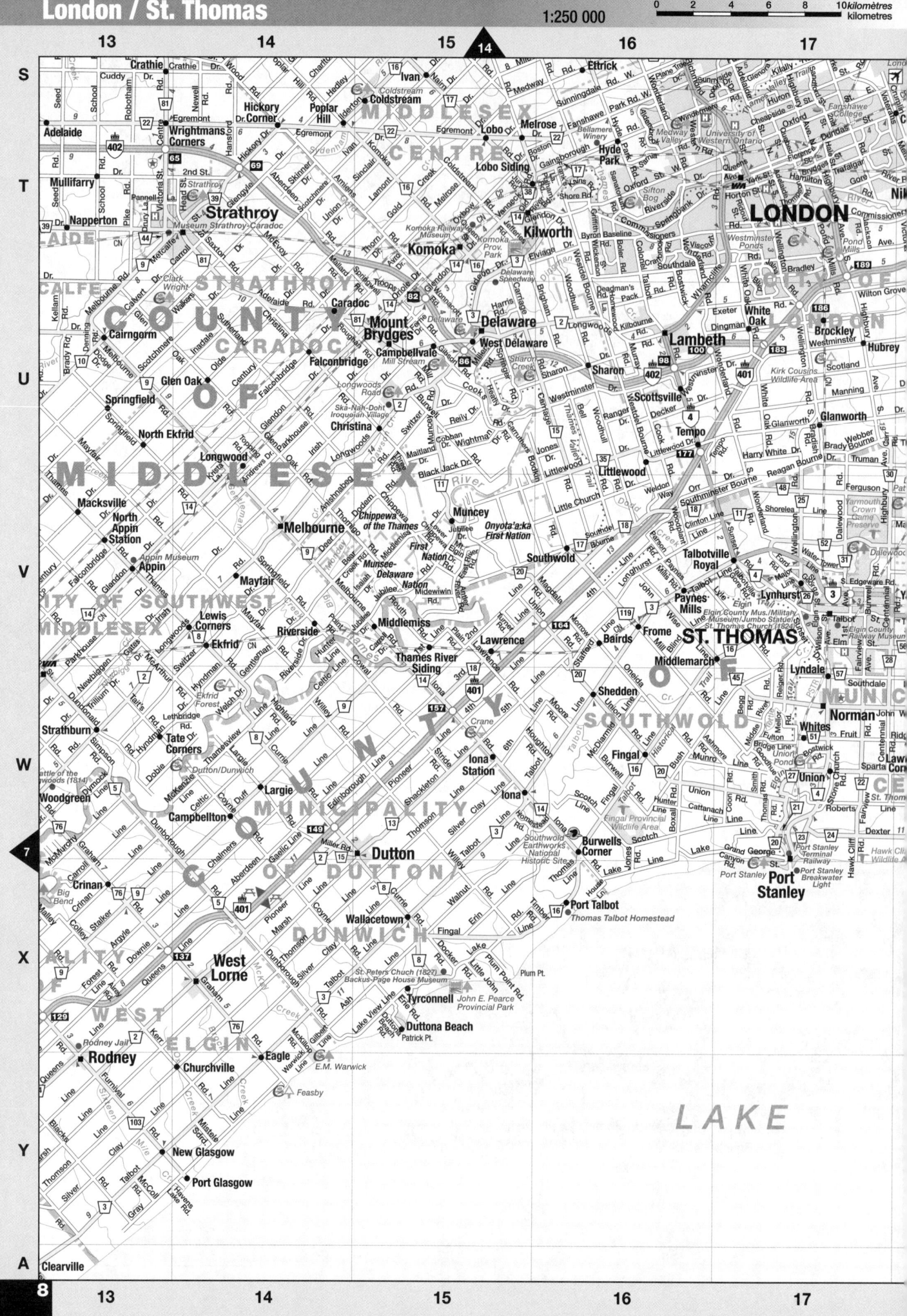

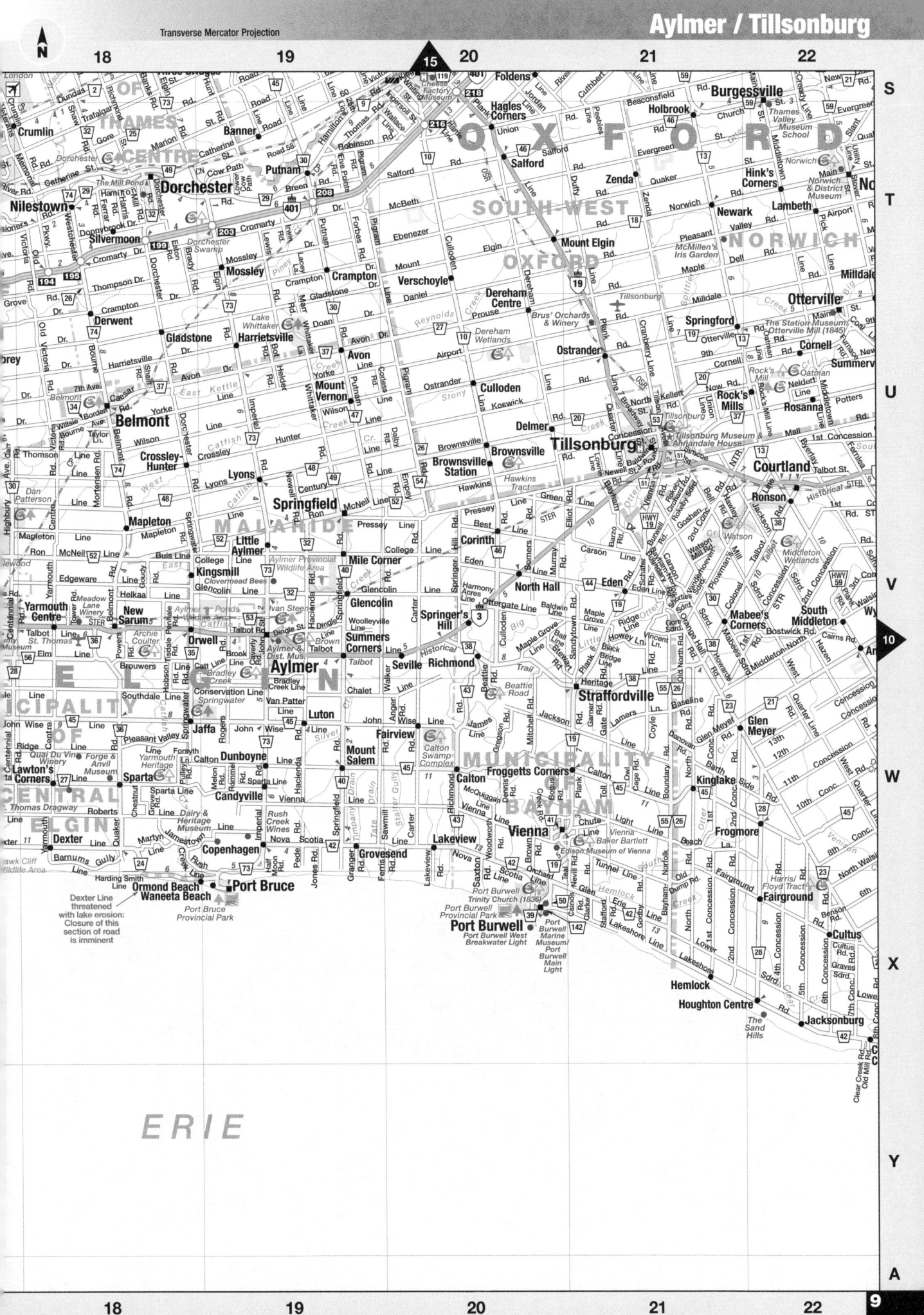

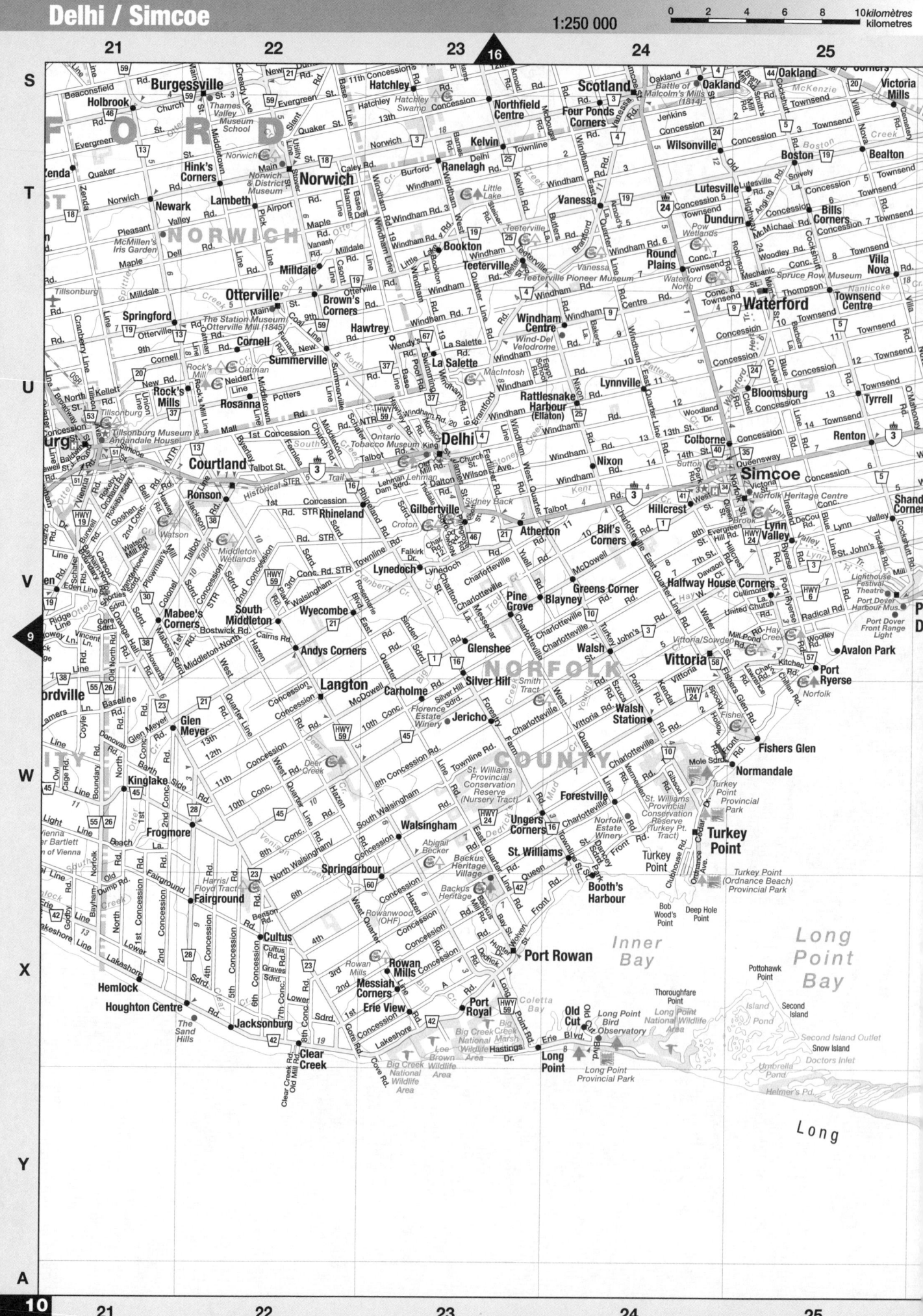

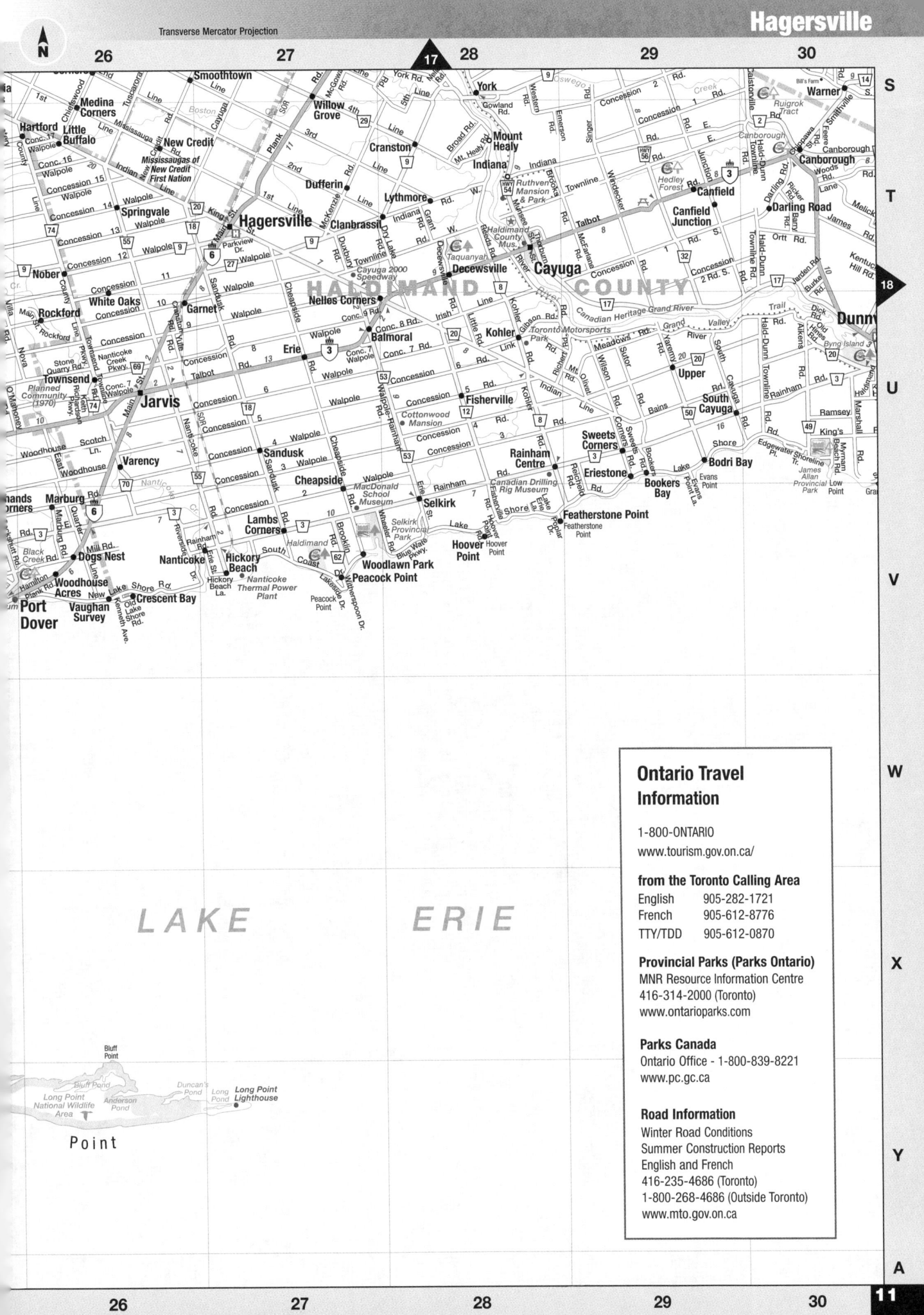

Ontario Travel Information

1-800-ONTARIO
www.tourism.gov.on.ca/

from the Toronto Calling Area
English   905-282-1721
French   905-612-8776
TTY/TDD   905-612-0870

Provincial Parks (Parks Ontario)
MNR Resource Information Centre
416-314-2000 (Toronto)
www.ontarioparks.com

Parks Canada
Ontario Office - 1-800-839-8221
www.pc.gc.ca

Road Information
Winter Road Conditions
Summer Construction Reports
English and French
416-235-4686 (Toronto)
1-800-268-4686 (Outside Toronto)
www.mto.gov.on.ca

1:250 000

0 2 4 6 8 10 *kilomètres*
kilometres

LAKE

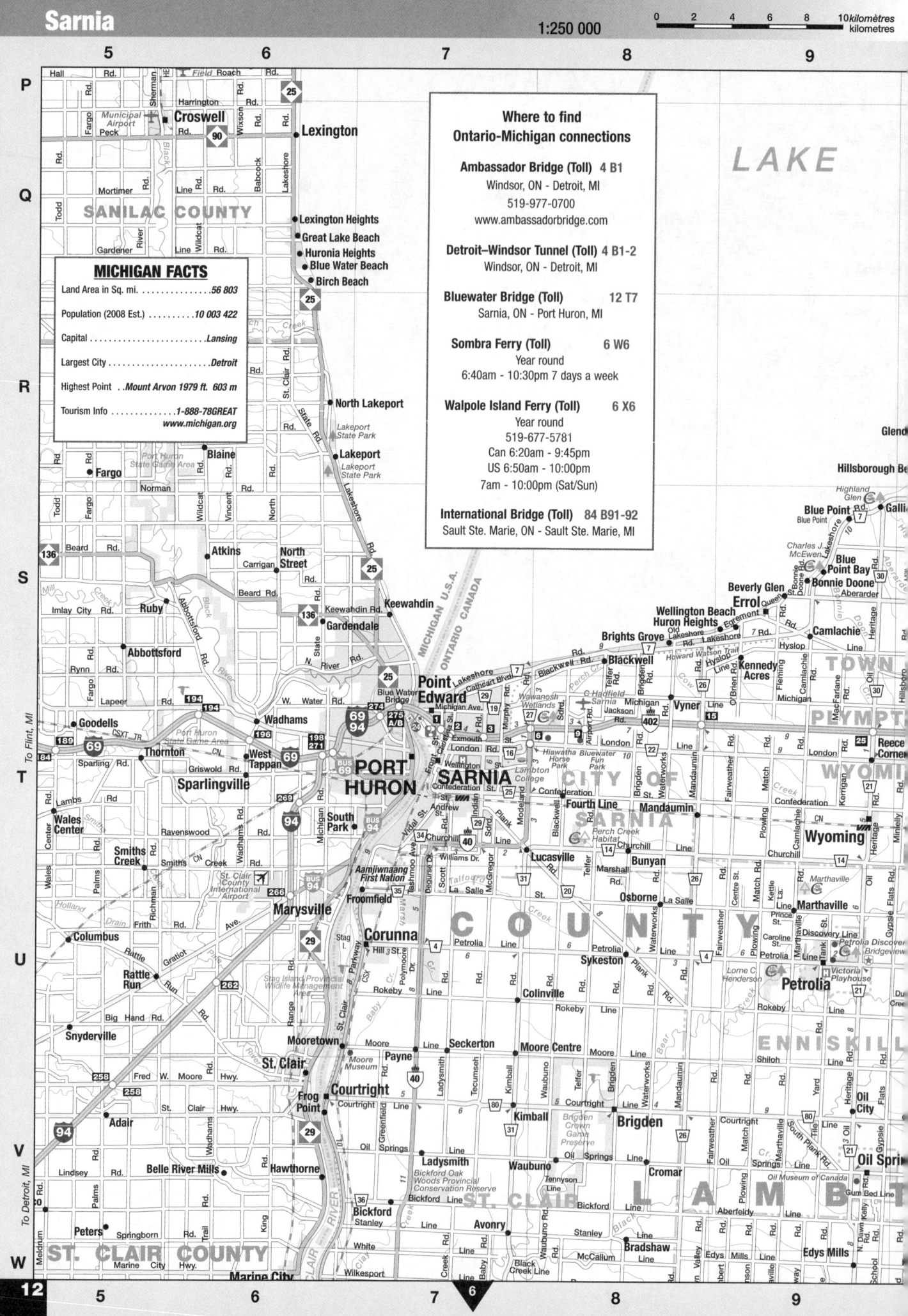

MICHIGAN FACTS

Land Area in Sq. mi. *56 803*

Population (2008 Est.) *10 003 422*

Capital . . . . *Lansing*

Largest City . . . . *Detroit*

Highest Point . . *Mount Arvon 1979 ft. 603 m*

Tourism Info *1-888-78GREAT*
www.michigan.org

Where to find Ontario-Michigan connections

Ambassador Bridge (Toll) 4 B1
Windsor, ON - Detroit, MI
519-977-0700
www.ambassadorbridge.com

Detroit–Windsor Tunnel (Toll) 4 B1-2
Windsor, ON - Detroit, MI

Bluewater Bridge (Toll) 12 T7
Sarnia, ON - Port Huron, MI

Sombra Ferry (Toll) 6 W6
Year round
6:40am - 10:30pm 7 days a week

Walpole Island Ferry (Toll) 6 X6
Year round
519-677-5781
Can 6:20am - 9:45pm
US 6:50am - 10:00pm
7am - 10:00pm (Sat/Sun)

International Bridge (Toll) 84 B91-92
Sault Ste. Marie, ON - Sault Ste. Marie, MI

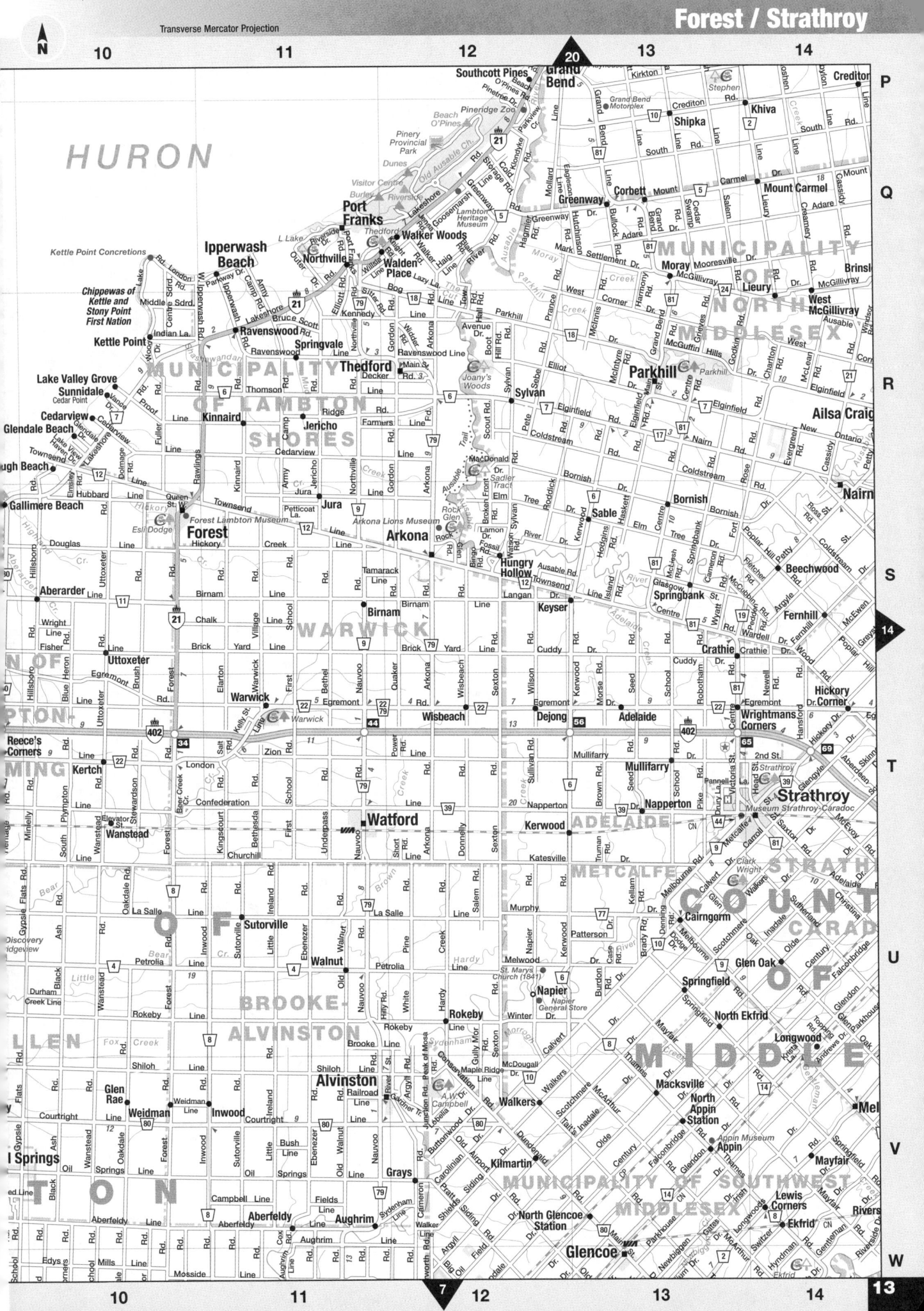

Transverse Mercator Projection

N

HURON

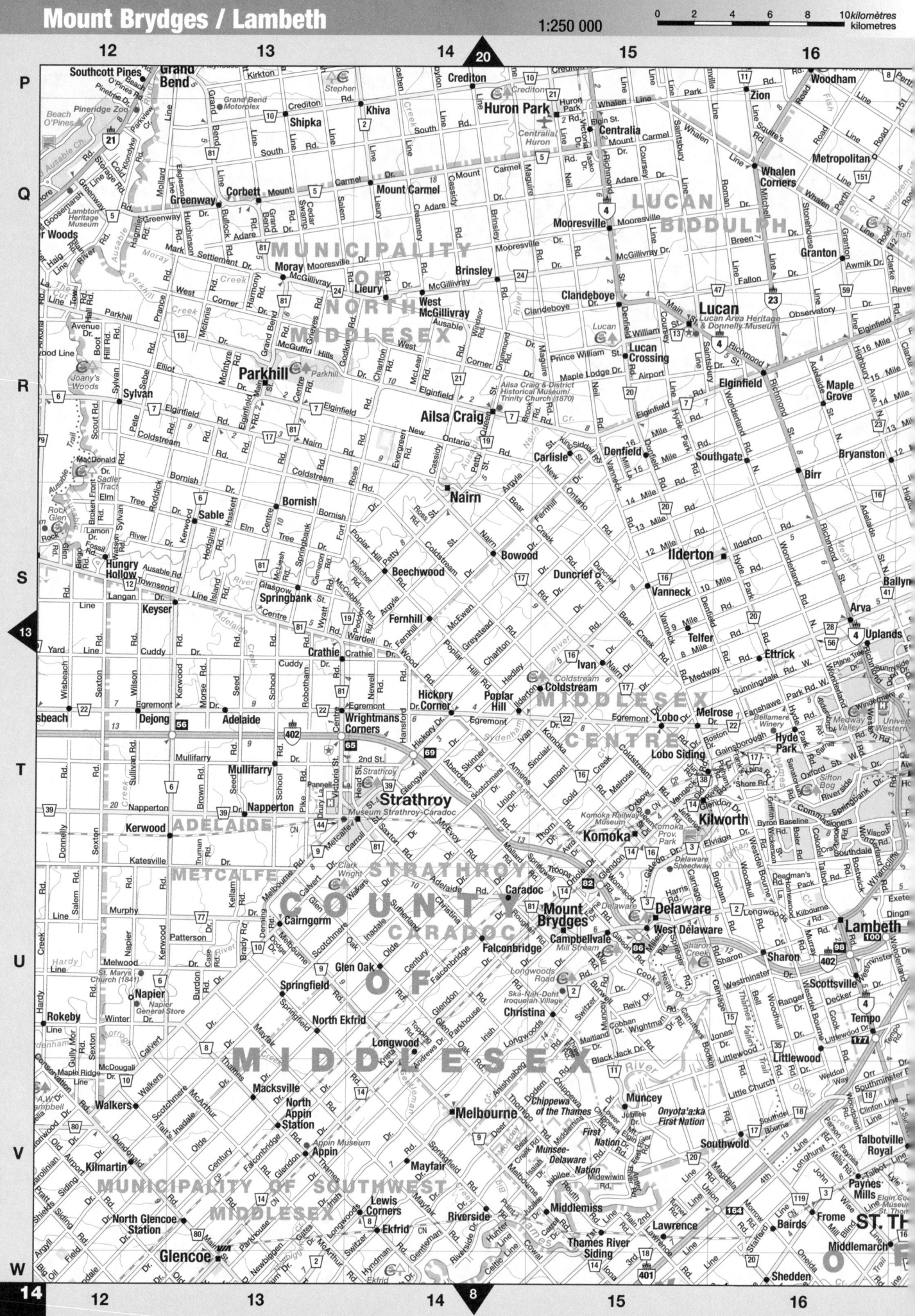

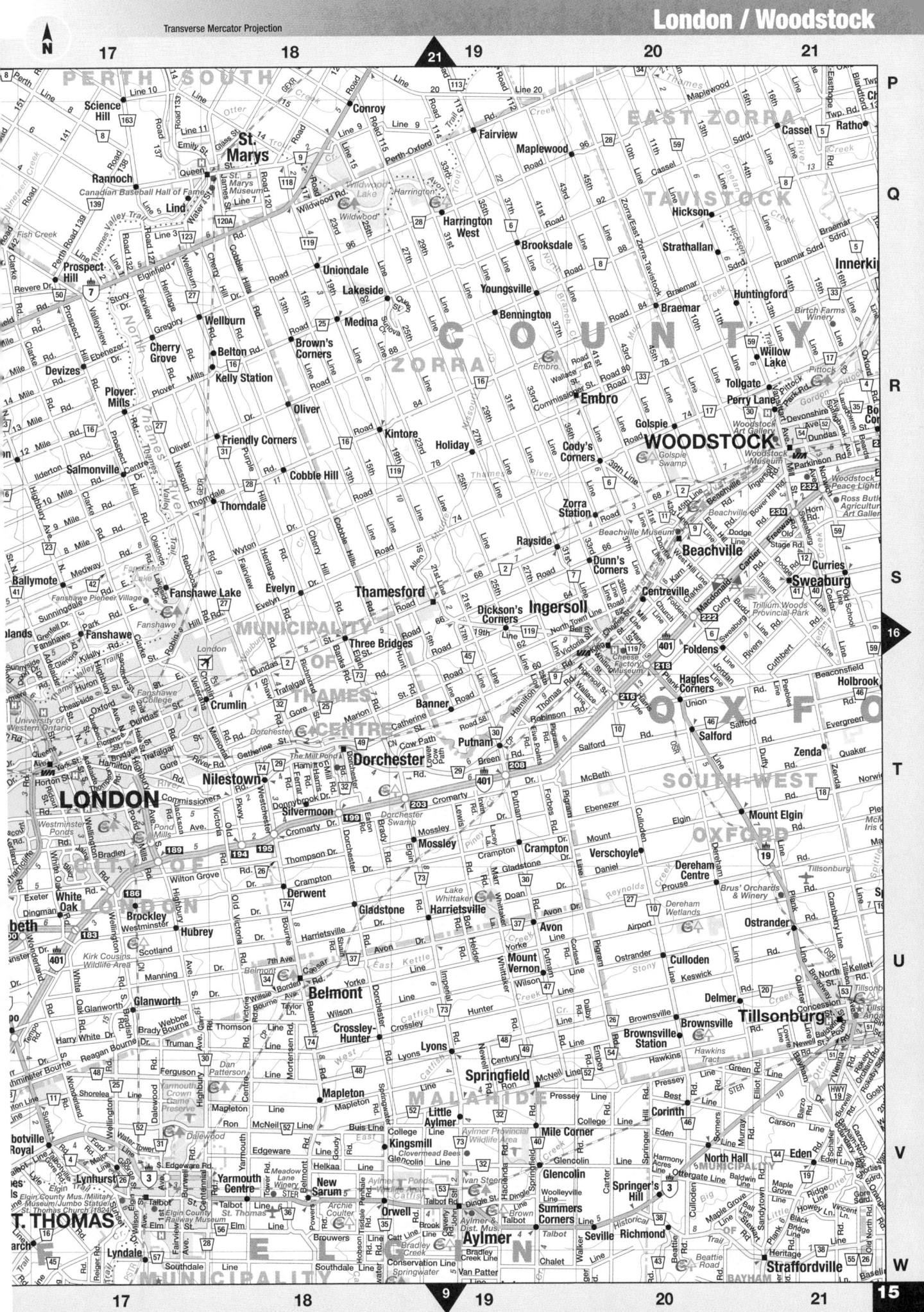

1:250 000

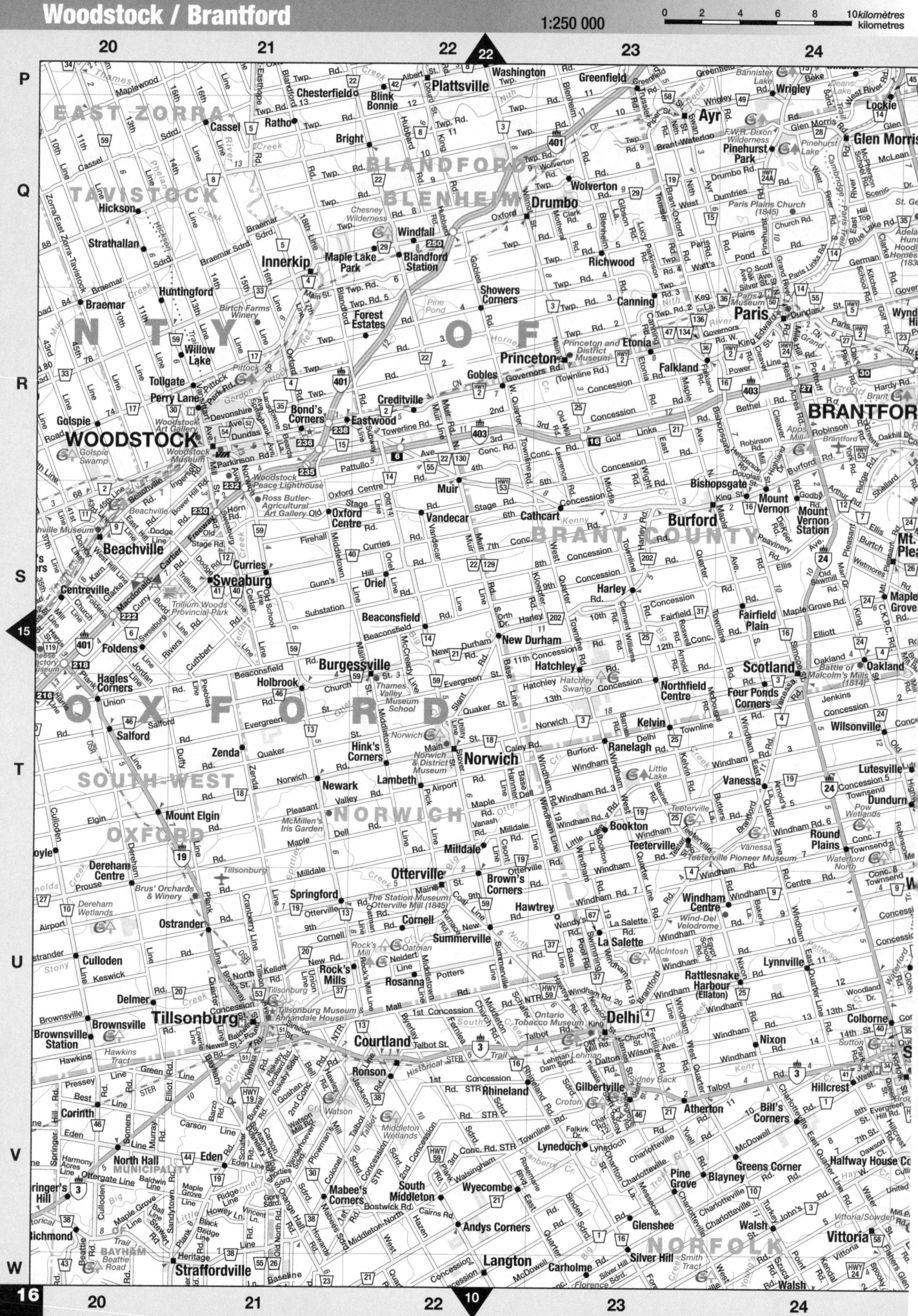

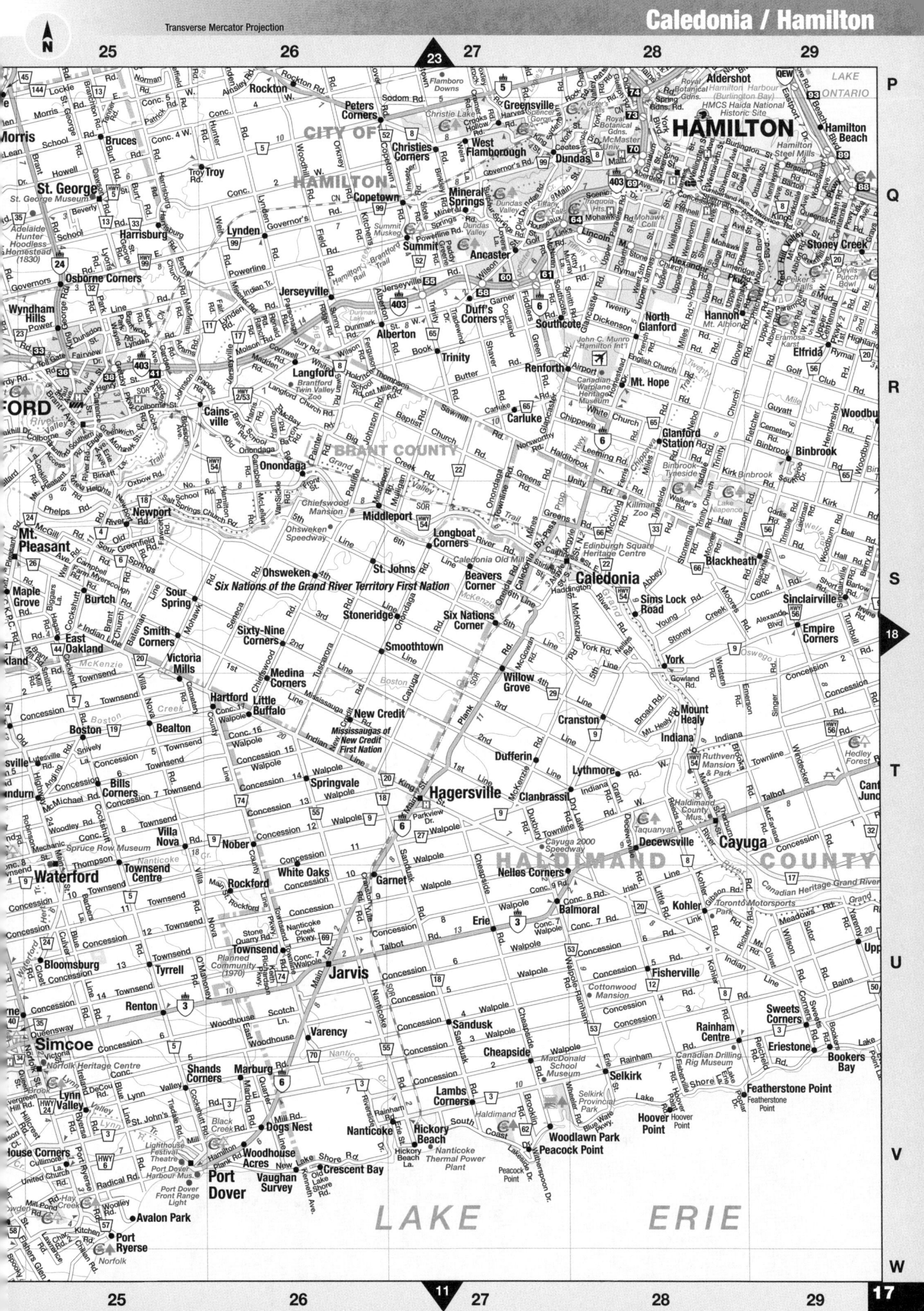

LAKE ERIE

LAKE ONTARIO

1:250 000

0 2 4 6 8 10 kilomètres / kilometres

Niagara Area Wineries - see red bullets on the map

1 Stoney Ridge Cellars 18 R32	25 Sunnybrook Farm 19 Q34	49 Angels Gate Winery 18 R31
2 Andrés Wines 18 Q30	26 Birchwood Estate 18 R32	50 Legends Estates 18 R31
3 Kittling Ridge 18 Q31	27 Creekside Estate 19 Q33	51 Frogpond farm 19 Q35
4 Thirty Bench 18 R31	28 Peller Estates 19 Q34	52 Kings Court 19 R33
5 EastDell Estates 18 R31	29 Caroline Cellars 19 Q35	53 Palatine Hills Estates ..19 Q34
6 Magnotta Cellars 18 R31	30 Royal DeMaria 19 Q35	54 Mountain Road Wine ..18 R31
7 De Sousa 18 R32	31 Puddicombe Estate ..18 Q30	55 Dom Vagners Winery ..19 Q34
8 Maplegrove Vinoteca ..18 R32	32 Hidden Bench 18 R31	56 Ridgepoint Wines 18 R32
9 Willow Heights 18 R32	33 Crown Bench 18 R32	57 Coyote's Run 19 R34
10 Lakeview Cellars 18 R32	34 Harbour Estates 18 R32	58 Flat Rock Cellars 18 R32
11 Vineland Estates 18 R32	35 Malivoire 18 R32	59 Niagara College Teaching Wines
12 Cave Spring Cellars ..18 R32	36 Peninsula Ridge 18 R31	................19 R34
13 Hernder Estates 18 R32	37 Thomas & Vaughan ..18 R32	
14 Henry of Pelham 19 R33	38 Kacaba 18 R32	60 Fielding Estate 18 R31
15 Stonechurch 19 Q34	39 Jackson-Triggs 19 Q35	61 Stratus 19 Q35
16 Konzelmann Estate ..19 Q34	40 Daniel Lenko Estate ..18 R31	62 Tawse Winery 18 R32
17 Strewn 19 Q34	41 Harvest Estate 19 R33	63 20 Bees 19 Q34
18 Pillitteri Estates 19 Q34	42 Lailey Vineyard 19 Q35	64 Cornerstone Estate ..18 R32
19 Joseph's Estate 19 Q35	43 Featherstone Estate ..18 R32	65 Calamus Estate 19 R32
20 Hillebrand Estates ..19 Q34	44 13th Street Winery ..19 R33	
21 Reif Estate 19 Q35	45 Trillium Hill 19 R33	For exact locations, see MapArt's
22 Inniskillin Wines 19 Q35	46 Rockway Glen 19 R33	Golden Horseshoe Street Atlas
23 Marynissen Estate ..19 Q35	47 Maleta Estate 19 R34	Erie North Shore Wineries – pg 5
24 Chateau des Charmes ..19 R34	48 Riverview Cellars 19 Q35	Prince Edward County Area Wineries – pg 34

Most of the wineries offer tours & tastings

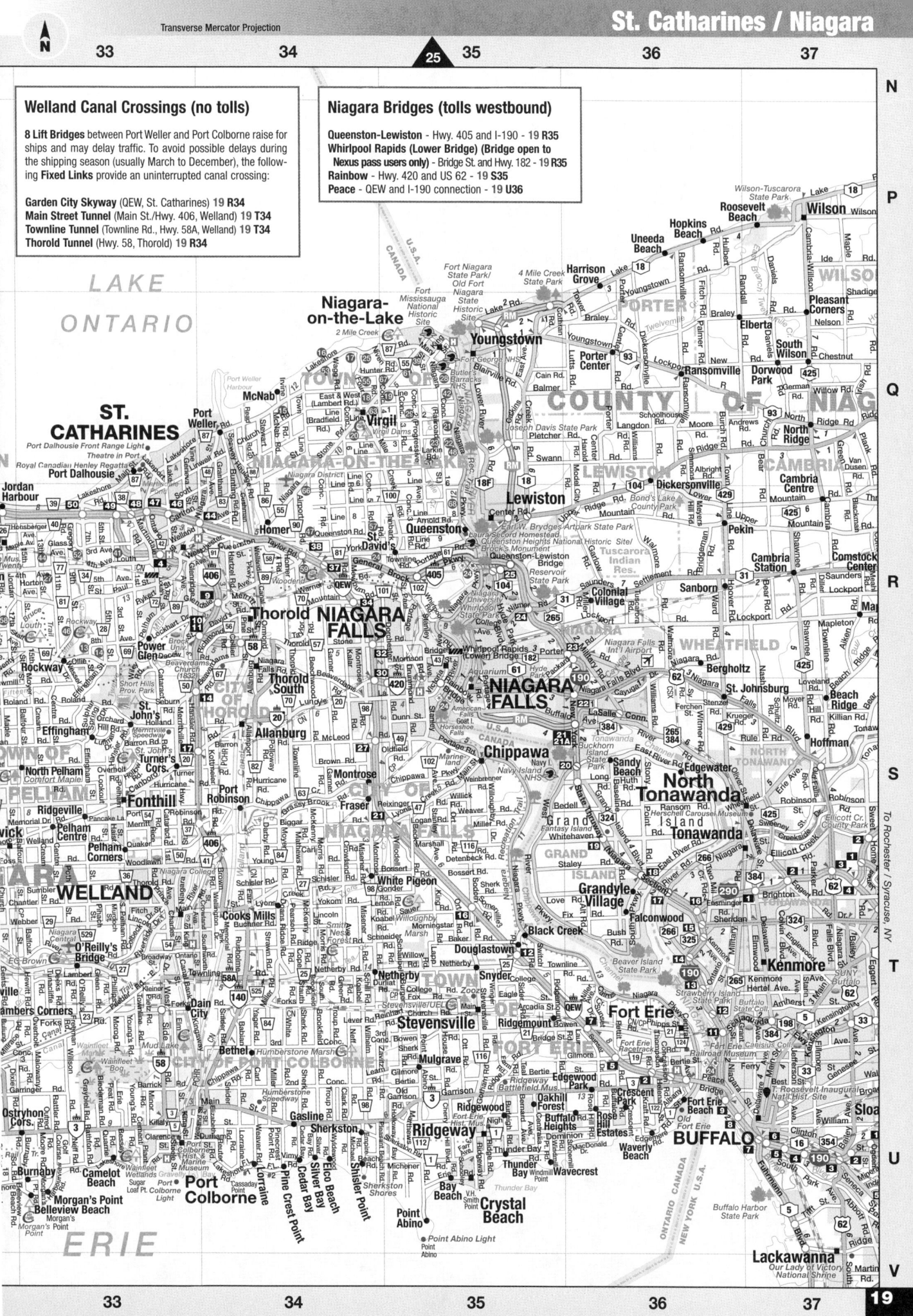

Welland Canal Crossings (no tolls)

8 Lift Bridges between Port Weller and Port Colborne raise for ships and may delay traffic. To avoid possible delays during the shipping season (usually March to December), the following **Fixed Links** provide an uninterrupted canal crossing:

Garden City Skyway (QEW, St. Catharines) 19 **R34**
Main Street Tunnel (Main St./Hwy. 406, Welland) 19 **T34**
Townline Tunnel (Townline Rd., Hwy. 58A, Welland) 19 **T34**
Thorold Tunnel (Hwy. 58, Thorold) 19 **R34**

Niagara Bridges (tolls westbound)

Queenston-Lewiston - Hwy. 405 and I-190 - 19 **R35**
Whirlpool Rapids (Lower Bridge) (Bridge open to **Nexus** pass users only) - Bridge St. and Hwy. 182 - 19 **R35**
Rainbow - Hwy. 420 and US 62 - 19 **S35**
Peace - QEW and I-190 connection - 19 **U36**

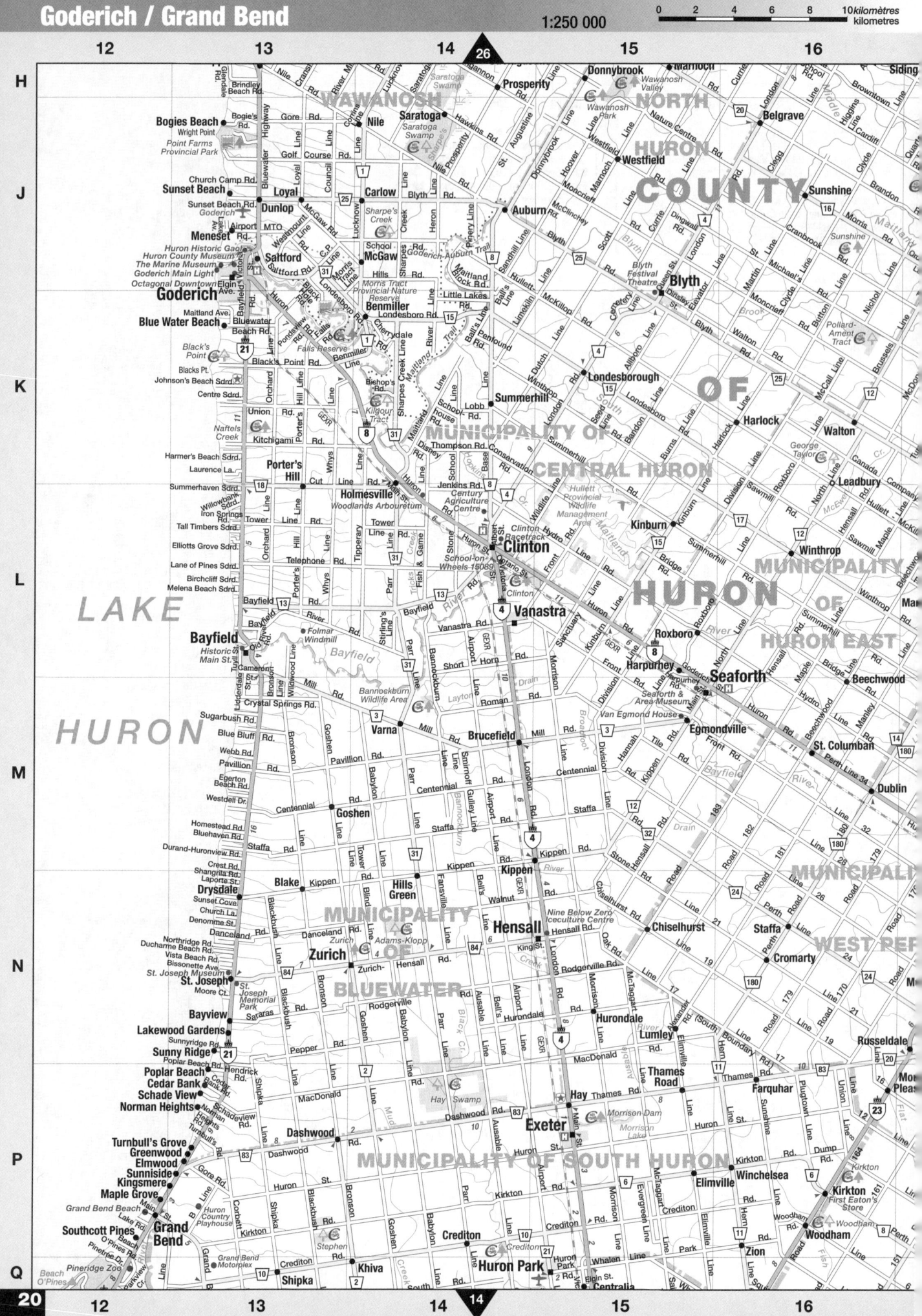

LAKE

HURON

WAWANOSH

NORTH

HURON

COUNTY

OF

MUNICIPALITY OF
CENTRAL HURON

MUNICIPALITY

OF

HURON

HURON EAST

Goderich

Bayfield

Bogies Beach
Sunset Beach
Meneset
Saltford
Blue Water Beach

Porter's
Hill

Holmesville

Drysdale
Zurich
St. Joseph
Bayview
Lakewood Gardens
Sunny Ridge
Poplar Beach
Cedar Bank
Schade View
Norman Heights
Turnbull's Grove
Greenwood
Elmwood
Sunniside
Kingsmere
Maple Grove
Southcott Pines
Grand Bend

MUNICIPALITY
OF
BLUEWATER

Blake
Kippen
Hills
Green
Dashwood

Varna
Brucefield
Kippen
Hensall
Cromarty
Staffa
Chiselhurst

Clinton
Vanastra
Harpurhey
Seaforth
Egmondville
St. Columban
Dublin

Summerhill
Londesborough
Harlock
Walton
Leadbury
Kinburn
Winthrop

Blyth
Belgrave
Westfield
Sunshine
Auburn

Prosperity
Donnybrook

MUNICIPALITY OF SOUTH HURON

Hurondale
Lumley
Thames
Road
Farquhar
Russeldale

Exeter
Hay
Winchelsea
Elimville
Kirkton
Woodham

Grand Bend Beach
Southcott Pines
Pineridge Zoo
Shipka
Khiva
Crediton
Huron Park
Zion
Woodham

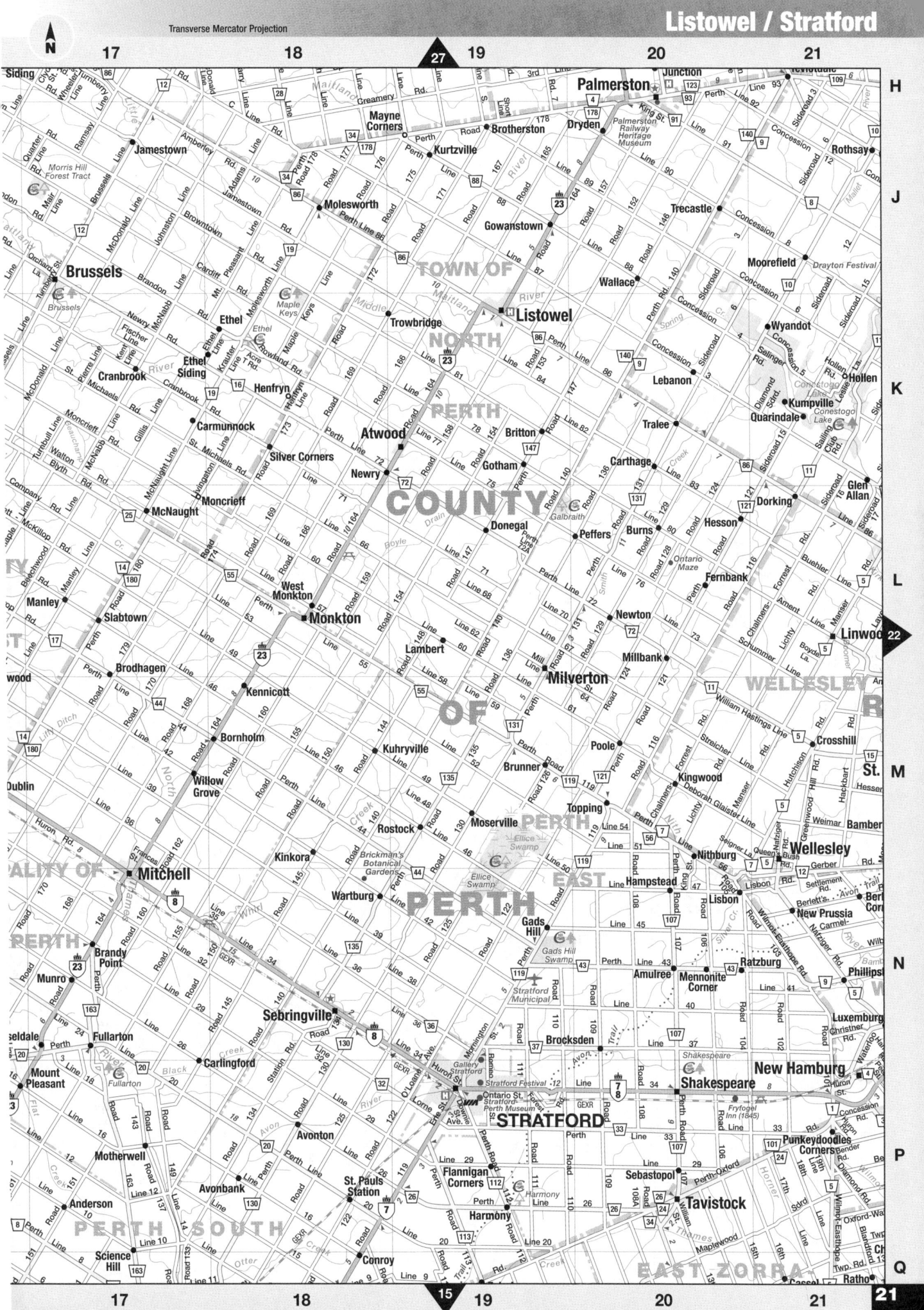

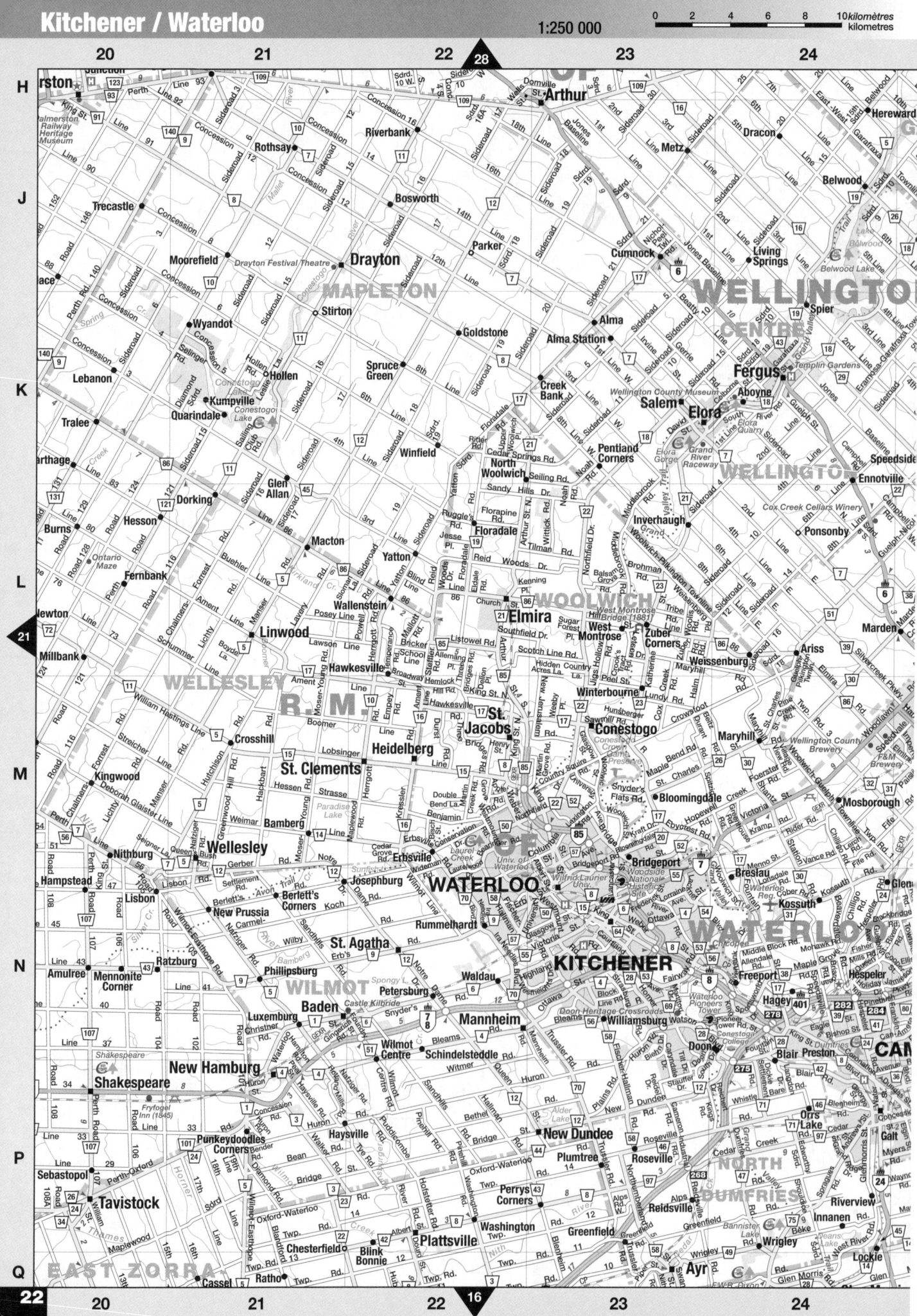

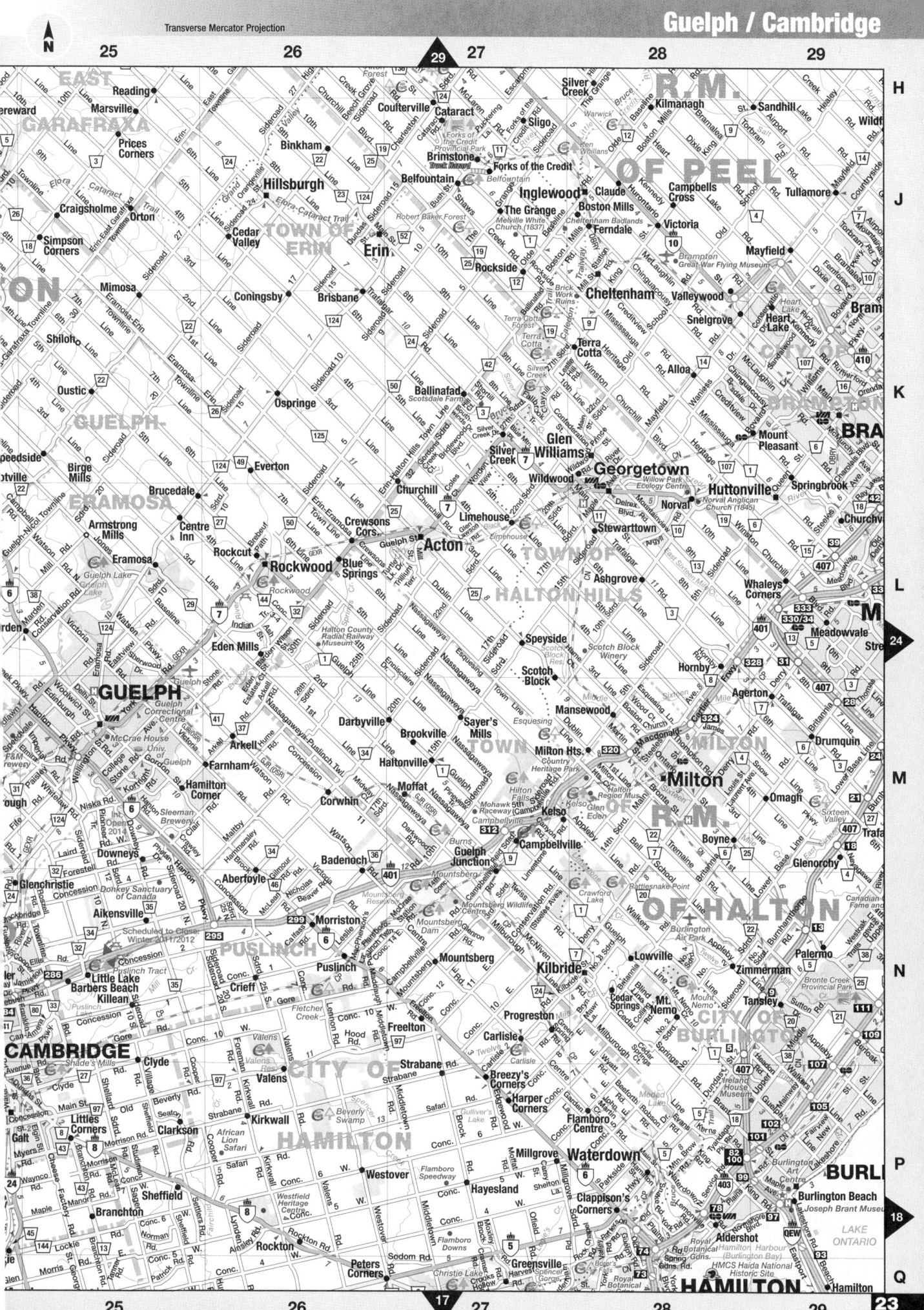

Transverse Mercator Projection

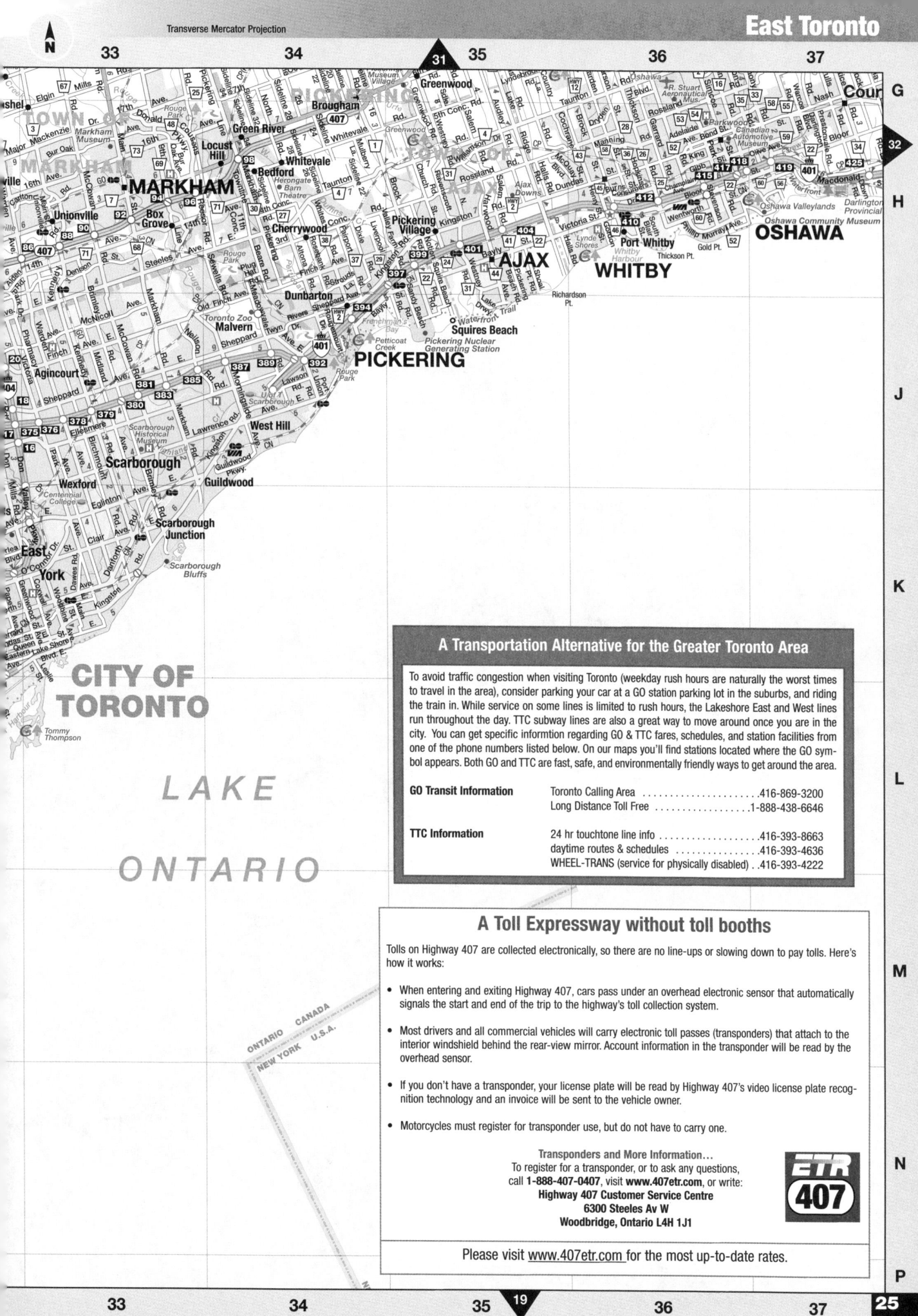

A Transportation Alternative for the Greater Toronto Area

To avoid traffic congestion when visiting Toronto (weekday rush hours are naturally the worst times to travel in the area), consider parking your car at a GO station parking lot in the suburbs, and riding the train in. While service on some lines is limited to rush hours, the Lakeshore East and West lines run throughout the day. TTC subway lines are also a great way to move around once you are in the city. You can get specific informtion regarding GO & TTC fares, schedules, and station facilities from one of the phone numbers listed below. On our maps you'll find stations located where the GO symbol appears. Both GO and TTC are fast, safe, and environmentally friendly ways to get around the area.

GO Transit Information	Toronto Calling Area	416-869-3200
	Long Distance Toll Free	1-888-438-6646
TTC Information	24 hr touchtone line info	416-393-8663
	daytime routes & schedules	416-393-4636
	WHEEL-TRANS (service for physically disabled) . .	416-393-4222

A Toll Expressway without toll booths

Tolls on Highway 407 are collected electronically, so there are no line-ups or slowing down to pay tolls. Here's how it works:

• When entering and exiting Highway 407, cars pass under an overhead electronic sensor that automatically signals the start and end of the trip to the highway's toll collection system.

• Most drivers and all commercial vehicles will carry electronic toll passes (transponders) that attach to the interior windshield behind the rear-view mirror. Account information in the transponder will be read by the overhead sensor.

• If you don't have a transponder, your license plate will be read by Highway 407's video license plate recognition technology and an invoice will be sent to the vehicle owner.

• Motorcycles must register for transponder use, but do not have to carry one.

Transponders and More Information...
To register for a transponder, or to ask any questions,
call **1-888-407-0407**, visit **www.407etr.com**, or write:
Highway 407 Customer Service Centre
6300 Steeles Av W
Woodbridge, Ontario L4H 1J1

ETR 407

Please visit www.407etr.com for the most up-to-date rates.

0 2 4 6 8 10 kilometres

LAKE HURON

Turners

North Bruce

Scott Pt.
MacPherson Pt.
Bruce Nuclear Plant A
Douglas Pt.
Baie Du Dore
Bruce Nuclear Plant B
Bruce Nuclear Power Visitor's Centre
Holmes Bay
Inverhuron Provincial Park
Inverhuron
Inverhuron Bay

Underwood

Paisley
Treasure Chest Museum

McRae Pt.

Tiverton

Lovat

MUNICIPALITY OF KINCARDINE

Bradley

Lorne Beach Rd.
Parkwood Rd.
Kinhuron Rd.
Lake Huron Highland
Kinhuron
Slade
Stoney Island
McConnell Dr.
Craig Dr.
Wickham Rd.
MacCastill Rd.
MacCaskill Rd.
Golf Links Rd.
Horton Pt.
Huron Ridge

Armow

Glammis

Portal
Pinkerton
Narva

Kincardine Rear Range Light & Museum
Bluewater Summer Festival Theatre
Kincardine
Boiler Beach
Penetangore

Millarton

Kingarf

Chepstow

Greenoch Swamp Wetland Complex
Schmidt Lake

Poplar Beach

Bervie

Bruce Beach Rd.

Pine River
Clarks Church

Purple Grove

Kinloss

Young's Conc.
Greenock Swamp Wetland Complex

Riversdale

Greenock

Lurgan Beach

HURON-KINLOSS

Little Egypt

Tinkertown

Point Clark
Point Clark Lighthouse National Historic Site
Point Clark Lighthouse Museum
Point Clark

Reid's Corners

Ripley

Verdun

Kinlough

Westford

Salem

Amberley

Clover Valley

Holyrood

Lochalsh

Lower Langside

Lothian

Langside

Teeswater
Hardwood Hills

Horizon View Rd.
MacKenzie Camp Rd.
Presbyterian Camp Rd.
Kintail
Huron Sands Rd.

Kintail School House

Lanes

Zion

Lucknow
Lucknow Waterworks

Belgrave

Kingsbridge

Belfast

Turnberry-Culross West

Huron Shores Rd.
Birch Beach Rd.

Mafeking

St. Helens

Whitechurch

Stapleton Tract

Wingham

Lakeland Estates Rd.
Mid-Huron Beach Rd.
Maple-Cedar Grove Rd.
Port Albert
Martin's Point
Quaid's Bay
Young's

Crewe

Lower Wingham
Turnberry Flood Plain
North Huron Museum/
Barn Dance Hall of Fame
Hutton Heights

Shoreline

Shepppardton

ASHFIELD-COLBORNE-WAWANOSH

Dungannon

St. Augustine

Mud Lake Forest Tract

Fordyce

Marnoch

Morris

Bluevale
Bluevale Siding

Bogies Beach
Bogie's Rd.

Nile

Saratoga
Saratoga Swamp

Prosperity

Donnybrook
Wawanosh Valley

NORTH

Belgrave

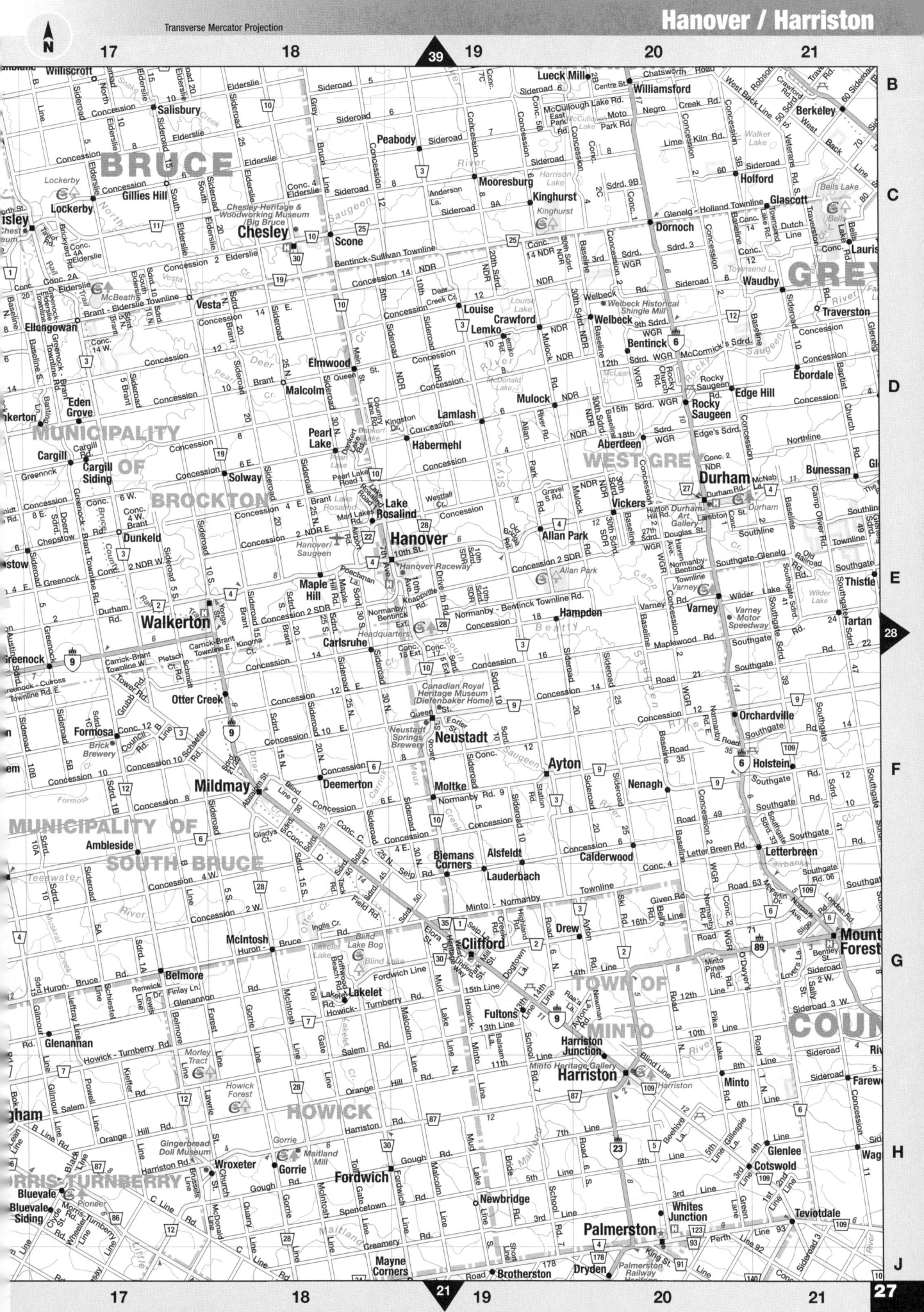

Transverse Mercator Projection

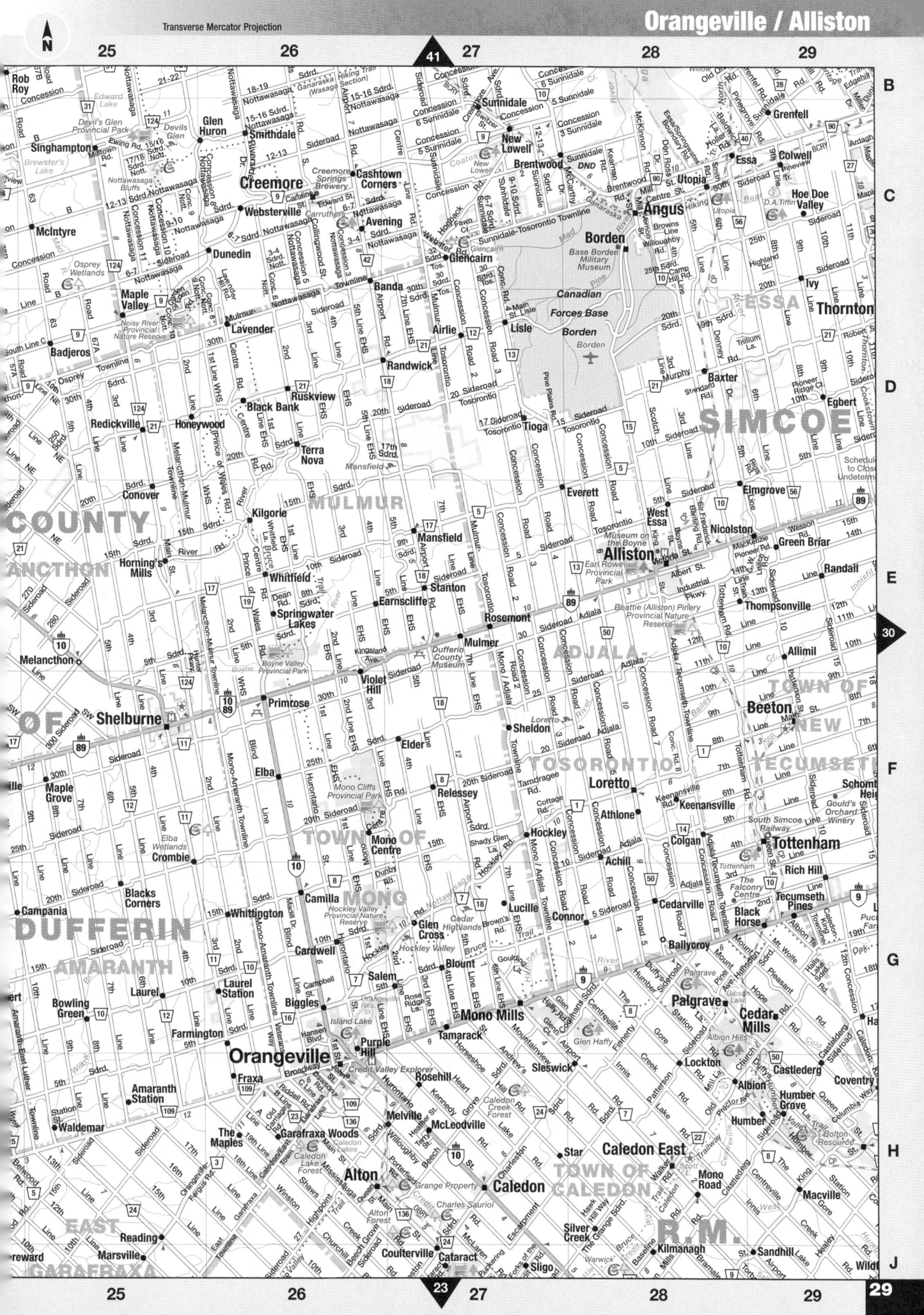

Transverse Mercator Projection

Transverse Mercator Projection

N

LAKE ONTARIO

COUNTY OF NORTHUMBERLAND

PETERBOROUGH

Cobourg

Port Hope

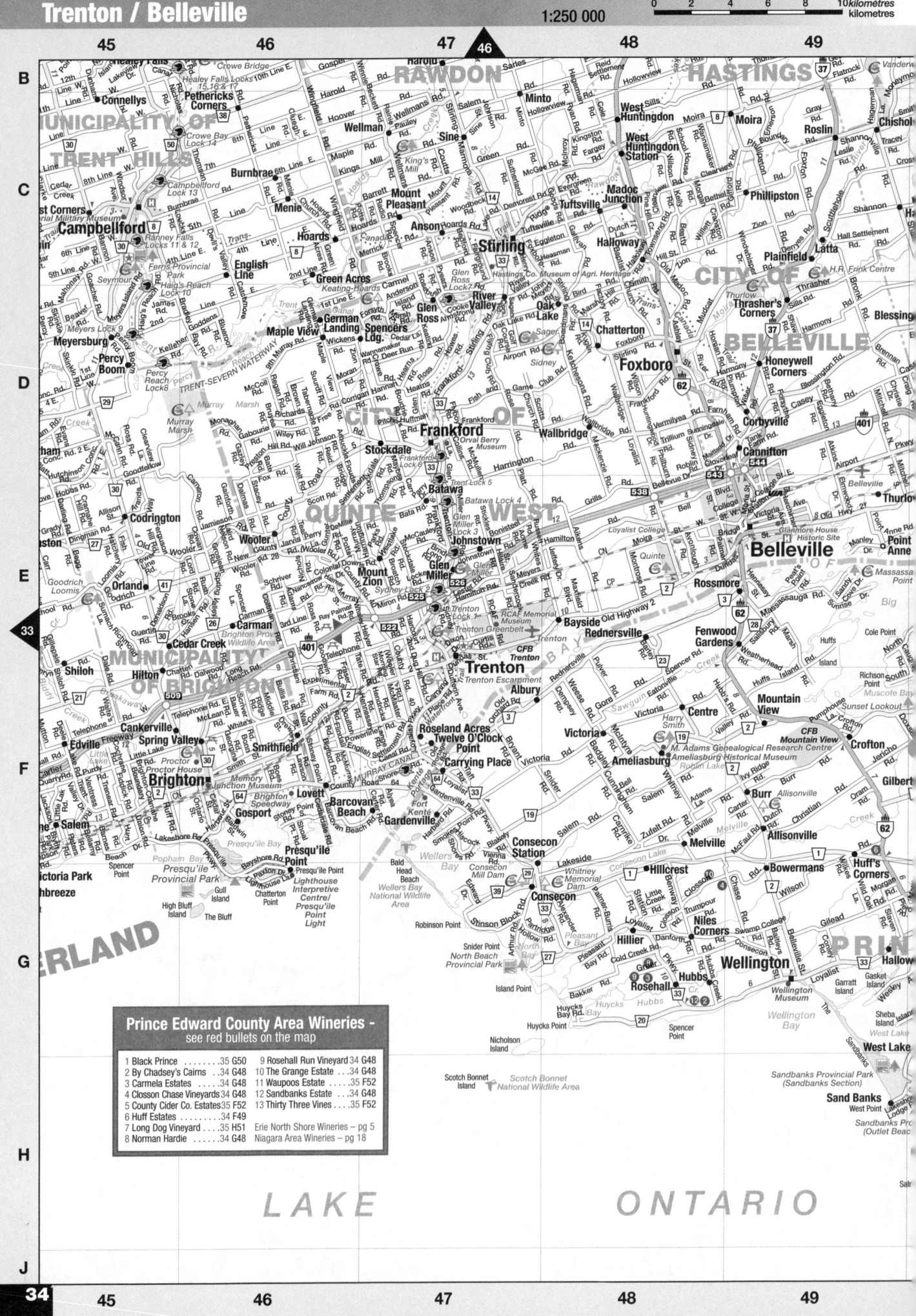

0   2   4   6   8   10 kilomètres
kilomètres

Prince Edward County Area Wineries –
see red bullets on the map

1 Black Prince 35 G50	9 Rosehall Run Vineyard 34 G48
2 By Chadsey's Cairns . .34 G48	10 The Grange Estate . . .34 G48
3 Carmela Estates 34 G48	11 Waupoos Estate 35 F52
4 Closson Chase Vineyards 34 G48	12 Sandbanks Estate 34 G48
5 County Cider Co. Estates 35 F52	13 Thirty Three Vines 35 F52
6 Huff Estates 34 F49	
7 Long Dog Vineyard . . .35 H51	Erie North Shore Wineries – pg 5
8 Norman Hardie 34 G48	Niagara Area Wineries – pg 18

LAKE   **ONTARIO**

34

45   46   47   48   49

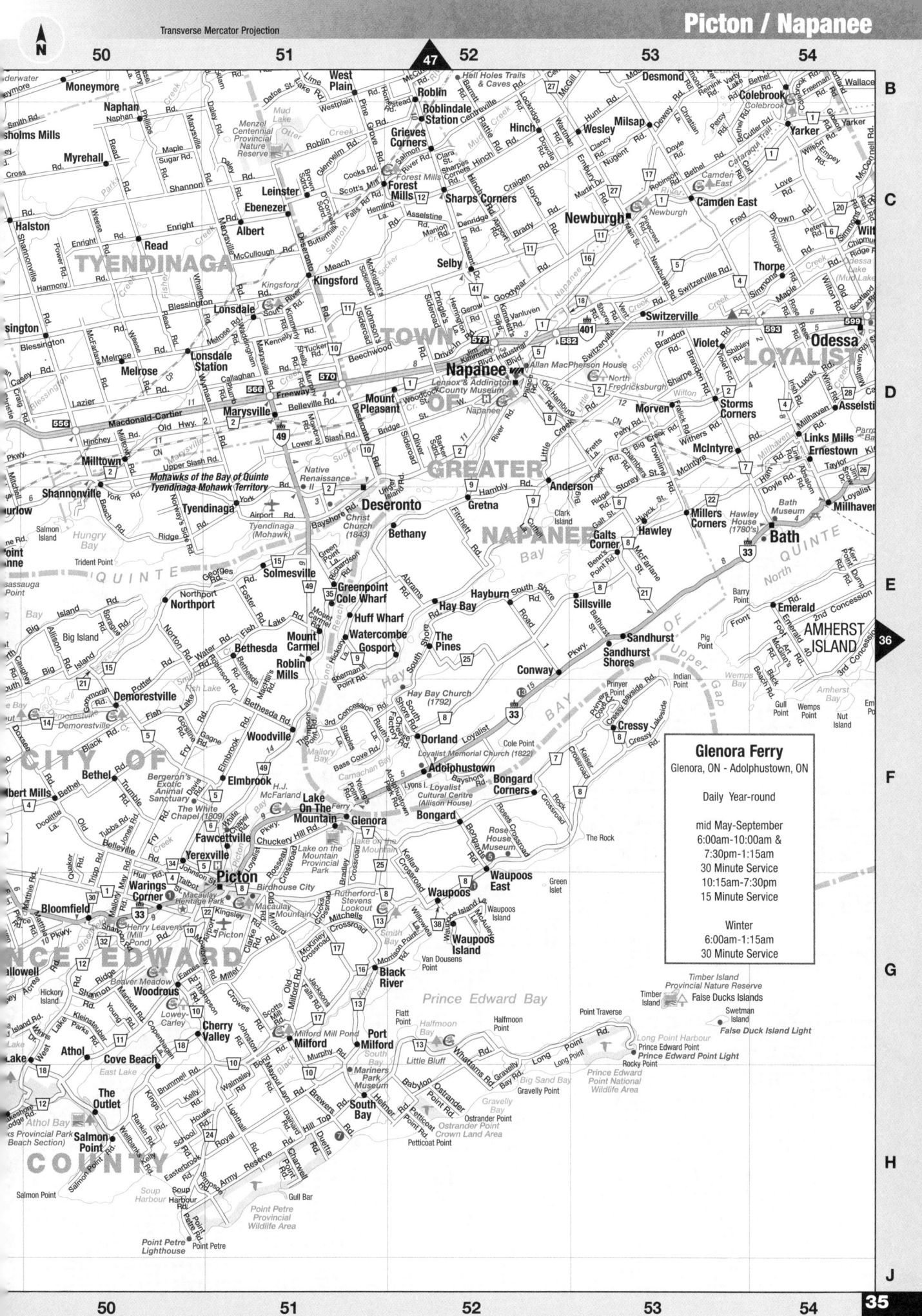

Transverse Mercator Projection

N

50　51　47　52　53　54

B

C

D

E
36

F

G

H

J

50　51　52　53　54

35

Glenora Ferry

Glenora, ON - Adolphustown, ON

Daily Year-round

mid May-September
6:00am-10:00am &
7:30pm-1:15am
30 Minute Service
10:15am-7:30pm
15 Minute Service

Winter
6:00am-1:15am
30 Minute Service

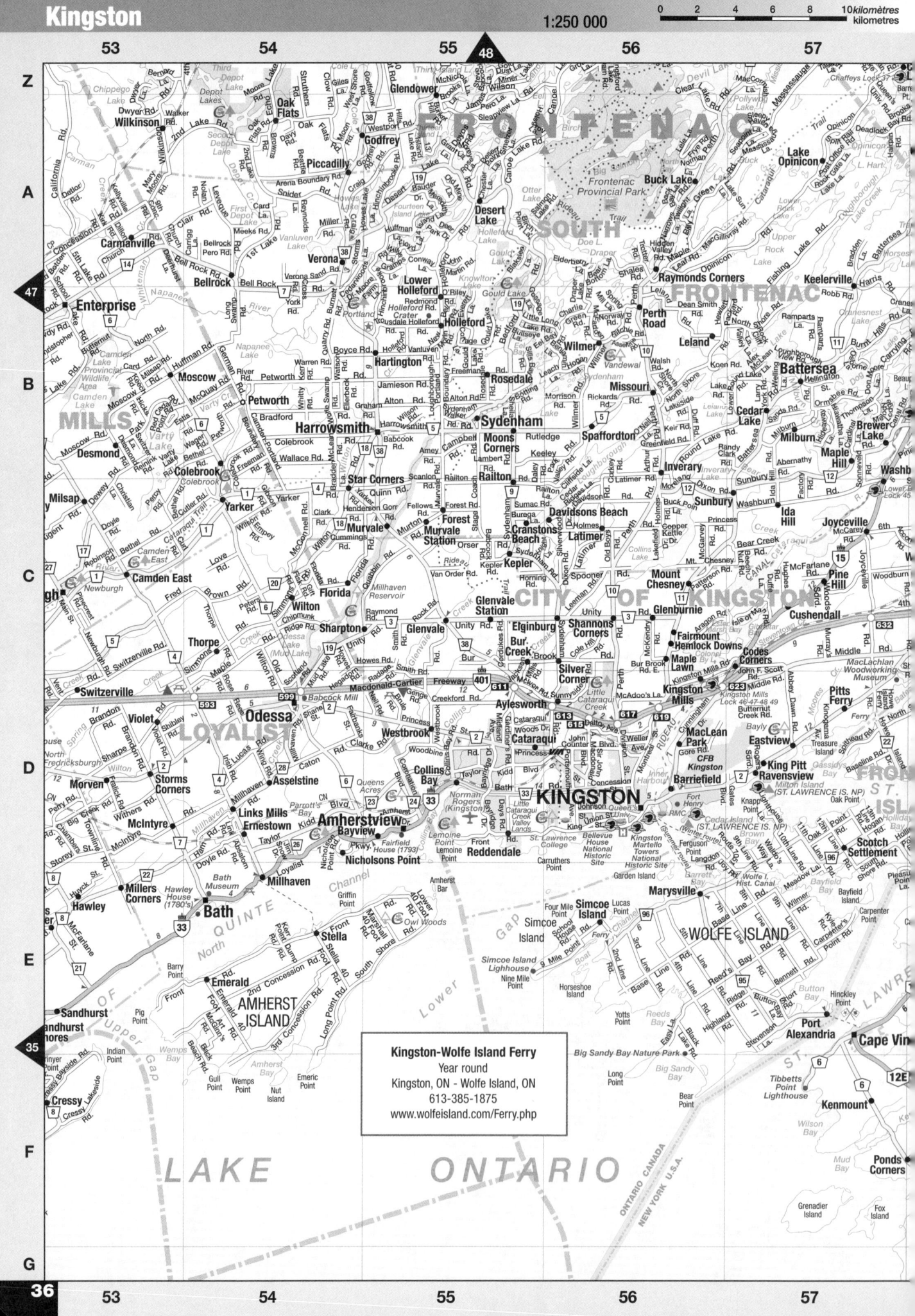

1:250 000

0 2 4 6 8 10 kilomètres
kilometres

FRONTENAC

SOUTH

FRONTENAC

CITY OF KINGSTON

LOYALIST

KINGSTON

WOLFE ISLAND

AMHERST ISLAND

LAKE ONTARIO

Kingston-Wolfe Island Ferry
Year round
Kingston, ON - Wolfe Island, ON
613-385-1875
www.wolfeisland.com/Ferry.php

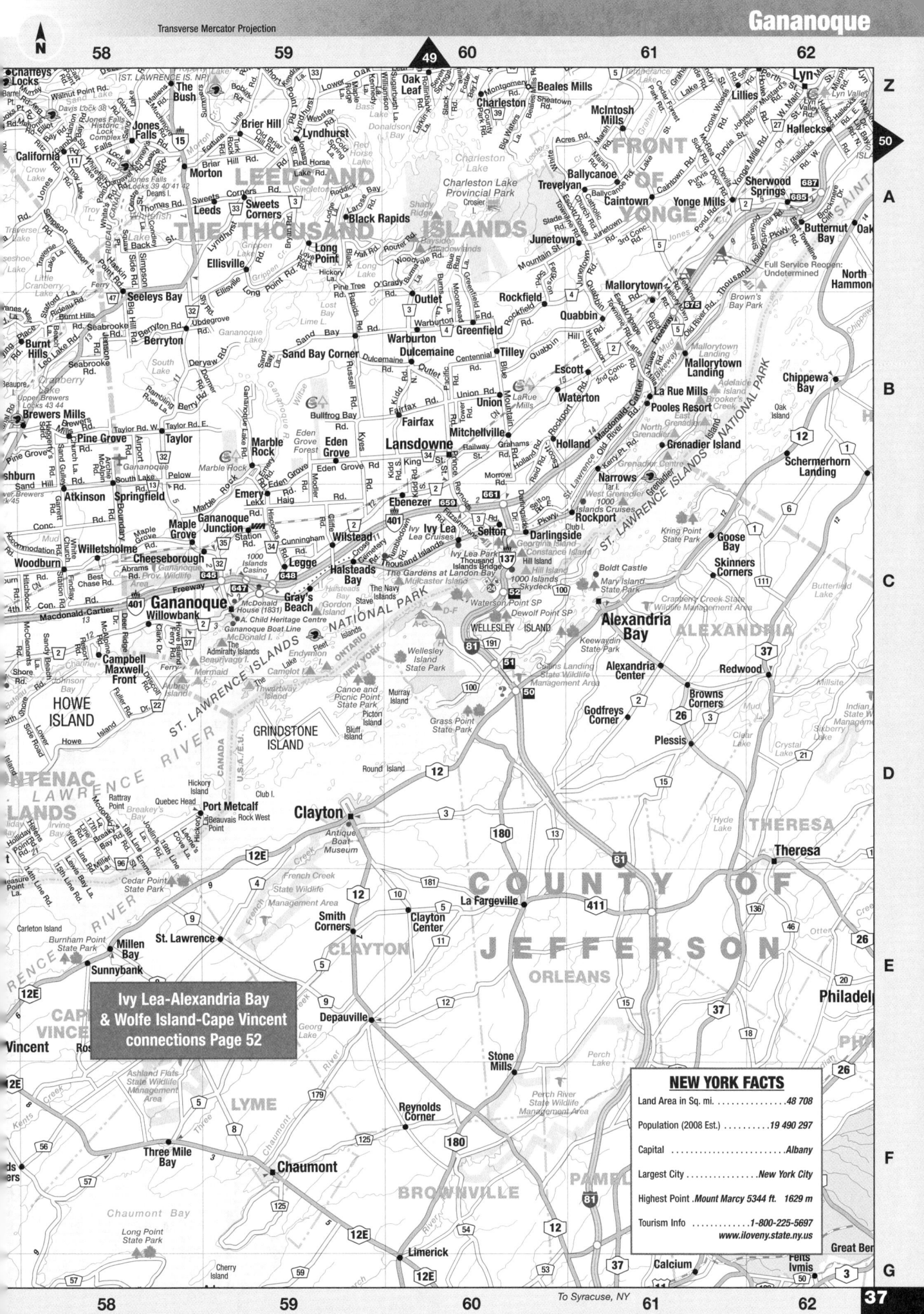

Transverse Mercator Projection

NEW YORK FACTS

Land Area in Sq. mi.	48 708
Population (2008 Est.)	19 490 297
Capital	Albany
Largest City	New York City
Highest Point	Mount Marcy 5344 ft. 1629 m
Tourism Info	1-800-225-5697
	www.iloveny.state.ny.us

Ivy Lea-Alexandria Bay & Wolfe Island-Cape Vincent connections Page 52

To Syracuse, NY

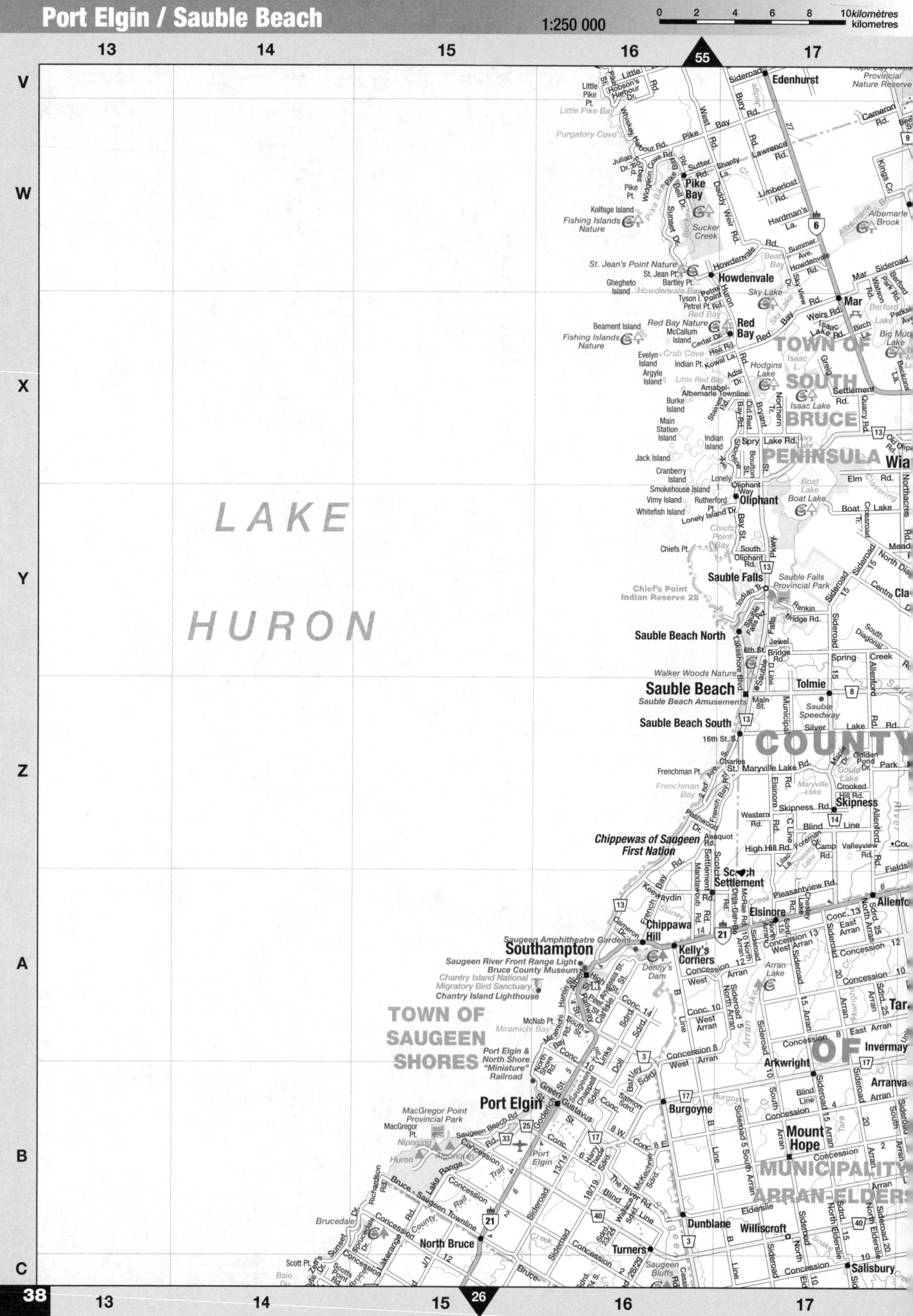

LAKE

HURON

TOWN OF
SOUTH
BRUCE
PENINSULA

COUNTY

OF

TOWN OF
SAUGEEN
SHORES

MUNICIPALITY
ARRAN-ELDERS

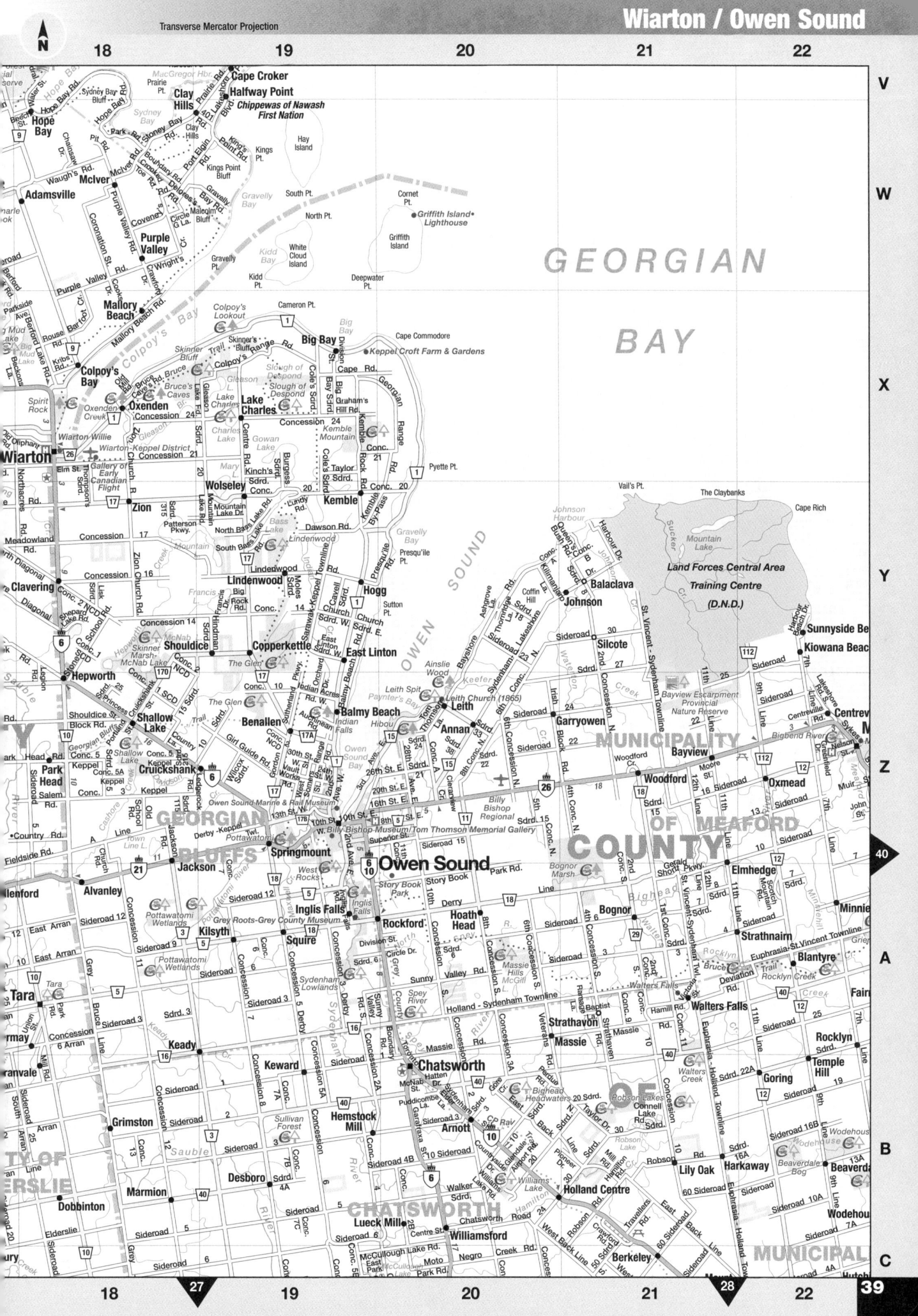

1:250 000

GEORGIAN   BAY

Nottawasaga

Bay

Hope

Daly
Point

Charity
Point

Christian

Blue
Point

Island   **Christia**
                Island

*West
Sand
Bay*

Vail's Pt.

The Claybanks

Cape Rich

*Mountain
Lake*

**Land Forces Central Area
Training Centre
(D.N.D.)**

clava

cote

39
30

27

Sunnyside Beach

Kiowana Beach

112

Bayview Escarpment
Provincial
Nature Reserve

Centreville

Centreville
Rd.

11th

25

Sideroad

9th Sideroad

Woodford
Cr.

Bayview

112

Moore
St.

3

Nelson
St.

Meaford

Meaford Museum/Christ Church (1862)

Christie
Beach

Georgian Trail

Christie Beach

*Lora
Bay*

26

MUNICIPALITY

Woodford

18

Sdr.

15

12

12th

16 11th

Sideroad

John
St.

13

Oxmead

Sideroad

3rd Line

35th

OF MEAFORD

COUNTY

gnor

Gerald
Short Pkwy.

12th

10

Conc. 9

St. Vincent-Sydenham Townline

Scotch
Mountain

Sideroad

7

12

Elmhedge

Sdr.

7

Sideroad

Thornbury

Thornbury Fish Lock

113

Peasmarsh
Nature

Clarksburg

Camperdown

Craigleith
Provincial Park

Delphi
Pt.

30th Sdr.

Clark
St.

13

40

Griersville

4

3rd Line

Old Mail

Griersville
Rd.

Slabtown
Rd.

Slabtown

24th

Sideroad

Clendenan
Dam

Minniehill

Sideroad

Strathnairn

Euphrasia-St Vincent Townline

Rocklyn
Bruce
Trail

Rocklyn Creek

Blantyre

Fairmount

Deviation
Rd.

40

Creek

Heathcote

21st
Sideroad

18th Sdr.

**Victoria
Corners**

Loree

18th Sdr.

Georgian
Peaks

Alpine

Blue
Mtn.

*Blue
Mountain*

Collingwood's
Scenic Caves

Sheffield
Park
Black
Cultural
Museum

*East
Black
Bass
Bay*

Nottawasaga
Island

Pigeon
Pt.

Craigleith

Blue Mtn.
Slide Ride

Monterra

26

Collingwood

Collingwood
Museum

Sunset

Hamill Rd.

Walters Falls

12

11th
Line

25

22B

Rocklyn

Sdr.

4th Line

Sideroad 22C

18th
Line

Sideroad

Banks

4th Line

12th

McMurchy
Settlement

**Mair
Mills**

Mountain Rd.

21 34

19 34

32

Bygone
Days
Heritage
Village

Nottawa

Massie
Rd.

10

40

Walters
Creek

22A

**Temple
Hill**

Sdr.

Goring

9th
Line

Epping John
Muir Lookout

Epping

13

Beaver

Ravenna

2

15th
Sideroad

119

6th

Castle Glen

3rd Line

Osler Bluff
Sideroad

36-37

Petun

**Batteaux
Rd.**

Robson Lakes
Rd.

Robson
Lake

30

12

Sdr.

Quiet
Valley
Rd.

Beaver

Sdr. 16C

Lowlands
Rd.

Sdr.
13B

13

Euphrasia Townline

**Red
Wing**

12th Sdr.

19

Sideroad

Gibraltar

Pretty River
Valley
Provincial Park

33-31

Bruce
Trail
Milepost

30-31

**Pretty River
Valley**

Collingwood
Classic
Aircraft
Foundation

Lily Oak

Harkaway

Beaverdale
Bog

13A

Sdr.

Wodehouse
Rd.

Wodehouse

7

Beaverdale

10B

Fox Ridge Rd.

Duncan

Duncan
Lake

Duncan
Crevice Caves
Provincial Nature
Reserve

Kolapore

Metcalfe Rock
& Caves

Kolapore
Uplands

3rd Sideroad

4th Line

Nottawasaga
Lookout Prov.
Nature
Reserve

26-27 Sdr.

Nottawasaga

Singhampton Cave

Duntroo

124

Berkeley

60 Sideroad

Sideroad

Wodehouse

7A

Sideroad

Kimberley

Beaver
Valley

Old
Baldy

4B Line

13

Talisman
Mountain

Sideroad 7B

7C

3rd Sdr.

Little Germany

3rd Sdr.

Kolapore Upland
Demonstration Forest

Little
Germany

Kolapore
Uplands

Osprey

The Blue Mountains

Reid's
Hill

Road 57D

91

21-22

**Rob
Roy**

Concession

31

*Edward
Lake*

Devil's Glen
Provincial Park

124

Gl

Devils

MUNICIPALITY OF

Lady Bank

Artemesia-Euphrasia

Bruce Townline

Rob Roy
Petting Farm

10th

31

40

21   **22**   **23**   28   **24**   **25**

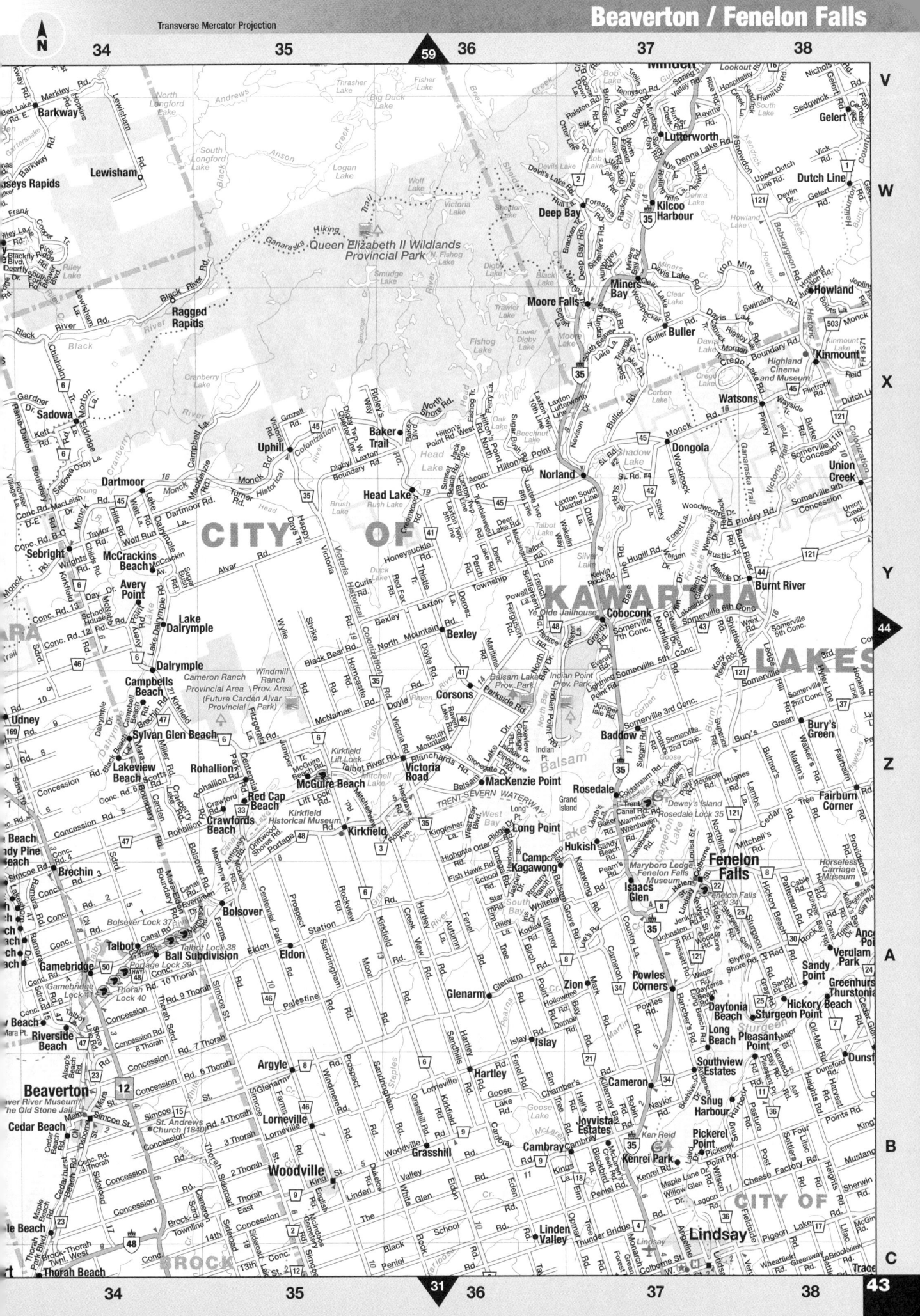

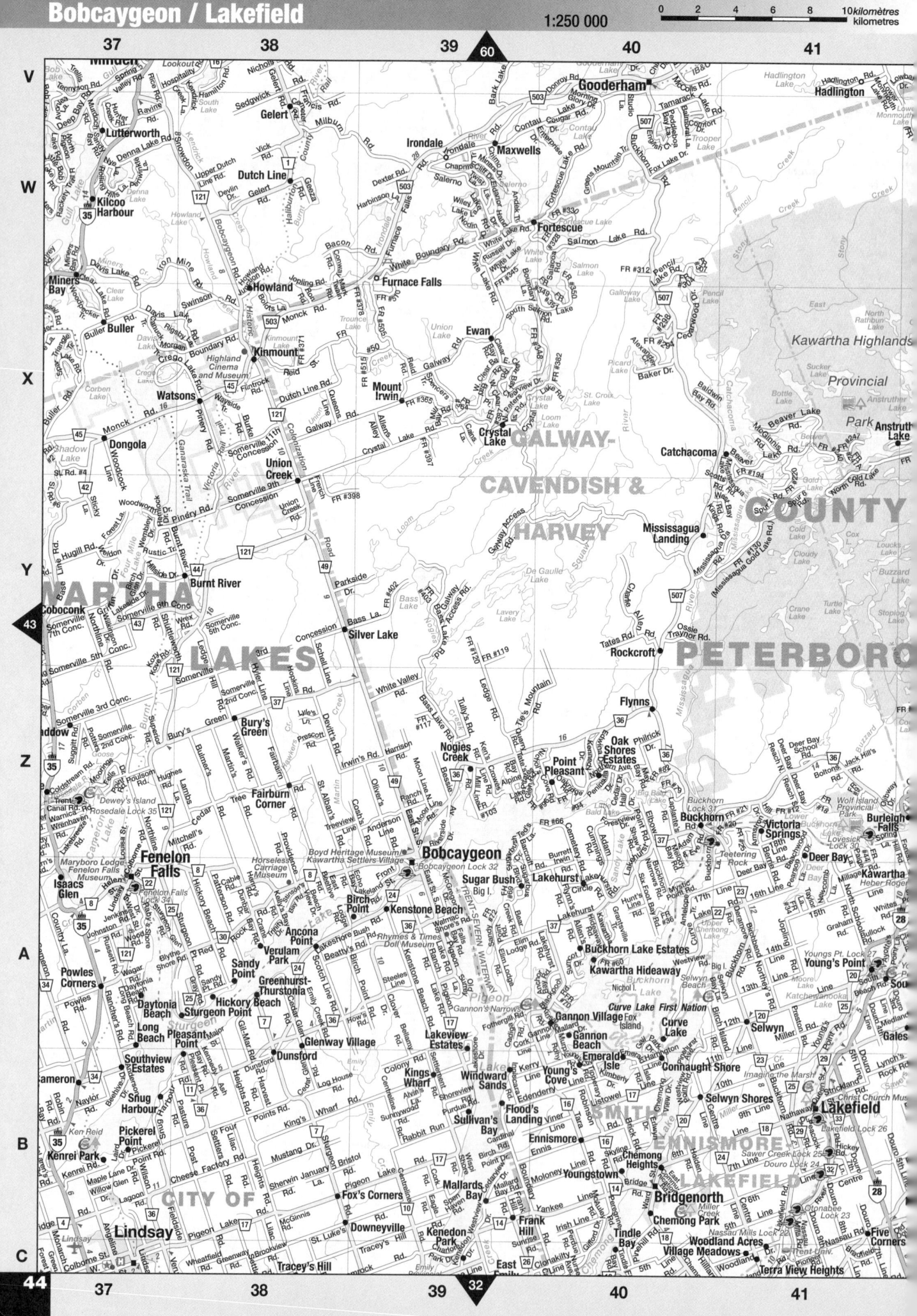

Bobcaygeon / Lakefield

Transverse Mercator Projection

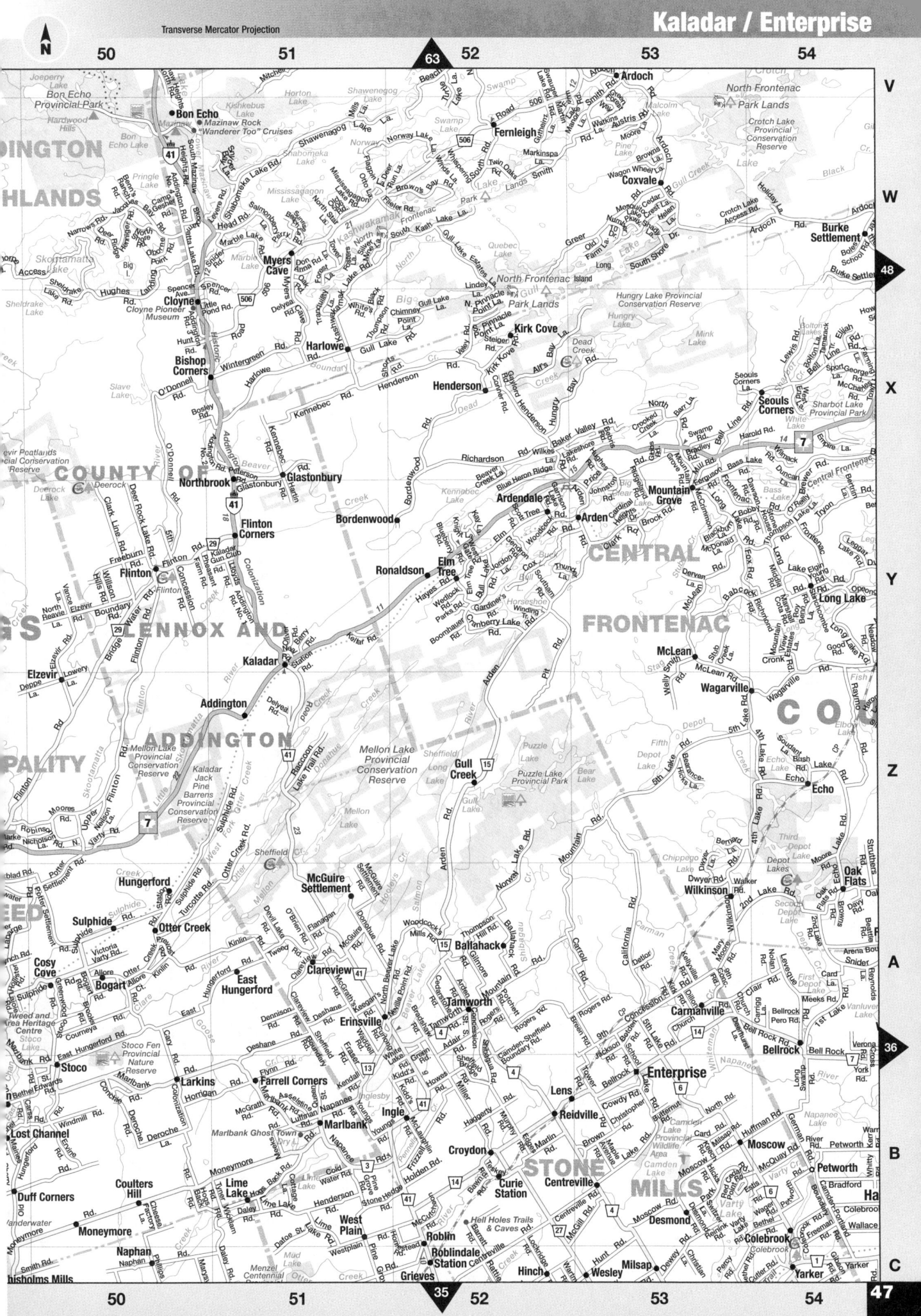

Transverse Mercator Projection

N

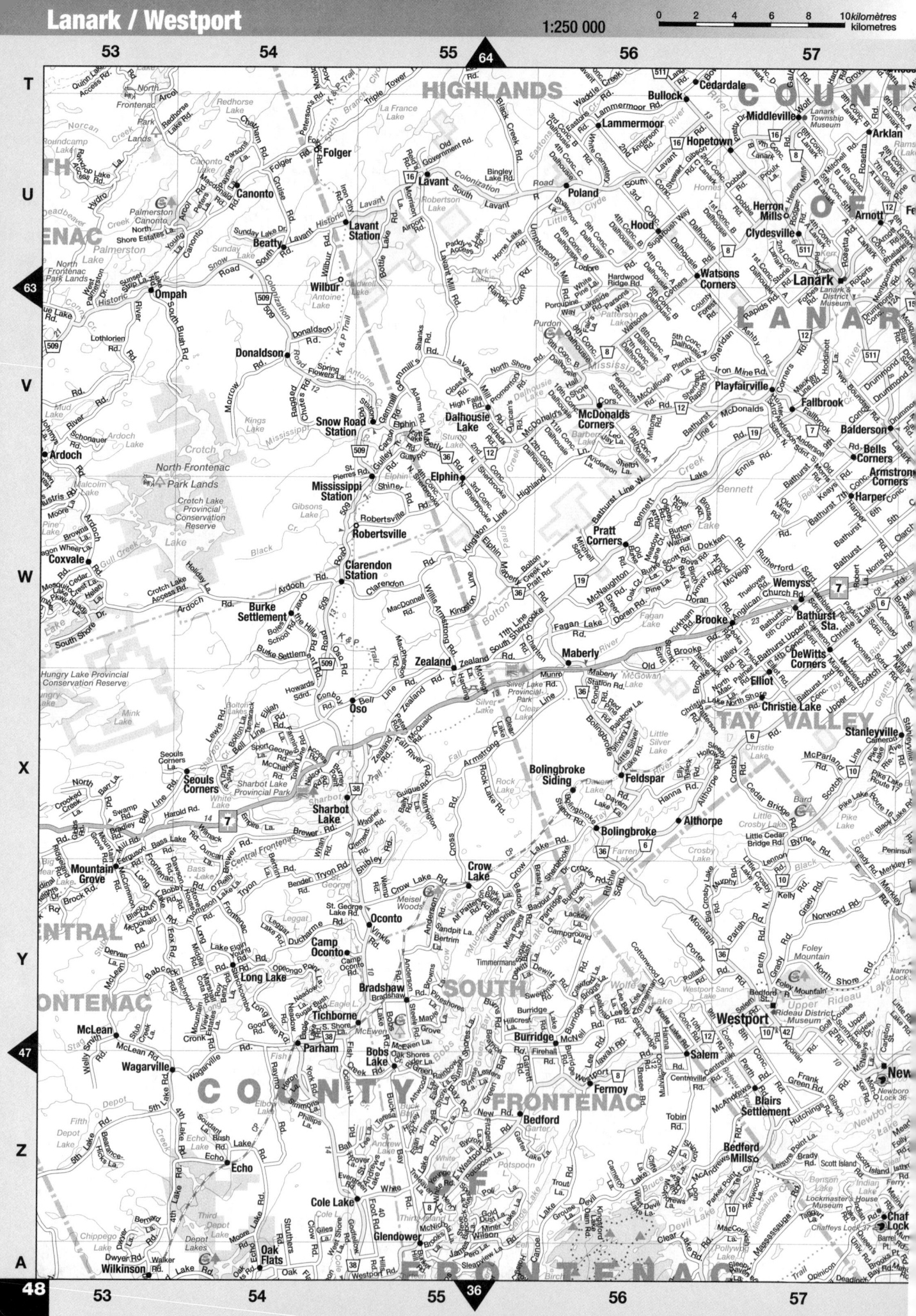

0 2 4 6 8 10 *kilomètres*
kilomètres

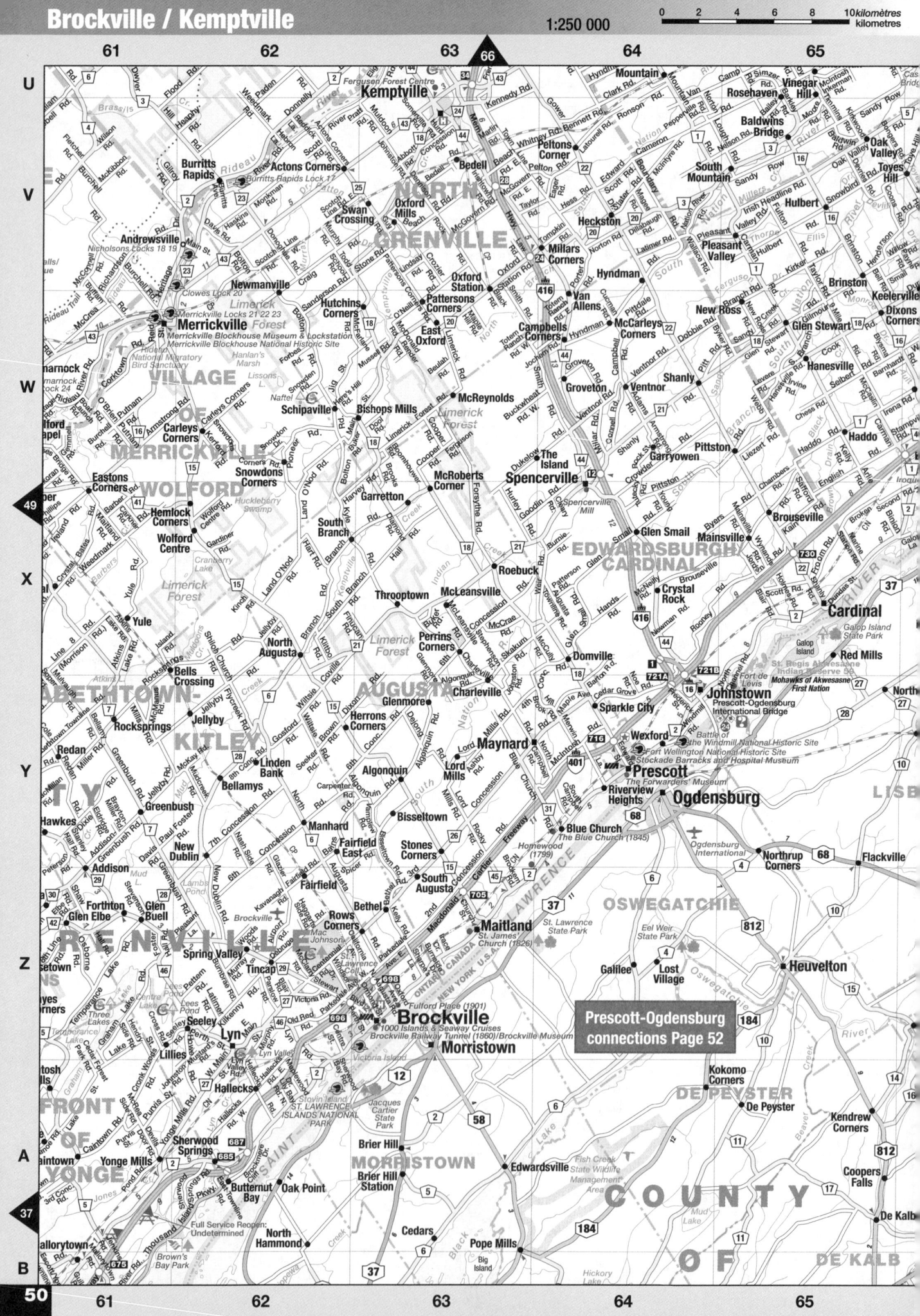

0 2 4 6 8 10 kilomètres
kilometres

Prescott-Ogdensburg
connections Page 52

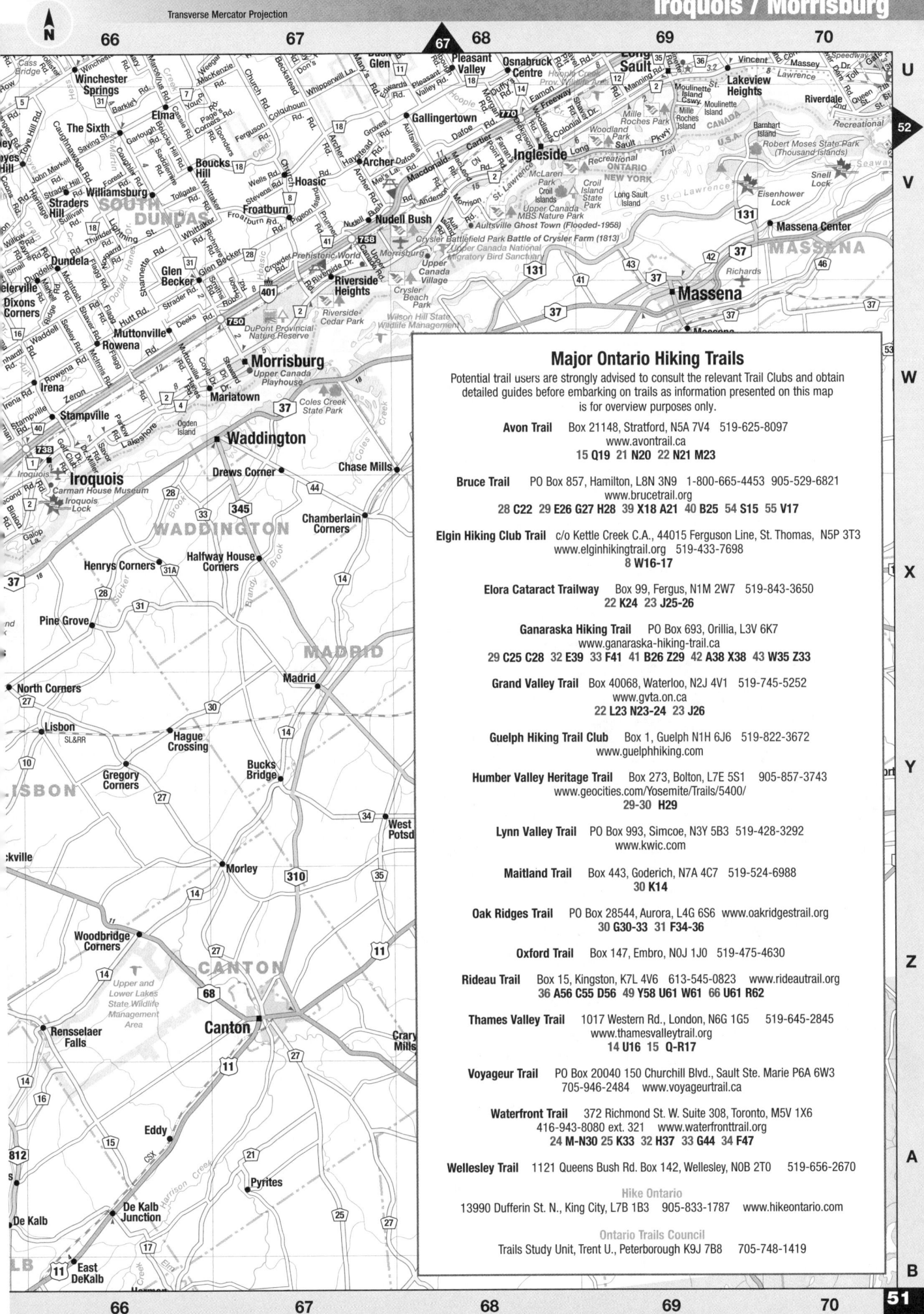

Major Ontario Hiking Trails

Potential trail users are strongly advised to consult the relevant Trail Clubs and obtain detailed guides before embarking on trails as information presented on this map is for overview purposes only.

Avon Trail   Box 21148, Stratford, N5A 7V4   519-625-8097
www.avontrail.ca
15 Q19   21 N20   22 N21 M23

Bruce Trail   PO Box 857, Hamilton, L8N 3N9   1-800-665-4453   905-529-6821
www.brucetrail.org
28 C22   29 E26 G27 H28   39 X18 A21   40 B25   54 S15   55 V17

Elgin Hiking Club Trail   c/o Kettle Creek C.A., 44015 Ferguson Line, St. Thomas,   N5P 3T3
www.elginhikingtrail.org   519-433-7698
8 W16-17

Elora Cataract Trailway   Box 99, Fergus, N1M 2W7   519-843-3650
22 K24   23 J25-26

Ganaraska Hiking Trail   PO Box 693, Orillia, L3V 6K7
www.ganaraska-hiking-trail.ca
29 C25 C28   32 E39   33 F41   41 B26 Z29   42 A38 X38   43 W35 Z33

Grand Valley Trail   Box 40068, Waterloo, N2J 4V1   519-745-5252
www.gvta.on.ca
22 L23 N23-24   23 J26

Guelph Hiking Trail Club   Box 1, Guelph N1H 6J6   519-822-3672
www.guelphhiking.com

Humber Valley Heritage Trail   Box 273, Bolton, L7E 5S1   905-857-3743
www.geocities.com/Yosemite/Trails/5400/
29-30 H29

Lynn Valley Trail   PO Box 993, Simcoe, N3Y 5B3   519-428-3292
www.kwic.com

Maitland Trail   Box 443, Goderich, N7A 4C7   519-524-6988
30 K14

Oak Ridges Trail   PO Box 28544, Aurora, L4G 6S6   www.oakridgestrail.org
30 G30-33   31 F34-36

Oxford Trail   Box 147, Embro, N0J 1J0   519-475-4630

Rideau Trail   Box 15, Kingston, K7L 4V6   613-545-0823   www.rideautrail.org
36 A56 C55 D56   49 Y58 U61 W61   66 U61 R62

Thames Valley Trail   1017 Western Rd., London, N6G 1G5   519-645-2845
www.thamesvalleytrail.org
14 U16   15 Q-R17

Voyageur Trail   PO Box 20040 150 Churchill Blvd., Sault Ste. Marie P6A 6W3
705-946-2484   www.voyageurtrail.ca

Waterfront Trail   372 Richmond St. W. Suite 308, Toronto, M5V 1X6
416-943-8080 ext. 321   www.waterfronttrail.org
24 M-N30   25 K33   32 H37   33 G44   34 F47

Wellesley Trail   1121 Queens Bush Rd. Box 142, Wellesley, N0B 2T0   519-656-2670

Hike Ontario
13990 Dufferin St. N., King City, L7B 1B3   905-833-1787   www.hikeontario.com

Ontario Trails Council
Trails Study Unit, Trent U., Peterborough K9J 7B8   705-748-1419

Where to find
Ontario-Upper New York State
connections

Seaway International Bridge (Toll)
52 V70
Cornwall, ON - Massena, NY
613-932-6601

Ogdensburg-Prescott Bridge (Toll)
50 Y64
Johnstown, ON - Ogdensburg, NY
315-393-4080
www.ogdensport.com/bridge.htm

Thousand Islands Bridge (Toll)
37 C60
Ivy Lea, ON - Alexandria Bay, NY
315-482-2501

Wolfe Island-Cape Vincent Ferry
(Toll)
36 E57
May-mid october
Wolfe Island, ON - Cape Vincent, NY
Can 613-385-2262
US 315-783-0638
www.wolfeisland.com/ferry.php

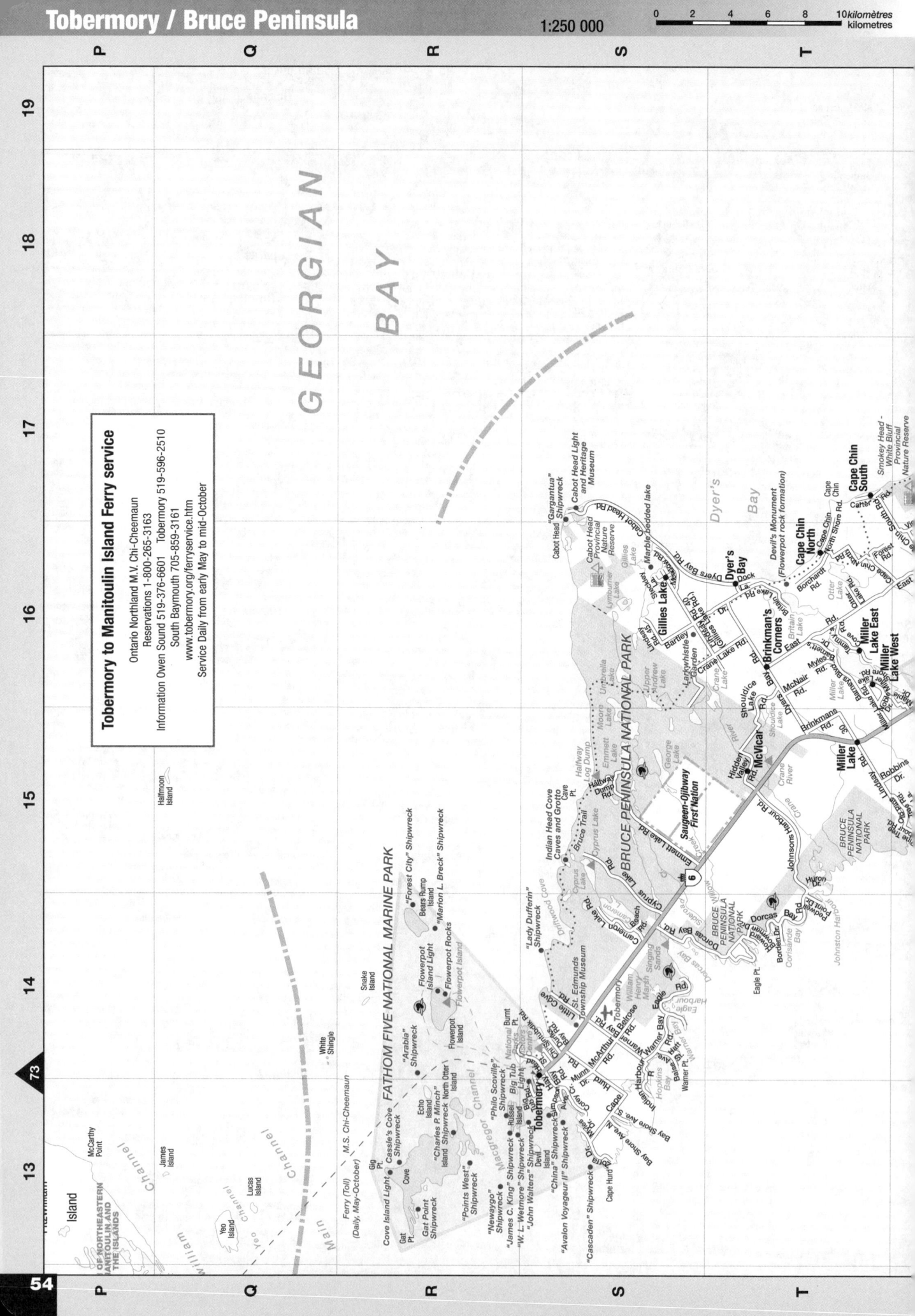

0 2 4 6 8 10 *kilomètres*
kilometres

GEORGIAN

BAY

Tobermory to Manitoulin Island Ferry service

Ontario Northland M.V. Chi-Cheemaun
Reservations 1-800-265-3163
Information Owen Sound 519-376-6601   Tobermory 519-596-2510
South Baymouth 705-859-3161
www.tobermory.org/ferryservice.htm
Service Daily from early May to mid-October

Halfmoon
Island

Cabot Head
"Gargantua"
Shipwreck

Cabot Head Light
and Heritage
Museum

Cabot Head Rd.

Cabot Head
Provincial
Nature
Reserve

Smokey Head -
White Bluff
Provincial
Nature Reserve

Marble Bedded lake

Gillies
Lake

Dyer's
Bay

Dyer's
Bay

Cape Chin
North

Cape Chin
South

Devil's Monument
(Flowerpot rock formation)

Lymburner
Lake

Gillies
Lake

Barley

Brinkman's
Corners

Miller
Lake East

Upper Andrew
Lake

Ladywhistle
Garden

Crane Lake Rd.

Shoulcice
Rd.

McNair
Rd.

Miller
Lake West

Moore
Lake

Umbrella
Lake

Emmett
Lake

Halfway
Log Dump

George
Lake

Hidden
Valley

McVical

Crane
River

Miller
Lake

Saugeen-Ojibway
First Nation

BRUCE PENINSULA NATIONAL PARK

Indian Head Cove
Caves and Grotto

Cave
Pt.

Halfway
Dump
Rd.

Bruce Trail

Cyprus
Lake

Cyprus
Lake

Emmett Lake Rd.

Johnstons
Bay

BRUCE
PENINSULA
NATIONAL
PARK

Harbour Rd.

"Forest City" Shipwreck

Bears Rump
Island

"Marion L. Breck" Shipwreck

Flowerpot
Island Light

Flowerpot Rocks

Flowerpot
Island

Snake
Island

"Lady Dufferin"
Shipwreck

Driftwood Cove

St. Edmunds
Township Museum

Cameron Lake Rd.

Cyprus Lake Rd.

Little Cove
Rd.

William
Henry
Marsh

Singing
Sands

Eagle
Rd.

Dorcas

Bay

Dorcas Bay Rd.

BRUCE
PENINSULA
NATIONAL
PARK

Dunks
Bay

Huron

White
Shingle

"Arabia"
Shipwreck

Cove Island Light

Cassle's Cove

Gig
Pt.

"Newaygo"
Shipwreck

"James C. King" Shipwreck

"W. L. Wetmore" Shipwreck

"John Walters" Shipwreck

"Avalon Voyageur II" Shipwreck

"Cascaden" Shipwreck

Echo
Island

"Charles P. Minch"
Island Shipwreck

North Otter
Island

Macgregor Channel

"Philo Scoville"
Shipwreck

Russel
Island

Big Tub
Light

Devil
Island

Tobermory

Cape Hurd

"China" Shipwreck

Bay Shore Ave. N.

Bay Shore Ave. S.

Cape
Hurd
Rd.

Hopkins
Bay

Indian Cove
Rd.

Warner Bay

Warner Bay
Rd.

Warner
Pt.

Eagle Pt.

Eagle
Harbour

Corisande
Bay

Borden Dr.

Dorcas

Johnston Hall

FATHOM FIVE NATIONAL MARINE PARK

FATHOM FIVE NATIONAL MARINE PARK

McCarthy
Point

James
Island

Lucas
Island

Yeo
Island

Channel

William

Yeo Channel

Main

Channel

Ferry (Toll)
(Daily, May–October)   M.S. Chi-Cheemaun

Island

MAP OF NORTHEASTERN
MANITOULIN AND
THE ISLANDS

"Points West"
Shipwreck

Gat Point
Shipwreck

Cove
Pt.

6

6

McVical

30

Brinkmans
Rd.

Robbins
Dr.

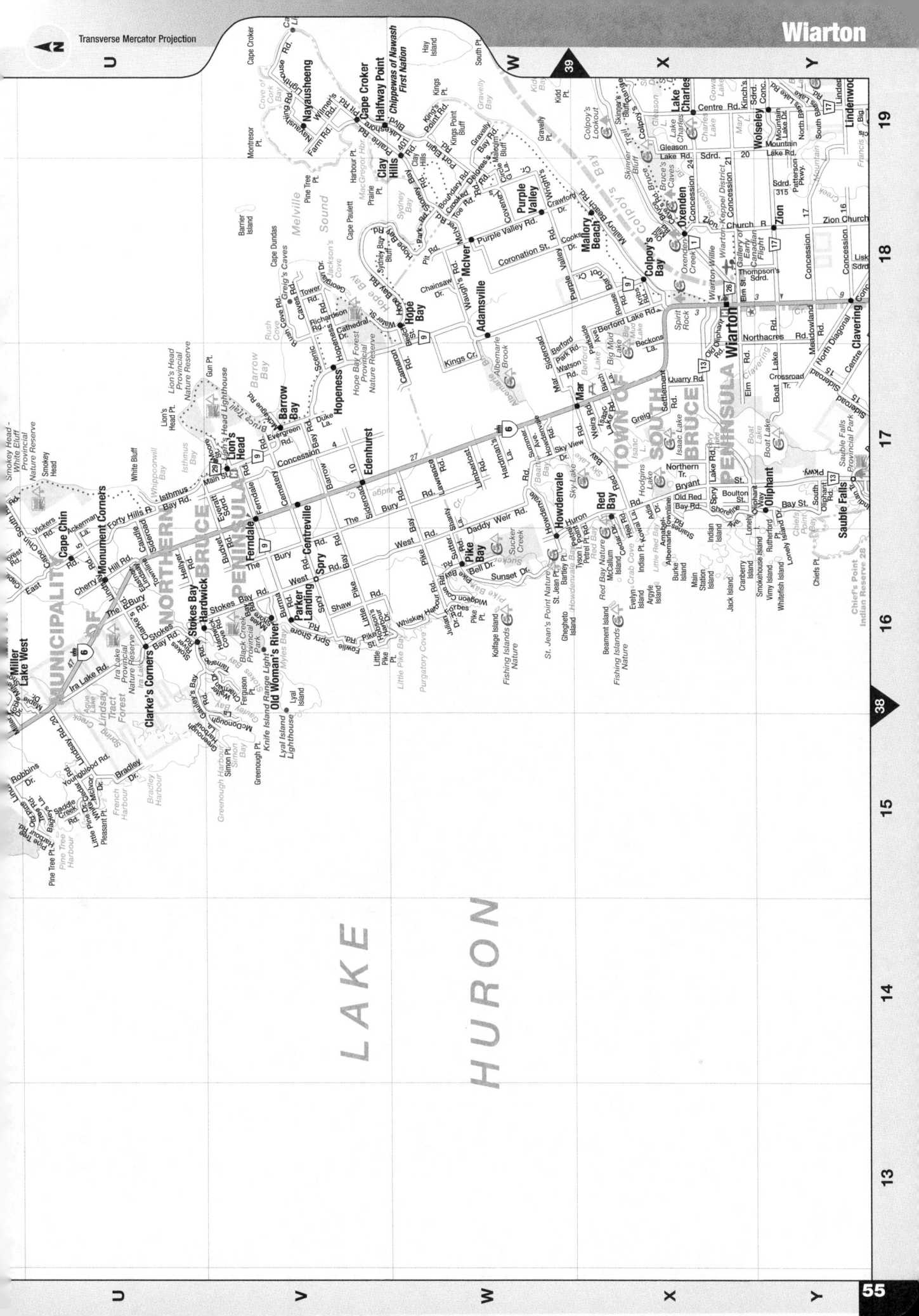

Transverse Mercator Projection

LAKE HURON

0 2 4 6 8 10 *kilomètres*
kilometres

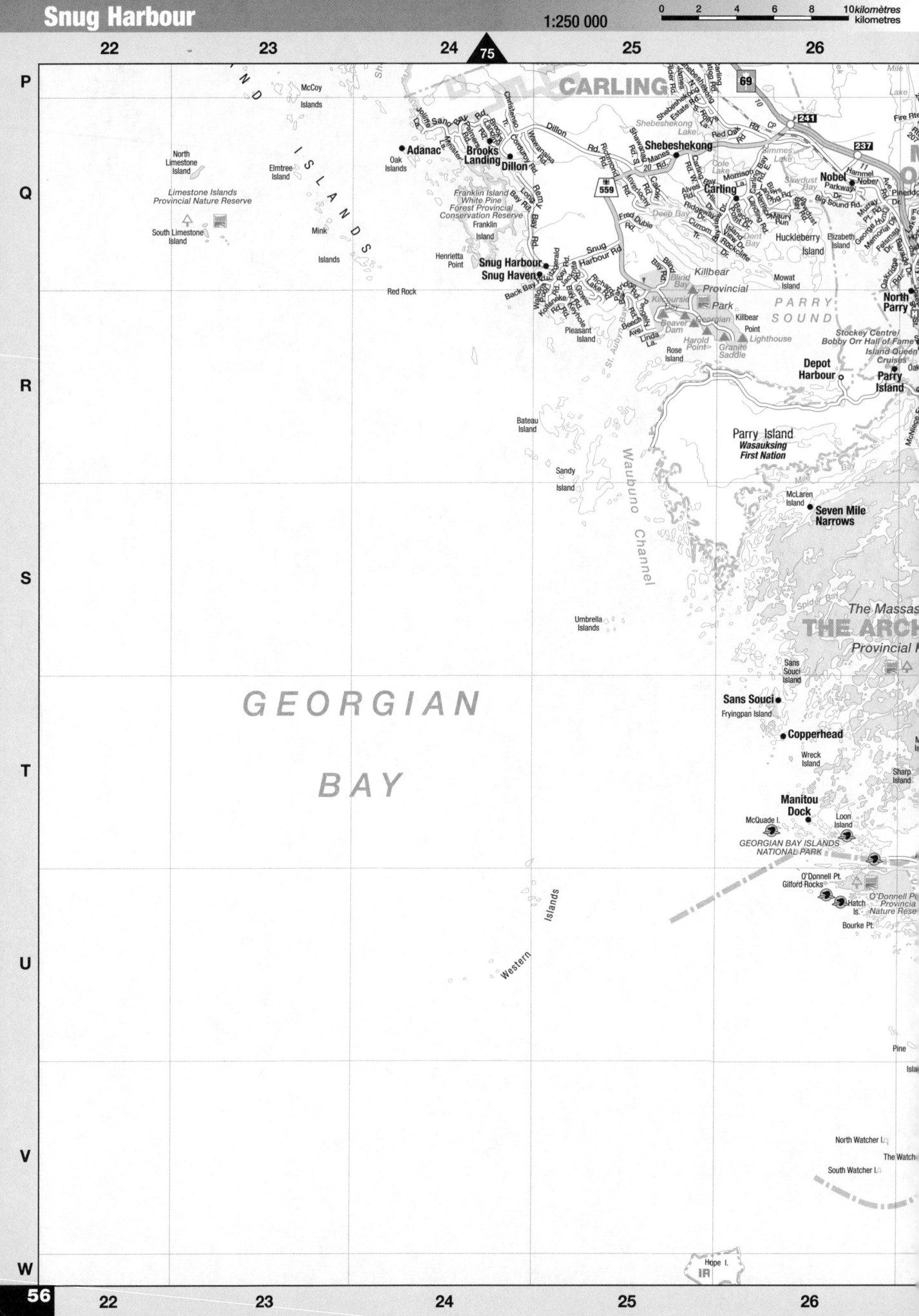

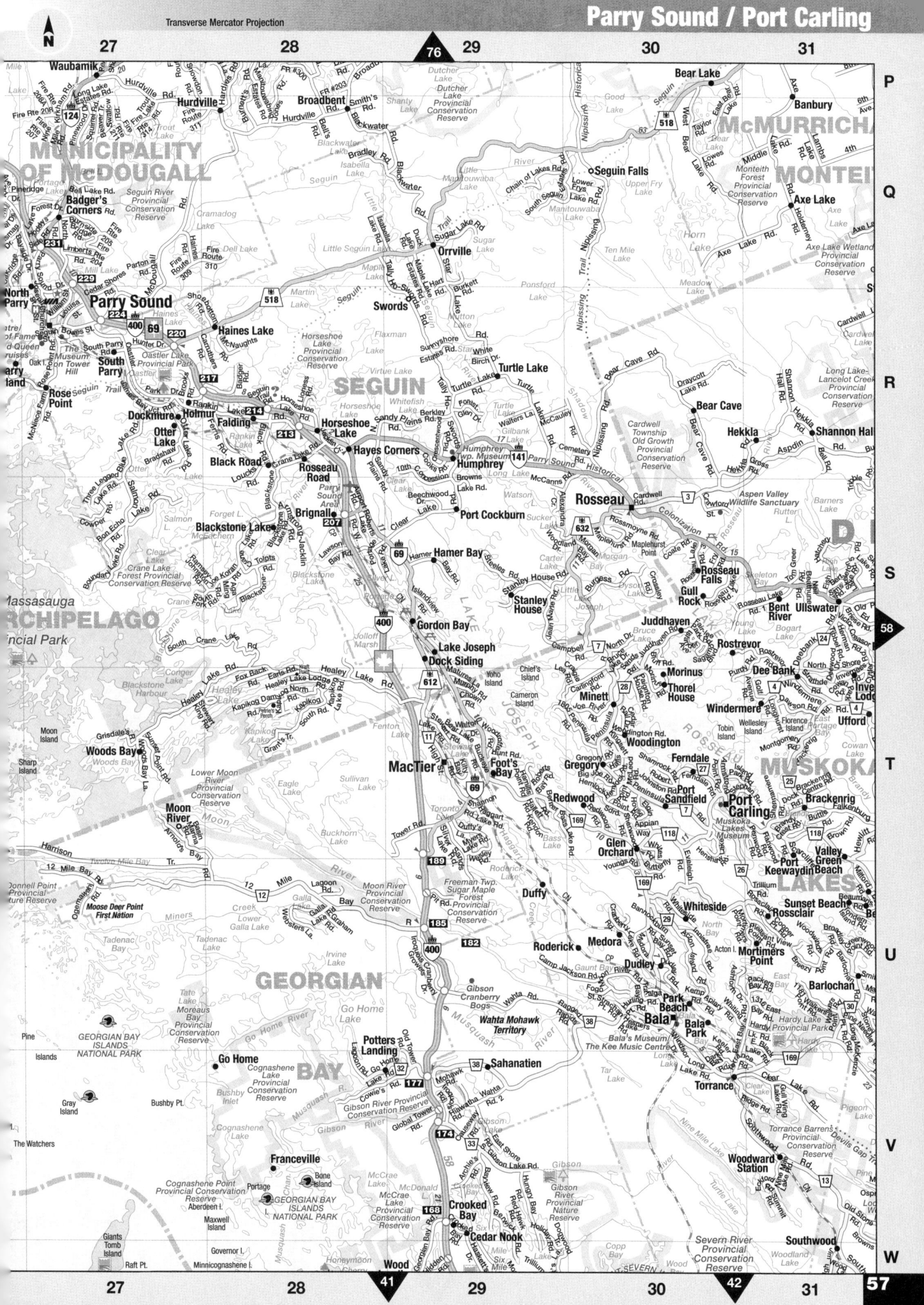

Transverse Mercator Projection

N

27 28 76 29 30 31

P

Q

R

S

58

T

U

V

W

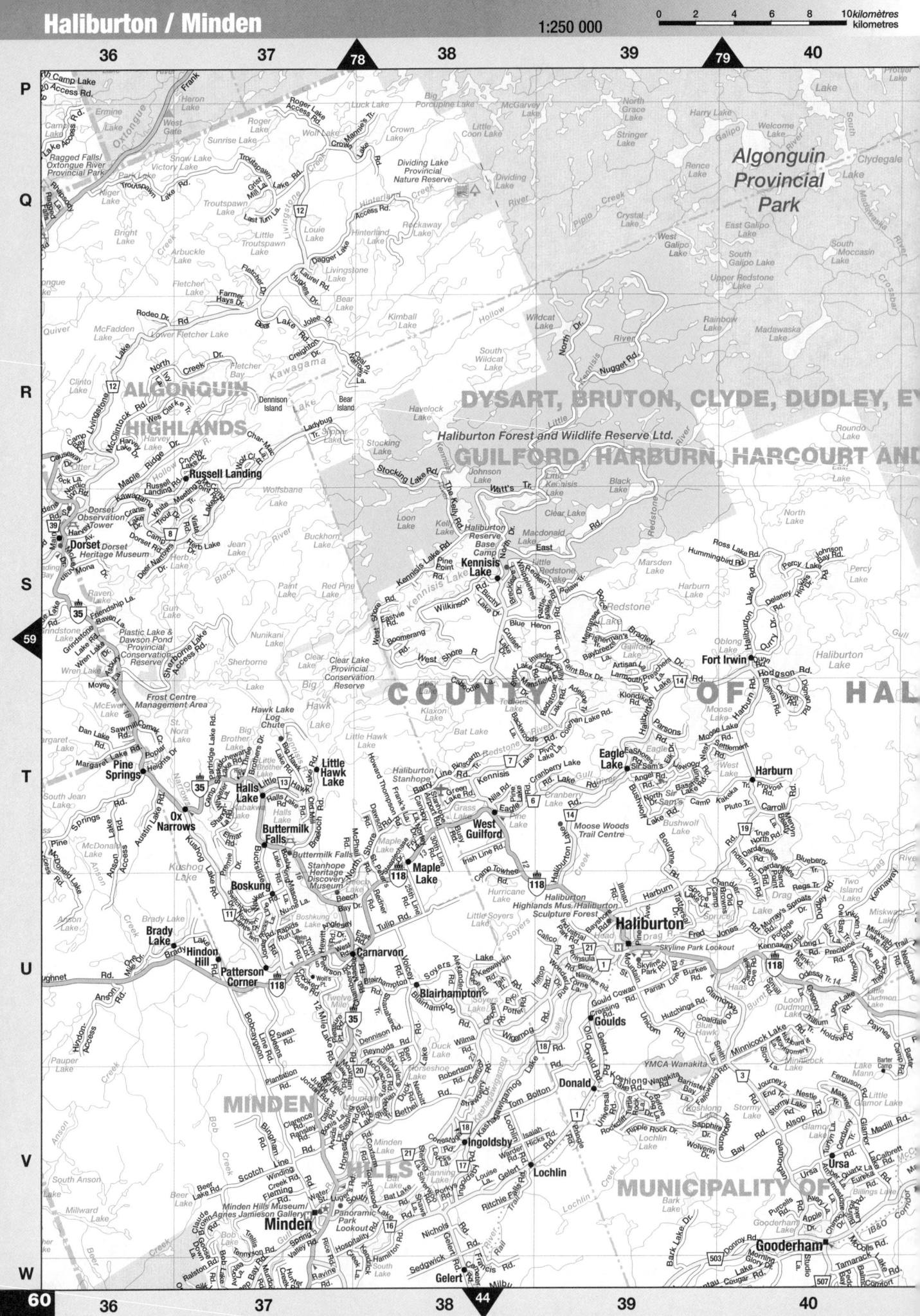

1:250 000

0 2 4 6 8 10 kilomètres
kilometres

44   **45**   **46** 80   **47**   **48**

P

Q

R

S

61

T

U

V

W

62   **44**   **45**   **46** 46   **47**   **48**

MUNICIPALITY OF HASTINGS HIGHLANDS

CARLOW/MAYO

TOWN OF BANCROFT

FARADAY

TUDOR AND CASHEL (Cashel Section)

LIMERICK

McKenzie Lake
Cross Lake
Bell Rapids
Centreview
Purdy
Scotch Bush
Maynooth Station
Maynooth
McAlpine Corners
Greenview
Maple Leaf
New Carlow
Burgess Mine
Scott Settlement
Graphite
Hickey Settlement
McGarry Flats
Hybla
Hughes
Baptiste
Birds Creek
York River
Maxwell
Musclow
Vardy
Monteagle Valley
Beechmount
Bancroft
Bronson
Bronson Station
Detlor
Egan Creek
L'Amable
Monck Road
Bow Lake
Paudash
Umfraville
Turriff
Nobbs Siding
Faraday
Brinklow
Ormsby

Kaszuby
Halfway
Rockingham
Barrymere
Combermere
Jewellville
Mayhews Landing
Palmer Rapids
Craigmont
Latchford Bridge
Schutt
Havergal
Boulter
Fort Stewart
Ireland
Rowland
McArthur Mills
Hermon
Hartsmere
Childs Mines
Bessemer
Bowen Corner
Caverlys Landing
Weslemkoon

Letterkenny
Rosenthal
Wingle

Lake St. Peter Provincial Park
Egan Chutes Provincial Park
Little Mississippi River Provincial Conservation Reserve
Conroys Marsh Provincial Conservation Reserve

Transverse Mercator Projection

N

49   50   81   51   52   53

P

Q

R

S   64

T

U   48

V

W

BRUDENELL,

LYNDOCH

AND RAGLAN

OF

BONNECHERE

VALLEY

GREATER

COUNTY OF

LENNOX

AND

ADDINGTON

NORTH

FRONTENAC

Brudenell
Harriets Corners
Lost Nation
Letterkenny
Rosenthal
Guiney
Quadeville
Wingle
Bruceton
Hardwood Lake
Massanoga
McCrae
Ferguson Corners
Denbigh
Rose Hill
Walkers Corners
Vennachar Junction
Vennachar
Buckshot
Glenfield
Matawatchan
Wilson
Bon Echo
Beech Corners
Plevna
Ardoch

Foymount
Highest settlement in Southern Ontario (502m)
Vanbrugh
Woermke
Wolfe

Clontarf
Newfoundout
Esmonde

Perrault
Perrault
Scotch Bush
Constant Creek
Balaclava
Dacre
Lower Dacre

Martins Corner
Moore
Mount St. P

Khartum
Balvenie
Griffith
Camel Chute
Slate Falls
Glenfield

Black Donald

Centennial Lake Provincial Park

Centennial Lake

Bon Echo Provincial Park

Lower Madawaska River Provincial Park

Matawatchan Provincial Park

North Frontenac Park Lands

Mosque Lake

0 2 4 6 8 10 kilomètres
kilometres

N **52** **53** **54** **82** **55** **56**

81

Mink Lake
Kellys Corner
Grist Mill Rd.
Grist Mill Rd.
Bromley
Haley Station
Garden of Eden
Station
Sand Bay
Ile Elliott
Baie Sand

P

Fourth Chute
Douglas
ADMASTON
Northcote
Rosebank
Payne
Castleford
HORTON
Castleford
Fergusons Beach
Castleford Station
Sand Po
Hyndford
Balsam Hill
BROMLEY
Cotieville
Renfrew
Mayhew
Lochwinnoch
Dewars
Martins Corner
Admaston
McDougall
Oakgrove
Renfrew Junction
Thompson Hill
Goshen
Glasgow Station
McI
Moores Lake
Perrault
Scotch Bush
Fremo Corners
Ferguslea
Lundys Corners
Stewartville
ERE
VALLEY

Q

Constant Creek
Balaclava
Shamrock
Belangers Corners
Hurds Lake
Burnstown
White Lake
Waba
Dacre
Lower Dacre
Mount St. Patrick
Ashdad
Springtown
Spruce Hedge
BRAE

R

63

Calabogie
Barryvale
Centennial Lake Provincial Park
GREATER MADAWASKA
Calabogie Peaks
White Lake

S

Big Limestone Lake
Black Donald
Barrett Chute
Wabalac
Lanark
California
Centennial Lake Provincial Park
White
Taltock

T

Flower Station
Marble Bluff
LANARK
Joes Lake
Clyde Forks
French Line
Brightside
HIGHLANDS
Bullock
Cedar
Lammermoor

NORTH
Lavant
Poland
Hood
Hopetow

U

Canonto
Beatty
Lavant Station
FRONTENAC
Ompah
Wilbur
Watson Corne

V

64 **52** **53** **54** **48** **55** **56**

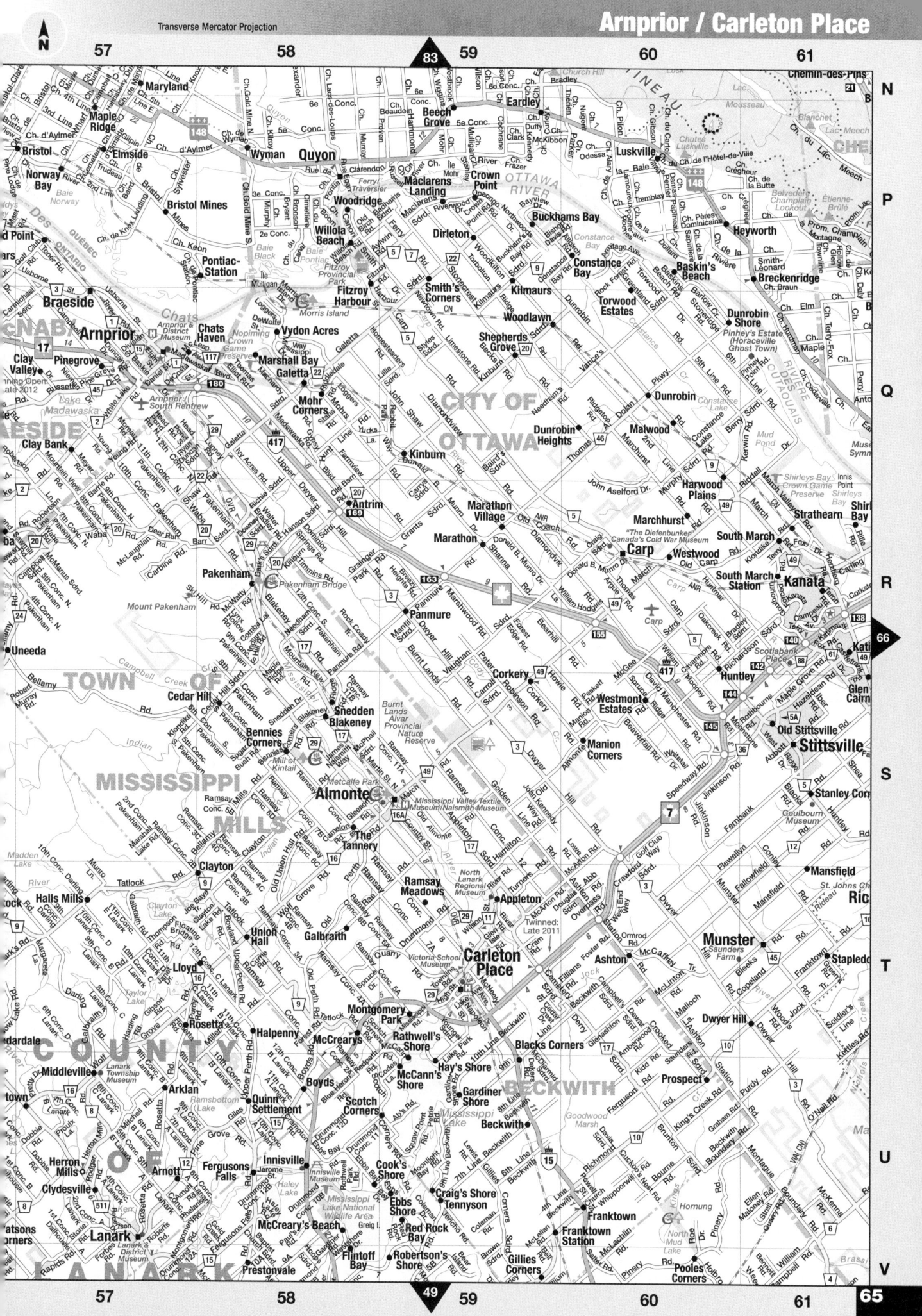

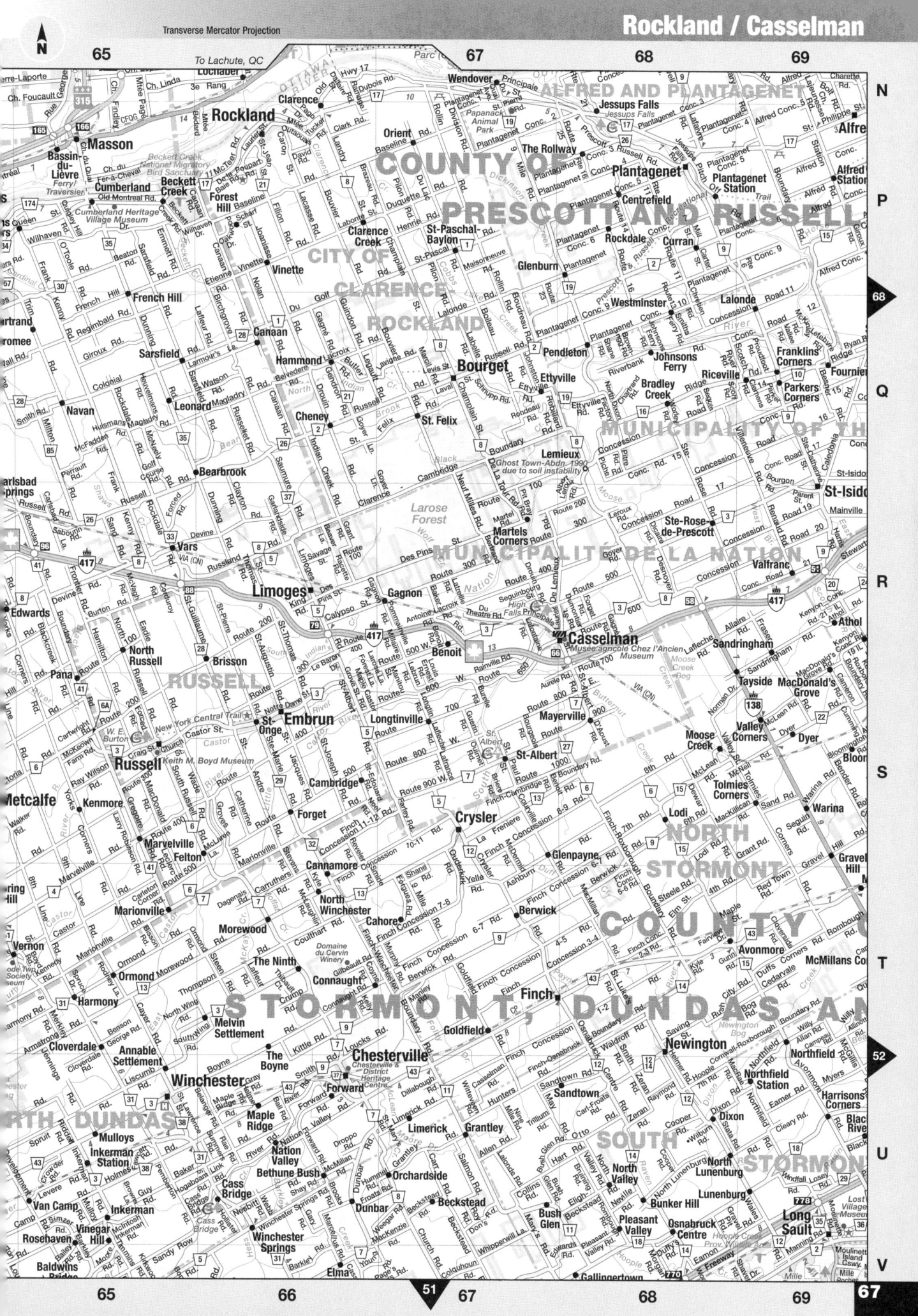

0 2 4 6 8 10 *kilomètres* / kilometres

98 99 1 87 2 3

G

DRUMMOND ISLAND

Glen Cove — Glen Point

ONTARIO CANADA / MICHIGAN U.S.A.

H Thompson Point — Monk Point — Pitman Point

Robb's Lake — Tolsma Lake — Ross Point

False Detour Channel

Herschell Island — Little Kitchener Island — Kitchener Island

Cockburn Island First Nation

14th Conc. — 12th Concession — 20th Sdrd. — 15th Sdrd. — 7th-8th Concession — McCaigs Hill — Scotch Block — 15th Sideroad — Lakeshore Rd. — Water St. — 10th Sideroad — 1st St. — L St. — W St.

Tolsmaville (Cockburn Island)

Devil's Horn — Robinson Bay — Big Bay

COCKBURN ISLAND / **COCKBURN ISLAND**

Wagoose Lake — Wagoose Bay — Station Point — Pulpwood Point — Hindman Bay — Sand Lake — Sand Creek — Sand Bay — Boom Point

Ricketts Harbour — Cinder Point — Mississagi Strait

There is no ferry service to Cockburn Island. Visitors must arrange their own transport.

Gravy Lake — Maggies Sdrd — Wasnage Rd. — Water St. — Meldrum Bay

Totten Lake — West Bass Lake — Young Lake — Wickett Lake — Carter Lake — Mississagi Rd. — Lighthouse Rd. — Cemetery Rd. — Joyce Rd. — Wlv/esea Rd.

Meldrum Bay — Net Shed Museum — Linda Lake — Pothole Lake — Burnett Lake — Maple Lake — Vidal Lake — Creasor Bight — Essins Rd. 28

Crescent Island — TOWN OF NORTHEAS MANITOULIN AND THE IS — Boat Harbour — Batture Island — West Point — Vidal Island — Arthur Point — Harold Point

J Mississagi Lighthouse Heritage Park & Museum — Falls — Falls Lake Rd. — Lily Lake Rd. — Lily Lake — Loon Lake — Kerr Lake — Dump Rd. — 540 — Hog Lake

Dawson — Beaver Meadow Lakes — Dormy Grant Rd. — The Queen Elizabeth / The Queen Mother M'Nidoo M'Nissing Provincial Park

K Quarry Bay — Twin Lakes — Steevens Island — Greene Island — Quarry Point — TOWN OF NORTHEASTERN MANITOULIN AND THE ISLANDS

West Belanger Bay — East Belanger Bay — Girouard Point — Rickley Point — Burnt Island Harbour — **Burn Islan**

ONTARIO MICHIGAN CANADA U.S.A.

Western Duck Island — Blake Point

TOWN OF NORTHEA MANITOULIN AND THE

98 99 1 2 L

Middle Duck Island — Bluff Point — Dese

Horseshoe Bay — Duck Island

M

ONTARIO MICHIGAN

N

P

Ontario
Distance Chart

How to use:
The distance is indicated in kilometres where the two place names intersect.

Example

	Parry Sound			
Owen Sound	220			
Ottawa	544	433		
North Bay	365	370	155	
Niagara Falls	455	530	260	335

Ontario Distance Chart (distances in kilometres):

	Windsor	Wawa	Toronto	Tobermory	Timmins	Thunder Bay	Sudbury	Stratford	Sault Ste. Marie	Sarnia	St. Thomas	St. Catharines	Peterborough	Pembroke	Parry Sound	Owen Sound	Ottawa	North Bay	Niagara Falls	London	Kitchener-Waterloo	Kirkland Lake	Kingston	Kenora	Kapuskasing	Huntsville	Hamilton	Fort Frances	Dryden	Cornwall	Brockville	Belleville
Wawa	1253																															
Toronto	911	370																														
Tobermory	300	1012	474																													
Timmins	785	680	333	1020																												
Thunder Bay	769	1480	1375	470	1715																											
Sudbury	997	290	495	390	530	724																										
Stratford	495	1485	790	270	150	1020	250																									
Sault Ste. Marie	796	305	690	441	796	690	225	1025																								
Sarnia	911	144	610	1600	900	340	280	1130	160																							
St. Thomas	111	860	89	560	1550	850	340	204	1080	188																						
St. Catharines	199	275	780	155	480	1470	775	350	109	1004	364																					
Peterborough	240	325	400	700	265	400	1390	687	385	135	920	490																				
Pembroke	250	490	575	650	650	520	344	1320	585	575	385	870	738																			
Parry Sound	330	240	321	399	450	465	330	165	1149	455	330	224	686	560																		
Owen Sound	220	466	277	240	240	255	685	158	384	1375	680	111	189	911	390																	
Ottawa	544	433	150	270	510	589	671	795	535	490	1466	730	650	400	1015	762																
North Bay	365	370	155	220	320	435	515	565	430	480	344	654	679																			
Niagara Falls	455	530	260	335	511	260	20	210	290	800	175	498	1490	790	370	130	1020	382														
London	190	494	569	210	375	555	300	180	30	99	840	60	539	1524	830	310	184	1059	190													
Kitchener-Waterloo	100	130	405	490	150	290	470	220	110	120	190	750	46	450	1441	742	160	105	972	288												
Kirkland Lake	649	740	700	250	610	614	400	464	566	680	760	811	580	696	315	880	142	719	590	475	928											
Kingston	705	350	430	390	460	175	430	415	245	180	370	450	529	876	396	582	1566	825	542	257	1099	620										
Kenora	2040	1355	1914	2004	1966	1580	1945	1850	1630	1800	1864	1946	2024	2075	1166	1960	1470	479	1250	1960	1855	950	2192									
Kapuskasing	1085	957	270	900	990	950	860	840	620	715	815	935	1011	1060	605	950	460	602	186	950	840	420	1182									
Huntsville	624	1710	350	369	280	365	333	129	350	240	88	244	195	308	390	443	544	325	250	1230	490	350	214	772	555							
Hamilton	269	888	1905	333	640	60	124	70	395	470	190	280	450	202	50	145	220	740	105	440	1432	730	300	70	960	312						
Fort Frances	1766	1566	940	214	1900	1214	1777	1860	1820	1443	1799	1711	1490	1655	1725	1805	1888	1663	1820	1711	1490	333	1105	1820	1715	811	2047					
Dryden	190	1770	945	140	1900	1220	1780	1867	1827	1444	1800	1711	1488	1663	1730	1811	1888	1940	1030	1820	1720	341	1111	1820	1715	811	2050					
Cornwall	1912	1904	499	450	960	2044	180	711	520	605	558	466	100	602	536	250	340	540	626	700	899	570	590	1567	830	715	435	1121	790			
Brockville	96	1862	1860	404	404	920	2000	80	666	424	510	464	420	111	511	465	206	255	444	530	605	850	470	530	1528	784	624	340	1075	695		
Belleville	154	250	1829	1828	254	280	899	1971	75	644	280	360	315	399	230	360	340	230	103	300	378	454	806	320	505	1496	763	471	189	1032	544	
Barrie	260	404	500	1624	1621	145	124	749	1762	330	499	180	260	220	251	430	120	134	350	160	198	264	316	595	200	300	1286	590	232	90	820	432

3

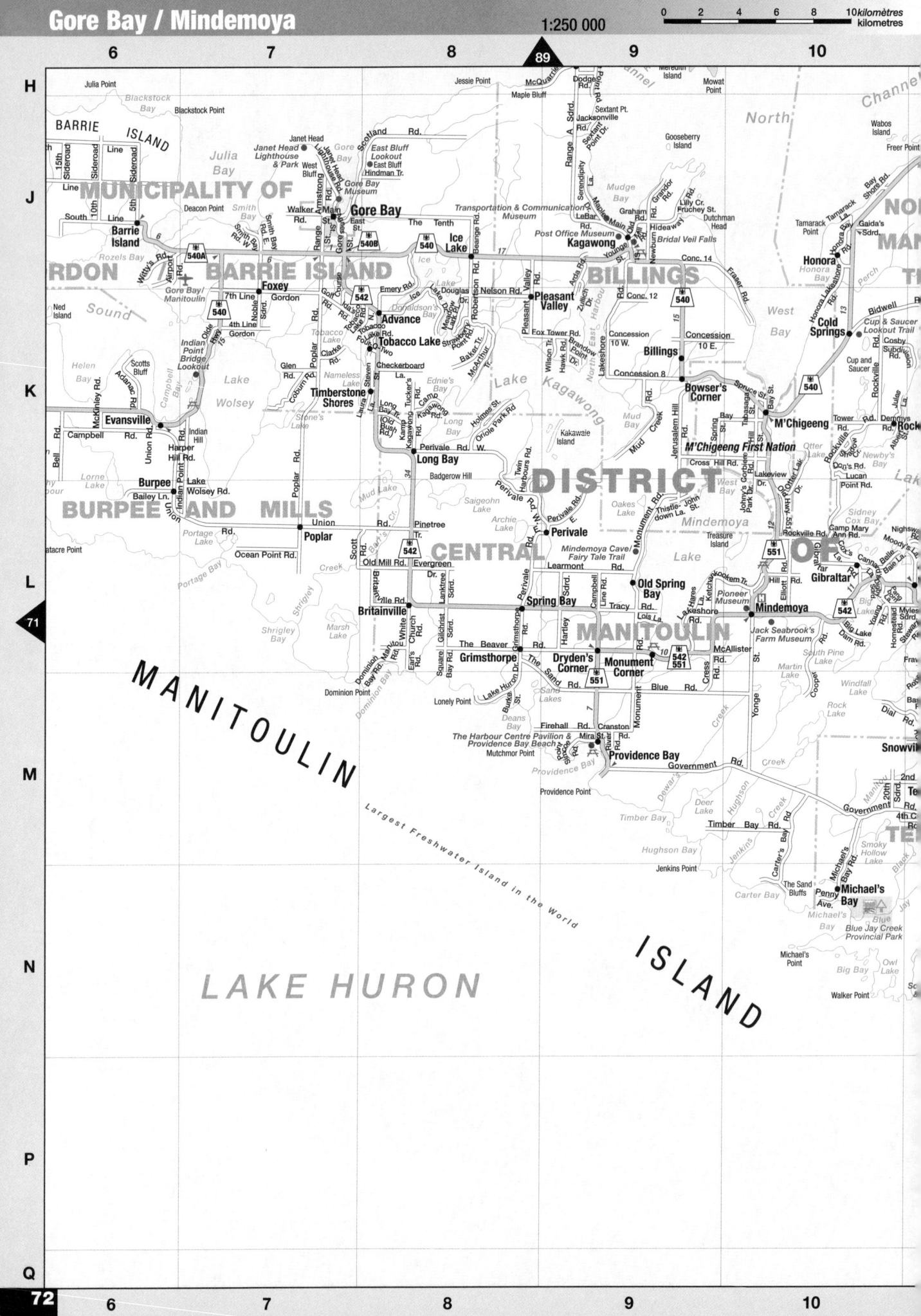

0 2 4 6 8 10 kilomètres
kilometres

89

6 7 8 9 10

H

Julia Point
Blackstock Bay
Blackstock Point
North Channel
Meredith Island
Mowat Point
Wabos Point
Freer Point
Jessie Point
McQuarrie
Maple Bluff
Dodge Rd.
Sextant Pt.
Sextant Point Dr.
Gooseberry Island

BARRIE ISLAND LINE
15th Sideroad
10th Sideroad
5th Sideroad
Line
Julia Bay
Janet Head
Janet Head Lighthouse & Park
West Bluff
Gore Bay
Scotland Rd.
East Bluff Lookout
East Bluff Hindman Tr.
Range A Sdrd.
Serendipity
Jacksonville
Mudge Bay
LeBar

J

MUNICIPALITY OF
South 10th Line
Deacon Point
Smith Bay
Walker Rd.
Main
Gore Bay Museum
Gore Bay
East St.
The Tenth
Transportation & Communication Museum
Post Office Museum
Kagawong
Meredith Main Rd.
Graham
Lilly Cr. Fruchey St.
Bridal Veil Falls
Dutchman Head
Hideaway
Newbury
Tamarack Point
Honora
Honora Bay
Tamarack
NO
MAN
T

Barrie Island
Rozels Bay
540A
Gore Bay / Manitoulin Airport
Foxey
540
7th Line
Gordon
4th Line
Gordon
542
Advance
Emery Rd.
Ice Lake Dr.
Douglas Lake Rd.
Nelson Rd.
Pleasant Valley
Robertson Rd.
Conc. 14
540
Conc. 12
West Bay
Cold Springs
Cup & Saucer Lookout Trail
Bidwell
Cosby Subdiv.
Rockville
Cup and Saucer
BARRIE ISLAND
540B
Ice Lake
540
Ned Island
Sound
Witty's Rd.
Smith Bay Rd. W.
Range
Gore St.

K

Helen Bay
Scotts Hill
Indian Point Bridge Lookout
Lake Wolsey
Timberstone Shores
Glen Rd.
Nameless Lake
Checkerboard La.
Ednie's Bay
Holmes St.
Lake Kagawong
Kakawaie Island
Concession 10 W.
Concession 10 E.
Billings
Concession 8
Bowser's Corner
540
M'Chigeeng
Tower Rd.
Rock
Demmys

McKinley Rd.
Evansville
Indian Hill
Harper Hill Rd.
Burpee
Bailey Ln.
Lake Wolsey Rd.
Union
Long Bay
Badgerow Hill
Saigeohn Lake
Perivale Rd. W.
Perivale
Oakes Lake
DISTRICT
Mud Bay
Mud Creek
Jerusalem Hill
M'Chigeeng First Nation
Cross Hill Rd.
Spring St.
Lakeview
Lucan Point Rd.

BURPEE AND MILLS
Lorne Lake
Portage Lake
Poplar
Union Rd.
Pinetree
542
Evergreen Dr.
Old Mill Rd.
CENTRAL
Archie Lake
Perivale
Mindemoya Cave / Fairy Tale Trail
Learmont
OF
551
Gibraltar
542
Camp Mary Ann Rd.
Moody's La.
Sidney Cox Bay

L

71

Portage Bay
Shrigley Lake
Marsh Lake
Britainville
Britainville Rd.
Lanktree Sdrd.
Church Rd.
Gilchrist Rd.
The Beaver
Grimsthorpe
Spring Bay
Hartley
MANITOULIN
Campbell Line Rd.
Tracy
Old Spring Bay
Pioneer Museum
Mindemoya
Lakeshore Rd.
542
551
Big Lake
Martin Lake
Windfall Lake
Dryden's Corner
551
Monument Corner
McAllister
Jack Seabrook's Farm Museum
South Pine Lake
Rock Lake
Dial Rd.
Snowvil

Dominion Point
Lonely Point
Lake Huron Rd.
Deans Bay
Firehall Rd.
Cranston Rd.
Mira St.
Providence Bay
Government Rd.
Dewar's Rd.
Hughson Rd.
Deer Lake
Timber Bay Rd.
Government Rd.
2nd Te
4th C

M

The Harbour Centre Pavilion & Providence Bay Beach
Mutchmor Point
Providence Point
Timber Bay
Hughson Bay
Jenkins Rd.
Carter Bay Rd.
Smoky Hollow Lake
The Sand Bluffs
Penny Ave.
Michael's Bay
Blue Jay Creek Provincial Park

Largest Freshwater Island in the World

MANITOULIN

N

LAKE HURON

ISLAND

Jenkins Point
Carter Bay
Michael's Bay
Michael's Point
Big Bay
Owl Lake
Walker Point

P

Q

0 2 4 6 8 10 *kilomètres*
kilometres

19   20   21   22   23

KILLARNEY

French River Provincial Park

Pickerel River

Visitors Centre

Wanikewin

Key Junction

Pickerel
Henvey Inlet First Nation

Nisbet Lake

Mowat Township Hemlock Forest Provincial Conservation Reserve

69

King's Island

Main Outlet French River

French River

French River Island

Fox Island

Pickerel River

Sand Bay

Jack Pine
Red Maple
White Birch
White Pine
Hemlock
White Spruce
Poplar

Grundy Lake Provincial Park

North Pickerel Access Rd.

Cantin Point

Northeast Passage

Whitebg Bay

Cranberry

Pakesley

522

Mowat

Bustard Islands

Tanvat I.

Dead Island

Key Harbour

Key Harbour

Key River

Key River

Ludgate

Ludgate Tr.

Key River

Henvey Inlet First Nation

Churchill Islands

Henvey Inlet First Nation

Henvey Inlet

Bekanon

Mowat

Mowat Township

Champlain Island

Still River

Old Still River Rd.

Still

Sandy Bay

Henvey

Britt Station

North Georgian Bay Islands and Shoreline Provincial Conservation Reserve

526

Riverside Dr.
Eastside Dr.
Britt
Tramway Ave.
Byng Inlet

Magnetawan River Rd.

645

529

Magnetawan First Nation

North Channel

Byng Inlet

South Channel

Giroux River

Giroux Lake

Wallbr

69

529

Foster Island

Naiscoot River

Shawanaga First Nation

Naiscoot

Wood

Harris La

North Georgian Bay Islands and Shoreline Provincial Conservation Reserve

Baby's Rd.

Manbert

529

Charles Inlet

Georgian Inlet

Bayfield Inlet

529A

Nares Inlet Rd.

Rattlebear Dr.

Granite

Sturgeon

Niv

Pointe au Baril Forests and Wetlands Provincial Conservation Reserve

Point au Baril Chann

GEORGIAN BAY

Bayfield

Pointe au Baril
Pointe au Baril Light

Lookout Island

Champlain Monument Island

Tonches L.

Th

THIRTY THOUSAND

Ojibway Island

Shawanaga Island

Shawanaga Island White Pine Forest Provincial Conservation Reserve

Hertzberg Island

McCoy Islands

19   20   21   22   23

H J K L M N P Q

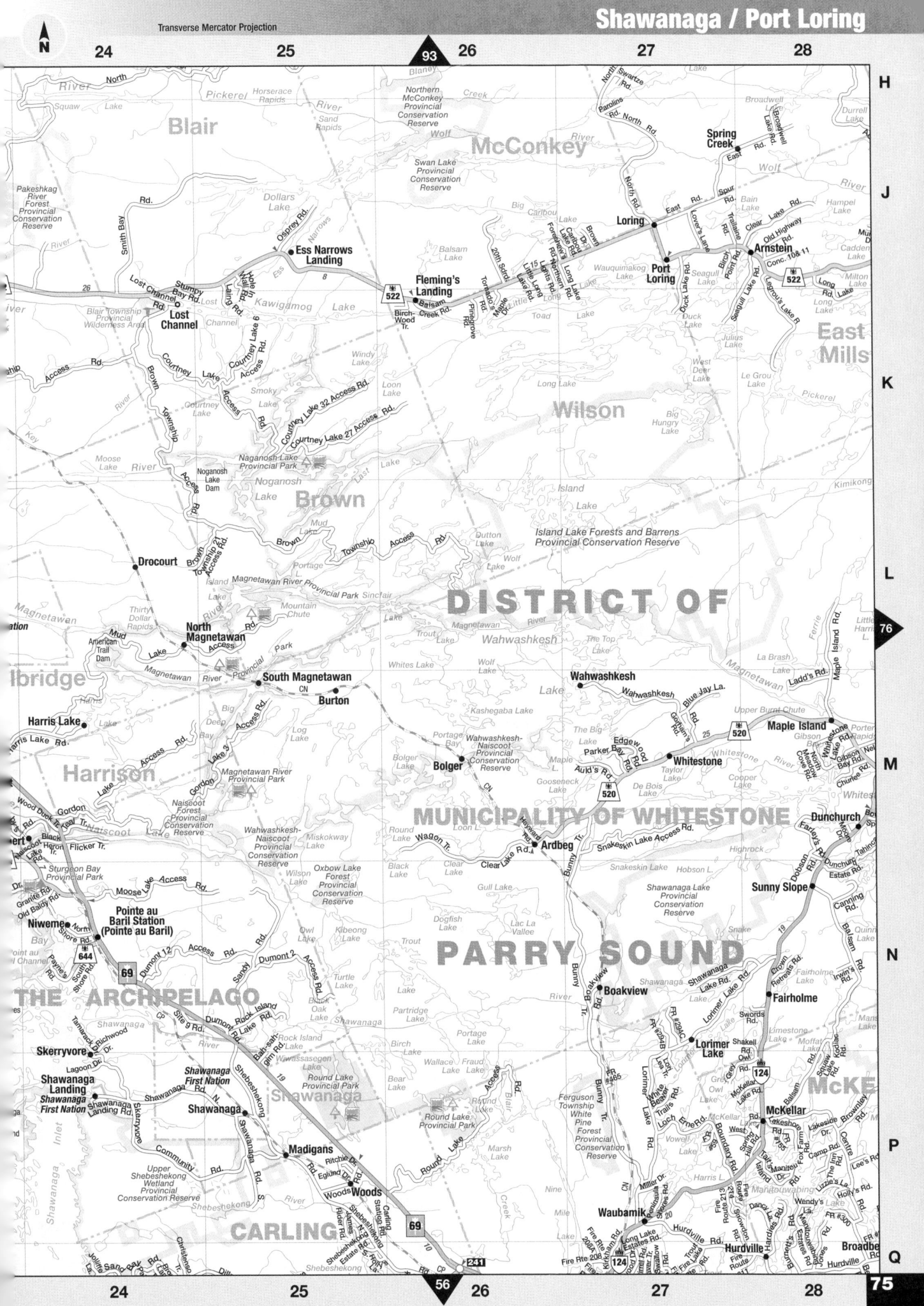

N

Transverse Mercator Projection

24   25   93   26   27   28

H

Blair

River
Squaw
Lake

North
River

Pickerel   Horserace
River   Rapids

Sand
Rapids

Northern
McConkey
Provincial
Conservation
Reserve

Wolf   Creek

McConkey

North Swartze
Rd.

Parolins
Rd. North Rd.

Broadwell
Rd.

Broadwell
Lake Rd.

Durrell
Lake

Spring
Creek

J

Pakeshkag
River
Forest
Provincial
Conservation
Reserve

Dollars
Lake

Osprey Rd.

Swan Lake
Provincial
Conservation
Reserve

Big
Caribou
Lake

North Rd.

East Rd.

Spur

Loring

Lover's Lane

Trailane

Bain Rd.

Clear Lake Rd.

Old Highway

Hampel
Lake

Cadden
Lake

Mill

River

Ess Narrows
Landing

Narrows

Balsam
Lake

522

Fleming's
Landing

20th Sdrd

Torbato's Rd.

Forester's Rd. Carlord Rd. Northern Rd.

Brown Rd.

Light's Rd.

Little Long

15 Long

Long Lake

Port
Loring

Wauquimakog
Lake

Birch
Point Rd.

Seagull
Lake

Duck Lake Rd.

Seagull Lake R

Arnstein
Conc. 10 & 11

522

Long
Rd.

Milton
Lake

Smith Bay

Stumpy
Bay Rd.

Hole in Wall Rd.

Laing Rd.

Ess

8

Kawigamog   Lake

Birch-
Wood
Tr.

Balsam
Creek Rd.

Pine
grove
Rd.

Maple
Little

Toad   Lake

Long

Julius Lake

West
Deer
Lake

Le Grou
Lake

East
Mills

Lost Channel

Blair Township
Provincial
Wilderness Area

Lost
Channel
Rd.

Courtney Lake 6

Windy
Lake

Loon
Lake

Long Lake

Big
Hungry
Lake

Pickerel

K

ship

Access
Rd.

Key

Moose
Lake

River

Courtney
Township
Rd.

Courtney
Lake

Smoky
Lake

Courtney Lake 32 Access Rd.

Courtney Lake 27 Access Rd.

Wilson

Island
Lake

Kimikong

Brown

Naganosh Lake
Provincial Park

Noganosh
Lake Dam

Noganosh
Lake

Township Rd.

Island
Lake

Access Rd.

Dutton
Lake

Wolf
Lake

Island Lake Forests and Barrens
Provincial Conservation Reserve

Drocourt

Mud
Lake

Brown Township

Access Rd.

Portage
Lake

Sinclair

DISTRICT OF

76

Magnetawan

station

Thirty
Dollar
Rapids

Island
Lake

River

Magnetawan River Provincial Park

Mountain
Chute

Magnetawan River

Lake

Trout
Lake

Wahwashkesh

The Top
Lake

La Brash

Ferrie

Maple Island Rd.

Little
Harris
L.

North
Magnetawan

American Trail
Dam

Mud
Lake

Access

Provincial   Park

Whites Lake

Wolf
Lake

Wahwashkesh
Lake

Blue Jay La.

Gahan's Rd.

25

Upper Burnt Chute

520

Maple Island

Gibson
Lake Rd.

Porter
Rapids

Gibson
Bay Rd.

North
Mead
Cove Rd.

ibridge

Magnetawan

River

South Magnetawan

CN

Burton

Access Rd.

Harris
Lake

Big
Deep
Bay

Bolger
Lake

Portage
Bay

Wahwashkesh-
Naiscoot
Provincial
Conservation
Reserve

Kashegaba Lake

Bolger

The Big
Lake

Maple
Lake

Parker
Bay

Edgewood
Rd.

Auld's Rd.

520

Taylor
Lake

Whitestone River

Whitestone

De Bois
Lake

Cooper
Lake

Churlet

Whites

Harris Lake

Harris Lake
Rd.

Harrison

Lake 3

Log
Lake

Magnetawan River
Provincial Park

Gooseneck
Lake

MUNICIPALITY OF WHITESTONE Rd.

Farley's

Dunchurch

Bob
Sp

M

Wood Duck Tr.

Gordon

Naiscoot Tr.

Rd.

Gordon
Lake

Naiscoot
Forest
Provincial
Conservation
Reserve

Wahwashkesh-
Naiscoot
Provincial
Conservation
Reserve

Miskokway
Lake

Round
Lake

Wagon Tr.

Loon L.

Hayward Tr.

Ardbeg

Clear Lake Rd.

Snakeskin Lake Access Rd.

Snakeskin L.

Hobson L.

Highrock

Dobson Rd.

Dunchurch
Estates Rd.

Sunny Slope

Canning
Rd.

Black
Heron Tr.

Flicker Tr.

Black

Snakeboot

Sturgeon Bay
Provincial Park

Granite Rd.

Old Baldy Rd.

Moose Lake Access Rd.

Oxbow Lake
Forest
Provincial
Conservation
Reserve

Wilson
Lake

Black
Lake

Clear
Lake

Gull Lake

Lac La
Vallee

Shawanaga Lake
Provincial
Conservation
Reserve

Snake
Lake

19

Bal
Quinn
Lake

N

Niweme

Shore Rd.

644

North

Pointe au
Baril Station
(Pointe au Baril)

69

Dumont 12

Sandy

Access Rd.

Dumont 2

Owl
Lake

Kibeong
Lake

Trout
Lake

Turtle
Lake

Dogfish
Lake

PARRY   SOUND

Bunny Tr.

River

Shawanaga

Shawanaga Lake Rd.

Oakview

Boakview

Lorimer Lake Rd.

Fairholme

Fairholme
Retreats Rd.

Irwin's Rd.

Crown
Rd.

Mans

Payne's
South
Shore Rd.

THE ARCHIPELAGO

CP

Dumont Rd.

Site 9 Rd.

Rock Island

Rock Island
Rd.

Babitah
Trim Rd.

Birch
Lake

Wallace
Lake

Fraud
Lake

Bear
Lake

Round
Lake

Blair
Lake

Access Rd.

Ferguson
Township
White
Pine
Forest
Provincial
Conservation
Reserve

Bunny Tr.

FR #294G

FR #294B

FR #465

Lorimer Tr.

White Beaver Tr.

Loch Erne Rd.

Lorimer
Lake

Swords
Rd.

Shakell
Lake

Limestone
Lake

124

Moffat
Lake

Squaw
Lake

Kodiac
Lake

McKE

Skerryvore

Lagoon Dr.

Tamarack
Dr.

Birchwood
Dr.

River

Wiwassegen
Lake

Round Lake
Provincial Park

Shawanaga
Landing

Shawanaga
First Nation

Shawanaga
First Nation
Rd.

Shawanaga Landing Rd.

Skerryvore

19

Shebeshekong

Shawanaga

Shawanaga

Round Lake
Provincial Park

Round
Lake

Marsh
Lake

Grey
Owl
Lake

McKellar
Lake

White
Tr.

Vowels
Lake

McKellar

Lakeshore
Rd.

Lakeside Rd.

Browley

Centre Rd.

McKE

Madigans

Ritchie Dr.

Eglund Dr.

Woods

Woods

69

Upper
Shebeshekong
Wetland
Provincial
Conservation
Reserve

Community Rd.

Shawanaga Landing Rd.

Shebeshekong Rd.

Shebeshekong Station Rd.

River

Shebeshekong

Shames
Rd.

Estate Rd.

River Rd.

Woods

Waubamik

Nine

Round Lake

Mile

Creek

Long Lake
Estates Rd.

Fire Rte 213

Fire Route 208

Kirkland Rd.

Shawanaga
Lake Rd.

Miller Rd.

Peninsula Rd.

CN

Harris Rd.

Hurdville Rd.

124

Fire
Route 213
Swallow

241

56   26

Christengo
Rd.

Joulie Sand Bay
Rd.

Diny

Boundary Rd.

Manitouwabing
Lake

Fox Rd.

Manitou
Rd.

Trails End
Tr.

Snowdon Rd.

Tait's Rd.

Vowel's
Rd.

Fire Route 213

Camp Rd.

Mansfield
Rd.

McKellar
Rd.

The Inn
Rd.

Lizzie's La.

Danler's Rd.

Wendy's
Rd.

Holly's Rd.

Hardies Rd.

Hurdville

Hurdville
Rd.

Broadbe

FR #30

Lee's Rd.

Q

CARLING

24   25   56   26   27   28

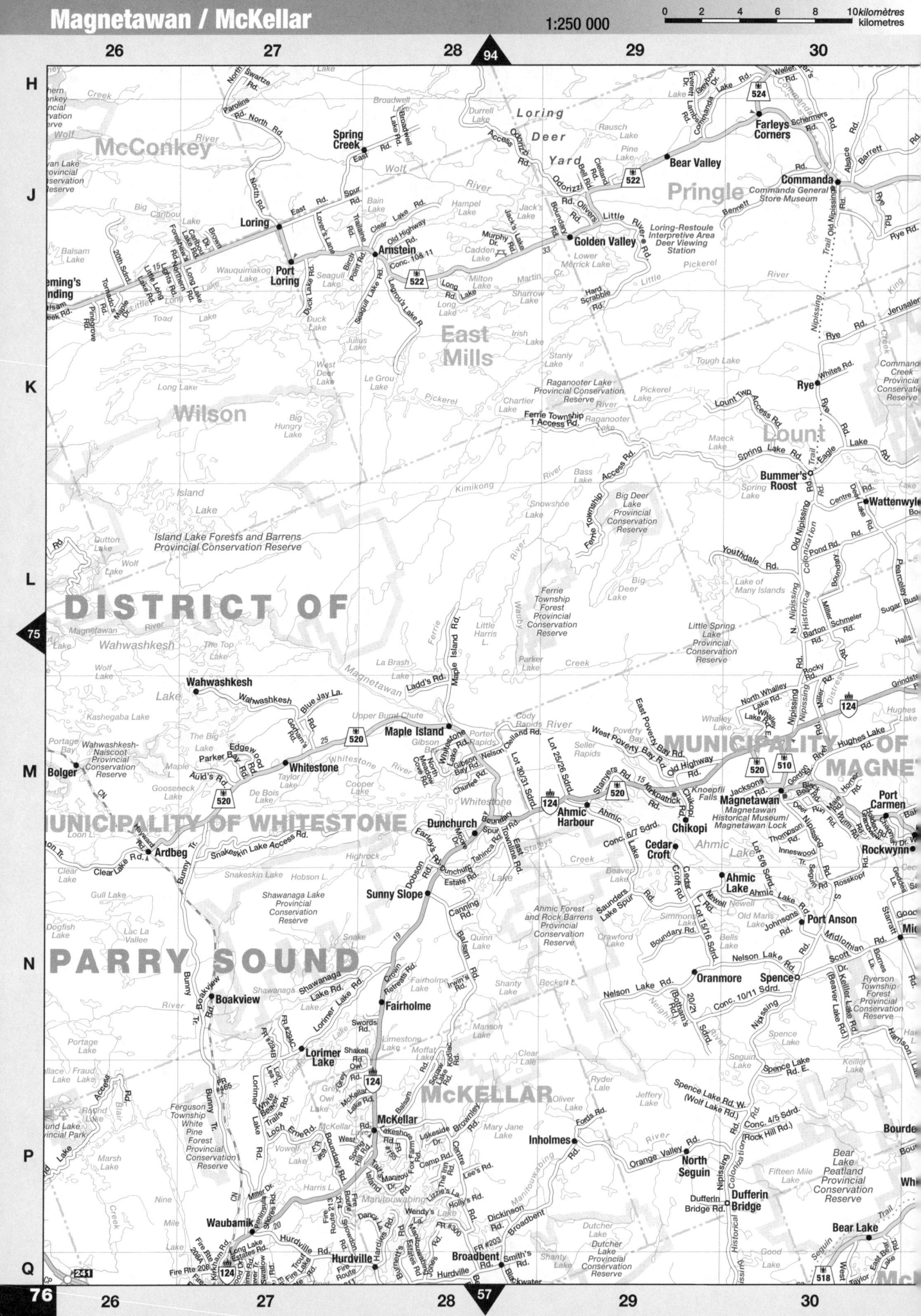

1:250 000

10 *kilomètres*
kilometres

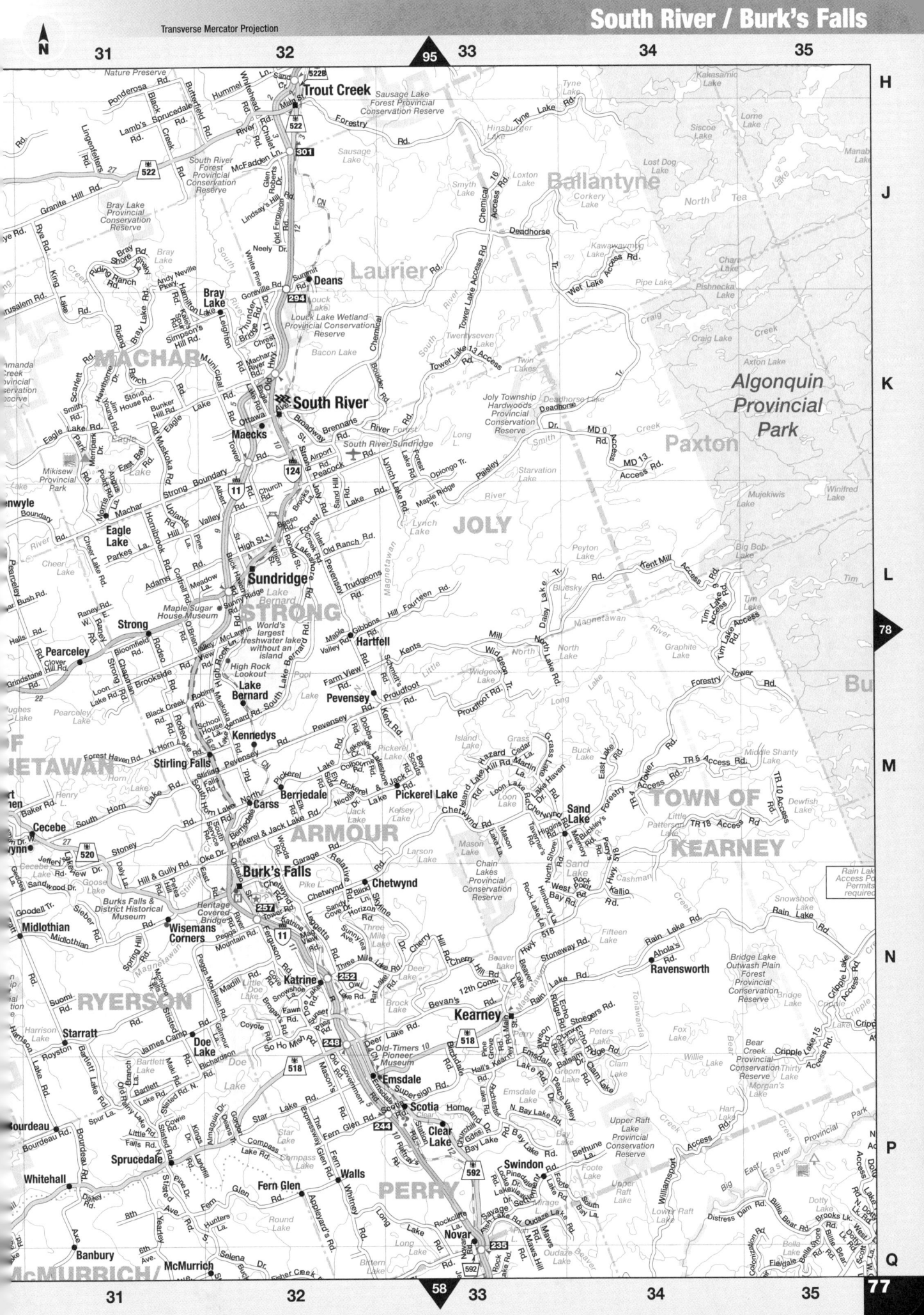

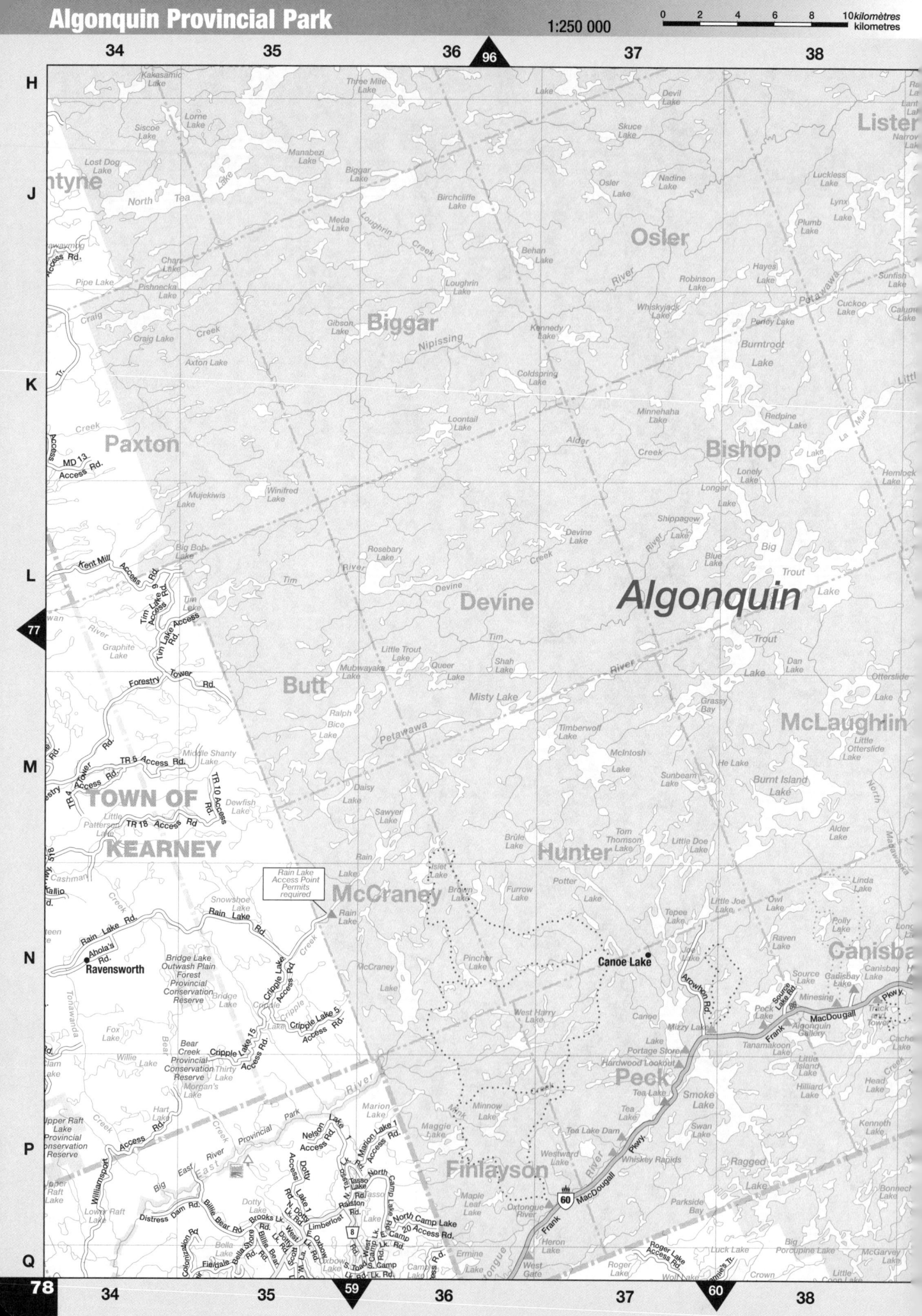

Transverse Mercator Projection

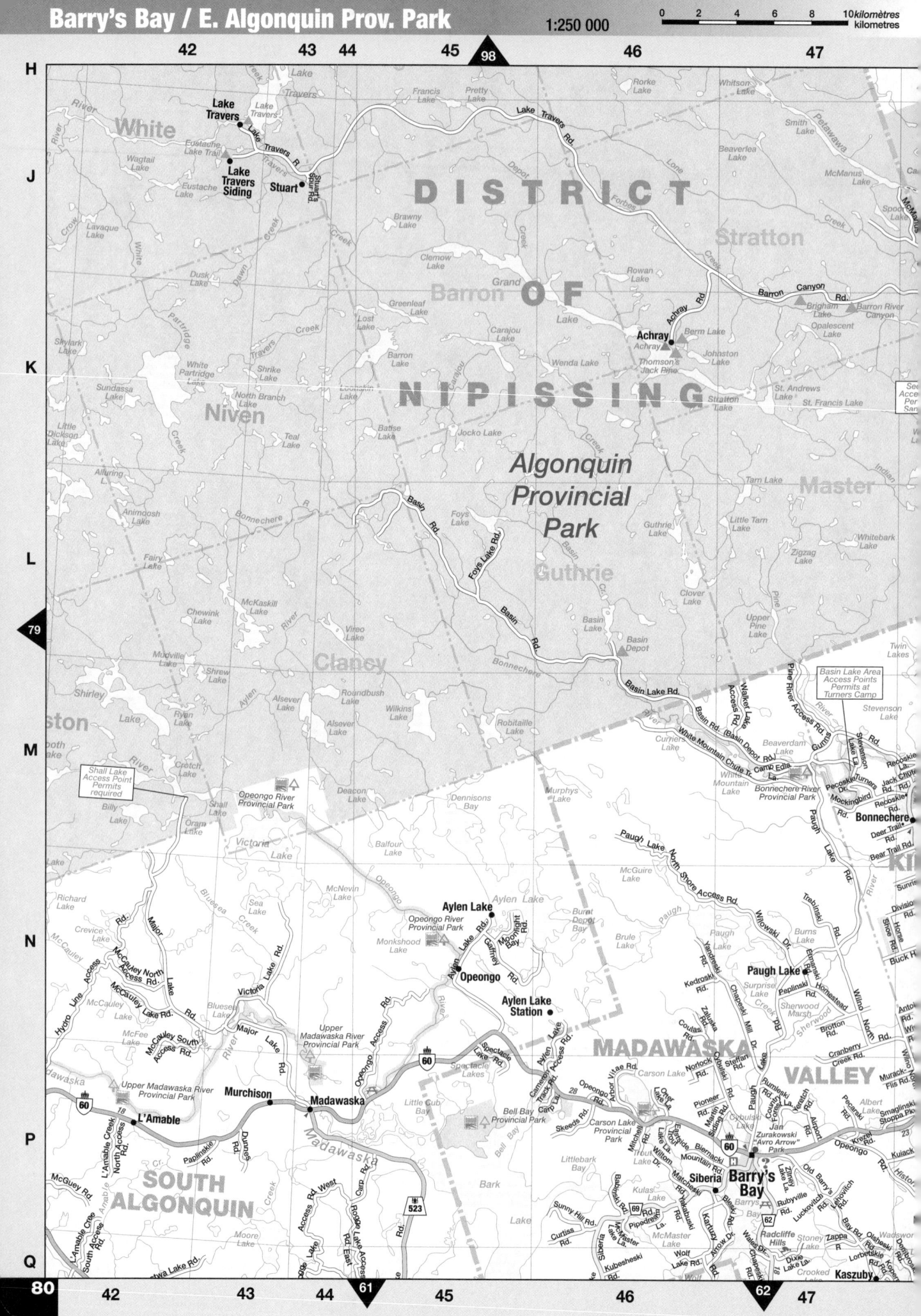

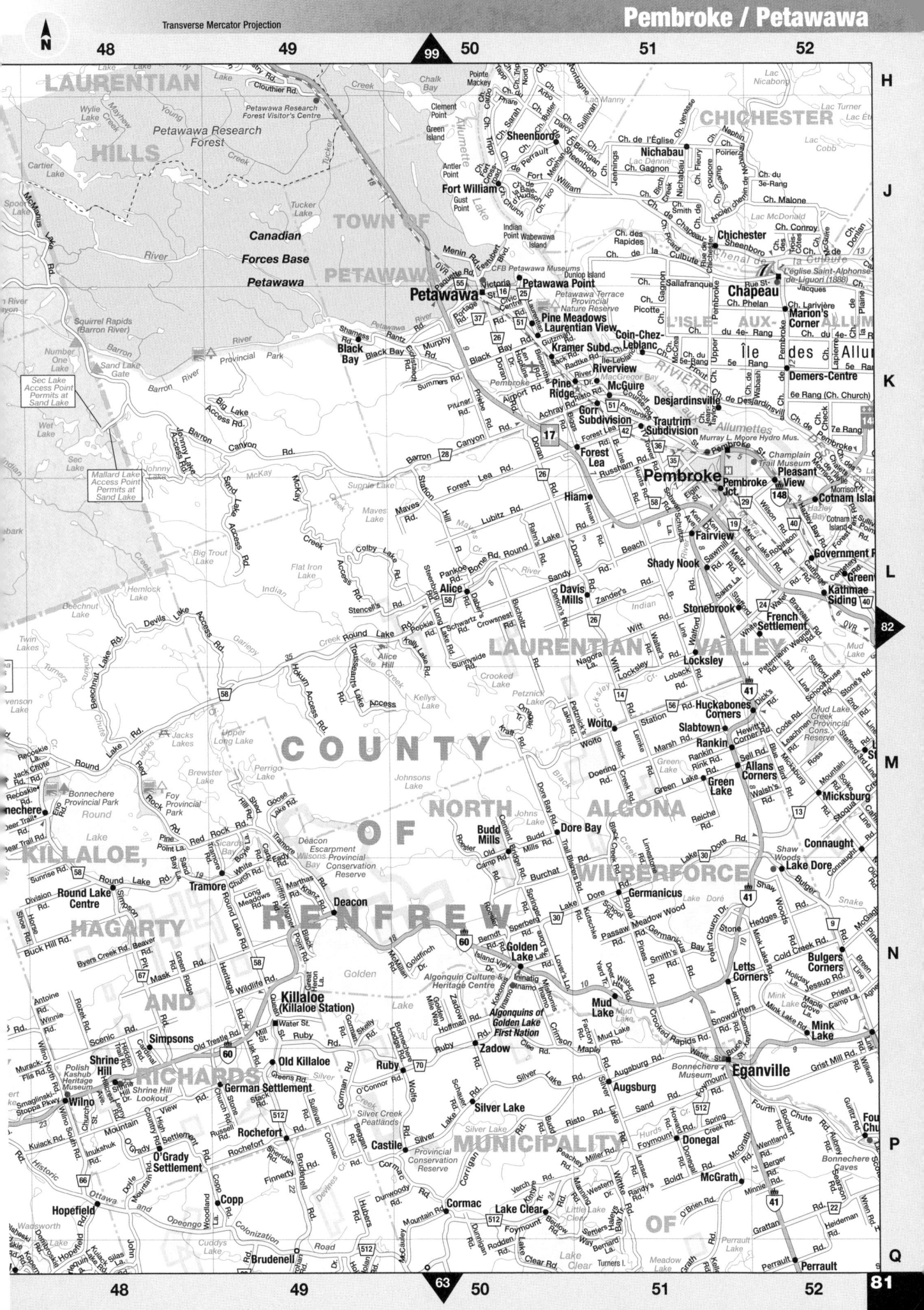

Transverse Mercator Projection

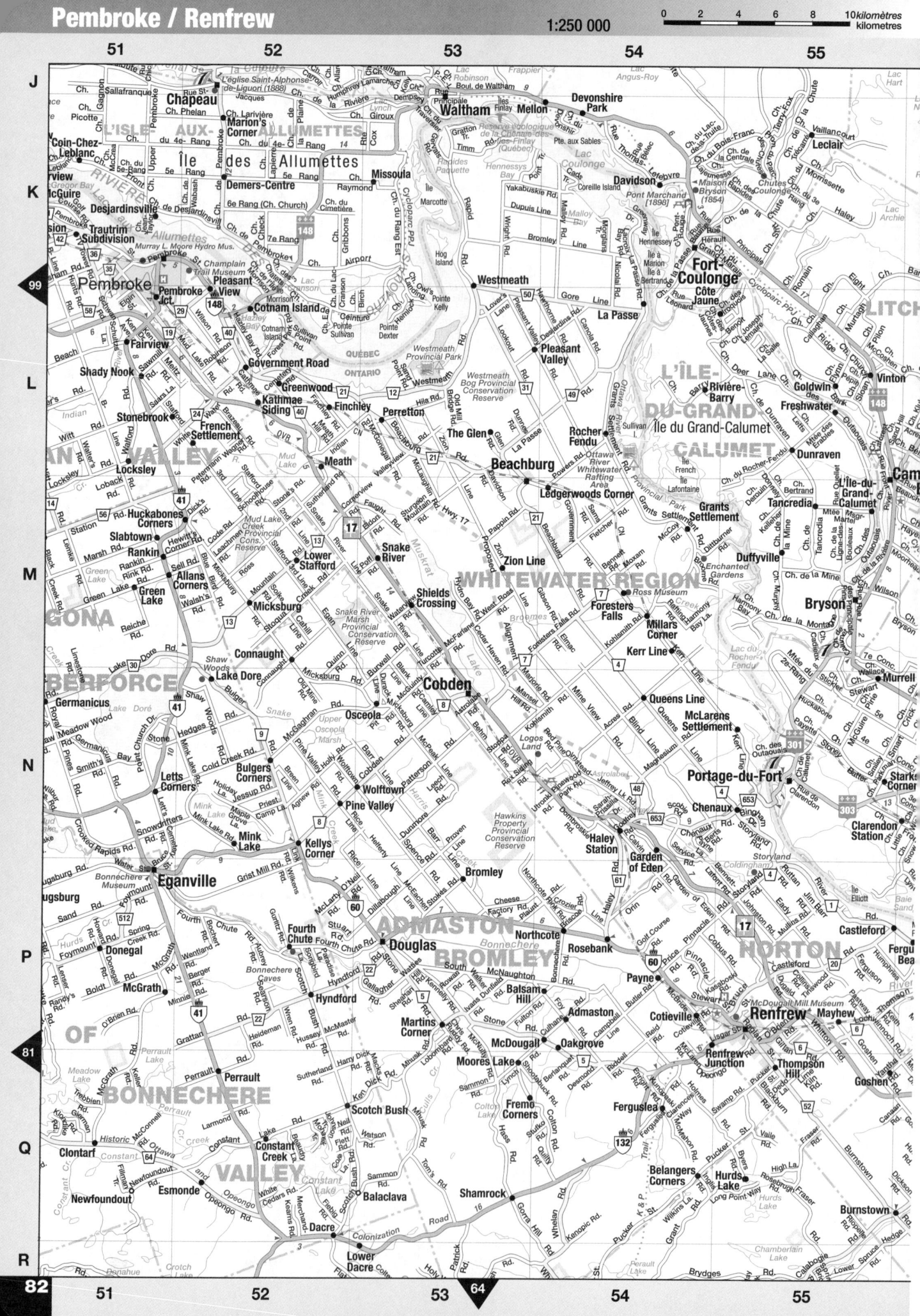

J

L'ISLE- AUX- ALLUMETTES

Chapeau
Coin-Chez-Leblanc
Île des Allumettes
Waltham
Mellon
Devonshire Park
Leclair

K

Desjardinsville
Demers-Centre
Missoula
Davidson
Fort-Coulonge
Côte Jaune

99

Pembroke
Pembroke Jct.
Pembroke View
Cotnam Island
QUÉBEC
ONTARIO
La Passe
LITCH

L

Fairview
Shady Nook
Government Road
Greenwood
Westmeath
Pleasant Valley
Rocher Fendu
Rivière-Barry
Freshwater
Goldwin
Vinton

Stonebrook
Kathmae Siding
Finchley
Perretton
The Glen
L'ÎLE-DU-GRAND-CALUMET
Île du Grand-Calumet
Dunraven

Locksley
French Settlement
Meath
Beachburg
Ledgerwoods Corner
Grants Settlement
Tancredia
Île-du-Grand-Calumet

M

Huckabones Corners
Slabtown
Rankin
Lower Stafford
Snake River
Zion Line
WHITEWATER REGION
Foresters Falls
Duffyville
Bryson

Allans Corners
Green Lake
Micksburg
Shields Crossing
Millars Corner
Kerr Line

N

Germanicus
Lake Dore
Connaught
Cobden
Osceola
Queens Line
McLarens Settlement
Portage-du-Fort
Murrell
Starks Corner

Letts Corners
Bulgers Corners
Wolftown
Pine Valley
Chenaux
Clarendon Station

Mink Lake
Kellys Corner
Haley Station
Garden of Eden
Castleford

P

Eganville
Douglas
Northcote
Rosebank
Payne
HORTON
Renfrew
Mayhew

Donegal
McGrath
Fourth Chute
Hyndford
Balsam Hill
Admaston
Cotieville
Renfrew Junction
Thompson Hill
Goshen

OF
BONNECHERE

Martins Corner
McDougall
Oakgrove
Moores Lake

81

Clontarf
Perrault
Scotch Bush
Fremo Corners
Ferguslea
Belangers Corners
Hurds Lake
Burnstown

Q

Newfoundout
Esmonde
Balaclava
Shamrock

Lower Dacre
Dacre

R

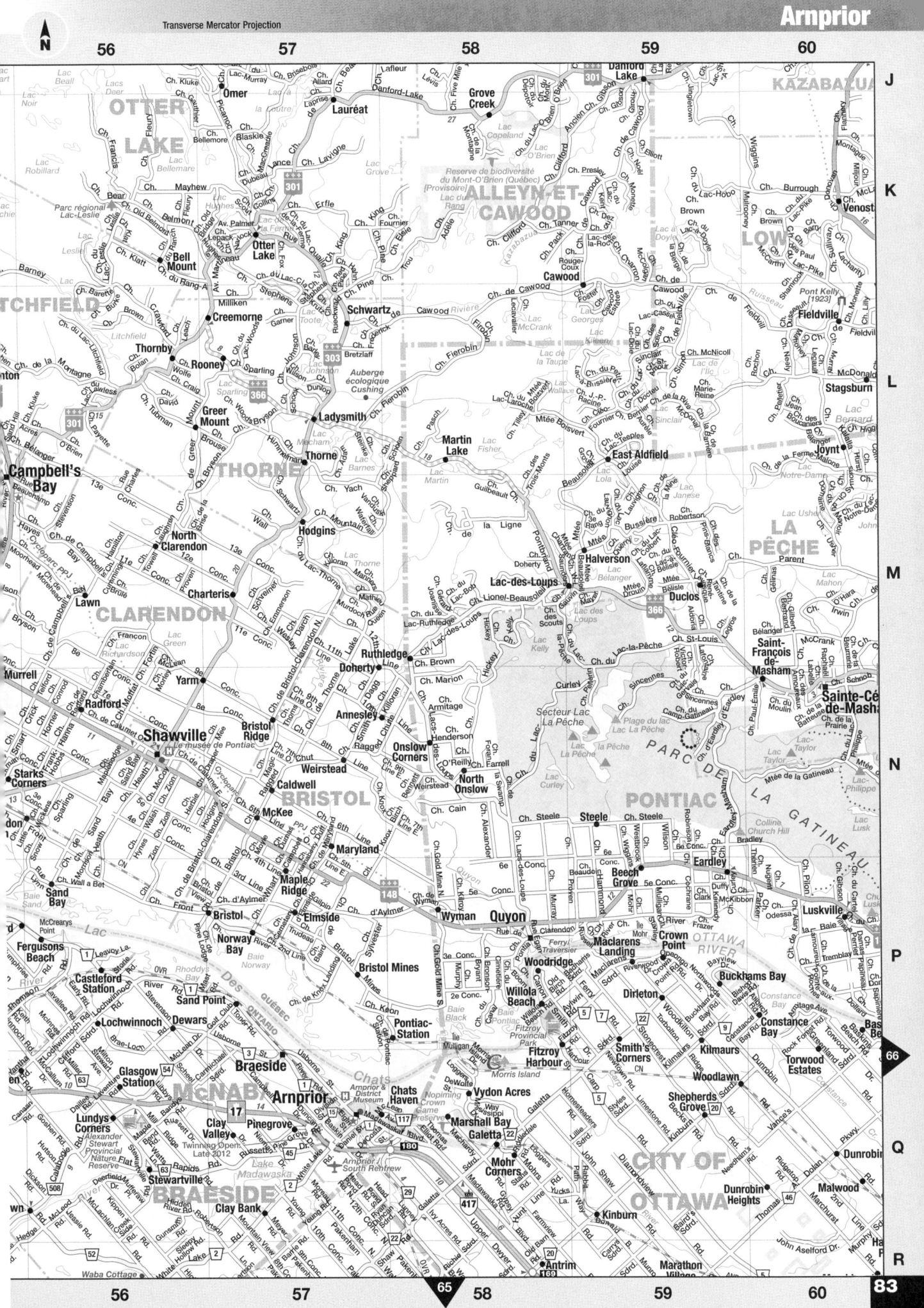

Transverse Mercator Projection

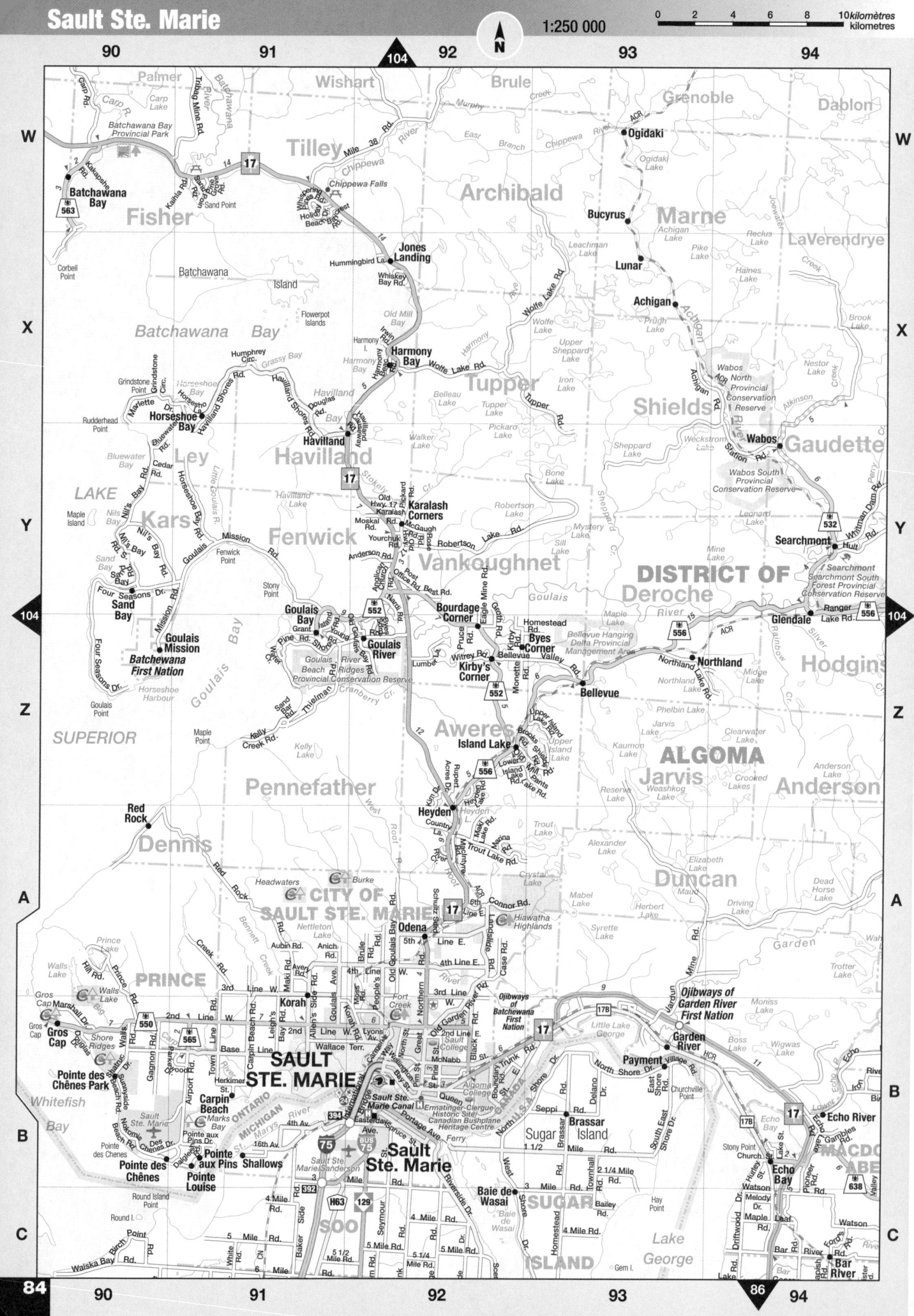

N

0 2 4 6 8 10 kilomètres

90 **91** 104 **92** **93** **94**

W ... W

Palmer
Wishart
Brule Creek
Grenoble
Dablon

Carp Rd.
Carp R.
Tribag Mine Rd.
Batchawana River
Tilley
Chippewa River
Mile 38 Rd.
Murphy
East Branch Chippewa
Ogidaki
Ogidak Lake
Marne
LaVerendrye

Kakenabo Dr.
Batchawana Bay Provincial Park
17
Chippewa Falls
Whiskering Rd.
Holloway Rd.
Sand Point
Jones Landing
Hummingbird La.
Bucyrus
Achigan Lake
Leachman Lake
Pike Lake
Reclus Lake
Haines Creek
Nestor Lake

Batchawana Bay
563
Fisher
14
Whiskey Bay Rd.
Lunar
Achigan River
ACR
Brook Lake

Corbell Point
Batchawana Island
Flowerpot Islands
Old Mill Bay
Harmony I.
Achigan
Prugh Lake
Upper Sheppard Lake
Wabos North Provincial Conservation Reserve
Weckstrom Lake

X ... X

Batchawana Bay
Humphrey Circ.
Grassy Bay
Harmony Circ.
Harmony Bay
Wolfe Lake Rd.
Wolfe Lake
Tupper
Belleau Lake
Iron Lake
Wabos
Gaudette

Grindstone Point
Grindstone Circ.
Horseshoe Shores Rd.
Havilland Shores Rd.
Douglas Rd.
Havilland Bay
Walker Lake
Tupper Lake
Pickard Lake
Bone Lake
Shields
Wabos Station Rd.
ACR
Leonard Lake

Horseshoe Bay
Rudderhead Point
Bluewater Bay
Cedar Rd.
Havilland
17
Havilland Lake
Stokely Cr.
Pickard Rd.
Robertson Lake
Sheppard Lake
Mine Lake
Wabos South Provincial Conservation Reserve

Y ... Y

LAKE
Ley
Kars
Bluewater Bay Rd.
Horseshoe Bay Rd.
Little Goulais R.
Fenwick
Karalash Corners
McGaugh Rd.
Robertson Lake Rd.
Mystery Lake
Sill Lake
532
Searchmont
Hult

Maple Island
Nils Bay Rd.
Nil's Bay
Mission Rd.
Fenwick Point
Moskal Rd.
Yourchuk Rd.
Anderson Rd.
Vankoughnet
DISTRICT OF
Searchmont Forest South Provincial Conservation Reserve

Sand Bay
Sand Bay Rd.
Goulais Rd.
Stony Point
Post Office Rd.
Best Rd.
Goulais River
Deroche
Searchmont South

Four Seasons Dr.
Sand Bay
Goulais Bay
552
Bourdage Corner
Eagle Mine Rd.
Groth Rd.
Homestead Rd.
Maple Lake
Bellevue Hanging Delta Provincial Management Area
Glendale
Ranger Lake Rd.
556

104 ... 104

Goulais Mission
Batchewana First Nation
Goulais River
Byes Corner
Bellevue
Kirby's Rd.
Valley
Goulais River
15
556
Northland
Hodgins

Horseshoe Harbour
Goulais Point
Goulais Beach Provincial Conservation Reserve
Goulais River Ridges Provincial Conservation Reserve
Lumber
552
Bellevue
Monette Rd.
Northland Lake Rd.
Northland Lake
Midge Lake
Rainbow
Silver

Z ... Z

SUPERIOR
Maple Point
Kelly Creek Rd.
Thielman Rd.
Cranberry Cr.
Sand Bar Rd.
Kelly Lake
Aweres
Island Lake
Brooks Shield Rd.
Upper Island Lake
Reserve Lake
Kaumon Lake
ALGOMA
Jarvis
Weashkog Lake
Clearwater Lake
Anderson Lake
Anderson

Pennefather
West Root River
12
556
Lower Island Lake
Upper Island Lake
Phelbin Lake
Jarvis Lake
Crooked Lakes

Red Rock
Heyden
Heyden
Maki Rd.
Trout Lake Rd.
Trout Lake
Duncan
Alexander Lake
Elizabeth Lake
Driving Lake
Dead Horse Lake

A ... A

Dennis
Red Rock Rd.
Rupert Acres Dr.
Heyden Country La.
McIntyre Rd.
ACR
Crystal Lake
Mabel Lake
Maud L.
Herbert Lake
Garden Rd.
Trotter Lake

Headwaters
Burke
CITY OF SAULT STE. MARIE
Schulz Sideroad
6th Line
17
Connor Rd.
Hiawatha Highlands
Syrette Lake
Moniss Lake

Prince Lake
Walls Lake
Nettleton Lake
Odena
5th Line E.
Line E.
4th Line E.
Case Rd.
Wah

PRINCE
Gros Cap
Walls Lake
Hill Rd.
Prince Rd.
Aubin Rd.
Anich Rd.
Goulais Ave.
3rd Line W.
Ojibways of Batchawana First Nation
9
Ojibways of Garden River First Nation
Little Lake George
Vardon Rd.
Moniss Lake
Boss Lake
Wigwas Lake

Gros Cap
Marshall Dr.
550
2nd Line W.
Korah
4th Line W.
Line W.
Lyons Ave.
Northern Ave.
17B
Garden River
Payment
17
Echo

Gros Cap
Shore Ridges
565
3rd Line
Maki Rd.
Leigh's St.
2nd Line
Base Line
Wallace Terr.
Great Northern Rd.
Sault College
17B
North Shore Dr.
East Shore Dr.
Churchville Point
Echo River

Pointe des Chênes Park
Carpin Beach
Airport Rd.
Gagnon Rd.
Carpin Beach Rd.
Allen's Side Rd.
People's Rd.
Old Garden River Rd.
Algoma College
Boundary Trunk Rd.
North Shore Rd.
17B
17
Echo Bay
Echo River
MACDO
ABE

B ... B

Whitefish Bay
Pointe des Chênes
Pointe aux Pins Dr.
Marks Bay
SAULT STE. MARIE
Sault Ste. Marie Canal
Ermatinger-Clergue Historic Site/ Canadian Bushplane Heritage Centre
Seppi Rd.
Brassar Island
South East Shore Dr.
Stony Point
Echo Bay
638

Pointe aux Pins
16th Ave.
Pointe Louise
Pointe
Shallows
394
Queen St.
Easterday Ave.
Ferry
Sugar 1 1/2
Brassar
Hay Rd.
Watson
Echo Bay

SOO
75
BUS 75
Sault Ste. Marie
Sanderson Ave.
Baie de Wasai
Sugar
Bailey Rd.
2 1/4 Mile
Melody Dr.
Maple Leaf Rd.
Bar River

Round Island Point
Baker Side Rd.
4 Mile Rd.
Spruce Rd.
Riverside Dr.
Baie de Wasai
Townhall
Homestead Rd.
4 Mile Rd.
Driftwood
Watson

Birch Point
Walska Bay
Round I.
H63
392
129
5 Mile Rd.
Seymour Rd.
4 Mile Rd.
5 1/4 Mile Rd.
Gem I.
SUGAR ISLAND
Lake George
Fords Rd.
Watson

C ... C

90 **91** **92** **93** **94**

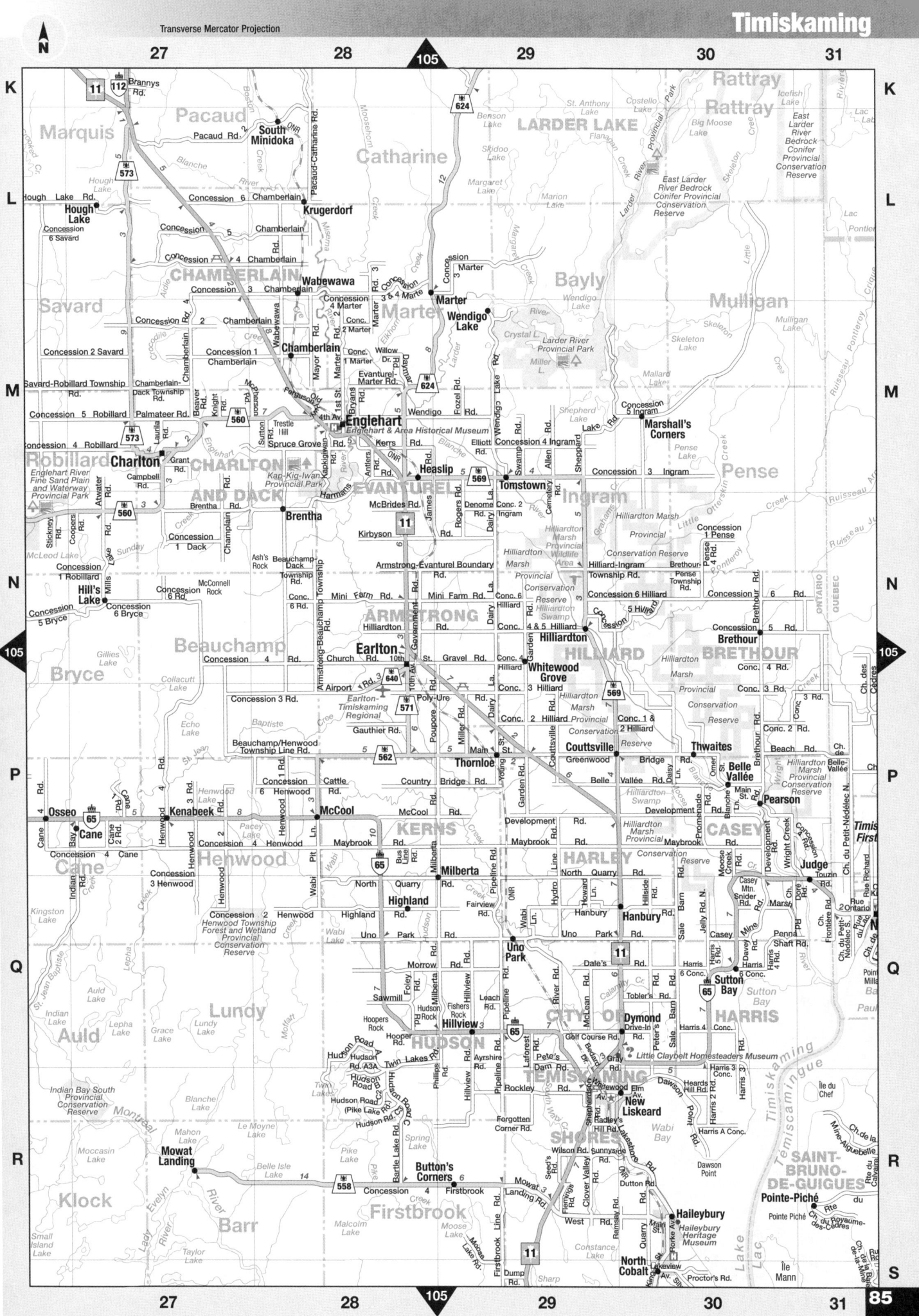

1:250 000

0 2 4 6 8 10 kilomètres
kilometres

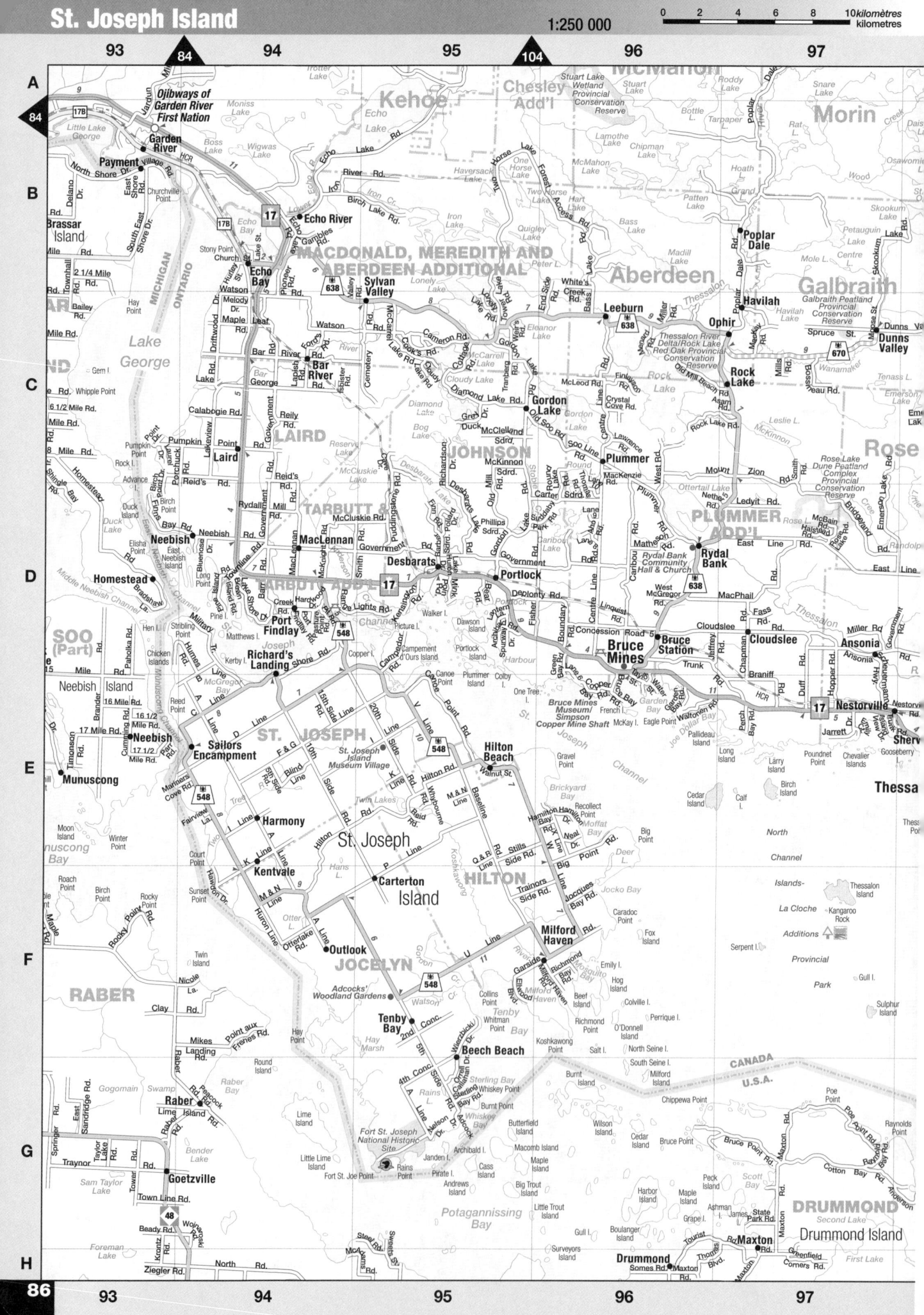

93 84 **94** **95** 104 **96** **97**

A

Ojibways of Garden River First Nation

Kehoe

McMahon

Chesley Add'l

Stuart Lake Wetland Provincial Conservation Reserve

Morin

Garden River

Payment

Echo Bay

Brassar Island

17B 17

Echo River

MACDONALD, MEREDITH AND ABERDEEN ADDITIONAL

Aberdeen

Poplar Dale

Galbraith

B

Echo Bay

638 Sylvan Valley

Leeburn 638

Ophir

Havilah

Galbraith Peatland Provincial Conservation Reserve

Dunns Valley

Lake George

670

Rock Lake

C

Bar River

LAIRD

Gordon Lake

JOHNSON

Plummer

Rose

Laird

Neebish

MacLennan

Desbarats

PLUMMER ADD'L

D

Homestead

TARBUTT &

Portlock

17

Rydal Bank

638

MacPhail

Ansonia

Port Findlay

548

Richard's Landing

Bruce Mines

Bruce Station

Cloudslee

Cloudslee

17 Nestorville

Sherv

E

Neebish Island

548

Neebish

Munuscong

ST. JOSEPH

Sailors Encampment

St. Joseph Island Museum Village

548

Hilton Beach

HILTON

Bruce Mines Museum/ Simpson Copper Mine Shaft

Thessa

Harmony

Kentvale

St. Joseph

Island

Carterton

Milford Haven

F

RABER

Outlook

JOCELYN

548

Adcocks' Woodland Gardens

Tenby Bay

Garside

Milford Haven

Provincial

Park

Raber

Beech Beach

CANADA

U.S.A.

G

Goetzville

Fort St. Joseph National Historic Site

DRUMMOND

Drummond Island

48

Maxton

H

Drummond

93 **94** **95** **96** **97**

N

98   99   104   1   2   3

Shelden Lake
Saunders Tower Rd.
Burden
Caribou   Caribou   Cr.   East   Narvik   Burns Lake   Regal L.
Lake   Caribou   Creek   Rd.   Lake   Caribou   Rd.   Endikai Lake

Wakomata Access Point Rd.
Sorenson Lake
Wakomata Dam Rd.
Otter   **Casson**
Pineland Lake
Dyment Lake
Highland Lake
Castra Lake
Wilson Lake
Little Dobie Lake

Daisy Mae Lake
Osawomick Lake
St Ouse Lake
okum Lake
Lake

Snowshoe Cr.
Wakomata Shores Rd.
Damn Lake
Jackson
Mississagi River Provincial Park
Mills Lake
Skirt Lake
Walsh Lake
Hoover Lake
Bull Lake
Waterhole L.
East Twin Lake
East Twin Lake
Mistaken L.
Canton Mine Rd.
Big Lake Rd.
Cashen
Rackey
Rackey

Haughton
Mississagi River
Pipe Lake
Huston Lake
14
Jobammageeshig
Chub Lake
Wawiyay Lake
Baird Lake
Little White River Provincial Park
Stringer Lake
Jess Lake
Rd.
Bull
Rd.

Dunns Valley Rd.   Shaw
Shaw
Pipe Lake Rd.
Footprint L.
Gould
Cummings Lake Rd.
Little Pickerel Lake Rd.
Grasett
Reception Lake
Echo Lake
Nouvel
15
Peple Lake Rd.
Hvg ing
Big Lake Rd.

Dunns Valley
Franklin Lake Rd.
Axe Camp Rd.
Cummings Lake
Jackpine Lake
Big Bear Lake
Varley Rd.
Provincial Park
Lajoule Creek
Peple Lake
Blind

enass L.
Emerson Lake
Wanamaker Lake   Shellrock Lake
Franklin Lakes
Burrows Lake
Appleby Lake
10
11
Kynoch
White River
Varley Rd.
Williamson Rd.
Crosby Lake
Boyea Lake
Pepler Lake
Blind River

Emerson Lake Rd.
Bridgland
Bailey Lake Rd.
Franklin Lake
Poverty La.
Wharncliffe
129
7
Woodrow Lake
Woodrow Lake Rd.
554
546
Constable Lake
Casselman's
Beecher Lake
Harvey Lake
Shoal Lake
Twin Mountains

ose Lake
Little Shaw
Bailey Lake
Byrnes Lake   White Birch
Byrnes Provincial Conservation Reserve
Prospect Lake
Wells
Wharncliffe Rd.
Wells Rd.
Bellingham Rd.
Willisville Rd.
Little Birch Lake
Pegamasai Lake
Howard Lake
68 Bay

Randolph L.
Shaw Dam Lake
14
Melwel Rd.
Mississagi
Bellingham
Casselman's Rd.
Montgomery
Smokey Lake
Copp Lake
Demorest Lake
Caribou Lake Rd.

East Line
Shaw Dam Lake
Beaver
Goldenburgh Rd.
Parkinson
Eakel Lake
11
Peake Lake
Mississauga First Nation
Little Chiblow Lake
Demorest West Rd.
Demorest Lake
Demorest East

Short Rd.
McCreight's Pond Rd.
Phillips Bay
McCallum
Parkinson
6
Gladstone Lake
546
Chiblow Lake Rd.
Horn Lake
The Big Island
Darrell Lake
Mississauga
Fox Point
Chiblow Lake

Government Rd.
129
Thessalon
Bead Perien Rd.
Phillips Bay
Boyles Bay
Basswood
Partridge Tr.
Basswood Lake Provincial Conservation Reserve
Red Rock
11
Chiblow Lake
Oscar Lake
Darrell Lake Rd.
Alma Lake
First
Holmes Lake
Lear Lake
Plump Lake

Little Rapids
Airport Rd.
McCreight's
Windmill Rd.
Basswood Lake Hemlock Provincial Conservation Reserve
Ridge Rd.
Oak Camp Rd.
Melwel
Red Rock
Skibo
Pitcher L.
Prospect Lake
Nation
Cherry Lake
Canoe

Nestorville Rd.
Thomas Rd.
Cranberry Lake
Ingram
Brownlee Lake
Sowerby
Cole Bay Rd.
Cavanagh Dr.
Portage St.
Demosta
Clear Lake
Bright
546 Rd.
Patton
Patton
Ryan Lake

Sherwood
Sherwood Rd.
Ferndam Rd.
Round Barn Rd.
Day Mills
Cullis
Cole St.
Mackay Rd.
Mosher
17
Watson Rd.
Red Rock River
Iron Bridge
Chiblow Bridge Rd.
Bay Lake

Gooseberry L.
2
Green La.
North Livingstone
Maple Ridge
Dumond Rd.
Dayton
Cameon Rd.
Hopkins Rd.
Sunset Beach
4
Eley Rd.
Tait Rd.
Huron Shores Museum
8

Thessalon
Bullhead Bay
Wawa I.
Walker Rd.
Livingstone Creek
Livingstone
Siguere Rd.
Maple Ridge Rd.
Pioneer
Thessalon First Nation
Pickard
Bright
Bolton River Rd.
Dayton Rd.
Chevis Rd.
Everett Lake
Mississauga

Thessalon Point
MUNICIPALITY
Dayton
Dayton
Horan Rd.
Baker Rd.
Dayton Rd.
Dean Rd.
Farmers Rd.
Old Mine Rd.
First

OF
North Channel Inshore Provincial Park
Lake Rd.
Eley Rd.
Eley
Camp Rd.
Willis Rd.
Lakeview Rd.
Hart Rd. Bay
15
Nation

HURON
Dobie Point
Bright Point
SHORES
Dean Lake
HCR
Woodside Rd.
Lavign Rd.
Mississagi
Maple Ridge Rd.

Sulphur Island
Bigsby Island
North Channel
North Channel Inshore
Dean Rd.
Provincial Park
Heather
Mississagi Delta Provincial Nature Reserve
Fox Island
Wolstan Island
Pigeon
Patrick Pt.

North Channel Islands- La Cloche Additions
Provincial Park
Burton Islands
Joliette Islands
De Roberval Pt.
Sayers I.
Sayers I.
La Salle Island
Tonty Island
Richelieu I.
Hennepin Island
Webber Island
Wolstan Pt.

Anchor I.   Bird I.
Fishery I.   East Grant Island
The French Islands

West Grant Island
Middle Grant I.
South Point
Herbert I.

Reynolds Point
ND

NORTH CHANNEL
North Point Shoal
West I.
Mississagi Island

Cotton Bay   Shoal Point
Anderson Rd.
ONTARIO
MICHIGAN

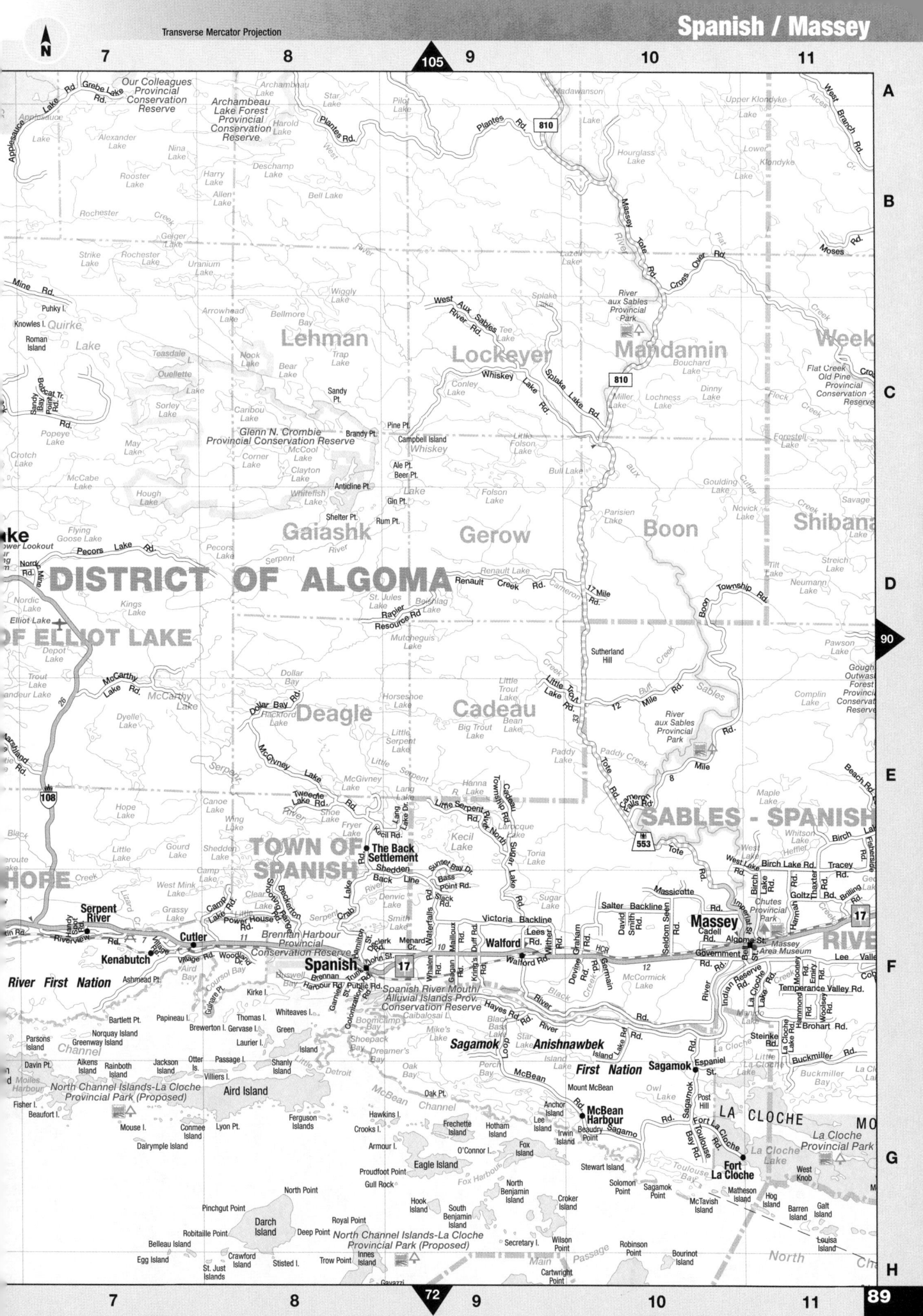

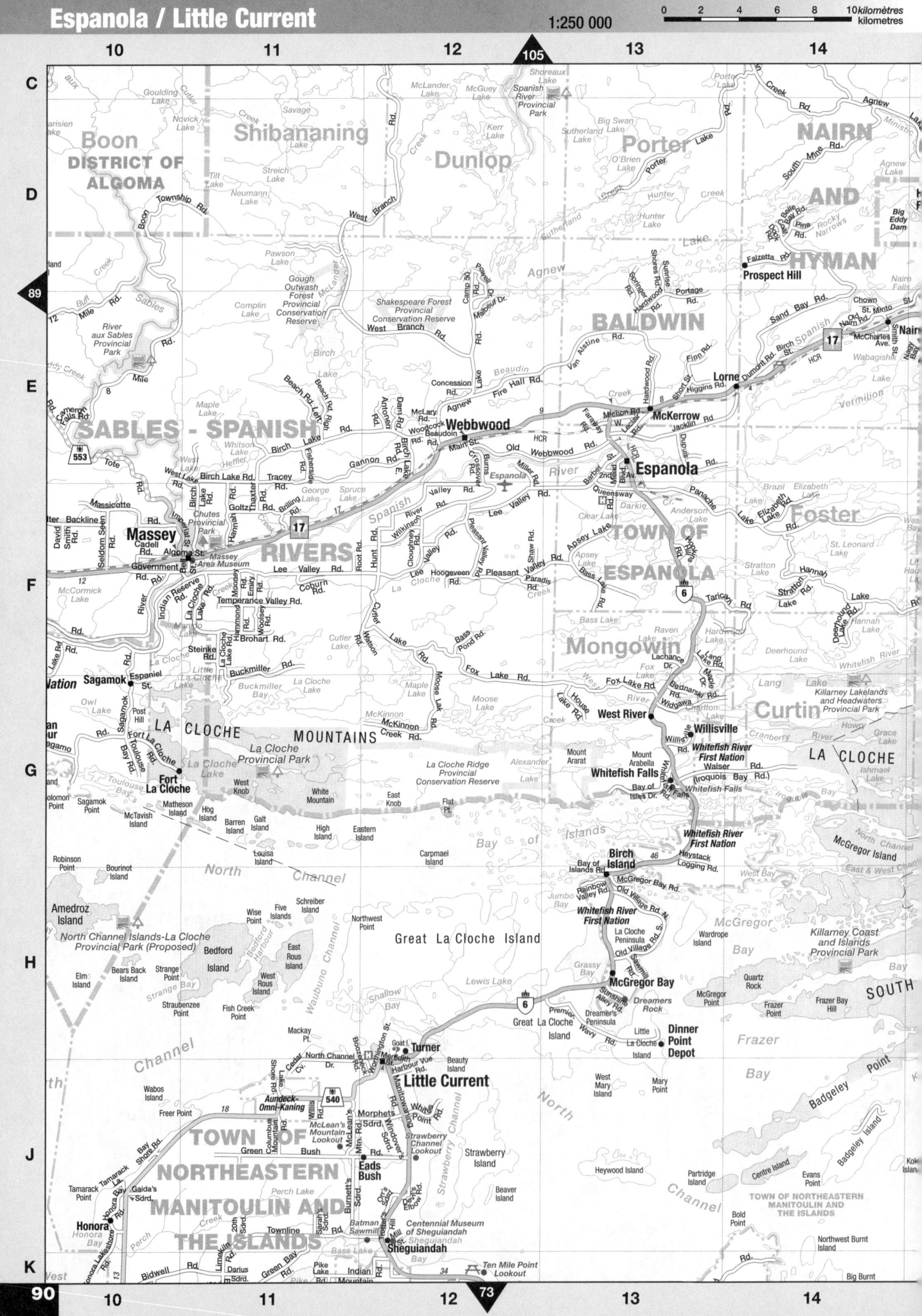

1:250 000

0 2 4 6 8 10 kilomètres
kilometres

C

Boon
DISTRICT OF ALGOMA

Shibananing

Dunlop

Porter

NAIRN

AND

D

HYMAN

Big Eddy Dam

Prospect Hill

Falzetta

Rocky Island

Nairn

89

River aux Sables Provincial Park

BALDWIN

17

McCharles Ave.

E

SABLES - SPANISH

553

Webbwood

Old Webbwood Rd.

Lorne

McKerrow

Espanola

Foster

F

Massey
Massey Area Museum

RIVERS

Lee Valley Rd.

TOWN OF ESPANOLA

6

Mongowin

Sagamok

LA CLOCHE   **MOUNTAINS**

La Cloche Provincial Park

West River

Willisville

Curtin

Killarney Lakelands and Headwaters Provincial Park

LA CLOCHE

G

Fort La Cloche

La Cloche Ridge Provincial Conservation Reserve

Whitefish Falls

Whitefish River First Nation

McGregor Island

H

Amedroz Island

North Channel Islands-La Cloche Provincial Park (Proposed)

Bedford Island

Great La Cloche Island

Birch Island

Whitefish River First Nation

McGregor Bay

Killarney Coast and Islands Provincial Park

SOUTH

6

Dinner Point Depot

Frazer Bay

Badgeley Point

Turner

Little Current

J

TOWN **OF**

540

McLean's Mountain Lookout

Strawberry Channel Lookout

Strawberry Island

NORTHEASTERN

Eads Bush

Beaver Island

Heywood Island

MANITOULIN AND

Honora

THE ISLANDS

Centennial Museum of Sheguiandah

TOWN OF NORTHEASTERN MANITOULIN AND THE ISLANDS

K

Sheguiandah

Ten Mile Point Lookout

73

90

10   11   12   13   14

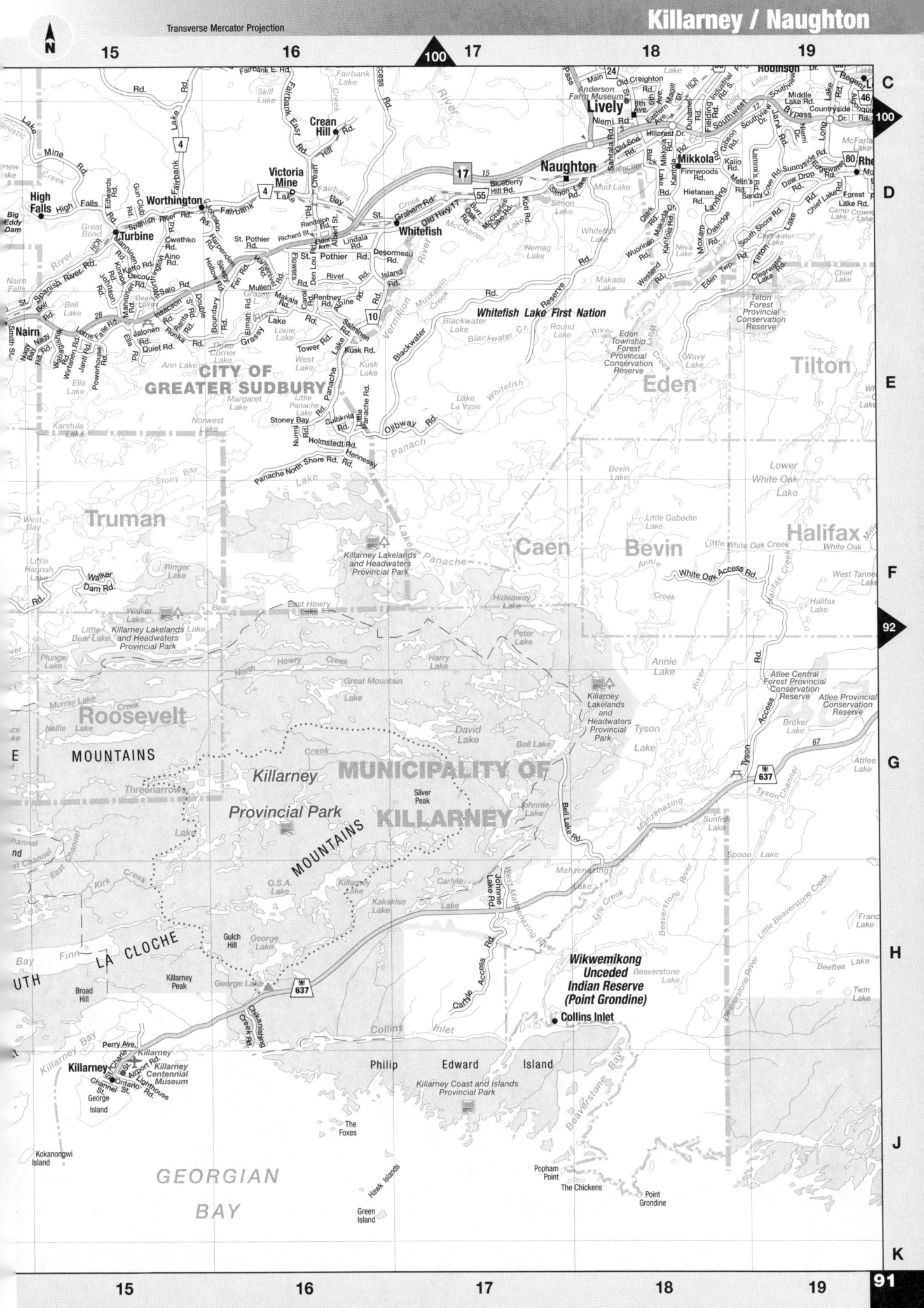

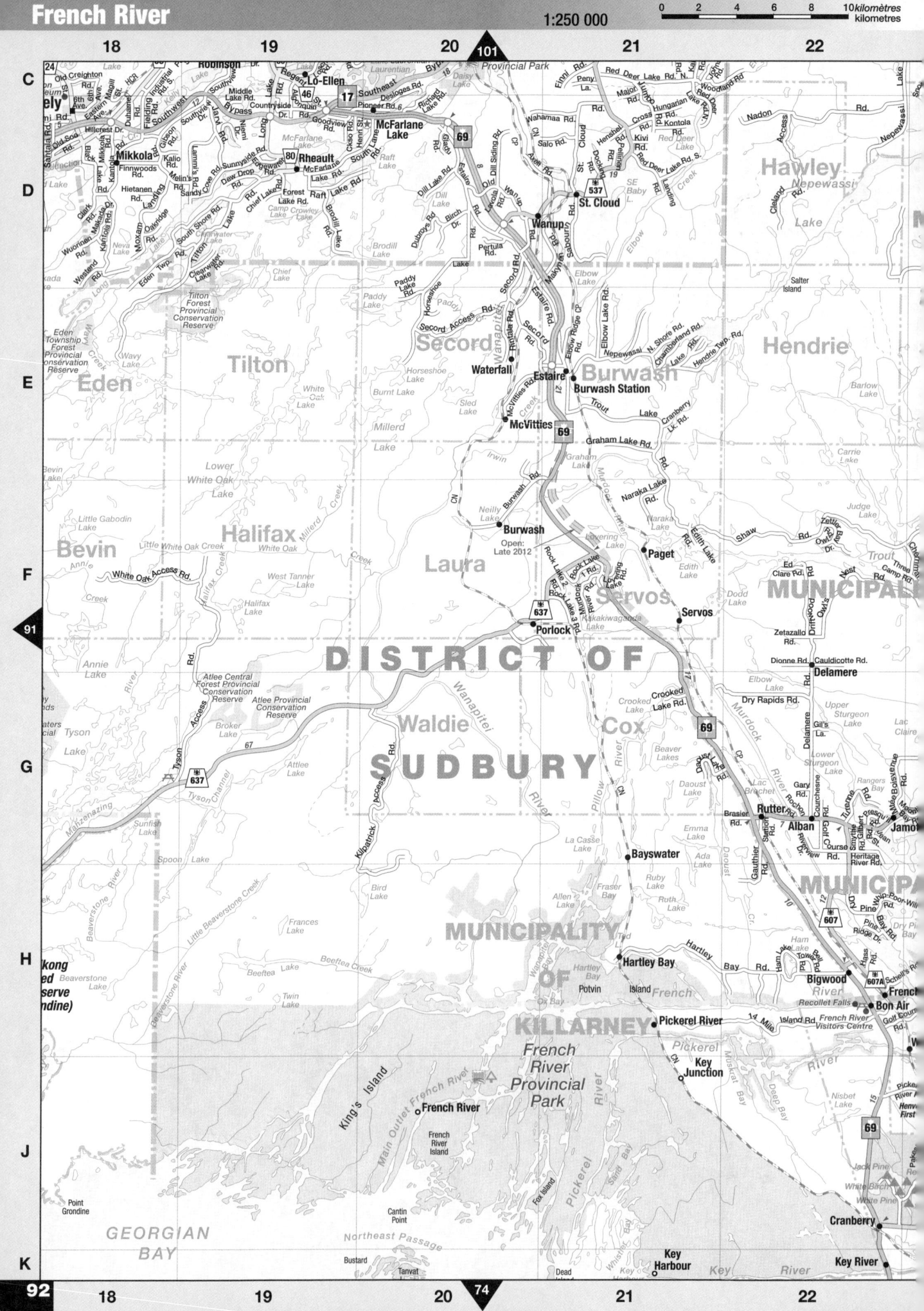

French River

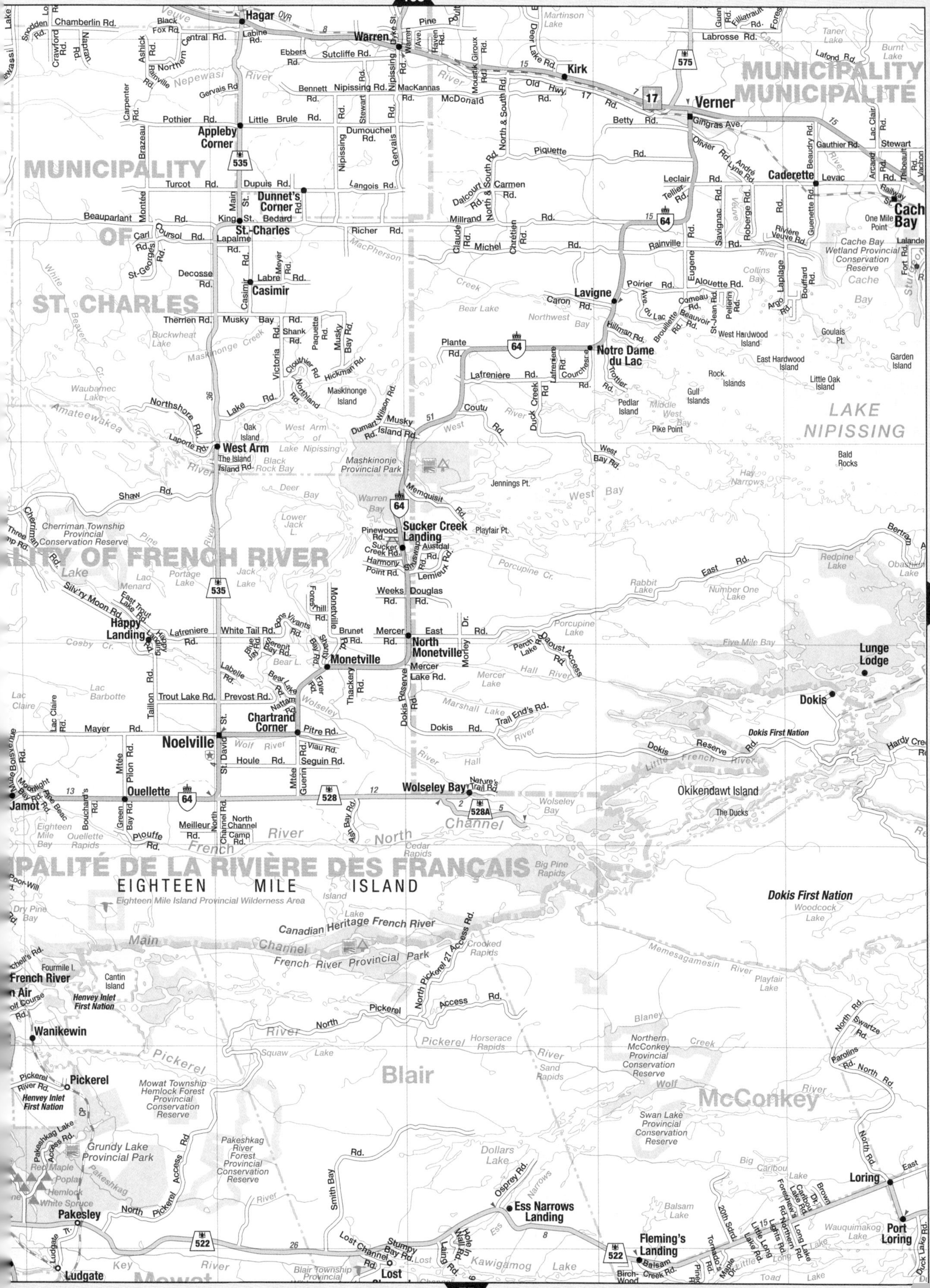
N
23
24
105
25
26
27
C
D
E
F
94
G
H
J
K
75
Hagar
Warren
Kirk
Verner
Appleby Corner
Dunnet's Corner
St.-Charles
Casimir
Caderette
Cache Bay
Lavigne
Notre Dame du Lac
West Arm
Sucker Creek Landing
Happy Landing
Monetville
North Monetville
Chartrand Corner
Noelville
Ouellette
Jamot
Wolseley Bay
Lunge Lodge
Dokis
Dokis First Nation
French River
Wanikewin
Pickerel
Pakesley
Ludgate
Lost Channel
Ess Narrows Landing
Fleming's Landing
Loring
Port Loring
MUNICIPALITY OF ST. CHARLES
MUNICIPALITY MUNICIPALITÉ
MUNICIPALITY OF FRENCH RIVER
MUNICIPALITÉ DE LA RIVIÈRE DES FRANÇAIS
LAKE NIPISSING
EIGHTEEN MILE ISLAND
Eighteen Mile Island Provincial Wilderness Area
Canadian Heritage French River
French River Provincial Park
Grundy Lake Provincial Park
Mashkinonje Provincial Park
Cherriman Township Provincial Conservation Reserve
Mowat Township Hemlock Forest Provincial Conservation Reserve
Pakeshkag River Forest Provincial Conservation Reserve
Northern McConkey Provincial Conservation Reserve
Swan Lake Provincial Conservation Reserve
Cache Bay Wetland Provincial Conservation Reserve
Henvey Inlet First Nation
Blair
McConkey
Okikendawt Island
17
64
535
575
528
528A
522

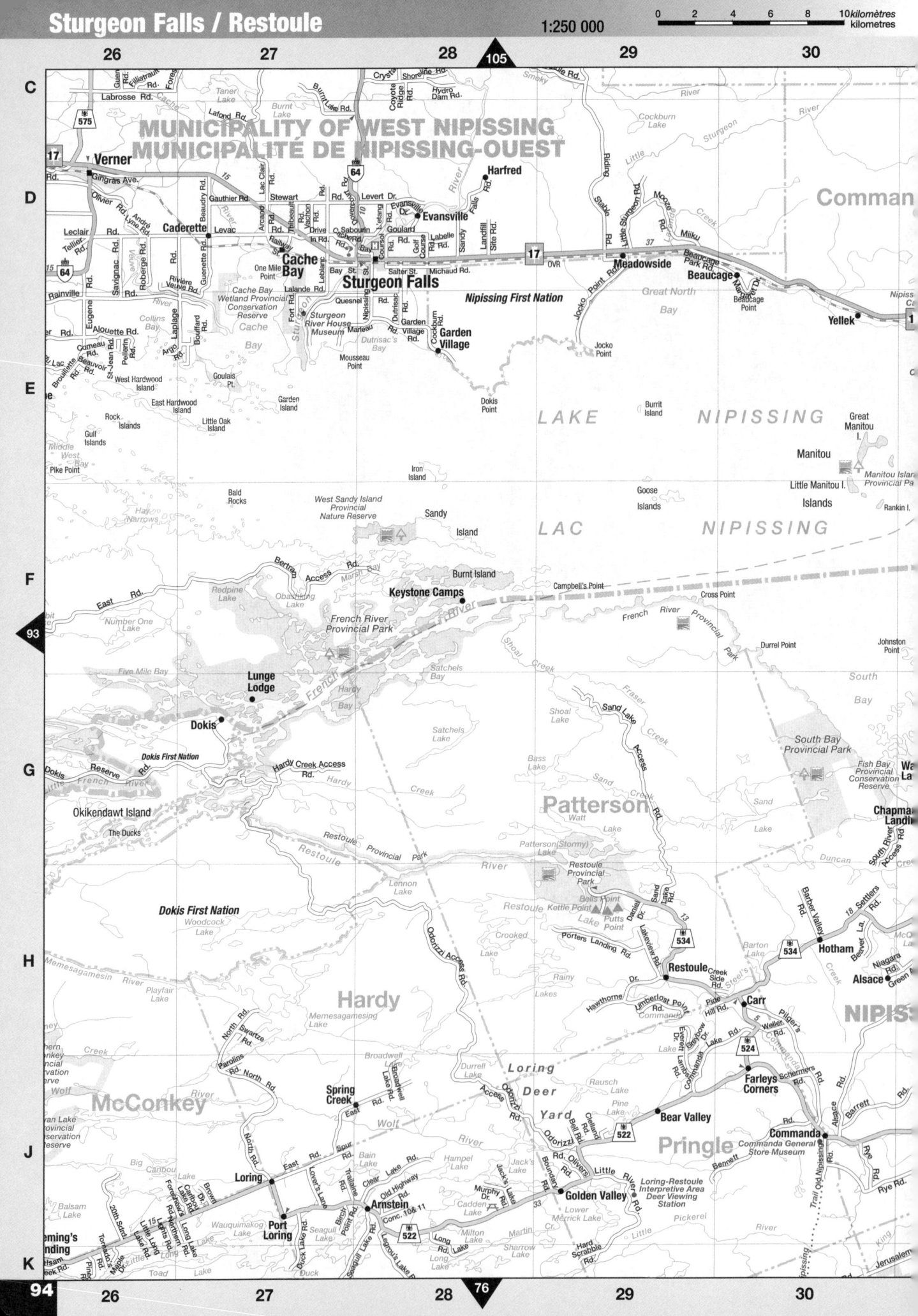

Transverse Mercator Projection

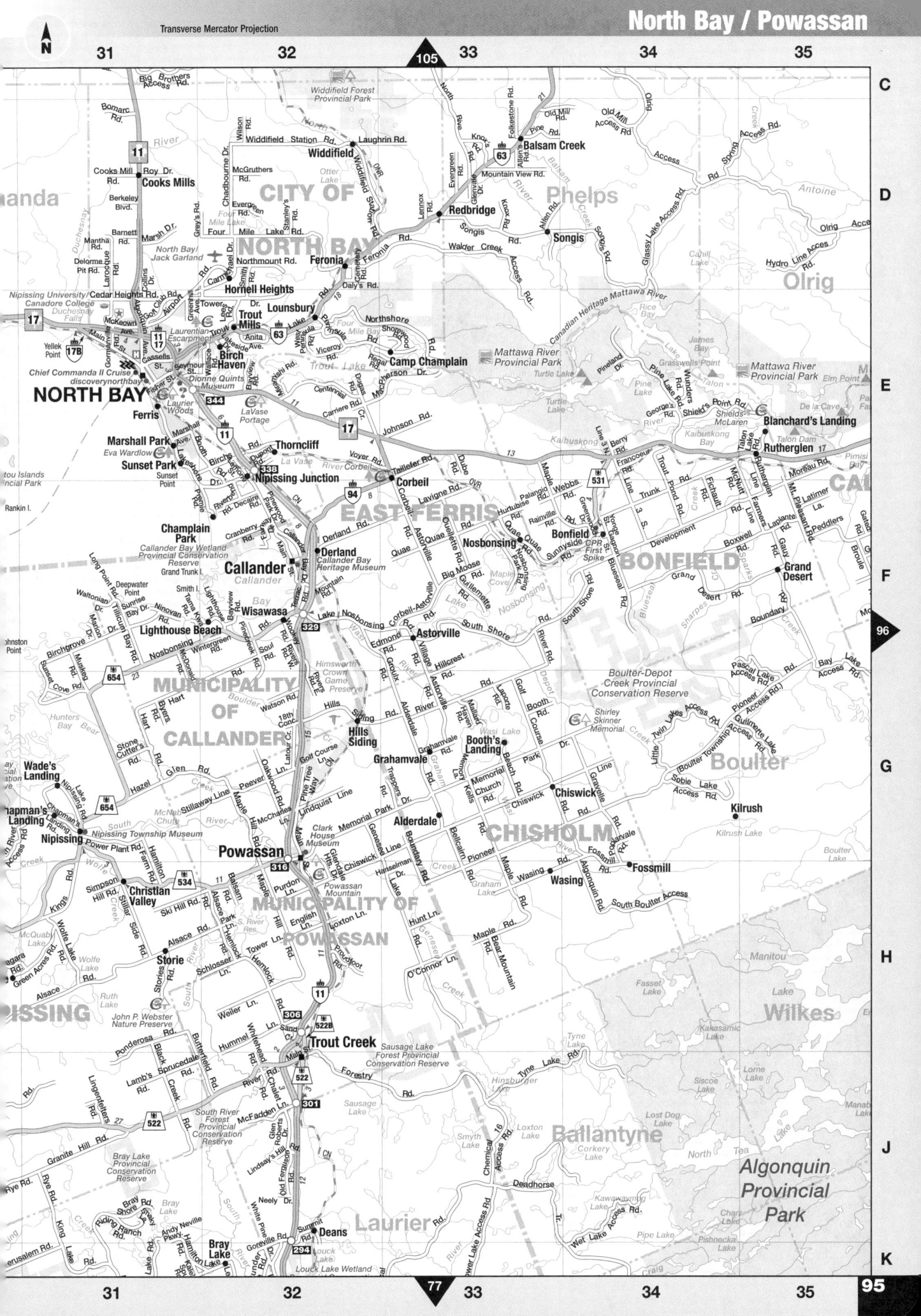

1:250 000

34 **35** **105** **36** **37** **38**

D
Olrig
Hydro Line Rd.
MATTAWAN
656
McCracken
Mattawa River
Rice Bay
Kearney Lake
Burke Dr.
Murphy's 5 Rd.
Mattawa Museum
Moose Head Rd.
Mattawa
RIVIÈRE DES OUTAO
James Bay
Grasswells Point
Samuel de Champlain Provincial Park
Mattawa River Provincial Park
Mattawa Island
17
Rankin

E
Pine Lake
Mattawa River Provincial Park
Canadian Ecology Centre
Champlain Provincial Park
Old Hwy. 17 Rd.
17 Rd.
Richard's Rd.
Pine Lake Rd.
Wunders Rd.
Point Rd.
Shield's Point Rd.
Blanchard's Landing
Voyageur Provincial Centre
Earls Lake
Jacbon Rd.
Chenier Rd.
Collins Rd.
Papineau
McMartin Rd.
Archambeault
Cameron Rd.
Janveau Rd.
Villeneuve Rd.
George's River
McLaren
Talon Dam
Eau Claire Station
Jingwakoki
18 Rd.
Vaughan Rd.
Papineau
Sturgeon Lake Rd.
Berry Francoeur
Kaibuskong Bay
Rutherglen
17
Amable du Fond River Provincial Park
Suzannes Rd.
Morel
Richard's Rd.
McDimond Rd.
Hazelwood Rd.
Boom Rd.

F
Trout Pond Line
McNutt Rd.
Farmers Line
Peddlers
Smith Lake
Eau Claire Gorge
Graham Rd.
Donalds Rd.
OVR Dr.
Daventry Rd.
Papineau Rd.
Papineau Rd.
Boutz Rd.
Little Pautois Lake
Papineau Rd.
Access Rd.
Cross Over Rd.
PAPINEAU-CAMER
Klock's Access
BONFIELD
Grand Desert
Grand Desert Rd.
Boxwell Rd.
Gauly Rd.
Galston Rd.
Beckett La.
Pratt Rd.
630
Bronson Lake Rd.
Floods Rd.
Stewarts Rd.
Landis Lake
Little Pautois Lake
Papineau Lake
Papineau Lake
East Thompson Lake
West Aumond Lake
Klock's Access

G
Boulter-Depot Creek Provincial Conservation Reserve
Pascal Lake Access Rd.
Pioneer Access Rd.
Guilmette Lake
Bay Lake Access Rd.
McBrian Access
Amable du Fond Provincial Park
Lauder
Thompson Lake
Lauder Lake
Daventry Rd.
Hurdman Creek
Brain Lake
Brain Lake
Boyd
Hurdman Lake
95
Sobie Lake Access Rd.
Kilrush
Kilrush Lake
Boulter Lake
Kiosk Access Point Permits required
Kiosk
Coristine
Kiosk
Kloshkokwi Lake
Brain Lake Access Point Permits at Mattawa Travel Information Centre
Bodri
Government Park

H
Fossmill
South Boulter Access
Pentland
Whitebirch Lake
Waterclear Lake
Maple Lake
Mink Lake
Club Lake
Mink Lake
Couchon Lake
Little Couchon Lake
Mouse Lake
Algonquin
Daventry
Gouinlock Lake
Carl Wilson Lake
Laurel Lake
Manitou Lake
Fasset Lake
Wilkes
Kakasamic Lake
Erables Lake
North Sylvia Lake
Ratrap Lake
N I P I S S I N G
Devil Lake
Lister

J
Lost Dog Lake
tyne
North Tea Lake
Siscoe Lake
Manabezi Lake
Lorne Lake
Three Mile Lake
Biggar Lake
Birchcliffe Lake
Meda Lake
Loughrin Creek
Behan Lake
Skuce Lake
Osler Lake
Nadine Lake
Osler
Luckless Lake
Lynx Lake
Plumb Lake

K
Chart Lake
Pipe Lake
Pishnecka Lake
Gibson Lake
Axton Lake
Biggar
Nipissing
Loughrin Creek
Kennedy Lake
Coldspring Lake
River
Whiskyjack Lake
Robinson Lake
Hayes Lake
Perley Lake
Burntroot Lake
Cuckoo Lake
Calume Lake
Craig Lake
Craig Creek

L
Paxton
MD 13 Access Rd.
Mujekiwis Lake
Winifred Lake
Loontail Lake
Minnehaha Lake
Alder Creek
Bishop
Redpine Lake
Lonely Lake
Longer Lake
Petawawa
Hemlock Lake
La Mur

34 **35** **36** **78** **37** **38**

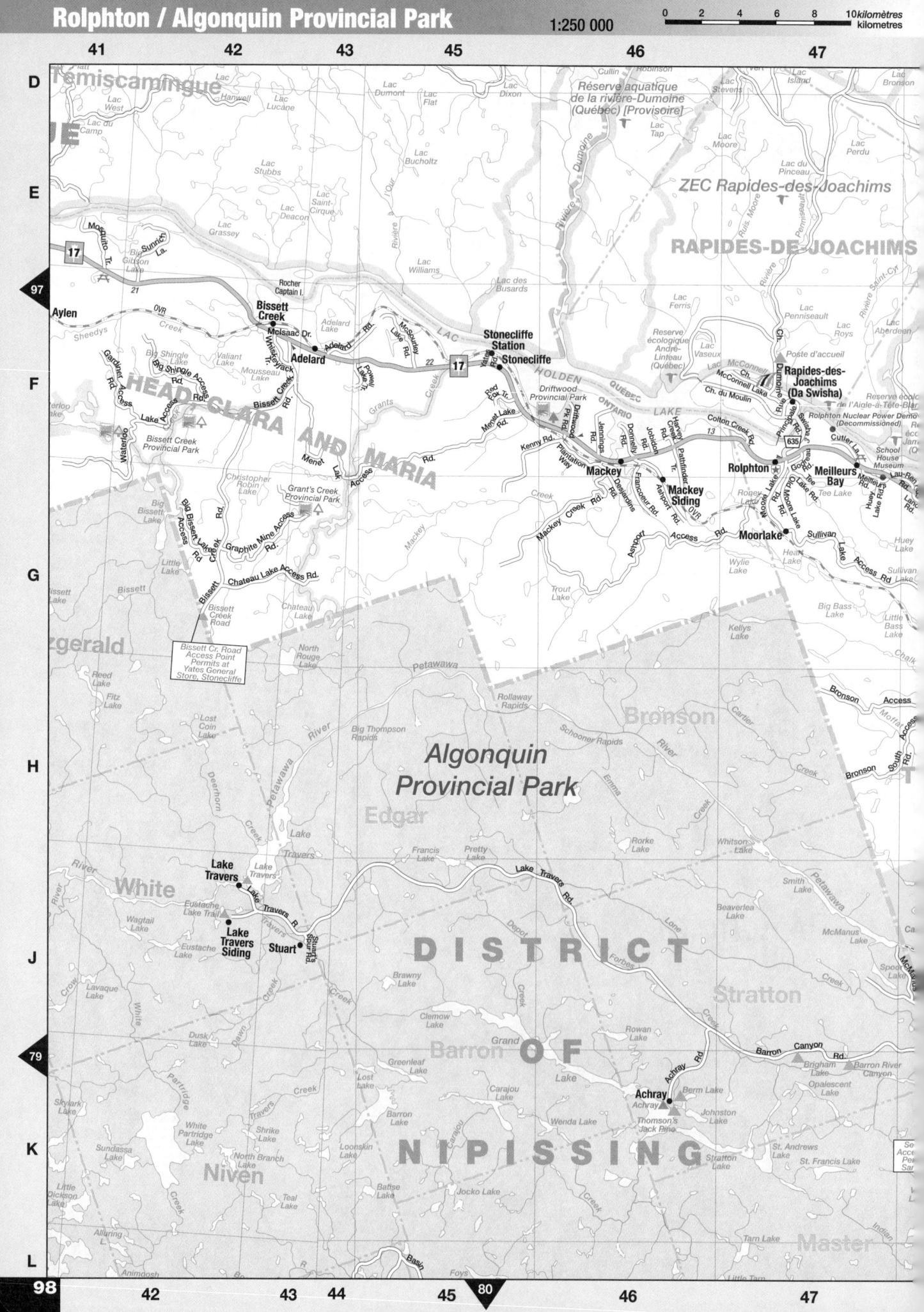

N

Transverse Mercator Projection

48   49   50   51   52

D
E
F
G
H
J
K
L

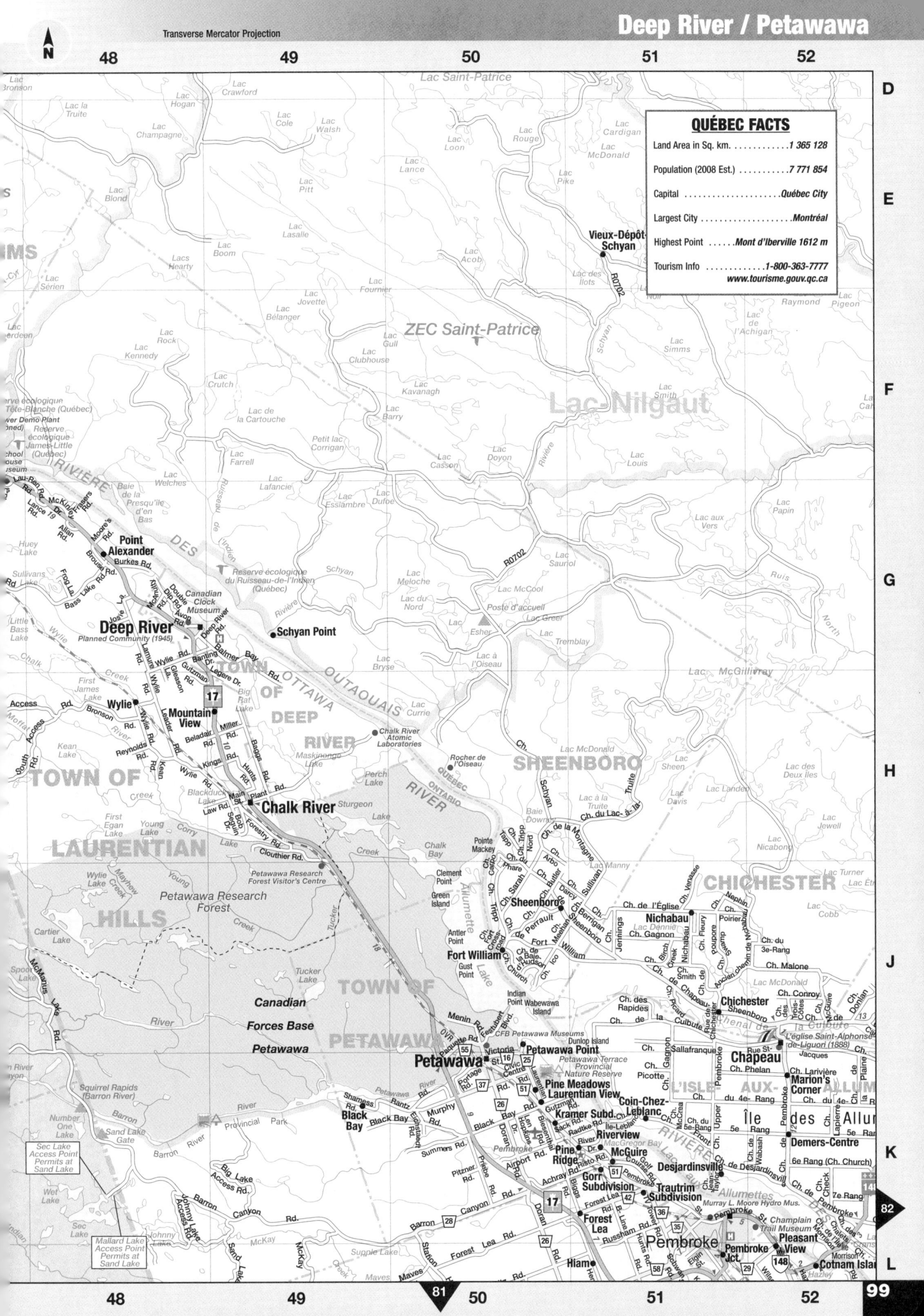

QUÉBEC FACTS

Land Area in Sq. km. *1 365 128*

Population (2008 Est.) *7 771 854*

Capital . . . . *Québec City*

Largest City . . . . *Montréal*

Highest Point . . . . . . *Mont d'Iberville 1612 m*

Tourism Info *1-800-363-7777*
www.tourisme.gouv.qc.ca

Lac Saint-Patrice

ZEC Saint-Patrice

Lac-Nilgaut

Vieux-Dépôt-Schyan

Reserve écologique
Tête-Blanche (Québec)

Reserve écologique
James-Little (Québec)

RIVIÈRE

DES

Point Alexander

Canadian Clock Museum

Deep River
Planned Community (1945)

OTTAWA

Schyan Point

SHEENBORO

CHICHESTER

TOWN OF
DEEP
RIVER

Nichabau

Chichester

Wylie

Mountain View

17

Chalk River Atomic Laboratories

Chalk River

Rocher de l'Oiseau

Poste d'accueil

Sheenboro

OUTAOUAIS

QUÉBEC
ONTARIO
RIVER

Chapeau

TOWN OF
LAURENTIAN
HILLS

Petawawa Research Forest Visitor's Centre

Petawawa Research Forest

Fort William

Marion's Corner

Île des Allumettes

L'ISLE
AUX-

**Canadian
Forces Base
Petawawa**

TOWN OF
PETAWAWA

CFB Petawawa Museums

Petawawa Point

RIVIÈRE

Demers-Centre

Petawawa

Pine Meadows
Laurentian View

Kramer Subd.

Coin-Chez-Leblanc

Black Bay

Riverview

Pine Ridge

McGuire

Desjardinsville

Trautrim Subdivision

Gorr Subdivision

17

82

Forest Lea

Murray L. Moore Hydro Mus.

Champlain Trail Museum

148

Pembroke

Pembroke Jct.

Pleasant View

Cotnam Island

Hiam

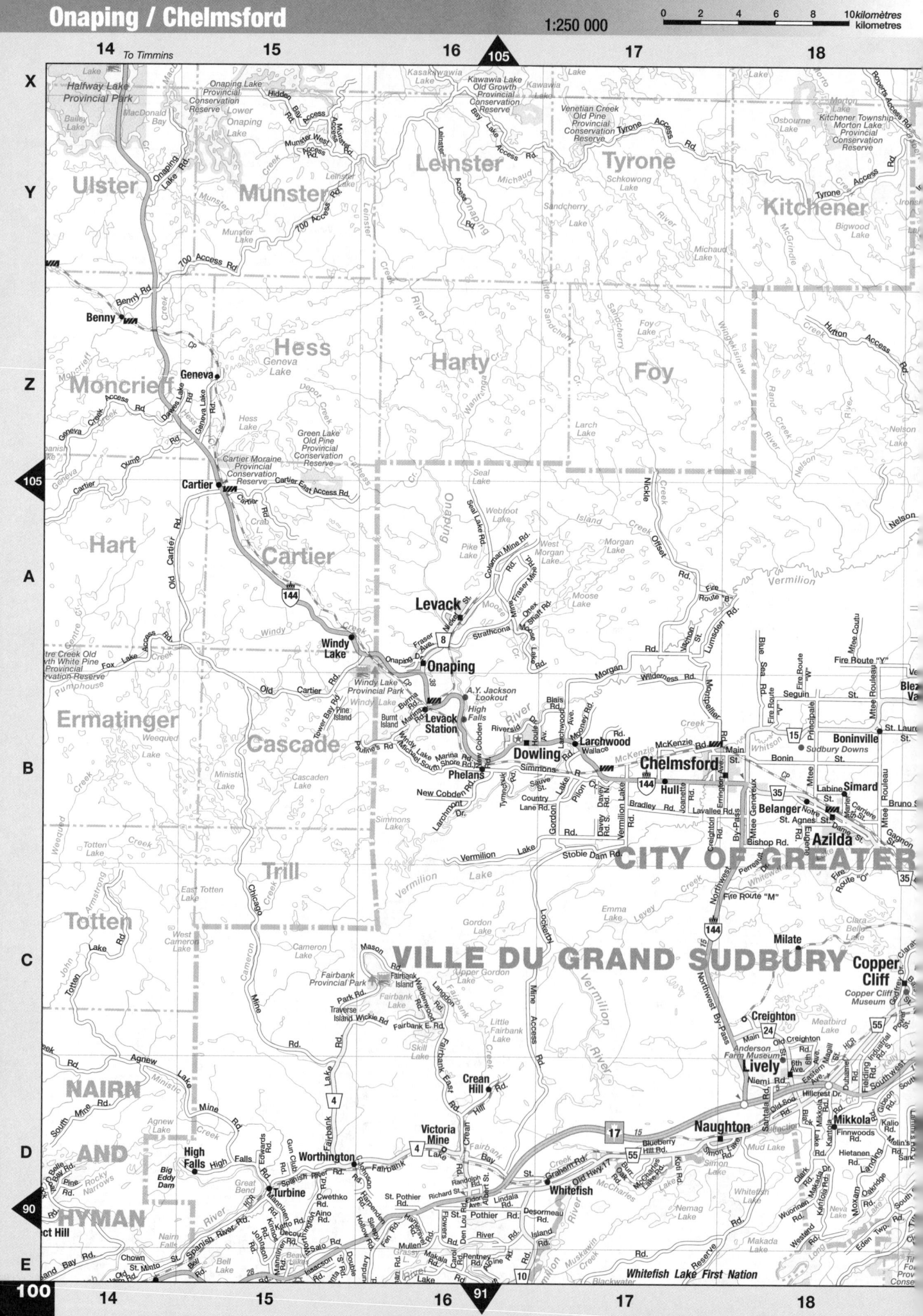

1:250 000

0 2 4 6 8 10 *kilomètres*
kilometres

14 To Timmins   **15**   **16** 105   **17**   **18**

X

Halfway Lake Provincial Park

MacDonald Bay

Bailey Lake

Onaping Lake Provincial Conservation Reserve

Lower Onaping Lake

Hidden Lake

Kasakawawia Lake

Kawawia Lake Old Growth Provincial Conservation Reserve

Venetian Creek Old Pine Provincial Conservation Reserve

Osbourne Lake

Morton Lake

Roberts Lake

Kitchener Township Morton Lake Provincial Conservation Reserve

Munster West Rd.

Leinster

Michaud Lake

Tyrone

Y

Ulster

Munster

700 Access Rd.

Leinster Access OnaPing Rd.

Tyrone

Sandcherry

Kitchener

Schkowong Lake

Bigwood Lake

McGrindle

Benny Rd.

Benny

Z

Moncrieff

Geneva

Hess

Geneva Lake

Hess Lake

Depot Creek

Harty

Wanitunga Cr.

Sandcherry River

Little Sandcherry

Foy

Larch Lake

Rand River

Nelson

Huton

Nelson

Access Rd.

105

Hart

Geneva Creek

Cartier

Cartier East Access Rd.

Green Lake Old Pine Provincial Conservation Reserve

Cartier Moraine Provincial Conservation Reserve

Seal Lake

Onaping

Webfoot Lake

Pike Lake

Island

Creek Offset

Morgan Lake

Moose Lake

Vermilion

Nickle Creek

A

Centre Creek Old Growth White Pine Provincial Conservation Reserve

Pumphouse

Old Cartier Rd.

144

Windy

Windy Lake

Fox Lake

Creek

Onaping Dr.

Fraser Ave.

8

Levack

Coleman Mine Rd.

Miller Fraser Mine Rd.

Onex Shaft Rd.

West Morgan Lake

Fire Route "B"

Lumsden Rd.

Blais Rd.

Bl...

B

Ermatinger

Weequed Lake

Cascade

Cascaden Lake

Ministic Lake

Old Cartier Rd.

Tower Bay Rd.

Pauline's Rd.

Windy Lake Provincial Park

Pine Island

Burnt Island

Levack Station

Windy Lake South

Michael

Marina Rd.

Mackey

Phelans

New Cobden Rd.

Larchmont Dr.

A.Y. Jackson Lookout

High Falls

Cobden

Riversid

Tymechuk

Country Lane Rd.

Riverside

Houle Dr.

Salve Rd.

Larchwood Ave.

Dowling

Simmons

Pilon Rd.

Davey Rd.

Davey Rd. S.

Morley Rd.

Larchwood

Wallace

McKenzie

McKenzie Rd.

Chelmsford

Hull

144

Bradley Rd.

Joanette

Lavallee Rd.

Vermilion Rd.

Mtee Generéux

Creighton Rd.

Wilderness Rd.

Montpellier

Whitson

Bonin

Sudbury Downs

Seguin St.

Fire Route "Y"

Principale

15

St. Laur...

Boninville

Mtee Rouleau

Simard

Belanger

Notre Dame

35

St. Agnes St.

Barre St.

Labine St.

Bruno St

Azilda

Gagnon

35

C

Totten

Totten Lake

John Lake

Totten Creek

West Cameron Lake

Chicago Creek

Cameron Lake

Trill

Mason Rd.

Fairbank Provincial Park

Fairbank Island

Upper Gordon Lake

Gordon Lake

VILLE DU GRAND SUDBURY

Mine Access Rd.

Emma Lake

Levey

Fire Route "M"

Northwest By-Pass

Vermilion River

144

CITY OF GREATER

Milate

Clara Bello Lake

Copper Cliff

Copper Cliff Museum

55

D

NAIRN

AND

Pine St.

Agnew Lake

Mine Creek

High Falls

Edwards

Big Eddy Dam

Spanish River Rd.

Great Bend

Turbine

Park Rd.

Fairbank Lake

Langdon

Traverse Island

Wickle Rd.

Waldenwood Rd.

Fairbank E. Rd.

Skill Lake

Little Fairbank Lake

Fairbank East Rd.

4

Crean Hill Rd.

Crean Hill

Victoria Mine

4

Fairbank Lake

Fairbank Bay

Graham Rd.

St.

Albert St.

Old Hwy 17

17

15

Blueberry Hill Rd.

55

Naughton

Mud Lake

Simon Lake

Creighton

24

Old Creighton Rd.

Anderson Farm Museum

Lively

Niemi Rd.

6th Av

Fielding Industrial Rd.

Mikkola

Finnwoods Rd.

Melin

Kalio Rd.

E

100

HYMAN

ct Hill

Chown

St. Minto

Bell Lake

Spanish River

Nairn Falls

Turbine

Cwethko Rd.

Aino Rd.

St. Pothier Rd.

Richard St.

Den Lou Rd.

Eldona Rd.

St. Pothier

Lindala Rd.

Desormeau Rd.

Whitefish

McCharles

Koti Rd.

Whitefish Lake

Nemag Lake

Makada Lake

Makada Rd.

Whitefish Lake First Nation

10

91

Eden Twp. Rd.

Mullen Rd.

Grassy Lake

Muskawin Creek

Blackwater

14   **15**   **16** 91   **17**   **18**

90

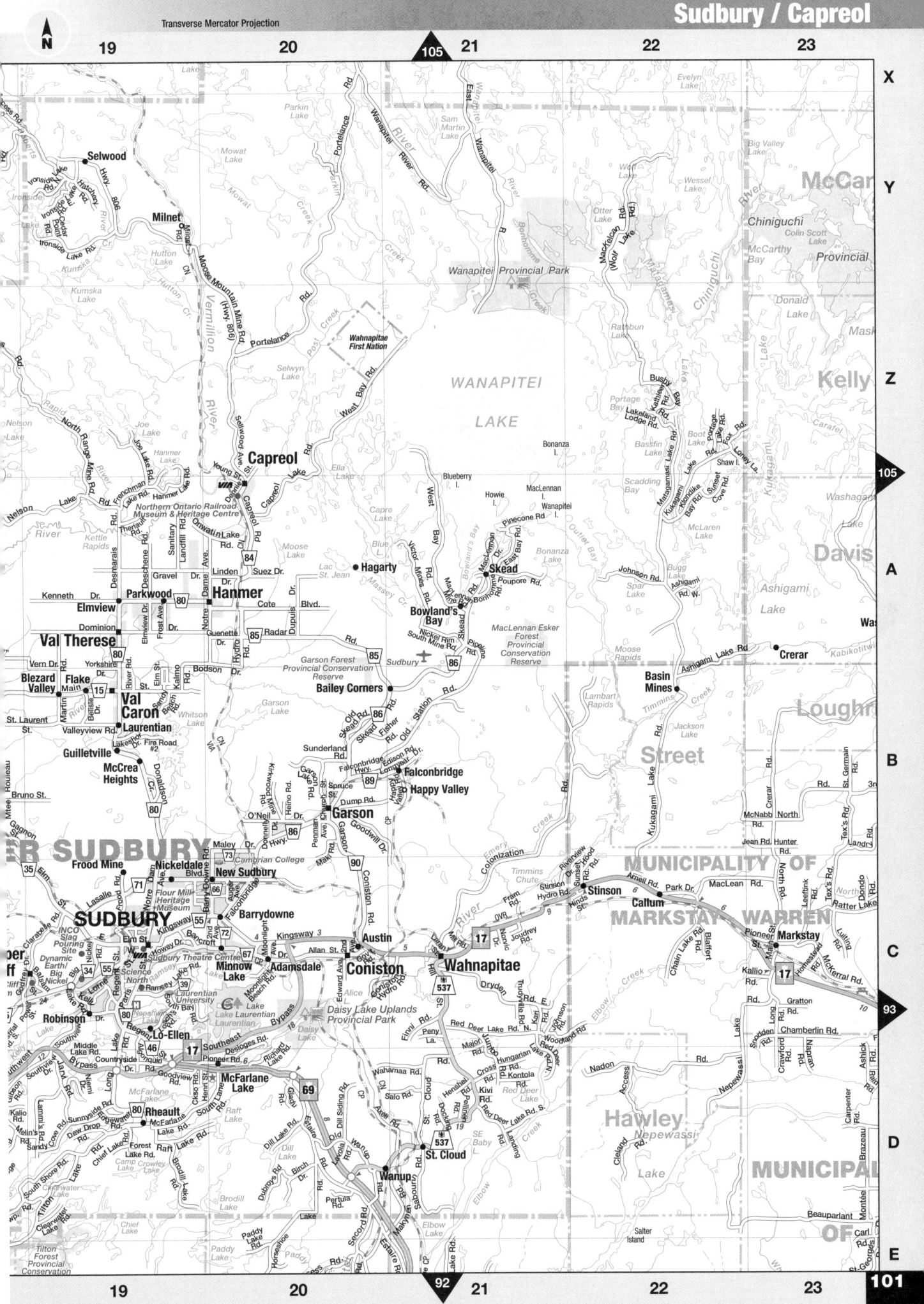

N

19   20   105   21   22   23

X
Y
Z
105
A
B
Street
C
93
D
E

McCarthy
Chiniguchi
Provincial
Kelly
Davis
Loughn
MUNICIPALITY OF
MARKSTAY WARREN
Hawley
Nepewassi
MUNICIPAL
OF

Selwood
Milnet
Capreol
Northern Ontario Railroad Museum & Heritage Centre
Hagarty
Parkwood
Hanmer
Elmview
Val Therese
Blezard Valley
Flake
Val Caron
Laurentian
Guilletville
McCrea Heights
Frood Mine
Nickeldale
New Sudbury
SUDBURY
Barrydowne
Flour Mill Heritage Museum
Sudbury Theatre Centre
Science North
Dynamic Earth
Big Nickel
Minnow Lake
Adamsdale
Robinson
Lo-Ellen
McFarlane Lake
Rheault
Coniston
Austin
Wahnapitae
St. Cloud
Wanup
Skead
Bowland's Bay
Bailey Corners
Falconbridge
Happy Valley
Garson
Stinson
Callum
Markstay
Crerar
Basin Mines
Timmins
Kenneth
WANAPITEI LAKE
Wanapitei Provincial Park
Wahnapitae First Nation
MacLennan Esker Forest Provincial Conservation Reserve
Garson Forest Provincial Conservation Reserve
Daisy Lake Uplands Provincial Park
Tilton Forest Provincial Conservation

SUDBURY

105   92   93   101

19   20   92   21   22   23

101

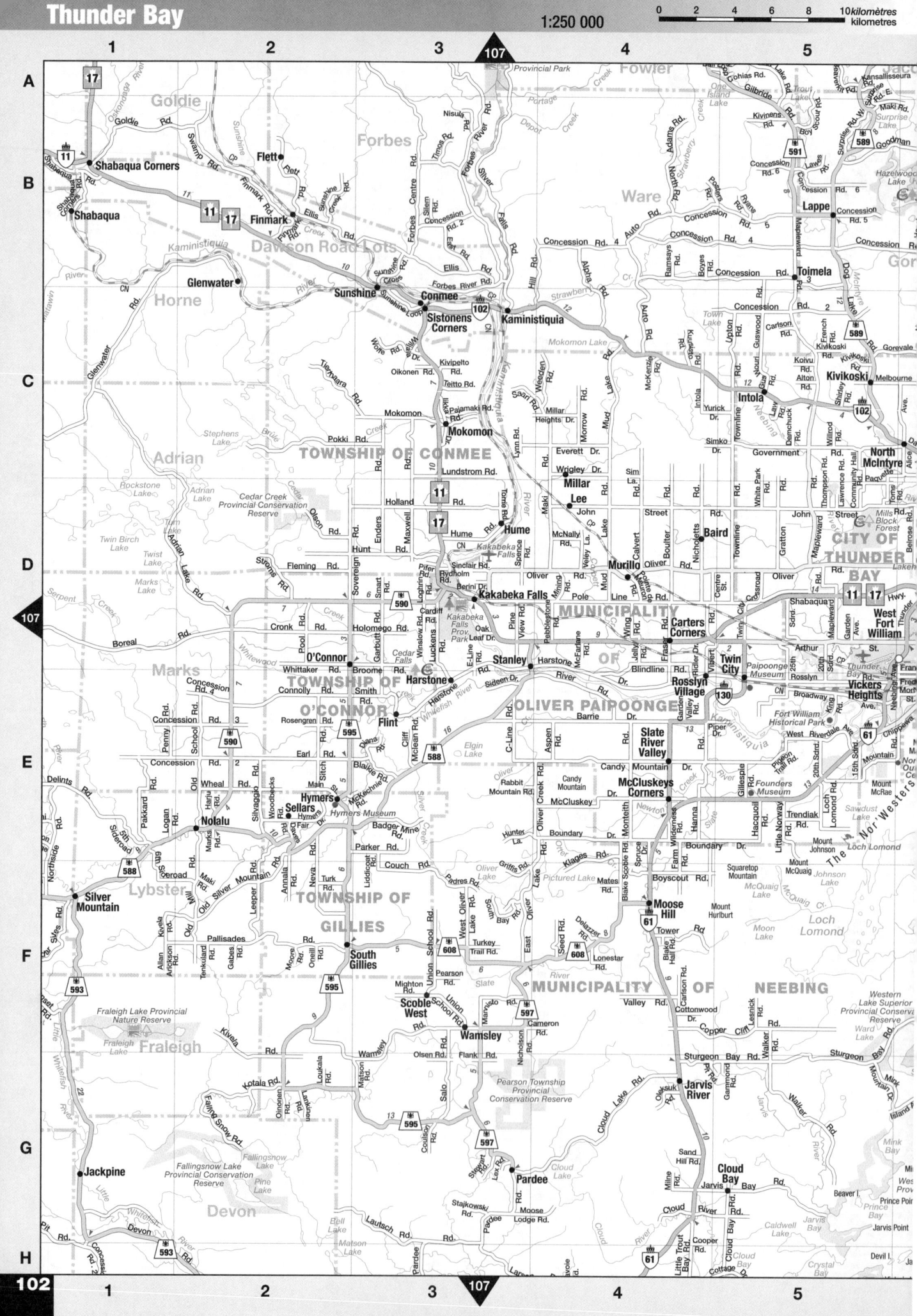

kilomètres
kilometres
0 2 4 6 8 10

Transverse Mercator Projection

N

6 7 107 8 9 10

A

Jacques
Misseura

Onion Lake
Walkinshaw Lake
Beaverlodge Lake

West Loon Rd.
Loon Lake
Silver Lake
Loon

A

Maki Rd.
Surprise Lake
Greenpike Lake
Pike Lake
Pike Lake Rd.

Southeast Onion Lake
Mogane Lake

CP
17
Deception Lake

Goodman
Maki Lake Rd.

Waller Lake

11
Blende Lake

B

Hazelwood Lake
Hazelwood Lake

Bentley Lake

Penassen Ct.
Penassen Lakes

Beck

MUNICIPALITY OF SHUNIAH

Matunina Rd.
Nelson Dr.
Birch
587

Pass Lake
CN
Commu

Mission Rd.
Gorham
Wishart Forest
Onila Rd.

527

Current River

Vigars Point
Bak Rd.

Passag Cross

Golding Lake
Millers Rd.
Evergreen
Pursiana

Stepstone
North Branch Rd.

Mackenzie

Walkinshaw Rd.
Scott Dr.
Amethyst Bay
Amethyst Harbour
Perry Point

Sour I.
Caribou Island

Sibley

B

Hazelwood Dr.
Ferguson

Silver Springs Rd.

Compressor Station Rd.

Mackenzie Creek
Otte Rd.
Amethyst Ave.
Lambert L.
Lambert I.

Hansen Rd.

Gorevale Rd.

Copenhagen Rd.
Mitchell Rd.
Isku Rd.
Mt. Baldy Rd.

Silver Harbour Dr.
Lakeshore
Silver Harbour Dr.
Mickelson
Conmee Point
Mackenzie Point

Milkshake Lake
Wiswell Lake

C

Melbourne Rd.
Fisher Rd.
Hilldale

Byers Rd.
Troutbridge Rd.
Mt. Baldy

Wild Goose Creek
13
CP

Silver Harbour
Mary Hbr.
Lefebvre I.
Silver Harbour

Mackenzie Bay

Poundsford Lake
Pounsford Lake
Lizard Lake
Lizard Lake

Joeboy Lake

North
Scenic Dr.

C

North McIntyre

Dawson
Alice
Sherwood
Wardrope

Cascades
Trowbridge Rd.
Navilus

Green White Point Rd.
Birch Rd.
Wild Goose
Wild Goose Pt.

Wild Goose

Mary Island

Thunder Bay Lookout
Clavet Point
Clavet Bay

Rita Lake
5
Rita Lake

D

Lancaster Ave.
Huron

17
11
Holden

Strathcona
Balsam

Bruce
Floral
CN

Bare Point

Sleeping Giant
Addison Lake
Twinpine Lake
587
Sifting Lake

Pickerel Lake

Mills Rd.
Block Forest

Balmoral
River
Riverdale

Boulward
Lake

THUNDER BAY

Sibley Peninsula

Provincial Park
Gardner Lake

North
Expressway
Belrose
Golf Links
Memorial

Oliver
Main St.

(LAKE SUPERIOR)

Hoorigan Bay
Marie Louise Dr.
Nanabosho
Ferns Lake

D

Hwy. Thunder
Confederation College

Lakehead Univ.

Thunder Bay North
(Port Arthur)

Marie Louise Lake
Marie Louise

107

West Fort William

James
Arthur
Waterloo
Edward

Pacific Ave.
Thunder Bay South
(Fort William)
Thunder Bay Historical Museum

McKellar Island
106th St.

Hoorigan Point
The Head
Sawyer Bay

Finlay Point
Finlay Bay

E

Francis
Frederica St.
Montreal St.
Neebing Ave.

Mission
City Rd.
CN

Welcome Islands

Mission Island Marsh
Mission Island

Thunder Mountain

Middlebrun Bay

Mt. McKay Scenic Lookout
Chippewa Park
Whiskeyjack Point

The Sleeping Giant

Silver Islet
Burnt I.
Skinaway I.

E

Mount Matchett
NorWest Outdoor Centre
Mount McRae

Fort William First Nation

Sandy Beach Rd.
Skeay

Grand Point
Brûlé Bay
McNab Point
Squaw I.
Squaw Bay

Tee Harbour
Lehtinen's Bay

Westers
Lomond

Lomond River

Thunder Cape

Shangoina Island

Trowbridge I.

LAKE
SUPERIOR

F

Russell Point
Birch I.

PIE ISLAND
Pie Island & Flatland Island Provincial General Use Area
Perch Lake

Turtle Head

F

Western Lake Superior Conservation Reserve

Pie Island & Flatland Island Provincial General Use Area
Flatland Island

Campbell I.
Keefer Point

Dawson Bay

Flatland Harbour
Margaret St.
Singleton I.
Wiley Point

Greenstone Point

Sturgeon Bay
Sturgeon Point

South McKellar I.

G

Mink Mountain Rd.
Island Ave.
Mink Bay

Windigo I.
White I.
Mink Island
Muskrat I.
Mink Point
Slipper I.

Thompson Island
Thompson Island Provincial Nature Reserve

G

Western Lake Superior Provincial Conservation Reserve
Prince Point
Prince Bay
Jarvis Point
Devil I.
Jarvis I.
Victoria Island

Spar Island

H

6 7 107 8 9 10

1:1 725 000

0 20 40 60 80 100 Kilometres
kilomètres

G

H

J

LAKE SUPERIOR

LAC SUPÉRIEUR

CANADA
U.S.A./É.-U.

MICHIGAN

K

L

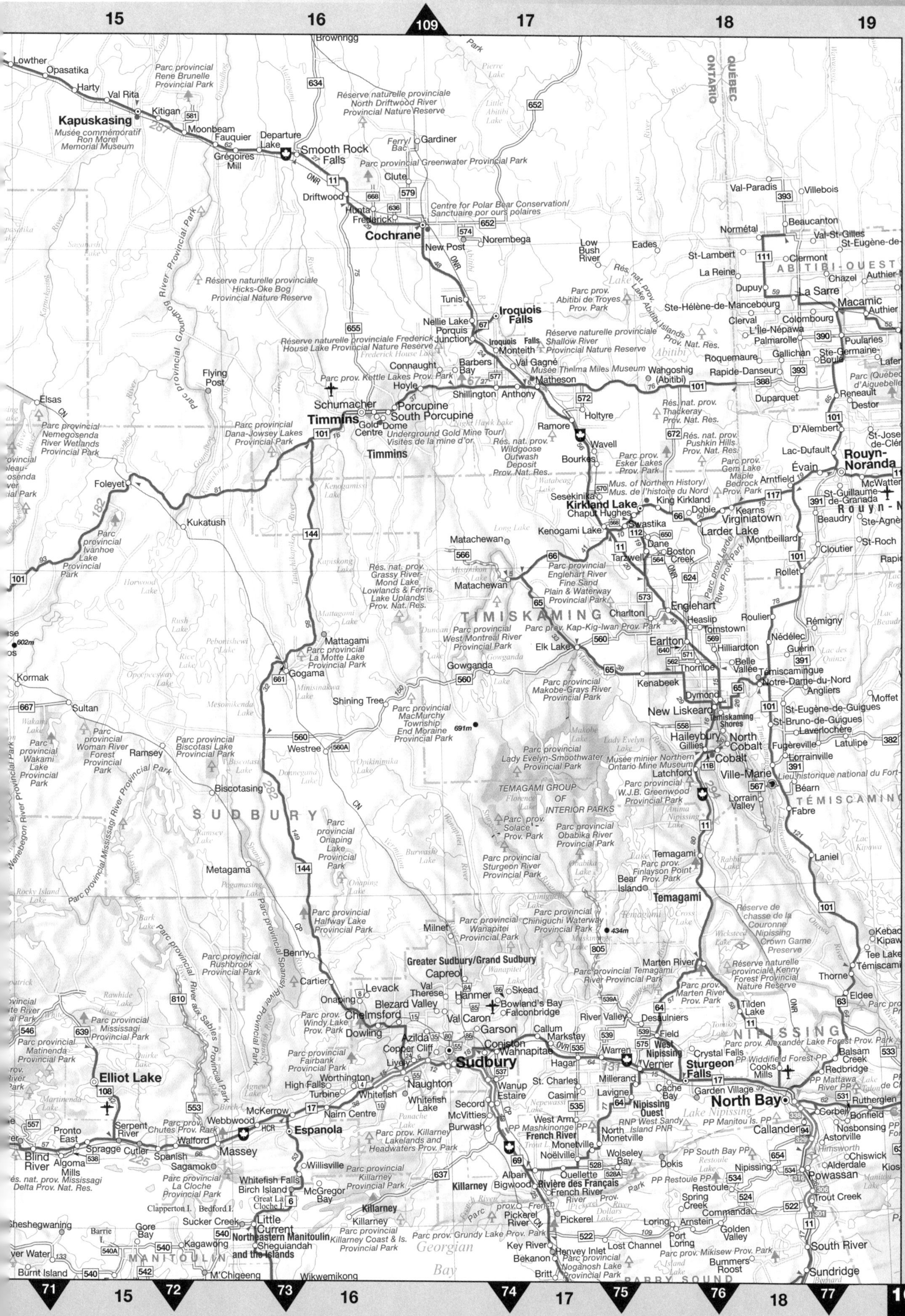

Lambert Conformal Projection

15 16 109 17 18 19

G

H

J

K

L

71 15 72 73 16 74 17 75 76 18 77

Lowther
Opasatika
Harty
Val Rita
Kitigan
Kapuskasing
Musée commémoratif Ron Morel Memorial Museum
Moonbeam
Fauquier
Grégoires Mill
Departure Lake
Smooth Rock Falls
Driftwood
Clute
Frederick
Hunta
Cochrane
New Post
Brownrigg
Gardiner
Ferry/Bac
Pierre Lake
Little Abitibi Lake
Norembega
Low Bush River
Val-Paradis
Villebois
Normétal
Beaucanton
Val-St-Gilles
St-Eugène-de-
St-Lambert
La Reine
Eades
Dupuy
Chazel
Authier-
ABITIBI-OUEST
La Sarre
Clerval
Colombourg
L'Île-Népawa
Palmarolle
Gallichan
Ste-Germaine-Boulé
Poularies
Macamic
Authier

Réserve naturelle provinciale North Driftwood River Provincial Nature Reserve
Parc provincial Rene Brunelle Provincial Park
Réserve naturelle provinciale Hicks-Oke Bog Provincial Nature Reserve
Parc provincial Greenwater Provincial Park
Centre for Polar Bear Conservation/ Sanctuaire por ours polaires

Tunis
Nellie Lake
Iroquois Falls
Iroquois Falls
Monteith
Barbers Bay
Val Gagné
Matheson
Musée Thelma Miles Museum
Wahgoshig (Abitibi)
Rapide-Danseur
Roquemaure
Duparquet
Reneault
Destor
D'Alembert
Lac-Dufault
Rouyn-Noranda
McWatter
Évain
St-Guillaume-de-Granada
Arntfield
Dobie
Kearns
Virginiatown
Larder Lake
Montbeillard
Beaudry
Ste-Agnès
St-Roch

Porquis Junction
Connaught
Hoyle
Shillington
Anthony
Holtyre
Ramore
Wavell
Bourkes
Kirkland Lake
Chaput Hughes
King Kirkland
Swastika
Kenogami Lake
Dane
Boston Creek
Tarzwell
Roulier
Rémigny
Nédélec
Guérin
Rollet

Timmins
Schumacher
Porcupine
South Porcupine
Gold Centre
Gold Dome
Underground Gold Mine Tour/ Visites de la mine d'or
Sesekinika
Matachewan
Matachewan
Charlton
Englehart
Heaslip
Tomstown
Earlton
Hilliardton
Thornloe
Belle Vallée
Dymond
New Liskeard
Témiskaming Shores
Haileybury
North Cobalt
Cobalt
Latchford
Gillies
Lorrain Valley
Ville-Marie
Fabre
Laniel

Foleyet
Kukatush
Mattagami
Gogama
Shining Tree
Gowganda
Elk Lake
Kenabeek
Westree
Biscotasing
Ramsey
Sultan
Kormak
Metagama
Benny
Cartier
Milnet
Levack
Onaping
Val Therese
Hanmer
Chelmsford
Val Caron
Capreol
Skead
Bowland's Bay
Falconbridge
Blezard Valley
Dowling
Azilda
Copper Cliff
Lively
Garson
Coniston
Wahnapitae
Markstay
Warren
Sudbury
Greater Sudbury/Grand Sudbury
Worthington
Naughton
Whitefish
Secord
Wanup
St. Charles
Verner
Sturgeon Falls
Crystal Falls
West Nipissing
North Bay
Callander

Elliot Lake
Pronto East
Spragge
Cutler
Blind River
Algoma Mills
Sagamok
Serpent River
Webbwood
Walford
Massey
Espanola
Nairn Centre
McKerrow
Whitefish
High Falls
Turbine
McVitties
Burwash
Estaire
Casimir
Lavigne
Milberand
Garden Village
Powassan
Trout Creek
South River

Little Current
Sucker Creek
Kagawong
Sheguiandah
Birch Island
McGregor Bay
Killarney
French River
Rivière des Français
Noëlville
Monetville
Wolseley Bay
Dokis
Nipissing
Restoule

SUDBURY
TIMISKAMING
NIPISSING
TÉMISCAMING
MANITOULIN
Georgian Bay
Lake Nipissing

To Amos, QC
To Val d'Or, QC
To Pembroke
To Petawawa

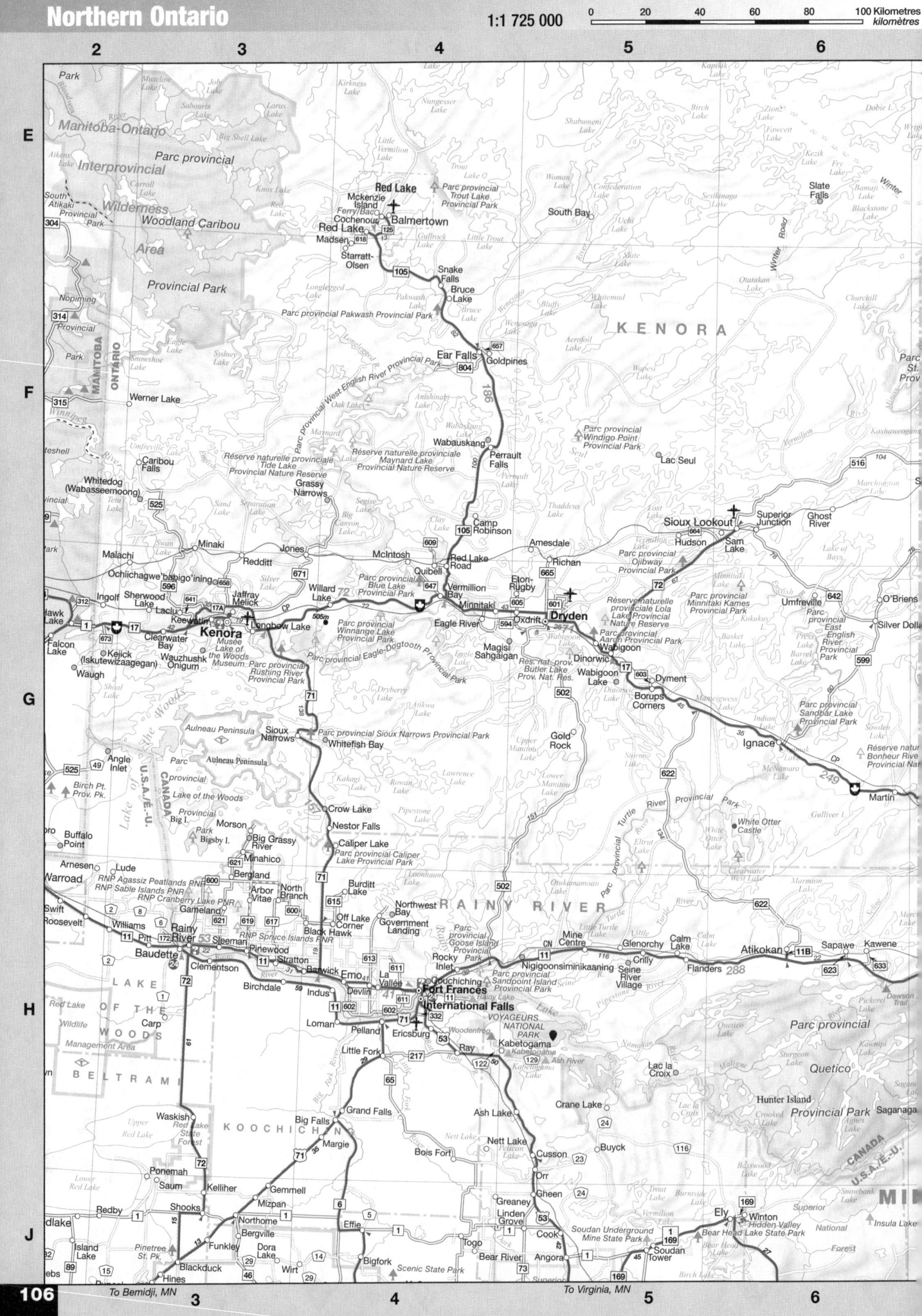

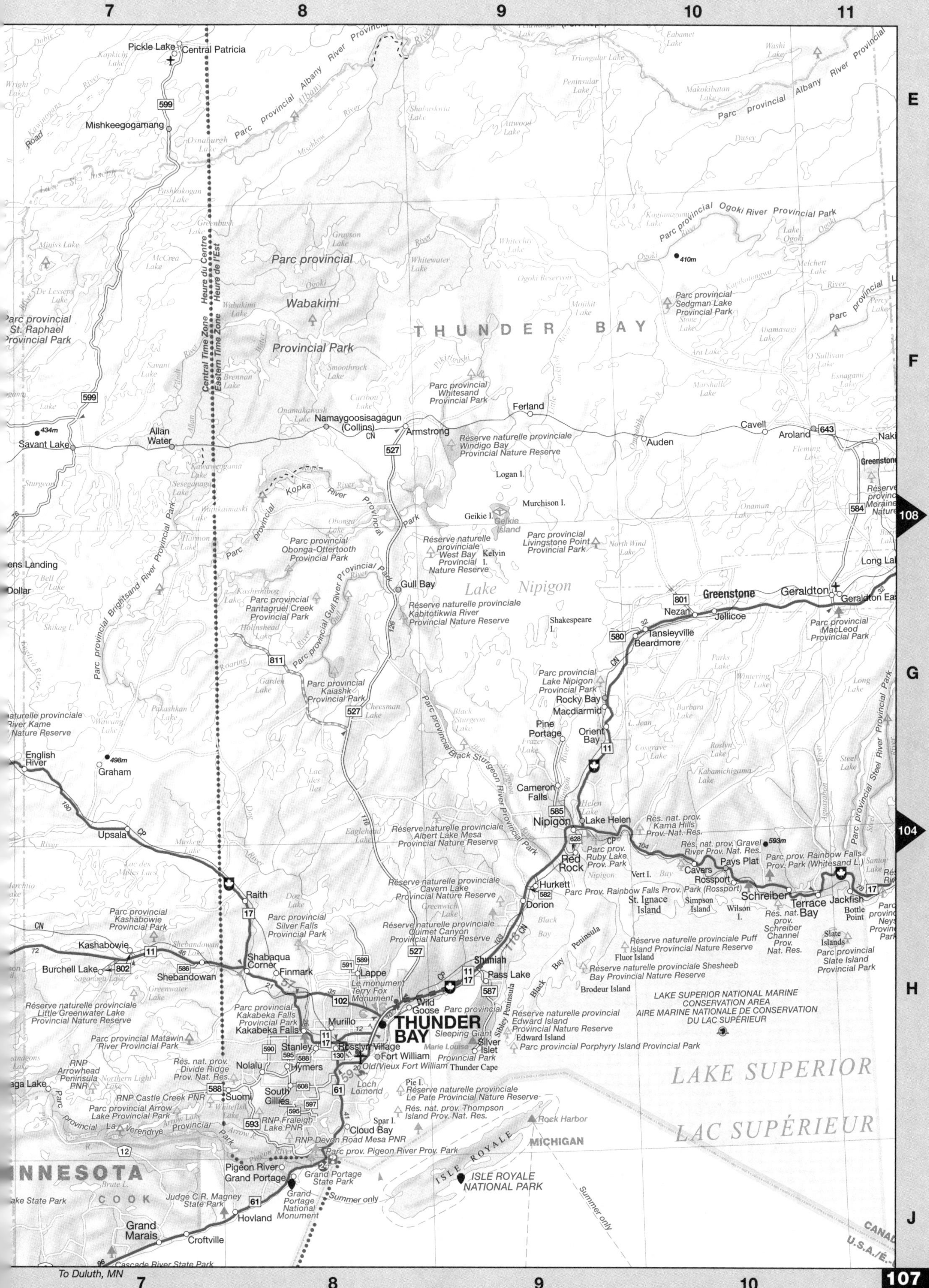

Lambert Conformal Projection

7   8   9   10   11

E

F

G

H

J

108

104

THUNDER BAY

Pickle Lake   Central Patricia

Mishkeegogamang

Parc provincial St. Raphael Provincial Park

Savant Lake   434m

Allan Water

Namaygoosisagagun (Collins)   Armstrong

Ferland   Cavell   Aroland   Naki

Greenstone

Parc provincial Wabakimi Provincial Park

Parc provincial Sedgman Lake Provincial Park

Parc provincial Whitesand Provincial Park

Reserve naturelle provinciale Windigo Bay Provincial Nature Reserve

Auden

410m

Logan I.

Murchison I.

Geikie I.   Geikie Island

Parc provincial Obonga-Ottertooth Provincial Park

Réserve naturelle provinciale West Bay Kelvin I. Provincial Nature Reserve

Parc provincial Livingstone Point Provincial Park

North Wind Lake

Long Lake

Gull Bay

Réserve naturelle provinciale Kabitotikwia River Provincial Nature Reserve

Lake Nipigon   Shakespeare I.

Greenstone   Geraldton   Geraldton East

Nezah   Jellicoe

Beardmore

Parc provincial MacLeod Provincial Park

Parc provincial Pantagruel Creek Provincial Park

Tansleyville

English River   498m

Graham

Upsala

Parc provincial Kaiashk Provincial Park

Cheesman Lake

Parc provincial Lake Nipigon Provincial Park

Rocky Bay   Macdiarmid

Pine Portage

Orient Bay

Black Sturgeon Lake

Cameron Falls

Nipigon   Lake Helen

Rés. nat. prov. Kama Hills Prov. Nat. Res.

593m   Rés. nat. prov. Gravel River Prov. Nat. Res.

Raith

Réserve naturelle provinciale Albert Lake Mesa Provincial Nature Reserve

Red Rock

Parc prov. Ruby Lake Prov. Park

Pays Plat

Cavers   Rossport (Rossport)

Schreiber   Terrace Bay   Jackfish

Parc provincial Kashabowie Provincial Park

Réserve naturelle provinciale Cavern Lake Provincial Nature Reserve

Hurkett

Dorion

Parc Prov. Rainbow Falls Prov. Park   St. Ignace Island

Simpson Island   Wilson I.

Rés. nat. prov. Schreiber Channel Prov. Nat. Res.

Parc prov. Rainbow Falls Prov. Park (Whitesand L.)

Slate Islands   Parc provincial Slate Island Provincial Park

Bottle Point

Kashabowie

Burchell Lake

Shebandowan

Shabaqua Corner   Finmark

Parc provincial Silver Falls Provincial Park

Réserve naturelle provinciale Quimet Canyon Provincial Nature Reserve

Greenwich Lake

Shuniah   Pass Lake

Réserve naturelle provinciale Puff Island Provincial Nature Reserve   Fluor Island

Réserve naturelle provinciale Shesheeb Bay Provincial Nature Reserve

Réserve naturelle provinciale Little Greenwater Lake Provincial Nature Reserve

Lappe   Le monument Terry Fox Monument

Wild Goose

Parc provincial Sibley Peninsula   Black Bay Peninsula

Réserve naturelle provincial Edward Island Provincial Nature Reserve   Edward Island

Brodeur Island

LAKE SUPERIOR NATIONAL MARINE CONSERVATION AREA / AIRE MARINE NATIONALE DE CONSERVATION DU LAC SUPÉRIEUR

Parc provincial Matawin River Provincial Park

Parc provincial Kakabeka Falls Provincial Park   Kakabeka Falls

Murillo

THUNDER BAY

Sleeping Giant

Marie Louise Lake Provincial Park

Silver Islet

Parc provincial Porphyry Island Provincial Park

RNP Arrowhead Peninsula PNR   Northern Light

Rosslyn Village   Fort William

Stanley

Nolalu   Hymers

Old/Vieux Fort William

Pie I.

Réserve naturelle provinciale Le Pate Provincial Nature Reserve

LAKE SUPERIOR / LAC SUPÉRIEUR

RNP Castle Creek PNR

Parc provincial Arrow Lake Provincial Park   La Verendrye Provincial

Suomi

South Gillies

RNP Fraleigh Lake PNR

Loch Lomond

Spar I.

Cloud Bay

Rés. nat. prov. Thompson Island Prov. Nat. Res.

Rock Harbor

MICHIGAN

RNP Devon Road Mesa PNR

Parc prov. Pigeon River Prov. Park

ISLE ROYALE

ISLE ROYALE NATIONAL PARK

MINNESOTA

COOK

Pigeon River   Grand Portage

Grand Portage State Park

Summer only

Judge C.R. Magney State Park

Grand Portage National Monument

Summer only

Lake State Park

Grand Marais

Croftville

Hovland

Cascade River State Park

To Duluth, MN

CANADA   U.S.A./É.-U.

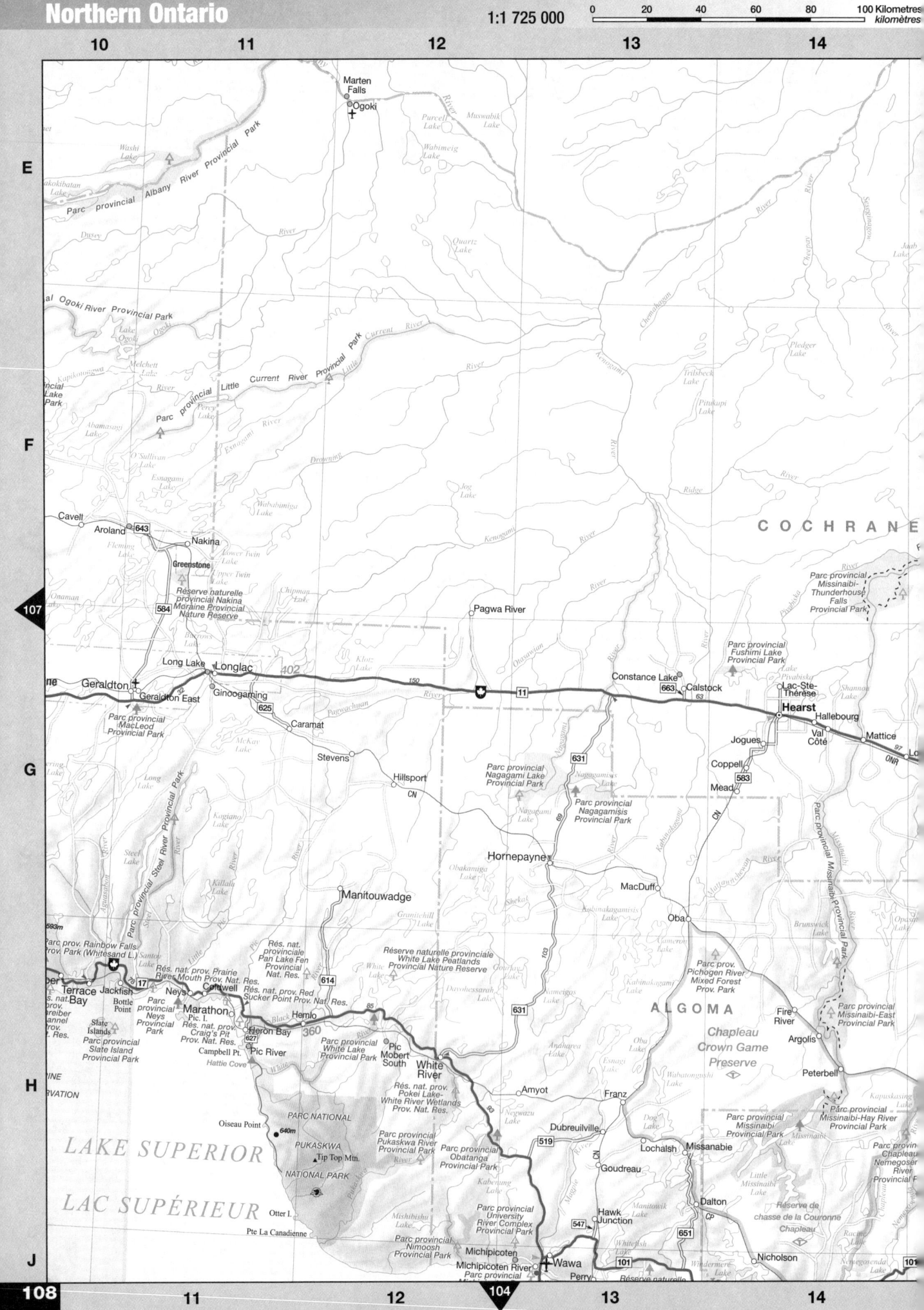

Marten Falls
Ogoki
Purcell Lake
Muswabik Lake
Wabimeig Lake
Quartz Lake

Washi Lake
Dusey River

Parc provincial Albany River Provincial Park

COCHRANE

Parc provincial Ogoki River Provincial Park
Lake Ogoki

Melchett Lake
Kapikanomiwa
Abamasagi Lake

Little Current River Provincial Park
Parc provincial

O'Sullivan Lake
Esnagami Lake
Wababimiga Lake
Drowning River

Jog Lake

Trilsbeck Lake
Pledger Lake
Pitukupi Lake

Cavell
Aroland 643
Nakina
Greenstone
Réserve naturelle provincial Nakina Moraine Provincial Nature Reserve
584
Fleming Lake
Lower Twin
Upper Twin
Chipman Lake

Parc provincial Missinaibi-Thunderhouse Falls Provincial Park

Pagwa River

Parc provincial Fushimi Lake Provincial Park

Long Lake
Longlac
402
150
11
Constance Lake
663
Calstock
53
Lac-Ste-Thérèse
Shannon Lake

Geraldton
Geraldton East
Ginoogaming
625
Caramat
Klotz Lake
Pagwachuan River

Hearst
Hallebourg
Jogues
Val Côté
Mattice
97
ONR
Lo

Parc provincial MacLeod Provincial Park
McKay Lake
Stevens

631
Coppell
583
Mead

Hillsport
CN

Parc provincial Nagagami Lake Provincial Park
Nagagamisus Lake
Parc provincial Nagagamisis Provincial Park
80

Long Lake
Kagiano Lake

Steel Lake

Parc Provincial Steel River Provincial Park

Killala Lake

Nagagami Lake
Horsepayne
MacDuff
Kabinakagamis Lake
CN

Oba

Brunswick Lake
Opasa

Manitouwadge
Granitehill Lake
Obakamiga Lake
Shekak
Kabinakagami Lake
Oba Lake
Cameron Lake

Parc prov. Rainbow Falls Prov. Park (Whitesand L.)
593m

Rés. nat. provinciale Pan Lake Fen Provincial Nat. Res.
Réserve naturelle provinciale White Lake Peatlands Provincial Nature Reserve
White Lake
Davohassarah Lake
631

Parc prov. Pichogen River Mixed Forest Prov. Park

ALGOMA

Fire River
Parc provincial Missinaibi-East Provincial Park
Argolis

Terrace Bay
Jackfish
Bottle Point
Neys
Coldwell
17
76
Rés. nat. prov. Prairie River Mouth Prov. Nat. Res.
614
Rés. nat. prov. Red Sucker Point Prov. Nat. Res.
85
Nameigos Lake

Chapleau Crown Game Preserve
Peterbell

Slate Islands
Parc provincial Neys Provincial Park
Pic I.
Marathon
Hemlo
Rés. nat. prov. Craig's Pit Prov. Nat. Res.
627
360
Heron Bay
Pic River
Pic Mobert South
White River
Anahareo Lake
Esnagi Lake

Parc provincial Slate Island Provincial Park
Campbell Pt.
Hattie Cove
Parc provincial White Lake Provincial Park
Rés. nat. prov. Pokei Lake-White River Wetlands Prov. Nat. Res.
83
Amyot
Franz
Dubreuilville
519
Wabatongushi Lake
Dog Lake

Parc provincial Missinaibi-Hay River Provincial Park

Oiseau Point
640m

PARC NATIONAL PUKASKWA
Tip Top Mtn.
NATIONAL PARK
Parc provincial Pukaskwa River Provincial Park
Parc provincial Obatanga Provincial Park
Negwazu Lake
CN
Lochalsh
Missanabie
Goudreau

Parc provincial Chapleau Nemegoser River Provincial P.
Little Missinaibi Lake
Réserve de chasse de la Couronne Chapleau

LAKE SUPERIOR
LAC SUPÉRIEUR

Otter I.
Pte La Canadienne
Mishibishu Lake

Kabenung Lake
Parc provincial University River Complex Provincial Park
Manitowik Lake
Dalton
547
Hawk Junction
651
Whitefish Lake

Parc provincial Nimoosh Provincial Park
Michipicoten
Michipicoten River
Parc provincial
Wawa
Perry
101
Nicholson
Windermere Lake
Nemegosenda Lake
101

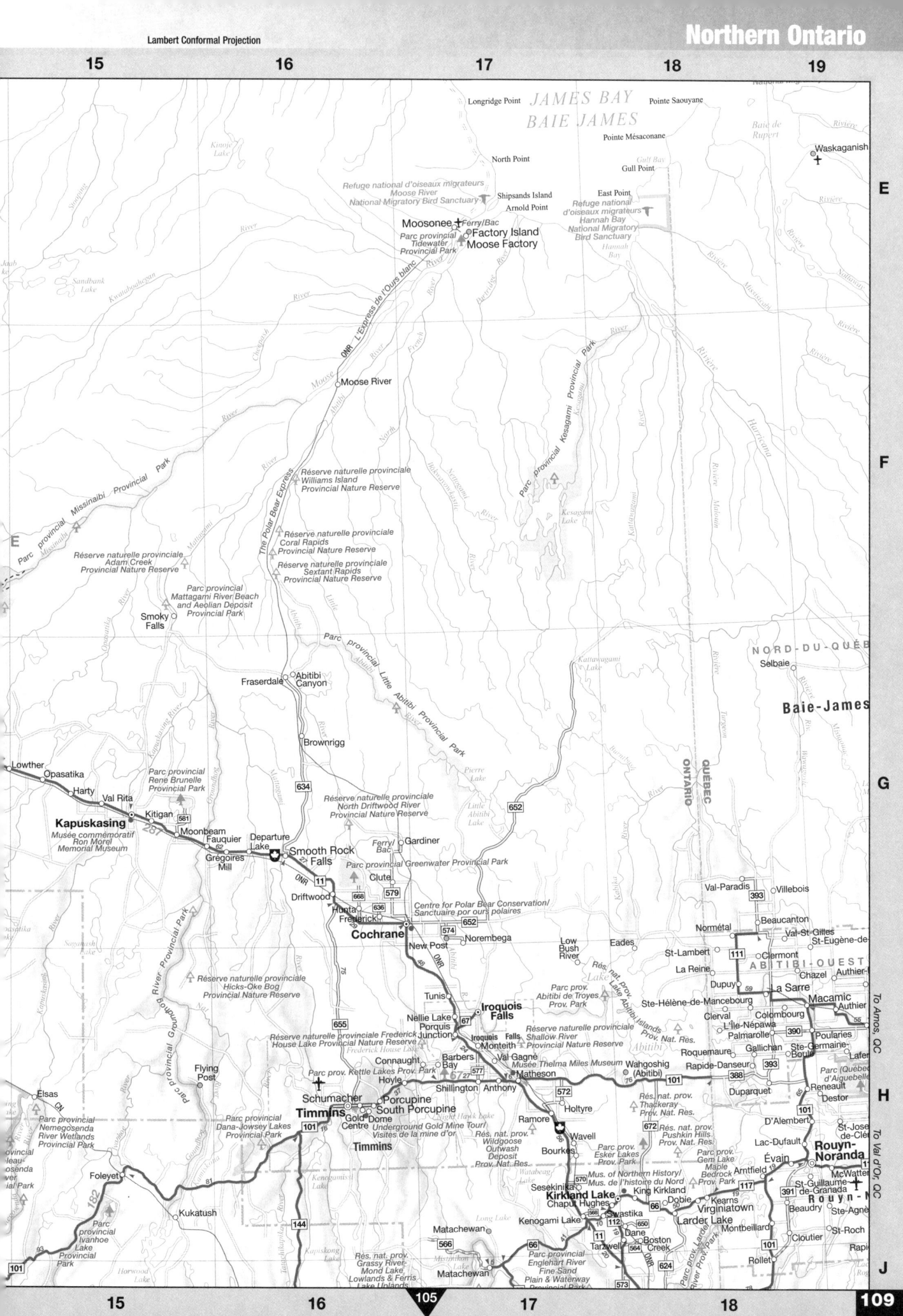

JAMES BAY
BAIE JAMES

Longridge Point   Pointe Saouyane

North Point

Refuge national d'oiseaux migrateurs
Moose River
National Migratory Bird Sanctuary

Shipsands Island
Arnold Point

Pointe Mésaconane

Baie de
Rupert

Waskaganish

Gull Bay
Gull Point

East Point
Refuge national
d'oiseaux migrateurs
Hannah Bay
National Migratory
Bird Sanctuary

Hannah Bay

Moosonee Ferry/Bac
Parc provincial   Factory Island
Tidewater   Moose Factory
Provincial Park

ONR L'Express de l'Ours blanc

Moose River

The Polar Bear Express

Réserve naturelle provinciale
Williams Island
Provincial Nature Reserve

Parc provincial Kesagami Provincial Park

Kesagami
Lake

NORD-DU-QUÉBEC

Réserve naturelle provinciale
Coral Rapids
Provincial Nature Reserve

Réserve naturelle provinciale
Sextant Rapids
Provincial Nature Reserve

Parc provincial Missinaibi Provincial Park

Parc
provincial
Missinaibi

Réserve naturelle provinciale
Adam Creek
Provincial Nature Reserve

Parc provincial
Mattagami River Beach
and Aeolian Deposit
Provincial Park

Smoky
Falls

Parc provincial Little Abitibi Provincial Park

Selbaie

Baie-James

Fraserdale   Abitibi
Canyon

Kattawagami
Lake

Brownrigg

Pierre
Lake

Lowther Opasatika
Harty Val Rita   Kitigan
Kapuskasing 581
Musée commémoratif Moonbeam
Ron Morel Fauquier
Memorial Museum Grégoires
Mill

Parc provincial
Rene Brunelle
Provincial Park

634

Réserve naturelle provinciale
North Driftwood River
Provincial Nature Reserve

652

Little
Abitibi
Lake

Val-Paradis Villebois

393

Departure
Lake Smooth Rock
Falls

Ferry/
Bac Gardiner

Parc provincial Greenwater Provincial Park

Normétal

Beaucanton
Val-St-Gilles
St-Eugène-de-

ONR 11
668 Clute
Driftwood 579
Hunta 636
Fredrickt 574
Cochrane 652
New Post

Centre for Polar Bear Conservation/
Sanctuaire pour ours polaires

Norembega

Low
Bush
River

St-Lambert
La Reine

Eades
Dupuy

111

Clermont

ABITIBI-OUEST

Chazel Authier-

La Sarre
Macamic

To Amos, QC

Tunis

655

Nellie Lake
Porquis
Junction

67
Iroquois
Falls

Iroquois Falls
Monteith

Réserve naturelle provinciale
Shallow River
Provincial Nature Reserve

Rés. nat. prov.
Abitibi de Troyes
Prov. Park

Ste-Hélène-de-Mancebourg
59

Réserve naturelle provinciale Frederick
House Lake Provincial Nature Reserve

Frederick House Lake

Réserve naturelle provinciale
Hicks-Oke Bog
Provincial Nature Reserve

Flying
Post

Elsas

Parc provincial
Nemegosenda
River Wetlands
Provincial Park

Parc provincial
Dana-Jowsey Lakes
Provincial Park

Connaught
Barbers
Bay

Val Gagné
Musée Thelma Miles Museum
Matheson

Parc prov. Kettle Lakes Prov. Park

Hoyle
577
27 Shillington Anthony

572

Clerval
L'Île-Népawa
Palmarolle
Roquemaure

Rés. nat. prov.
Abitibi-Islands
Prov. Res.

Abitibi

Colombourg
390
Gallichan

Poularies
Authier
55

Ste-Germaine-
Boulé
393

Lafer

Parc (Québec)
d'Aiguebelle

Schumacher
Timmins Gold
Centre
101 16
Timmins South Porcupine
Underground Gold Mine Tour/
Visites de la mine d'or

Porcupine

Wahgoshig
(Abitibi)

Rapide-Danseur

388

101

Duparquet

Reneault
Destor
101

D'Alembert

Lac-Dufault

McWatter

Ramore

Rés. nat. prov.
Wildgoose
Outwash
Deposit
Prov. Nat. Res.

Holtyre

Rés. nat. prov.
Thackeray
Prov. Nat. Res.

672 Rés. nat. prov.
Pushkin Hills
Prov. Nat. Res.

Parc prov.
Esker Lakes
Prov. Nat. Res.

St-Jose-
de-Clé-

Rouyn-
Noranda

Évain Amtfield

To Val d'Or, QC

Foleyet
182

Parc provincial
Ivanhoe
Lake
Provincial Park

Kukatush

144

Sesekinika
Wavell
Bourkes
Mus. of Northern History/
Mus. de l'histoire du Nord

Kirkland Lake
Chapul Hughes   King Kirkland

Parc prov.
Gem Lake
Maple
Bedrock Park

117

St-Guillaume-
de-Granada

391

Gallagher

Beaudry

Virginiatown
66 Dobie Larder Lake
Swastika
Kenogami Lake 112 650

Montbeillard

Ste-Agnè-

Rouyn-N

101

Matachewan
566

Matachewan

11
Tarzwell
564

Dane Boston
Creek

Parc provincial
Englehart River
Fine Sand
Plain & Waterway
Provincial Park

Rés. nat. prov.
Grassy River-
Mond Lake,
Lowlands & Ferris
Lake Uplands

624

573

Cloutier
St-Roch

Rollet
Rapi

E

F

G

H

J

Place Name Index

How to use this index

To find a place, search through the alphabetically arranged columns. Note the page number and reference square to the right of the place name. For example, to find the location of Hendrie:

Hendrie **41** A28

Place name / Page number / Reference Square

Chercher le nom de la localité dans la première colonne. Noter le Numéro de page et les coordonnées à côté du nom. Par exemple, pour trouver Mattice:

Mattice **108** G14

Localités / Numéro de page / Coordonnées

Aberarder 13 S10
Aberdeen (Grey) . . 27 D20
Aberdeen (Prescott & Russell) 68 P71
Aberfeldy 13 V11
Aberfoyle 23 N26
Abingdon 18 S30
Abitibi 105 H18
Abitibi Canyon . . 109 G16
Aboyne 22 K24
Acanthus 97 H40
Achigan . . 84 X93 104 K13
Achill 29 F-G28
Achray 80 K46
Actinolite 46 A49
Acton 23 L27
Actons Corners . . 50 V62
Adamsdale 101 C20
Adamsville 39 W18
Adanac 56 O24
Addington 47 Z50-51
Addison 49 Y-Z61
Adelaide 13 T13
Adelard 97 F43
Admaston 82 P54
Adolphustown . . . 35 F52
Advance 72 K8
Agawa Bay 104 J13
Agerton . . 23 M28 24 M29
Agincourt 25 J33
Ahmic Harbour . . 76 M29
Ahmic Lake 76 N30
Aikensville 23 N25
Ailsa Craig 14 R14
Airlie 29 D27
Ajax 25 H35
Alban . . 92 G22 105 K17
Albert 35 C51
Alberton 17 R26-27
Albion . . 24 H29 29 H28
Albuna 5 D5
Albury 34 F47
Alcona 30 C31
Alder 30 E32
Alderdale 95 G33
Aldershot . . 18 P29 23 P28
Alderslea 30 C31
Alderville 33 D-E43
Aldreds Beach . . 31 E36
Alexandria 52 R71
Alfred 68 P69
Alfred Station . . 68 P69
Algoma Mills . 88 F5 105 K15
Algonquin 50 Y63
Alice 81 L50
Allan Mills 46 B46
Allan Park 27 E19-20
Allan Water . . . 107 F7
Allanburg 19 S34
Allans Corners . . . .
. . . . 81 M51 82 M52
Allen 46 Z48
Allenford . . 38 A17 39 A18
Allens Corner . . 18 S30-31
Allensville . 58 S32 59 S33
Allenwood 41 Z27-28
Allenwood Beach . 41 Z27
Allimil 30 E29
Allisonville 34 F49
Alliston 29 E28
Alloa 23 K28
Alma 22 K23
Alma Station . . . 22 K23
Almira 30 G32
Almonte 65 S58
Alport 58 U32
Alsace 94 H30
Alsfelder 27 F19
Althorpe 48 X56-57
Alton 29 H26
Altona 31 G33
Alvanley 39 A18
Alvinston 13 V11
Amaranth Station . 29 H25
Amberley 26 F13
Ambleside 27 F17
Ameliasburg . . . 34 F48
Amesdale 106 F5
Amethyst Harbour . . . . . .
. . . . 103 B-C9
Amherst Pointe . . . 4 E1
Amherstburg 4 D1
Amherstview . . 36 D54-55
Amigo Beach . . . 42 Y32
Amulree 21 N20
Amyot 104 H13
Ancaster 17 O27
Ancona Point . . 44 A38
Anderson (Lennox & Addington) . 35 D52 E52-53
Anderson (Perth) . 21 P17
Andrewsville . 49 V61 50 V62
Andys Corners . 10 V22-23

Angus 29 C28
Annable Settlement . . . .
. . . . 67 T-U65
Annan 39 Z20
Anoma Lea 49 Z61
Ansnorveldt 30 F31
Anson 34 C47
Ansonia 86 D97
Anstruther Lake . . . . . .
. . . . . . 44 X41 45 X42
Anten Mills . . . 41 A28-29
Anthony 105 H17
Antrim 65 R58-59
Appin 13 V13
Apple Hill 52 S70
Appleby Corner . . 93 D24
Appledore 6 Y9
Appleton 65 T59
Apsley 45 X43
Apto 41 A29
Arbor Vitae . . . 106 H3
Archer 51 V67-68
Archipelago, The . . . . . .
. . . . . . 74 N23 75 N24
Ardbeg 75 M26-27
Arden 47 Y53
Ardendale . . . 47 Y52-53
Ardmore Beach . . 41 Y27
Ardoch 47 V53
Ardtrea 42 Y32
Argolis 104 H14
Argyle 43 B35
Ariss 22 L24
Arkell 23 M26
Arklan 48 U57
Arkona 13 S12
Arkwood 6 Y9
Arkwright . . . 38 A-B17
Armow 26 D15
Armstrong . . . 107 F8-9
Armstrong Mills . 23 L25
Armstrongs Corners . . . .
. . . . 49 V-W58
Arner 4 E3
Arnott 48 U57
Arnott 39 B20
Arnprior 65 Q57
Arnstein 76 J28
Aroland . . 107 F10 108 F11
Arranvale . . 38 B17 39 B18
Arthur 22 K23
Arva 14 S16
Ashburn 31 G35
Ashby Mill 45 A45
Ashdad 64 R54
Ashgrove 23 L28
Ashton 65 T60
Ashworth 58 R32
Aspdin 58 R32
Asseltine 36 D54
Assumption 33 C41
Astorville 95 F33
Atha Road 31 G34
Athens 47 Z60-61
Atherley 42 Z32
Atherton 10 V23-24
Athlone 29 F28
Athol 35 G50
Athol (Stormont, Dundas,
& Glengarry) . . 52 R69
Atikokan 106 H6
Atironto 49 W60
Atkinson 37 C58
Attercliffe . . . 18 T30-31
Attercliffe Station . 18 T31
Atwood 21 K18-19
Auburn 20 J14-15
Auden 107 F10
Aughrim 13 V11
Augsburg 81 P51
Auld K14
Aurora 30 G31-32
Austin 101 C20-21
Avalon Park . . . 10 V25
Avening 29 C26-27
Avery Point . . . 43 Y34
Avon 9 U19
Avonbank . . . 21 P17-18
Avondale . . . 52 S70-71
Avonmore 52 T69
Avonry 12 V7-8
Avonton 21 P18
Axe Lake 58 Q31
Aylen 97 F41
Aylen Lake . . 80 N45-46
Aylen Lake Station . . . . .
. . . . 80 N45-46
Aylesworth . . 36 D55-56
Aylmer 9 V19
Ayr 16 O23
Ayton 27 F19-20
Azilda . 100 B18 105 K16-17

Babys Point 6 W-X6
Back Settlement, The . . . .
. . . . 89 E8-9
Baddow 43 Z37
Baden 22 N21
Badenoch 23 N26
Badgers Corners . 57 Q27
Badjeros 29 D25
Bagnall 5 B7
Baie Du Dore . 26 C14-15
Bailey Corners . 101 B20
Bailieboro 33 E41
Bainsville 53 T73
Baird 102 D4-5
Bairds 8 V16
Baker Trail . . 43 X35-36
Bala 57 U30
Bala Park 57 U30
Balaclava (Grey) . 39 Y21
Balaclava (Renfrew) 64 Q53
Balderson 48 V57
Baldoon 6 Y7-8
Baldwin 30 D32
Baldwins Bridge . 50 V65
Ball Subdivision . 43 A34
Ballahack 47 A52
Ballantrae 30 F32
Ballinafad 23 K27
Ballycanoe 37 A61
Ballycroy 29 G28
Ballyduff 32 E38
Ballymote . . 14 S16 15 S17
Balm Beach . . . 41 Y27
Balmertown . . . 106 E4
Balmoral . . 11 U27-28
Balmy Beach . . . 39 Z19
Balsam 31 G34
Balsam Creek . . . .
. . . . . . 95 D33 105 K18
Balsam Hill . . 82 P53-54
Baltics Corners . 52 R70
Baltimore 33 F42
Balvenie 63 S51-52
Bamberg . . . 22 M21-22
Banbury 58 Q31
Bancroft . . 61 U45 62 U46
Banda 29 C26-27
Bangor Lodge . . 58 U32
Banks 40 A24
Banner 19 T19
Bannockburn . . . 46 Y47
Baptiste 61 T44
Bar Point 4 E1
Bar River 86 C94
Barb 68 P72
Barbers Bay . . 105 H17
Barbers Beach . 23 N25
Barclay 30 C30
Barcovan Beach . 34 F46-47
Bardsville . . 58 T31-32
Barhead 28 C22
Barkway 43 W34
Barlochan 58 U31
Barrett Chute . . 64 S54
Barretville 4 E3
Barrhaven 66 S62
Barrie 42 B30
Barrie Island . . . 71 J6
Barriefield 36 D56
Barrilla Park . . . 42 B31
Barrow Bay 55 V17
Barrydowne . . . 101 C20
Barrymere 62 U47
Barrys Bay 80 P47
Barryvale 64 S54
Barwick 106 H4
Basin Mines . . 101 B22
Basingstoke . . 18 R-S30
Baskin's Beach . 65 P60
Bass Creek 73 K11
Bass Lake Park . 42 Z31
Batawa 34 E47
Batchawana Bay . . . . . .
. . . . 84 W90 104 K13
Batchewana First Nation . .
. . . . 84 Z90-91
Bates Subdivision . 7 B12
Bath 36 E54
Bathurst Station . 48 W57
Batteaux 41 A26
Battersea 36 B57
Baxter 29 D28
Baxters Corners . 22 N21
Bay Beach 19 U35
Bayfield 20 L13
Bayfield Inlet . 74 M-N23
Bayshore Estates . 30 C30
Bayshore Village 42 A33 Z33
Bayside 34 E48
Baysville 59 T34
Bayswater . . . 92 G-H21
Bayview (Grey) . . 39 Z21
Bayview (Huron) 20 N12-13

Bayview (Lennox & Addington) . . 36 D54-55
Bayview Beach . . . .
. . . . . . 42 A33 43 A34
Bayview Park . . . 41 W28
Baywood Park . . 42 A31-32
Beachburg . 82 L53-54 M53
Beachville 15 S20
Beaconsfield . . . 16 S22
Beales Mills . . 49 Z60-61
Bealton 10 T25
Beamsville . . . 18 R31-32
Bear Cave . . 57 R30 58 R31
Bear Island . . 105 J-K17
Bear Lake 76 P30
Bear Point 42 B31
Bear Valley 76 J29
Bearbrook 67 Q66
Bearline 6 A8
Beatrice 58 T32
Beatty 48 U54
Beaucage . . . 94 D29-30
Beaumaris 58 U31
Beaver Meadow . . 6 W8-9
Beaverbrook . . . 65 R61
Beaverdale 40 B22
Beavers Corner . 17 S27
Beaverton . 42 B33 43 B34
Becher 6 X7-8
Beck 103 B9
Beckett Creek . 67 P65-66
Becketts Bridge . 18 T32
Becketts Landing 66 U62-63
Beckstead 67 U67
Beckwith 49 U59
Bedell 50 V63
Bedford (Durham) . 25 H34
Bedford (Frontenac) . . . .
. . . . 48 Z55-56
Bedford Mills . . . 48 Z57
Beech Beach . 86 F-G95
Beech Corners . 47 V51-52
Beechmount . . 61 U44-45
Beechwood (Chatham-Kent) . . 7 A11 Y11
Beechwood (Huron) . . . . .
. . . . . . 20 M16 21 M17
Beechwood (Middlesex) . . .
. . . . 14 S14
Beeton 30 F29
Bekanon . . . 74 K22-23
Belanger 100 B18
Belangers Corners . 64 Q54
Belfast 26 G-H14
Belfountain 23 J27
Belgrave 20 J16
Belhaven 30 D32
Bell's Corners 65 R61 66 R62
Bell Ewart . . 30 C30-31
Bell Rapids 62 Q46
Bellamys 50 Y62
Bellamys Mills . . 49 Y60
Belle-Eau-Claire Beach . . . .
. . . . 41 Y26
Belle Air Beach . 30 C-D31
Belle River 4 E4
Belle Vallée . 85 P30 105 J18
Belleview Beach . . . . . .
. . . . . . 18 U32 19 U33
Belleville 34 E49
Bellevue 84 Z93
Bellingham 87 D1
Bellrock 36 A-B54
Bells Corners . . 48 V57
Bells Crossing . 50 X-Y62
Belmeade 66 T64
Belmont 9 U18
Belmore 27 G17
Belton 15 R18
Belwood 22 J24
Benallen 39 Z19
Benmiller 20 K14
Bennies Corners . 65 S58
Bennington 15 T19
Benny . . 100 Z14 105 K16
Benoit 67 R67
Bensfort 33 D-E41
Bensfort Bridge . 33 D41
Bent River 58 S31
Bentinck 27 D20
Bentpath 6 W9
Bergland 106 H3
Berkeley 28 C21
Berlett's Corners . 22 N21
Berriedale 77 M32
Berryton 37 B58-59
Bervie 26 E15
Berwick 67 T67
Bessemer 62 U47
Bethany (Kawartha Lakes) . .
. . . . 32 D38-39
Bethany (Lennox & Addington) 35 E52

Bethel (Leeds & Grenville) . .
. . . . 50 Z63
Bethel (Niagara) . . 19 T34
Bethel (Prince Edward) . . . .
. . . . 35 F50
Bethel (Victoria) . . 32 C39
Bethesda (Prince Edward) . .
. . . . 35 E51
Bethesda (Simcoe) . . . . . .
. . . . 30 D29-30
Bethesda (York) . . 30 G32
Bethune Bush . . 67 U66
Beveridge Locks . 49 W59
Beverly Glen . . . 12 S9
Bewdley 33 F41
Bexley 43 Y36
Bickford 12 V7
Bidwell 73 K11
Biemans Corners . 27 F-G19
Big Bay 39 X19
Big Bay Point . . 42 B31
Big Cedar 45 Z42
Big Cedar Point . 30 C31
Big Chute 42 W30
Big Grassy River . 106 G3
Big Lake 73 L11
Biggles 29 G26
Bigwin 59 S35
Bigwood 92 H22
Bill's Corners . . 10 V24
Billings 105 J15-16
Bills Corners . . . 10 T25
Binbrook . . 17 R28 18 R29
Binkham 23 J26
Birch Haven . . . 95 E32
Birch Island . . . 90 H13
Birch Point 44 A38
Birdell 28 E23
Birdhouse City . . 35 G51
Birds Creek . . . 61 T45
Birdsalls 33 C43
Birdsalls Station . 33 C43
Birge Mills . . 23 K-L25
Birkendale . . 59 R35-36
Birnam 13 S11-12
Birr 14 R16
Biscotasing . 105 J15-16
Bishop Corners . 47 X51
Bishops Mills . . 50 W63
Bishopsgate . . 16 R-S23
Bismarck . . 18 S31-32
Bisselton 50 Y63
Bissett Creek . 97 F42-43
Black Bank . . . 29 D26
Black Bay 81 K49
Black Creek (Niagara) . . . .
. . . . 19 T35
Black Donald . . 64 S53
Black Hawk . . 106 H4
Black Horse . 29 G28 30 G29
Black Rapids . . 37 A59
Black River (Prince Edward) . . 35 G51-52
Black River (Stormont,
Dundas, & Glengarry) . . . .
. . . . 52 U69
Black Road 87 C94
Blackburn Hamlet . 66 Q64
Blackheath . 17 S28 18 S29
Blacks Corners (Dufferin) . .
. . . . 29 G25
Blacks Corners (Lanark) . . .
. . . . . 49 U59 65 T59
Blackstock . . 31 E36 32 E37
Blackstone Lake . . . . . .
. . . . 57 S27-28
Blackwater . . 31 D34-35
Blackwell 12 S8
Blair 22 P24
Blairhampton . . 60 U38
Blairs Settlement . 48 P47
Blairton 46 A46
Blairton Station . . . . . .
. . . . . . 45 B45 46 B46
Blake 20 N13
Blakeney 65 S58
Blanchard's Landing . . . .
. . . . . 95 E34 96 E35
Blanchards Hill . . 49 X59
Blandford Station . 16 Q22
Blantyre 40 A22
Blayney 10 V24
Blenheim . . . 7 B10-11
Blenheim Junction . 7 B10
Blessington . 34 D49 35 D50
Blezard 33 C42-43
Blezard Valley . . . .
. . 100 B18 101 B19 105 K16
Blind River . . 88 F4 105 K15
Blink Bonnie . 16 Q22 22 P22
Bloomfield 35 G50
Bloomfield Mill Pond . . . .
. . . . 35 G50
Bloomingdale . 22 M23-24

Bloomington (Stormont,
Dundas, & Glengarry) . . .
. . . . 52 S69
Bloomington (York) . 31 G33
Bloomsburg . . . 10 U25
Blossom Park . . 66 R63
Blount 29 C27
Blue Church . . . 50 Y64
Blue Corners . . 68 N70
Blue Mountain . . 45 Y44
Blue Mountain . 40 B23-24
Blue Mountain, The . . . . .
. . . . 40 B23-24
Blue Point 12 S9
Blue Point Bay . . 12 S9
Blue Springs . . 23 L26
Blue Water Beach . . . . .
. . . . . . 20 K12-13
Bluevale . 26 H16 27 H17
Bluevale Siding . . . .
. . . . . 26 H16 27 H17
Bluewater Beach . 41 Z27
Blyth 20 J15
Blytheswood . . . 5 D5
Boakview 75 N27
Bobcaygeon . . . 44 Z39
Bobs Lake . . 48 Y-Z55
Bodri Bay 11 U29
Bogart 47 A50
Bogarttown . . . 30 F32
Bogies Beach . 20 J12-13
Bognor 39 A21
Bolger 75 M26
Bolingbroke . . . 48 X56
Bolingbroke Siding . . . . .
. . . . 48 X55-56
Bolsover 43 A35
Bolton 24 H29
Bon Air 92 H22
Bon Echo . . 47 W50-51
Bona Vista 59 S34
Bonarlaw 46 B46-47
Bond Head (Durham) . . . .
. . . . 32 H39
Bond Head (Simcoe) 30 F29
Bondi Village . . 59 R35
Bonds Corners . 15 R21
Bonfield 95 F33-34
Bongard 35 F52
Bongard Corners . 35 F52
Boninville 100 B18
Bonnechere . 80 M47 81 M48
Bonnie Beach . . 42 Z33
Bonnie Doone . . 12 S9
Bonville 52 T69-70
Bookers Bay . . 11 U29
Bookton 10 T23
Booth's Landing . 95 G33
Booths Harbour . 10 X24
Boothville 28 E22
Borden 29 C28
Bordenwood . . 47 Y51-52
Bornholm 21 M18
Bornish 13 S13
Borups Corners . 106 G5
Boskung 60 U37
Boston 10 T25
Boston Creek . . 105 H18
Boston Mills . . . 23 J28
Bosworth 22 J22
Botany 7 Y10
Bothwell 7 X11
Bothwell Station . 7 X11
Boucks Hill . . 51 V66-67
Boulter 62 S47
Bourdage Corner 84 Y-Z92
Bourget 67 Q67
Bourkes 105 H17
Bow Lake 61 U44
Bowen Corner . 62 T-U46
Bowermans . . . 34 G49
Bowers Beach . . 41 A26
Bowland's Bay . . . .
. . . . 101 A21 105 K17
Bowling Green . 29 G25
Bowmanville . 32 G37-38
Bowood 14 S14-15
Bowser's Corner . 72 K9
Box Grove . . 25 H33-34
Boyds 49 U58
Boyle 18 S32
Boyne 67 T-U66
Boyne 23 M24
Boyne, The . . 67 T-U66
Bracebridge 58 U32 59 U33
Brackenrig 58 T31
Bradford 30 E-F30
Bradford West Gwillimbury . .
. . . . 30 D30
Bradley (Bruce) . 26 D16
Bradley (Chatham-Kent) . . .
. . . . 5 B7
Bradley Creek . . 67 Q68

Bradshaw (Frontenac) . . . .
. . . . 48 Y55
Bradshaw (Lambton) . . . . .
. . . . 6 W8 12 V8
Brady Lake . . . 60 U37
Braemar 15 R20
Braeside 65 Q57
Bramalea 24 K29
Brampton 24 K29
Branchton 23 P25
Brandy Point . . 21 N17
Brantford . 16 R24 17 R25
Bray Lake 77 J-K32
Breadalbane . . . 68 Q71
Brechin 43 A34
Brechin Beach . 42 A33
Brechin Point . . 42 A33
Breezy's Corners . 23 P27
Brent 97 H39
Brentha 85 N28
Brentwood 29 C27
Breslau 22 M23
Brethour 85 N30
Brewer Lake . . . 36 B53
Brewers Mills . . 37 B58
Briars Park . . . 30 C32
Briarwood Estates . 7 X11
Brickley 33 D44
Bridge End 53 S73
Bridgenorth . . 44 B40-41
Bridgeport . . 22 M-N23
Brier Hill 37 A59
Brigden 12 V8
Bright . . . 15 Q21 16 Q22
Brighton . . 33 F45 34 F46
Brights Grove . . 12 S8
Brightside 64 T56
Brignall 57 S28
Brimstone 23 J27
Brinklow . . 45 W46 46 W47
Brinkman's Corners 54 T16
Brinsley 14 Q14
Brinston 50 W65
Brisbane 23 K26
Brisson 67 R66
Britainville 72 L12
Britannia 59 R34
Britannia Road . 59 S34
Britt 74 L22
Britt Station . . 74 L22-23
Britton 21 K19
Broadbent 57 Q28
Brockley 8 U17
Brocksden . . 21 N19-20
Brockville . . 50 Z62-63
Brodhagen . . . 21 L-M17
Brodie 68 Q72
Bromley 82 P53
Bronson . . 61 U45 62 U46
Bronson Station . . . . . .
. . . . . 61 U45 62 U46
Bronte 24 N29-30
Brooke 48 W56-57
Brooklin 31 G36
Brooks Landing . 56 J23
Brooks Mills . . . 59 Q35
Brooksdale 15 Q19
Brookville 23 M27
Brotherston . . . 21 J19
Brougham . . . 25 H34
Brouseville . . . 50 X65
Brown's Corners (Norwich) . .
. . . . 10 U22
Brown's Corners (Zorra) . . .
. . . . 15 R18
Brown Hill 30 D32
Brown House Corner . . . . .
. . . . 52 S72
Browning Island . 58 U-V32
Brownrigg . . . 109 G16
Browns Brae . . 59 S35
Brownsville (Durham) . . . .
. . . . 32 G39
Brownsville (Oxford) . 9 U20
Brownsville Station 9 U20-21
Bruce Lake . . . 106 F4
Bruce Mines . . 104 K14
Bruce Mines . 86 D-E96
Bruce Station . . . .
. . . . . 86 D96 104 K14
Brucefield 20 M14
Bruces 17 Q25
Bruceton 63 S49
Bruces 63 S49
Bruner 21 M19-20
Brunswick 32 D38-39
Brunswick House . 104 J13
Brussels 21 J17
Bryanston 14 R16
Buck Lake 36 A56
Buckhams Bay . 83 P59
Buckhorn . . 44 Z40-41
Buckhorn Lake Estates . . . .
. . . . 44 A40

Buckskin 42 W30
Bucyrus 84 W93
Budd Mills 81 M50
Buena Vista Park . . 42 Y32
Buffalo Heights . . 19 U35-36
Bulgers Corners . . 82 N52
Buller (Haliburton) . 43 X37
Buller (Hastings) . . 48 B49
Bullock . . 48 U56 64 T56
Bummer's Roost . . 76 K-L30
Bunessan 28 D21
Bunker Hill 67 U68
Bunyan 12 T-U8
Bur Creek 36 C55
Burchell Lake 107 H7
Burditt Lake 106 H4
Burford 16 S23-24
Burgess Mine 62 R46
Burgessville . . 15 S21 16 S22
Burgoyne 38 B16
Burk's Falls 77 N32
Burketon 32 F37
Burleigh Centre . . 45 Y42
Burleigh Falls . 44 Z41 45 Z42
Burlington 18 P29-30
Burlington Beach . 18 P29
Burnaby 19 U33
Burnbrae 34 C46
Burnley 33 E43
Burns 21 L20
Burnside 42 X31
Burnstown 64 Q55
Burnt Hills . 36 B57 37 B58
Burnt Island . . 70 K3 71 K4
Burnt River . 43 Y37 44 Y38
Burpee 71 K-L6
Burr 34 F49
Burridge 48 Y-Z56
Burritts Rapids . . . 50 V62
Burromee . . 66 Q64 67 Q65
Burtch 17 S25
Burton (Durham) . . 32 E37
Burton (Parry Sound) 75 M25
Burwash 92 F20-21 105 K16-17
Burwash . . . .
Burwash Station . . 92 E21
Burwells Corner . . 8 W16
Bury's Green 44 Z38
Bush 49 Z58
Bush Glen . . . 67 U67-68
Buttermilk Falls . . 60 T37
Butternut Bay . . . 50 A62
Button's Corners . 85 R28-29
Buttonville 24 H32
Buzwah 73 L13
Byes Corner . . . 84 Z92-93
Byng 18 U30
Byng Inlet . . . 74 L22-23
Byrnedale 5 C5

Cache Bay
. . . . 94 D27 105 K17-18
Caderette . . 93 D26 94 D27
Cadmus 32 E37
Caesarea . 31 E36 32 E37
Cahore 67 T66-67
Cainsville 17 R26
Caintown 37 A61
Cairngorm 13 U13
Cairo 7 W11
Caistor Centre . . . 18 S30
Caistorville . . . 18 S29-30
Calabogie . . 64 R54-55
Calderwood . . 27 F-G20
Caledon 29 H27
Caledon East . . . 29 H28
Caledonia 17 S28
Caledonia Springs . 68 P70
California (Lanark) . 64 S56
California (Leeds & Grenville) 37 A58
Caliper Lake . . . 106 G4
Callander 95 F32
Callum . . . 101 C22 105 K17
Calm Lake 106 H5
Calstock 108 G13-14
Calton 9 W20
Camborne 33 C43
Cambray 43 B36-37
Cambridge (Prescott & Russell) 67 S66
Cambridge (Waterloo) 22 N24 23 N25
Camden East . 35 C53 36 C54
Camel Chute . . . 63 S51
Camelot Beach . . 19 U33
Cameron (Peterborough) 33 C43
Cameron (Victoria) . 43 B37
Cameron Falls . . 107 G9
Camerons Point . . 52 U72
Camilla 29 G26
Camlachie 12 S9
Camp Champlain . 95 E33
Camp Kagawong 43 A36 Z36
Camp Oconto . . . 48 Y54
Camp Robinson . . 106 F4
Campania . . 28 G24 29 G25
Campbell Maxwell Front 37 C-D58
Campbellcroft 32 F40 33 F41
Campbellford . . . 34 C46
Campbells Beach . 43 Z34
Campbells Corners 50 W63-64
Campbells Cross . 23 J28
Campbellton . 7 W13 8 W14

Campbelltown . . . 33 D41
Campbellvale . . . 8 U15
Campbellville . . . 23 M27
Campden 18 R32
Camperdown . . . 40 A24
Canaan 67 Q66
Canal 59 R34
Canborough . . . 18 T30
Candyville 9 W19
Cane 85 P27
Canfield 11 T29
Canfield Junction . 11 T29
Cankerville 33 F45
Cannamore . . 67 S-T66
Cannifton 34 D49
Canning 16 R23
Cannington . . . 31 C35
Canoe Lake . . . 78 N37
Canonto 48 U54
Cape Chin . . 55 U16-17
Cape Chin North . 54 T16-17
Cape Chin South . 54 T17
Cape Croker . . . 55 V19
Capreol . . 101 C22 105 K17
Caradoc 8 U14-15
Caramat 108 G11-12
Cardiff 61 U43
Cardinal 50 X65
Cardwell 29 G26
Cargill 27 D17
Cargill Siding . . 27 D-E17
Carholme 10 W23
Cariboo Falls . . 106 F3
Carleton Place . . 65 T59
Carley 42 Z30
Carleys Corners 49 W61 50 W62
Carling 56 Q25-26
Carlingford . . . 21 P17-18
Carlisle (Hamilton) . 23 N27
Carlisle (Middlesex) . 14 R15
Carlow 20 J14
Carlsbad Springs . 66 R64
Carlsruhe 27 E18
Carluke 17 R27
Carlyon 42 Y31
Carman 34 E46
Carmanville . . . 47 A53
Carmel (Northumberland) 33 E44
Carmel (Peterborough) 32 E40
Carmunnock . . 21 K17-18
Carnarvon 60 U38
Carnegie Beach 31 D36 32 D37
Carp 65 R60
Carpin Beach . . 84 B91
Carr 94 H30
Carrying Place . . 34 F47
Carsonby 66 T62
Carss 77 M32
Carters Corners . 102 D4
Carterton 86 F95
Carthage 21 K20
Carthew Bay . . 42 A32
Cartier . . 100 A15 105 K16
Casborne 29 C26-27
Casimir . . 93 E24 105 K17
Cass Bridge . . 67 U66
Cassburn . . . 68 N70-71
Cassel 15 Q21
Casselman . . 67 R68
Castile 81 P49-50
Castle Glen Estates 40 A-B24
Castleberg . . . 24 H29
Castleford 82 P55
Castleford Station . 83 P56
Castlemore . . . 24 J30
Castleton 33 E44
Cat Lake 106 E6
Cataract 23 J27
Cataraqui . . 36 D55-56
Catchacoma . . 44 X40
Cathcart . . . 16 S22-23
Cavan 32 D39-40
Cavell 107 F10
Caverlys Landing 63 U48-49
Cavers 107 H10
Cawaja Beach . 41 Y27
Cayuga 11 T28-29
Cecebe 77 M31
Cedar Bank . . 20 P12-13
Cedar Bay . . . 19 U34
Cedar Beach (Durham) 42 B33 43 B34
Cedar Beach (Essex) . 5 D7-8
Cedar Creek . 33 E45 34 E46
Cedar Croft . . 78 M29
Cedar Hill . . 65 S57-58
Cedar Island . . 4 F4
Cedar Lake . . 36 B57
Cedar Mills . 29 G28 30 G29
Cedar Mount . 42 B30-31
Cedar Nook . 41 W29 57 V29
Cedar Point . . 41 X26
Cedar Shores . 31 E36
Cedar Springs (Chatham-Kent) 7 C10
Cedar Springs (Halton) 23 N28
Cedar Valley (Victoria) 32 E40
Cedar Valley (Wellington) 23 J26
Cedar Valley (York) . 30 F32
Cedar Village . . 58 U32
Cedarbrae . . . 31 D33

Cedardale (Lanark) 64 T56 65 T57
Cedardale (Ottawa) . 66 R63
Cedarhurst Park . . 4 F4
Cedarmont Beach . 42 A32
Cedarview 13 R10
Cedarville (Grey) . 28 F22
Cedarville (Simcoe) . 28 F25
Centralia 14 Q15
Centre 34 F48
Centre Dummer . 45 A43
Centre Inn . . . 23 L25
Centrefield . . . 67 P68
Centreton . . 33 E-F43
Centreview . . . 62 Q46
Centreville (Bruce) 55 V16-17
Centreville (Grey) . 40 Z22
Centreville (Lennox & Addington) . . . 47 B52-53
Centreville (Oxford) . 15 S20
Centurion . . . 58 Q32
Ceylon 28 D22
Chaffeys Locks 48 Z57 49 Z58
Chalk River . . 99 H49
Chamberlain . . 85 M28
Chambers Corners 18 T32 19 T33
Champlain Park . 95 F32
Chandos Lake . 45 X42-43
Chantry 47 Y59
Chapleau . . . 104 J14
Chapman . . . 46 B49
Chapman's Landing 94 G30 95 G31
Chaput Hughes . 105 H17
Charing Cross . 6 B9
Charlemont . . 6 X8
Charleston . 37 A60 49 Z60
Charlton . 85 M27 105 J17-18
Chartrand . 66 Q64 67 Q65
Chartrand Corner . 93 G24
Chase Corners . 45 A45
Chatham . . 6 A8-9
Chats Haven . 65 Q58
Chatsworth . . 39 B20
Chatterton . . 34 D48
Cheapside . . 11 U-V27
Cheddar . . 61 U-V42
Cheeseborough . 37 C58-59
Chelmsford 100 B17 105 K16
Cheltenham . 23 J-K28
Chemong Heights 44 B40-41
Chemong Park . 44 B40-41
Chenaux . . 82 N54-55
Cheney . . . 67 Q66
Chepstow . . 27 E17
Cherry Beach . 18 Q29
Cherry Grove . 15 R17
Cherry Lane Estates 5 E-F5
Cherry Valley . 35 G50-51
Cherrywood . 25 H34
Chesley . . . 27 D19
Chesterfield . 15 Q21 22 P21
Chesterville 67 T66-67 U66-67
Chetwynd . . 77 N32-33
Chevrier . . . 69 Q73
Chikopi . . . 76 M29
Childs Mines . 62 U47
Chippawa . . 19 S35
Chippawa Hill . 38 A16
Chippewas of Beausoleil First Nation . 41 W26
Chippewas of Georgina Island First Nation 30 C31 31 C33 42 B33
Chiselhurst . . 20 N15
Chisholms Mills 34 C49 35 C50
Chiswick . . 95 G33-34
Christian Island . 40 W25
Christian Valley . 95 H31
Christie Beach . 40 Z23
Christie Lake . 48 X57
Christies Corners . 17 Q27
Christina . . 8 U14-15
Churchill (Simcoe) . 30 D30
Churchill (Wellington) 23 K-L27
Churchill Heights . 52 U70
Churchville (Elgin) . 9 W20
Churchville (Peel) . 24 L29
Chute à Blondeau . 68 N72
Clachan . . . 7 X12
Claireville . . 24 J30
Clanbrassil . 11 T32-33
Clandeboye . 14 Q-R15
Clappison's Corners 23 P28
Clare 28 G22
Claremont . 25 H34
Clarence . 67 N-P66
Clarence Creek . 67 P66-67
Clarendon Station 48 W54-55
Clareview . 47 A51
Clarina . . . 45 Z43
Clarington . 32 G37-38
Clarke . . . 32 G39
Clarke's Corners . 55 U15-16
Clarks Church . 26 E14
Clarksburg . 40 A23-24
Clarkson (Peel) . 24 M30
Clarkson (Waterloo) 23 P25
Claude . . . 23 J26
Clavering . 38 Y17 39 Y18
Clay Bank . 65 Q57
Clay Hills . 39 W18 55 V18

Clay Valley . . 64 Q56 65 Q57
Clayton . . . 65 T58
Clear Creek . 10 X-Y22
Clear Lake (Muskoka) 59 U35
Clear Lake (Parry Sound) 77 P33
Clearville . . . 7 A13
Clearwater Bay . 106 G3
Clearwater Beach . 41 W28
Clifford . . . 27 G19
Clinton . . 20 L14-15
Clontarf . . 63 Q51
Cloud Bay . 102 G5 107 H8
Cloudslee . . 86 D97
Clover Valley (Bruce) 26 F14
Clover Valley (Manitoulin) 73 M12-13
Cloverdale . 67 U-65
Cloyne . . . 47 X50-51
Clute 109 G16
Clyde 23 N25
Clyde Forks . 64 T55
Clydesville . 48 U57
Coatsworth . 5 D7-8
Cobalt . . . 105 J18
Cobden . . . 82 N53
Cobble Hill . 15 R18
Coboconk . . 43 Y37
Cobourg . . . 33 G42
Cochenour . 106 E4
Cochrane . . 109 G16
Codes Corners . 36 C57
Codrington . 33 E45
Codys Corners . 15 R19-20
Coe Hill . . 45 W45
Coin Gratton . 68 N69
Colbeck . . . 28 G24
Colborne (Norfolk) . 10 U25
Colborne (Northumberland) . . 33 F44
Colchester . . . 4 F2
Cold Springs (Manitoulin) 72 K10
Cold Springs (Northumberland) . 33 F42
Cold Springs (Peterborough) . . . 33 D41
Coldstream . . 8 T15
Coldwater . . 42 Y30
Coldwell . . 104 H11
Cole Lake . 48 Z54-55
Cole Wharf . 35 E51
Colebrook . 36 B54 47 B53
Coleraine . 24 J30
Colgan . . 29 F28
Colinville . 12 U7-8
Collingwood . 40 A25
Collins . . . 107 F8
Collins Bay . 36 D55
Collins Inlet . 91 H17-18
Colpoy's Bay . 39 X18
Columbus . 31 G36
Colwell . . 30 C29
Comber . . . 5 C6
Combermere . 62 Q47
Comet 4 E2
Commanda . 76 J30
Concord Point . 42 A33
Conestogo . 22 M23
Coningsby . 23 K26
Coniston . . 105 K17
Coniston . 101 C20-21
Conmee . . 102 C3
Conn 28 G22
Connaught . 105 H16-17
Connaught (Renfrew) 82 M52
Connaught (Stormont, Dundas, & Glengarry) 67 T66
Connaught Shore . 44 B40
Connellys . . 33 C45
Connor . . 29 G27-28
Conover . . 29 G25
Consecon . 34 G47-48
Consecon Station 34 F47-48
Constance Lake . 108 G13
Constant Creek . 63 Q52
Conway . . 35 E-F52
Cook's Dock . 71 J5
Cooks Mills . 105 K18
Cooks Mills (Niagara) 19 T34
Cooks Mills (Nipissing) 95 D31
Cooks Shore . 58 U58-59
Cookstown . 30 E29-30
Cooksville . 24 L30
Cooper . . 46 Y48
Coopers Falls . 42 X33
Copenhagen . 9 W19
Copetown . 17 Q26-27
Copp . . . 81 P49
Coppell . . 108 G14
Copper Cliff 100 C18 101 C19 105 K16
Copperhead . 56 T26
Copperkettle . 39 Y19
Coppins Corners . 31 F34
Corbeil . . 95 E-F33
Corbett . . 13 Q13
Corbetton . 28 E24 29 E25
Corbyville . 34 D49
Cordova Mines 45 A45 46 A46
Corinth . . . 9 V20
Coristine . . 9 W18
Corkery . . 65 R-S59
Cormac . . 81 P50
Cornell . . 10 U22

Cornwall . . 52 U70-71
Cornwall Centre . 52 U70
Cornwall Island . 52 V71
Corsons . . 43 Z36
Corwhin . . 23 N26
Cosy Cove . 47 A50
Cotieville . 82 P54
Cotnam Island . 82 L52
Cotswold . 28 H21
Cottam . . 4 D4
Cottesloe . 45 B43
Couchiching . 106 H4
Coulson (Bradford-West Gwillimbury) . . . 30 E30
Coulson (Oro-Medonte) 42 Z32
Coulters Hill . 47 B50
Coulterville . 23 J26-27
Courtice . . 32 G37
Courtland . 10 U22
Courtright . 12 V6-7
Coutenac Beach . 41 W28
Coutts ville . 85 P29
Cove Beach (Prince Edward) . 35 G50-51 H50-51
Cove Beach (Simcoe) 41 X26
Coventry . . 24 H29
Cowans Bay . 32 C39
Coxvale . . 47 W53
Craighurst . 41 A29 42 A30
Craiglethn . 40 A24-25
Craigmont . 62 R47
Craigs Shore . 49 U59
Craigsholme . 23 J25
Crampton . 9 T19
Cranberry . 74 J22
Cranbrook . 21 K17
Cranston . 11 T27-28
Cranstons Beach 36 C55-56
Crathie . . 13 S13
Crawford . 27 D19
Crawfords Beach . 43 Z35
Crean Hill . 91 D16
Crediton . 20 P14
Creditville . 16 R22
Creek Bank . 22 K23
Creemore . 29 D26
Creighton (Simcoe) 42 Z30-31
Creighton (Sudbury) 100 C18
Creighton Heights . 33 F42
Creightons Corners . 31 C34
Crerar . . 101 A23
Crescent Bay . 11 V26
Crescent Beach (Simcoe) 41 W28
Crescent Beach (York) 30 C31
Crescent Park . 31 C35-36
Cresswell . 31 C35
Cressy . . 35 F53
Crewe . . 26 H13
Crewsons Corners 23 L26-27
Crieff . . 23 N26
Crilly . . 106 H5
Crinan . . 7 X13
Crofton . 34 F49
Cromar . 12 V8
Cromarty . 20 N16
Crombie . 29 F-G25
Crooked Bay . 57 V29
Crooked Creek . 32 G39
Crooks . . 102 G4
Crookston . 46 B48
Crosby . . 49 Z58
Cross Lake . 61 Q45
Crosshill . 22 M21
Crossley-Hunter . 9 U18
Croton . . 7 X10
Crow Lake . 48 Y55
Crow Lake IR . 106 G4
Crowe Bridge . 46 B46
Crowes Landing . 45 Z43
Crown Hill . 42 B30
Crown Point . 83 P59
Croydon . 35 B52
Cruickshank . 39 Z18
Crumlin . 9 T18
Crysler . 67 S67
Crystal . 49 X61
Crystal Bay . 65 R61
Crystal Beach . 19 U35
Crystal Falls . 105 K18
Crystal Lake . 44 X39
Crystal Rock . 50 X64
Culloden . 9 U20
Cultus . 10 X22
Cumberland (Ottawa) 67 P65
Cumberland (Simcoe) 42 Y32
Cumnock . 22 J23
Cunningham's Corners 32 C38
Curie Station . 47 B52
Curran . . 67 P68
Curries . 95 E-F33
Curry Hill . 53 S-T73
Curve Lake . 44 A40
Cushendall . 36 C57
Cutler . . 89 F7-8 105 K15

Dacre
. . . . 63 Q52
Dain City . 19 T33-34
Dale . . . 33 G41
Dalhousie Lake . 48 V55

Dalhousie Mills . . 52 R72
Dalkeith . . 68 Q71-72
Dalmeny . 66 T64
Dalrymple . 43 Z34-35
Dalston . . 42 A30
Dalton . 104 H13-14
Drummond . 33 D41-42
Dane . . 105 H18
Darbyville . 23 M26
Darling Road . 18 T30
Darlingside . 37 C60-61
Darrell . . 6 Y9
Dartford . 33 D44
Dartmoor . 43 X-Y34
Dashwood . 20 P13
Daventry . 96 H37-38
Davidsons Beach . 36 C56
Davidsons Corners . 33 F41
Davis Mills . 81 L50-51
Dawn Valley . 6 X8-9
Day Mills . 87 E99 104 K14
Dayton . . 87 E99
Daytonia Beach . 43 A37
Daytown . 49 Z59
Dealtown . 6 C9 7 C10
Dean Lake . 87 F2
Deanlea Beach . 41 Z27
Deans . . 77 J32
Decewsville . 11 T28
Dee Bank . 58 T31
Deemerton . 27 F18
Deep Bay . 43 W37
Deep River . 99 G48
Deer Bay . 44 Z41
Deer Lake . 61 U43
Deerbrook . 5 B-C5
Deerhurst . 30 E30
DeGrassi Point . 30 D31
Dejong . . 13 T12
Delamere . 92 F-G22
Delaware . 8 U15
Delhi . . 10 U23
Delmer . . 9 U20
Delta . . 49 Z59
Demorestville . 35 F50
Demorestville Dam . 35 F50
Denbigh . 63 T50
Denfield . 14 R15
Departure Lake . 109 G16
Depot Harbour . 56 R26
Dereham Centre . 9 U20-21
Derland . 95 F32
Derrynane . 28 G22
Derryville . 31 C34
Derwent . 9 U18
Desaulniers . 105 K17-18
Desbarats . 104 K13-14
Desbarats . 86 D95
Desboro . 39 B19
Deseronto . 35 E51-52
Desert Lake . 36 A55
Desmond . 47 B53
Detlor . . 62 U46
Deux-Rivières . 97 F-G41
Devizes . 15 R17
Dewars . 83 P56-57
DeWitts Corners . 48 W-X57
Dexter . . 9 W18
Dicksons Corners . 15 S19
Dicksons Hill . 31 G33
Dillon . . 56 Q24
Dinner Point Depot 73 J13 90 H-I13
Dinorwic . 106 G5
Dirleton . 83 P59
Dixon . . 67 U68
Dixons Corners 50 W65 51 W66
Dobbinton . 39 B18
Dobie . . 105 H16
Dock Siding . 57 S28-29
Dockmure . 57 R27-28
Doe Lake . 77 N31-32
Dogs Nest . 11 V26
Dokis . . 94 G27
Dome . . 105 H16
Dominionville . 52 S70
Domville . 50 X64
Don Mills . 24 K32
Donald . 60 V39
Donaldson . 48 V54
Donegal (Perth) . 21 L19
Donegal (Renfrew) . 81 P51
Dongola . 43 X37
Donnybrook . 26 H15
Donwood . 33 C41
Doon . . 22 N23-24
Dorchester . 9 T18-19
Dore Bay . 81 M50-51
Dorion . 107 H9
Dorion's Corner . 41 X27
Dorking . 22 L21
Dorland . 35 F52
Dornie . 52 R71
Dornoch . 27 C20
Dorset . 59 S36
Douglas . 82 P53
Douglastown . 19 T35-36
Douro . . 45 B42
Dover Bay . 7 C10
Dowling . 100 B16-17 105 K16
Downeys . 23 M25
Downeyville . 44 B38
Downsview . 24 K31
Doyles . . 6 B9
Dracon . 22 J24
Drayton . 22 J21-22
Dresden . 6 X9

Drew . . 27 G20
Driftwood . 109 G16
Drocourt . 75 L24
Dromore . 28 E22
Drumbo . 16 Q22-23
Drummond . 33 D41-42
Drummond Centre 49 V58-59
Drumquin . 24 M29
Dryden (Kenora) . 106 G5
Dryden (Perth) . 21 J20
Dryden's Corner . 72 L-M9
Drysdale . 20 N13
Duart . . 7 Y12-13
Dublin . . 20 M16 21 M17
Dubreuilville . 104 H13
Duclos Point . 31 C33
Dudley . . 57 U30
Duff's Corners . 11 T27
Duff Corners . 46 B49 47 B50
Dufferin . 11 T27
Dufferin Bridge . 76 P30
Duffy . . 57 U29
Dulcemaine . 37 B60
Dunbar . 67 U66-67
Dunbarton . 25 H-J34
Dunblane . 38 B16-17
Dunboyne . 9 W19
Duncan . 40 B23
Dunchurch . 76 M28
Duncrief . 14 S15
Dundalk . 28 E23-24
Dundas . 17 Q27-28
Dundela . 51 V66
Dundonald . 33 F44-45
Dundurn . 10 T24-25
Dunedin . 29 C26
Dungannon . 26 H14
Dunkeld . 27 E17
Dunkerron . 30 E30
Dunlop . 20 J13
Dunnet's Corner . 93 D24
Dunnette Landing 33 D42-43
Dunns Corners . 15 S20
Dunns Valley 86 C97 87 C98 104 K14
Dunnville . 18 U30
Dunrobin . 65 Q60
Dunrobin Shore . 65 Q60-61
Dunsford . 44 B38
Duntroon . 40 B25
Dunvegan . 52 R69-70
Duphuston . 31 E33
Durham . 27 D20 28 D21
Dutch Line . 44 W38
Duthill . . 6 W7
Dutton . 8 W-X15
Duttona Beach . 8 X15
Dwight . 59 R35
Dwyer Hill . 65 T60-61
Dyer . . 52 S69
Dyer's Bay . 54 T16
Dyment . 106 G5
Dyno Estates . 61 V42-43

E
Ebametoong . 107 E9-10
Eades . . 105 H18
Eads Bush . 73 J11-12
Eady . . 42 Y30
Eagle . . 8 X-Y14
Eagle Lake (Haliburton) 60 T39
Eagle Lake (Parry Sound) 77 L31
Eagle River . 106 G4
Eagles Nest . 73 L12
Eamers Corners . 52 U70
Ear Falls . 106 F4
Earlton . 85 N28 105 J18
Earnscliffe . 29 E26-27
East Colborne . 33 F45
East Emily . 32 C39
East Gwillimbury . 30 E31-32
East Hungerford . 47 A51
East Linton . 39 Y19-20
East Oakland . 17 S25
East Oro . 42 A31
East Oxford . 50 W63
East Tay Point . 41 X28
East York . 24 K32 25 K33
Eastons Corners . 49 W-X61
Eastview . 36 D57
Eastwood . 15 R21 16 R22
Eatonville . 7 B11-12
Eau Claire . 96 F36
Eau Claire Station . 96 E36
Ebbs Shore . 49 U59
Ebenezer (Hastings) . 35 C51
Ebenezer (Leeds & Grenville) 37 C60
Ebenezer (Peel) . 24 J29-30
Ebenezer (Simcoe) 41 Y28-29
Eberts . . 6 Y9
Ebordale . 28 D21
Echo . . 48 Z54
Echo Bay . 86 B94 104 K13-14
Echo Beach . 58 S31-32
Echo River . 86 B94
Eden . . 9 V21
Eden Grove (Bruce) . 27 D17
Eden Grove (Leeds & Grenville) 37 B59
Eden Mills . 23 L26
Edenhurst . 55 V17
Edenvale . 41 B28
Edgar . . 42 A30
Edgars . 43 Z35
Edge Hill . 27 D20 28 D21

Edgewater Beach 4 D1
Edgewood Park . 19 U35-36
Edmore Beach 41 Z27
Edville 33 F45
Edwards . . 66 R64 67 R65
Edys Mills . . . 6 W9 12 V9
Effingham 19 S33
Egan Creek 62 U46
Eganville . . 81 P51 82 P52
Egerton 28 G23
Egmondville . . 20 M15-16
Egypt 31 D33
Eight Mile Point . . 42 A32
Ekfrid 8 V14
Elba 29 F26
Elcho 18 T31
Elco Beach 19 U34
Eldee 105 K18
Elder 29 F27
Elder Mills 24 J30
Eldon 43 A35
Eldorado 46 Z48
Electric 6 Y7-8
Eley 87 E-F1
Elford 4 E3
Elfrida 18 R29
Elgin 49 Z58
Elginburg . . . 36 C55-56
Elginfield 14 R16
Elimville 20 P15-16
Elizabeth Bay . . 71 K5-6
Elizabethville . 32 F39-40
Elk Lake 105 J17
Ellaton 10 U23-24
Ellengowan 27 D17
Elliot 48 X57
Elliot Lake 10 K-L51
Elliot Lake . . . 88 D6 89 D7
Elliots Corners . . . 41 Y29
Ellisville 37 A59
Elm Tree 51 V66
Elma 51 V66
Elmbrook 35 F51
Elmdale 5 E6
Elmgrove (Lanark) . 49 X58
Elmgrove (Simcoe) . 30 D29
Elmhedge . . 39 A21 40 A22
Elmhurst Beach . . 30 D31
Elmira 22 L22
Elmstead 4 B-C3
Elmvale 41 Z28
Elmview 101 A19
Elmwood (Grey) . 27 D18-19
Elmwood (Huron) 20 P12-13
Eloida 49 Y60
Elora 22 K23-24
Elphin 48 V55
Elsas 105 H15
Elsinore 38 A17
Elzevir 47 Y-Z50
Embro 15 R20
Embrun 67 S66
Emerald 36 E54
Emerald Isle 44 B40
Emery 37 C59
Emeryville 4 B4
Emo 106 H4
Empire Corners . . 18 S29
Emsdale . . . 77 P32-33
Enfield . . 31 F36 32 F37
Englehart . 85 M28 105 J18
English Line 34 C46
English River . . . 107 G7
Enniskillen 32 F37
Ennismore 44 B39-40
Ennotville . 22 K24 23 K25
Enterprise 47 B53
Epping 40 A-B22
Epsom 31 F35
Eramosa 23 L25
Erbsville 22 M22
Erie 11 U27
Erie Beach 7 C10
Erie View 10 X23
Erieau 7 C11
Eriestone 11 U29
Erin 23 J26
Erin Mills 24 M30
Erinsville 47 A51
Ernestown 36 D54
Errol 12 S9
Escott 37 B60-61
Esmonde 63 Q51-52
Espanola . 90 E13 105 K16
Ess Narrows Landing . . . .
Essa . . 29 C28 30 C29
Essex 4 D3-4
Essonville 61 U41
Estaire 105 K17
Estaire 92 E20-21
Ethel 21 K18
Ethel Siding . . 21 K17-18
Etobicoke . . . 24 K-L31
Eton-Rugby . . . 106 G5
Etonia 16 R23
Ettrick 14 S16
Ettyville 67 Q67-68
Etwell 58 R32
Eugenia 27 D18
Evansville (Manitoulin) 71 K6
Evansville (West Nipissing) 94 D28
Evanturel 68 N70
Evelyn 15 S18
Everett 29 E28
Eversley 30 G31
Everton 23 K26
Ewan 44 X39
Exeter 20 P14-15
Eyre Corners . . . 49 Y59

Factory Island 109 E17
Fair Valley . . . 42 Y30-31
Fairburn Corner . . . 44 Z38
Fairfax 37 B60
Fairfield 50 Z62
Fairfield East . . 50 Y62-63
Fairfield Plain . . . 16 S24
Fairground 10 X22
Fairholme 76 N28
Fairmount (Frontenac) 36 C56
Fairmount (Grey) . 40 A22-23
Fairplay 4 C2-3
Fairview (Elgin) . . 9 W19-20
Fairview (Leeds & Grenville) 52 R70
Fairview (Oxford) . . 15 Q19
Fairview (Renfrew) . 81 L51
Falconbridge . . . 105 K17
Falconbridge (Middlesex) 8 U14-15
Falconbridge (Sudbury) 101 B21
Falding 57 R28
Falkenburg Station 58 T32 59 T33
Falkland 16 R23
Fallbrook 48 V57
Fallowfield 66 S62
Fanshawe 15 S17
Fanshawe Lake . 15 S17-18
Faraday 45 V45
Farewell 28 H21
Fargo Station 7 B10
Farleys Corners . . 76 J30
Farmington . . 29 G-H26
Farnham 23 M26
Farquhar 20 P16
Farrell Corners . . 47 B51
Fassifern 42 Z31
Fauquier 109 G15-16
Fawcettville . . 35 F50-51
Fawkham 42 Y33
Featherstone . . . 11 V28
Featherstone Point . 11 V28
Feir Mill 32 C-D38
Feldspar 48 X56
Felton 67 S65-66
Fenaghvale . . . 68 P69-70
Fenella 33 E42-43
Fenelon Falls . 43 A37 44 A38
Fennell 20 P16
Fenwick 18 S32
Fenwood Gardens 34 E48-49
Fergus 22 K24
Fergus Hill Estate . 42 Z31
Ferguslea 64 Q54
Ferguson Corners 63 U49-50
Fergusons Beach 82 P55 83 P56
Fergusons Falls . . 49 U58
Fergusonvale . . . 41 A28
Ferland 107 F9
Fermoy 48 Z56
Fern Glen 77 P32
Fernbank 21 L20
Ferndale (Bruce) . 55 V16-17
Ferndale (Muskoka) 57 T30
Ferndale (Peel) . . 23 J28
Fernhill 14 S14
Fernlee 71 K5
Fernleigh 47 W52
Feronia 95 D32
Ferris 95 E31
Fesserton 42 X30
Feversham 28 C24
Ficko 66 S63
Field 105 K17-18
Fifes Bay 32 C40
Finch 67 T67-68
Finchley . . . 82 L52-53
Fingal 8 W16
Fingerboard . . . 31 D36
Finmark 102 B2
Finmark 107 H8
Fire River 104 H14
Fishers Glen . . . 10 W25
Fisherville 11 U28
Fiskes Corners 52 R70 68 Q70
Fitzroy Harbour . . 66 R67
Five Corners . 44 B41 45 B42
Flake 101 B19
Flamboro Centre 23 P27-28
Flamborough . . 23 P26-27
Flanders 106 H5-6
Flannigan Corners . 21 P19
Fleetwood 32 D38
Fleetwood Station 32 D38-39
Fleming's Landing 75 J-K26
Flesherton . . . 28 D22
Fletcher 5 C8
Flett 102 B2
Flint 102 E3
Flintoff Bay . . 49 V58-59
Flinton 47 Y50
Flinton Corners . . 47 Y51
Floods Landing 44 B39-40
Floradale 22 L22
Floral Park . . 42 Y32-33
Florence . . . 7 X10-11
Florida 36 C54
Flower Station . . 64 T55
Flying Post . . 105 H15
Flynns 44 Z40
Foldens 15 S20
Foleyet 105 H15
Folger 48 U54
Fonthill 19 S33

Foots Bay 57 T29
Fordwich 27 H18
Fordyce 26 H15
Forest (Frontenac) . 36 C55
Forest (Lambton) 13 S10-11
Forest Estates 15 R21 16 R22
Forest Harbour . . 41 X29
Forest Hill 67 P66
Forest Hill 24 K32
Forest Home . 42 Z31-32
Forest Lea . . . 81 K-L51
Forest Mills 35 C52
Foresters Falls . . 80 M34
Forestville 10 W24
Forfar 49 Y58
Forfar Station . 49 Z58-59
Forget 67 S66
Forks of the Credit . 27 F17
Formosa 27 F17
Fort Erie Beach . 19 U36
Fort Frances . . . 106 H4
Fort Hope . . . 107 E9-10
Fort Irwin . . 60 S39-40
Fort La Cloche 89 G10 90 G11
Fort Stewart . . . 62 T47
Fort William 103 D6 107 H8-9
Fort William First Nation 103 E6
Fortescue 44 W40
Forthton 49 Z61
Forward 67 U66
Fossmill 95 H34
Fountain Beach . 42 Z33
Four Ponds Corners 10 T24
Fournier 68 Q69
Fourth Chute . . 82 P52
Fourth Line 12 T8
Fowlers Corners . 32 C40
Fox's Corners . 44 B38-39
Fox Corners . . . 46 Z48
Fox Point 59 S35
Foxboro 34 D48
Foxey 71 J-K7
Foxmead 42 Y30
Foymount 63 Q50
Fralicks Beach . . 31 D36
Franceville 57 V28
Frank Hill 44 B39
Frankford 34 D47
Franklin 32 D39
Franklin Beach . . 57 V28
Franklins Corners . 68 Q69
Franktown . . . 49 U60
Franktown Station 49 U-V59
Frankville . . . 49 Y60-61
Franz 104 H13
Fraser 19 S34-35
Fraserburg . . . 59 U34
Fraserdale . . 109 G16
Fraserville 32 D40
Frater 104 J13
Fraxa 29 H26
Frederick . . . 109 G16
Freeland 49 Y58
Freelton 23 N27
Freeman Corners 45 A45 46 A46
Freeport 22 N24
Fremo Corners . 64 Q54
French Hill 67 Q65
French Line . . . 64 T56
French River . . 105 K17
French River (Brant) 16 Q24 17 Q25
French River (Mun. of French River) 92 H22 93 H23
French River (Parry Sound) 74 J20
French Settlement . 82 L52
Friendly Corners . 15 R18
Froatburn 51 V67
Frog Point 12 V6
Froggetts Corners 9 W20-21
Frogmore . . 9 W21 10 W22
Frome 8 V16
Frood Mine . . 101 C19
Froomfield . . . 12 U6-7
Fruitland . . . 18 Q29-30
Fullarton 21 N17
Fulton 18 R30
Fultons 27 G19
Furnace Falls . 44 W-X39

Gads Hill 21 N19
Gagnon 67 R67
Galbraith 65 T58
Galesburg 45 A42
Galetta 65 Q58
Gallimere Beach 12 S9 13 S10
Gallingertown . . 51 V68
Galt 22 P24 23 P25
Galts Corner . . 35 E53
Gamebridge . . . 43 A34
Gamebridge Beach . 42 A33
Gameland . . . 106 H3
Gananoque . . 37 C58-59
Gananoque Junction 37 C58-59
Gannon Beach . . 44 A40
Gannon Village . . 44 A40
Garafraxa Woods . 29 H26
Garden Hill . . . 32 F40
Garden of Eden . 82 N-P54
Garden River 86 B93 104 K13-14
Garden Village 94 E28 105 K18
Gardenville . . . 34 F47
Gardiner . . . 109 G16-17
Gardiner Shore . 49 U59

Garnet 11 U26-27
Garretton 50 X63
Garryowen (Grey) 39 Z20-21
Garryowen (Leeds & Grenville) 50 W64
Garson . . 101 B20 105 K17
Gasline 19 U34
Gelert 44 W38
Geneva 100 Z15
Geneva Park . . 42 Y32
Georgetown . . 23 K-L28
Georgian Heights . 41 Z27
Georgian Highlands 41 X26
Georgian Inlet . . 74 M-N23
Georgian Sands Beach 41 X-Y26
Georgina 31 D33
Georgina Beach . 41 Z27
Geraldton . 107 G10 108 G11
Geraldton East . . 108 G11
German Landing . 34 D46
German Settlement . 81 P49
Germania . . 59 V33-34
Germanicus . . 81 N51
Gerrows Beach . 31 E36
Gesto 4 D3
Ghost River . . 106 F6
Gibraltar (Grey) . 40 B24
Gibraltar (Manitoulin) 72 L10
Gibson 41 Z27
Gilbert Mills . . 35 F50
Gilbertville . . . 10 V23
Gilchrist Bay . 45 Z42-43
Gildale 28 F23
Gilford 30 D31
Gilford Beach . . 95 D31
Gillies 105 J18
Gillies Corners . 49 V59
Gillies Hill . . . 27 C17
Gillies Lake . . 54 S16
Gillsons Point . 31 D36
Gilmour 46 W47
Ginoogaming . 108 G11
Gladstone . . 9 U18-19
Glammis . . 26 D15-16
Glamorgan . . . 32 E39
Glandine . 31 C36 32 C37
Glanford Station . 17 S28
Glanmire . 45 X46 46 X47
Glanworth . . . 8 U17
Glascott 28 C21
Glasgow 31 G33
Glasgow Station 64 Q56
Glastonbury . 47 X-Y51
Glen 82 L53
Glen 28 D21
Glen, The . . . 82 L53
Glen Alda . . . 45 W44
Glen Allan . 22 K-L21
Glen Andrew . . 68 Q72
Glen Becker . 51 V-W66
Glen Brook . . 52 T71
Glen Buell . . 49 Z61
Glen Cairn . . 65 S61
Glen Cross . . 29 G27
Glen Donald . 52 U71
Glen Eden . . 4 E1
Glen Elbe . . 49 Z61
Glen Falloch . 52 U71
Glen Huron . 29 C26
Glen Major . 31 F-G34
Glen Meyer . 10 W22
Glen Miller . 34 E47
Glen Morris (Brant) 16 Q24 17 Q25
Glen Morris (Leeds & Grenville) . 49 Z60-61
Glen Nevis . . 52 S72
Glen Norman . 52 R-S72
Glen Oak . . 8 U14 13 U13
Glen Orchard . 57 T-U30
Glen Rae . . 13 V10
Glen Robertson 52 R72
Glen Ross . . 34 D47
Glen Sandfield . 68 Q72
Glen Smail . . 50 X64
Glen Stewart . 50 W65
Glen Tay . . . 49 W58
Glen Walter . 52 U71
Glen Williams 23 K27-28
Glenannan . . 27 G17
Glenarm . . . 43 A36
Glenburn . . 67 P68
Glencairn . . 29 C27
Glenchristie . 22 N24 23 N25
Glencoe . . . 7 W12-13
Glencolin . . 9 V19-20
Glendale . . 52 U71
Glendale . . 84 Y-Z94
Glendale Beach 12 R9 13 R10
Glendower . . 36 A55
Glenelg Centre . 28 D21
Glenfield . . . 63 T51
Glenhaven Beach . 42 B31
Glenlee 28 D21
Glenmore . . 50 Y63
Glenmount . . 59 S35
Glenora . . . 35 D51
Glenorchy (Halton) . 24 M29
Glenorchy (Rainy River) 106 H5
Glenpayne . . 67 S67-68
Glenrest Beach . 42 Z33
Glenroy . . . 52 S71
Glenshee . . 10 V23
Glenvale . . . 36 C55
Glenvale Station . 36 C55
Glenview . . 49 V59
Glenview Heights . 52 U-V71
Glenville . . 30 F31

Glenwater . . 102 B-C2
Glenway Village . 44 A38
Glenwood . . . 5 C8
Glenwood Beach . 30 C31
Gloucester . . 66 R64
Gloucester Glen . 66 R63
Go Home . . . 57 V28
Gobles 16 R22
Goderich . . 20 K12-13
Godfrey . . . 36 A55
Godolphin . . 33 C45
Gogama . . 105 J16
Gold Centre . 105 H16
Gold Rock . . 106 G5
Golden Beach . 58 U32
Golden Hill . 68 P71-72
Golden Lake . 81 N50
Golden Valley . 76 Q29
Goldenburgh . 87 D1 D99
Goldfield . . 67 T67
Goldpines . 106 F4-5
Goldsmith . . 5 D6
Goldstone . . 22 K22
Golspie . . . 15 R20
Gooderham . 44 W40 60 V40
Goodstown . 65 T61 66 T62
Goodwood . 31 F33
Gordon Bay . 57 S28-29
Gordon Lake . 86 C95-96
Gordonville . 22 P23
Gore Bay . 71 J7 72 J8
Gores Landing . 33 E42
Goring . . . 40 B22
Gormley . . 30 G32
Gorr Subdivision . 81 K51
Gorrie . . . 27 H18
Goshen (Huron) . 20 M13-14
Goshen (Renfrew) . 64 Q55
Gosport (Lennox & Addington) . 35 E51-52
Gosport (Northumberland) 34 F46
Gotham . . . 21 K19
Goudreau . . 104 H13
Goulais Bay 84 Y-Z91 104 K13
Goulais Mission . 84 Z90-91
Goulais River 84 Z92 104 K13
Goulds . . . 60 U39
Government Landing 106 H4
Government Park 96 H38 97 H39
Government Road . 82 L52
Gowanstown . 21 J19
Gowganda . 105 J17
Grafton . . . 33 G43
Graham . . 107 G7
Grahamvale . 95 G32-33
Grand Bend . 20 P12-13
Grand Desert . 96 F35
Grand Valley . 28 H24
Grande Pointe . 6 A7-8
Grandview . 59 S35
Grange . . . 23 J27
Grange, The . 23 J27
Grantley . . 67 U67
Granton . . . 14 Q16
Grants Corners . 52 U71
Grants Settlement 82 M54-55
Graphite . . 61 S45
Grasshill . . 23 R28
Grassie . . . 18 R30
Grassmere . 59 Q34
Grassy Narrows 106 F3-4
Gravel Hill . 52 S-T69
Gravenhurst . 58 V32
Grays . . . 13 V11-12
Grays Bay . 42 Z32
Grays Beach . 37 C59
Greater Sudbury 105 K16-17
Greely . . . 66 S63-64
Green Acres . 34 C-D46
Green Bay . 73 K11
Green Briar . 30 E29
Green Lake . 81 M51
Green Lane . 68 N71
Green Park . 28 H23
Green River . 25 H34
Green Valley . 52 S71
Greenbank . 31 E35
Greenbush . 49 Y61 50 Y62
Greenfield (Leeds & Grenville) . . 37 B60
Greenfield (Prescott & Russell) . 52 R-S70
Greenfield (Waterloo) 22 P23
Greenhurst-Thurstonia 44 A38
Greenleys Corners . 33 F44
Greenock . 26 E16 27 E17
Greenpoint . 35 E51-52
Greens Corner . 10 L-M15
Greenstone 107 G10 108 F11
Greensville . 17 Q27
Greenview . 62 S46
Greenway . 13 Q12-13
Greenwood (Durham) 31 G35
Greenwood (Huron) 20 P12-13
Greenwood (Renfrew) 82 L52
Grégoires Mill . 109 G15-16
Gregory . . 57 T30
Grenadier Island . 37 B61
Grenfell . . 11 T26
Gretna . . . 35 E52
Griersville . 40 A22-23
Grieves Corners . 35 E52

Griffis Corners . . 33 F44
Griffith 63 S51
Grimsby . . . 18 Q31
Grimsby Beach . 18 Q-R31
Grimsby Centre . 18 R31
Grimsthorpe . . 72 L8
Grimston . . . 39 B18
Gros Cap . . 104 K13
Gros Cap . . 84 B90
Grove Park . 59 S35
Grovesend . . 9 W19-20
Groveton . . 50 W63-64
Guaytown . . 52 R71
Guelph . . . 23 M25
Guelph Junction . 23 M-N27
Guerin . . . 33 C42
Guilds 7 B11
Guildwood . 25 J-K34
Guilletville . 101 B19
Guiney . . . 63 R49
Gull Bay . . 107 G8-9
Gull Creek . 47 Z52
Gull Rock . 57 S30
Gully, The . 33 F43
Gunter . . . 46 W47-48
Gunters . . 61 Q42-43
Guthrie . . . 42 A30

Haakland Esates . 88 E4
Habermehl . . . 27 D19
Haddo . . . 50 W65
Hadlington . 60 V-W41
Hagar . . . 105 K17
Hagarsville . 11 T27
Hagersville . 11 T27
Hagey . . . 22 N24
Hagles Corners 9 T20 15 S20
Haileybury . 85 R30 105 J18
Haines Lake . 57 R28
Haldane Hill . 58 Q31-32
Haldimand . 11 T28
Haley Station . 82 N-P54
Halfway . . 62 Q48
Halfway House Corners 10 V24-25
Halfway Point . 55 V19
Haliburton . 60 U39
Hall's Glen . 45 A42
Hall Landing . 33 E41
Hallebourg . 108 G14
Hallecks . . 50 A62
Halloway . . 34 C48
Hallowell . 34 G49 35 G50
Halls Lake . 60 T37
Halls Mills . 65 T57
Hallville . . 66 U64
Halpenny . 65 T58
Halstead Beach . 33 E41
Halsteads Bay . 37 C59
Halston . . 34 C49 35 C50
Halton Hills . 23 L27-28
Haltonville . 23 M26-27
Hamer Bay . 57 S29
Hamilton . 17 Q28 18 Q29
Hamilton Beach . 18 Q29
Hamilton Corner . 23 M25
Hamlet . . . 42 X32
Hammertown . 30 G29
Hammond . 67 R66
Hampden . 27 E19-20
Hampshire Mills . 42 Y31
Hampstead . 21 N20
Hampton . 32 G37-38
Hanbury . . 85 P30
Hanesville . 50 W65
Hanmer . 101 A20 105 K17
Hanover . . 27 E19
Happy Hollow . 68 P71
Happy Landing . 93 F23
Happy Valley (Sudbury) 101 B21
Happy Valley (York) . 30 G30
Happyland . 42 Y32
Harburn . . 60 T40
Harcourt . . 61 T42
Hardwick . 55 U-V16
Hardwood Lake . 63 S49
Harfred . . 94 D28
Harkaway . 39 B21 40 B22
Harlem . . 49 Y59
Harley . . 16 S23
Harlock . . 20 K16
Harlowe . 47 X51-52
Harmony . 86 E94
Harmony (Perth) . 21 P19
Harmony (Stormont, Dundas, & Glengarry) 52 R70
Harmony Bay . 84 X92
Harold . . 46 B47
Harper . . 48 W57
Harper Corners . 23 P27
Harpurhey . 20 L-M15
Harriets Corners . 63 Q49
Harrietsville . 9 U19
Harrington West . 15 U19
Harris Lake . 75 M24
Harrisburg . 17 Q27
Harrisons Corners . 52 U69
Harriston . . 27 H19-20
Harriston Junction 27 G19-20
Harrow . . 4 E3
Harrowsmith . 36 B54-55
Harstone . . 102 E3
Hartfell . . 77 L32-33
Hartford . . 11 T26
Hartington . 36 B55
Hartley . . 43 B36
Hartley Bay . 92 H21

Hartsmere . . 62 T49
Harty . . . 109 G15
Harwood . . 33 E42
Harwood Plains . 65 Q-R60
Hastings . . 33 C44
Hatchley . . 16 S23
Hatherton . 28 C-D24
Haultain . . 45 Z42
Havelock . . 45 A45
Havergal . . 62 S47
Havilah . . 86 C97
Havilland . 84 Y91
Hawk Junction . 104 H13
Hawkes . . 49 Y61
Hawkesbury . 68 N71
Hawkestone . 42 A31-32
Hawkesbury Beach 42 A31-32
Hawkesville . 22 L21-22
Hawkins Corner . 42 Y32
Hawley . . 35 E53
Hawtrey . . 10 U22-23
Hay . . . 20 P15
Hay Bay . . 35 E52
Hayburn . . 35 E52
Haycroft . 5 C5-6
Haydon . . 32 F37
Hayes Corners (Leeds & Grenville) . 49 Y61
Hayes Corners (Parry Sound) . 57 R28-29
Hayesland . 23 P27
Hays Shore . 49 U59
Haysville . . 22 P21-22
Hazzards Corners . 46 X47
Head Lake . 43 X-Y36
Healey Falls . 45 A45 46 A46
Hearst . . . 108 G14
Heart Lake . 24 K29
Hearts Desire . 66 S62
Heaslip . 85 M28-29 105 J18
Heathcote . 40 A23
Heather . . 87 F2 88 F3
Heckston . 50 V64
Heidelberg . 22 M22
Hekkla . . 57 R30 58 R31
Hemlo . . 104 H11-12
Hemlock . 9 X21
Hemlock Corners 49 X61 50 X62
Hemlock Downs . 36 C56-57
Hemstock Mill . 39 B19
Hendershot Corners 18 T32
Henderson . 47 X52
Hendrie . . 41 A28
Henfryn . . 21 K18
Henrys Corners . 68 N-P71
Hensall . 20 N14-15
Henvey Inlet First Nation . 74 J23 K22 93 H23
Hepworth . 39 Z18
Herbert Corners . 66 S64
Hereward . 22 J24 23 J25
Hermon . . 62 T47
Heron Bay . 104 H11
Heron Mills . 48 U57
Herrons Corners . 50 Y62-63
Hespeler . 22 N24 23 N25
Hesson . . 21 L20
Heyden . 84 A92 104 K13
Hiam . . 81 L50-51
Hiawatha . 33 D-E42
Hickey Settlement 61 S-T45
Hickory Beach (Haldimand) . 11 V27
Hickory Beach (Kawartha Lakes) . 44 A38
Hickory Corner . 8 T14
Hickson . . 15 Q20
Hidden Valley . 59 Q-R34
High Falls . 91 D15 105 K16
Highgate . 7 Y12
Highland Beach . 31 E35
Highland Estates 28 D21-22
Highland Grove . 61 U42
Hill's Lake . 85 N27
Hillcrest (Norfolk) . 10 V24
Hillcrest (Prince Edward) . . . 34 G48
Hillhead Corners . 32 C38
Hilliardton . 85 N30 105 J18
Hillier . . 34 G48
Hills Green . 20 N14
Hills Siding . 95 G32
Hillsborough Beach 12 R9 13 R10
Hillsburgh . 23 J26
Hillsdale . 41 Z29
Hillside . 59 R34-35
Hillsport . 108 G12
Hillview . 85 Q28
Hilly Grove . 73 M12
Hilton . . 33 F-G45
Hilton Beach . 104 K14
Hilton Beach . 86 B96
Hinch . . 35 C52
Hindon Hill . 60 U37
Hinks Corners . 9 T21 10 T22
Hoards . . 34 C46
Hoasic . . 51 W67
Hoath Head . 39 A20
Hobart . 41 Z29 42 Z30
Hockley . 29 F27
Hodgson . 97 A30-99
Hoe Doe Valley . 30 C29
Hogg . . 39 Y19-20
Holbrook . 9 T21
Holford . 27 C20 28 C21
Holiday . . 15 R19
Holiday Harbour . 5 E6-7
Holland . 37 B60-61
Holland Centre . 39 B21

Holland Landing . . . 30 E31
Holleford 36 B55
Hollen 22 K21
Holly 30 C29
Holly Park . . . 30 G29
Holmes Point . . . 31 C33
Holmesville . . . 20 L13-14
Holmur . . . 57 R27-28
Holstein . . . 28 F21
Holt . . . 30 E32
Holtyre . . . 105 H17
Holyrood . . . 26 F15
Homer . . . 19 R34
Honey Beach . . . 31 E36
Honey Harbour . 41 W28-29
Honeygables . . . 66 S63
Honeywell Corners . 34 D49
Honeywood . . . 29 D25
Honora . . . 72 J10
Hood . . . 48 U56
Hoover Point . . 11 V28
Hope . . . 24 H31
Hope Bay . . . 39 W18
Hopefield . . . 81 P48
Hopeness . . . 55 V17
Hopetown . . . 48 U57
Hopeville . . . 28 E22
Hopkins Bay . . . 42 Y-Z32
Hornby . . . 23 L28
Hornell Heights . . 35 E36
Hornepayne . 108 G12-13
Horning's Mills . . . 29 D25
Horseshoe Bay 84 X90-91 Y90
Horseshoe Lake . 57 R28-29
Horseshoe Valley 42 A30 Z30
Hotham . . . 94 H30
Hotspur . . . 61 V41
Hough Lake . . 85 L26-27
Houghton Centre . . . 9 X21 10 X22
Houseys Rapids 42 W33 43 W34
Howdenvale . . 38 W16-17
Howland . . . 44 X38
Hoyle . . . 105 H16
Hubbs . . . 34 G48-49
Hubrey . 8 U17 9 U18
Huckabones Corners . . . 81 M51 82 M52
Hudson . . . 106 F5
Huff Wharf . . 35 E51-52
Huffman Corners . 7 B10
Huffs Corners (Lambton) . . 7 W-X10
Huffs Corners (Prince Edward) . . . 34 F-G49
Hughes . . . 61 T44
Hukish . . . 43 Z37
Hulbert . . . 50 V65
Hull . . . 100 B17
Humber . . . 24 H29 29 H28
Humber Grove . . 24 H29
Hume . . . 102 D3
Humphrey . . . 57 R29
Hungerford . . . 47 A50
Hungry Hollow . . 13 S12
Hunta . . . 109 G16
Huntingford . . 15 R20-21
Huntley . . 65 S60-61
Huntsville . . . 59 R33
Hurds Lake . . . 64 Q55
Hurdville . . 57 Q27-28
Hurkett . . . 107 H9
Huron Estates . . 88 F4
Huron Heights . . 12 S8
Huron Park . . . 14 Q15
Huron Ridge . . 26 D14
Hurondale . . . 20 N15
Hutchins Corners 50 W62-63
Hutchisons Corners 28 C22
Hutton . . . 49 X60
Hutton Heights . . 26 H16
Huttonville . . 23 L28 24 L29
Hybla . . . 61 T45
Hyde Park . . . 8 T16
Hydro Glen . . . 42 W31
Hymers . . . 102 E2
Hymers . . . 107 H8
Hyndford . . 82 P52-53
Hyndman . . . 50 V64

Ice Lake . . . 72 J8
Ida . . . 32 D39-40
Ida Hill . . . 36 C57
Ignace . . . 106 G6
Ilderton . . . 14 S15
Ilfracombe . . . 58 Q32
Indian River . . . 33 C42
Indiana . . . 11 T28
Ingersoll . . 15 S19-20
Ingle . . . 47 B51-52
Ingleside . . . 51 V68
Inglewood . . 23 J27-28
Inglis Falls . . . 39 A19
Ingoldsby . . . 60 V38
Ingolf . . . 106 G2
Inholmes . . 76 P28-29
Inkerman . . . 67 U65
Inkerman Station . 67 U65
Innanen . . . 22 P24
Innerkip . . . 15 Q21
Innisfil . . 30 C-D30
Innisfil Heights . 30 C-D30
Innisville . . . 49 U58
Intola . . . 102 C5
Inverary . . . 36 B-C56
Inverhaugh . . . 22 L23
Inverhuron . . . 26 C14
Invermay . . 38 A17 39 A18
Inverness Lodge . 58 T31

Inwood . . . 13 V11
Iona . . . 8 W15
Iona Station . . . 8 W15
Ipperwash Beach . 13 Q11
Ireland . . . 62 T48
Irena . . . 51 W66
Irish Lake . . . 28 D22
Iron Bridge . 104 K14
Iron Bridge . . . 87 E2
Irondale . . . 44 W39
Ironsides . . . 61 U42
Iroquois . . 51 W-X66
Iroquois Falls . . 105 H17
Isaacs Glen . . . 43 A37
Ishpiming Beach . 41 X26
Iskutewizaagegan 106 G2-3
Island . . . 50 W64
Island, The . . . 50 W64
Island Grove . . . 30 C31
Island Lake . 84 Z92 104 K13
Island View Beach . 31 C33
Islay . . . 43 A36
Islington . . . 24 L31
Ivan . . . 14 S15
Ivanhoe . . . 46 B48
Ivy . . . 30 C-D29
Ivy Lea . . . 37 C60

Jack Lake (Peterborough) . . 45 X-Y43
Jackpine . . . 102 G1
Jackson . . 39 A18-19
Jacksonburg . . 10 X22
Jacksons Point . . 30 C32
Jaffa . . 9 W18-19
Jaffray Melick . 106 G3
Jamestown . . . 21 J17
Jamot . . 92 G22 93 G23
Janetville . . . 32 D37
Jarratt . . . 42 Z31
Jarvis . . . 11 U26
Jarvis River . . 102 G4
Jasper . . . 49 X61
Jeannette . . . 32 C42
Jeannettes Creek . 5 B7
Jefferson . . . 24 H32
Jellicoe . . . 107 G10
Jellyby . . . 50 Y62
Jericho . . . 10 W23
Jericho . . . 13 R11
Jermyn . . . 33 C42
Jerseyville . . 17 Q-R26
Jessopville . . . 28 F24
Jessups Falls . . 67 N-P68
Jevins . . . 42 W32
Jewellville . . . 62 R48
Joes Lake . . . 64 T55
Johnson . . . 39 Y21
Johnsons Ferry . 67 Q68
Johnston Corners . 66 S63
Johnstown (Hastings) . . . 34 E47
Johnstown (Leeds & Grenville) . 50 Y64-65
Jones . . . 106 F-G3
Jones Falls . . . 37 A58
Jones Landing . . 84 X92
Jordan . . . 18 R32
Jordan Harbour . . . 18 R32 19 R33
Jordan Station . . . 18 R32 19 R33
Josephburg . . 22 N22
Joyceville . . . 36 C56
Joyland Beach . 42 A32 Z32
Joyvista Estates . 43 B37
Juddhaven . . 57 S30
Judge . . . 85 P-Q31
Judgeville . . . 47 X60
Junetown . . 37 A60-61
Juniper Island . . 43 Z42
Jura . . . 13 S11

Kaboni . . . 73 L13
Kagawong . . . 72 J9
Kahshe Lake . 42 W33
Kakabeka Falls . . . 102 D3-4 107 H8
Kaladar . . . 47 Y51
Kaministiquia . 102 C3-4
Kanata . . 65 R60-61
Kapuskasing . 109 G15
Karalash Corners . . . 84 Y92 104 K13
Kars . . . 66 T63
Kashabowie . . 107 H7
Kaszuby . . . 62 Q47
Kathmae Siding . 82 L52
Katimavik . . . 65 R61
Katrine . . . 77 N32
Kawartha Hideaway 44 A40
Kawartha Park . . . 44 A41 45 A42
Kawene . . . 106 H6
Keady . . . 39 A18
Kearney . . . 77 N33
Kearns . . . 105 H18
Kedron . . . 31 G36
Keelerville (Frontenac) . . 36 A-B57
Keelerville (Stormont, Dundas, & Glengarry) . . 50 W65 51 W66
Keenansville . . 29 F28
Keene . . . 33 D42
Keewatin . . . 106 G3
Kejick . . 106 G2-3
Keldon . . . 28 F24
Keller Bridge . . 46 Z48

Kellers . . . 45 B45
Kelleys Island . . 4 B4
Kelly's Corners . 38 A16
Kelly Station . . 15 R18
Kellys Corner . 82 N-P52
Kelso . . . 23 M27
Kelvin . . . 10 T23
Kemble . . . 39 Y19
Kempark . . . 66 R63
Kemptville . 50 V63 66 U63
Kenabeek 85 P27 105 J17-18
Kenabutch . . . 89 F7
Kendal . . . 32 F39
Kenedon Park 32 C39 44 B39
Kenilworth . . 28 H21-22
Kenmore . . . 67 S65
Kennaway . . 61 S-T42
Kennedy Acres . . 12 S9
Kennedys . . . 77 M32
Kennicott . . . 21 M18
Kennisis Lake . 60 S38-39
Kenogami Lake . 105 H17
Kenora . . . 106 G3
Kenrei Park . . . 43 B37
Kenstone Beach . 44 A38-39
Kent . . . 40 Z22
Kent Bridge . . . 7 Y10
Kent Centre . . . 7 B10
Kentvale 86 E-F94 104 K13-14
Kepler . . . 36 C55
Kerr Line . . . 82 M54
Kerwood . . . 13 T12
Keswick . . . 30 D31
Kettle's Beach . 41 W27
Kettle Point . . 13 R10
Kettleby . . . 30 D31
Keward . . . 39 B19
Key Harbour . 74 J-K21
Key Junction . 74 J21-22
Key River . . . 74 K22
Keyser . . . 13 S12
Keystone Camps . 94 F28-29
Khartum . . . 63 S51
Khiva . . . 14 Q14
Kilbride . . 23 N27-28
Kilcoo Harbour . 43 W37
Kilgorie . . . 29 E26
Killaloe (Killaloe Station) . . 81 N49
Killarney . . . 73 J15
Killarney Beach . 30 D31
Killean . . . 23 N25
Kilmanagh . 23 J28 29 H28
Kilmarnock . . 49 W61
Kilmartin . . . 13 V12
Kilmaurs . . . 65 Q59
Kilrush . . 95 G34 96 G35
Kilsyth . . . 39 A19
Kilworth . . 8 T15-16
Kilworthy . . . 42 W32
Kimball . . . 12 V7-8
Kimberley . . . 40 B23
Kimbo . . . 18 R30
Kinburn (Huron) . 20 L15
Kinburn (Ottawa) . 65 Q59
Kincardine . . 26 E13
King City . . . 30 G31
King Creek . . . 24 H30
King Kirkland . 105 H18
King Pitt . . . 35 D57
Kingarf . . . 26 E15
Kinghorn . . . 24 H31
Kinghurst . . 27 C19-20
Kinglake . . . 9 W21
Kings Wharf . . 44 B39
Kingsbridge . . 26 G13
Kingscote . . . 26 F23
Kingscross Estates . 30 G30
Kingsford . . . 35 C51
Kingsmere . . 20 H22
Kingsmill . . 9 V18-19
Kingston . . 36 D55-56
Kingston Mills . 36 D56
Kingsville . . . 4 E4
Kingwood . . . 21 M20
Kingwood Acres . 41 X26
Kinhurn . . . 26 D14
Kinkora . . . 21 M18
Kinloss . . . 26 E15
Kinlough . . . 26 F15
Kinmount . . . 44 X38
Kinnaird . . . 13 R11
Kinsale . . . 31 G35
Kintail . . . 26 G13
Kintore . . 15 R18-19
Kintyre . . . 7 X12
Kiosk . . . 96 G36
Kiowana Beach . 40 Y22
Kippen . . 20 M-N14
Kirby . . 32 F38-39
Kirbys Corner . 104 K13
Kirk . . . 93 D25
Kirk Cove . . . 47 X52
Kirkfield . . . 43 Z35
Kirkhill . . . 68 Q71
Kirkland Lake . 105 H17
Kirkton . . . 20 P16
Kirkwall . . . 23 P26
Kirby's Corner . 84 Z92
Kitchener . . . 22 N23
Kitigan . . . 109 G15
Kivikoski . . . 102 C5
Kleinburg . . . 24 H30
Klies Beach . . 4 F2-3
Klock . . . 97 E39
Klondyke . . 20 K-L16
Klueys Bay . . 44 W33
Kohler . . . 11 U28
Kolapore . . . 40 B24
Komoka . . . 8 T15

Korah . . . 84 A-B91
Kormak . . 105 J15
Kossuth . . . 22 N24
Kramer Subdivision . . . 81 K50-51
Krugerdorf . . 85 L28
Kuhryville . . 21 M18-19
Kukatush . . . 105 H15
Kumpville . 21 K20 22 K21
Kurtzville . . . 21 J19
Kynoch . . . 87 D1

L'Amable (Nipissing) 79 P42
L'Amable . . . 62 U46
L'Ange-Gardien . . 68 N70
L'Orignal . . 68 N70-71
La Passe . . . 82 L54
La Salette . . . 10 U23
La Vallee . . . 106 H4
Lac-Sainte-Thérèse 108 G14
Lac La Croix . . 106 H5
Lac Seul . . . 106 F5
Laclu . . . 106 G3
Lady Bank . . 28 C23-24
Ladysmith . . . 12 V7
Lafontaine . . . 41 X26
Lafontaine Beach . 41 X26
Laggan . . . 68 Q71
Lagoon City . . 42 A33
Laird . . . 86 C94
Lake . . . 84 X45
Lake Bernard . . 77 M32
Lake Charles . . 39 X19
Lake Clear . . 81 P50
Lake Dalrymple . 43 Y34-35
Lake Dore . . 82 N52
Lake Helen . . 107 G9
Lake Huron Highland . . . 26 D13-14
Lake Joseph . . 57 S29
Lake Morningstar . 7 A10
Lake On The Mountain . . . 35 F51
Lake Opinicon . 36 A57
Lake Rosalind . . 27 E18-19
Lake Saint Peter . 61 R43
Lake Travers . . 79 J42
Lake Travers Siding . 79 J42
Lake Valley Grove . 13 R10
Lakefield . . . 44 B41
Lakehurst . . . 44 A40
Lakelet . . . 27 G18
Lakeport . . 33 G44-45
Lakeside Beach . 31 E36
Lakeview (Elgin) . 9 W20
Lakeview (Peel) . 24 L31
Lakeview (Simcoe) . 42 B31
Lakeview Beach . 43 Z34
Lakeview Estates . 43 A39
Lakeview Heights . . . 51 V69 52 U69
Lakewood . . 59 U-V34
Lakewood Beach . 4 E1
Lakewood Gardens . . . 20 N12-13
Lalonde . 67 Q68 68 Q69
Lamable . 61 U45 62 U46
Lambert . . . 21 L19
Lambeth (Middlesex) . . . 8 U16-17
Lambeth (Oxford) . 10 T22
Lambs Corners . 11 V27
Lamlash . . . 21 D19
Lammermoor . . 48 U56
Lanark . . 48 U-V57
Lancaster . . . 52 T72
Lancaster Bay . 32 C40
Lancelot . . 58 S32
Landerkin . . . 28 G22
Lanes . . . 33 C-D42
Lang . . . 33 C-D42
Langford . . . 17 R26
Langman . . . 41 A27
Langside . . 26 G15-16
Langton . . 10 W22-23
Lansdowne . . 37 B60
Lappe . . 102 B5 107 H8
Larchwood . . 100 B17
Larder Lake . . 105 H18
LaRenouche . . 68 P72
Largie . . 8 W14
Larkins . . 47 B50-51
LaRue Mills . . 37 B61
Laskay . . . 24 H30
Lasswade . . 45 X44-45
Latchford . . 105 J18
Latchford Bridge . . . 62 R48 63 R49
Latimer . . . 36 C56
Latta . . . 34 C49
Lauderbach . . 27 G19
Lauderdale Point . 42 X32
Laurel . . . 29 G25
Laurel Station . 29 G26
Laurentian . . . 11 V27
Laurentian View . 81 K50-51
Lauriston . . . 28 C21
Lavant . . . 48 U55
Lavant Station . 48 U54-55
Lavender . . . 29 D26
Lavigne . . 93 E25-26
Lavigne . . . 105 K17
Lawrence . . . 8 V15
Lawtons Corners . 9 W18
Layton . . . 31 D35
Leadbury . . 20 K-L16
Leamington . . 5 E5-6
Leaside . . . 24 K32
Leaskdale . . . 31 D34
Lebanon . . 21 K20-21

Ledgerwoods Corner . . . 82 M54
Lee . . . 102 D4
Leeburn . 86 C96 104 K14
Leeds . . . 37 S58-59
Lefaivre . . . 68 N69
Lefroy . . 30 D-31
Leggatt . . . 28 G24
Legge . . . 37 C59
Lehighs Corners . 49 Y61
Leinster . . . 35 C51
Leith . . . 39 Z20
Leitrim . . 66 R63-64
Leland . . . 38 B56
Lemieux . . 67 Q67-68
Lemonville . . 31 G33
Leonard . . 67 Q65-66
Leskard . . 32 F38
Leslies Corner . 4 D-E2
Letterbreen . . 28 F21
Letterkenny 62 Q48 63 Q49
Letts Corners 81 N51 82 N52
Levack . . . 105 K16
Levack . . 100 A16
Levack Station . 100 B16
Lewis Corners . 8 V14
Lewisham . . 43 W34
Lieury . 14 Q-R14
Lifford . . 32 D-E38
Lighthouse Beach . 95 F32
Lighthouse Cove . 5 R6-7
Lily Oak . . . 39 B21
Limberlost Lodge . 59 Q35
Limbank . . . 66 S63
Limerick . . 67 U67
Limges . . 67 R66
Lincoln . . 18 Q32
Lind . . . 15 Q17
Linden Bank . . 50 Y62
Linden Beach . . 4 E-F4
Linden Valley . 43 B36-37
Lindenwood . . 39 Y19
Lindsay . 43 B37 44 B38
Links Mills . . 36 D54
Linton . . . 30 G30
Linwood . . 22 L21
Lion's Head . . 55 V17
Lisbon . . . 21 N20
Lisle . . . 29 D27
Listowel . . 21 K19-20
Little Aylmer . 9 V19
Little Britain . 31 C36
Little Brockville . 49 Z59
Little Buffalo . . 11 T26
Little Current . 90 H11-12
Little Egypt . . 26 F16
Little Falls . . 42 X32-33
Little Germany (Grey) . . . 40 B23-24
Little Germany (Northumberland) . . . 33 D42-43
Little Hawk Lake . 60 T37-38
Little Lake . . 23 N25
Little Rapids . . . 87 D-E98 104 K14
Littles Corners . 23 P25
Littlewood . . 8 U-V16
Lively 91 D18 100 C18 105 K16
Living Springs . 22 J24
Livingstone . . 87 E98-99
Livingstone Creek 87 E98-99
Lloyd . . . 65 T57
Lloydtown . . 30 G29
Lo-Ellen . . 101 C19
Lobo . . . 8 T15
Lobo Siding . . 8 T16
Lochalsh (Algoma) 104 H13
Lochalsh (Huron) 26 F13-14
Lochiel . . . 52 R71
Lochinvar . . . 52 R71
Lochlin . . 60 V38-39
Lochwinnoch . . 83 P56
Lockerby . . . 27 C17
Lockie . . . 16 Q24
Locksley . . 81 L-M51
Lockton . . 29 H28
Lodgeroom Corners 46 A49
Lodi . . . 67 S68
Loiselleville . . 4 D1-2
Lombardy . . 49 X59
Londesborough . 20 K15
London . . . 8 T17
Long Bay . . . 72 K8
Long Beach (Kawartha Lakes) . . . 43 A37
Long Beach (Niagara) . . . 18 U32
Long Lake (Frontenac) . . . 48 Y54
Long Lake (Thunder Bay) . . 108 G11
Long Point (Kawartha Lakes) . . . 43 Z36
Long Point (Leeds & Grenville) . . . 37 A59
Long Point (Norfolk) . . . 10 X-Y24
Longboat Corners . 17 S27
Longbow Lake . 106 G3
Longford . . . 42 Y32
Longlac . . . 108 G11
Longtinville . 67 S66-67
Longwood . . 8 U14

Lonsdale . . . 35 D51
Lonsdale Station 35 D50-51
Loon Island . . 52 U72
Loree . . . 40 A24
Loretto . . . 29 F28
Lorimer Lake . . 75 N27
Loring . . . 75 J27
Lorne (Stormont, Dundas, & Glengarry) . 68 Q71-72
Lorne (Sudbury) . 90 E13-14
Lorne Park . . . 24 M30
Lorneville . . . 43 B35
Lorrain Valley . 105 J18
Lorraine . . . 19 U34
Lost Channel (Manitoulin) . . 46 B49 47 B50
Lost Channel (Parry Sound) . . 75 K24-25
Lost Nation . . 63 Q49
Lothian . . . 26 G14
Lotus . . . 32 E38
Loughbreeze . 33 G45
Louise . . . 27 D19
Louisville . 6 A9 7 A10
Lounsbury . . . 95 E32
Lovat . . . 26 D16
Lovering . . . 42 X30
Lovett . . . 34 F46
Low Bush River . . . 105 H17 109 G17
Lowbanks . . 18 U31-32
Lower Dacre . 63 R52 64 R53
Lower Holleford . 36 A-B55
Lower Langside . 26 G15
Lower Stafford . 82 M52
Lower Wingham . 26 H16
Lowther . . 109 G15
Lowville . . . 23 N28
Loyal . . . 20 J13
Lucan . . . 14 R15-16
Lucan Crossing . 14 R15
Lucasville . . 12 T8
Lucille . . . 29 G27
Lucknow . . . 26 G14
Ludgate . . . 74 K23
Lueck Mill . . 39 B20
Lukerville . . 4 D2
Lumina . . 59 R35
Lumley . . 20 N15
Lunar . . . 84 X93
Lundys Corners . 94 G56
Lunenburg . 52 U69 67 U68
Lunge Lodge . 94 F-G27
Luquan Beach . 26 E-F13
Lutesville . . 10 T24-25
Luton . . . 10 V19
Lutterworth . . 43 W37
Luxemburg . . 22 N21
Lyn . . . 50 Z62
Lyndale . . . 8 V17
Lynden . . . 17 Q26
Lyndhurst . . 37 A59
Lynedoch . . 10 V23
Lynhurst . . 8 V17
Lynn Valley . . 10 V25
Lynnville . . 10 U24
Lyons . . . 9 U19
Lythmore . . 11 T28

M'Chigeeng . 72 K10
Mabee's Corners . . . 9 V21 10 V22
Maberly . . . 48 W56
Macdiarmid . 107 G9
MacDonald's Grove . . . 52 R-S69
MacDonald Bay . 45 Y44-45
MacDuff . . 108 G13
Macey Bay . . 41 W29
MacGillivrays Bridge 52 T71
Mackenzie . . 103 B8
MacKenzie Point . 43 Z36
Mackey . . 98 F-G46
Mackey Siding . 98 G46
Macksville . . 13 V13
MacLarens Landing 83 P59
MacLean Park . 11 T26
MacLennan . . 86 D94
MacTier . . . 57 T29
Macton . . 22 L21
Macville . . 24 H29
Madawaska . 80 P44-45
Madigans . . 75 P25
Madoc . . 46 A48
Madsen . . 106 F3-4
Maecks . . 77 K32
Magisi Sahgaigan . 106 H4
Magnetawan . 76 M29-30
Magnetawan First Nation . . . 72 L13 75 L24
Maiangowi Settlement . . . 73 L13
Maidstone . . 4 C3
Mainville . 50 X64-65
Mair Mills . . 40 A25
Maitland . . 50 Z63
Malachi . . 106 G2-3
Malakoff . . 66 T-U62
Malcolm . . 27 D18
Malden Centre . 4 E1-2
Mallards Bay . 44 B39
Mallory Beach . 39 X18
Mallorytown . 37 A-B61
Mallorytown Landing . . . 37 B61
Malone . . 46 Z47
Malton . . 24 L30
Malvern . . 25 J34
Malwood . . 65 Q60

Manbert . . 74 M23 75 M24
Manchester . . 31 F35
Mandaumin . . 12 T8
Manhard . . 9 Y62
Manilla . . 31 C35
Manion Corners . 65 S60
Manitou Dock . 56 T26
Manitouwadge . 108 G12
Manitowaning . 73 L12
Manley . . 21 L17
Mannheim . . 22 N22
Manotick . . 66 S63
Manotick Station . 66 S63
Mansewood . 23 M27-28
Mansfield (Dufferin) . 29 E27
Mansfield (Ottawa) 65 S-T61
Manvers . . 32 E39
Many . . 24 H31
Maple Beach . 42 B33 43 B34
Maple Grove (Brant) . . . 16 S24 17 S25
Maple Grove (Dufferin) . . . 29 F25
Maple Grove (Durham) . . . 32 H37-38
Maple Grove (Huron) 20 P12
Maple Grove (Leeds & Grenville) . . 37 C58
Maple Grove (Middlesex) . . 14 R16
Maple Hill (Bruce) . 27 E18
Maple Hill (Frontenac) . . . 36 B57
Maple Hill (York) . 30 G32
Maple Island . . 76 M28
Maple Lake . 60 T-U38
Maple Lake Park . . . 15 Q21 16 Q22
Maple Lane . . 28 C22
Maple Lawn . 36 C-D56
Maple Leaf . 61 R45 62 R46
Maple Ridge . 87 E99
Maple Ridge (Muskoka) . . . 59 S35-36
Maple Ridge (Stormont, Dundas, & Glengarry) . . 67 U66
Maple Row . . 68 P72
Maple Valley (Clearview) . . 29 D25
Maple Valley (Severn) . . . 42 Y33
Maple View . . 34 D46
Maplegrove . . 42 B31
Maples . . 29 H26
Maples, The . 29 H26
Maplewood . 15 Q19-20
Mar . . . 38 X17
Mara Beach . . 42 A33
Marathon (Ottawa) . 65 R59
Marathon (Thunder Bay) . . 104 H11
Marble Bluff . . 64 T56
Marble Rock . . 37 B59
Marburg . . 11 V26
Marchhurst . . 65 R60
Marchmont . . 42 Z31
Marden . . 22 L24 23 L25
Marentette Beach . 5 F6
Mariatown . . 51 W67
Marina Estates . 31 C33
Marionville . . 67 T65
Mariposa . . 31 C36
Mariposa Beach . 42 Y32
Markdale . . 28 C22
Markham . . 25 H33
Markstay . 101 C23 105 K17
Marlbank . . 47 B51
Marmion . . 39 B18
Marmora . . 46 A46-47
Marmora Station . 46 A46-47
Marnoch . . 26 H15
Marsh Hill . . 31 E34-35
Marshall's Corners . 85 M30
Marshall Bay . . 65 Q58
Marshall Park . 95 E31
Marshfield . . 4 E3
Marsville . . 18 T32 19 T33
Marsville . . 23 J25
Marten Falls . 108 E12
Martel Corners . 67 R67
Marten River . 105 K17-18
Marter . . 85 L-M29
Marthaville . . 12 U9
Martin . . . 106 G6
Martins . . 59 R33
Martins Corner . 82 P53
Martins Corners . 66 P64
Martins Landing . 46 W47
Martintown . . 52 T71
Martinville . 41 Z29 42 Z30
Martland . . 67 S65
Marvelville . . 67 S65
Mary Grove . 41 W27-28
Maryhill . . 22 M24
Marysville (Frontenac) . . . 36 E56
Marysville (Hastings) 35 D52
Massanoga . 47 V50 63 V49
Massassauga Point . . . 34 E49 35 E50
Massey . 89 F10 105 K15-16
Massie . . 39 A20-21
Matachewan . 105 J17
Matachewan (IR) . 105 H17
Matawatchan . 63 T51
Mathers Corners . 33 D42
Matheson . 105 H17
Mattagami . . 105 H17
Mattawa . 96 E37-38
Mattice . . 108 G14

Plantagenet Station . . . .
. . . . 67 P68 68 P69
Plattsville . . 16 Q22 22 P22
Playfairville . . . 48 V56-57
Pleasant Corners . . 68 P71
Pleasant Park 4 C3
Pleasant Point 44 B38
Pleasant Valley
(Manitoulin) 72 K8-9
Pleasant Valley (Renfrew) . .
. . . . 82 L54
Pleasant Valley (South
Dundas) 50 V64-65
Pleasant Valley (South
Stormont) 67 U68
Pleasant View 82 K-L52
Pleasantville 30 F32
Plevna 63 V52
Plover Mills 15 R17
Plum Hollow 49 Z60
Plummer 86 C96
Plumtree 22 P23
Point Abino 19 U35
Point Alexander . . . 99 G48
Point Anne . . 34 E49 35 E50
Point Clark 26 F13
Point Edward 12 T7
Point of Mara Beach 42 A33
Point Pleasant 44 Z40
Pointe au Baril 74 N23
Pointe au Baril Station . . .
. . . . 75 N24
Pointe aux Pins . . . . . .
. . . . . 84 B91 104 K13
Pointe des Chênes . 84 B90
Pointe des Chênes Park . . .
. . . . 84 B90
Pointe Louise 84 D91
Puland 48 U56
Pomona 28 D21-22
Ponsonby 22 L24
Pontypool 32 E38
Poole 21 M20
Pooles Corners . . . 49 V60
Pooles Resort 37 B61
Poplar 71 L7
Poplar Beach . . 20 P12-13
Poplar Dale . 86 B97 104 K14
Poplar Hill 8 T14
Porcupine . . 105 H16-17
Porlock 92 F20-21
Porquis Junction . . 105 H17
Port Albert 26 H13
Port Alexandria . . . 36 E57
Port Alma 5 D8
Port Anson 76 N30
Port Arthur 103 D6
Port Bolster 31 C33
Port Britain . . 32 G40 33 G41
Port Bruce 9 X19
Port Burwell 9 X20
Port Carling . . 57 T30 58 T31
Port Carmen 76 M30
Port Cockburn 57 S29
Port Colborne . . 19 U33-34
Port Credit 24 L-M31
Port Crewe 6 D9
Port Cunnington . 59 S34-35
Port Dalhousie 19 Q33
Port Darlington . . . 32 H38
Port Davidson 18 T31
Port Dover 11 V26
Port Elgin 38 B15
Port Elmsley 49 W59
Port Findlay 86 D94
Port Franks . . . 13 Q11-12
Port Glasgow 8 Y14
Port Granby . . . 32 G-H40
Port Hope 33 G41
Port Keewaydin . . 58 T-U31
Port Lambton 6 W6-7
Port Law 28 D23
Port Loring 75 J27
Port Maitland (East) 18 U31
Port Maitland (West) . . . .
. . . . 18 U30-31
Port McNicoll . . . 41 X28-29
Port Metcalf 37 D58
Port Milford . . . 35 G51-52
Port Perry 31 E35-36
Port Robinson 19 U34
Port Rowan . . . 10 X23-24
Port Royal 10 X23
Port Ryerse . . . 10 V-W25
Port Sandfield 57 T30
Port Severn 41 X29
Port Stanley 8 X17
Port Stanton . . 42 X31-32
Port Sydney 59 S33
Port Talbot 8 X16
Port View Beach . . 31 E-F36
Port Weller . . . 19 Q33-34
Port Whitby 25 H36
Portal 26 D16
Porter's Hill 26 H13
Portland 49 Y58-59
Portlock 86 D95-96
Pottageville 30 G30
Potters Landing . 57 V28-29
Powassan 95 G32
Power Glen 19 R33
Powles Corners . . . 43 A37
Prairie Siding 5 B8
Pratt Corners . . . 48 W56
Precious Corners . . 33 F42
Preneveau 45 B45
Prescott 50 Y64
Presquile Point . . 34 F-G46
Preston 22 N24
Preston Lake 30 G32
Prestonvale 49 V58
Pretty River Valley . . 40 B25

Prices Corners (Dufferin) . .
. . . . 23 J25
Prices Corners (Simcoe) . .
. . . . 42 Z31
Priceville 28 D22
Primrose 29 F26
Prince Albert 31 F35
Princeton 16 R23
Progreston 23 N27
Pronto 88 F5
Pronto East . . 88 F5-6 105 K15
Prophet Beach . . . 42 A33
Prospect (Durham) . 31 F35
Prospect (Lanark) . . 49 U60
Prospect Hill (Perth) 15 Q17
Prospect Hill (Sudbury) . . .
. . . . 90 D14
Prosperity 26 H14-15
Proton Station 28 D23
Proulx 68 Q70
Providence Bay . . . 72 M9
Puce 4 B4
Punkeydoodles Corners . .
. . . . 22 P21
Purbrook 59 U34
Purdy 62 R46
Purdy Corners 33 F44
Purple Grove . . 26 F14-15
Purple Hill (Dufferin) . . .
. . . . 29 G-H26
Purple Hill (Durham) 31 F36
Purple Valley 39 W18
Purpleville 24 H30
Pusey 61 U41-42
Puslinch 23 N26
Putnam 9 T19

Quabbin 37 B61
Quadeville 63 R49
Quarindale . . 21 K20 22 K21
Queens Line 82 N54
Queensborough . . 46 Z49
Queenston 19 R35
Queensville 30 E32
Queenswood Village 66 P64
Quibell 106 G4
Quinn 5 C7
Quinn Settlement . . 49 U58

Radiant 97 H41
Ragged Rapids . 43 X34-35
Raglan (Chatham-Kent) . .
. . . . 7 B11
Raglan (Durham) . . 31 F36
Railton 36 B-C55
Rainham Centre . . 11 U28
Rainy River 106 H3
Raith 107 H8
Rama Road 42 Y32
Ramore 105 H17
Ramsay Meadows . 65 T59
Ramsayville . . 66 R63-64
Ramsey 105 J15
Randall 30 E29
Randwick 29 D27
Ranelagh 10 T23
Ranger Lake 104 K14
Rankin (Nipissing) . 96 E38
Rankin (Renfrew) . 81 M51
Rannoch 15 Q17
Rathburn 42 Y33
Ratho 15 Q21
Rathwells Shore . . 65 T59
Rattlesnake Harbour . . . .
. . . . 10 U23-24
Ratzburg . . 21 N20 22 N21
Ravenna 40 A23-24
Ravenscliffe . 58 Q32 59 Q33
Ravenshoe 30 D32
Ravensview 36 D57
Ravenswood 13 R11
Ravensworth 77 N34
Raymond 58 S32
Raymonds Corners . . . . .
. . . . 36 A56-57
Rayside 15 S19
Rayside-Balfour 100 B17-18
Reaboro 32 C38
Read 35 D50
Reading 23 J25 29 H25
Red Bay 38 X17
Red Cap Beach . . . 43 Z35
Red Lake 106 E3-4
Red Lake Road . 106 F-G4
Red Rock 84 A90
Red Rock (Algoma) 104 K13
Red Rock (Thunder Bay) . .
. . . . 107 H9
Red Rock Bay 49 U59
Red Wing 40 B23
Redan 49 Y61
Redbridge . . 95 D33 105 K18
Reddendale 36 D55
Redditt 106 G3
Redickville 29 D25
Rednersville 34 E48
Redwood 57 T29-30
Reeces Corners . . . .
. . . . . 12 T9 13 T10
Reevecraig 66 U63
Reid's Corners . . . 26 F13
Reids Mills 66 U64
Reidsville 22 P23
Relessey 29 F27
Renfort 17 R27
Renfrew 82 P55
Renfrew Junction . . . .
. . . . 64 Q54-55 82 P54-55
Renton 10 U25
Renwick 5 D7
Restoule 94 H29

Rexdale 24 K30-31
Rheault 92 D19
Rhineland 10 V22-23
Rhodes 5 B8 6 B9
Riceville . . . 67 Q68 68 Q69
Rich Hill 30 G29
Richan 106 F-G5
Richard's Landing 86 D-E94
Richards Landing . . . . . .
. . . . 104 K13-14
Richardson 49 V59
Richmond (Elgin) . . . 9 V20
Richmond (Ottawa) . 65 T61
Richmond Hill . . 24 H31-32
Richwood 16 Q23
Rideau Ferry 49 W59
Rideau Glen . . . 66 R62-63
Ridge 45 X45-46
Ridgemount 15 T24
Ridgetown 7 A11-12
Ridgeville 19 S33
Ridgeway 19 U35
Riley Lake 42 W33
Rimington 46 Z48
Ringold 5 B8
Ringwood 31 G33
Ripley 26 F14
Ritchance 68 P69-70
River Canard . . . 4 C-D1
River Drive Park . . 30 E31
River Valley (Hastings) . .
. . . . 34 C-D47
River Valley (Nipissing) . .
. . . . 105 K17
Riverbank 22 J22
Riverdale 52 V70
Riversdale 26 F14
Riverside (Middlesex) 8 V14
Riverside (Simcoe) . 41 Y29
Riverside Beach . . 43 A34
Riverside Heights 51 V-W67
Riverstown . . . 28 G-H21
Riverview (Dufferin) . 28 F24
Riverview (Renfrew) 81 K51
Riverview (Waterloo) 22 P24
Riverview Heights . 50 Y64
Riviera Estate 68 N71
Rivière Veuve . . 101 B23
Rob Roy 22 N24
Robbtown . . . 28 F21-22
Robertsons Shore . 49 V59
Robertsville . . 48 W54-55
Robin Landing . 33 D42-43
Robinson 101 C19
Roblin 47 B52
Roblin Mills 35 E-F51
Roblindale Station . 35 C52
Rochefort 81 P49
Rocher Fendu 82 L54
Roches Point 30 D31
Rock Lake 86 C97
Rock Lake (Algoma) . . . . .
. . . . 104 K14
Rock Lake (Haliburton) . . .
. . . . 79 P40
Rock Mills 28 C23
Rockcliffe Park . . . 66 Q63
Rockcroft 44 Y40
Rockcut 23 L26
Rockdale 67 P68
Rockfield . . . 37 A-B60
Rockford (Grey) . 39 A19-20
Rockford (Norfolk) . 11 U26
Rockingham . 62 Q48 63 Q49
Rockland 67 P66
Rocklyn 40 A22
Rockport 37 C61
Rocks Mills . . 9 U21 10 U22
Rockside 23 J27
Rocksprings 49 Y61
Rockton 23 P26
Rockville 72 K10
Rockway 19 R33
Rockwood 23 L26
Rockwynn . 76 M30 77 M31
Rocky Bay 107 G9
Rocky Inlet 106 H4
Rocky Saugeen . . 27 D20
Roderick 57 U29-30
Rodney 7 Y13
Roebeck Park 42 B31
Roebuck 50 X63-64
Rohallion 43 Z35
Rokeby 13 U12
Rollway 9 V20
Rollway, The . . . 67 P67-68
Rolphton 98 F-G47
Ronaldson . . . 47 Y51-52
Rondeau Bay Estates . . . .
. . . . 7 B11-12
Rondeau Park 7 B12
Ronson 10 V22
Rosanna 28 D24
Rose Hill 63 T50-51
Rose Hill Estates . . 19 U36
Rose House Museum . . . .
. . . . 47 B52
Rose Island . . . 45 W44-45
Rose Point 57 R27
Rosebank 82 P54
Rosedale (Frontenac) . . . .
. . . . 22 K23
Rosedale (Kawartha
Lakes) 43 Z37
Rosedale (Lanark) . . . . . .
. . . . 49 W60-61
Rosedale Terrace . 52 U70
Rosedene 18 S32
Rosehall 34 G48
Rosehaven . . 50 V65 67 U65
Rosehill 29 H27
Roseland Acres . . 34 F47

Rosemont 29 E27
Roseneath 33 D43
Rosenthal . . 62 H48 63 H49
Rosetta 65 T57-58
Roseville (Durham) . . . . .
. . . . 31 F33-34
Roseville (Waterloo) 22 P23
Roslin 34 C49
Rossclair 58 U31
Rosseau 57 S30
Rosseau Falls . . . 57 S30
Rosseau Road . . 57 R-S28
Rosslyn 5 D5
Rosslyn Village . . . .
. . . . . . 102 E4 107 H8
Rossmore . . . 34 E48-49
Rossmount 33 F41
Rossport 107 H10
Rostock 21 M18-19
Rostrevor . . 57 S30 58 S31
Rothsay 22 L21
Round Lake . . . 45 A44-45
Round Lake Centre 81 N48
Round Plains 10 T24
Routhier 68 Q70
Rowan Mills 10 X23
Rowena 51 W66
Rowland 62 T47
Rowntree Beach . 41 Y26-27
Rows Corners . . 50 Z62-63
Roxboro 20 L15
Roxborough 59 U33
Ruby 81 P49-50
Rugby 42 Z31
Rummelhardt . . . 22 N22
Rush Point . . . 45 A44-45
Ruskview 29 D26
Russeldale . . 20 N16 21 N17
Russell 67 S65
Russell Landing . . 60 R37
Rutherford 6 W-X9
Rutherglen 96 E35
Ruthven 5 E5
Rutter 92 G22
Rydal Bank . . . .
. . . . . 86 D96-97 104 K14
Rye 76 K30
Rylstone 46 B46

Sable 13 S13
Sabourins Crossing 66 U63
Sadowa 43 X34
Sagamok . . . .
. . . . . 89 F-G10 105 K15
Saganaga Lake . . . .
. . . . . 106 H6 107 H7
Saginaw 31 C34-35
Sahanatien 57 V29
Sailor's Encampment . . . .
. . . . 86 E94
St-Isidore-de-Prescott . . .
. . . . . 52 R69 68 Q69
St. Agatha 22 N22
St. Albert 67 S67
St. Amour . . . 68 Q69-70
St. Andrews 52 U70
St. Anns 18 S31
St. Augustine . . 26 H14-15
St. Bernardin . . . 68 Q70
St. Catharines . . 19 Q33
St. Charles 105 K17
St. Charles 93 D24
St. Clair Beach . 4 B3-4
St. Clements . . 22 M21-22
St. Cloud 92 D21
St. Columban . . 20 M16
St. Davids (Niagara) . . . .
. . . . 19 R34-35
St. Davids (Prescott &
Russell) . . 68 P72 69 P73
St. Elmo (Muskoka) . 58 U32
St. Elmo (Stormont,
Dundas, & Glengarry) . .
. . . . 52 R69
St. Eugene 68 P72
St. Felix 67 Q67
St. George 17 Q25
St. Helens 26 H15
St. Jacobs 22 M22
St. Joachim 5 C5
St. Joachim Station . 5 C5
St. Johns (Brant) . 17 S26-27
St. Johns (Niagara) 19 S33
St. Joseph 20 N13
St. Marys 15 Q18
St. Ola 46 W47
St. Onge 67 S66
St. Pascal Baylon . 67 P67
St. Pauls 30 Q30
St. Pauls Station . 21 P18
St. Raphaels . . 52 S71-72
St. Thomas 8 X17
St. Williams . . 10 W23-24
Ste-Anne-de-Prescott . . .
. . . . 68 Q72
Ste-Rose-de-Prescott . . .
. . . . 67 R68
Saintfield . . . 31 D-E35
Salem (Centre Wellington)
. . . . 22 K23
Salem (Dufferin) . 29 G26-27
Salem (Durham) . 32 G37-38
Salem (Frontenac) . . . . .
. . . . 48 Z56-57
Salem (Northumberland)
. . . . 33 F45
Salem (South Bruce) 26 F16
Salford 9 T20
Salisbury 27 C17
Salmon Point . . . 35 H50
Salmonville 15 R17

Saltford 20 J13
Sam Lake 106 F6
Sand Banks 33 H49
Sand Bay 84 Y-Z90
Sand Bay Corner . 37 B59
Sand Castle Beach 41 X26
Sand Lake 77 M33
Sand Point . . . 83 P56-57
Sandfield 73 M11
Sandfield Mills . . 52 T70
Sandford 31 E33
Sandhill 24 J29
Sandhurst 35 E53
Sandhurst Shores 35 E53
Sandison 6 C9
Sandown 68 Q69-70
Sandringham 52 R69 67 R68
Sandtown . . . 67 U67-68
Sandusk 11 U27
Sandy Bay 41 X26
Sandy Beach (Ramara) . . .
. . . . 42 Z32
Sandy Beach (Springwater)
. . . . 41 Z28-29
Sandy Cove 30 C31
Sandy Cove Acres . . . . .
. . . . 30 C30-31
Sandy Hill 68 N71
Sandy Pine Beach . . . . .
. . . . 42 Z33 43 Z34
Sandy Point 44 A38
Sans Souci 56 T26
Sapawe 106 H6
Saratoga 20 J14
Sarnia 12 T7
Sarsfield 67 Q65
Sauble Beach . 38 Z16-17
Sauble Beach North . . . . .
. . . . 38 Y16-17
Sauble Beach South . . . .
. . . . 38 Z16-17
Sauble Falls 38 Y17
Saugeen 28 D23
Saugeen Shores . 38 A-B15
Saurin 41 Z28
Savant Lake . . . 107 F7
Sawlog Bay . . . 41 W27-28
Sayer's Mills . . . 23 M27
Scarborough . . . 25 J33
Scarborough Junction . . .
. . . . 25 K33-34
Scarlet Park 42 Y32
Schade View . . 20 P12-13
Schindelsteddle . 22 N22
Schipaville 50 W62
Schomberg 30 G30
Schomberg Heights 30 F29
Schreiber 107 H10
Schumacher . . . 105 H16
Schutt 62 S48
Science Hill 15 Q17
Scoble West . . . 102 F3
Scone 27 C18
Scotch Block (Halton) . . .
. . . . 23 L-M27
Scotch Block (Manitoulin)
. . . . 70 J1
Scotch Bush (Hastings) . .
. . . . 61 S44
Scotch Bush (Renfrew) . .
. . . . 64 Q53
Scotch Corners . . 49 U58
Scotch Line 49 W58
Scotch Point . . . 49 X59
Scotch Settlement (Bruce)
. . . . 38 A16-17
Scotch Settlement
(Frontenac) . 36 D57 37 D58
Scotia 77 P33
Scotland 16 S24
Scott Settlement
(Hastings) . . 61 S44-45
Scott Settlement
(Peterborough) 45 W42-43
Scotts Landing . . 45 X43
Scottsville 8 U16
Scudder 5 H5
Scugog 31 E36
Scugog Centre . . 31 E36
Scugog Point . 32 D-E37
Sea Breeze 59 R35
Seacliffe 5 E5
Seaforth 20 L-M16
Seagrave . . 31 D35-36
Searchmont . . . .
. . . . 84 Y94 104 K13-14
Sebastopol 21 P20
Sebright 43 Y34
Sebringville 21 N18
Seckerton 12 U7
Secord 105 K17
Seeley 50 Z62
Seeleys Bay . . . 37 B58
Seguin Falls 57 Q30
Seine River Village 106 H5
Selby 35 C52
Selkirk 11 V28
Sellars 102 E2
Selton (Chatham-Kent) . .
. . . . 7 Y11
Selton (Leeds & Grenville)
. . . . 37 C60
Selwood 101 Y19
Selwyn 44 A41
Selwyn Shores . . 44 B40
Senecal 67 N68
Seouls Corners . . . .
. . . . . 47 X53 48 X54
Serpent River . . 105 K15
Serpent River . . 89 F7

Serpent River First Nation
. . . . 88 F6 89 F7
Servos 92 F21
Sesekinika 105 H17
Seven Mile Narrows 56 S26
Severn Bridge . 42 X32-33
Severn Falls 42 W30
Seville 9 V20
Shabaqua 102 B1
Shabaqua Corner . 107 H8
Shabaqua Corners 102 B1-2
Shady Nook 81 L51
Shakespeare . 21 P20 22 P21
Shallow Lake . . . 39 Z18
Shamrock 64 Q53
Shands Corners . . 10 V25
Shanes 49 X60
Shanly 50 W64
Shannon Hall . . . 58 R31
Shannons Corners 36 C56
Shannonville . . . 35 D50
Shanty Bay . . 42 B30-31
Sharbot Lake . . 48 X54
Sharon (Middlesex) . 8 U16
Sharon (York) . . 30 E-F32
Sharps Corners . 35 C52
Sharpton 28 D24
Shawanaga . . . 75 P24-25
Shawanaga First Nation . .
. . . . . 74 M23 75 P24-25
Shawanaga Landing 75 P24
Shebandowan . 107 H/
Shebeshekong . . 56 Q25
Shedden 8 W16
Sheffield 23 P25
Sheguiandah . 73 J-K12
Shelburne 29 E25
Sheldon 37 B59
Sheldon's Corners 49 Z60
Sheperds Grove . 65 Q59
Sheppardton . . . 26 H13
Sherkston 19 U34
Sherwood . 86 E97 87 E98
Sherwood Lake . 106 G3
Sherwood Springs 50 A62
Sheshegwaning . 71 J4-5
Shetland 6 D9
Shields Crossing . 82 M53
Shillington 105 H17
Shiloh (Northumberland) .
. . . . 33 E-F45
Shiloh (Wellington) . 23 K25
Shining Tree . . . 105 J16
Shipka 13 Q13
Shirley 31 F36
Shirleys Bay . . . 65 R61
Shisler Point . 19 U34-35
Shouldice 39 Y19
Showers Corners 16 Q-R22
Shrewsbury 7 C11
Shrigley 28 D24
Shrine Hill 81 P48
Siberia 80 P46-47
Signet 28 F23
Silcote 39 Y21
Sillsville 35 E53
Siloam 31 F33
Silver Bay 19 U34
Silver Birch Beach . . . . .
. . . . 41 W26-27
Silver Corner . 36 C-D56
Silver Corners . 21 K18
Silver Creek (Halton) 23 K27
Silver Creek (Peel) . . . . .
. . . . 29 H27-28
Silver Dollar . 106 G6 107 G7
Silver Harbour . . 103 C8
Silver Islet . 103 E9 107 H9
Silver Lake (Kawartha
Lakes) 44 Y38-39
Silver Lake (Renfrew) . . .
. . . . 81 P50
Silver Mountain . 102 F1
Silver Water 71 K4
Silverdale 18 S32
Silvermoon 9 T18
Silverwood 20 U-V24
Simard 100 B18
Simcoe 10 U-V24
Simcoe Island . 36 E55-56
Simcoeside . . 42 A31-32
Simpson Corners . 23 J25
Simpsons 81 N-P48
Sims Lock 17 S28
Sinclairville 18 S29
Sine 34 C47
Singhampton . . 29 C25
Sioux Lookout . 106 F5-6
Sioux Narrows . 106 G3
Sistonens Corners 102 C3
Six Nations Corner 17 S27
Six Nations of the Grand
River Territory First Nat. . .
. . . . 17 S26-27
Sixth 51 V66
Sixth, The 51 V66
Sixty-Nine Corners 17 S26
Skead . . 101 A21 105 K17
Skerryvore . . . 75 N-P24
Skibo 87 E2
Skipness 38 Z17
Skye 68 Q70
Slabtown (Grey) . 40 A23
Slabtown (Perth) . 21 L17
Slabtown (Renfrew) 81 M51
Slash 38 D14
Slash, The 73 M11
Slate Falls . . . 63 S-T50
Slate River Valley . 102 E4
Sleeman 106 H3
Sleswick 29 H27-28

Sligo 23 J27
Sloane Point . . 41 W-X28
Smith Corners . . 17 S25
Smithdale 29 C26
Smithfield 34 F46
Smiths Corners . . . .
. . . . . 65 Q59 83 P59
Smiths Falls . . . 49 W60
Smithville 18 S31
Smoky Falls . . . 109 F15
Smooth Rock Falls 109 G16
Smoothtown . . . 17 S27
Snake Falls . . . 106 F4
Snake River . . . 82 M53
Snedden 65 S58
Snelgrove 23 K28
Snow Road Station . . . . .
. . . . 48 V54-55
Snow Valley . . . 41 B29
Snowball 30 G31
Snowdons Corners . . . . . .
. . . . 50 W-X62
Snowville . 72 M10 73 M11
Snug Harbour (Kawartha
Lakes) 43 B37
Snug Harbour (Parry
Sound) 56 Q24-25
Snug Haven . . 56 Q24-25
Snyder 19 T35
Solina 32 G37
Solmesville . . . 35 E51
Solway 27 D-E18
Sombra 6 W6-7
Songis 95 D33-34
Sonya 31 D36
Soperton 49 Z60
Sophers Landing . 42 W32
Sour Spring . . . 17 S25
South Augusta . 50 Z63
South Bay (Kenora) 106 E5
South Bay (Muskoka) . . . .
. . . . 41 W29
South Bay (Prince Edward)
. . . . 35 H51
South Baymouth . 73 N11
South Beach . 44 A41 45 A42
South Branch . . 50 X62
South Buxton . . . 6 C9
South Cayuga . 11 U29
South Dummer . 45 B43
South Gillies 102 F2-3 107 H8
South Gloucester . 66 S64
South Lancaster . . . .
. . . . . 52 T72 53 T73
South Magnetawan 75 M25
South March . 65 R60-61
South March Station . . . .
. . . . 65 R60-61
South Middleton . 10 V22
South Minidoka . 85 L28
South Monaghan . . . .
. . . . . 32 E40 33 E41
South Mountain . 50 V64-65
South Parry 57 R27
South Porcupine 105 H16-17
South Portage . 59 R34-35
South River 77 K32
South Wilberforce . . . . . .
. . . . 61 U41-42
South Woodslee . 4 D4
Southampton . 38 A15-16
Southcote . . . 17 R27-28
Southcott Pines . 20 P12
Southern Bruce Peninsula
. . . . 38 X17
Southgate 14 H16
Southview Cove 42 A33 Z33
Southview Estates 43 B37
Southwold 8 V15-16
Southwood . . 42 W33 58 V33
Sowerby . . 87 E99 104 K14
Spaffordton 36 B56
Spanish . . . 89 F8 105 K15
Sparkle City . . . 50 Y64
Sparrow Lake . . 42 X32
Speedside . . 22 K24 23 K25
Spence 76 N30
Spencers Landing 34 D47
Spencerville . . 50 W63-64
Speyside 23 L27
Spier 22 K24
Spragge 105 K15
Spragge 88 P7
Spring Bay . . . 72 L8-9
Spring Brook . . . 46 B47
Spring Creek . 75 J27 76 J23
Spring Hill . . 66 T64 67 T65
Spring Valley (Leeds &
Grenville) . . . 50 Z62
Spring Valley
(Northumberland) . . . . . .
. . . . . 33 F45 34 F46
Springarbour . . 10 X22-23
Springbank . . . 13 S13
Springbrook . . 24 K-L29
Springdale Park . 59 T33
Springers Hill . . 9 T33
Springfield (Elgin) 9 V19
Springfield (Frontenac) . .
. . . . 37 C58
Springfield (Middlesex) . .
. . . . 13 U13
Springford 9 U21
Springhill 68 P71
Springmount . . . 39 Z19
Springtown . . . 64 R55
Springvale (Haldimand) . .
. . . . 11 T26
Springvale (Lambton) . . . .
. . . . 13 R11
Springville 32 D40

Springwater Lakes . 29 E26
Spruce Green 22 K22
Spruce Hedge 64 R55
Sprucedale 77 P31
Spry 55 V16
Squire 39 A19
Squires Beach 25 J35
Squirrel Town 73 M12
Staffa 20 N16
Stampville 51 W66
Stanley 102 D3 107 H8
Stanley Corners . . . 65 S61
Stanley House 57 S29
Stanleydale 58 Q-R31
Stanleyville . . 48 X57 49 X58
Stanton 29 E27
Stanwood . . 45 B45 46 B46
Stapledon 65 T61
Staples 5 D5
Star 29 H27-28
Star Corners . 36 B54-55 C54
Stardale 68 P72
Starkville 32 G39
Starr's Beach . 31 D36 32 D37
Starratt 77 N31
Starratt-Olsen . . . 106 F4
State Falls 106 E6
Stayner 41 B26
Stella 36 E54
Stephens Bay 58 U32
Stepstone 103 B6
Stevens 108 G12
Stevenson 5 D7-8
Stevensville 19 T35
Stewart 5 C7
Stewart Hall 33 D41
Stewart Heights . . . 32 C40
Stewarts Glen . . 52 R69-70
Stewarttown 23 L28
Stewartville 64 Q56
Still River 74 K22
Stinson 101 C22
Stirling 34 C47
Stirling Falls . . 77 M31-32
Stirton 22 K21-22
Stittsville 65 S61
Stockdale 34 D47
Stoco 47 B50
Stokes Bay 55 U-V16
Stonebrook . 81 L51 82 L52
Stonecliffe 98 F45
Stonecliffe Station . 98 F45
Stoneleigh 59 T33
Stoneridge . . . 17 S26-27
Stones Corners . . . 50 Y63
Stoney Creek 18 Q29
Stoney Point 5 B5-6
Stonyridge 45 Z43
Storie 95 H31
Storms Corners . . . .
. . . . 35 D53 36 D54
Stouffville 31 G33
Strabane 23 N-P27
Straders Hill 51 V66
Straffordville 9 W21
Stralak 100 Y14
Strange 24 H30
Strangfield 5 D6
Stratford 21 P19-20
Strathallan 15 Q20
Strathavon 39 A20-21
Strathburn 7 W13
Strathearn 65 R61
Strathmore 52 T70
Strathnairn 40 A22
Strathroy 8 T14
Stratton 106 H3-4
Streetsville 24 L29
Stromness 18 U31
Strong 77 L31
Strongville 41 B27
Stroud 30 C30
Stuart 80 J43
Sturgeon Bay . . . 41 X-Y29
Sturgeon Falls . . . .
. . . . . 94 D27-28 105 K18
Sturgeon Point . . . 44 A38
Sucker Creek Landing . . . . .
. . . . 93 F24-25
Sudbury 101 C19 105 K16-17
Sugar Bush (Peterborough) . . .
. . . . 44 A39
Sugar Bush (Simcoe) . . . . . .
. . . . 42 Z30
Sullivans Bay 44 B39
Sulphide 47 A50
Sultan 105 J15
Summerhill 20 K14-15
Summers Corners 9 V19-20
Summerstown . . 52 U71-72
Summerstown Station . . . . .
. . . . 52 U71-72
Summerville 10 U22
Summit 17 O27
Sunbury 36 C56-57
Sunderland 31 D35
Sundridge 77 L32
Sunnidale (Lambton) 13 R10
Sunnidale (Simcoe) . 29 C27
Sunnidale Corners . 41 B27
Sunniside 20 P12-13
Sunny Ridge . . . 20 N12-13
Sunny Slope 76 N28
Sunnybrae 33 C44
Sunnyside 41 X28
Sunnyside Beach . . 40 Y22
Sunrise Beach . . . 31 E36
Sunset Bay Estates 41 W27
Sunset Beach 87 E1
Sunset Beach (Essex) 4 E1
Sunset Beach (Huron) . . . . .
. . . . 20 J12-13

Sunset Beach (Muskoka) . . . .
. . . . 58 U31
Sunset Beach (Simcoe) . . . . .
. . . . 41 X29
Sunset Corners . . . 24 J30
Sunset Lookout . . . 34 F49
Sunset Park 95 E31
Sunshine 102 C2-3
Sunshine 20 J16
Suomi 107 H8
Superior Junction . 106 F6
Sutorville 7 B11
Sutton 30 C32
Sutton Bay 85 Q30
Swan Crossing . . 50 V62-63
Swansea 24 K-L31
Swastika 105 H17-18
Sweaburg 15 S21
Sweets Corners
(Haldimand) 11 U29
Sweets Corners (Leeds &
Grenville) 37 A59
Swift Rapids 42 W31
Swindon 77 P33
Swinton Park 28 E22
Switzerville 35 D53
Swords 57 R28-29
Sydenham 36 B55
Sykeston 12 U8
Sylvan 13 R12
Sylvan Glen Beach . . . .
. . . . 43 Z34-35
Sylvan Valley . . . 86 B-C95

Taits Beach 33 E41
Talbot 43 A34
Talbotville Royal . . . 8 V17
Taltock 64 T56
Tamarack 29 G27
Tamworth 47 A52
Tanglewood Beach . 42 Y32
Tannery 65 S58
Tansley 23 N28 24 N29
Tansleyville 107 G10
Tapley 32 E39
Tapleytown 18 R29-30
Tara 38 A17 39 A18
Tarbert 28 G24
Tartan 28 E21
Tarzwell 105 H17-18
Tate Corners . 7 W13 8 W14
Taunton 32 G37
Tavistock 21 P20
Taylor 37 B58
Taylor Corners . . . .
. . . . 31 C36 32 C37
Tayside . . 52 S69 67 S68
Tecumseh 4 B3
Tecumseh Pines . . 30 G29
Teeswater 26 F-G16
Teeterville 10 T23-24
Tehkummah 73 M11
Telfer 14 S15
Temagami 105 J18
Temiskaming Shores . . . . . .
. . . . 105 J18
Temperanceville . . 30 G31
Temple Hill 40 B22
Tempo 8 U16
Tenby Bay 86 F95
Tennyson 49 U59
Terra Cotta 23 K28
Terra Nova 29 D26
Terra View Heights . 33 C41
Terrace Bay 104 H11 107 H10
Teston 24 H31
Teviotdale 28 H21
Thames River Siding . . . . . .
. . . . 8 V-W15
Thames Road 20 P15
Thamesford 15 S18-19
Thamesville 7 Y11
Thanet 46 W46
Thedford 13 R11-12
Thessalon . . . .
. . 86 E97 87 E98 104 K14
Thessalon First Nation . . . . .
. . . . 87 E99
Thistle 28 E21
Thomasburg 46 B49
Thompson Hill . . . 64 Q55
Thompsonville 29 E28 30 E29
Thomstown 32 F40
Thorah Beach . . 31 C33-34
Thorel House 57 T30
Thornbury 40 Z23-24
Thorncliff 95 E32
Thorncliffe 6 Y9
Thorndale 15 S18
Thorne 105 K18
Thornhill 24 J31-32
Thornloe 85 P29
Thornloe 105 J18
Thornton 30 D29
Thornyhurst 6 W6-7
Thorold 19 R34
Thorold South . . 19 R-S34
Thorpe 36 C54
Thrashers Corners . 34 D49
Three Bridges . . 15 S18-19
Throoptown . . 50 X62-63
Thunder Bay (Niagara) . . . . .
. . . . 19 U35
Thunder Bay (Thunder
Bay) 107 H8-9
Thunder Beach . 41 X26-27
Thurlow 34 E49 35 E50
Thwaites 85 P30
Tichborne . . . 48 Y54-55
Tilbury 7 Y10
Tilden Lake 105 K18
Tilley 37 B60

Tillsonburg 9 U20-21
Timberstone Shores . 72 K8
Timmins 105 H16
Tincap 50 Z62
Tindle Bay 32 C40
Tinkertown 26 F16
Tintern 18 R-S32
Tiny Beach 41 Y26
Tioga 29 D27
Tiverton 26 D14-15
Tobacco Lake 72 K8
Tobermory 54 S13-14
Toimela 102 B5
Toledo 49 Y60
Tollendal . . . 30 C32 42 D32
Tollgate 15 R20-21
Tolmie 38 Z17
Tolmies Corners . . . .
. . . . 52 S69 67 S68
Tolsmaville 70 H-J1
Tomelin Bluffs . . 58 S31-32
Tomstown 85 M29
Tomstown 105 J18
Topcliff 28 E22
Topping 21 M19-20
Tormore 24 H30
Toronto 24 K32
Torrance 57 V30
Torwood Estates . . 65 Q60
Tory Hill 61 V41
Tottenham 30 F29
Townsend 11 U26
Townsend Centre . . 10 T-U25
Toyes Hill 50 V65
Traceys Hill 32 C38
Trafalgar 24 M29
Tralee 21 K20
Tramore 81 N48-49
Trautrim Subdivision 81 K51
Traverston 28 D21
Treadwell 67 N68
Trecastle 21 J20
Trent River 45 B45
Trenton 34 E-F47
Trevelyan 37 A60-61
Trillium Estates . . 49 W58
Trinity 17 R27
Triple Bay Park . . . 41 X28
Trout Creek 95 H32
Trout Mills 95 E32
Trowbridge 21 K19
Troy (Chatham-Kent) . 7 B11
Troy (Hamilton-Wentworth) . . .
. . . . 17 Q25
Tubbs Corners . . . 33 F44
Tuftsville 34 C48
Tullamore 24 J29
Tunis 105 H17
Tupperville 6 X8
Turbine . . . 91 D15 105 K16
Turin 7 Y11-12
Turkey Point . . . 10 W24-25
Turnbulls Grove . 20 P12-13
Turner 90 H12
Turners . . . 26 C16 38 B16
Turners Corners . . 19 S33
Turnerville 6 Y9
Turriff 45 V46
Turtle Lake 57 R29
Tweed 46 A49
Tweedside 18 R30
Twelve O'Clock Point . . . . . .
. . . . 34 F47
Twin City 102 D-E5
Twin Elm 66 S62
Twin Valleys 7 X12-13
Two O'Clock 73 L13
Tyendinaga . . . 35 E50-51
Tyotown 52 U71
Tyrconnell 8 X15
Tyrone 32 F37-38
Tyrrell 10 U25

Udney 42 Z33 43 Z34
Udora 31 D34
Uffington 59 V33-34
Ufford 58 T31
Uhthoff 42 Y31
Ullswater 58 T30
Umfraville 61 V46
Umfreville 106 G6
Underwood 26 C15
Uneeda 64 R56 65 R57
Ungers Corners . . 10 W24
Union (Elgin) 8 W17
Union (Essex) 5 E5
Union (Leeds & Grenville) . . . .
. . . . 37 B60
Union Creek . . . 44 X-Y38
Union Hall 65 T58
Uniondale 15 Q18
Unionville . . . 24 H32 25 H33
Uno Park 85 Q29
Uphill 43 X35
Uplands 14 S16 15 S17
Upper 11 U29
Upper Paudash . . . 61 V43
Uppergrove 42 Z33
Ursa 50 V40
Utica 31 F35
Utopia 29 C29
Utterson 58 S32
Uttoxeter 13 S10
Uxbridge 31 E34

Val Caron . . . .
. . 101 B19 105 K16-17
Val Côté 108 G14
Val Gagné 105 H17
Val Rita 109 G15

Val Therese 101 A19 105 K16
Valens 23 P26
Valentia 32 D37
Valetta 5 C7
Valfranc 52 R69
Vallentyne 31 D34
Valley Corners . . . .
. . . . . . 52 S69 67 S68
Valley East 100 A18 101 A19
Valley Green Beach . . . .
. . . . 58 T-U31
Valleywood . 23 J28 24 J29
Van Horne . . . 6 A9 7 A10
VanAllens 50 W64
Vanastra 20 L14-15
Vanbrugh 63 Q50
VanCamp 67 U65
Vandecar 16 S22
Vandeleur 28 C22-23
Vandorf 30 G32
Vanessa 10 T24
Vanier 66 Q63
Vankleek Hill 68 P71
Vankleek Hill Station 68 P71
Vankoughnet . . . 59 V34-35
Vanneck 14 S15
Vansickle 45 Z45
Vanzant's Point . . . 73 L12
Vardy 62 T46
Varency 11 U26
Varna 20 M14
Varney . . . 27 E20 28 E21
Vars 67 R65-66
Vasey 41 Y29
Vaughan (Niagara) . 18 S31
Vaughan (York) . 24 H30-31
Vaughan Survey . . 11 V26
Vellore 24 H30-31
Vennachar 63 U50-51
Vennachar Junction . . . . . .
. . . . 63 T-U50
Ventnor 50 W64
Ventry 28 E23
Verdun 26 F13-14
Vermillion Bay . . . 106 G4
Verner . . 93 D26 105 K17-18
Vernon 67 T65
Vernon Shores . . . .
. . . . . . 58 R32 59 R33
Vernonville 33 F44
Verona 36 A54
Verschoyle 9 T20
Verulam Park 44 A38
Vesta 27 D17-18
Vickers 27 E20
Vickers Heights . . 102 E5
Victoria (Peel) . . . 23 J27
Victoria (Prince Edward) . . . .
. . . . 34 F48
Victoria Corners (Durham) . . .
. . . . 31 E34-35
Victoria Corners (Grey) . . . . .
. . . . 40 A24
Victoria Harbour . . 41 X29
Victoria Mills . 10 T25 17 S25
Victoria Mine 91 D16
Victoria Park 33 G45
Victoria Road 43 Z36
Victoria Springs . . 44 Z41
Victoria Square . . . 24 J29
Vienna 9 W20
Viewlake 32 D37
Vigo 41 A28
Villa Nova 10 T25
Village Lanthier . . 68 N70
Village Meadows . . . .
. . . . . . 32 C40 33 C41
Villiers 33 C42-43
Vinegar Hill . 50 V65 67 U65
Vineland 18 R32
Vineland Station . . 18 R32
Vinemount 18 Q-R30
Vinette 67 P66
Violet 35 D53 36 D54
Violet Hill 29 F26-27
Virgil 19 Q34-35
Virginia 31 C33
Virginiatown 105 H18
Vittoria 10 V24
Vivian 31 F33
Vosburg 6 A9 7 A10
Vroomanton 31 D34
Vydon Acres 65 Q58
Vyner 12 T8

Waba 64 R56
Wabash 7 B10
Wabasseemoong . 106 F2-3
Wabauskang 106 F4
Wabewawa 85 L28
Wabigoon 106 G5
Wabigoon Lake . . 106 G5
Wabos 84 Y94 104 K13
Wabozominissing 73 K13-14
Waddington Beach . . . .
. . . . 42 A31-32
Wade's Landing . . . 95 G31
Wagar 9 X20-21
Wagarville 47 Z53
Wagram 28 H21
Wahawin 59 S34-35
Wahgoshig 105 H18
Wahnapitae 101 C21 105 K17
Wahnapitae First Nation . . . . .
. . . . 101 B20-21
Wahnekewaning Beach . . . . .
. . . . 41 Y26-27
Wahwashkesh . . . 75 M27
Wainfleet 18 T32
Waldau 22 N23
Waldemar 29 H25
Walden 91 E15-16

Walden Place . . . 13 Q12
Walford . . 89 F9 105 K15
Walker Woods . . . 31 E34
Walkers 13 V12-13
Walkers Corners . 63 T50-51
Walkers Point . . 58 U31-32
Walkerton . . . 27 E17-18
Wallace (Nipissing) . . . .
. . . . 61 Q42-43
Wallace (Perth) . . . 21 J20
Wallace Point 33 D41
Wallaceburg 6 X6-7
Wallbridge 34 D47-48
Wallenstein 22 L21-22
Walls 77 P32
Walnut 13 U11
Walpole Island . . . 6 X6
Walsh 10 V24
Walsh Station 10 W24
Walsingham 10 W23
Walters Falls . 39 A21 40 A22
Walton 20 K16
Wamsley 102 F3
Waneeta Beach . 9 X18-19
Wanikewin 92 H22 93 H23
Wanstead 13 T10
Wanup 105 K17
Wanup 92 D20-21
Warburton 37 B60
Ward 61 V41
Warina 52 S69
Warings Corner . . 35 Q50
Warkworth 33 D44
Warminster . . . 42 Z30-31
Warner 18 S30
Warren . . 93 D24 105 K17
Warsaw 45 B42
Wartburg 21 N18
Warwick 13 T11
Wasa Beach . . 41 A26-27
Wasagaming . . . 101 A23
Washago 42 X32-33
Washburn 36 B57 C57 37 B58
Washburn Island . . 32 D37
Washburns Corners 49 Z60
Washington 22 P22-23
Wasing 95 H33-34
Watercombe 35 E51-52
Waterdown 23 P27-28
Waterfall 92 E20
Waterford 10 U25
Waterloo 22 N22-23
Waterton 37 B60-61
Watertown 49 Z61
Watford 13 T11-12
Watsons . . . 43 X37 44 X38
Watsons Corners 48 U56-57
Wattenwyle . 76 L30 77 L31
Watterson Corners 66 S-T53
Waubamik 75 P27
Waubaushene 41 X22 42 X30
Waubuno 12 V7-8
Waudby . . . 27 C20 28 C21
Waupoos 35 G52
Waupoos East . . . 35 F-G52
Waupoos Island . . 35 G52
Wauzhushk Onigum 106 G3
Wavecrest . . . 19 U35-36
Wavell 105 H17
Waverley 41 Z28-29
Waverly Beach . . . 19 U36
Wawa 104 J13
Wayside 49 V58
Webbwood . . . .
. . . 90 E12 105 K15-16
Websterville 29 C26
Weidman 13 V10
Weissenburg . . 22 L23-24
Welbeck 27 D20
Welcome . . 32 G40 33 G41
Welland 19 T33
Wellandport . . . 18 T31-32
Wellburn 15 R18
Wellesley 22 M21
Wellington 34 G48-49
Wellington Beach . 12 S8-9
Wellman 34 C46-47
Welmer 49 V60
Wemyss 48 W57
Wendake Beach . . 41 Y27
Wendigo Lake . . . 85 M29
Wendover 67 N67
Werner Lake 106 F3
Weslemkoon 63 V49
Wesley 35 C53
Wesley Corners . 30 F-G32
Wesleyville 32 G40
West Arm . . 93 F24 105 K17
West Becher 6 W7
West Corners 33 C45
West Delaware . 8 U15-16
West Essa 29 C29
West Flamborough . 17 Q27
West Fort William . . . .
. . . . . . 102 D5 103 D6
West Franklin 31 E33
West Gravenhurst . 58 V32
West Guilford . . . 60 T38-39
West Hill 25 J34
West Huntingdon . 34 C48
West Huntingdon Station . . . .
. . . . 34 C48
West Lake . . 34 G49 35 G50
West Lorne 8 X14
West McGillivray . . 14 R14
West Monkton . . . 21 L18
West Montrose . . . 22 L23
West Nipissing . . . .
. . 94 D27-29 105 K17-18
West Osgoode . . . 66 T64

West Plain 47 B51
West River 90 G13
West Side Beach . . 32 H38
Westbrook 36 D55
Westfield 20 J15
Westford 26 F16
Westmeath 82 K-L53
Westminster 67 Q68
Westmont Estates . 65 S60
Weston 24 K31
Westover 23 P26-27
Westport 48 Y57
Westree 105 J16
Westview 33 C44-45
Westwick Corners . . . 5 C6
Westwood (Ottawa) . 65 R60
Westwood (Peterborough) . . . .
. . . . 33 C43
Wexford (Leeds &
Grenville) 50 Y64
Wexford (Toronto) . 25 J-K33
Whaleys Corners . . . .
. . . . 23 L28 24 L29
Wharncliffe . 87 C99 104 K14
Wheatley 5 E6
Whitby 25 H36
Whitchurch-Stouffville . . . . . .
. . . . 30 G32 31 G33
White 64 T55-56
White Lake 64 R56
White Oak 8 U17
White Oaks 11 T26
White Pigeon . . . 19 T34-35
White River 104 H12
Whitebread 6 X6-7
Whitechurch 26 F16
Whitedog 106 F2-3
Whitefish . . 91 D17 105 K16
Whitefish Bay . . . 106 G4
Whitefish Falls . . . .
. . . . . . 90 G13 105 K16
Whitefish Lake . . 105 K16
Whitefish Lake First Nation . . .
. . . . 91 E17-18
Whitehall 77 P31
Whites 8 W17
Whites Junction . . 27 H20
Whiteside 57 U30
Whitestone 75 M27
Whitevale 25 H34
Whitewood Grove . 85 N29
Whitfield 29 E26
Whitney 79 P41
Whittington 29 G26
Wiarton 39 X18
Wick 31 D35
Wicklow 33 F-G44
Widdifield 95 D32-33
Wigens Corners . 49 Z60-61
Wikwemikong . 73 L13-14
Wikwemikonsing . 73 L14
Wilberforce 61 U41-42
Wilbur 48 U-V54
Wilcox Corners . . 18 S30
Wilcox Lake 30 G31
Wild Goose . . . .
. . 103 C7-8 107 H8-9
Wildfield 24 J29
Wildwood 23 K27-28
Wilfrid 31 C34
Wilkesport 6 W7
Wilkinson 47 A53
Willard Lake . . . 106 G3-4
Willetsholme 37 C58
Williams Point . . . 32 E37
Williamsburg (Stormont,
Dundas, & Glengarry) . . . . . .
. . . . 51 V66
Williamsburg (Waterloo) . . . .
. . . . 22 N23
Williamsford 39 B20
Williamsport 59 Q34
Williamstown 52 T72
Williscroft 38 Y18
Willisville . 90 G13-14 105 K16
Willola Beach . . . 83 P58
Willow Bay 18 U32
Willow Beach (Durham) . 4 E1
Willow Beach (Muskoka) . . . .
. . . . 58 U31-32
Willow Beach (York) 30 C32
Willow Grove (Haldimand) . . . .
. . . . . . 11 T27 17 S27
Willow Grove (Perth) . . . .
. . . . 21 M17-18
Willow Lake 15 R21
Willowbank 37 C58
Willowdale 24 J32
Willowood 4 E1
Wilmer 36 B56
Wilmot Centre . . . 22 N22
Wilmot Creek . . . 32 H38
Wilno 81 P48
Wilson 83 T51
Wilson Point 42 Z32
Wilsons Bush 6 A9
Wilsonville 10 T24
Wilstead 37 C59
Wilton 36 C54
Wiltsetown 49 Z61
Winchelsea 20 P16
Winchester . . . 67 U65-66
Winchester Springs . . . .
. . . . . . 51 V66 67 U66
Windermere . 57 T30 58 T31
Windfall (Essex) . . . 5 D6
Windfall (Oxford) . . 16 Q22
Windham Centre 10 U23-24
Windsor 4 B1-2
Windward Sands . . 44 B39
Windy Lake 100 A15
Winfield 22 K22

Winger 18 T32
Wingham . . 26 H16 27 H17
Wingle 62 R48 S48 63 R49 S49
Winona 18 Q-R30
Winona Park 18 Q30
Winslow 18 S31
Winterbourne . . . 22 M23
Winthrop 20 L16
Wisawasa 95 F32
Wishart 13 T12
Wisemans Corners . . . .
. . . . 77 N31-32
Wodehouse 40 B22
Woermke 63 Q50
Woito 81 M51
Wolfe 63 R50
Wolford Centre . . . 50 X62
Wolford Chapel . . 49 W61
Wolftown 82 N53
Wolseley 39 Y19
Wolseley Bay . . . .
. . . . . . 93 G25 105 K16
Wolverine Beach . . 41 W29
Wolverton 16 Q23
Wood Landing . . 41 W28-29
Woodbridge 24 J30
Woodburn (Hamilton) . . . . . .
. . . . 18 R29
Woodburn (Kingston) . . . . . .
. . . . 37 C58
Woodford 39 Z21
Woodgreen 7 W13
Woodham 20 P16
Woodhouse Acres . 11 V26
Woodington 57 T30
Woodland . . 45 B45 46 B46
Woodland Acres . . . .
. . . . 33 C41 44 B41
Woodland Beach . . 41 Z27
Woodlawn 65 Q59
Woodlawn Park . 11 V27-28
Woodridge 83 P58-59
Woodrous 35 Q50
Woods 75 P25
Woods Bay 57 T27
Woodstock 15 R20-21
Woodview (North
Kawartha) 45 Z42
Woodview (Otonabee-
South Monaghan) . . . .
. . . . 33 C41-42
Woodville (Kawartha
Lakes) 43 B35-36
Woodville (Prince Edward) . . . .
. . . . 35 F51
Woodward Station . . . .
. . . . . . 57 V30 58 V31
Wooler 34 E46
Worthington 105 K16
Worthington 91 D15
Wrightmans Corners . . . .
. . . . . . 8 T14 13 T13
Wrigley 22 P24
Wroxeter 27 H17
Wyandot 22 K21
Wybridge 41 Y28
Wycombe 10 V22
Wyevale 41 Y28
Wylie 99 H48
Wymbolwood Beach 41 Y27
Wyndham Hills . . . 17 R25
Wyoming 12 T9

Yarker 36 C53
Yarmouth Centre . . 9 V18
Yatton 22 L22
Yearley 58 Q31-32
Yellek 94 E30
Yelverton 32 E38
Yeovil 28 F21
Yerexville 35 F50-51
Yonge Mills 37 A61
York (Haldimand-Norfolk) . . . .
. . . . 17 S28
York (Toronto) . . 24 K31-32
York River 61 V44
Young's Cove 44 B40
Young's Point 44 A41
Youngstown 44 B40
Youngsville . . . 15 Q-R19
Yule 94 X61

Zadow 81 P50
Zealand 48 W55
Zenda 9 T21
Zephyr 31 D33
Zimmerman 22 N28 24 N29
Zion (Ashfield-Colborne-
Wawanosh) 20 P16
Zion (Grey) 39 Y18
Zion (Huron) 26 G14
Zion (Kawartha Lakes) . . . . . .
. . . . 43 A37
Zion (Northumberland) . . . . . .
. . . . 32 G40
Zion (Peterborough) 33 D41
Zion Line 82 M53-54
Ziska 58 U32
Zorra Station . . . 15 S19-20
Zuber Corners . . . 22 L23
Zurich 20 N13

Road Index

How to use the index

All road names are followed by a County Code which indicates the county, district, or region that the road is in. A list of the County Codes is provided below. To find a road, search through the alphabetically arranged columns. Note the page number and the reference square.

For example, to find the location of Motheral Road in the County of Oxford:

Motheral Rd *OX*...... 16 Q23

Turn to page 16 and locate the square Q23. Scan through the squares to find the road.

Duplicated Road Names

When two or more roads in a county share the same name, a local name in brackets following the street name indicates in which part of the county the street is located.

Numbered Roads

All numbered roads are grouped together at the beginning of the index–they do not appear in the alphabetical listings that follow. This is the case even if the name is normally spelled out. For example Twenty-Third Line will be found as 23rd Ln.

Index des chemins

Comment utiliser l'index

Les noms de chemin sont classés par ordre alphabétique. Chacun est suivi d'un code qui indique le comté, le district ou la région où se trouve le chemin. Voir la liste des codes ci-dessous. Pour trouver un chemin, prenedre note du numéro de page et des coordonnées qui suivent le nom.

Par example, pour trouver le chemin Tucker à Northumberland:

Tucker Rd *NR*...... 33 E43

Tourner à la page 33 et chercher le carré E43. Regarder dans le carré pour trouver le chemin.

Noms de chemin identiques

Lorsque deux ou plusieurs chemins dans un comté portent le même nom, la localité où se trouve chaque chemin est indiquée entre crochets.

Chemins numérotés

Toutes les chemins numérotés sont classés par ordre alphabétique au début de l'index. Ils ne font pas partie de la liste alphabétique même si le nom est normalement écrit en toutes lettres. Par exemple, pour trouver Twenty-Third Line, voir 23rd Ln.

County Codes

Codes des comtés

ALGOMA, DISTRICT OF ....A	LAMBTON, COUNTY OF ....LM
BRANT, COUNTY OF ....BT	LANARK, COUNTY OF ....LN
BRUCE, COUNTY OF ....BR	LEEDS & GRENVILLE, COUNTY OF ...LG
CHATHAM-KENT, MUNICIPALITY OF ...C	LENNOX & ADDINGTON, COUNTY OF .LA
DUFFERIN, COUNTY OF ....DF	MANITOULIN, DISTRICT OF ....MA
DURHAM, REGIONAL MUNICIPALITY OF ..DH	MIDDLESEX, COUNTY OF ....MD
ELGIN, COUNTY OF ....EL	MUSKOKA, DISTRICT MUNICIPALITY OF . MK
ESSEX, COUNTY OF ....EX	NIAGARA, REGIONAL MUNICIPALITY OF ..NI
FRONTENAC, COUNTY OF ....F	NIPISSING, DISTRICT OF ....NP
GREY, COUNTY OF ....G	NORFOLK, COUNTY OF ....NF
HALDIMAND, COUNTY OF ....HD	NORTHUMBERLAND, COUNTY OF ....NR
HALIBURTON, COUNTY OF ....HL	OTTAWA, CITY OF ....OT
HALTON, REGIONAL MUNICIPALITY OF ..HT	OXFORD, COUNTY OF ....OX
HAMILTON, CITY OF ....HM	PARRY SOUND, DISTRICT OF ....PS
HASTINGS, COUNTY OF ....HS	PEEL, REGIONAL MUNICIPALITY OF ....PL
HURON, COUNTY OF ....HU	PERTH, COUNTY OF ....PT
KAWARTHA LAKES, CITY OF ....K	PETERBOROUGH, COUNTY OF ......PB

PRESCOTT & RUSSELL, COUNTY OF ..PR
PRINCE EDWARD, COUNTY (CITY) OF ..PE
RENFREW, COUNTY OF ....R
SIMCOE, COUNTY OF ....SM
STORMONT, DUNDAS & GLENGARRY, COUNTY OF ....SDG
SUDBURY, DISTRICT OF ....SD
SUDBURY, CITY OF GREATER ....CS
TIMISKAMING, DISTRICT OF ....TM
THUNDER BAY, CITY OF ....TB
TORONTO, CITY OF ....T
WATERLOO, REGIONAL MUNICIPALITY OF ....WT
WELLINGTON, COUNTY OF ....WL
YORK, REGIONAL MUNICIPALITY OF .....Y

Numbered Roads

Chemins numérotés

1, Addington Rd *LA* 47 Y51
1, Alfred Concession *PR* . 67 N68 68 N69-70
1, Belmont Township Concession *PB* .. . 45 A45 Z45
1, Charlotteville Rd *NF* 10 W24
1, Concession *DH* 31 D33
1, Concession *WL* 23 N25-26
1, Concession (Chatsworth) *G* ... 27 C20
1, Concession (SCD) *G* 39 Y18 Z18
1, Concession (West Grey) *G* ... 27 E20
1, Concession Rd *SDG* 68 T72
1, Concession Rd *SM* 43 A34
1, Concession Rd (Brock) *DH*. . 43 B34-35
1, Concession Rd (Clarington) *DH* 32 G39-40
1, Concession Rd (East Hawkesbury) *PR* 68 P72 69 P73
1, Concession Rd (Nation) *PR*.. . 68 P70
1, County Rd *LM*............ 6 W6
1, Dalhousie Concession *LN*...... 48 V57
1, Drummond Concession *LN* . 49 V59 W58
1, Fire Lane *NI* 19 U34
1, Fire Rte *PB* 45 Z42
1, Kenyon Concession Rd *SDG* 68 S70-71 T70
1, Lake Rosalind Rd *BR*........ 27 E18
1, Line *NI* 19 O34-35
1, Ln *PT* 15 Q17
1, Mersea Rd *EX*............ 5 E5-6
1, Pearl Lake Rd *BR* 27 D18
1, Pike Lake Rte *LN* 48 X57
1, Plantagenet Concession *PR* . 67 N-P67
1, Ramsay Concession *LN*.... 65 T-U58
1, Range Rd *NI* 18 S30-31
1, Road *LA* 35 E52
1, Rosseau Lake Rd *MK*........ 58 S30-31
1, Sideroad *G* 39 B18-20
1, Skeleton Lake Rd *MK* 58 S32
1, Township Rd *WL*........ 22 M24
1 Chamberlain , Concession *TM* 85 M27-28
1 Dack , Concession *TM*...... 85 N27
1 E , Concession Rd *NR* 33 D45
1 E , Stephenson Rd *MK*.... 59 T33

1 Marter , Concession *TM* 85 M28
1 N , Line *SM* 41 A29 42 A-B30
1 N , Road *WL* 28 G-H21
1 Pense , Concession *TM*...... 85 N30
1 Robillard , Concession *TM* .. 85 N26-27
1 S , Line *SM* 42 B30
1 W , Concession Rd *NR*...... 33 E44
1 W , Stephenson Rd *MK*...... 58 T32
1 Rd, Cane *TM* 85 P27
1 Rd, Concession *HD* 18 T29
1 Rd, Concession (Wainfleet) *NI* .. 18 U32
1 Rd, Concession (West Lincoln) *NI*.... ...... 18 S29 S32
1 Rd, Henwood *TM* 85 P28
1 Rd, Line *LG* 49 W-X60 X59
1 Rd, Zone *C* 7 X10
1 Rd S , Concession *HD* 18 T29
1 Sdrd, No. *HT* 23 N-P28
1 Woodhouse, Concession *HD*... 17 V26
1-2 Rd, Finch Concession *SDG* . 67 T67-68
1 & 2 Hilliard , Concession *TM* 85 P29
1 4 Ln, Digby Township W *K*.... 43 X35
1A, Sideroad *BR* 27 G17
1B, Sideroad *BR* 27 F17
1C, Sideroad *BR* 27 F17
1st Av *EL* 15 V17
1st Av *SM* 41 X28-29
1st Av (Lincoln) *NI* 18 R32
1st Av (Welland) *NI* 19 S33
1st Concession *G* 39 A21
1st Concession Lavant *LN*...... 64 T56
1st Concession Rd *EX*...... 6 B6-7
1st Concession A Dalhousie *LN* . 65 U57
1st Concession B Dalhousie *LN* 64 U56 65 U57
1st Concession Ln *C*.......... 6 B7
1st Concession Rd *NF*.. 9 W-X21 10 X22-23
1st Concession Rd NTR *NF*..... 16 U22
1st Concession Rd STR *NF*.. 16 V21-22
1st Lake Rd *F*............ 36 A54
1st Line, Douro *PB* 45 A42 B42
1st Line Rd *OT* 66 T63
1st Ln *BT* 17 S-T26
1st Ln *C* 6 B7
1st Ln *EL* 14 V15

1st Ln *HD* 17 T27
1st Ln *NR* 33 D-E43 E42-43
1st Ln (Centre Wellington) *WL* 22 J23-24 K24
1st Ln (EHS (Mono)) *DF* 29 F-G26
1st Ln (EHS (Mulmur)) *DF* 29 D26
1st Ln (Erin) *WL*.... 23 K25-26 L26
1st Ln (Minto) *WL*.......... 28 H21
1st Ln (WHS (Mulmur)) *DF*...... 29 D26
1st Ln, Challice *TM* 32 E40
1st Ln, Eagleson *NR* 32 E40
1st Ln E *NR*.......... 34 D46
1st Ln Nassagaweya *HT* 23 M26 M-N27 M-N28
1st Ln W *NR* 33 D45
1st Ln W *WL* 22 K23
1st Rd E *HM* 18 Q-R29
1st Rd W *HM* 18 Q-R29
1st St *DF* 29 G-H26
1st St *NI* 19 R33
1st St *SM* 40 A25
1st St *TM* 85 M28
1st Line Rd *SDG* 68 R-T72

2, Addington Rd *LA* 47 X50-51 Y51
2, Alfred Concession *PR* 68 N69
2, Concession *HD*...... 17 U-V27
2, Concession *SM* 41 Z28
2, Concession (Brock) *DH* ... 31 D34-35
2, Concession (Brockton) *BR*... 26 E16
2, Concession (Chatsworth) *G* 27 C20 39 A-B20
2, Concession (Huron-Kinloss) *BR* . 26 F14
2, Concession (Kincardine) *BR* .. 26 D15
2, Concession (NCD) *G*.... 39 Y-Z18 Z19
2, Concession (NDR) *G*...... 27 D20 E19
2, Concession (Puslinch) *WL*.. 23 N25-26
2, Concession (Saugeen Shores) *BR* 26 C16 38 B16
2, Concession (SDR) *BR* 27 E18
2, Concession (SDR) *G*...... 27 E19-20
2, Concession (South Bruce) *BR* .. 27 G17
2, Concession (Uxbridge) *DH*... 31 D-F33
2, Concession (Wellington North) *WL*... ...... 28 G22

2, Concession (West Grey [Bentinck]]) *G*. 27 C-E20
2, Concession (West Grey [Glenelg]) *G*. 27 C-D20 28 E21
2, Concession (West Grey [Normanby]) *G* 27 E-G20
2, Concession Rd *DH* 43 B34-35
2, Concession Rd *NR* 33 D45
2, Concession Rd *SM* 41 Z28
2, Concession Rd (Adjala-Tosorontio) *SM* 29 D27 E-G27
2, Concession Rd (Brechin) *SM* ... 43 A34
2, Concession Rd (Devon) *TB*..... 102 G1
2, Concession Rd (East Hawkesbury) *PR* 68 P72 69 P73
2, Concession Rd (Forbes) *TB* 102 B3
2, Concession Rd (Marks) *TB*... 102 E1-2
2, Concession Rd (Nation) *PR* .. 68 P70-71
2, Concession Rd (O'Connell) *SM* 42 Y32-33
2, Concession Rd (Ware-Gorham) *TB* ...
2, County Rd *HS* 34 F46-47
2, Drummond Concession *LN* . 49 V59 W58
2, Fire Lane *NI* 19 U34
2, Fire Rd *CS* 101 B19
2, Line *NI*...... 19 O34-35 O35
2, Line *SM*...... 30 F30
2, Line *WL* 28 H23
2, Ln *PT* 14 Q16 15 Q17
2, Marter Rd *TM* 85 M28
2, Medonte Sdrd *SM* 42 Y30
2, Mersea Rd *EX* 5 D-E5
2, Old Highway *HS*... 34 E48-49 35 D50
2, Pacaud Rd *TM*...... 85 L27-28
2, Plantagenet Concession *PR* ... 67 P67
2, Range Rd *NI*...... 18 R30
2, Road *EX* 4 E3-4
2, Rosseau Lake Rd *MK* 58 S70
2, Scugog Ln *DH*...... 31 F35-36
2, Sideroad *G* 39 B18-19
2, Sideroad *SM* 28 H23
2, Skeleton Lake Rd *MK* 58 S31
2, SL Rd *K* 43 X37
2, South Grimsby Rd *NI* 18 R-S31
2, Township Rd *OX* 16 R21-23

2, Windham Rd *NF* 16 T23-24
2 Arran , Concession *BR*........ 38 B17
2 Chamberlain , Concession *TM* 85 M27 M27-28
2 E , Concession (NDR) *BR*..... 27 E18
2 E , Concession Rd *NR* 33 D45
2 E , Concession Rd *SM* 41 Z28
2 E , Kenyon Concession Rd *SDG* . 68 S71
2 E , Sideroad *WL* 28 G22
2 E , Stephenson Rd *MK* 59 S-T33
2 Elderslie , Concession *BR*.... 27 C17-18
2 Henwood , Concession *TM* .. 85 Q27 Q28
2 Hilliard , Concession *TM* 85 P29
2 Ingram , Concession *TM* 85 N29
2 Marter , Concession *TM* 85 M28
2 N , Concession *EX* 4 D1
2 N , Line *SM*.......... 41 Y-Z29 42 A-B30
2 S , Line *SM* 42 B30
2 Savard , Concession *TM*.... 85 M26-27
2 Sunnidale , Concession *SM* .. 29 C27-28
2 W , Concession *HM* 17 U26
2 W , Concession (NDR) *BR* 27 E17
2 W , Concession (South Bruce) *BR*27 G18
2 W , Concession Rd *NR* 33 D-E44
2 W , Concession Rd *SM* 41 Z28
2 W , Kenyon Concession Rd *SDG* . 68 S70
2 W , Sideroad *WL* 28 G21
2 W , Stephenson Rd *MK* 58 T32
2 Concession Rd, Charlotteville Rd *NF* 10 W24
2 Rd, Cane *TM*...... 85 P27
2 Rd, Concession *HD* 18 S29
2 Rd, Concession *TM* 85 P30-31
2 Rd, Concession (Wainfleet) *NI*.. 18 U32
2 Rd, Concession (West Lincoln) *NI* 18 S30
2 Rd, Harris *TM* 85 N29
2 Rd, Henwood *TM*...... 85 P-Q27
2 Rd, Line *LG* 49 X60
2 Rd, Zone *C* 7 X10
2 Rd S , Concession *HD*.... 18 S29
2 Sdrd, No. *HT* 23 N28 24 N29
2 Townsend, Concession *NF* 16 T24 17 T25
2&3 Rd W/Newholm , Concession *MK*.. ...... 59 S34
2-3, Concession Rd *DF* 28 N24

2-3 Rd, Finch Concession SDG . . . 67 T68
2A, Concession G. 39 A-B19
2A, Drummond Concession LN. . . 49 V59
2A, Ramsay Concession LN. 65 T-U58
2A Elderslie , Concession BR 27 C17
2B, Ramsay Concession LN. 65 S-T57
2C, Concession G 27 C20
2nd N , Old SM 41 A29 Z30
2nd S , Old SM 41 A29 42 B30
2nd Av CS. 101 C20
2nd Av NI 18 R32
2nd Av PS 58 Q32
2nd Av SD. 90 E13
2nd Av E G 39 A19 Z19
2nd Av S BR 38 Z16-17
2nd Concession A 86 F95
2nd Concession B 28 D22
2nd Concession HM 17 Q25-26
2nd Concession LA 47 A-B51
2nd Concession NI 19 U34
2nd Concession Y 30 E-F31
2nd Concession, Bathurst LN . . 48 W-X57
2nd Concession, Somerville K . . 43 Z37
2nd Concession Dalhousie LN
. . . . 64 U56 65 U57
2nd Concession N G 39 Y-Z21
2nd Concession North/Sherbrooke LN .
. . . . 48 V-W55
2nd Concession S G. 39 A21 Z21
2nd Concession Rd BT. . . . 16 R22-23
2nd Concession Rd LA 36 E54
2nd Concession Rd SM. 29 C27-28 D27 E27
2nd Concession Rd (Augusta) LG 50 Y-Z63
2nd Concession Rd (Leeds and the
Thousand Islands) LG 37 B61
2nd Concession Rd NTR NF. . 16 U-V21
2nd Concession Rd STR NF . . 16 V22-23
2nd Lake Rd F. 36 A54 47 A53
2nd Line (Otonabee-South Monaghan)
PB 33 E41
2nd Line (Smith-Ennismore-Lakefield) PB
. . . . 32 C40
2nd Line, Asphodel PB 33 C43
2nd Line, Belmont Township PB. . . . . .
. . . . 45 A45 46 B46
2nd Line, Douro PB 45 A42 B42
2nd Line Rd OT 66 T63
2nd Line Rd (Ottawa[Kanata]) OT . 65 Q60
2nd Line Rd (Ottawa[Osgoode]) OT . . . .
. . . . 66 T63-64
2nd Ln BT 17 S-T26
2nd Ln C 6 B7-8
2nd Ln DF 29 F-G26
2nd Ln EL 14 V15
2nd Ln G. 40 B24
2nd Ln HD 17 T27
2nd Ln NR 33 D43-44
2nd Ln (Centre Wellington) WL . . . .
. . . . 22 J23-24 K24
2nd Ln (EHS (Mono)) DF . . 29 E-F26 G27
2nd Ln (EHS (Mulmur)) DF. . . . 29 D26
2nd Ln (Erin) WL 23 K25-26
2nd Ln (Innisfil) SM 30 D30-31
2nd Ln (Minto) WL 28 H21
2nd Ln (New Tecumseth) SM. . . . .
. . . . 29 G28 30 F29-30 G29
2nd Ln, (WHS) DF 29 D25-26 E-F26
2nd Ln, Stafford R 82 L-M52
2nd Ln E A 84 B92
2nd Ln E NR. 33 D45 34 C46 D46
2nd Ln E WL 22 K-L24
2nd Ln E K-L24
2nd Ln Nassagaweya HT. . 23 L-M26 M27
2nd Ln NE DF 28 E24
2nd Ln SW DF 28 E24 29 F25
2nd Ln W A 84 B90-92
2nd Rd E HM 18 Q-R29
2nd Rd W HM 18 R29
2nd St SDG 52 U71 V70
2nd St (London) MD. 15 T17
2nd St (Strathroy-Caradoc) MD. . . 14 T14
2nd Dug Hill Rd HS. 34 E-F47
3-4 Sdrd SDG 68 R-S72 T72 69 T73

3, Addington Rd LA 47 X50
3, Alfred Concession PR 68 N69
3, Concession DH 31 D-E33 F-G34
3, Concession HD 17 U27
3, Concession WL 28 K20 22 K21
3, Concession Rd PR . . . 68 P70 P72 69 P73
3, Concession Rd SDG . . 68 T72 69 T73
3, Concession Rd (Adjala-Tosorontio) SM
. . . . 29 D-F27 F-G28
3, Concession Rd (Brechin) SM. . 43 A34
3, Concession Rd (Brock) DH. . . 43 B34-35
3, Concession Rd (Clarington) DH . . . . .
. . . . 32 G38 G39-40
3, Concession Rd (Marks) TB. . 102 E1-2
3, Concession Rd (O'Connell) SM. 42 Y33
3, Concession Rd (Ware-Gorham) TB . . . .
. . . . 102 B4-5
3, Kenyon Concession Rd SDG . . 68 S70
3, Line NI 19 Q34-35
3, Line SM. 30 F30
3, Ln PT 15 Q17
3, Marter Rd TM 85 L-M28
3, Mersea Rd EX 5 E5
3, Plantagenet Concession PR. . . . .
. . . . 67 N68 P67-68
3, Road EX 4 E3-4
3, Rosseau Lake Rd MK 58 S30
3, Scugog Ln DH 31 F35-36
3, Sideroad G 28 E-F22
3, Sideroad (Chatsworth) G. . . . .
3, Sideroad (Georgian Bluffs [Derby]) G.. .
. . . . 39 A18 A19
3, Sideroad (Mapleton) WL . . . .
. . . . 21 J-K20 22 J21 28 H21
3, Sideroad (Meaford) G. 39 A20-21
3, Sideroad (Wellington North) WL . 28 G23
3, Sideroad (West Grey) G. 27 C20

3, Skeleton Lake Rd MK. 58 S31
3, South Grimsby Rd NI. 18 R31
3, Township Rd OX. 16 Q23 R21-23
3, Township Rd WL. 22 M24
3, Windham Rd NF 16 T23-24
3 Chamberlain , Concession TM 85 L27-28
3 Derby , Concession G 39 A19
3 E , Flos Rd SM 41 A29
3 E , Sideroad WL 28 G22
3 Henwood , Concession TM. . . 85 P-Q27
3 Hilliard , Concession TM 85 N-P29
3 Ingram , Concession LA . . . 85 M29-30
3 Keppel , Concession G. 39 Z18
3 Marter , Concession TM 85 L29
3 N , Concession EX 4 D1
3 N , Line NP 95 E34
3 N , Line SM 41 Y-Z29 42 A30
3 N , Road WL 27 G20
3 Nottawasaga , Concession SM . 29 C26
3 S , Concession EX 4 E1
3 S , Line NP 95 E-F34
3 S , Line SM 42 B30
3 Sunnidale , Concession SM . 29 C27-28
3 W , Concession Rd NR. 33 D44
3 W , Concession Rd SM . . . 41 Y27-28
3 W , Flos Rd SM 41 A28 A-B28
3 W , Sideroad SM 28 G21
3 Concession, Harris TM 85 Q-R30
3 Rd, Concession HD . . . 17 U28 18 U29
3 Rd, Concession NI. 18 S30
3 Rd, Concession NI. 19 Q-R35
3 Rd, Concession PR. 67 R68
3 Rd, Concession (Beauchamp) TM . . . .
. . . . 85 P27-28
3 Rd, Concession (Brethour) TM. . . . . . .
. . . . 85 P30 P30-31
3 Rd, Concession (Wainfleet) NI. . 19 T-U33
3 Rd, Harris TM. 85 Q-R30
3 Rd, Henwood 85 P27
3 Rd, Line LG. 45 X59-60
3 Townsend, Concession NF 16 T24 17 T25
3-4, Concession WL. 23 L26
3-4, Concession DF 28 H24
3-4, Finch Concession SDG . 67 T67-68
3-4 Sdrd Sunnidale SM . . 29 C27 41 B27
3 & 4 Marter , Concession TM. . 85 L-M28
3A, Concession G 27 C20 39 B19
3A, Ramsay Concession LN . . . 65 T58
3B, Concession G 27 C20 39 A-B20
3C, Ramsay Concession LN. . . . 65 S57
3rd Av NI 19 R32 19 R33
3rd Av W G 39 Z19
3rd Concession DH 31 D34
3rd Concession G . . . 28 C24 D23-24 29 C25
3rd Concession NI. 64 R56
3rd Concession NI 19 T34-35
3rd Concession, Somerville K . . . .
. . . . 43 Z37 44 Y-Z38
3rd Concession Dalhousie LN . . . .
. . . . 64 R54 U56
3rd Concession North/Sherbrooke LN . .
. . . . 48 V-W55
3rd Concession Rd (Essex) EX . . 4 E2-3
3rd Concession Rd (Leamington) EX . 5 E5
3rd Concession Rd B Dalhousie LN . 64 U56
3rd Concession Ln C. 5 D7-8
3rd Concession Rd BT 16 R22 R23
3rd Concession Rd DH 31 H34
3rd Concession Rd NF . . 10 W-X22 X22-23
3rd Concession Rd SD 101 B23
3rd Concession Rd (Augusta) LG. 50 Y-Z63
3rd Concession Rd (Front of Yonge) LG
. . . . 37 A61
3rd Concession Rd (Greater Napanee) LA
. . . . 35 F51-52
3rd Concession Rd (Loyalist) LA. . 36 E54
3rd Concession Rd STR NF. . . 16 V22
3rd Line (Otonabee-South Monaghan) PB
. . . . 33 E41
3rd Line (Smith-Ennismore-Lakefield) PB
. . . . 32 C40
3rd Line, Asphodel PB 33 C43 45 B43
3rd Line, Belmont Township PB . . . 45 A45
3rd Line, Douro PB . . . 44 A41 45 A42 B42
3rd Line W PL 29 H26
3rd Line Rd OT 66 T-U64
3rd Line Rd N OT 66 T62
3rd Line Rd S OT 66 T-U63
3rd Line Rd F 36 E56
3rd Line Rd LN. 65 U60
3rd Line Rd Mid Dummer PB . . 45 B42-43
3rd Line Rd North/Dummer PB . . 45 A42
3rd Line Rd South/Dummer PB. 45 B42-43
3rd Ln BT 17 S26
3rd Ln C 5 D7-8
3rd Ln EL 8 W15 14 V15
3rd Ln HD 17 T27-28
3rd Ln NR 33 D-E42
3rd Ln (Amaranth) DF 29 G26
3rd Ln (Centre Wellington) WL . . . .
. . . . 22 J23-24 K24
3rd Ln (EHS (Mono)) DF. . 29 F26-27 G27
3rd Ln (EHS (Mulmur)) DF. . . . 29 D-E26
3rd Ln (Erin) WL 23 K25-26 K26
3rd Ln (Essa) SM 29 D28
3rd Ln (Guelph-Eramosa) WL. . . . .
. . . . 23 K25 L25-26
3rd Ln (Halton Hills) HT . . . 23 L27 L-M28
3rd Ln (Innisfil) SM 30 D30-31
3rd Ln (Mapleton) WL 22 L22
3rd Ln (Meaford) G. 40 Z23
3rd Ln (Melancthon) DF 29 D-F25
3rd Ln (Milton) HT . . . 23 M28 24 M29
3rd Ln (Minto) WL 27 H20 28 H21
3rd Ln (New Tecumseth) SM 29 G28 30 F29
3rd Ln (Oakville) HT. 24 M28
3rd Ln (The Blue Mountain) G. . 40 A24 B24
3rd Ln, Stafford R 82 L-M52
3rd Ln A G 40 B23
3rd Ln B G 40 B23
3rd Ln C G 40 A23
3rd Ln D G 40 A23 B23
3rd Ln W A 84 A91 A-B92
3rd Ln W NR 22 K23
3rd Rd, Little SDG 68 R71
3rd Rd E HM 18 Q-R29
3rd Sdrd G 40 B23 B24
3rd Sdrd HT. 23 M27 N27
3rd Sdrd (WGR) G 27 C20

3rd St NI 19 R33
3rd Line HS 34 E46
3rd Line Rd SDG . . . 68 R72 69 R-S73

4, Addington Rd LA 47 W50
4, Alfred Concession PR . . . 68 N69-70
4, Chamberlain Concession TM . 85 M27
4, Concession HD 17 U27
4, Concession (Brock) DH 31 D34-35
4, Concession (Huron-Kinloss) BR . 26 F14
4, Concession (Kincardine) BR. . 26 C14-15
4, Concession (Mapleton) WL. . . 21 K20
4, Concession (NDR) G 27 D19
4, Concession (Northern Bruce
Peninsula) BR 55 V17
4, Concession (Puslinch) WL . . 23 N25
4, Concession (Saugeen Shores) BR . . . .
. . . . 38 B15
4, Concession (South Bruce) . . . .
. . . . 26 G16 27 G17
4, Concession (Uxbridge) DH . . . .
. . . . 31 D-E33 F34
4, Concession (West Grey [Glenelg]) G
. . . . 28 D21
4, Concession (West Grey [Normanby]) G
. . . . 27 G20
4, Concession Rd PR. 68 P70
4, Concession Rd SDG . 68 S72 69 S73
4, Concession Rd SM . . . 43 A34 Z34
4, Concession Rd (Adjala-Tosorontio) SM
. . . . 29 D-E27 F-G28
4, Concession Rd (Brock) DH. . 43 B34-35
4, Concession Rd (Clarington) DH . . . . .
. . . . 32 G38 G39-40
4, Concession Rd (Marks) TB . . 102 E2
4, Concession Rd (Ware-Gorham) TB . . .
. . . . . . 102 B4-5 103 B6
4, Fire Rte PB 57 Z42
4, Kenyon Concession Rd SDG. . . . .
. . . . 68 R71 S70-71
4, Line NI 19 Q34-35
4, Line SM. 30 F30
4, Line WL 28 H23
4, Ln PT 14 Q16 15 Q17
4, Mersea Rd EX 5 E5
4, North Kawartha Concession PB . 45 X42
4, Plantagenet Concession PR. . . . .
. . . . 67 P67-68 P68 68 P69
4, Road EX 4 E3-4
4, Scugog Ln DH 31 F35
4, Sideline DH 31 G35
4, Sideroad (Wellington North) WL . . . . .
. . . . 28 G-H21
4, Skeleton Lake Rd MK 58 S31
4, Southgate Township Rd G . . . .
. . . . . . 28 F22-24 G21-22
4, Stephenson Rd MK. . . 58 S32 59 S33
4, Township Rd OX 16 Q23 R21-22
4, Windham Rd NF. 16 T23
4 Arran , Concession BR 38 B17
4 Cane , Concession TM 85 P26
4 Chamberlain , Concession TM 85 L27-28
4 E, Concession EX. . . 26 E16 27 E17 E18
4 E, Concession (South Bruce) . . . .
. . . . 27 F18-19
4 E, Concession Rd NR 33 D45
4 E, Flos Rd SM 41 A29 Z29
4 E, Sideroad WL 22 L23-24
4 Elderslie , Concession BR 27 C18
4 Firstbrook , Concession TM . . 85 R28-29
4 Henwood , Concession TM . . 85 P27-28
4 Hilliard , Concession TM 85 N29
4 Ingram , Concession LA 85 M28
4 Marter , Concession TM 85 L-M28
4 N , Concession EX 4 D1
4 N , Concession WL 28 G22
4 N , Line SM 41 Y-Z29 42 A30
4 Robillard , Concession TM . . 85 M26-27
4 S , Concession EX 4 D1
4 S , Concession WL. . . 22 J22 28 H22
4 S , Line SM. 42 B30-31
4 W , Concession HM. . 17 Q26 23 P26 P27
4 W , Concession (Brockton) BR . . . .
. . . . 26 E15 27 E17
4 W , Concession (South Bruce) . . . .
. . . . 27 G17-18
4 W , Concession Rd NR. 33 D44
4 W , Concession Rd SM 41 A28-29
4 W , Flos Rd SM 41 A27-28
4 Concession, Harris TM 85 Q30
4 Rd, Cane TM 85 P26
4 Rd, Concession HD . . 17 U28 18 S29
4 Rd, Concession PR. 67 R66
4 Rd, Concession SDG 68 Q-R72
4 Rd, Concession (Beauchamp) TM . . . .
. . . . 85 N30 P31
4 Rd, Concession (Brethour) TM. . . . . . .
4 Rd, Concession (Niagara-on-the-Lake)
NI 19 Q34-35
4 Rd, Concession (West Lincoln) NI. . . . .
. . . . 18 S31 S32
4 Rd, Harris TM 85 Q30
4 Rd, Henwood TM 85 P27
4 Rd, Line LG. 49 X60-61
4 Rd, Pense TM 85 P26
4 Rd, Shadow Lake K 43 X-Y37
4 Rd, Zone C 7 X11
4 Sdrd G 39 A21 40 A22-23
4 Sdrd, No. HT 23 N28
4&5 Rd E/Newholm , Concession MK . . .
. . . . 59 S34
4&5 Rd W/Newholm , Concession MK. . .
. . . . 59 S33-34
4-5, Concession DF 28 H24
4-5, Concession PT 21 N20
4-5, Finch Concession SDG . 67 T67-68
4-5 Sdrd, Concession (Rock Hill Rd) PS
. . . . 76 P30
4 & 5 Hilliard , Concession TM . . 85 N29
4A, Concession G 39 A19
4A, Drummond Concession LN . . 49 V58
4A, Ramsay Concession LN. . . . 65 T58
4A, Sideroad (Chatsworth) G . . . 39 B19
4A, Sideroad (Grey Highlands) G. . 28 C22
4A, Sideroad (The Blue Mountain) G . . . .
. . . . 40 B23
4A Elderslie , Concession BR. . . 27 C17
4A, Drummond Concession LN. . 49 V58

4B, Ramsay Concession LN 65 T58
4B, Sideroad (Chatsworth) G . . 39 R19-20
4B, Sideroad (Grey Highlands) G . 28 C22
4C, Drummond Concession LN . . 49 V58-59
4C, Ramsay Concession LN. . . . 65 S-T58
4D, Drummond Concession LN . . 49 V59
4D, Ramsay Concession LN 65 S58
4th Av NI 18 R32 19 R33
4th Av PS 58 Q31
4th Av SM. 85 M28
4th Concession A 86 G95
4th Concession B 65 R57
4th Concession, Bathurst Upper LN . . . .
. . . . 48 W-X57
4th Concession A G 28 D22
4th Concession B G. . 28 C24 C-D23 29 C25
4th Concession Dalhousie LN . . . .
. . . . 48 V56 64 U56
4th Concession N G 39 Z21
4th Concession N G 39 Z21
4th Concession North/Sherbrooke LN . .
. . . . 48 V-W55
4th Concession S G 39 A21
4th Concession Rd EX 4 E2-3
4th Concession Rd MA . . 72 M10 73 M11
4th Concession A Lanark LN. . . . 65 U57
4th Concession B Dalhousie LN . 64 U56
4th Concession B Lanark LN. . . . 65 U57
4th Concession D Dalhousie LN . 64 U56
4th Concession Ln C. 5 D7
4th Concession Rd BT. . . . 16 R22-23
4th Concession Rd DH 31 H34
4th Concession Rd F . . . 36 C57 37 C58
4th Concession Rd HM 17 Q25
4th Concession Rd LG. 50 Y63
4th Concession Rd NF . . . 10 X22-23
4th Lake Rd F. 48 Z54
4th Line PB. 33 D41
4th Line, Asphodel PB . . 33 C43 45 B43
4th Line, Belmont Township PB . . 45 B45
4th Line, Douro PB. . 33 C42 44 A41 45 B42
4th Line Rd OT 66 T64
4th Line Rd (Ottawa[Rideau]) OT . . . . . .
. . . . 66 T62 U63
4th Line Rd F 36 E56
4th Line Rd PB 45 B43
4th Line Rd North/Dummer PB . . 45 A42
4th Ln A 87 E1
4th Ln BT 17 S26-27
4th Ln EL 8 W15 14 V15 V16
4th Ln HD. 17 T27-28
4th Ln (Alnwick-Haldimand) NR . . 33 D43
4th Ln (Amaranth) DF 29 F-G25
4th Ln (Centre Wellington) WL . . . .
4th Ln (EHS (Mono)) DF. . . . 29 F-G27
4th Ln (EHS (Mulmur)) DF. . . . 29 D-E26
4th Ln (Erin) WL . . . 23 J25-26 K26-27
4th Ln (Essa) SM 29 D28
4th Ln (Guelph-Eramosa) WL. . 23 K25 L26
4th Ln (Halton Hills) HT 23 L27-28
4th Ln (Innisfil) SM 30 D29-30
4th Ln (Mapleton) WL 22 K21-22
4th Ln (Melancthon) DF 29 D-F25
4th Ln (Milton) HT . . . 23 M28 24 M29
4th Ln (Minto) WL 28 H20 28 H21
4th Ln (New Tecumseth) SM. 29 F28 30 F29
4th Ln (Oakville) HT 24 N29 N30
4th Ln, Blind C. 7 A10
4th Ln, East PB 33 D41
4th Ln A G 28 C20 40 B23
4th Ln B G 28 C23-24 29 C25
4th Ln Beckwith LN 65 U59-60
4th Ln E A 84 A92
4th Ln E NR 33 C45 34 C46
4th Ln E WL 22 L24
4th Ln Gordon MA 72 K7
4th Ln Nassagaweya HT. 23 L26
4th Ln NE DF . . . 28 D24 E24 29 E25
4th Ln SW DF 28 E-F24
4th Ln SW A G 28 E24
4th Ln W A 84 A91-92
4th Rd SDG 67 T68
4th St SM 41 X28
4th Line Rd SDG. . . . 68 R72 69 S-T73

5 E , Concession Rd SM. . . . 41 Y27-28
5 E , Flos Rd SM 41 A28 Z29
5 E , Kenyon Concession Rd SDG . . . . . .
. . . . 68 R70-71
5 E , Sideroad WL 28 G22
5 Elderslie , Sideroad BR . . 27 C17 38 B17
5 Ext , Sideroad G. 27 E-F19
5 Hilliard , Concession TM . . . 85 N29-30
5 Ingram , Concession TM 85 M30
5 Keppel , Concession G. 39 Z18
5 N , Line SM 41 Y-Z29 42 A30 Z30
5 N , Sideroad (Kincardine) BR . . 26 D14
5 North Arran , Sideroad BR . . . 38 A17
5 Nottawasaga , Concession SM . 29 C26
5 Robillard , Concession TM . . 85 M26-27
5 S , Concession EX 4 E1
5 S , Line SM. 42 A-B31
5 S , Sideroad (Brockton) BR. . . 27 E17
5 S , Sideroad (Kincardine) BR . . 26 D14
5 S , Sideroad (South Bruce) BR . 27 F-G18
5 South Arran , Sideroad BR . . . 38 B17
5 Strange , Concession TB 102 E1
5 Sunnidale , Concession SM . 41 B27-28
5 W , Concession HM 23 P26
5 W , Concession Rd SM. . . . 41 Y-Z27
5 W , Flos Rd SM 41 A27-28
5 W , Kenyon Concession Rd SDG . . . . . .
. . . . 68 R-S70
5 W , Road EX. 4 E3-4
5 W , Sideroad SM. 28 G21
5 Rd, Cane TM 85 P26
5 Rd, Concession HD 17 U28
5 Rd, Concession NI. 18 R-S30
5 Rd, Concession NI. 19 Q-R34
5 Rd, Concession SDG 68 Q72
5 Rd, Concession TM 85 N30-31
5 Rd, Harris TM 85 Q30
5 Rd, Line LG 49 X60-61 X-Y60
5 Rd, Zone C 7 X11
5 Sdrd Adjala SM 29 G28
5 Sdrd Tosorontio SM 29 E27-28
5 Townsend, Concession NF. . . 17 T25
5 Woodhouse, Concession NF . 17 U26 V25
5-6, Sdrd (Ramara) SM 42 Y33
5-6, Finch Concession SDG . . . 67 T66-67
5-6 Sdrd (Oro-Medonte) SM. . . 42 B30
5-6 Sdrd, Lot P 76 M-N30
5A, Concession G. 39 A19
5A, Drummond Concession LN. 49 V-W58
5A, Ramsay Concession LN. . . 65 T58-59
5A, Sideroad BR 27 C17
5A Keppel , Concession G . . . 39 Z18
5B, Concession G 27 C19 39 B19
5B, Drummond Concession LN. 49 V58-59
5B, Ramsay Concession LN 65 S58
5B, Sideroad BR. 27 F17
5th Av HU 20 L14
5th Av NI 19 R33
5th Concession, Bathurst LN . . . .
. . . . 48 W57 49 W58
5th Concession, Somerville K. . . 43 Y-Z37
5th Concession Darling LN . . . 64 T56
5th Concession N G 39 Z20
5th Concession Rd (Essex) EX . . 4 E2-3
5th Concession Rd (Lakeshore[Tilbury
North]) EX. 6 C6
5th Concession A Dalhousie LN . 48 V56
5th Concession A Lanark LN. . . . 65 U57
5th Concession B Dalhousie LN . 48 V56
5th Concession B Lanark LN. . . . 65 U57
5th Concession C Dalhousie LN . . . .
. . . . 48 V56 64 U56
5th Concession Ln C 5 D7
5th Concession Rd BT R-S23
5th Concession Rd HM. . . 17 Q25 23 P25
5th Concession Rd LG. 47 Y50
5th Concession Rd (Ajax) DH . . 31 E34
5th Lake Rd F. 48 Z53
5th Line (Cavan-Millbrook-North
Monaghan) PB. 32 E39-40
5th Line (Otonabee-South Monaghan) . . .
. . . . 32 D-E40
5th Line (Smith-Ennismore-Lakefield) PB
. . . . 32 C40 44 B41
5th Line, Asphodel PB . . 33 C43 45 B43
5th Line, Douro PB . 33 C42 44 A-B41 45 B42
5th Line, Laxton Township K. . . 43 Y36
5th Line Rd (Ottawa[Kanata]) OT . 65 Q60
5th Line Rd (Ottawa[Osgoode]) OT. 66 T64
5th Line Rd F 36 E56
5th Line Rd North/Dummer PB . . 45 A42
5th Line Rd South/Dummer PB. . 45 B43
5th Ln BT 17 S26-27
5th Ln EL 8 W15-16
5th Ln G 40 A24
5th Ln HD 17 S27
5th Ln (Alnwick-Haldimand) NR . . 33 D43
5th Ln (Amaranth) DF 29 F25
5th Ln (Centre Wellington) WL . . . .
. . . . 22 J24 23 K25
5th Ln (EHS (Mono)) DF . . 29 F27 G27
5th Ln (EHS (Mulmur)) DF . . . 29 D26 E27
5th Ln (Erin) WL 23 J25-26 K27
5th Ln (Essa) SM 29 C-D28
5th Ln (Guelph-Eramosa) WL. . . 23 L25
5th Ln (Halton Hills) HT 23 L27-28
5th Ln (Innisfil) SM 30 D29-30
5th Ln (Melancthon) DF 29 D-F25
5th Ln (Milton) HT 24 M29
5th Ln (Minto) WL 27 H19-20
5th Ln (New Tecumseth) SM. 29 F28 30 F29
5th Ln (Port Hope) NR. . . 32 G40 33 F41
5th Ln E A 84 A92
5th Ln E C 6 B8
5th Ln E NR 34 C46
5th Ln Nassagaweya HT. . . . 23 L26-27
5th Ln W NR 33 C45
5th Rd, Little SDG 68 S72
5th Rd E HM 18 R29
5th Rd E SM 23 L-M28 M27
5th Sdrd TB 102 E1
5th Sdrd (Amaranth) DF . . 29 G25-26 H25
5th Sdrd (Barrie Island) MA . . . 71 J6
5th Sdrd (Bradford West Gwillimbury) SM
. . . . 30 E-F30
5th Sdrd (Essa) SM . . . 29 E28 30 D29
5th Sdrd (Innisfil) SM 30 C-D30
5th Sdrd (Melancthon) DF . . 29 G26-27
5th Sdrd (Mono) DF 29 G26-27
5th Sdrd (Mulmur) DF 29 E26
5th Sdrd (Tehkummah) MA. . . 73 N11

5th Sdrd NDR G 27 D18-19
5th St NI 19 R33
5th St, West HM 17 Q-R28
5th Line Rd SDG 69 S-T73
5th Side Rd A 86 E94 F-G95

6 (Proposed) HM 17 R27
6, Addington Rd LA 63 U50
6, Concession G 39 A19
6, Concession HD 17 U26-27
6, Concession LA 63 T50
6, Concession WL 21 J20 22 J-K21
6, Concession (Brock) DH . . 31 D35
6, Concession (Brockton) . . . .
. . . . 26 E15-16 27 E17
6, Concession (Chatsworth) . . . . .
. . . . 27 C19 28 C21 39 B19
6, Concession (Kincardine) BR . . 26 C15
6, Concession (NDR) G 27 D19-20
6, Concession (Saugeen Shores) BR . .
. . . . 38 B16
6, Concession (Uxbridge) DH . . 31 D-F34
6, Concession (West Grey) G . . 28 D21
6, Concession (West Grey [Normanby]) G .
. . . . 27 F19-20
6, Concession Rd EX 4 E3-4
6, Concession Rd SDG . . . 68 S72 69 S73
6, Concession Rd TB 102 B5
6, Concession Rd (Adjala-Tosorontio) SM
. . . . 29 D-E28
6, Concession Rd (Brock) DH . . 43 B34-35
6, Concession Rd (Clarington) DH . . . . .
. . . . 32 F-G39 G37
6, Concession Rd (East Hawkesbury) PR
. . . . 68 P72 Q72 69 P73 Q73
6, Concession Rd (Nation) PR . . 68 Q70
6, Concession Rd (Ramara) . . . . . .
. . . . 42 Z33 43 Z34
6, Fire Rte PB 45 A45
6, Kenyon Concession Rd SDG . 68 R70-71
6, Lane A 86 D-E96
6, Line NI 19 Q34-35 R34-35
6, Line SM 30 T30
6, Line WL 28 H23
6, Ln PT 14 Q16 15 Q17
6, Mersea Rd EX 5 E5-6
6, Plantagenet Concession PR . . 67 P68
6, Route PR 67 P68 68 P69
6, Scugog Ln DH 31 F35
6, Sideline DH 31 G35
6, Sideroad WL 21 K20 22 J21
6, Sideroad (Chatsworth) G . . 27 C18-19
6, Sideroad (Georgian Bluffs) G . 39 A19
6, Sideroad (Meaford) G 39 A20-21
6, Sideroad (Southgate) G 28 E21
6, Sideroad (West Grey) G . . . 27 C-D20
6, South Grimsby Rd NI 18 R-S31
6, Southgate Township Rd G . . 28 G21
6, Township Rd OX 16 Q21-23
6, Windham Rd NF 16 T23-24
6 Arran , Concession BR 39 A18
6 Bryce , Concession TM 85 N27
6 Chamberlain , Concession TM . . . . . .
. . . . 85 L27-28
6 E , Concession HM 23 P27
6 E , Concession (Brockton) BR . 27 D18
6 E , Concession (Huron-Kinloss) BR . . .
. . . . 26 F14
6 E , Concession (South Bruce) BR . . . .
. . . . 27 F18-19
6 E , Concession Rd NR 33 D45
6 E , Concession Rd SM 41 Y28
6 E , Road EX 4 E4 E5 E5
6 E , Sideroad WL 28 D22
6 Elderslie , Concession BR . . 27 C17-18
6 Henwood , Concession TM . . 85 P28
6 Hilliard , Concession TM . . 85 N29 N29-30
6 N , Concession WL 4 D2
6 N , Concession WL 28 G21-22
6 N , Line SM . . . 41 Y29 42 A30-31 Y30
6 N , Road WL 27 G19
6 N , Sideroad WL 22 K-L24
6 Nottawasaga , Concession SM . . . . .
. . . . 29 C-D26 41 B26
6 S , Concession EX 4 E1
6 S , Concession WL 28 H22
6 S , Line SM 42 A-B31
6 S , Road WL 27 H20
6 S , Sideroad WL 22 L24
6 Savard , Concession TM . . . 85 L26-27
6 Sunnidale , Concession SM . . 41 B27-28
6 W , Concession HM 23 P26-27
6 W , Concession (Brockton) BR . 27 D17
6 W , Concession (Huron-Kinloss) BR . . .
. . . . 26 E13
6 W , Concession Rd SM 41 Y27
6 W , Flos Rd SM 41 A28
6 W , Road EX 4 E3-4
6 W , Sideroad WL 28 H21-22
6 Concession, Harris TM 85 Q30
6 Rd, Concession HD 17 U28
6 Rd, Concession NI 19 Q-R34
6 Rd, Concession (Beauchamp) . . . . . .
. . . . 85 N27 N28
6 Rd, Concession (Brethour) TM . . . . . .
. . . . 85 N30-31
6 Rd, Concession (Wainfleet) NI . 18 T31-32
6 Rd, Line LG 49 Y60
6 Rd, Shadow Lake K 43 Y37
6 Rd, Zone C 7 X11
6 School Rd, No. BT 17 R-S25
6 Townsend, Concession NF . . 17 T25
6 Woodhouse, Concession NF . . 17 U-V25
6-7, Concession Rd DF 28 G24
6-7 Rd, Finch Concession SDG . . . .
. . . . 67 S-T68 T67
6-7 Sdrd, Concession PS 76 M29
6-7 Sdrd Nottawasaga SM . . 29 C25-27
6-7 Sdrd Sunnidale SM . . 29 C27 41 B27
6 Mile Channel Rd MK . . 41 W29 42 W30
6A, Drummond Concession LN . . 49 V58
6A, Ramsay Concession LN . . 65 T58-59
6B, Drummond Concession LN . . 49 V58
6B, Ramsay Concession LN . . 65 T58
6C, Ramsay Concession LN . . 65 S-T58
6C, Ramsay Concession LN . . 65 S-T58
6th Av CS 100 C-D18 D18
6th Av NI 18 R32
6th Av PS 58 Q31
6th Concession LN 65 S57-58
6th Concession, Bathurst LN . . . .
. . . . 48 W57 49 W58
6th Concession, Somerville K . . 43 Y37
6th Concession Darling LN . . 64 T56
6th Concession N G 39 Y-Z20

6th Concession S G 39 A20
6th Concession Rd (Essex) EX . . 4 E2-3
6th Concession Rd (Lakeshore[Tilbury
North]) EX 5 C5 6 C6
6th Concession Rd E MA 73 M-N11
6th Concession Rd W MA . . . 73 M-N11
6th Concession A Dalhousie LN . 48 V56
6th Concession A Lanark LN . . 65 U57-58
6th Concession B Dalhousie LN . . . . . .
. . . . 48 V56 64 U56
6th Concession B Lanark LN . . 65 U57
6th Concession C Lanark LN . . 65 T57
6th Concession Ln C 5 D6-7
6th Concession Rd BT 16 S22-23
6th Concession Rd DH 31 G35
6th Concession Rd F . . 36 C57 37 C58
6th Concession Rd HM 23 P25
6th Concession Rd NF 10 W23 X22
6th Concession Rd (Augusta) LG . 50 X-Y63
6th Concession Rd (Elizabethtown-Kitley)
. . . . 50 Y-Z62
6th Line (Asphodel-Norwood) PB . . . . . .
. . . . 33 C44 45 B43
6th Line (Otonabee-South Monaghan) PB
. . . . 32 D40
6th Line (Smith-Ennismore-Lakefield) PB
. . . . 44 B41
6th Line, Belmont Township PB . 45 A-B45
6th Line, Laxton Township K . . 43 X-Y36
6th Line Rd OT 66 T64
6th Line Rd (Ottawa[Kanata]) OT . 66 Q61
6th Line Rd (Ottawa[Osgoode]) OT . 66 T64
6th Line Rd LN 65 T-U60
6th Line Rd North/Dummer PB . . 45 242
6th Line Rd South/Dummer PB . . 45 B43
6th Ln DF 29 F-G25
6th Ln EL 8 W15-16
6th Ln G 40 A24 B24
6th Ln HD 17 S27
6th Ln LN 65 U58
6th Ln NR 32 F-G40 33 F41
6th Ln (Centre Wellington) WL . . . .
. . . . 22 .I24 K L24 23 J25
6th I n (EHS) DF 29 G27
6th Ln (Erin) WL 23 J25-26 K26-27
6th Ln (Essa) SM 29 C28 30 D29
6th Ln (Guelph-Eramosa) WL . 23 K25 L26
6th Ln (Halton Hills) HT . . 23 K-L27 L28
6th Ln (Innisfil) SM . . . 30 C30-31 D29-30
6th Ln (Mapleton) WL 22 K22
6th Ln (Milton) HT 24 M29
6th Ln (Minto) WL 27 H20 28 H21
6th Ln (New Tecumseth) SM . 29 F28 30 F29
6th Ln Beckwith LN 65 U59
6th Ln E A 84 A92
6th Ln E C 6 B8-9
6th Ln E NR 34 C46
6th Ln E WL 22 L24
6th Ln Nassagaweya HT . . 23 L26-27 M27
6th Ln NE DF 28 D24 29 D-E25
6th Ln W C 6 B8
6th Ln W NR 33 C45
6th Rd SDG 67 S68
6th Rd E HM 18 R29-30
6th Sdrd G 40 B23 B24
6th Sdrd TB 102 E1 F1-2
6th St NI 55 Y17
6th St SM 40 A25

7, Addington Rd LA 63 T50
7, Alfred Concession PR 68 P69
7, Charlotteville Rd NF . . . 16 U23 V24
7, Concession BR 26 D14-15
7, Concession G 39 A19 Z19
7, Concession (Brock) DH 31 D34
7, Concession (Puslinch) WL . . 23 N26
7, Concession (Uxbridge) DH . . 31 F34
7, Concession (Wellington North) WL . . .
. . . . 28 H22
7, Concession Rd NI 18 R30
7, Concession Rd SDG . . . 68 S72 69 S73
7, Concession Rd SM . . . 42 Z33 43 Z34
7, Concession Rd (Adjala-Tosorontio) SM
. . . . 29 D-E28 E-G28
7, Concession Rd (Brock) DH . . . .
. . . . 43 A34-35 B34
7, Concession Rd (Clarington) DH . . . . .
. . . . . . 32 F38 F-G37 F-G38
7, Concession Rd (Nation) PR . . 68 Q69-70
7, Drummond Concession LN . 49 V58-59
7, Kenyon Concession Rd SDG . 68 R70
7, Line NI 19 R34-35
7, Ln PT 15 Q18
7, Mersea Rd EX 5 E5-6
7, Plantagenet Concession PR . 67 P68
7, School Rd WL 27 G-H19
7, Sideroad G 27 C19
7, Sideroad WL 28 G-H23
7, South Grimsby Rd NI 18 R-S31
7, Southgate Township Sdrd G . 28 F22
7, Windham Rd NF 16 T24 U23
7 E , Concession HM 23 P27-28
7 E , Flos Rd SM 41 Z28-29
7 E , Road EX 4 D4 5 D5
7 E , Sideroad WL 28 H22
7 N , Line SM . . . 41 Y29 42 A30-31 Y30 Z30
7 S , Concession EX 4 E2
7 S , Line SM 42 A31
7 Sunnidale , Concession SM . . 41 B27
7 W , Concession HM 23 P25
7 W , Concession Rd NR 33 D44
7 W , Concession Rd SM 41 Y27
7 W , Flos Rd SM 41 A28 Z28
7 W , Road EX 4 D3-4
7 W , Sideroad WL 28 H21-22
7 W , Stephenson Rd MK . 58 S32 59 S33
7 Walpole , Concession HD . . . 17 U28
7 Rd, Concession HD 17 U27 U28
7 Rd, Concession NI 19 Q-R34
7 Rd, Concession Rd (East Hawkesbury)
PR 68 P-Q72 69 P73
7 Rd, Line LG 49 Y60-61
7 Rd, Zone C 7 X11
7 Sdrd G 39 A21 40 A22 Z29
7 Townsend, Concession NF . . 17 T25
7-8 Rd, Finch Concession SDG . 67 T66-67
7 Mile Island Rd DH 31 E36
7A, Concession G 39 B19
7A, Ramsay Concession LN . . 65 S58
7A, Sideroad G 40 B22
7B, Concession G 39 B19
7B, Ramsay Concession LN . . 65 S58
7B, Sideroad G 40 B23
7C, Concession G 39 B19

7C, Sideroad G 40 B23
7th Av EL 15 U18
7th Av NI 27 E18
7th Av HU 20 L14
7th Av NI 18 R32 19 R33
7th Av SM 41 X28
7th Concession LN 65 R57 S58
7th Concession Y. 30 G30
7th Concession, Bathurst LN . . 48 V-W57
7th Concession, Somerville K . . 43 Y37
7th Concession Dalhousie LN . . 48 V56
7th Concession Darling LN . . 64 S-T56
7th Concession Rd (Essex) EX . . 4 E2-3
7th Concession Rd (Lakeshore[Tilbury
North]) EX 5 C5 6 C6
7th Concession Rd (LaSalle) EX . . 4 C2
7th Concession A Lanark LN . . 65 U57
7th Concession Rd BT 16 S22-23
7th Concession Rd DH 31 G34-35
7th Concession Rd HM 23 P25
7th Concession Rd LG 50 Y62
7th Concession Rd NF . . 10 W23 W-X22
7th Line (Asphodel-Norwood) PB . . . . . .
. . . . 33 C44 45 B43
7th Line (Smith-Ennismore-Lakefield) PB
. . . . 44 B40-41
7th Line, Douro PB 33 C41 44 B41
7th Line, Mid Belmont Township PB . . . .
. . . . 45 A-B45
7th Line, South Belmont Township PB . . .
. . . . 45 B45
7th Line Rd F 36 E56-57
7th Line Rd Mid Dummer PB . . 45 B43
7th Line Rd North/Dummer PB . . 45 A43
7th Line Rd South/Dummer PB . 45 B43
7th Ln DF 29 F-G25
7th Ln (Alnwick-Haldimand) NR . . 33 D43
7th Ln (Centre Wellington) WL . . . .
. . . . 22 J24 28 H24
7th Ln (EHS (Mono)) DF . 29 E-F27 G27
7th Ln (EHS (Mulmur)) DF . . 29 D27 E27
7th Ln (Grey Highlands) G . . 40 A-B22
7th Ln (Guelph-Eramosa) WL . . 23 K25
7th Ln (Innisfil) SM . . 30 C30-31 D29-30
7th Ln (Meaford) G 40 Y-Z22
7th Ln (Minto) WL 27 H19-20
7th Ln (New Tecumseth) SM . 29 F28 30 F29
7th Ln (Port Hope) NR . . 32 F40 33 F41
7th Ln (The Blue Mountain) G . . 40 A24
7th Ln, Mid Belmont Township PB . . . . .
. . . . 45 A-B45
7th Ln E C 6 B9
7th Ln E NR 34 C46
7th Ln Gordon MA 72 J-K7
7th Ln SW DF 28 F24
7th Ln W C 6 B8
7th Rd SDG 67 S68
7th Rd, Hoople SDG 67 U68
7th Rd E HM 18 R30
7th St NF 16 V24
7th St NI 19 R33
7th St SDG 52 V70
7th Line Beckwith LN . . . 65 T60 U59

8, Addington Rd LA 63 T50
8, Alfred Concession PR 68 P69
8, Belmont Township Concession PB . . .
. . . . 45 B45
8, Charlotteville Rd NF . . 16 V23-24
8, Concession HD 17 U26-27
8, Concession MA 72 K9
8, Concession (Brock) DH 31 D34
8, Concession (Brockton) BR . 27 D17-18
8, Concession (Chatsworth) G . . . .
. . . . 27 C19 39 B19
8, Concession (Kincardine) BR . 26 C16
8, Concession (Mapleton) WL . . 22 J21
8, Concession (NDR) G 27 D19
8, Concession (South Bruce) . . . .
. . . . 26 F16 27 F17 F18
8, Concession (Uxbridge) DH 31 E34 F34-35
8, Concession (Wellington North) WL . . .
. . . . 28 G21
8, Concession (West Grey [Gilenelg]) G . .
. . . . 28 D21
8, Concession (West Grey [Normanby]) G .
. . . . 27 F19-20
8, Concession Rd PR 68 Q69-70
8, Concession Rd SDG 68 R-S72
8, Concession Rd (Adjala-Tosorontio) SM
. . . . 29 F-G28
8, Concession Rd (Brock) DH . . 43 A34
8, Concession Rd (Clarington) DH . . . . .
. . . . 32 F37-39
8, Concession Rd (Ramara) SM . . . .
. . . . 42 Z33 Z33 43 Z34
8, Dalhousie Concession LN . 48 V56 64 U56
8, Fire Rte PB 45 A45
8, Kenyon Concession Rd SDG . 68 R69-70
8, Lane A 86 D96
8, Line NI 19 R34-35
8, Line SM 30 E30
8, Line WL 28 G23
8, Mersea Rd EX 5 D5-6
8, Perth Ln PT 15 Q17 21 P17
8, Plantagenet Concession PR . . . .
. . . . . . 67 P68 P68 68 P69
8, Ramsay Concession LN . . 65 S58 T59
8, Scugog Ln DH 31 E35
8, Sideline DH 31 G35
8, Sideroad (Chatsworth) G . . 27 C18-20
8, Sideroad (Meaford) G 39 Y21
8, South Grimsby Rd NI 18 R-S31
8, Southgate Township Rd G . . 28 F21-23
8, Township Rd OX 16 Q21-23
8 E , Concession HM 23 N28 P27
8 E , Concession (Brockton) . . . .
. . . . 26 E16 27 E17
8 E , Concession (Saugeen Shores) BR . .
. . . . 38 B16
8 E , Concession Rd NR 33 D43
8 E , Concession Rd SM 41 Y27-28
8 E , Flos Rd SM 41 Z28
8 E , Road EX 4 D4 5 D5
8 E , Stephenson Rd MK . . . 59 S33
8 East Arran , Concession BR . 38 A17
8 Elderslie , Concession BR . . 27 C17
8 N , Concession EX 4 D2
8 N , Line SM . . 41 Y29 42 A31 Y30 Z30

8 Nottawasaga , Concession SM . 29 C26
8 S , Line SM 42 A31
8 W , Concession (Brockton) BR . 26 E15
8 W , Concession (Saugeen Shores) BR . .
. . . . 38 B16
8 W , Concession Rd NR 33 D44
8 W , Concession Rd SM . . . 41 Y27
8 W , Flos Rd SM 41 A27-28 Z28
8 W , Road EX 4 D3-4
8 W , Sideroad WL 28 H21-22
8 West Arran , Concession BR . 38 A16-17
8 Rd, Concession HD 17 U27-28
8 Rd, Concession SDG 68 Q72
8 Rd, Zone C 7 X11
8 Sdrd G 39 A21
8 Sdrd, No. HT 23 N28
8 Townsend, Concession NF 16 T24 17 T25
8-9, Concession PT 21 N17
8-9, Concession SM 29 C27
8-9 Rd, Finch Concession SDG . 67 S67-68
8 Mile Rd MD 14 S16 15 S17
8 Mile Rd SD 90 E10
8A, Drummond Concession LN . . . .
. . . . 48 V57 49 V58
8B, Drummond Concession LN . . 49 V58
8th Av NI 18 R32 19 R33
8th Av PS 77 P31
8th Concession G 28 C23
8th Concession LN 65 R57 R-S58
8th Concession (East Gwillimbury) Y . . .
. . . . 30 D32
8th Concession (King) Y. . . 30 G-H30
8th Concession, North Burgess LN . . . . .
. . . . 49 W-X58
8th Concession A G 28 C23-24
8th Concession B G 28 C24 29 C25
8th Concession Dalhousie LN . . 48 V56
8th Concession N G 39 Y-Z20
8th Concession S G 39 A20
8th Concession Rd (Essex) EX . . 4 E3
8th Concession Rd (Lakeshore[Tilbury
North]) EX . . . .
8th Concession Rd (Tecumseh) EX . 4 C-D2
8th Concession A Lanark LN . . 65 U57-58
8th Concession B Lanark LN . . 65 U57
8th Concession C Lanark LN . . 65 T57
8th Concession Rd BT 16 S22-23
8th Concession Rd DH 31 G34-35
8th Concession Rd NF . . 10 W22-23 X22
8th Concession Rd (Elizabethtown-Kitley)
LG 50 Y62
8th Concession Rd (Rideau Lakes) LG . . .
. . . . 48 Y-Z57
8th Line PB 44 B40-41
8th Line, Asphodel PB . . . 33 C44 45 B44
8th Line, Douro PB 33 C41 44 B41
8th Line, Laxton Township K . . 43 Y36
8th Line Rd (Ottawa[Gloucester]) OT . . .
. . . . 66 R64
8th Line Rd (Ottawa[Osgoode]) OT . 67 T65
8th Line Rd F 36 E57
8th Line Rd LG 49 Z61
8th Line Rd North/Dummer PB . 45 A43 Z43
8th Line Rd South/Dummer PB . 45 A-B43
8th Ln C 6 B8-9
8th Ln DF 29 F-H25
8th Ln (Erin) WL 23 J26 K27
8th Ln (Essa) SM 30 D29
8th Ln (Halton Hills) HT . . 23 K27 L28
8th Ln (Mapleton) WL 22 K22
8th Ln (Milton) HT 24 M-N29
8th Ln (Minto) WL 27 H20 28 H21
8th Ln (New Tecumseth) SM . 29 F28 30 F29
8th Ln (Oakville) HT 24 M29-30
8th Ln E NR 34 C46
8th Ln NE DF 28 D24 29 D25
8th Ln SW DF 28 F24
8th Ln W NR 33 C45
8th Ln W WL 22 K23
8th Rd SDG 67 S68
8th Rd E HM 18 R30
8th Sdrd E G 39 C19-20
8th St NF 16 V24
8th Line Beckwith LN . . . 65 T60 U59

9, Alfred Concession PR 68 P69
9, Concession BR 26 D15
9, Concession DH 31 C34 C35
9, Concession HD 17 U26-27
9, Concession WL 28 H21
9, Concession Rd SDG 68 R-S72
9, Concession Rd SM . . . 42 Z33 43 Z34
9, Concession Rd (Brock) DH . . 43 A34-35
9, Concession Rd (Clarington) DH . . . . .
. . . . 31 F36 32 F37
9, Concession Rd (East Hawkesbury) PR
. . . . 68 Q72
9, Concession Rd (Nation) PR . 68 Q69-70
9, Fire Rte PB 44 Z41
9, Lane A 86 D96
9, Line NI 19 R35
9, Line SM 30 E30
9, Ln PT 15 Q18-19
9, Mersea Rd EX 5 D5-6
9, Normanby Rd G 27 F19
9, Plantagenet Concession PR . . . .
. . . . . 67 P68 Q67-68 68 P69
9, Scugog Ln DH 31 E35
9, Sideroad (Centre Wellington) WL 22 J24
9, Sideroad (Erin) WL 23 K26-27
9, Township Rd OX 16 Q21-23
9, Windham Rd NF 16 U23-24
9 E , Concession HM 23 N28 P27
9 E , Concession Rd SM . . . 41 Y27-28
9 E , Sideroad WL 28 H22
9 N , Line SM . . . 42 A31 Y30 Z30
9 Nottawasaga , Concession SM . . . . . .
. . . . 29 C-D25 40 B25
9 S , Concession EX 4 D2
9 S , Line SM 42 A31
9 Sunnidale , Concession SM . . 41 B27
9 W , Concession Rd NR . . 33 D43 D44
9 W , Road EX 4 D3-4
9 W , Sideroad WL 28 H22
9 Concession, Saugeen Shores BR . 39 A21

9 Rd, Concession HD 17 U27
9 Rd, Line LG 49 Y60-61
9 Rd, Zone C 7 X11
9 Sdrd, Sideroad (Georgian Bluffs) G . . .
. . . . 39 A18
9 Sdrd, Sideroad (Meaford) G . 39 A21
9-10 Sdrd Nottawasaga SM . 29 C27 41 B27
9-10 Sdrd Sunnidale SM . . 29 C27 41 B27
9 Mile Rd MD 14 S16 15 S17
9 Mile Rd PR 67 P67
9 Mile Rd (North Stormont) SDG . 67 T67
9 Mile Rd (South Dundas) SDG . 50 W65
9 Mile Rd (South Glengarry) SDG . 68 T71
9 Mile Point Rd F 36 E56
9A, Drummond Concession LN . . . .
. . . . 48 V57 49 V58
9A, Sdrd, Sideroad G 27 C19
9B Sdrd, Sideroad G 27 C20
9th Av NI 18 R-S32
9th Concession LN 65 R57 R-S58
9th Concession, Bathurst LN . . 48 V-W57
9th Concession, Somerville K . . 44 Y38
9th Concession Darling LN . . 65 T57
9th Concession (Essex) EX 4 D3
9th Concession Rd (Lakeshore[Tilbury
North]) EX 5 D6 6 C6
9th Concession Rd (Tecumseh) EX . 4 C-D2
9th Concession A Dalhousie LN . 48 V56
9th Concession A Lanark LN . . 65 U57-58
9th Concession B Dalhousie LN . 48 V56
9th Concession B Lanark LN . . 65 T57
9th Concession Rd BT 16 S22-23
9th Concession Rd DH 31 G34-35
9th Concession RJ LA 47 A53
9th Concession Rd LG . . . 48 Y56-57 Z57
9th Line PB 45 B44
9th Line, Douro PB 33 C41 44 B41
9th Line Rd (Ottawa[Gloucester]) OT . . .
. . . . 66 R64
9th Line Rd (Ottawa[Osgoode]) OT . 67 T65
9th Line Rd F 36 E57
9th Line Rd LN 65 T59-60 U59
9th Ln C 6 C8
9th Ln LN 65 U57-58
9th Ln NR 33 F41
9th Ln PL 24 L-M29
9th Ln WL 23 J26 J-K27
9th Ln Y 31 E-H33
9th Ln (Amaranth) DF 29 F-H25
9th Ln (East Garafraxa) DF . 23 J25 28 H24
9th Ln (Essa) SM 30 C-D29
9th Ln (Grey Highlands) G . 28 C22 40 B22
9th Ln (Halton Hills) HT . . 23 K27 L28
9th Ln (Innisfil) SM . . 30 C29 C30-31
9th Ln (Meaford) G 40 Z22
9th Ln (New Tecumseth) SM . . . .
. . . . 29 F28 30 E29 F29
9th Ln (Oakville) HT 24 M29-30
9th Ln W NR 33 C45
9th Rd OX 16 U21-23
9th Rd, Little OX 41 Z28
9th Rd, Line NI 18 R30
9th Sdrd DF 29 E27
9th Sdrd G 40 B23-24
9th Sdrd (WGR) G 27 D20
9th St NI 19 R33
9th St SDG 52 U70
9th Murray Rd HS 34 D46

10, Alfred Concession PR 68 P69
10, Charlotteville Rd NF . . 16 V23-24
10, Concession DH 31 C34 C35
10, Concession G 39 Z19
10, Concession HD 17 U26
10, Concession (Brockton) DH . . . .
. . . . 26 D-E16 27 D17-18
10, Concession (Chatsworth) G . 39 A-B21
10, Concession (Huron-Kinloss) BR . . . . .
. . . . 26 E14
10, Concession (Kincardine) BR . 26 C15-16
10, Concession (NDR) G 27 D19
10, Concession (Saugeen Shores) BR . . .
. . . . 38 A-B16
10, Concession (South Bruce) . . . .
. . . . 26 F16 27 F17
10, Concession (Southgate [Proton]) G . .
. . . . 28 E23 F22
10, Concession (West Grey) G . 28 C21-22
10, Concession Rd PR . . . 67 Q68 68 P69
10, Concession Rd SM . . . 42 Z33 43 Z34
10, Concession Rd (Brock) DH . . 43 A34
10, Concession Rd (Clarington) DH . . . . .
. . . . 32 F37 F38
10, Fire Rte PB 45 Z42
10, Lane A 86 D96
10, Line SM 30 E30
10, Line WL 28 G22-23
10, Ln PT 21 P17
10, Mersea Rd EX 5 D5-6
10, North Belmont Township PB . 45 A44
10, Plantagenet Concession PR . 67 Q68
10, Road EX 4 D4 5 D5
10, Scugog Ln DH 31 E35
10, Sdrd (New Tecumseth) SM 30 E29 F-G29
10, Sdrd (Ramara) SM . . . 42 Z33 43 Z34
10, Sideroad WL 23 L25 L26
10, Sideroad (Brockton) BR . . . 26 D16
10, Sideroad (Centre Wellington) . . . . . .
. . . . 22 K23 L23-24
10, Sideroad (Erin) WL . . 23 J-K27 K26
10, Sideroad (Kincardine) BR . 26 D14
10, Sideroad (Northern Bruce Peninsula)
BR 55 V17
10, Sideroad (Saugeen Shores) BR . . . . .
. . . . 26 C16 38 B16
10, Sideroad (South Bruce) G . 27 G17
10, Sideroad (West Grey [Glenelg]) G . . .
. . . . 28 D21
10, Sideroad (West Grey [Normanby]) G . .
. . . . 27 F19
10, South Belmont Township PB . . . . . .
. . . . 45 B44-45
10, South Grimsby Rd NI . . . 18 R30-31
10, Southgate Township Rd G . 28 F21-23
10, Township Rd OX 16 Q21-23
10, Windham Rd NF 16 U23-24
10 E , Concession MA 72 K9-10
10 E , Concession (South Bruce) . . . .
. . . . 27 F18

10 E , Flos Rd SM 41 Z28-29
10 E , Sideroad WL 28 H22-23
10 East Arran , Concession BR . . .
. . . . 38 A17 39 A18
10 Elderslie , Concession BR . . . . .
. . . . 27 C17 38 B17 39 B18
10 N , Line SM 42 A31 Y-Z30
10 N , Sideroad WL 23 M-N25
10 N , Sideroad (Brockton) BR . . 27 D17
10 N , Sideroad (Huron-Kinloss) BR . .
. . . . 26 E14-15
10 North Arran , Sideroad BR . . 38 A17
10 North Elderslie , Sideroad BR . . .
. . . . 27 C17 38 B17
10 Nottawasaga , Concession SM . . .
. . . . 29 C25 D25 40 B25
10 S , Line SM 42 A31
10 S , Sideroad WL 23 N25
10 S , Sideroad (Brockton) BR . 27 E17-18
10 S , Sideroad (Huron-Kinloss) BR . . .
. . . . 26 F14
10 South Arran , Sideroad BR . . 38 A-B17
10 South Elderslie , Sideroad BR . . .
. . . . 27 C-D17
10 Sunnidale , Concession SM . . 41 B27
10 W , Concession HM 23 N26-27
10 W , Concession MA 41 X27
10 W , Concession SM 41 Y27
10 W , Flos Rd SM 41 Z27-28
10 W , Sideroad WL 28 H22
10 West Arran , Concession BR . 38 A16-17
10 Rd, Zone C 7 X12
10 Sdrd (Chatsworth) G 39 B20
10 Sdrd (Georgian Bluffs) G . . . 39 Z19
10 Sdrd (Grey Highlands) G . . . 28 D22
10 Sdrd (Meaford) G 40 B22
10 Sdrd Adjala SM 29 F28
10 Townsend , Concession NF . . . .
. . . . 16 U24 17 U25
10-11 , Concession DF 28 G24
10-11 Rd, Finch Concession SDG . . .
. . . . 67 S67 T66
10-11 Sdrd, Concession PS . . 76 N29-30
10 & 11 , Concession PS . . . .
10 Mile Rd MD 14 S16 15 S17
10 Mile Point Rd S MA 73 K12
10 Mile Point Rd W MA 73 K12
10A, Drummond Concession LN . . .
. . . . 48 V57 49 V58
10A, Fire Rte PB 45 Z42
10A, Sideroad BR 27 F-G17
10A, Sideroad G 40 B22
10B, Drummond Concession LN . 65 U58
10B, Sideroad BR 26 F16 27 F17
10B, Sideroad G 40 B22-23
10C, Sdrd G 40 B23
10D, Sdrd G 40 B23
10th Av G 27 E19
10th Av TM 85 N-P26
10th Concession HM 23 N25-26
10th Concession LN 65 Q-R57
10th Concession PS 57 R28 58 S29
10th Concession Y 30 G29-30
10th Concession (Grey Highlands) G . .
. . . . 28 C23-24 40 B25
10th Concession (Meaford) G . . 39 A20
10th Concession Dalhousie LN . . 48 V56
10th Concession Darling LN . . 65 S-T57
10th Concession Rd (Essex) EX . . 4 C3
10th Concession Rd (Lakeshore[Tilbury
West]) EX 5 D5-6
10th Concession Rd (Tecumseh) EX . .
. . . . 4 C-D2
10th Concession A Lanark LN . . 65 U58
10th Concession B Lanark LN . . 65 U58
10th Concession C Lanark LN . . 65 T57
10th Concession D Lanark LN . . 65 T57
10th Concession BT 16 S23-24
10th Concession EX 4 C3
10th Concession Rd LG 48 Y56
10th Concession Rd NF . . . 10 W22-23
10th Line PB 44 B41
10th Line, Asphodel PB 45 B44
10th Line, Laxton Township L . . 43 X36
10th Line Rd (Ottawa[Gloucester]) OT . .
. . . . 66 Q64
10th Line Rd (Ottawa[Osgoode] OT 67 S65
10th Line Rd F 36 D-E57
10th Line Rd LG 49 Z60
10th Line Rd South/Dummer PB . 45 B44
10th Ln C 6 C8
10th Ln HT 23 K27-28 L28
10th Ln LN 65 U58
10th Ln NR 32 E40
10th Ln OX 15 Q-R20
10th Ln PL 24 L-M29
10th Ln SM 40 A25
10th Ln Y 31 G33
10th Ln Beckwith LN . . . 65 T60 T-U59
10th Ln E NR 45 B46
10th Ln NE DF 29 D25
10th Ln SW DF 28 F24
10th Ln W NR 33 C45
10th Rd E HM 18 R30
10th Sdrd HT 23 L28 M27
10th Sdrd (Amaranth) DF . . . 29 G25-26
10th Sdrd (Barrie Island) MA . . 71 J6
10th Sdrd (Bradford West Gwillimbury)
SM 38 G23
10th Sdrd (Cockburn Island) MA . 70 J1
10th Sdrd (East Garafraxa) DF . . .
. . . . 23 J25 29 H25
10th Sdrd (Essa) SM . . 29 D30 30 D30
10th Sdrd (Innisfil) SM 30 D30
10th Sdrd (Mono) DF 29 E26
10th Sdrd (Mulmur) DF 29 E26
10th Sdrd (NDR) G 27 D19
10th Sdrd (SDR) G 27 E19
10th Sdrd (The Blue Mountain) G . . .
. . . . 40 A-B23 Z23
10th St G 27 E19

10th St SDG 52 U70-71
10th St TM 85 M28
10th St E G 39 Z19
10th St W G 39 Z19
10th Side Rd A 86 E94

11 TB 102 B2 D3 D5 103 B10 C6
11 , Alfred Concession PR . . . 68 P69
11 , Charlotteville Rd NF 16 V23
11 , Concession BR 26 D15
11 , Concession DH 31 C35
11 , Concession HD 17 T26-27
11 , Concession (Chatsworth) G . 39 A21
11 , Concession (Georgian Bluffs) G 39 A18
11 , Concession (Puslinch) WL . 23 M26
11 , Concession (Wellington North) . .
. . . . 28 H21
11 , Concession Rd PR . . 67 Q68 68 Q69
11 , Concession Rd SM 42 Z33
11 , Drummond Concession LN . 65 U58-59
11 , Line SM 30 E30
11 , Ln PT 15 Q17-18
11 , Mersea Rd EX 5 D5-6
11 , Old Highway PS 95 J32
11 , Old Hwy A 77 K32
11 , Road EX 4 D4 5 D5
11 , Route PR 67 P-Q68
11 , Sideroad WL 22 K23
11 , South Grimsby Rd NI 18 R30
11 , Southgate Township Sdrd G . 28 F23
11 , Township Rd OX 16 Q22-23
11 , Windham Rd NF 16 U23-24
11 E , Concession HM 23 N27
11 E , Concession Rd NR 33 C44
11 E , Concession Rd SM 41 Y27
11 E , Flos Rd SM 41 Z28
11 N , Line SM 42 A31 Y-Z30
11 Nottawasaga , Concession SM . . .
. . . . 29 C25 40 B25
11 S , Line SM 42 A31
11 Thorah , Concession DH . . . 43 X38
11 W , Concession Rd NR 33 C44
11 W , Concession Rd SM 41 Y27
11 W , Flos Rd SM 41 Z27-28
11 Walpole , Concession HD . . 17 T26
11 Townsend , Concession NF . . . .
. . . . 16 U24 17 U25
11-12 Rd, Finch Concession SDG . . .
. . . . 67 S66-67
11A, Ramsay Concession LN . . 65 S58-59
11B, Ramsay Concession LN . . 65 S58
11th Concession Y . . . 30 G-H29 31 H34
11th Concession (Mississippi Mills) . .
. . . . 65 Q-R57
11th Concession, Sunnidale K . 44 X38
11th Concession Dalhousie LN . 48 V55-56
11th Concession Rd (Essex) EX . . 4 D2
11th Concession Rd (Lakeshore) EX . 5 D5-6
11th Concession Rd (Tecumseh) EX 4 C-D3
11th Concession A Lanark LN . . 65 U58
11th Concession B Lanark LN . . 65 T58
11th Concession C Lanark LN . . 65 T58
11th Concession D Lanark LN . . 65 T57
11th Concession E Lanark LN . . 65 T57
11th Concession Rd BT . . . 16 S22-23
11th Concession Rd NF 16 W22
11th Line PB 44 A41 B40-41
11th Line (Tay Valley) LN . . 48 W55-56
11th Line, Asphodel PB 45 B44
11th Line, Belmont Township PB . 45 B44
11th Line Rd F 36 D-E57
11th Line Rd Mid Dummer PB . 45 A-B44
11th Line Rd North/Dummer PB . 45 Z43
11th Line Rd South/Dummer PB . . .
. . . . 45 A-B44 B44
11th Ln C 6 C8-9
11th Ln DF 28 H24 29 H25
11th Ln OX 15 Q-R20
11th Ln WL 27 H19
11th Ln (Essa) SM 30 C-D29
11th Ln (Grey Highlands) G . . . 40 A22
11th Ln (Meaford) G . 39 A21 Y-Z21 40 A22
11th Ln (New Tecumseth) SM . . . .
. . . . 29 E28 30 E29
11th Ln (The Blue Mountain) G . 40 B23
11th Ln E NR 45 B46
11th Ln N W NR 33 C45 45 B45
11th Rd E HM 18 R30
11th Sdrd G 40 Z23
11th St NI 19 R33

12 , Charlotteville Rd NF . . . 16 V23
12 , Concession MA 72 K9
12 , Concession G 22 J21
12 , Concession (Brockton) BR . 27 D17-18
12 , Concession (Chatsworth) G . . .
. . . . 27 C18 39 B18
12 , Concession (Huron-Kinloss) BR 26 E14
12 , Concession (Kincardine) BR . 26 C15-16
12 , Concession (NDR) G 27 C-D19
12 , Concession (South Bruce) BR . .
. . . . 26 F16 27 F17
12 , Concession (Southgate) G . 28 E24
12 , Concession (West Grey [Glenelg])
G 27 C20-21
12 , Concession (West Grey [Normanby])
G 27 F19-20
12 , Concession Rd PR . . 67 Q68 68 Q69
12 , Concession Rd SM . . . .
. . . 42 Y-Z33 Z32-33 43 Y34
12 , Dalhousie Concession LN . 48 V55-56
12 , Fire Rte PB 45 Z41 45 A45
12 , Huntley Concession Rd OT . 65 S59
12 , Line HU 20 P16
12 , Line SM 30 E30
12 , Line WL 28 H20
12 , Ln PT 20 P16 21 P17
12 , Mersea Rd EX 5 E5 E-F6
12 , Ramsay Concession LN . . 65 S-T59
12 , Scugog Ln DH 31 E34-35
12 , Sideline DH 31 G34
12 , Sideroad (Centre Wellington) WL . .
. . . . 22 L24
12 , Sideroad (Puslinch) WL . . . . .
. . . . 22 J-K21 23 M-N25
12 , South Grimsby Rd NI 18 R30
12 , Southgate Township Rd G . . . .
. . . . 28 E-F23 F21-22

12 , Stephenson Rd MK 59 R-S33
12 , Township Rd OX . . 16 Q21-22 22 P22-23
12 , Windham Rd NF 16 U23-24
12 E , Concession HM 23 N27
12 E , Concession (South Bruce) BR . .
. . . . 27 F18
12 E , Concession Rd NR . . . 33 C44-45
12 E , Concession Rd SM 41 Y27
12 East Arran , Concession BR . . . .
. . . . 38 A17 39 A18
12 IL , Kenyon Concession Rd SDG . . .
. . . . 68 S-T70
12 N , Line SM . . . 42 A31 Y-Z30 43 A31
12 S , Line SM 42 A31
12 Sunnidale , Concession SM . 41 A-B27
12 W , Concession Rd SM 41 Y27
12 Walpole , Concession HD . . 17 T26
12 West Arran , Concession BR . 38 A16-17
12 Rd, Concession F 48 Z56
12 Townsend , Concession NF . . . .
. . . . 16 U23-24 17 U25
12-13 , Concession DF 28 F-G24
12-13 Sdrd Nottawasaga SM . . 29 C25-27
12-13 Sdrd Sunnidale SM . . . 29 C27
12 Mile Rd SD 90 E10
12 Mile Bay Rd MK 57 U28
12 Mile Lake Rd HL 60 U-V37
12A, Drummond Concession LN . 48 V57
12D, Drummond Concession LN . 65 U58
12th Concession LN 65 Q57 R58
12th Concession MA 70 H1
12th Concession PS 77 N33
12th Concession Y 30 G29
12th Concession A G 28 C22
12th Concession B G . 28 C23-24 40 B25
12th Concession Dalhousie LN . 48 V55-56
12th Concession Rd (Essex) EX . . 4 D2
12th Concession Rd (Tecumseh) EX 4 C-D3
12th Concession B Lanark LN . . 65 U58
12th Concession C Lanark LN . . 65 T57-58
12th Concession Rd BT . . . 16 S23-24
12th Concession Rd NF 10 W22
12th Line (Smith-Ennismore-Lakefield)
PB 44 A41
12th Line, Asphodel PB 45 B44
12th Line Rd F 36 D-E57
12th Line Rd Dummer PB . . . 45 A-B44
12th Ln DF 23 J25 29 H25
12th Ln G 27 D19
12th Ln SM 29 E28 30 E29
12th Ln (Mapleton) WL 22 J22
12th Ln (Minto) WL 27 G20
12th Ln E NR 45 B46
12th Sdrd EX 5 D-E6
12th Sdrd (The Blue Mountain) . . .
. . . . . 40 A24-25 B23-24
12th Sdrd (West Grey) G 27 D20

13 , Concession DH 31 C34-35
13 , Concession G 39 B18
13 , Concession HD 17 T26
13 , Concession Rd SM . . 42 Y33 43 Y34
13 , Line SM 30 E30
13 , Route PR 67 P-Q68
13 , Sideroad (Wellington North) WL . .
. . . . 28 G23 H23
13 , South Grimsby Rd NI 18 R30
13 , Southgate Township Sdrd G 28 E23 F23
13 , Township Rd OX 16 Q21
13 , Windham Rd NF 16 U24
13 E , Concession Rd NR . . . 33 C44-45
13 E , Concession Rd SM 41 X27
13 East Arran , Concession BR . 38 A17
13 N , Line SM 42 A31
13 W , Concession Rd SM . . 41 X-Y27 Y27
13 West Arran , Concession BR . 38 A17
13 Sdrd G 40 Z22
13 Townsend , Concession NF . . 17 U25
13 14 , Sideroad BR 38 B15-16
13 Island Lake Rd F 36 A55
13 Mile Rd MD 14 R-S16
13A, Sideroad 40 B22
13B, Sideroad 40 B23
13th Concession Rd EX 4 D2-3
13th Concession Rd BT 16 T23
13th Concession Rd NF 10 W22
13th Line PB 44 A41
13th Line Rd F 36 D57
13th Ln C 6 C9
13th Ln DF 29 H25
13th Ln WL 27 G19
13th Ln (East Zorra-Tavistock) OX . .
. . . . 15 Q20 16 Q-R21
13th Ln (Innisfil) SM 30 C29
13th Ln (New Tecumseth) SM 29 E28 30 E29
13th Ln (Zorra) OX 15 R-S19
13th Ln E NR 45 B46
13th Ln W NR 45 B45
13th St NF 16 U24 17 U25
13th St NI 19 R33
13th St SDG 52 U70
13th St W G 39 Z19

14 , Concession DH 31 C34
14 , Concession G 27 C20 28 C21
14 , Concession HD 17 T26
14 , Concession MA 72 J9
14 , Concession WL 22 J21
14 , Concession (Brockton) BR . 26 D16
14 , Concession (Georgian Bluffs) G . .
. . . . 39 Y18-19
14 , Concession (NDR) G . . . 27 C18-19
14 , Concession (Saugeen Shores) BR . .
. . . . 38 A16
14 , Concession (South Bruce) BR . .
. . . . 26 F16 27 E-F18
14 , Concession (West Grey) G . 27 F19-20
14 , Concession Rd PR 67 Q68
14 , Ln PT 15 Q18 21 P17
14 , Route PR 67 P68
14 , Scugog Ln DH 31 D-E35
14 , Sideline DH 31 G34-35
14 , Sideroad WL 22 L24
14 , South Grimsby Rd NI 18 R30
14 , Southgate Township Rd G . . . .
. . . . . 27 F20 28 E23 F21-22
14 , Township Rd OX . . 22 P21-22 22 P22-23
14 , Windham Rd NF 16 U24

14 E , Concession BR 27 D18
14 E , Concession HM 23 N26-27
14 E , Concession Rd NR . . . 33 C44-45
14 E , Concession Rd SM 41 X27
14 IL , Kenyon Concession Rd SDG . . .
. . . . 68 S70
14 N , Line SM 42 Z31
14 S , Line SM 42 A31-32
14 W , Concession BR 27 D17
14 W , Concession Rd SM . . 41 X-Y27
14 Ln, Old OX 16 S22
14 Townsend, Concession NF . . 17 U25
14 Island La F 36 A55
14 Mile Rd MD 14 R16 15 R17
14th Av Y 31 H33
14th Concession MA 70 H1
14th Line PB 44 A41
14th Line Rd F 36 D-E57
14th Ln OX 15 Q20 16 Q21 R21
14th Ln (Innisfil) SM 30 D-E30
14th Ln (Mapleton) WL 22 J22
14th Ln (Minto) WL 27 G19-20
14th Ln (New Tecumseth) SM 29 E28 30 E29
14th Ln E NR 45 B45-46
14th Ln W NR 45 B45
14th Sdrd HT 23 M28

15 , Concession HD 17 T26
15 , Concession Rd PR . . 67 Q68 68 Q69
15 , Ln PT 15 Q18 21 P18
15 , Mersea Rd EX 5 E6
15 , Old Highway LG 49 X59
15 , Sdrd (New Tecumseth) SM . 30 E-G29
15 , Sdrd (Ramara) SM . 42 Y-Z33 43 A34
15 , Sideroad (Brockton) BR . 26 D16 27 E18
15 , Sideroad (Centre Wellington) WL . .
. . . . 22 J24 K23-24
15 , Sideroad (Erin) WL . . 23 J26-27 K26
15 , Sideroad (Georgian Bluffs) G . 39 Z18
15 , Sideroad (Kincardine) BR . 26 C15
15 , Sideroad (Meaford) G . 39 Z20 Z21
15 , Sideroad (Puslinch) WL . . 23 M26
15 , Sideroad (South Bruce) BR . 27 G17
15 , Sideroad (South Bruce Peninsula) BR
. . . . 55 Y17
15 , Sideroad (Wellington North) WL . .
. . . . . 28 F-G23 H23-24
15 , Southgate Township Sdrd G . 28 E-F23
15 Arran , Sideroad BR . . . 38 A-B17
15 IL , Kenyon Concession Rd SDG . . .
. . . . 68 S70
15 N , Line SM 42 Z31
15 N , Sideroad (Kincardine) BR . . .
. . . . 26 D15 E14
15 N , Sideroad (South Bruce) . 27 F18
15 North Arran , Sideroad BR . . 38 A17
15 North Elderslie , Sideroad BR . 38 B17
15 S , Line SM 42 A32 Z32
15 S , Sideroad (Arran-Elderslie) BR . .
. . . . 27 C17
15 S , Sideroad (Huron-Kinloss) BR 26 E14
15 S , Sideroad (South Bruce) BR 27 F-G18
15 South Elderslie , Sideroad BR . 27 C17
15 W , Concession Rd SM . . 41 X26-27
15 Rd NI 18 S32
15 Sdrd G 28 C22
15 Sdrd Tosorontio SM . . . 29 D27-28
15-16 Sdrd G 42 A30-31
15-16 Sdrd, Lot 75 . . . . 76 N29
15-16 Sdrd Nottawasaga SM . . 29 C25
15-16 Sdrd Sunnidale SM . . . 41 B27
15 Mile Rd A 44 R15-16
15th Line Rd F 37 D-E58
15th Ln C 6 C9 7 C10
15th Ln DF 29 H25
15th Ln SM 30 E29
15th Ln WL 27 G19
15th Ln (East Zorra-Tavistock) OX . .
. . . . 16 Q-R21 22 P21
15th Ln (Zorra) OX 15 Q-S18 S-T19
15th Sdrd EX 22 J24
15th Sdrd HT 23 L27-28 M27
15th Sdrd TB 102 E5
15th Sdrd Y 30 G31 G-H30
15th Sdrd (Amaranth) DF . . . 29 G25-26
15th Sdrd (Barrie Island) MA . . 71 J6
15th Sdrd (Cockburn Island) MA . 70 J1
15th Sdrd (East Garafraxa) DF . 29 H25
15th Sdrd (Melancthon) DF . . 29 E25
15th Sdrd (Mono) DF 29 E25
15th Sdrd (Mulmur) DF 29 E25
15th Sdrd (Tehkummah) MA . . 73 M11
15th Sdrd (The Blue Mountain) G . 40 A24
15th Sdrd (WGR) G 27 D20
15th St NI 19 R33
15th Side Rd A 86 E94

16 , Concession BR 26 D16
16 , Concession HD 17 T26
16 , Concession WL . . . 22 J22 28 H22
16 , Concession (Georgian Bluffs) G . .
. . . . 39 Y18
16 , Concession (West Grey) G . 27 E-F19
16 , Concession Rd PR 67 Q-R68
16 , Fire Rte PB 45 Z42-43
16 , Ln PT 20 N-P16 21 P17-18
16 , Pike Lake Rte LN 48 X57
16 , Route PR 67 P-Q68
16 , Sideline DH 31 G34 H34-35
16 , Sideroad (Mapleton) WL . 22 J22 K-L21
16 , South Grimsby Rd NI 18 R30
16 E , Concession Rd SM 41 X27
16 IL , Kenyon Concession Rd SDG . . .
. . . . 68 S69-70
16 N , Sideroad . 18 R-S30 S31-32 19 S33
16 Sdrd G 39 Z21 40 Z22
16 Mile Rd MD 14 R16
16A, Sideroad 39 B21 40 B22
16A, Sideroad WL 40 B22
16B, Sideroad 40 B22
16C, Sideroad 40 B22
16th Av Y 30 H32 31 H33-34
16th Line PB 44 A41
16th Line Rd F 37 D-E58
16th Ln C 6 C9 7 C10
16th Ln OX 16 Q-R21 22 P21
16th Ln (Mapleton) WL 22 J22-23
16th Ln (Minto) WL 27 G20
16th Sdrd Y 30 G29-31

16th St E G 39 Z19-20
16th St S BR 38 Z16-17

17 A 84 A92 W01 Y91-92
. . 86 B93 B94 E95 E97 E7 E1 E8 F3 F6 E8 F9
17 TB 102 B2 D3 D5 103 B10 C6
17 , Concession HD 17 T26
17 , Concession (Georgian Bluffs) G 39 Y18
17 , Concession (West Grey) G . 27 E19
17 , Concession Rd PR . . 67 R68 68 Q69
17 , County Rd EX 4 C3
17 , Line HU 20 N15-16
17 , Ln PT 20 N15-16
17 , Old Highway CS 100 D16-17
17 , Old Hwy A 84 Y92
17 , Pike Lake Rte LN . . . 48 X57 X9 X58
17 , Sideroad DH . . . 31 C-D34 43 A34
17 , Sideroad (Erin) WL . . . 23 J-K26
17 , Sideroad (Mapleton) WL . 22 K21-22
17 E , Concession Rd SM 41 X27
17 IL , Kenyon Concession Rd SDG . . .
. . . . 68 S69
17 W , Concession Rd SM . . 41 X26-27
17 Sdrd Tosorontio SM 29 D27
17-18 Sdrd SM 29 C25
17 Mile Rd A 89 D10
17A, Sideroad DH 31 D34
17B A 84 Y92
17th Av Y G-H33
17th Line Rd E SM . . 41 W27-28 X27
17th Line PB 44 A40-41
17th Line Rd F 37 D-E58
17th Ln C 7 C10
17th Ln DF 29 H25
17th Ln (East Zorra-Tavistock) OX . .
. . . . 16 R21 22 P21
17th Ln (Zorra) OX 15 S-T19
17th Sdrd DF 29 D26-27
17th Sdrd EX 4 C3
17th Sdrd HT 23 L27-28 M26
17th Sdrd Y 30 G29-31
17th St NI 18 R32

18 , Concession BR 26 D16
18 , Concession G 27 E19
18 , Fire Rte PB . . 44 Z41 45 A45 Z45
18 , Ln PT 21 N-P17
18 , North Kawartha Concession PB . .
. . . . 45 W42
18 , Sdrd SM 30 E-F29
18 , Side Rd NI 18 U32
18 , Sideroad BR 38 F16
18 , Sideroad DH 31 C-D35 43 B35
18 , Sideroad G 39 Y20
18 , Sideroad (Mapleton) WL . . 22 J-K22
18 , South Grimsby Rd NI 18 R30
18 W , Concession Rd SM . . . 41 X26
18 Ext, Concession 27 E19
18-19 , Sideroad BR 26 C15
18-19 Sdrd Nottawasaga SM . . 41 B28
18-19 Sdrd Sunnidale SM . . . 41 B28
18A, Sideroad DH 31 C35 43 B35
18th Concession PS 95 G32
18th Line Rd F 37 D58
18th Ln OX 16 Q21 22 P21
18th Ln PB 44 Z41
18th Ln WL 22 J22-23
18th Sdrd Y 30 G29-31
18th Sdrd (WGR) G 27 D20

19 , Concession Rd PR . . 67 R68 68 R69
19 , Ln PT 20 N15-16
19 , Mersea Rd EX 5 E-F6
19 , Sideroad G 40 B22
19 , Sideroad (Centre Wellington) WL . .
. . . . 22 K24
19 , Sideroad (Mapleton) WL . 22 J23 K-L22
19 , South Grimsby Rd NI 18 R30
19 , Southgate Township Sdrd G 28 E23 F23
19 , Windham Rd NF 16 T-U23
19 E , Concession Rd SM 41 X27
19 IL , Kenyon Concession Rd SDG 68 R69
19 W , Concession Rd SM . . . 41 X28
19th Av Y 30 H32 31 G33
19th Ln C 29 H26
19th Ln (East Zorra-Tavistock) OX . 22 P21
19th Ln (Zorra) OX . . . 15 Q-R18 R-S19
19th Sdrd Y . . . 30 F31 F-G30 G29-30
19th St NI 18 R32
19th Line Rd F 37 D58

20 , Concession BR 27 C-D17
20 , Concession G 39 Y19-20
20 , Concession Rd PR . . 67 R68 68 R69
20 , Fire Rte PB 44 Z41
20 , Ln PT 20 N-P16 21 P19
20 , Perth Ln PT 21 N-P17
20 , Sdrd G 39 X-Y19
20 , Sdrd (New Tecumseth) SM . . .
. . . . 30 E29 F29-30
20 , Sdrd (Ramara) SM 42 Z33
20 , Side Rd NI 18 U32
20 , Sideline 31 G34
20 , Sideroad G 27 E19 F20
20 , Sideroad (Brockton) BR . . 27 D18
20 , Sideroad (Centre Wellington) WL . .
. . . . 22 J23-24
20 , Sideroad (Guelph-Eramosa) WL . .
. . . . 23 K25
20 , Sideroad (Kincardine) BR . 26 D15
20 , Sideroad (Mapleton) WL . 22 J-K23
20 , Sideroad (Saugeen Shores) BR 26 C16
20 , Sideroad (South Bruce) BR . 26 G16
20 , Windham Rd NF 16 U23
20 Arran , Sideroad BR . . . 38 A-B17
20 E , Concession Rd SM . . 41 W-X27
20 N , Sideroad WL 23 N25
20 N , Sideroad (Brockton) BR . 26 D-E16
20 N , Sideroad (Huron-Kinloss) BR . .
. . . . 26 E-F14
20 N , Sideroad (South Bruce) BR . 27 F18
20 North Elderslie , Sideroad BR . . .
. . . . 27 C17 38 B17
20 S , Sideroad WL 23 N26
20 S , Sideroad (Brockton) BR . . . .
. . . . 26 E-F16 27 E18
20 S , Sideroad (Huron-Kinloss) BR . .
. . . . 26 F13-14
20 South Elderslie , Sideroad BR . . .
. . . . 27 C17-18
20 W , Concession Rd SM . . . 41 X26

A, Concession / Bartley

A, Concession G . . . 39 Y-Z20
A, Concession Rd NF . . . 10 X23
A, Concession Rd SM . . . 43 A34
A, Scotch Line Sdrd LN . . 65 U58-59
A Concession, Harris TM . . 85 R30
A Ln A . . . 86 E94 E-F94 F94 G95
A Ln DF . . . 29 H26
A Ln G . . . 39 Z18
A&B Rd C . . . 6 C8
A Guy Wilson Rd HS . . . 62 S47
Ab's Rd LN . . . 65 U59
Abb Rd OT . . . 65 T60
Abbey Rd HD . . . 17 S28
Abbey Rd NI . . . 18 U32
Abbey Dawn Rd F . . . 36 D57
Abbott Rd LG . . . 50 V63
Abbott Rd OT . . . 66 S61
Aberarder Ln LM . . . 12 S9 13 S10
Aberdeen Av HM . . . 17 Q28
Aberdeen Ln EL . . . 8 W-X14
Aberdeen Rd MD . . . 14 T14
Aberdeen Rd NI . . . 18 R32
Aberdeen Rd PR . . . 68 P71
Aberdeen Rd SDG . . . 68 P-Q71
Aberfeldy Ln LM . . . 12 V9 13 V10-11
Abernathy Rd F . . . 36 B57
Abernott Rd A . . . 88 E-F4
Abingdon Rd NI . . . 18 R-S30
Abraham Ln HU . . . 26 H16 27 H17
Abrams Rd HL . . . 61 V43
Abrams Rd LA . . . 35 E52
Abrams Rd LG . . . 37 C58
Absalom Rd LA . . . 36 D-E54
Absalom St BR . . . 27 F18
Academy Hill Rd NR . . . 33 F43
Access Rd F . . . 48 X54
Accommodation Rd F 36 C57 37 C58
Achigan Rd A . . . 84 X93-94
Achray Rd NP . . . 98 K46
Ackerman La BR . . . 55 U16-17
Ackison Rd PB . . . 32 C40
Acme Rd HS . . . 34 E47
Acorn Rd K . . . 43 X-Y36
Acres Rd DH . . . 32 F-G38
Acres Rd MK . . . 59 S35-36
Acres Rd OT . . . 66 T64
Acres Rd R . . . 82 N54
Acrevale Rd K . . . 32 C39
Acton Dr LN . . . 49 W60
Acton Rd DH . . . 31 D-E34
Acton Island Rd MK . . . 58 U30
Actons Corner Rd LG . . . 50 V62
AD Shadd Rd C . . . 6 B8 C9
Adair Rd LA . . . 47 A-B52
Adam & Eve Rd PB . . . 44 Z40
Adam Cummings Rd PB 44 A40 Z40
Adams La PE . . . 34 F48
Adams Ln HU . . . 21 J17 J18
Adams Rd BT . . . 17 R25
Adams Rd DH . . . 32 G39
Adams Rd LN . . . 48 V55
Adams Rd LG . . . 50 W64
Adams Rd NP . . . 96 F35-36
Adams Rd PS . . . 77 L31-32
Adams Rd TB . . . 102 B4
Adams Rd (Carlow Mayo) HS 62 T47
Adams Rd (Quinte West) HS 34 E46
Adanac Rd HL . . . 61 U42
Adanac Rd MA . . . 71 K6
Adare Dr MD . . . 14 Q13-15
Adcock Dr A . . . 86 G95
Adcock La R . . . 63 R49
Addington Rd F . . . 47 W50
Addington Rd R . . . 63 R49
Addison-Greenbush Rd LG 49 Y-Z61
Adelaide Av DH . . . 31 H36
Adelaide Rd MD . . . 14 U14
Adelaide St N MD 14 R-S16 15 S-T17
Adelaide St S MD . . . 15 T17
Adelard Rd R . . . 98 F45
Adeline Tr HL . . . 60 T39
Adirondack La HL . . . 61 V43
Adis Dr BR . . . 55 X17
Adjala-Tecumseth Townline SM . . . 29 E-G28
Admiral Dr MD . . . 15 T17
Adolphustown Park Rd LA . . 35 F52
Adrian Lake Rd TB . . . 102 D1-2
Africa Tr HL . . . 61 T42
Aga Ming Rd PS . . . 57 S28
Agar Rd NR . . . 32 F40
Agnes St MA . . . 72 J7
Agnew Ln HU . . . 26 H15
Agnew Rd R . . . 82 N52
Agnew Rd SM . . . 42 X32
Agnew Lake Rd SD . . . 90 E12
Agnew Lake Mine Rd SD 100 D14-15
Ahmic Lake Rd PS . . . 76 M-N29 N30
Aho Rd A . . . 86 D96
Ahola's Rd PS . . . 77 N34
Aide Rd LA . . . 62 U48
Aide Lake Access Rd HS . . . 62 U47-48 V47
Aikens Rd HS . . . 34 E48
Aikens Rd HD . . . 18 U30
Aino Rd CS . . . 100 D15
Aino Beach Rd K . . . 32 D37
Ainsley Rd HM . . . 23 P26
Ainslie Rd MA . . . 71 K5
Air Service Rd A . . . 88 F4-5
Aird Ct Y . . . 30 D32
Airds Lake Rd R . . . 63 T51-52
Airey Rd EL . . . 7 X13
Airport Dr MD . . . 14 R15-16
Airport La PE . . . 35 G50-51
Airport Ln HU 14 Q15 20 M14 N14 P15
Airport Pkwy HS . . . 34 D49 35 D50
Airport Pkwy OT . . . 66 R63
Airport Rd BR . . . 27 E18
Airport Rd DF . . . 29 D26 E-G27
Airport Rd HL . . . 61 U43
Airport Rd HS . . . 35 E51
Airport Rd HM . . . 17 R28
Airport Rd HU . . . 20 J13
Airport Rd LA . . . 35 C52
Airport Rd LM . . . 12 T8
Airport Rd LN . . . 64 U55
Airport Rd MA . . . 91 J15
Airport Rd NP . . . 95 D32 E31
Airport Rd NI . . . 19 R34
Airport Rd PB . . . 32 D40 33 D41
Airport Rd PL . 24 J29 K30 29 G27 H28
Airport Rd R . . . 80 P47
Airport Rd SDG . . . 52 U72
Airport Rd TM . . . 85 N-P28
Airport Rd (Clearview) SM . . . 29 C26 41 B26
Airport Rd (Elizabethtown-Kitley) LG . . . 50 Z62
Airport Rd (Faraday) HS . 61 U43-44
Airport Rd (Gordon) MA . 71 J6 72 J7
Airport Rd (Joly) PS . . . 77 K32
Airport Rd (Leeds and the Thousand Islands) LG . . . 37 B58
Airport Rd (Little Rapids) A . 87 D98
Airport Rd (Norwich) OX . . . 16 T22
Airport Rd (Quinte West) HS . . . 34 D47-48
Airport Rd (Ramara) SM . 42 Y32-33
Airport Rd (Sault Ste Marie) A . . . 84 B91
Airport Rd (Seguin) PS . . . 57 S28
Airport Rd (South-West Oxford) OX . . . 15 U20 16 U21
Airy Rd NP . . . 79 P41
Aked Rd DH . . . 32 F38
Akins Rd OT . . . 66 S61
Albany St NI . . . 19 U36
Albert Rd BR . . . 26 C14
Albert Rd HS . . . 45 W45
Albert St CS . . . 100 D16
Albert St HU . . . 20 L14
Albert St MA . . . 72 K10
Albert St OX . . . 22 P22
Albert St PS . . . 77 L32
Albert St SM . . . 29 E28
Albert St WT . . . 22 M-N22
Albert St (Saugeen Shores) BR . . . 38 A16
Albert St E SM . . . 41 Z29
Albert St S DH . . . 31 D35
Albert Leroux Rd PR . . . 67 Q-R68
Alberton Rd HM . . . 17 Q-R26
Albion Rd OT . . . 66 R63
Albion Rd T . . . 24 J30 K31
Albion Tr PL . . . 30 G29
Albion Lake Dr HS . . . 61 U44
Albright Rd DH . . . 31 F34
Albuna Townline Rd EX . . . 5 D-E5
Alden Rd Y . . . 24 I-J32 30 H32
Alder La F . . . 48 Y55
Alderdale Rd NP . . . 95 G33
Aldersbrook Rd MD . . . 14 T16
Aldred Dr DH . . . 31 E36
Alex McLean La F . . . 36 B56
Alexander Ct PB . . . 44 X40
Alexander Rd HL . . . 60 U38
Alexander Rd PE . . . 34 G48
Alexander Sdrd HU . . . 20 N15
Alexandra Cr PS . . . 58 S29-30
Alf's Bay La F . . . 47 X52
Alf Patterson Rd F . . . 48 Y55
Algoma St SD . . . 90 F10-11
Algoma St TB . . . 103 D6
Algonquin Av NP . . . 95 E31
Algonquin Rd CS . . . 101 D19
Algonquin Rd K . . . 31 D36
Algonquin Rd LG . . . 50 Y62-63
Algonquin Rd NP . . . 95 G-H34
Algonquin St NP . . . 79 Q46
Algonquin Outfitters Rd HL . 59 Q36
Alice Av TB . . . 103 C6
Allaire Rd SDG . . . 67 R68 68 R69
Allan Rd R . . . 99 G48
Allan St CS . . . 101 C20
Allan's Sdrd LN . . . 49 W58
Allan's Mill Rd LN . . 48 W57 49 X58
Allan Arickson Rd TB . . . 102 F1-2
Allan Carricks Rd SM . . . 42 Y33
Allan Mills Rd NR . . . 45 B46
Allan Park Rd G . . . 27 D-E19
Allanburg Rd NI . . . 19 R-S34
Allanport Rd NI . . . 19 S34
Allbirch Rd OT . . . 65 P60
Allboro Ln HU . . . 20 K15
Allemang Pl WT . . . 22 L22
Allen Rd NP . . . 95 D33
Allen Rd PR . . . 68 N-P70
Allen Rd TM . . . 85 M29
Allen Rd T . . . 24 J31 K32
Allen Rd (Grimsby) NI . . 18 R30-31
Allen Rd (North Dundas) SDG . . . 66 U64
Allen Rd (South Stormont) SDG . . . 67 U67
Allen Rd (West Lincoln) NI . . 18 S30
Allen St A . . . 87 E1-2
Allen St OX . . . 15 S19
Allen's Rd NP . . . 95 D33
Allen's Rd PB . . . 44 A40
Allendale Rd WT . . . 22 N24
Allenford Rd BR . . . 38 Z17
Allens Alley PB . . . 44 X39
Allens Side Rd A . . . 84 A-B91
Allensville Rd MK . . . 59 S33
Allin Rd DH . . . 32 F38
Allington Rd LN . . . 49 W61
Allinotte Rd SDG . . . 68 T69
Allison La HS . . . 62 S46
Allison Ln C . . . 7 B10
Allison Rd PE . . . 35 E50
Allison St NR . . . 33 E45
Allnut Rd SDG . . . 68 S69
Allore Ct HS . . . 47 A50
Allore Rd HS . . . 47 A50
Allport Rd SM . . . 41 W-X27
Alma St EX . . . 4 D1
Almaguin Dr PS . . . 77 P32
Alnwick Hill Rd NR . . . 33 F42
Alouette Rd NP . . . 93 E26
Alp La HS . . . 61 T44
Alpha Rd TB . . . 102 B-C4
Alpine Rd CS . . . 91 E16
Alpine Rd SDG . . . 68 T71-72
Alps Rd WT . . . 22 P23-24
Alps Rd W WT . . . 22 P23
Alsace Rd PS . . . 94 J30 95 H31-32
Alsop Rd HL . . . 60 V40
Alsop's Beach Rd DH . . . 43 B34
Alta Vista Dr OT . . . 66 Q63
Althorpe Rd LN . . . 48 X56
Altman Rd LM . . . 6 X6
Alton Rd TB . . . 102 C5
Alton Rd (South Frontenac) F . . . 36 B55
Altona Rd DH . . . 31 H34
Alvar Rd K . . . 43 Y35
Alves Rd PS . . . 56 Q25
Alvin's La K . . . 44 B39
Alvin Williams Rd SM . . . 41 X28
Alway Rd NI . . . 18 R30
Alyea Rd HS . . . 34 F46
Amabel-Albemarle Townline BR . . . 55 X16-17
Amaranth-East Luther Townline DF . . . 28 F-G24 29 H25
Amberley Rd BR . . . 26 F13-14
Amberley Rd HU . . . 21 J17-18 26 G14 H16 27 H17
Amberley Beach Rd HU . . . 26 F13
Amberwood Rd LN . . . 65 T60
Ambleside La MK . . . 58 T31
Amell & Ranald George Rd SDG . . . 68 T70
Ament Ln WT . . . 22 L21 M21-22
Amethyst Av TB . . . 103 B9
Amethyst Harbour Rd TB . . . 103 B9
Amey Rd F . . . 36 B55
Amherst Dr LA . . . 36 D55
Amiens Rd MD . . . 14 T14-15
Amilia Dr SM . . . 42 Z33
Amyot Rd LN . . . 48 W56
Anaquot Rd BR . . . 38 Z16-17
Anchor Bay Rd PB . . . 44 A40
Andek Tr HL . . . 44 W39
Ander Dr K . . . 43 B37
Anderson La G . . . 27 C19
Anderson La HS . . . 46 Y49
Anderson La LN . . . 48 V-W56
Anderson Ln K . . . 44 Z39
Anderson Ln SM . . . 42 Y30
Anderson Rd A . . . 84 Y91-92
Anderson Rd F . . . 48 Y55
Anderson Rd HL . . . 61 V41
Anderson Rd LN . . . 64 U56
Anderson Rd NR . . . 32 F-G40
Anderson Rd NI . . . 18 T31
Anderson Rd OT . . . 66 R64
Anderson Rd PB . . . 45 A45
Anderson Rd SDG . . . 51 V68
Anderson Sdrd LN . . . 48 V57
Anderson Sdrd S LN . . . 48 V57
Anderson St DH . . . 31 G-H36
André Lyne Rd NP . . . 93 D26
Andrew Dr SM . . . 41 X27
Andrews Dr MD . . . 14 U-V14
Andrews Dr SM . . . 30 F29-30
Andrews Rd DH . . . 32 F39
Andy Neville Pkwy PS . . . 95 J31
Angel Rd HL . . . 60 T39
Angel Rd SDG . . . 68 S-T70
Angela S Foster Rd SM . . . 41 Y28
Angeline St K . . . 32 C37 43 B37
Anger Rd EL . . . 9 W20
Angle Lake Rd MK . . . 59 R35
Angler Ln C . . . 6 A7 Y7
Anglesey dr HL . . . 60 U37-38
Anglesia St BR . . . 38 A16
Anglican Church Rd A . . . 84 Y92
Anglican Church Rd LN . . . 48 W57
Anglican Church Rd LG . . . 49 X59
Angling Rd NF . . . 17 T25
Angus Rd SDG . . . 68 T71
Angus Point Rd PS . . . 77 K-L31
Anich Rd A . . . 84 A91
Anita Av NP . . . 95 E32
Annala Rd TB . . . 102 F2
Anne St N SM . . . 41 B29
Annett Rd LM . . . 7 W11
Anson La HS . . . 45 W45
Anson Rd HS . . . 34 C47
Anson Lake Access Rd HL 59 T-U36
Ansonia Rd A . . . 86 D97 87 D98
Anstruther Lake Rd PB . . . 45 X42
Antelope Tr PB . . . 44 A41
Anthony St SDG . . . 52 U-V71
Antiquary Rd K . . . 43 A35 Z35
Antlers Rd TM . . . 85 M28
Antoine Rd PR . . . 67 R67
Antoine Rd R . . . 81 N48
Antonen Rd SD . . . 90 E12
Antrim Rd C . . . 7 A-B12
Apiary Rd MK . . . 58 U30
Appel La R . . . 64 R54
Apple Dr HL . . . 60 V40
Apple Grove Rd WT . . . 22 M22
Apple Hill Rd SDG . . . 68 S-T70
Apple Orchard Rd NR . . . 33 G42
Apple Orchard Rd OT . . . 66 S63
Appleby Ln HT . . . 18 P29 23 M27-28 24 N29
Applesauce Lake Rd A . 88 B6 89 B7
Appleton Sdrd LN . . . 65 S-T59
Appleyard's Rd PS . . 58 Q32 77 P32
Apsey Lake Rd SD . . . 90 F13
Aragon Rd F . . . 36 C56
Aranda Way NR . . . 33 D-E45
Arbor Vitae Rd R . . . 80 P46
Arbuckle Rd HS . . . 34 D46
Arcadia St NI . . . 19 T35
Arcand Rd LG . . . 66 U63
Arcand Rd NP . . . 94 D29
Archambault Rd SDG . 52 U70 68 T70
Archambeault Rd NP . . . 96 E38
Archer Rd NR . . . 33 G43
Archer Rd SDG . . . 51 V67
Archibald Rd A . . . 86 D95
Archie's Rd MK . . . 58 V29
Archie McAlpin Rd F . . . 37 B58
Arcol Rd F . . . 64 T53-54 U54
Arda Rd MA . . . 72 J9
ARDA Access Rd LN . . . 64 T54-55
Ardagh Rd SM . . . 30 C29
Arden Rd F . . . 47 Y-Z52 48 Y53
Arden Rd LA . . . 47 A52 Z52
Ardoch Rd F . . . 48 W53-54
Arena Boundary Rd F . . . 36 A54
Argo Rd NP . . . 93 E26 94 E27
Argyle Ln EL . . . 7 X13 8 X14
Argyle St MD . . . 14 R-S14
Argyle St N HD . . . 17 S27-28
Argyle St S HD . . . 17 S27-28
Argyll Dr MD . . . 7 W12 13 V12
Argyll Rd LM . . . 13 U-V12
Arkell Rd WL . . . 23 M26
Arkona Rd LM . . . 13 R-T12
Arlwood Rd C . . . 6 Y9
Arlie Rd SDG . . . 50 W-X65
Arlington Blvd EX . . . 4 B3
Arlington Rd SDG . . . 68 T72
Armanda St EX . . . 4 C1
Armitage Av OT . . . 65 P60
Armour Rd LN . . . 49 X58
Armour Rd NP . . . 93 D25-26
Armour Rd PB . . . 33 C41
Armstrong La PB . . 44 Z41 45 Z42-43
Armstrong Ln F . . . 48 X55-56
Armstrong Rd LN . . . 49 V-W59
Armstrong Rd MA . . . 71 J4
Armstrong Rd MA . . . 72 J7
Armstrong Rd SDG . . . 67 T65
Armstrong Rd (Edwardsburgh Cardinal) LG . . . 50 W64
Armstrong Rd (Merrickville-Wolford) LG . . . 49 W61 50 W62
Armstrong Sdrd LN . . . 49 V58
Armstrong-Beauchamp Township Rd TM . . . 85 N-P28
Armstrong-Evanturel Boundary Rd TM . . . 85 N28-29
Armstrong-Jacklin Rd PS . . . 57 S28
Armstrong Point Rd MK . . . 58 T30
Army Camp Rd LM . . . 13 R-S11
Army Reserve Rd PE . . . 35 H51
Arnald La EX . . . 4 C3
Arnell Rd SD . . . 101 C22
Arner Townline Rd EX . . . 4 E-F3
Arnold Rd BT . . . 16 S-T23
Arnold Rd C . . . 6 X7
Arnold Rd LG . . . 49 X61
Arnold Rd NI . . . 19 R35
Arnold's La NF . . . 16 T24
Arnold's Bay Rd MK . . . 57 T27
Arnold T Dr LN . . . 48 W56-57
Arnott Rd LN . . . 64 T56
Arnott Lake Access Rd LA . . 63 U49
Arowhon Rd NP . . . 78 N37
Arrow Dr R . . . 62 Q47 80 P47
Arrowhead Rd G . . . 40 A24
Art's La MK . . . 41 W29
Art Barton La HL . . . 61 T-U41
Art Lang Rd NR . . . 33 F41
Art McGinn's Rd LA . . . 36 E54
Artemesia-Euphrasia Twnln G . . . 28 C22 C23
Artemesia-Glenelg Twnln G . 28 D22
Artemesia-Southgate Twnln G . . . 28 D23 E22
Artesian Industrial Pkwy SM 30 E31
Arthur Rd BT . . . 16 R-S24
Arthur Rd F . . . 36 B56
Arthur Rd HS . . . 46 B47
Arthur Rd LN . . . 48 W56
Arthur Rd PE . . . 34 G47
Arthur St DH . . . 32 G39
Arthur St MA . . . 73 L12-13
Arthur St TB . . . 102 D5 103 D6
Arthur St N WT . . . 22 L22-23
Arthur St S WT . . . 22 L-M22
Arthur Evans Cr SM . . . 30 E30
Arthur Schultz Rd MK . . . 42 W32
Artisan La HL . . . 60 S39
Arundel St TB . . . 103 C6
Arundel Lodge Rd MK . . . 58 U31
Arvids La HL . . . 60 V37
Asam Rd A . . . 86 C96-97
Asbury La HL . . . 59 S-T36
Ash Ln EL . . . 8 X14-15
Ash Rd HS . . . 46 A47
Ash Rd K . . . 44 B38
Ash St WL . . . 23 L26
Ash Bay Rd SD . . . 93 G24
Ashburn Rd DH . . . 37 F-G35
Ashburn Rd SDG . . . 67 S68 T67
Ashburnham Dr PB . . . 33 C41
Ashburton Rd NP . . . 94 C27
Ashby Rd LN . . . 48 V57
Ashby Rd LG . . . 50 Y63
Ashby-Trout Lake Access Rd LA . . . 63 T-U49
Ashby Lake Rd LA . . . 63 U49-50
Ashby White Lake Rd LA . . . 63 T49
Ashdad Rd R . . . 64 R54
Ashfield-Huron Townline BR . 26 F13
Ashforth Dr MK . . . 58 U30-31
Ashgrove La G . . . 39 Y20
Ashick Rd SD . . . 101 C-D23
Ashigami Rd W CS . . . 101 A22
Ashigami Lake Rd CS . . . 101 A-B22
Ashkaby Rd LM . . . 6 X6
Ashley La MK . . . 59 U-V34
Ashley St HS . . . 34 D48
Ashmore Rd EL . . . 8 W16-17
Ashport Rd R . . . 98 G46
Ashport Access Rd R . . . 98 G46-47
Ashton Station Rd OT . . . 65 T-U60
Ashworth Rd DH . . . 31 E33-34
Ashworth Rd MK . . . 58 Q-R32
Askew Rd C . . . 5 D8
Aspdin Rd MK . . . 58 R31-32
Aspen Rd R . . . 64 R55
Aspen Rd TB . . . 102 E4
Asphodel-Seymour Boundary Ln NR . . . 45 B44
Asselstine Rd HS . . . 47 B51
Asselstine Rd LA . . . 35 C52
Asseltine Rd F . . . 36 B56
Assiginack Tr MA . . . 73 L12
Assumption Rd PB . . . 33 D41
Astles Rd A . . . 88 E3
Astorville Rd NP . . . 95 F-G33
Astrolake Rd R . . . 82 N53
Atchison Rd PB . . . 32 D40
Atchison Rd SDG . . . 52 U70
Athabaska Rd HL . . . 61 U41-42
Atherley Rd SM . . . 42 Z32
Athol Rd SDG . . . 68 R69
Atkins Rd HS . . . 34 D49
Atkins Lake Rd LG . . . 49 X61
Atkinson Rd HS . . . 46 A48
Atkinson Rd SM . . . 41 A-B27
Attwood La F . . . 48 Z55
Atwater Rd TM . . . 85 M-N27
Aubin Rd A . . . 84 A91
Aubrey Rd R . . . 82 P52
Auchinean Rd G . . . 39 Z19
Audley Rd DH . . . 31 G-H35
Audubon Way Y . . . 30 C-D32
Auger Av CS . . . 101 C20
Aughrim Ln LM . . . 7 W11 13 V11
Augsburg Rd R . . . 81 P51
Augusta Townline Rd LG . . . 50 X64
Augustine Rd NR . . . 33 G41
Augustine Rd NI . . . 18 U32
Auld's Rd PS . . . 76 M27
Auld MacMillan Rd SDG . . . 68 S71
Ault Island Rd SDG . . . 51 V68
Aultsville Rd SDG . . . 51 V68
Aumond Creek Access Rd NP . . . 97 E39-40 F39-40
Aurele Rd PR . . . 67 S67-68
Aurora Rd Y . . . 30 F32 31 F33
Ausable Dr MD . . . 14 R14-15
Ausable Ln HU . 14 Q14 20 N-P14 P14
Ausable Rd MD . . . 13 S12 14 S13
Austdal Rd NP . . . 93 F25
Austin Ln C . . . 7 X12
Austin Rd HS . . . 46 A46
Austin Rd LM . . . 6 X6
Austin Sdrd BR . . . 26 E-F16
Austin Lake Rd HL . . . 59 T36
Austris Rd F . . . 48 W53
Auto Rd TB . . . 102 B4 C4
Autumn La K . . . 43 A36
Autumn Hill Blvd Y . . . 30 H31
Ava Cr PB . . . 32 E40
Avalon La NF . . . 17 V25
Avenue Dr MD . . . 13 R12
Avenue Rd T . . . 24 K32
Avenue Rd WT . . . 23 N-P25
Avery La HL . . . 60 V40
Avery Rd A . . . 84 A91
Avery Rd DH . . . 32 F37
Avery Point Rd K . . . 43 Y34
Aviation Pkwy OT . . . 66 Q63
Avon Dr MD . . . 15 U18-19
Avon Rd R . . . 99 G48
Avonlea La HL . . . 43 W37
Avonlough Rd HS . . . 34 E48
Avonmore Rd SDG . . . 52 U69
Avro Dr MD . . . 14 T15
Awenda Park Rd SM . . . 41 X27
Awmik Dr MD . . . 14 Q16
Axe Lake Rd A . . . 87 B-C99
Axe Lake Rd PS . . . 58 Q30-31 Q31 P31
Axe Lake Rd R . . . 62 Q48
Axe Lake Camp Rd A . . . 87 B-C99
Axeli Rd CS . . . 101 D20-21
Aylen Lake Rd NP . . . 80 N45
Aylen Lake Access Rd R . . 80 N-P46
Aylwin Rd OT . . . 83 P59
Ayotte Rd PB . . . 45 W43
Ayotte's Point La PB . . . 44 A41
Ayr Rd BT . . . 16 Q23-24
Ayrshire Rd TM . . . 85 Q-R29
Ayton Rd WL . . . 27 G20
B, Concession G . . . 39 Y21
B, Concession Rd SM . . . 43 A34
B, Fire Rte CS . . . 100 A17-18
B, Mersea Rd EX . . . 5 E-F6
B, Scotch Line Sdrd LN . . . 65 U58
B Ln A . . . 86 E94
B Ln DF . . . 29 H26
B Ln HU . . . 20 P13
B Ln (Arran-Elderslie) BR . . . 27 C17 38 A-B16 B17
B Ln (South Bruce) BR . . . 27 F-G17
B-C, Concession Rd SM . . . 42 Y33 43 Y34
B-C, Sideroad BR . . . 26 C14-15
B-Line Rd R . . . 81 L-M51 99 K51
B B Beach Rd PB . . . 33 E41
B Line Rd HU . . . 27 H17
Babcock Blvd Y . . . 30 G32
Babcock Rd (Central Frontenac) F . . . 48 Y53
Babcock Rd (Kingston) F . . . 36 C55
Babcook Rd F . . . 36 B55
Babian Rd NI . . . 19 T-U34
Babinski Rd R . . . 80 P46
Baby Rd LM . . . 6 W7 12 V7
Babylon Ln HU . . . 14 Q14 20 M13-14 N-P14
Babylon Rd PE . . . 35 H52
Bacchus Island Rd LG . . 49 W59-60
Back St LG . . . 37 A58
Back Bay La F . . . 36 A56
Back Bay Rd PS . . . 56 Q24-25
Back Beach Rd LA . . . 36 E-F54
Backus Mill Rd NF . . . 10 X23
Backwoods La HL . . . 44 W40
Bacon Rd HL . . . 44 W38-39
Badder Ln C . . . 5 D8 6 C8
Badger Rd PS . . . 57 R28
Badger Mine Rd TB . . . 102 E3
Badgley Rd PE . . . 34 F48
Badhams Sdrd OT . . . 83 P59
Badour La F . . . 48 Y56
Badour Rd F . . . 48 Y55
Baert Rd C . . . 6 B7
Baggs Rd R . . . 99 H49
Bagley Rd NR . . . 33 D44
Bagley Rd SM . . . 42 X32
Bagot Long Lake Rd R . . . 64 S55
Baguley Rd SM . . . 41 X29
Bah-sah-gim Rd PS . . . 75 N-P25
Bailey Ln MA . . . 71 L6
Bailey Rd HS . . . 46 Y48
Bailey Lake Rd A . . . 87 C-D98
Bains Rd HD . . . 18 U29
Bains Rd LG . . . 50 Y62-63
Baird's Sdrd OT . . . 83 Q59
Baise Av BR . . . 54 S14
Baitleys Rd PE . . . 34 G49
Bak Rd TB . . . 103 B10
Baker Blvd K . . . 43 X36
Baker Dr PB . . . 44 X40
Baker Rd K . . . 43 Z37
Baker Rd NR . . . 33 F42
Baker Rd PB . . . 45 B44
Baker Rd PR . . . 67 R67
Baker Rd PS . . . 76 M30 77 M31
Baker Rd SDG . . . 67 U65-66
Baker Rd (Grimsby) NI . . . 18 R31
Baker Rd (Niagara Falls) NI . 19 T35
Baker Rd (Rideau Lakes) LG . . . 49 X-Y59
Baker Sdrd MK . . . 59 T33
Baker St A . . . 87 E1
Baker Tr MA . . . 72 K8
Baker's La NF . . . 16 U24
Baker's Rd (Elizabethtown-Kitley) LG . . . 49 Y60
Baker School Rd DH . . . 32 G37
Baker Valley Rd F . . . 47 X52 48 X53
Bakker Rd PE . . . 34 G48
Baldoon Rd C . . . 6 A8 Y7-8
Baldwick La SM . . . 29 C28
Baldwin Ln EL . . . 15 V20
Baldwin Rd C . . . 6 A7
Baldwin Rd MK . . . 58 U32
Baldwin Rd NI . . . 18 S-T31
Baldwin Rd SDG . . . 51 V68
Baldwin Rd Y . . . 30 D32
Baldwin St NR . . . 33 F42
Baldwin St OX . . . 16 U21
Baldwin Bay Rd PB . . . 44 X40
Bales Dr Y . . . 30 F32
Balfour St NI . . . 19 S-T33
Balkwill Ln SM . . . 42 X30-31 Y31
Ball Ln EL . . . 15 V20 16 V21
Ball Rd DH . . . 31 E34
Ball Rd F . . . 48 Z54-55
Ball Rd HL . . . 60 V38
Ball Rd NR . . . 33 F42
Ball Rd SDG . . . 67 U66
Ball's Ln HU . . . 20 K14
Ball Point Rd K . . . 32 D37
Ballahack Rd LA . . . 47 A52
Ballinafad Rd PL . . . 23 K27
Ballycanoe Rd LG . . . 37 A60-61
Ballyduff Rd K . . . 32 E38
Balm Beach Rd SM . . . 41 Y27
Balmer Rd PB . . . 45 X43
Balmer Bay Rd R . . . 99 G-H49
Balmoral Dr PL . . . 24 K29-30
Balmoral La HL . . . 44 W40
Balmoral Ln C . . . 6 B7
Balmoral St TB . . . 103 D6
Balmy Beach Rd G . . . 39 Y-Z19
Balsam Dr PS . . . 77 N-P34
Balsam La WL . . . 27 G-H19
Balsam Rd DH . . . 31 G35
Balsam Rd (McKellar) PS . . . 76 P28
Balsam Rd (Powassan) PS . . . 95 H32
Balsam Rd (Whitestone) PS . 76 N28
Balsam St CS . . . 101 C19
Balsam St TB . . . 103 C-D6
Balsam Chutes Rd MK . . . 59 T33
Balsam Creek Rd PS . . . 75 K26
Balsam Grove Rd K . . . 43 A36-37
Balsam Grove Rd WT . . . 22 L23
Balsam Lake Dr K . . . 43 Z36
Bancroft Dr CS . . . 101 C19-20
Bandon Ln HU . . . 20 K15
Bandys Rd R . . . 83 Q56
Bangs Rd PR . . . 68 N71
Bank St OT . 66 Q63 R63-64 S64 S-T64
Bankfield Rd OT . . . 66 S62-63
Banks Rd MD . . . 15 S18
Bannockburn Ln HU . . . 20 M14
Bannockburn Rd HS . . . 46 Y47-48
Bannockburn Rd MK . . . 58 U30
Bannon Rd NR . . . 33 C45
Banta Rd NR . . . 33 D44
Banting Dr R . . . 99 G48
Banting Ln BR . . . 27 D17
Banwell Rd EX . . . 4 B3
Baptist La G . . . 39 A21
Baptist Rd NR . . . 33 F43
Baptist Church Rd BT . . . 17 R27
Baptist Church Rd G . . . 28 D21
Baptist Church Rd HS . . . 34 C-D48
Baptist Church Rd R . . . 63 Q50-51
Baptist Church Sdrd LN . . . 49 V58 65 U58
Baptiste Rd C . . . 6 B-C7
Bar River Rd A . . . 86 C94
Baragars Rd HS . . . 61 R43
Barber Rd LG . . . 49 X61
Barber Sdrd A . . . 86 D95
Barber St SD . . . 90 E-F13
Barber Valley Rd PS . . . 94 H30
Barbers La NF . . . 17 U25
Barcovan Beach Rd HS . . . 34 F46
Barcroft Rd PB . . . 44 A39 Z39
Barden St WL . . . 23 L26
Barfoot Cr BR . . . 55 X18
Bark Lake Dr HL . . . 44 W39 60 V39
Bark Lake Rd HS . . . 62 Q45
Bark Lake Dam Rd R . . . 62 Q46
Barker Rd HS . . . 46 Z48
Barker Sdrd LA . . . 35 D52
Barker Lake Access Rd LA . 63 T49
Barkley Rd SDG . . . 50 V65 51 V66 67 U65
Barkway Rd MK . . . 42 W33 43 W34 59 V34
Barley Rd PE . . . 34 E48
Barlochan Rd MK . . . 58 U31
Barlow Cr OT . . . 65 Q60
Barlow Rd HM . . . 18 S29
Barlow Rd NR . . . 33 E44
Barnes Rd BT . . . 16 T23
Barnes Rd MK . . . 58 V32
Barnes Rd NR . . . 33 F45
Barnett Rd NP . . . 95 D31
Barnett's Dr BR . . . 54 T16
Barneys Blvd BR . . . 54 T16
Barnhardt Rd SDG . . 50 W65 51 W66
Barnsdale Rd OT . . . 66 S62
Barnums Gully Ln EL . . . 9 W18
Barr La F . . . 48 X53
Barr Ln R . . . 82 N-P53
Barr Rd A . . . 86 D94
Barr Sdrd LN . . . 65 R57-58
Barrett Rd HS . . . 34 C47
Barrett Rd LA . . . 47 B52
Barrett Rd PS . . . 94 J30 95 J31
Barrett Chute Rd R . . . 64 S54
Barrick Rd NI . . . 19 U33
Barridge Rd F . . . 48 Y56
Barrie Dr TB . . . 102 E4
Barrie Rd LN . . . 65 Q-R57
Barrie Rd NR . . . 33 F-G41
Barrie Rd SM . . . 42 A30
Barrie Rd SM . . . 42 Z32
Barrie St SM . . . 30 D29 E31
Barrie Hill Rd SM . . . 41 B29
Barries Sdrd LN . . . 49 V58
Barrister Bay La HL . . . 60 V39
Barron Rd NI . . . 19 S33 S34
Barron Canyon Rd NP . . . 98 J-K47
Barron Canyon Rd R . . . 99 K48 K50
Barrow Bay Rd BR . . . 55 V17
Barrs La F . . . 48 Z55
Barry Rd HS . . . 46 Z48
Barry Rd HD . . . 18 T30
Barry's Rd K . . . 31 C36
Barry Downe Rd CS . . . 101 C19-20
Barry Lake Tr R . . . 64 S54
Barry Line Rd HL . . . 60 T38
Barrymere Dr HS . . . 62 Q47
Barryvale Rd R . . . 64 S54-55
Barter Camp Rd HL . . . 60 U-V40 61 U-V41
Barth Side Rd NF . . . 9 W21 10 W22
Bartle Lake Rd TM . . . 85 R28
Bartlett Av NI . . . 18 Q-R31
Bartlett Rd HS . . . 62 S46
Bartlett Rd HD . . . 18 T30-31
Bartlett Rd NI . . . 18 R32
Bartlett Rd PB . . . 32 D40
Bartlett St HS . . . 61 T44
Bartlett Lake Rd PS . . . 77 N-P31
Bartley Dr BR . . . 54 S16

Bartley / Blueberry

Bartley Sdrd BR 38 B16
Barton Rd BT 17 R26
Barton Rd DH 32 F37
Barton Rd LG 50 X-Y64
Barton Rd PR 68 P71
Barton Rd PS 76 L30
Barton St HM 18 Q29-30
Barzo Rd EL 16 V21
Base Ln A 84 B91
Base Ln BT 16 S-T22
Base Ln C 6 X7-9 7 X10-11
Base Ln HU 20 K14
Base Ln OX 16 T-U23
Base Ln PB 33 C-D42 D41
Base Rd C 7 A-B11
Base Line Rd F 36 E56-57
Base Line Rd K 43 Y37
Base Line Rd MK 42 X32
Base Line Rd Y 30 C32
Baseline BR 26 E13
Baseline (Grey Highlands) G 28 D22
Baseline (West Grey) G 27 C-E20
Baseline N BR 26 D16 27 D17
Baseline S BR 27 D17
Baseline Rd A 86 E95
Baseline Rd DH 32 H37-38
Baseline Rd EX 4 C2-3
Baseline Rd F 36 D57
Baseline Rd LM 6 W6
Baseline Rd NF 9 W21
Baseline Rd OT 66 R62
Baseline Rd PR 67 P66-67
Baseline Rd SM 41 Y-Z28 Z29
Basin Rd NP 80 L45
Basin Rd R 80 M46-47
Basin Depot Rd R 80 M46-47
Basin Lake Rd NP 80 L-M46
Basin Marina Rd MK 57 T27
Baskin Dr R 83 Q57
Baskins Beach Rd OT 65 P-Q60
Bass La PB 44 Y38-39
Bass Ln SM 42 Z31
Bass Rd LG 49 X59
Bass Bay Rd LN 49 X-Y58
Bass Bay Rd MK 41 W-X29
Bass Cove Rd LA 35 F51
Bass Creek Rd MA 73 K-L11
Bass Lake Rd F 48 X53-54
Bass Lake Rd LG 49 W-X59
Bass Lake Rd MK 58 T29-30
Bass Lake Rd PB 44 Y-Z39
Bass Lake Rd R 99 G48
Bass Lake Rd SD 90 F13
Bass Lake Rd (Blind River) A 88 F4
Bass Lake Rd (Leeburn) A 86 B-C96
Bass Lake Sdrd SM 42 A30 Z30-31
Bass Point Rd SD 89 F9
Bass Pond Rd SD 90 F12
Bassette Ln C 6 Y7
Basshaunt Lake Rd HL 60 T39
Basso Rd PS 77 L32
Basswood Lake Rd A 87 D98-99
Basswood Lake Camp Rd A 87 D-E99
Bastien Rd MA 73 M11
Bat Lake Rd HL 60 V38
Bata Rd HS 34 E47
Bate Rd HS 34 D46
Bateman Ln BT 17 S25
Bateman Rd HS 46 B47
Bates Rd LG 49 X61
Bath Rd F 36 D55-56
Bathurst Ln E LN 48 V56
Bathurst Ln W LN 48 W56
Bathurst St LA 35 E53
Bathurst St T 24 J-K32
Bathurst St Y 24 I-J31 30 E-H31
Battams Rd LG 49 Z58
Batteaux Rd SM 40 B25 41 B26
Batten La PB 45 A42
Batten Rd EX 4 D3
Battersea Rd F 36 A57 B57 37 A58
Battle Point Rd A 88 E4
Bauder Dr F 36 A55
Baulch Rd NR 33 G41
Baver Rd NR 34 F46
Bawn Rd LA 47 B52
Baxter Rd NR 33 D43
Baxter Loop Rd MK 41 W28-29
Bay Ln C 6 Y7
Bay Rd LG 49 W59
Bay Rd MK 57 T27
Bay Rd PR 68 N70
Bay St A 84 B92
Bay St BR 55 Y17
Bay St CS 100 D16
Bay St MA 72 K10
Bay St MK 58 V32
Bay St NF 10 X23
Bay St NP 94 D27
Bay St SM 42 B30
Bay Estate Rd MA 73 K12
Bay Estate Rd N MA 73 K12
Bay Estate Rd S MA 73 K12-13
Bay Lake Rd HS 62 U45-46
Bay Lake Rd PS 77 P33
Bay Lake Access Rd NP 96 F-G35
Bay Lake Access Rd SD 100 Y16
Bay Meadows Rd MK 59 R33-34
Bay of Islands Rd MA 90 H13
Bay of Islands Rd MA 90 H13
Bay of Gis Dr SD 90 G13
Bay Shore Av N BR 54 S13
Bay Shore Av S BR 54 S13
Bay Shore Dr HS 62 U45
Bay Shore Rd MA 90 J10
Baybreeze La HL 60 S39
Baycrest Rd A 84 W91
Bayfield Rd HU 20 J-K13 L13-14
Bayfield St SM 41 B29 42 B30
Bayfield River Rd HU 20 L13-14
Bayham Dr OX 16 U-V21
Bayham-Norfolk Boundary Rd EL 9 W-X21 16 V21
Bayly St DH 25 J34-35 31 H35
Bayou Rd SM 42 Y32
Bayridge Dr F 36 D55
Bayshore Dr SM 42 Z33
Bayshore Rd G 39 Y20
Bayshore Rd HL 60 U39
Bayshore Rd HS 35 E51
Bayshore Rd LA 35 F52
Bayshore Rd NR 34 G46
Bayshore Rd PB 45 W44
Bayside Dr PS 56 Q26 57 Q27
Bayview Av MK 59 S36
Bayview Av SM 41 X28
Bayview Av T 24 J-K32
Bayview Av Y 24 I-J32 30 G-H32
Bayview Dr OT 83 P59
Bayview Dr PS 56 Q25-26
Bayview Dr SM 30 C30
Bayview Rd MK 58 V29
Bayview Rd NP 95 E32
Bayview Rd PS 95 F32
Bayview Lodge Rd LN 64 R56
Beach Blvd HM 18 Q29
Beach Dr A 84 W91
Beach Dr NR 33 F45 G44
Beach La F 37 B58
Beach La NF 9 W21 10 W22
Beach Rd EX 5 E-F7
Beach Rd HS 35 E50
Beach Rd K 32 D37
Beach Rd LG 50 V63
Beach Rd MA 71 K5
Beach Rd MA 73 K14
Beach Rd NP 95 G33
Beach Rd NI 19 U34
Beach Rd TM 85 P30-31
Beach Rd E LG 50 V63
Beach Rd Left SD 90 E11
Beach Rd Right SD 90 E11
Beach View Dr K 44 A38
Beachburg Rd R 82 L53 M54
Beaches Rd LG 49 Z58
Beachin Rd NI 18 T32
Beachville Rd OX 15 S20 16 S21
Beachwood Dr PB 44 A41 Z41
Beacock Rd DH 31 E36 32 E37
Beacon Point Dr PS 56 Q26
Beaconsfield Rd OX 16 S22 S-T21
Beagle Club Rd NR 33 E42-43
Beales Mills Rd LG 37 A60 49 Z60
Beamish Rd NR 33 G44
Bean Rd WT 22 P21
Beange Rd MA 72 J8
Bear Rd A 86 D95
Bear Bottom La F 36 A56
Bear Cave Rd MK 58 R30
Bear Creek Rd C 7 X10
Bear Creek Rd F 36 C57
Bear Creek Rd MD 14 S14-15
Bear Creek Rd PB 44 A39
Bear Island Rd LN 49 V59 65 U59
Bear Lake Rd HL 60 R37
Bear Lake Rd MK 58 T29
Bear Lake Rd SD 93 G24
Bear Line Rd C 6 A8 Y7-8
Bear Mountain Rd NP 95 H33
Bear Point Tr HS 62 U47
Bear Ponds Access Rd LA 63 U49-50
Bear Shanty La HS 62 V46
Bear Trail Rd R 80 M47 81 M48
Bearance-Hicks La F 48 Z53
Bearbrook Rd OT 66 Q64
Bearcamp Rd TB 102 G1
Bearcroft Rd K 31 D36
Beard Farm Tr SM 42 X30-31
Beards La OX 16 R21
Beardsmore Rd PB 32 D40 33 D41
Beare Rd T 25 H34
Bearhead Lake Rd A 88 E4
Bearhill Rd OT 65 R59-60
Bearinger Rd WT 22 M22
Bearsfield Dr SM 30 E30
Beaton Rd A 87 E1
Beaton Rd OT 67 P65
Beatrice La F 48 Y-Z55
Beatrice Townline Rd MK 58 T31-32
Beattie Ln EL 7 X12
Beattie Rd EL 9 W20 15 V20
Beattie Rd F 36 A54
Beatty La NR 32 F40
Beatty Ln WL 22 K23-24
Beatty Rd HS 34 C48
Beatty's Rd K 44 A38-39
Beaucage Park Rd NP 94 D29
Beauchamp-Dack Township Rd TM 85 N28
Beauchamp-Henwood Township Line Rd TM 85 P27-28
Beauchesne Rd PR 68 P70-71
Beaudette Lake Access Rd LA 63 V49
Beaudoin Rd SD 90 E12
Beaudry La R 82 Q52
Beaudry Rd NP 94 D27
Beaudry Rd R 64 R56
Beaumaris Rd MK 58 U31
Beaumont Dr MK 58 U32
Beaumont Farm Rd MK 58 U32
Beauparlant Rd SD 101 D23
Beaupre Rd SDG 68 S71-72
Beauvoir Rd NP 93 E26
Beaver Blvd MK 43 W34
Beaver La PB 45 X42
Beaver La PR 67 R66
Beaver La PS 94 H30
Beaver La SM 41 A29
Beaver Rd K 32 C39
Beaver Rd NR 33 D45
Beaver Rd R 81 N48
Beaver Rd TM 85 M27
Beaver Rd, The MA 72 L8-9
Beaver St NI 18 R-S32
Beaver Tr PS 57 Q27
Beaver Brook Rd SDG 68 T71
Beaver Creek Dr MK 59 V33
Beaver Creek La F 47 X-Y52
Beaver Creek La HS 46 X47
Beaver Creek Rd HS 46 A46
Beaver Lake Dr HL 61 U-V43
Beaver Lake Dr HS 61 U-V44
Beaver Lake La PS 77 N33
Beaver Lake Rd PB 44 X41
Beaver Meadow Rd MK 59 S33
Beaver Ridge Rd MK 42 W32
Beaverdale Rd WT 22 N24
Beaverdams Rd NI 19 R-S34
Beavermeadow Rd (Hamilton) NR 33 E-F42
Beavermeadow Rd (Port Hope) NR 32 F39-40
Beavertail Rd OT 65 S60
Bebris Rd F 48 X53
Bechard Rd C 6 A-B8
Beck Rd NI 19 S35
Beck's Dr MK 42 W31
Beckerton Shooting Range Rd A 89 F8
Beckett La NP 96 F35-36
Beckett Rd HS 34 C47 46 B47
Beckett Creek Rd OT 67 P65
Becketts Sdrd SM 41 X-Y29
Beckons La BR 55 X17-18
Becks Rd OT 83 Q59
Beckstead Rd SDG 51 V67 67 U67
Beckwith Boundary Rd LN 65 U60 66 U61
Bedard Dr TM 85 Q29
Bedard Rd HU 20 N13
Bedard Rd SD 93 D24
Bedard St PR 68 N71
Bedell Rd LG 50 V63
Bedford Rd C 6 A9
Bedford Rd F 36 A-B55
Bedford Rd HS 34 C47
Bedford St LG 48 Y57
Bednarski Rd SD 90 G13
Bedwell Dr PB 45 Z43
Bee Dr PB 32 E40
Bee Hill Rd NR 33 F41
Beech Av PS 56 R25
Beech Dr A 88 F4
Beech St BR 55 W17-18
Beech Bay Dr HL 60 U37-38
Beech Grove Sdrd PL 29 H26-27
Beech Hill Rd NR 32 F40
Beech Nut Rd F 36 C57
Beecham Rd HS 62 T45-46
Beechnut Lake Rd R 81 M48
Beechwood Dr PS 58 S29
Beechwood Ln C 7 A11
Beechwood Ln HU 20 L16 21 L17
Beechwood Rd LA 35 D51-52
Beechwood Rd NI 19 R-S34
Beecroft Ln HU 26 H15
Beeforth Rd HM 23 P28
Beehive Dr K 43 B37
Beehive La WL 27 H20
Beer Creek Cr LM 13 T10
Beer Lake Rd HL 60 V37
Beers Rd K 32 D-E38
Before Long La HL 60 V39
Begg Rd EL 8 W17
Begg Rd NR 33 E45
Beggan Rd R 81 P49
Behm Rd R 82 N53
Beiers Rd MK 42 W32
Beitz Rd WT 22 M23-24
Beke Rd WT 22 P24
Beladair Rd R 99 H48-49
Belanger Rd NP 96 E37
Belanger Rd SDG 67 U65-66
Belfast Rd HU 26 G13-14 H15-16
Belfield Rd T 24 K30
Belgrave Rd HU 20 J16 26 G13 H15
Belisle Dr CS 101 B19
Belknap La F 48 Y56
Bell Blvd HS 34 E48-49
Bell Dr (Huron-Kinloss) BR 26 E13
Bell Dr (Northern Bruce Peninsula) BR 55 W16
Bell Rd CS 91 E15
Bell Rd EX 4 F3
Bell Rd F 36 B55
Bell Rd HS 46 B48
Bell Rd HM 18 S29
Bell Rd LN 49 V59 65 U59
Bell Rd MA 71 K6
Bell Rd MD 14 U-V16
Bell Rd MK 58 R31
Bell Rd NI 18 T-U32
Bell Rd PE 34 F48
Bell Rd PS 94 J29
Bell Rd SDG 50 V-W65
Bell St OX 15 S19-20
Bell St SD 90 F10-11
Bell's Ln HU 20 N14
Bell's Rd PS 57 Q28
Bell's Rd WL 27 G20
Bell's Hill Rd NR 32 F40
Bell's Lake Rd G 28 C21
Bell Lake Rd MA 91 G17-18
Bell Lake Rd PS 57 Q27
Bell Line Rd F 48 W-X55 X53-54
Bell Mill Sdrd NF 16 V21-22
Bell Rock Rd F 36 A54 B54 47 A53
Bell School Ln HT 23 M-N28
Bell Tower Rd SD 92 H22
Bella Shores Rd MK 59 Q35 78 P35
Bellamy Rd DH 32 G-H39
Bellamy Rd K 44 A-B39
Bellamy Rd LN 64 R56 65 R57 S57
Bellamy Rd LG 49 Y61
Bellamy Rd NR 33 F45
Bellamy Rd R 64 R56
Bellamy Mills Rd LN 65 S57-58
Bellas La R 63 R49
Bellcairn Rd NP 95 G-H33
Bellcreft Dr EX 4 F2
Belle Aire Beach Rd SM 30 D30-31
Belle Baie La MA 72 L10
Belle Bay Rd SD 100 D14
Belle River Rd EX 4 C-D4
Belle Rose Ln C 6 A-B7
Belle Vallée Rd TM 85 P29-30
Belleview Beach Rd NI 18 U32 19 U33
Belleville Rd HS 35 D51
Belleville St PE 34 G49
Bellevue Dr HS 46 Z48
Bellevue Valley Rd A 84 Z92-93
Bellingham Rd A 87 D1
Bellrock Rd LA 47 A-B53
Bells Park Rd SM 41 A27
Bellwood Acres Rd MK 59 S35-36
Belmeade Rd OT 66 T-U64
Belmont Rd EL 15 U-V18
Belmore Ln HU 27 G-H17
Belrose Rd BR 54 S14
Belrose Rd TB 103 D6
Belton Rd HS 62 T47
Belvedere Rd PR 67 Q66
Belwood Rd DF 22 J24 28 H24
Ben Rd HL 60 U38
Ben & Jean Rd A 88 E4
Ben Lake Rd E MK 42 W33 43 W34
Ben Lake Rd W MK 42 W33
Bend Rd WT 22 M23
Bender Rd F 48 Y54
Bender Rd SDG 68 S-T69
Bender Rd WT 22 P21
Benfield Rd HS 46 W46
Benjamin La F 36 B56
Benjamin Rd WT 22 M22
Benmiller Ln HU 20 K13-14
Benn's Point Rd LA 35 E53
Benn's Ranch Rd LA 47 W50
Bennett Rd DH 32 H38
Bennett Rd F 36 E57
Bennett Rd LN 49 V61 66 U61
Bennett Rd NR 33 E45
Bennett Rd NI 18 S31
Bennett Rd PS 94 J29-30
Bennett Rd SD 93 D24
Bennett Rd (Elizabethtown-Kitley) LG 49 X60
Bennett Rd (North Grenville) LG 50 V64
Bennett-Lafont Rd R 82 M54
Bennett Lake Rd HS 62 Q-R47
Bennett Lake Rd LN 48 V56-57 W56
Bennies Corners Rd LN 65 S58
Benny Rd SD 100 Z14
Benoir Lake Rd HL 61 S42
Benoit Rd PR 67 R67
Benoit Rd SDG 67 S67
Bensfort Rd PB 33 D-E41
Benson Rd NF 10 X22
Benson Rd NR 33 F41
Benson Sdrd SM 42 Y32
Benson George Rd SDG 67 T65
Bentinck-Sullivan Twnln G 27 C18-19
Bentley St WL 28 G21
Bentpath Ln LM 6 W6-9 7 W10-12
Benway Rd PE 34 G48
Benzinger Rd MK 42 W33
Berford Lake Rd BR 55 X18
Berford Park Rd BR 55 W17-18
Berger Rd R 82 P52
Berini Dr TB 102 D3
Berkeley Blvd NP 95 D31
Berkley Rd PS 58 R29
Berlanquet Rd R 82 Q54
Berletts Rd WT 22 N21
Bernard Av NI 19 U35
Bernard La F 48 Z53
Bernard La R 63 Q51 81 P51
Bernard Long Rd HS 34 E47
Berndt Rd R 81 N50
Berners Rd MK 58 T29
Bernice Cr LN 49 W58
Bernique Rd PR 68 Q70
Berrie Rd PB 44 A41 Z41
Berriedale Rd PS 77 M32
Berry Rd HM 18 S29
Berry Rd LA 47 Y51
Berry Rd LG 37 B58
Berry Rd NP 95 E34
Berry Sdrd OT 66 Q61
Berryton Rd LG 37 B58
Bert Sims Rd MK 58 S31
Bertie St NI 19 U35-36
Bertram Access Rd NP 94 F27
Bertram Industrial Pkwy SM 41 A29
Bertrand Rd PR 67 R66
Bertrim La (Central Frontenac) F 48 Y54
Bertrim La (South Frontenac) F 48 Y55
Berts Rd R 82 N54
Bervie Sdrd BR 26 E15
Berwick Rd MK 58 V29
Berwick Rd SDG 67 S-T68 T67
Besner Rd PR 68 Q69
Bessemer La HS 62 U46-47
Bessemer Rd HS 62 U47
Bessey Rd NI 19 U33
Bessie Av PB 44 Z39
Best Ln EL 15 V20
Best Rd A 84 Y92
Best Rd DH 32 F-G38
Best Rd HS 62 S45
Best Rd LN 49 W59
Best Rd PB 32 C-D39
Best's Rd NR 32 G40
Best Chase Rd F 37 C58
Bethany Rd HS 34 D49
Bethany Hills Rd K 32 D38-39
Bethel Rd BT 16 R24
Bethel Rd HL 60 V38
Bethel Rd K 32 C39-40
Bethel Rd LA 35 C53 36 B54
Bethel Rd LM 13 S-T11
Bethel Rd LG 50 Z63
Bethel Rd PE 35 F50
Bethel Rd WT 22 P23
Bethel Rd (Belleville) HS 34 C48-49
Bethel Rd (Tweed) HS 46 B49 47 B50
Bethel Sdrd Y 30 D32
Bethel Church Rd BT 17 Q-R25
Bethel Church Rd HM 17 Q25
Bethel Grove Rd NR 33 F41
Bethesda Rd DH 32 F-G38
Bethesda Rd LM 13 T11
Bethesda Rd NI 18 R32
Bethesda Rd PE 35 E-F51
Bethesda Sdrd Y 30 G32 31 G33
Bethune Dr MK 58 V32
Bethune La PS 77 P34
Bethune Rd MK 59 R33
Betty La HS 45 W-X45
Betty Rd HL 61 S-T42
Betty Rd NP 93 D26
Beulah Rd LG 50 W63
Beulow Rd R 81 P50
Bevan's Rd PS 77 N33
Bevan Ridge Rd NR 33 F43
Bevel Line Rd EX 5 E-F5
Beverly St BT 17 Q25
Bexley-Laxton Township Ln K 43 Y36-37
Bickford Ln LM 12 V7-8
Bickle Hill Rd NR 33 F41-42
Bidwell Rd MA 72 K10 73 K11 L11-12
Bidwell Rd SM 41 A29 42 A30
Bieber Rd C 7 A12-13
Biederman Rd NI 19 U33
Biehn Dr WT 22 N-P23
Biernacki Mountain Rd R 80 P46-47
Bierworth Rd HS 62 U45
Biesenthal Rd R 99 K50
Big Bay Sdrd G 39 X19
Big Bay Point Rd SM 30 C30 42 B30-31
Big Bend Rd MD 7 W12
Big Bissett Lake Access Rd R 98 G42
Big Burnt Lake Access Rd HS 46 Y46
Big Cedar Lake Rd PB 45 Z42
Big Chief Rd SM 42 Y32
Big Creek Rd BT 17 R26-27
Big Creek Rd LA 35 D53
Big Crosby Lake Rd LG 48 Y56-57
Big Hawk Lake Rd HL 60 T37
Big Hill Rd LG 37 B58
Big Island Rd HS 46 A46
Big Island Rd PB 46 A46
Big Joe Rd MK 58 T30
Big Lake Rd A 88 B3
Big Lake Access Rd R 99 K49
Big Lake Dam Rd MA 72 L10
Big Lighthouse Tr HS 61 S44
Big McGarry Lake Access Rd HS 61 S42-43
Big Moose Rd NP 95 F33
Big Nickel Rd CS 101 C19
Big Point Rd A 86 E-F96
Big Point Rd HS 62 R45-46
Big Pointe Rd C 6 A7-8
Big Rideau Lake Rd LG 49 Y58
Big Rideau North Shore LN 49 Y58
Big Rock Rd G 39 Y19
Big Shingle Access Rd R 98 F42
Big Sound Rd PS 56 Q26
Big Waters La LG 37 A60
Bigford Rd HS 34 F46
Biggar Rd NI 19 S34
Biggars La BT 17 S25
Biggs Rd R 99 K50-51
Bigwind Lake Rd MK 59 U35
Bill Lang Rd NR 33 G42
Bill McLaren Tr HL 61 T42
Billie Bear Rd MK 59 Q35 78 P35
Billings Lake Rd HL 60 V40
Billy Green Rd F 36 A56-57
Bilton Ln LM 7 W11
Binbrook Rd HM 18 R29
Binette Rd SDG 68 Q72
Bingham Dr R 82 N55
Bingham Rd HL 60 V37
Bingley Rd SDG 68 T70
Bingley Lake Rd LN 64 U55
Bingo La HS 62 S-T47
Bingo Rd LM 13 S12
Binion Rd SDG 50 X65
Binkley Rd HM 17 Q27
Binnie Dr SM 41 A28-29
Binscarth Tr HL 60 T38
Birch Dr CS 101 D20
Birch Dr SM 42 X33
Birch La BR 55 X17
Birch Rd NR 33 F-G42
Birch St A 88 F3
Birch St MA 73 M12-13
Birch St PB 45 B44
Birch St SD 90 E14
Birch Bay La LN 48 W56
Birch Beach Rd HU 26 G13
Birch Beach Rd TB 103 B9
Birch Glen Dr K 43 Y37
Birch Island Rd PB 44 A40-41
Birch Lake Rd A 86 B94-95
Birch Lake Rd SD 90 E11-12 F11
Birch Lake Rd E SD 90 E12
Birch Narrows Rd HL 60 U39
Birch Point Dr A 86 C-D93
Birch Point Dr K 44 B39
Birch Point La F 36 A55
Birch Point Rd NR 45 B45
Birch Point Rd PS 94 J27-28
Birch Point Rd (Kawartha Lakes[Bobcaygeon Verulam]) K 44 A38-39
Birch Point Rd (Kawartha Lakes[Fenelon]) K 43 A36
Birchbend Rd PB 44 A41
Birchcliff Sdrd HU 20 L13
Birchcroft Rd MK 59 R35
Birchdale Rd PS 77 N-P33
Birchgrove Dr PS 95 F31
Birchgrove Rd OT 67 Q66
Birchmount Rd T 25 J-K33
Birchs Rd NP 95 E31-32 E32
Birchview Rd PB 45 A42
Birchwood Cir A 88 F4
Birchwood Tr PS 75 K26
Birchy Lake Dr HL 60 S38
Bird Rd HS 34 D48
Bird Rd HD 18 T30 U31
Bird Lake Rd MK 59 U35
Bird Song La MK 41 X29
Birdsall Ln PB 33 C-D43
Birkett La BT 17 R-S25
Birnam Ln LM 13 S10-11
Bisch St WT 22 M22
Bishop Rd CS 100 B18
Bishop St WT 22 N24
Bishop's Rd HU 20 K14
Bishop Davis Rd OT 65 P60 83 P59
Bishopsgate Rd BT 16 R-S24
Bismarck Rd NI 18 S31-32
Bisnett Ln C 7 C10-11
Bisselltown Rd LG 50 Y-Z63
Bissett Creek Rd R 98 F-G42
Bisson Rd SDG 67 T65
Bissonette Av HU 20 N12-13
Bissonnette La EX 4 C4
Bitter Lake Rd HL 60 S-T38
Black Ln HU 27 H17
Black Rd A 84 B92
Black Rd F 47 W-X51
Black Rd LG 50 W63
Black Rd PE 35 F50
Black Rd PS 57 R-S28
Black Rd SDG 68 Q70
Black's Point Rd HU 20 K13
Black Ance Pt LN 49 X58
Black Ash Rd LM 13 U-V10
Black Bay Rd R 99 K50
Black Beach La SM 43 Z34
Black Bear Rd K 43 X36
Black Bear Rd PS 76 M30
Black Church Rd LG 49 Z60
Black Creek Dr T 24 K31
Black Creek Ln LM 6 W7 12 V7
Black Creek Rd LN 64 T-U55
Black Creek Rd R 81 M51
Black Creek Rd (Nipissing) PS 95 H-J31
Black Creek Rd (Strong) PS 77 M31
Black Creek Tr NI 19 T35
Black Donald Rd R 64 S53
Black Fly Blvd MK 42 W33 43 W34
Black Fox Rd SD 101 C23
Black Heron Tr PS 75 M24
Black Hole Rd HU 20 J-K13
Black Jack Dr MD 14 U-V15
Black Lake Rd CS 100 D18
Black Lake Rd LN 48 X57 49 X58
Black Mountain Rd R 63 T52
Black Point Rd R 81 N49
Black Pool Rd PB 44 A39-40
Black Rapids Rd LG 37 A-B59
Black River Rd HL 59 T35-36
Black River Rd HS 46 A49 Z49
Black River Rd K 43 X34
Black River Rd MK 59 U35
Black River Rd SDG 52 U69
Black River Rd Y 30 C32 31 C33
Black School Rd K 43 B35-36
Blackbass Lake Access Rd LA 63 T49
Blackbird Rd K 43 B37
Blackbridge Rd WT 22 N24 23 N25
Blackburn La F 48 Y53
Blackburn Rd MA 71 K5
Blackburn Rd R 82 Q55
Blackburn Hamlet By-Pass OT 66 Q64
Blackbush Ln HU 14 Q13 20 N-P13
Blackcreek Rd OT 67 R-S65
Blackfish Bay Rd R 62 Q47
Blackheath Rd HD 18 S29
Blackmore Rd MK 59 V33-34
Blacks Rd EL 7 X12 Y13
Blacks Rd OT 66 S61
Blackstone-Crane Lake Rd PS 57 R28 S28
Blackstone Lake Rd PS 57 S28
Blackwater Rd DH 31 D35
Blackwater Rd PS 57 Q28 58 Q29
Blackwater Rd SD 91 E17
Blackwell Rd LM 12 S-T8
Blackwell Sdrd LM 12 T8
Blaffert Rd SD 101 C22
Blain Rd LM 13 Q12
Blaine Rd SDG 67 U67
Blair La R 64 R53
Blair Rd OT 66 Q63
Blair Rd WT 22 P24
Blair Rd (Edwardsburgh Cardinal) LG 50 X65
Blair Rd (Elizabethtown-Kitley) LG 50 Z62
Blairhampton Rd HL 60 U38
Blairs Tr BR 26 F13
Blairs Landing Rd PS 56 Q26
Blairton Rd PB 46 A46
Blais Rd CS 100 B16-17
Blais Rd OT 66 R64
Blake Av Y 30 D32
Blake Rd NR 32 F40
Blake St SM 42 B30
Blake Hall Rd TB 102 F4
Blake Scoble Rd TB 102 E-F4
Blakely La HS 46 A48
Blakely Rd HS 46 Z47
Blakely Rd PE 34 F47
Blakeney Rd LN 65 R-S58
Blakslee La F 36 A55
Blanchard's Rd LG 49 X59
Blanchards Rd K 43 Z36
Blanche Ln TM 85 P30
Blanchfield Rd OT 66 T63-64
Bland Ln PB 32 D39
Blandford Rd OX 16 Q-R21 22 P21
Blaney Sdrd PR 68 P70
Blank Ln R 82 M-N53
Bleeks Rd OT 65 T60 66 T61
Blenheim Rd OX 16 Q-R23 22 P23
Blenheim Rd WT 22 P24
Bleski Rd R 80 P47
Blessington Rd HS 34 D49 35 D50-51
Blezard Ln PB 33 C42-43
Blind Ln A 86 E94
Blind Ln DF 29 F-G26
Blind Ln EL 14 V16
Blind Ln HT 23 N28
Blind Ln HU 20 N14
Blind Ln PS 77 N32
Blind Ln R 82 N54
Blind Ln (Arran-Elderslie) BR 38 B17
Blind Ln (Mapleton) WL 22 L22
Blind Ln (Minto) WL 27 G-H20
Blind Ln (Saugeen Shores) BR 38 B16
Blind Ln (South Bruce Peninsula) BR 38 Z17
Blind Ln C BR 27 F18
Blind Rd SDG 68 Q71
Blind Bay Rd PS 56 Q25
Blindline Rd TB 102 D-E4
Block Ln C 7 Y10-11
Block Line Rd WT 22 N23
Bloomfield Rd C 6 A-B8 B9
Bloomfield Rd PS 77 L31
Bloomingdale Rd WT 22 M23
Bloomington Rd SDG 68 S69
Bloomington Rd Y 30 G31-32 31 G33
Bloor St DH 31 H36 32 H37
Bloor St W PL 24 L30-31
Bloor St W T 24 K32 L30-31
Blossom Av BT 17 R25
Blue Rd MA 72 M9
Blue Bird Rd R 82 M52
Blue Bluff Rd HU 20 M13
Blue Chalk Lake Rd MK 59 S35-36
Blue Church Rd LG 50 Y63
Blue Corner Rd PR 68 N-P70
Blue Heron Dr HL 60 S38-39
Blue Heron La PB 45 X43
Blue Heron Rd LM 13 S-T10
Blue Heron Rd LN 65 U58
Blue Heron Ridge F 47 X-Y52
Blue Jay La PS 76 M27
Blue Jay Rd SD 93 F-G24
Blue Lake Rd BT 16 Q24
Blue Lake Rd MK 59 Q36
Blue Lake Rd PS 57 R27
Blue Line Rd NF 17 U-V25
Blue Mountain Pl HT 23 K27
Blue Mountain Rd DH 31 E34 E35
Blue Mountain Rd LG 37 B60
Blue Mountain Rd PB 45 Z44
Blue Mountains-Clearview Twnln, The G 40 A-B25
Blue Mountains-Euphrasia Twnln, The G 40 A-B23
Blue Mountains-Meaford Twnln, The G 40 A-B23
Blue Run La LG 37 A60
Blue Sea Rd CS 100 A-B18
Blue Spruce Rd HL 59 Q35-36
Blue Water Pkwy HD 17 V28
Blueberry Rd F 47 Y52

Blueberry / Byers

Blueberry Tr HL 60 T-U40
Blueberry Hill Rd CS 100 D17
Blueberry Marsh Rd SM 41 Z29
Bluehaven Rd HU 20 M13
Bluenose Dr A 86 D94
Blueroof Rd NR 34 D46
Blueseal Rd NP 95 F34
Bluewater Hwy HU 20 J13
Bluewater Ln C 6 X6-7
Bluewater Rd A 84 Y90-91
Bluewater Beach Rd HU 20 K13
Bluff Ln C 5 D-E7
Bluff Rd MK 58 S-T30
Bluff Point Dr R 64 R54
Blysma Rd SDG 50 W65
Blyth Rd HU 20 J14 J15 K15-16 21 K-L17
Blyth Rd SDG 68 R69
Blyth Park Rd NR 33 F45
Blythe Shore Rd K 43 A37 44 A38
Boag Rd Y 30 D32 E31-32
Boakview Rd PS 76 N27
Boar Farm Rd G 28 D-E23
Boardmans Rd HS 34 D48
Boat Lake Rd BR 55 Y17-18
Boat Launch Rd LN 49 W61
Boat Launch Rd (Blind River) A 88 E4
Boat Launch Rd (Huron Shores) A 87 D98
Bob Carr Rd NR 33 G42
Bob Lake Rd HL 43 W37 60 V37 V37
Bob Seguin Dr R 99 H49
Bobby Rd F 48 Y53-54
Bobcat Tr A 89 C7
Bobcaygeon Rd HL 60 U-V37
Bobiak Rd LG 49 Z59
Bobs Lake Rd F 48 Y-Z55
Bobshire Rd MK 59 R-S36
Bochert Rd R 82 P52
Bodkin Rd MD 14 U15-16 V16
Bodson Dr CS 101 A19-20
Boe Bay Rd MK 59 U34-35
Boegel Rd F 47 X51
Boes Rd NR 34 F46
Bog Ln LM 13 Q-R12
Bogart Rd HS 47 A50
Bogart Rd MK 58 T32
Bogie's Beach Rd HU 20 J13
Bogus Rd EL 9 W20-21
Boice Bradley Dr HL 60 S39
Boileau Rd PR 67 Q67
Boiler Beach Rd BR 26 E13
Boisvenue Dr SDG 52 U71
Boisvenue Rd SD 92 G22
Bok Ln HU 26 H16
Boldt Rd R 81 P51
Boldts La HL 44 X38
Boler Rd MD 14 T16
Boles School Rd F 48 W54
Bolingbroke Rd LN 48 X56
Bolingbroke Station Rd LN 48 X56
Bolsover Rd K 43 A34-35 Z34
Bolt Rd PR 68 N-P69
Boltim Rd A 88 D5-6
Bolton La F 48 X54
Bolton Rd LG 50 V-X62
Bolton Rd NR 33 C44
Bolton Creek La LN 48 W55-56
Bolton Point Rd HL 61 V42
Bolton River Rd A 87 E1
Boltons Rd PB 44 Z41
Bomanton Rd NR 33 E42-43
Bomarc Rd NP 95 D31
Bon Echo Rd PS 57 S27
Bon Echo Creek Loop LA 63 V49
Bond Rd PE 35 G-H51
Bond St DH 31 H36
Bongards Rd PE 35 F52
Bongers Rd SDG 50 V65
Bonhomme Rd CS 101 A21
Bonin St CS 100 B18
Bonis La HL 60 V37
Bonisteel Rd HS 34 E47-48
Bonn Rd NR 34 F46
Bonneau Ln C 6 C7
Bonnechere Rd R 82 P54
Bonnechere Lodge Rd R 81 N-P50
Bonnell Rd MK 58 U32 59 U33
Bonner Rd R 64 S53
Bonnett Rd NR 33 E45
Bonneville Rd MK 41 X29
Bonnie Doone Rd LM 12 S9
Bonnie Lake Rd MK 59 T33
Bonnie Lake Camp Rd MK 59 T33
Bons Vivants Rd SD 93 F-G24
Book Rd HM 17 R27
Book Rd NI 18 S32
Booker Rd HD 18 U31
Bookers Rd HD 18 U29
Bookton La NF 16 T23
Boomer Ln WT 22 M21-22
Boomerang Rd HL 60 S38
Boomerang Rd NR 33 F43
Boomhauer Rd F 47 Y52
Boomhouwer Rd LG 50 W63
Boon Township Rd A 89 D10-11
Booster Park Rd HS 46 A46
Boot Hill Rd MD 13 R12
Boot Jack Ranch Rd G 28 D-E22
Booth Rd C 6 X7-8
Booth Rd (Chisholm) NP 95 G33
Booth Rd (North Bay) NP 95 E31-32
Boozeneck Rd MA 90 H-J11
Borchardt Rd BR 54 T16
Borden Av EL 15 U18
Borden Dr BR 54 T14
Bordenwood Rd F 47 X-Y52
Border Rd C 6 X7
Boreal Rd TB 102 D1-2
Borland Ln PB 33 C42
Borne Rd R 81 L50
Borne Rd R 81 L50
Bornes La PS 76 N30
Bornish Dr MD 13 R12 14 S13-14
Borris Rd PR 68 P70 P71
Boshkung Lake Rd HL 60 T-U37
Bosley Rd HS 46 Z49
Bosley Rd LA 47 X50-51
Bossert Rd NI 19 T35
Bossineau Rd A 86 C97
Boston Dr MD 14 T15-16
Boston Church Rd HT 23 M28
Boston Mills Rd PL 23 J27 J28 29 H28
Bostwick Rd EL 8 W17
Bostwick Rd MD 14 T-U16
Bot Rd MD 15 U19
Botany Ln C 7 A10 Y10-11
Botden Rd LA 47 A53
Botham Rd LG 49 X-Y60
Botham's Rd PS 76 N29
Botting Rd C 6 X8
Botting Rd F 36 B55
Botting Rd MK 58 R32
Bottle Lake Rd LN 64 U54-55
Bouchard's Rd SD 93 G23
Boucks Hill Rd SDG 51 V66
Boudreau Rd PR 67 P-Q67
Boudreau Rd R 64 R53
Bouffard Rd EX 4 C1-2
Bouffard Rd NP 94 E27
Boughner Rd HL 60 T-U39
Bougie Sdrd PR 68 Q70
Boulder Rd PS 77 K32-33
Boulder St K 32 D37
Boulter Rd HS 62 R46 S46-47 T47
Boulter Rd TB 102 D4
Boulter Lake Rd HS 61 R43
Boulter Township Access Rd NP 95 G34 96 G35
Boulton Rd HS 34 F46
Boulton St BR 55 X17
Boundary Dr TB 102 E4-5
Boundary La PB 44 W-X39
Boundary Ln C 7 A10
Boundary Rd CS 91 E16
Boundary Rd DH 31 F36 32 E-F39 F37-38
Boundary Rd F 37 B-C58
Boundary Rd G 39 A-B20
Boundary Rd K 44 X38
Boundary Rd LG 50 V64 66 U63-64
Boundary Rd OT 67 R65
Boundary Rd PB 44 B39-40
Boundary Rd PR 68 N-P69
Boundary Rd SDG 52 U70-71
Boundary Rd (Bonfield) NP 96 F35
Boundary Rd (Calvin) NP 96 E-F36
Boundary Rd (Centre Hastings) HS 34 C49
Boundary Rd (Chisholm) NP 95 G-H33
Boundary Rd (Johnson) A 86 D96
Boundary Rd (Lount) PS 77 L31
Boundary Rd (Magnetawan) PS 76 N29
Boundary Rd (McKellar) PS 76 P27
Boundary Rd (Perry) PS 58 Q32 59 Q33
Boundary Rd (Pringle) PS 94 J28-29
Boundary Rd (Sault Ste Marie) A 84 B92
Boundary Rd (Wollaston) HS 45 W44 61 V44
Boundary Spur Rd PS 76 M28
Bourdeau Rd PS 77 P31
Bourdeau Rd SDG 68 S-T72
Bourgeois Rd PR 67 S67
Bourgeois Beach Rd SM 41 X29
Bourgon Rd PR 68 Q-R69
Bourne Rd LN 65 U60
Boutz Rd NP 96 E-F37
Bouvier Rd PR 67 P66 Q67
Bova Rd LN 48 W56
Bovaird Dr PL 24 J-K29
Bow St Y 30 F32
Bow Lake Rd LN 64 T56
Bowen Rd HS 61 T44
Bowen Rd K 32 D37
Bowen Rd NI 19 T35
Bowen Rd PB 45 A45 46 A46
Bower Hill Rd OX 16 R-S21
Bowers Ln C 5 D8 6 C8
Bowers Tr HS 62 U47
Bowers Point Rd HS 61 T43
Bowes Sdrd LN 48 W57 49 W58
Bowes St PS 57 R27
Bowesville Rd OT 66 R-S63
Bowland Rd LN 65 T58
Bowles Rd DH 31 F34-35
Bowles Bluff Rd G 28 C22
Bowman Rd NR 33 F41-42
Bowslaugh Rd NI 18 R30
Bowyer Rd MK 59 Q33-34
Boxall Rd EL 8 W16
Boxton Rd HL 61 T-U42
Boxwell Rd NP 95 F34 96 F35
Boy Scout Rd SDG 68 S70
Boy Scout Rd TB 102 B5
Boy Scouts Rd PS 77 M33
Boyce Rd F 36 B54-55
Boyce Rd NR 33 F44
Boyces Rd MK 59 R35
Boychuk Rd A 88 C6
Boyd Rd HS 46 A46
Boyd Rd OT 67 T65
Boyd Rd SM 42 X32
Boyde La WT 22 L21
Boyer Rd LN 65 T-U58
Boyers Sdrd Y 30 D31-32
Boyes Rd TB 102 B4
Boyes Heritage Rd MK 59 U34-35
Boyle La R 81 M49
Boyle Rd NR 33 F43
Boyle Rd NI 18 S-T32
Boyne Rd SDG 67 T-U66
Boyne St SM 29 E28
Bozeneck Rd TB 102 F4
Bracken Av LN 49 W59
Bracken Rd F 36 B-C54
Bracken Tr HL 43 W37
Brackenridge Dr PB 32 E40
Brackenrig Centre Rd MK 58 T31
Bradburn Rd DH 32 F37
Bradden La F 36 A57
Bradfield Rd NI 19 Q34
Bradfield Rd PB 33 C41
Bradford Rd F 36 B54
Bradford St SM 41 B29 42 B30
Bradish Rd MD 15 U17
Bradley Av MD 15 T17
Bradley Crossroad PE 35 F-G51
Bradley Dr BR 55 U15
Bradley La HS 62 T47-48
Bradley Ln C 6 B7
Bradley Rd CS 100 B17
Bradley Rd F 48 X53
Bradley Rd MK 58 U31
Bradley Rd PS 57 Q28 58 Q29
Bradley Sdrd OT 66 R61
Bradley Sdrd PR 68 P-Q70
Bradley Bay Rd NR 33 D45 34 D46
Bradley Creek Ln EL 9 W19 15 V19
Bradley Hollow Rd NR 33 E-F43
Bradshaw Rd F 48 Y55
Bradshaw Rd HS 62 U46
Bradshaw Rd LA 47 A52
Bradshaw Rd NI 18 T32
Bradshaw Rd PS 57 R27
Brady Dr MD 15 U17
Brady Rd LA 35 C52
Brady Rd LG 48 Z57
Brady Rd (Adelaide Metcalfe) MD. 14 U13
Brady Rd (Thames Centre) MD 15 T18
Brady St NI 18 S32
Brady Lake Rd HL 59 U36 60 U37
Brae-Loch Rd R 83 P56
Braeloch Rd HL 60 T37
Braemar Sdrd OX 15 Q20 16 Q21
Braemore Ln C 7 Y11-12
Bragg Rd DH 32 G38
Bragmore Bay La MA 73 L11
Bramalea Rd PL 23 J28 24 J-K29
Brambel Rd SM 42 B31
Brampton Rd HM 18 Q29
Branch La PS 77 P31
Branch Rd LG 50 X62-63
Branch Rd SDG 50 V-W65
Branchton Rd BT 17 P-Q25
Branchton Rd WT 23 P25
Brand Rd NR 33 G41
Brandon Rd HU 20 J16 21 J-K17
Brandon Rd LA 35 D53
Brandow Point Dr MA 72 K9
Brandy Crest Rd MK 58 T31
Braniff Rd A 86 D-E97
Branson Rd HL 60 U37
Brant Av BT 17 R25
Brant Rd BT 17 Q25
Brant St HT 23 P28
Brant-Elderslie Townline BR 27 D17
Brant-Oxford Rd BT 16 Q23
Brant Church Rd BT 17 S25
Brant Mill Rd BT 17 S25
Brant School Rd BT 17 R26
Brant Waterloo Rd WT 22 P24 23 P25
Brantford Rd NF 16 T24 U23
Brantford Southern Access Rd BT 17 R25
Brantwood Park Rd BT 17 R25
Brash La F 48 Y55-56
Brasier Rd SD 92 G22
Brawley Rd DH 31 G35
Brawn Rd NI 18 U32
Bray Lake Rd PS 77 K31 95 J31
Bray Shore Rd PS 95 J31
Brayton-Miller Rd LG 49 Y61
Brazeau, Mtée SD 101 D23
Brazeau Rd PR 67 P66
Brazeau Rd R 82 L52
Breadalbane Rd SDG 68 P72 Q71
Breaky's Bay Rd F 37 D58
Brealey Dr PB 32 C-D40
Brebeuf Path WL 23 L26
Brebeuf Rd SM 41 Y28
Brechin Rd K 43 Z34
Breckles Dr HL 60 S38
Breen Dr MD 14 Q15-16
Breen Rd LA 47 A52-53
Breen Rd MD 15 T19
Breezeway Rd K 32 C38
Breezy Heights Rd OT 65 R59
Breezy Point Rd MK 58 U31
Breisacher Rd MK 58 Q32 59 Q33
Brenda's Rd DH 32 E37
Brennan Cir MK 58 R32
Brennan Ln SM 42 X-Y32
Brennan Rd HS 34 D49
Brennan Harbour Rd A 89 F8
Brennans Rd PS 77 K32
Brent Rd R 97 F-G40
Brentha Rd TM 85 N27
Brentwood Rd SM 29 C28
Bresee Rd F 48 Z56
Brethour Rd HS 61 T-U44
Brethour Rd TM 85 N-P30
Brethour-Pense Township Rd TM 85 N30
Brewer Rd F 48 X54
Brewers Rd PE 35 H51
Brewers Mills Rd F 37 B58
Brewster Rd DH 31 D33
Brewster Lake Rd G 28 C24
Briar Hill Rd LG 37 A59
Briardean Rd WT 22 N24
Brick Rd C 7 X10
Brick Rd PB 44 B40
Brick Yard Ln LM 13 S10-11
Bricker School Ln WT 22 L22
Brickyard Rd BR 27 C17
Bride Rd WL 27 H19
Bridge Rd HU 20 L16
Bridge Rd PB 44 B40
Bridge St LA 63 T50
Bridge St NI 19 T35-36
Bridge St OT 66 S63
Bridge St SM 30 E31
Bridge St (Fort Erie) NI 19 T35-36
Bridge St (Niagara Falls) NI 19 R35
Bridge St (Waterloo) WT 22 M23
Bridge St (Wilmot) WT 22 P21-22
Bridge St W HS 34 E48-49
Bridge St W LA 35 D51-52
Bridge Water Rd LA 47 Y50
Bridgeland Rd A 86 D97
Bridgeport Rd WT 22 M23
Bridgewater Rd HS 46 A49
Bridle Path Y 30 E32
Bridle Rd DH 31 G36
Bridle Rd K 32 C37
Bridlewood Blvd HT 23 K27
Briere Rd PR 67 S67
Brigden Rd C 6 X8
Brigden Rd LM 12 S-V8
Briggs La F 48 Y56
Brigham Rd MD 14 T-U16
Bright Rd NR 33 E44
Bright Lake Rd A 87 E1
Brighton Rd EX 4 B3
Brighton-Cramahe Boundary Rd NR 33 F45
Brights La NR 33 C44 D43
Brilling Rd SD 90 F11
Brimley Rd NR 33 F-G43
Brimley Rd T 25 J33
Brindley Beach Rd HU 26 H13
Brinklow Rd HS 46 W46
Brinkmans Rd BR 54 T15
Brinsley Rd MD 14 Q-R14
Brinson Rd HS 46 A49
Brinston Rd SDG 50 V65 51 W66
Briscoe Rd R 82 P54
Bristol Rd K 44 B38-39
Bristol Rd PL 24 L30
Bristol Sands Cr DH 31 F33
Britain Lake Rd BR 54 T16
Britainville Rd MA 72 L8
Britannia Rd HT 23 M-N28 24 L-M29
Britannia Rd MK 59 R34
Britannia Rd PL 24 K-L30 L29
Briton Rd EX 4 E2
Briton-Houghton Bay Rd LG 49 X58-59
Broad Ln C 6 X8
Broad Rd HD 17 T28
Broad St HD 18 U30
Broadbent Rd PS 76 P28-29
Broadley Rd MK 58 U31
Broadview Av LN 49 W60
Broadview Av T 24 K32
Broadway DF 29 H26
Broadway Av TB 102 E5
Broadway St BR 26 D-E14
Broadway St EX 4 C1
Broadway St NI 19 T33
Broadway St OX 16 U21
Broadway St PS 77 K32
Broadway St WT 22 L-M22
Broadwell Lake Rd PS 94 J28
Broadworth Rd NR 33 D44
Broatch Rd HS 34 E47
Brock Rd DH 25 I-J35 31 C-D34 F-H34 H35
Brock Rd F 48 Y53 Y54
Brock Rd HM 17 Q27 23 P27
Brock Rd WL 23 M-N26
Brock St (Uxbridge) DH 31 E34
Brock St (Whitby) DH 31 H36
Brock-Scugog Townline Rd DH 31 D35
Brock-Thorah Townline E DH 43 B34-35
Brock-Thorah Townline W DH 31 C34
Brockem Rd LG 50 Y-Z63
Brockmere Cliff Dr LG 50 A62
Brockville St LN 49 W60
Broderick Rd EX 4 C-D2
Brodie Dr SM 42 Y-Z32
Brodie Rd SDG 68 Q71-72
Brodill Lake Rd CS 101 D19
Brodofske Rd R 63 S49
Brogan's Rd PS 77 N32
Brohart Rd SD 90 F11
Broken Front Rd MD 13 S12
Broken Second Rd SDG 50 X65 51 X66
Bromley Ln R 82 K53-54
Bronk Rd HS 34 D49
Bronson Av OT 66 Q-R63
Bronson Ln HU 14 Q14 20 M-P13 P14
Bronson Rd HS 46 Z47 62 U46
Bronson Rd R 99 H48
Bronson Access Rd R 98 H47 99 H48
Bronson Lake Rd NP 96 F36
Bronson Rapids Rd HS 46 A-B47
Bronson South Access Rd R 98 H47 99 H48
Bronte Rd HT 24 N29
Bronte St HT 23 M28
Brook Ln C 6 A8 Y8
Brook Ln EL 15 V19
Brook Ln NR 33 F42-43
Brook Rd MD 14 R14
Brook Rd (Alnwick-Haldimand) NR 33 E42
Brook Rd (Cobourg) NR 33 G42
Brookdale Av SDG 52 U-V70
Brookdale Rd DH 31 F34
Brooke Ln LM 13 U11-12
Brooke Valley Rd LN 48 W57 X56
Brookfield Rd NI 19 T-U34
Brooklin Rd HD 17 V27
Brooks Cr NR 33 E45 34 E46
Brooks La F 36 A55 48 Z55
Brooks La HS 46 W46
Brooks La PS 77 L32
Brooks Rd A 84 Z92-93
Brooks Rd HS 34 C47 47 A50
Brooks Rd HD 17 T28 18 T29
Brooks Rd LG 50 W-X63
Brooks Rd PS 57 R27
Brooks Rd SDG 67 U66
Brooks Sdrd SM 42 X33
Brooks Lake Rd MK 78 P35
Brooks Landing Rd PS 56 Q24
Brooks Point Rd LG 37 A58
Brookside Rd NR 33 G43
Brookside Rd PS 77 L-M31
Brookview Rd K 32 C38
Broome Rd R 82 M54
Broome Rd TB 102 D-E3
Broomfield Rd NR 33 E-F43
Brophy Rd OT 66 S-T62
Brottan Rd R 80 N47
Brouillette Rd NP 93 E26
Broule Rd NP 96 F35
Brouse Rd LN 48 W56
Brouse Rd R 99 G48
Brouseville Rd LG 50 X64-65
Brouwers Ln EL 15 V18
Brown Dr PS 94 J27
Brown La HS 62 U47
Brown Ln PB 32 D40
Brown Rd DH 32 F38
Brown Rd EL 9 W20
Brown Rd HS 34 D48
Brown Rd LA 47 B53
Brown Rd LN 49 V60
Brown Rd LG 50 Y62
Brown Rd MD 14 T13
Brown Rd MK 58 T31
Brown Rd NR 33 F42
Brown Rd NI 19 S-T34
Brown Rd SM 42 A-B30
Brown Sdrd LA 35 C51
Brown Sdrd LN 49 V59 65 U59
Brown's Rd DF 29 G27
Brown's Rd EX 5 H5
Brown's Rd R 62 S47-48
Brown's Rd (Port Hope) NR 33 F41
Brown's Bay Rd F 47 W52
Brown Island Rd A 86 D94
Brown Township 21 Access Rd PS 75 L24-25
Brown Township Access Rd PS 75 K24 L24-26
Brownlee Rd A 87 E99
Brownlee Rd OT 66 S61
Brownley Rd PS 76 P28-29
Brownrigg Rd PR 67 Q68
Browns La SDG 67 U65
Browns La (North Frontenac) F 48 W53
Browns La (South Frontenac) F 48 Y55
Browns Ln SM 29 C28
Browns Ln T 24 L31
Browns Rd F 36 A54
Browns Rd (Alnwick-Haldimand) NR 33 E43
Browns Rd E MK 59 R34
Browns Way MK 42 W31 58 V31
Browns Brae Rd MK 59 S35
Browns Lake Rd PS 58 R-S29
Browns Lake Access Rd LA 63 U50-51
Browns Line Rd PB 45 B45
Brownson Rd HS 46 Z47
Brownsville Rd DH 32 G39
Brownsville Rd OX 15 U20 16 U21
Browntown Rd HU 20 J16 21 J17-18 26 H16
Bruce Av R 82 P55
Bruce Dr C 6 B7
Bruce Dr K 32 D38
Bruce Rd HS 62 T47
Bruce Rd PS 77 M32
Bruce St R 81 P51
Bruce-Greenock Rd BR 26 C16
Bruce-Saugeen Twnln BR 26 C15-16
Bruce-Saugeen Townline Rd BR 38 B15
Bruce Bay Rd A 86 E96
Bruce Beach Rd BR 26 E13
Bruce Cave's Rd G 39 X18
Bruce Lake Rd MK 58 S-T30
Bruce Scott Rd LM 13 R11
Bruceton Rd R 63 S49
Brudenell Rd R 81 P49
Brule Rd A 84 A92
Brule Rd F 36 D55
Brule Tr Y 30 F30
Brule Lake Rd F 63 U-V52
Brule View La F 63 U52
Brummell Rd PE 35 H50
Brunel Rd MK 59 R33-34 S-T34
Brunelle Sdrd SM 41 X28
Bruner Sdrd EX 5 E5
Brunet Rd SDG 52 U69
Brunet Rd SD 93 F-G24
Bruno St CS 100 B18 101 B19
Brunon Av K 31 D-E36
Brunton Sdrd LN 65 U60
Brush Ln C 7 B10-11
Brush Rd EX 4 D2-3
Brush Rd LM 13 S-T10
Brussels Ln HU 20 K16 21 J17 K17
Bruyea Rd HS 34 D46
Bryan Rd LG 37 A59
Bryan's Rd HL 61 V41
Bryans Rd TM 85 M28
Bryant Rd PE 34 F47
Bryant Sdrd DH 31 F35
Bryant St BR 55 X17
Brydges Rd R 64 R54-55
Brydges St MD 15 T17
Brydons Bay Rd MK 58 V32
Bryn Mawr La HT 23 N28
Buchler Rd MK 41 W29
Buchner Rd NI 19 T34
Bucholtz Rd R 81 L50
Buck Bay Rd F 48 Z55
Buck Haven Rd PS 77 L32
Buck Hill Rd HS 62 T45
Buck Hill Rd R 81 N48
Buck Lake Landing Rd MK 59 Q35
Buck Point La F 36 C56
Buckeye Rd MK 58 T29
Buckham's Bay Rd OT 83 P59
Buckhorn La PB 44 A40-41 Z40
Buckhorn Rd HL 44 W40
Buckhorn Rd MK 58 Q-R32
Buckhorn Rd PB 44 A-B41
Buckhorn Narrows Rd PB 44 A40 Z40
Buckingham Rd LM 6 X7
Buckles St OT 66 T63
Buckley's Rd PS 77 M34
Buckmiller Rd SD 90 F-G11
Buckner Rd NI 18 T31
Buckshot Creek Access Rd LA 63 V51
Buckshot Lake Rd F 63 V53
Buckshot Lake Rd LA 63 U-V51
Buckskin Lake Rd HL 61 V41-42
Buckslide Rd HL 60 T-U37
Buckvale Dr PS 58 Q32
Buckwheat Rd W LG 50 W63-64
Budarick Rd HS 62 S47
Budd Ln OX 15 S20 16 S21
Budd Rd R 81 P50
Budd Mills Rd R 81 M50
Budvet Rd BR 55 V16
Buehler Ln WT 22 L21
Buelow Rd HS 62 R46
Buffalo Rd NI 19 U36
Buffam Rd LN 49 V-W61
Buis Ln EL 15 V18
Buker Rd LG 50 W62-63
Buker Rd LG 50 X63
Bulger Rd R 82 N52
Buliung Rd NI 18 T32
Bull Rd NR 33 F42-43
Bull Lake Rd F 47 Y52
Buller Rd HL 43 X37
Buller Rd K 43 X37
Bullfrog Bay Rd LG 37 B59
Bullis Rd NR 34 F46
Bullock Rd MD 14 Q13
Bullock Rd PB 44 A41
Bulls Rd NR 33 D44
Bulls Mill Rd NR 33 F42-43
Bullseye La F 36 B55
Bulmer's Rd K 44 Z38
Bunker Hill Rd F 36 A55
Bunker Hill Rd PS 77 K31
Bunny Tr PS 76 N-P27
Bunting Rd NI 19 Q-R34
Bur Brook Rd F 36 C55-56
Bur Brook Rd E F 36 C-D56
Bur Oak Av Y 31 H33
Burbridge Rd NR 33 F44
Burchat Rd R 81 N50
Burchell Rd LN 49 V-W61
Burchell Rd LG 49 W61
Burdon Rd MD 14 U13
Bureau Rd SDG 68 R72
Burega La F 36 C55-56
Burelle Rd PR 67 S67
Burford Rd BT 16 R24
Burford-Delhi Townline Rd NF 16 T23-24
Burger Rd NI 19 U35
Burgess Rd HS 62 R46
Burgess Rd PS 58 S30
Burgess Sdrd G 39 X-Y19
Burk Ln C 7 A10
Burke Dr NP 96 E37
Burke La LN 48 W56
Burke Rd HD 18 T-U30
Burke Rd K 44 X38
Burke St MA 72 M8
Burke Settlement Rd F 48 W54
Burkes Rd HL 60 U39
Burkes Rd R 99 G48
Burkett Rd NI 18 U32
Burkett Rd PS 58 Q-R29
Burkic La HS 62 S47
Burlanyett Rd HS 62 R45
Burleigh Rd HL 61 T-U41
Burleigh Rd NI 19 U35
Burleigh St PB 45 X42-43
Burleigh Access Rd PB 45 Y43
Burlington St HM 17 Q28 18 Q29
Burlmarie Rd MK 59 T34
Burloak Dr HT 24 N29
Burma La LG 37 A60
Burma Rd BR 55 V16
Burma Rd CS 100 B16
Burman Ln LM 6 W8
Burnaby Rd NI 19 U33
Burnbrae Rd LG 50 Z62
Burnbrae Rd NR 34 C46
Burnett Rd F 36 B54
Burnett's Rd PS 57 Q28 76 P28
Burnett's Sdrd MA 90 J11-12
Burney Point Rd F 48 X54
Burnham Rd PB 33 C41
Burnham St NR 33 F-G42
Burnhamthorpe Rd HT 24 M-N29
Burnhamthorpe Rd PL 24 L-M30
Burnie Rd LG 50 X64
Burnley Rd NR 33 E44
Burns La LG 37 A-B60
Burns Ln HU 20 K15
Burns Rd F 48 Y55
Burns Rd LN 49 V59
Burns Rd NI 18 R-S29
Burns St DH 31 H36
Burns Crossover Rd SD 90 E-F12
Burns Lake Tr R 63 R51
Burnside Dr LG 50 Z63
Burnside Ln SM 42 Y31
Burnside Bridge Rd PS 57 Q27
Burnstown Rd R 82 Q55
Burnt Bridge Rd R 62 R-S48
Burnt Dam Rd PB 45 A45
Burnt Hills Rd F 36 B57 37 B58
Burnt Island Rd MA 71 K4
Burnt Lake Rd NP 94 D27
Burnt Lands Rd OT 65 R-S59
Burnt River Rd K 43 Y37 44 Y38
Burr Rd LM 7 W11 13 V11
Burr Rd PE 34 F49
Burr Oak Rd CS 100 D17
Burrett Irwin Rd PB 44 A40 Z40
Burridge Rd F 48 Z56
Burridge Lake Rd F 48 Y55-56
Burritt's Rd NP 96 E38
Burritts Av OT 50 V62
Burrows La LN 48 Y56
Burt Rd BT 17 Q25
Burt St BR 26 F15
Burtch Rd BT 16 S24 17 S25
Burton Av SM 30 C30 42 B30
Burton Rd LN 48 W56
Burton Rd OT 67 R65
Burwash Rd SD 92 F20
Burwell Rd MD 14 U15
Burwell Rd NF 16 V21
Burwell Rd (Southwold) EL 8 W16
Burwell Rd (St Thomas) EL 15 V17
Bury Rd C 7 A12 Y12
Bury Rd, The BR 55 U16
Bury's Green Rd K 43 Z37 44 Z38
Bus Line Rd TM 85 P28
Bush Ln C 6 Y8
Bush Ln EL 8 W16-17
Bush Ln LM 13 V11
Bush Rd F 48 Z54
Bush Rd LG 49 Z58
Bush Rd PB 45 W44
Bush Rd SDG 68 R71-72
Bush Rd SM 41 W27-28
Bush Rd (Bobcaygeon) K 44 A39
Bush Rd (Oakwood) K 31 C36 32 C37
Bush St PL 23 J27
Bush Glen Rd SDG 67 U67-68
Bushell St BR 26 E-F15
Bushwolf Lake Rd HL 60 T39
Bushy Bay Rd CS 101 Z22
Busy Rd HL 60 T38
Butler Dr PB 45 Z42
Butler Rd PR 67 Q66
Butler Rd R 82 P54
Butler Mill Rd MK 58 R31
Butlers La NF 16 T23-24
Buttar-Blezard Rd NR 33 E-F42
Butter Rd HM 17 R27
Butter & Egg Rd MK 58 T-U31
Butterfield Rd PS 95 H31 J32
Butterfly Rd MK 58 U30
Buttermilk La HS 46 Z46
Buttermilk Falls Rd LA 35 C51
Buttermilk Hill Rd LN 49 V59
Butternut Rd LA 47 B53
Butternut Creek Rd F 36 D57
Buttler Rd MK 58 T31
Button Ln HU 20 J-K16
Button St BR 26 G14
Button Bay La F 36 E57
Buttonwood Dr MD 13 V12
Bycroft La F 48 Z55
Byerlay Sdrd NF 16 U-V22
Byers Rd DH 32 F37

Byers Rd HS 62 Q46
Byers Rd LG 50 X64-65
Byers Rd NR. 33 E41-42
Byers Rd PS 95 G31
Byers Rd R 82 Q55
Byers Rd TB 103 C6
Byers Creek Rd R. 81 N48
Byes Sdrd A 84 Z92
Byker Rd LG 50 W64-65
Byrnedale Rd EX 5 C5
Byrnes Rd LG 48 X57
Byron Baseline Rd MD . . . 14 T16

C, Concession BR 27 F18
C Ln A 5 F6
C, Mersea Rd EX 5 F6
C Ln A 86 E94
C Ln BR. 38 Z17
C Ln DF 29 H26
C-Line Rd TB. 102 E3
C Johnson Rd CS 100 D15-16
C Line Rd HU . . . 21 J18 27 H17-18
C W Leach Rd SM 30 E29
Cabana Rd EX 4 C2
Caber Rd SDG 68 S71
Cabin Rd OT 66 T63
Cable Rd K 44 A38
Caboodle La HL 60 S38
Cabot Head Rd BR 54 S16-17
Cache Bay Rd NP. 94 D28
Cadell Rd OT 90 F10
Cadieux Ch PR 68 N69
Cadieux Rd SDG 68 Q71
Cadigan Rd PB 44 A39
Cadillac Blvd K 32 C40
Cads Tr R 82 K54
Caesar Rd NI 15 U18
Cahiague Rd SM 42 Y30-31
Cahill Ln R 82 M52
Caille Av EX 4 B4
Cailloux La SDG 68 P71
Cains La PB. 44 X39
Caintown Rd LG 37 A61
Cairn View Rd SDG 68 T72
Cairns Cr NI 19 T36
Cairns Rd NF 16 V22
Cairo Rd LM 7 W11
Caister La K 43 Y37
Caister-Gainsborough Townline Rd
NI 18 S31
Caistor Centre Rd NI . . 18 R-S30
Caistorville Rd NI 18 S-T30
Caistorville Rd NI . . 18 S29-30
Caithness St E HD . . 17 S27-28
Calabogie Rd A 86 C94
Calabogie Rd R . . 64 R54-55 S53
Calahan Rd LM 6 W7
Calbrett Rd HL 60 V40 61 V41
Caldwell La LN 64 T56
Caldwell Rd PB 45 W43
Caledon-King Townline Y. . 30 H29
Caledon East Garafraxa Townline
DF. 29 H26
Caledonia By-Pass HL. . . 17 S27
Caledonia Rd C 6 A9 Y9
Caledonia Springs Rd PR 88 N-P70
Caley Rd OX 16 T22-23
Calfass Rd WL 23 N26
Calico Rd HL. 60 U39
California Av LG 57 Z62-63
California Rd LA 47 A53
California Rd LN 64 S56
Callaghan Rd HS 35 D51
Callaghan Rapids Rd HS . . 46 B46
Callander Bay Dr PS 95 F32
Callendor Rd OT 66 U63
Calow Rd PS. 56 Q25
Calton Ln EL 9 W18-21
Calvert Dr MD . . . 13 U12 14 T-U13
Calvert Rd HD 14 T31
Calvert Rd TB 102 D4
Calvin Rd R 82 N-P54
Calypso St PR 67 R66
Cambray Rd K 43 B37
Cambrian Rd DH. 32 F37
Cambrian Rd OT. 66 S62
Cambrian Rd SM . . 42 X32 Y31-32
Camden-Portland Boundary Rd F. .
. . . . 36 B-C54
Camel Lake Rd MK. 58 T32
Camelon Rd LN. 65 S58
Cameron Av LN . . . 48 X57 49 X58
Cameron La F 48 Z56
Cameron Ln PB 44 X39
Cameron Rd BR 55 W17
Cameron Rd HS 35 D52
Cameron Rd K 43 A37
Cameron Rd LM . . 7 W-X12 13 V12
Cameron Rd MD 14 S13
Cameron Rd NP 95 D32
Cameron Rd NR 34 E46
Cameron Rd SDG 68 T70
Cameron Rd TB 102 F3-4
Cameron Rd WT 22 P23
Cameron Rd (Huron Shores) A . . .
. . . . 87 E99
Cameron Rd (MacDonald,
Meredith, & Aberdeen) A . . 86 C95
Cameron Rd (North Dundas) SDG.
. . . . 50 V64-65
Cameron Rd (North Stormont)
SDG. 68 R-S69
Cameron Sdrd DH 43 B34
Cameron Sdrd EX 4 D4
Cameron Sdrd LN 48 W57
Cameron St DH 31 C35
Cameron St HU 20 L13
Cameron St PR. 68 N71
Cameron Falls Rd SD . . . 90 E10
Cameron Lake Rd BR. . . . 54 S14
Cameron Lake Rd HL 63 R49
Cameron Track Rd R 88 D67
Camlachie Rd LM 12 S-T9
Camley Ln R 82 N53
Camp La HS 46 A49
Camp Rd A 87 C99
Camp Rd BR 38 Z17
Camp Rd HS 46 A49
Camp Rd PS 76 P28
Camp 50 Rd SD 90 D-E12
Camp Bay Dr HL 59 R36
Camp Dorset Rd HL 59 S36
Camp Edlau La R 80 M47
Camp Eley Rd A. 87 E-F1
Camp Gesher Rd LA 47 W50
Camp Hill Rd SM 29 C28
Camp Jackson Rd MK. . 58 U29-30
Camp Kagawong Rd MA . . 72 K8

Camp Kakeka Tr HL 60 T39-40
Camp Lake Rd A 89 F8
Camp Lake Rd MK. . 59 Q36 78 P36
Camp Line Rd PB 45 A42
Camp Mary Ann Rd MA . . 72 L10
Camp Newport Rd MK . . . 58 S32
Camp Oconto Rd F 48 Y54-55
Camp Oliver Rd K 28 E21
Camp Towhee Rd HL . . . 60 T-U38
Camp Wheeler La HL 60 T37
Campbell Dr R 49 X60
Campbell Dr R 83 Q57
Campbell La K 43 X34-35
Campbell Ln C 7 B10-11
Campbell Ln LM 13 V11
Campbell Ln R 82 P54
Campbell Rd BT 17 R-S26
Campbell Rd C 5 D7
Campbell Rd DF 29 G26
Campbell Rd F 4 D3
Campbell Rd F 36 B55
Campbell Rd LG. 50 W64
Campbell Rd MA 71 K6
Campbell Rd MK. 59 V33
Campbell Rd PR. 68 Q70
Campbell Rd SDG. 68 T69
Campbell Rd TM. 85 M27
Campbell Rd WL. . . 22 L24 23 L25
Campbell Rd (Alnwick-Haldimand)
NR 33 D43
Campbell Rd (Cramahe) NR. 33 E44
Campbell Rd (Percy) NR . . 33 D44
Campbell Rd (Port Hope) NR. . . . .
. . . . 32 F40 33 F41
Campbell Sdrd LN . . 64 R56 65 R57
Campbell's Hill G 28 C23
Campbell's Rd LN 64 S-T55
Campbell's Sdrd Beckwith . . . .
. . . . 65 T60
Campbell Beach Rd K . . . 43 Z34
Campbell Farm Rd BT . . . 17 S25
Campbell Line Rd MA 72 L9
Campbellcroft Rd OT 66 T64
Campbells Rd MK 58 S29-30
Campbells Creek Access Rd F . . . .
. . . . 63 V51
Campbellton Rd PR 33 D41
Campbellville Rd HM. . . 23 N26-27
Campbellville Rd HT. . . 23 M-N27
Campden Rd NI 18 R-S32
Campeau Dr OT 66 R61
Campeau Rd SDG. 68 T69
Campedor Rd A 86 D95
Camperdown Rd G 40 A24
Campers Cove Rd C 5 E7
Campground La F 48 Y56
Campground Sdrd R . . . 64 R53-54
Can-Amera Pkwy WT . . 22 N24 23 N25
Canaan Rd A 6 W7
Canaan Rd OT 67 P65-66 Q66
Canaan Rd R 82 Q55 83 Q56
Canada Company Rd HU . . . .
. . . . 20 K-L16 21 L17
Canal Rd F 36 B57
Canal Rd HS 34 F46-47
Canal Rd K 43 A34-35
Canal Rd MK 59 R34
Canal Rd NR. 45 B45
Canal Rd (Bradford West
Gwillimbury) SM 30 F30-31
Canal Rd (Ramara) SM . . . 43 A34
Canal Rd (Severn) SM . . . 42 X32
Canal St C 5 E7
Canal Bank Rd HD 18 U31
Canal Bank La LN 49 W58
Canal Bank St NI. 19 T33
Canard Dr EX 4 C-D1
Canboro Rd NI. . . 18 S32 19 S33-34
Canborough Rd NI 18 T30
Canborough Rd NI. 18 T31-32
Candy Mountain Dr TB. . . 102 E4
Candytown La MK 59 S33
Cannard's La MA. 72 L10
Canning Rd MK. 42 X32
Canning Rd NR 33 E-F41
Canning Rd OX 16 R23
Canning Rd PS 76 N28
Cannon Mine Rd A 88 B-C3
Canoe Lake Rd A 88 E3
Canoe Lake Rd F . . 36 A56 48 Z56
Canoe Point Rd A 86 E95
Canola Rd LN 82 L54
Canon Smith Dr OT . . . 83 P58-59
Canonto Rd R 64 U53-54
Canonto Hydroline Access Rd F. . .
. . . . 64 T54
Canopy La HL 60 T38
Canrobert St G 28 C23
Canuck Tr HL 43 X37
Canyon Rd HL 60 T40
Canyon Rd HT 23 M27
Cape G 39 X19-20
Cape Chin North Rd BR . . 54 T16
Cape Chin North Shore Rd BR . . . .
. . . . 54 T16-17
Cape Chin South Rd BR . . . .
. . . . 54 T17 55 U16
Cape Hurd Rd BR 54 S13
Cape Smith Rd MA 73 L14
Capreol Rd CS 101 A20
Capreol Lake Rd CS . . 101 A20 Z20
Captains Rd R 64 R55
Caradoc Rd NR. 33 E43
Carbine Rd LN 65 R57
Card Rd LA 36 A54
Card Rd LA 47 B53
Card Lake Rd HS . . 61 U44 62 U45
Cardico Dr Y 30 G32
Cardiff Rd HU . . 20 J16 21 J17-18
Cardiff Rd TB 102 D3
Cardiff Access Rd HL. . . . 61 V42
Cardiff Lake Rd HL 61 T-U42
Cardinal Rd K 43 X36
Cardinal Rd R 81 N-P48
Cardinal Heights Dr F. . . . 48 Y53
Cardwell Rd PB. 58 S30
Cardwell St MA 73 L13
Cardwell Lake Rd MK . . . 58 R31
Cargill Rd R 27 D17
Caribou Rd A 86 D96
Caribou Rd HL 60 V38
Caribou Rd MK. 59 U34
Caribou Creek Rd R . . . 87 B1-2
Caribou Lake Rd PS . . 93 J26 94 J27
Carkner Rd LG 49 X61
Carl Rd (Niagara Falls) NI. . 19 S34
Carl Rd (Port Colborne) NI. . 19 U34
Carl-Froats Rd SDG 67 U68

Carlas La A 88 E4
Carless Rd C. 5 D7 6 C7
Carleton St LG 48 Y57
Carleton Corner Rd OT. . . 67 T65
Carley Rd Y. 30 G32
Carleys Corners Rd LG . . 50 W62
Carling Av OT . . 66 Q-R62 R61 T65
Carling Bay Rd E PS 56 Q26
Carling Bay Rd W PS. . . 56 Q25-26
Carling Station Rd PS . . 75 P25-26
Carlingford Rd MK 58 T30
Carlingview Rd T. 24 K30
Carlisle Rd HM. 23 N-P27
Carlisle St BR 38 A16
Carlow Ln PB 45 B42
Carlsbad La OT 67 R65
Carlsmount Rd SM 59 U33-34
Carlson Rd (Neebing) TB . . 102 F4
Carlson Rd (Ware) TB. . . 100 D-E32
Carlton Rd Y. . . . 30 H32 31 H33
Carlton St N. 19 R33-34
Carlton St T. 24 K32
Carluke Rd HM 15 T18-19
Carlyle Access Rd MA . . . 91 H17
Carlyon Ln SM 42 Y31
Carman Rd NR 34 E46
Carman St MD. 15 T18-19
Carmel Cr PB 32 E40
Carmel Ln PB 32 E39-40
Carmel Rd HS 6 C-D47
Carmel Rd NI 33 E43
Carmel-Koch Rd WT . . 22 N21-22
Carmen Rd NP 93 D25
Carmens Way A 84 B92
Carmichael Dr NP . . . 95 D-E32
Carmichael Sdrd R 83 Q57
Carnarvon Rd HS 59 R36
Carnrike Rd PE. 34 F48
Carol Rd CS 91 E16
Caroline Ct HS 62 U45
Caroline St LM 12 U9
Caroline St SM 29 C26
Carolinian Dr MD 13 V12
Caron Rd F. 93 E25-26
Caron St PR 67 P06
Carp La R 80 P46
Carp Rd NP 84 W90
Carp Rd OT 65 R60 83 Q59
Carpenter Rd LG. 50 Y62
Carpenter Rd SD. 101 D23
Carpenter Sdrd SM . . . 41 Y-Z28
Carpenter's Point Rd F. . . 36 E57
Carpin Beach Rd A 84 B91
Carr Av EX 5 E6
Carr Rd EL 15 U17-18
Carr Rd NR 33 E45
Carr Rd SDG 67 U67
Carr Rd (Hastings Highlands) HS . .
. . . . 62 T46
Carr Rd (Quinte West) HS. . 34 E47
Carriage Rd MD . . 14 T-U15 U-V16
Carrick-Brant Townline Rd E BR . .
. . . . 27 E17-18
Carrick-Brant Townline Rd W BR. . .
. . . . 27 E-F17
Carriere Rd NP 95 E32
Carriere St CS 100 B18
Carrigg La F 36 A54
Carroll Dr MD 14 V15
Carroll Ln EL 7 W-X13
Carroll Rd HL 60 T40
Carroll Rd LA 47 A52-53
Carroll Rd LN 49 V59-60
Carroll Sdrd OT 14 T55
Carroll St MD 14 T13-14
Carruthers Rd MD. 14 U18-21
Carruthers Rd NR 33 F-G43
Carruthers Rd PS. 57 R27-28
Carruthers Rd SDG. 67 T66
Carrville Rd Y 30 H31-32
Carrying Place Rd F. . 36 B57 37 B58
Carrying Place Rd HS . . . 34 F47
Carrying Place Tr Y 30 G30
Carrys Sdrd OT . . . 65 R59 83 Q59
Carscadden Rd DH 32 F39
Carscadden Rd K 32 E39
Carson Dr HS 46 Z48
Carson Ln EL 16 V21
Carson Rd HS . . . 34 C49 46 B48
Carson Rd W SM 41 B29
Carson Sdrd NF 16 V21
Carson Tr F 48 V55
Carsonby Rd E OT. 66 T63
Carsonby Rd W OT 66 T63
Carss Rd HS. . . 46 B49 47 B50
Carter La DH 31 E36
Carter Rd BR 54 T17
Carter Rd EL 9 W20 15 W21
Carter Rd HS 34 F46
Carter Rd HD 18 T30-31
Carter Rd PE. 34 F48-49
Carter Sdrd A 86 D95-96
Carter St PR 67 P68
Carter's Bay Rd MA . . 72 M-N10
Carter Dump Rd SD . . . 100 A14
Carter East Access Rd SD . . . .
. . . . 100 A15 Z15
Cartier Rd SD 100 A15
Cartwright Rd OT 67 S65
Cartwright East Quarter Ln DH . . . .
. . . . 32 E-F37
Cartwright West Quarter Ln DH . . .
. . . . 31 E-F36 32 F37
Carty Rd R 81 M-N49
Carveth Dr PB. 32 E40
Casablanca Blvd NI 18 Q30
Case Rd A 84 A92
Case Rd MA 73 M11
Case Rd NI. 14 U13
Case Rd NI. 18 T-U32
Casey Rd HS 34 D49
Casey Mine Rd TM. 85 Q30
Cashion Rd SDG. 52 U71
Cashmere Rd MD 7 X12
Casimir Rd SD. 93 E24
Cass Bridge Rd SDG . . 67 U65-66
Cassburn Rd PR 68 N-P71
Cassel Sdrd OX . . . 15 Q20 16 Q21
Cassell Dr SM 41 Z29
Casselman Rd SDG 67 U67
Cassels St NP 95 E31
Cassidy Rd BR 26 D15
Cassidy Rd MD 14 Q-R14
Cassie Rd SDG 51 V66
Casteels Rd NR 33 E-F43

Castle Harbour Dr DH. . . . 31 E36
Castleberg Sdrd PL. . . . 30 G-H29
Castleford Rd R 82 P55
Castlefrank Rd OT 66 R61
Castlehill Dr NR 33 F-G42
Castlemore Rd PL 24 J29-30
Castor Rd OT 67 T65
Castor Rd PR 67 S66
Castor St PR 67 S65-66
Castors Rd PR 69 Q73
Cataract Rd NI 19 R-S33
Cataract Rd PL 23 J27
Cataract River Rd A 88 E3-4
Catchmore Rd NR 34 D46
Catering Rd Y 30 C32 D-E32
Cathcart Blvd LM 12 T7
Cathcart Cr PB 32 E40
Cathedral Dr BR 55 V18
Catherine Rd PR. 67 S66
Catherine St MD. 15 T18-19
Cathmae Rd R. 82 L52
Catholic Church Rd LG . . 37 A61
Caton Rd LA. 36 D54
Catt Ln EL 15 V18-19
Cattanach Ln EL 8 W16-17
Cattle Rd TM. 85 P28
Caudle Sdrd R. 55 U16-17
Caughey Rd PE. . . . 34 E49 35 E50
Caughnawaga Rd SDG. . . 51 V66
Cauldicotte Rd SD 92 F22
Causeway Rd A 59 R36
Causeway Rd MK 58 T29
Causley St A 88 F3-4
Cavan Rd R 33 E-F41
Cavanagh Dr A 87 D-E99
Cavanmore Rd OT 65 R60
Cave Dr A 86 C95
Cavell Srdrd G 39 V19
Caverly Rd EL 15 V19
Caves Rd PB 45 A42
Cawthra Rd PL. 24 L30
Cayer Rd SDG. 67 T65
Cayouette Rd NP 94 C27
Cayuga Rd BT 17 S-T27
Cazabon La EX. 5 C5
Cecil's Rd LG 49 X61
Cedar Cr PB 32 E40
Cedar Cr PB 32 E40
Cedar Cv MA 90 H-J11
Cedar Dr BR 55 X16-17
Cedar Rd HS . . . 61 T44 62 T45
Cedar Rd NF 10 W24
Cedar Rd PB 44 Z40
Cedar Gt LN 49 X58
Cedar La MK 58 U33
Cedar La MK 59 U33
Cedar St NR 34 F46
Cedar St WT 22 P24
Cedar Bank Rd HU. 20 P13
Cedar Bank Rd PB . . 32 D40 33 D41
Cedar Bay Rd MA. 19 U34
Cedar Beach Rd DH 43 B34
Cedar Beach Rd MK. 58 U32
Cedar Bridge Rd LG 48 X57
Cedar Cove Rd LN 64 S56
Cedar Creek Rd WT 22 P24
Cedar Creek La LN 65 T59
Cedar Croft Rd PS 76 N29
Cedar Crest Rd LN 65 T59
Cedar Cross Rd PB 45 B42
Cedar Forest Park Rd LG . . . .
. . . . 37 A61 49 Z61
Cedar Glen Rd K 44 A38
Cedar Grove Rd K. 50 Y64
Cedar Grove Rd R. . 62 S48 63 S49
Cedar Grove Rd SDG 68 T72
Cedar Grove Tr MA 73 M13
Cedar Haven Rd R. 82 M-N53
Cedar Heights Rd NP . . . 95 D32
Cedar Hill Side Rd LN . . 65 S57-58
Cedar Lake Rd HL 61 U41
Cedar Park Rd DH. 32 F-G37
Cedar Point Ln LM 13 R10-12
Cedar Point Rd CS 101 Y19
Cedar Point Rd SM . . . 41 X26-27
Cedar Rail Dr MK. 58 T30
Cedar Ridge Tr HS 62 U45
Cedar Ridges La F 36 C56
Cedar Sands Rdwy LG . . . 49 Z59
Cedar School Rd HS. 46 Z48
Cedar Shores Rd PS . . . 57 Q-R27
Cedar Spring Rd WT . . . 22 K22-23
Cedar Springs Ct HT. . . 23 N-P28
Cedar Springs Rd HT . . . 23 N28
Cedar Swamp Rd MD . . . 14 Q13
Cedar Tree Rd K 43 Z38
Cedar Valley Rd DH 32 G39
Cedar Valley Rd PS 32 D-E40
Cedarbrook Dr Y 31 G35-36
Cedarbrook Tr DH. 31 G35-36
Cedardale Rd DH 32 D-E37
Cedardale Rd HS 34 F46
Cedarhurst Beach Rd DH. . 43 B34
Cedarstone Rd LA 47 A52
Cedarvale Dr SM 30 C31
Cedarvale Rd SDG 68 T69
Cedarview Dr K 32 C39
Cedarview Rd OT 66 R-S62
Cedarwood Rd DH 32 D-E37
Cedarwoods Dr F 36 A-B54
Celtic Ln EL 8 W14 14 V14
Cement Bridge Rd R 81 N50
Cement Plant Rd NI 19 U33
Cemetary Rd HS 62 T48
Cemetery Ln HU. 20 K15
Cemetery Rd A 86 C95
Cemetery Rd DH 31 E-F34
Cemetery Rd HA 44 W38
Cemetery Rd HA 18 R29
Cemetery Rd MA 70 J2
Cemetery Rd NF. 17 T25
Cemetery Rd NR 33 E44
Cemetery Rd PB 44 A40 Z40
Cemetery Rd PS 58 R29-30
Cemetery Rd SDG 68 T70

Cemetery Rd TM. 85 M-N29
Cemetery Rd (Wallaceburg) C. . 6 X7
Cemetery Rd (Wheatley) C. . 5 E7
Cemetery Sdrd LN . . . 65 T59-60
Centennial Cr NP 95 E32
Centennial La LN 64 S56
Centennial La NR 45 B45
Centennial Pkwy HM 18 Q30
Centennial Rd EL . . . 8 W17 15 V17
Centennial Rd HU 20 M14-15
Centennial Rd (Elizabethtown-
Kitley) LG 50 Z62-63
Centennial Rd (Leeds and the
Thousand Islands) LG . . . 37 B60
Centennial Lake Rd V . . . .
. . . . 63 S-T52 T52 64 S53
Centennial Lake Access Rd F . . . .
. . . . 63 S-T52
Centennial Park Rd K . . 43 A35 Z35
Centennial Ridges Rd NP . 79 N40
Central Av EX 4 B2
Central Rd A 19 U-36
Central Pkwy 24 L30
Centralia Rd NI 19 U35
Centre Diagonal BR. . . . 55 Y17-18
Centre Dr MD. 15 R-S17
Centre Ln (Asphodel-Norwood) PB
. . . . 33 C43-44 45 B44
Centre Ln (Smith-Ennismore-
Lakefield) PB. 44 B40-41
Centre Ln A G . . 28 D23-24 29 D25
Centre Ln B G 28 D24 29 D25
Centre Rd DH 29 D-E26
Centre Rd G 39 X19
Centre Rd HM 23 N-P27 P28
Centre Rd LM 14 R-T13
Centre Rd MK 58 T31
Centre Sdrd LM 13 Q-R10
Centre Rd SM 29 C28
Centre St LM 12 U9
Centre St SM. 19 S-T33
Centre St TB 102 D4-5
Centre St (Brockville) LG . . 50 Z62
Centre St (East Gwillimbury) Y. . . .
. . . . 31 E33
Centre St (Leeds and the
Thousand Islands) LG. . . 37 A58
Centre St (Vaughan) Y . . 24 J31-32
Centre Dummer Rd PB. . 45 A-B43
Centre Dyke Rd EX 5 H43
Centre Line Rd A . . . 86 Q96 D96
Centre Line Rd HS . . 46 A46 Z46-47
Centre Line Rd SM 29 C27
Centre Millbridge Rd HS . . 46 Y47
Centre Side Rd C . . . 6 X-Y8 Y9
Centreline Rd K. 44 B39
Centreview Dr HS 62 Q46
Centreville Dr MD . . 7 W12-13 X12
Centreville Rd F 48 Z56
Centreville Rd G 39 X19
Centreville Rd LA . . 35 C52 47 B52
Centreville Rd LG 48 Z56-57
Centreville Creek Rd PL. . . . .
. . . . . . 24 J-29 29 G-H28 30 H28
Centurian Tr MK. . . 58 Q32 59 Q33
Centurion Rd OT . . . 14 U14 V13
Century Ln EL 15 U-V19
Century Rd E OT 66 T62-63
Century Rd W OT 66 T62
Century Farm Rd K 32 E38
Ceramic Mine Rd MK 59 Q33
CGIT Camp Rd MK 42 W33
Chadbourne Dr NP 95 D32
Chaffey Twp Rd MK. . . 59 R33-34
Chaffeys Lock Rd LG 49 Z58
Chain Lake Rd SD. 101 C22
Chain of Lakes Rd PS . . 58 Q29-30
Chainsaw Dr DH 55 W18
Chainy Lakes Access Rd HS 61 S42
Chalet Ln EL 9 W19-20
Chalk Lake Rd DH 31 F35
Chalk Rd MK 59 V33
Challice Ln PB. 32 E40
Challice La R 8 W-X14
Chalmers-Forrest Rd WT. . 28 C27
Chamber's Rd K 43 B36-37
Chamberlain-Dack Township Rd
TM. 85 M27
Chamberland Rd SD. 92 E21
Chamberlin Rd SD 101 C23
Chambers Rd HL. 60 U37-38
Chambers Rd LA 35 D53
Chambers Rd LG 50 W-X65
Champlain Av DH 31 H36
Champlain Rd SM 41 W-X27
Champlain Rd TM. 85 M-N27
Champlain St OT 67 P-Q67
Champlain Provincial Park Rd NP.
. . . . 96 E36
Chancellor Dr Y 24 J31
Chandler Dr DH. 31 E36
Chandler Dr HL. 60 U40
Chandos-Wollaston Rd PB. . . . . . .
. . . . . . 45 W44 61 V44 62 V45
Channel St MA 91 J15
Chanonhouse Rd R 62 U47
Chant Rd LG 49 Y60
Chantler Rd NI . . 18 T32 19 T33
Chantry Rd LG 43 Y-Z59
Chapel Rd SDG. 68 S70
Chapel Hill Rd SDG . . 58 T69-70
Chapeski Rd R 80 N47
Chapeski Mill Dr R 80 N47
Chapeskie Rd R. 80 N47
Chapman Dr W PS. . 76 M30 77 M31
Chapman Rd A 86 D97
Chapman Rd HS 46 B49

Chapman Rd NR. 33 F45
Chapman Tr HL 59 S36
Chapman's Landing Rd PS . . 95 G31
Chapman Strong Rd PS . . 77 L-M31
Chappell Sdrd BR. 38 B16
Char-Mac La HL 60 R37
Charbonneau Rd PR. 68 N71
Charette Rd PR 68 N69
Charing Cross Rd C . . . 6 B9 7 B10
Charland Rd G. 39 W19
Charlemagne Blvd OT 66 P64
Charlemont Ln LM 6 X8
Charles Rd HS 62 T45
Charles Rd MK 58 V31
Charles St BR 38 Z17
Charles St K 15 S20
Charleston Sdrd PL . . 23 J27 29 H27
Charleston School Rd LG. . 49 Z60
Charleville Rd LG 50 X-Y63
Charlie Allen Rd PB 44 Y40
Charlie Green Rd F 36 B56
Charlie Thompson Rd MK. . 59 R35
Charlies La MK 58 S32
Charlies Bay Rd NP 94 C29
Charlore Park Dr K 32 C39
Charlotteville East Quarter Line Rd
NF. 16 V24
Charlotteville West Quarter Line
Rd NF. 10 W24 16 V23
Charlton Dr MD. 14 S14-15
Charlton Rd LN. 48 W55-56
Charlton Rd K 14 R14
Charlton St NF 16 V23
Charlton Access Rd NP. . . 94 C29
Charolais Blvd PL. 24 K29
Charran Line Rd EX 4 B-C4
Chartrand Rd PR 67 Q68
Chartrand St PR 68 N70
Chartwell Rd HT 24 N30
Charwell Point Rd PE. . . . 35 H51
Chase Rd K. 34 G49
Chateau Lake Access Rd R. . . . . .
. . . . 98 G42-43
Chatham Rd K 64 U54
Chatson Dr LA. 63 T50
Chatten Rd NR . . . 33 F45 34 F46
Chatterton Rd HS 62 T47
Chatterton Rd TB 10 U27
Cheapside Rd LA 15 T17
Cheapside St MD. 15 T17
Cheapside Rd K 34 C28
Chebouteguon Dr PB . . . 45 Z43
Checkerboard La MA . . . 72 K8
Cheddar Rd HL. 61 U-V42
Cheer Lake Rd PS 77 L31
Cheese Factory La HS . . . 47 B50
Cheese Factory Rd K 44 X38
Cheese Factory Rd LA . . . 35 F52
Cheese Factory Rd R 82 P53
Cheese Factory Rd WT . . . 23 P25
Cheethams Rd LG 49 Y58
Chemical 16 Access Rd PS. . 95 J33
Chemin du Loup Rd SM. . . 41 X27
Chemong Rd PB . . . 32 C40 33 C41
Chemong View Dr PB. . . . 44 B40
Chenal Rd C 6 X7
Chenaux Rd R 82 N54-55
Chenier Rd NP 96 E37
Chepstow Rd BR 27 E17
Cherriman Rd SD 93 F23
Cherry Av NI 18 R32
Cherry La NR. 33 F42
Cherry St T 24 L32
Cherry St Y 31 F33
Cherry Hill Blvd NI 19 U35
Cherry Hill Rd HS 55 U16
Cherry Hill Rd MD 15 R-S18
Cherry Hill Rd PS 77 N33
Cherrydale Rd HU. 20 K14
Chesley Lake Rd BR. 38 A17
Chess Rd SDG 50 W65
Chester La F 36 A55
Chestnut Grove Rd EL. . . . 9 W18
Chetwynd Rd PS 77 M33 N32
Chevis Rd A 87 E2
Chi-Cheemaun Rd SDG . . 52 U72
Chiblow Lake Rd A. . 87 D2 D-E2 E2
Chicago Mine Rd CS . . . 100 C15
Chickadee La MK 42 W32-33
Chief's Rd LM 6 X-Y6
Chief's Rd LM 101 D19
Chiefswood Rd BT 17 S-T26
Chikanishing Creek Rd MA 91 H16
Chikopi Rd PS 76 M29
Childerhouse Rd HS. 62 R45
Childs Rd K 43 Y34
Chilian Rd NF. 10 W25 17 V25
Chilligo Rd WT 22 M-N24
Chimney Point La F 47 X52
Chimo Dr HL. 44 W39
Chimo Rd N R 64 S53
Chimo Rd N S R 64 S53
Chinguacousy Rd PL23 J-K28 24 K29
Chinook Dr HL. 60 V40
Chipmunk Rd K 32 D38
Chipmunk Ridge Rd A. . . . 36 C54
Chippawa Pkwy NI 19 S35
Chippawa Rd A 62 Q47
Chippawa Rd (Port Colborne) NI. . .
. . . . 19 U34
Chippawa Rd (West Lincoln) NI. . .
. . . . 18 T32
Chippawa St B 18 T30
Chippawa Creek Rd NI . . . 19 S34
Chippewa Rd HM. 17 R27-28
Chippewa Rd TB . . . 102 E5 103 E6
Chiselhurst Rd HU. 20 N15
Chisholm Rd SDG. 52 U70
Chiswick Ln NP 95 G33-34
Chiswick Ln PS . . . 95 G33-34 G-H32
Choate St PR 33 G41
Cholette St PR. 68 N69
Chown Rd MK 58 T29
Chown Rd SD. 90 E14
Chrest Dr PS 77 K32
Chretien Rd PR. 67 Q68
Chrétien Rd NP 93 D-E25
Chris Ruddy Rd R 82 P53
Christener Rd WT 22 N21
Christenson Tr PR. 56 Q24
Christian La LA 35 C53

Christian / Cross Cemetery

Christian Rd PE 34 F49
Christian Cemetery Rd PB 45 X44
Christiani Rd HS 34 E-F46
Christie Dr HS 34 D49
Christie St G 28 E23
Christie St NI 18 Q31
Christie Beach Rd G 40 Z23
Christie Lake Rd LN 48 W57 49 W58
Christie Lake North Shore Rd LN 48 X56-57
Christina Rd MD 14 U14-15
Christina St LM 12 T7
Christine Rd HL 61 S42
Christner Rd WT 22 N21
Christopher Rd LA 47 B53
Chrysler Rd MK 59 V34-35
Chubb Lake Rd MK 59 R33
Chuckery Hill Rd PE 35 F51
Church La F 37 B58
Church La HU 20 N13
Church Ln OX 15 S20
Church Ln SM 42 X30-31
Church Rd BT 16 Q24
Church Rd F 47 A53
Church Rd G 39 A18 Z18
Church Rd HS 62 R-S45
Church Rd HM 17 Q-R25
Church Rd LA 47 A53
Church Rd MA 73 M-N11
Church Rd NP 95 G33
Church Rd PB 45 A44-45
Church Rd PS 77 L32
Church Rd TM 85 N28
Church Rd (Fort Erie) NI 19 T35
Church Rd (Grimsby) NI 18 R31
Church Rd (Niagara-on-the-Lake) NI 19 Q34
Church Rd (North Dundas) SDG 66 U64
Church Rd (South Dundas) SDG 51 V-W67 67 U67
Church Rd (West Lincoln) NI 18 S-T30
Church Sdrd E G 39 Y19-20
Church Sdrd W G 39 Y19
Church St A 86 B94
Church St CS 101 B20
Church St HU 27 H18
Church St LN 65 U60
Church St NF 16 U23
Church St NI 18 T32
Church St OT 66 T62
Church St OX 16 T21-22
Church St PR 67 S65
Church St PS 57 R27
Church St R 81 P48
Church St (Ajax) DH 31 H35
Church St (Georgina) Y 30 D31
Church St (Innisfil) SM 30 D29-30
Church St (King) Y 30 G30
Church St (Maitland) LG 50 Z63
Church St (Penetanguishene) SM 41 X28
Church St (Scugog) DH 31 E-F36
Church Camp Rd HU 20 J13
Church Farm Rd R 64 S54
Churchill Av Y 30 G30
Churchill Dr HU 26 F-G13
Churchill Gdns PS 77 P33
Churchill Ln LM 12 T8-9 13 T10-12
Churchill Rd HT 23 L27
Churchill Rd LN 49 W59
Churlee Rd PS 76 M28
Chute Ln EL 9 W21
Chutes Rd MK 59 T33
Cider Mill Ln C 7 X10
Cilica Dr HS 62 U45
Cinder Lake Rd A 88 C6
Cinder Lake Access Rd HL 59 U35-36
Circle Dr G 39 A20
Circle G La BR 55 W18
City Rd TB 103 E6
Civic Centre Rd R 99 K50
Civic Centre Rd Y 30 C32
CKPC Rd BT 16 S24 17 S25
Ckso Rd CS 101 D19
Clachan Rd C 7 X-Y12
Clachan Rd EL 7 X-Y12
Clair Rd F 36 A54 47 A53
Clair Rd WL 23 M25
Clam Lake Rd PS 77 P34
Clancy Rd LA 35 C53
Clandeboye Dr MD 14 R14-15
Clansman Dr HL 59 T35
Clapperton Rd NR 33 F42
Clara St LA 35 C52
Clarabelle Rd CS 101 C19
Clarchris Rd LN 48 W57 49 W58
Clare Newnhams Rd PB 45 X44
Clarence Rd HL 60 V37
Clarence St BT 17 R25
Clarence St NI 19 U33
Clarence St Y 24 J30
Clarence-Cambridge Boundary Rd PR 67 Q67 R66-67
Clarences Way R 82 Q54
Clarendon Rd F 48 W55
Clarendon St NI 18 T32 U32 19 T33
Clareview Rd LA 47 A51
Clark Av Y 24 J31-32
Clark Blvd PL 24 K29-30
Clark Dr LG 37 C58
Clark Rd CS 100 D18
Clark Rd NR 33 D43
Clark Rd NI 19 U34
Clark Rd OX 16 Q23
Clark Rd PR 67 P66
Clark Rd R 64 R53
Clark Rd SDG 50 V64 66 U64
Clark Rd (Central Frontenac) F 48 Y53
Clark Rd (South Frontenac) F 36 C54
Clark St G 40 A23
Clark Hill Rd HL 61 U41
Clark Lake Rd HS 62 T-U45
Clark Line Rd LA 47 Y50
Clarke Rd BT 16 Q24
Clarke Rd EL 9 W-X21
Clarke Rd HL 61 T42
Clarke Rd K 32 E39
Clarke Rd LA 36 D54-55
Clarke Rd MA 72 K7
Clarke Rd MD 14 Q-R16 15 R-T17
Clarke Rd OX 15 S20
Clarke Rd PE 35 G51
Clarke Rd (Cramahe) NR 33 E45
Clarke Rd (Hastings Highlands) HS 61 T43
Clarke Rd (Trent Hills) NR 33 C45
Clarke Rd (Tweed) HS 46 Z49
Clarke's Rd BR 55 U16
Clarkes La MK 58 S32
Clarkson Rd NR 33 E44
Clarkson Rd PL 24 M30
Clarkway Dr PL 24 J29-30
Claude Rd HS 46 B46
Claude Rd NP 93 D-E25
Claude Brown Rd HL 60 V37
Claude Duval Sdrd PR 68 P70
Claus Rd NI 18 R32
Clayhill Rd HT 23 K27
Claymore Ln C 6 Y8-9
Clayton La HS 62 R46
Clayton Rd LN 65 S-T58
Clayton Rd OT 67 Q-R66
Clayton Cove Rd HS 45 W45
Clayton Lake Rd LN 65 T57-58
Clear Rd MK 42 X33
Clear Bay Rd PB 44 X39
Clear Creek Rd NF 10 X-Y22
Clear Lake La F 48 X55
Clear Lake La HS 62 V48
Clear Lake Rd F 36 A56 48 Z56
Clear Lake Rd HL 43 W-X37
Clear Lake Rd HS 62 T-U46
Clear Lake Rd LA 63 S-T50
Clear Lake Rd LG 49 Z58
Clear Lake Rd PB 45 A42
Clear Lake Rd (Bracebridge) MK 59 U35
Clear Lake Rd (East Mills) PS 94 J28
Clear Lake Rd (Muskoka Lakes) MK 58 V31
Clear Lake Rd (Seguin) PS 58 S29
Clear Lake Rd (Whitestone) PS 75 M26
Clear Lake Rd N MK 59 U35
Clear Lake Rd S MK 59 U35
Cleareview Rd LA 47 A51
Clearview Cr G 39 Z20
Clearview Dr PB 44 X39
Clearview La NR 33 D45
Clearview Rd HS 34 C48
Clearville Rd C 7 A13
Clearwater Lake Rd CS 101 D19
Clearwater Lake Rd MK 59 S33
Cleary Rd LG 50 X64
Cleary Rd SDG 52 U69
Cleaver Rd BT 16 R-S24
Clee Rd R 81 N50
Cleeves Ln C 7 A12
Clegg Ln HU 20 J16 26 H16
Cleland Ct HS 62 V45
Cleland Access Rd SD 101 D22
Clelland Rd PS 94 J29
Clemenger Rd HS 46 Z46
Clemens Rd DH 32 F-G38
Clemens Rd PR 68 Q69
Clement Rd BT 16 S23
Clement Rd F 48 X54-55
Clement Rd PR 68 P72
Clement Lake Rd HL 61 U41
Clements Rd DH 31 E35-36
Clermont Rd PR 69 Q73
Cleveland Rd HS 46 Y47-48
Cliff Mclean Rd TB 102 E3
Cliffdene Rd MK 59 S36
Cliffe La F 48 Z56
Cliffe Rd LG 37 C59
Cliffe Rd NR 33 E44-45
Clifford Ln PB 32 D40
Clifford Rd PB 45 B42-43
Clifford Sdrd R 83 P-Q56
Cliffside La F 36 B-C56
Clinton Ln EL 14 V16 15 V17
Cloet Rd NF 16 U24 17 U25
Clonakilty Ln PB 32 C40
Clonsilla Av PB 32 C40 33 C41
Closs Dr HL 61 U-V43
Closs's Rd LN 48 V55
Closson Rd PE 34 G48-49
Cloud Bay Rd TB 102 G5
Cloud Lake Rd TB 102 G4
Cloud River Rd TB 102 G4-5
Cloudslee Rd A 86 D96-97
Cloudy Lake Rd A 86 C95
Cloughney Rd SD 90 F12
Clouston Rd NR 33 F43
Clouthier Rd R 99 H-J49
Clouthier Rd SD 93 E24
Clovelly Cv Y 31 C34
Clover Dr K 44 A39
Clover Hill Rd PS 77 L31
Clover Valley Rd MA 73 L-M12
Clover Valley Rd TM 85 R29
Clover Valley Rd E MA 73 M12-13
Clover Valley Rd W MA 73 M12
Cloverdale Ln PB 33 D41
Cloverdale Rd (North Dundas) SDG 67 U65
Cloverdale Rd (South Glengarry) SDG 68 T71
Cloverleaf Dr HS 34 D48
Cloverside Rd SDG 68 T69
Clow Rd F 36 A54 48 Z54
Clubhouse Rd NF 10 W-X24 16 V24
Cluegh Rd NR 34 C46
Clutton Rd EX 5 H5
Clyde Ln HU 20 J-K16 26 H16
Clyde Rd WT 23 P25
Clyde St HU 27 H17
Clyde Forks Rd LN 64 T55
Clyde Lake Rd LN 64 T54
Clydesdale Rd PB 45 W43-44
Coal Ln OX 16 U22
Coal Dock Rd SD 100 D14
Coaldale Dr HL 60 U39-40
Coate Rd MK 58 S30
Coates Rd DH 31 E34
Coatsworth Rd C 5 D7 6 C7
Cobban Dr MD 14 U15
Cobble Hills Rd MD 15 R-S18
Cobbledick Rd DH 32 H38-39
Cobden Rd R 82 N53
Cober Rd WT 22 N24
Coburn Rd MA 72 K7
Coburn Rd SD 90 F11
Cobus Rd R 82 P54-55
Cochrane Ln C 7 A12 Y12
Cochrane Rd DH 31 F36
Cochrane Rd (Cramahe) NR 33 F45
Cochrane Rd (Hamilton) NR 33 F42
Cochrane St DH 31 G35 H35-36
Cockburn Rd NP 94 E28
Cockshutt Rd BT 17 S-T25
Cockshutt Rd NF 17 T-V25
Code Rd R 82 M52
Code Rd (Drummond-North Elmsley) LN 49 V58-59
Code Rd (Montague) LN 49 V-W60
Codes La LN 65 U59
Coe Island Lake Rd HS 62 U45
Cofell Ln C 7 A11
Coffey Rd SM 30 F30
Colbeck Dr NI 19 T33
Colborne St BT 16 R24 17 R25
Colborne St C 6 A9
Colborne St K 43 A37 Z37
Colborne St WL 22 K23-24
Colborne St W K 32 C37
Colborne Creek Rd HL 61 V43
Colbourne Rd HS 62 U46
Colbourne Rd PS 77 M32
Colby Rd C 7 A11
Colby Lake Rd R 81 L49-50
Cold Creek Rd PE 34 G48
Cold Creek Rd R 82 N52
Cold Creek Rd Y 30 H29-30
Cold Spring La LG 37 A59
Cold Springs Camp Rd DH 32 F39
Cold Storage Rd LM 13 Q12
Cold Water Rd LA 47 B51
Coldstream Rd K 43 Z37
Coldstream Rd MD 13 R12 14 R13 S14 T15
Coldwater Rd (Orillia) SM 42 Z32
Coldwater Rd (Severn) SM 42 Y30
Cole La R 82 Q52
Cole Rd DH 32 G38
Cole Rd HS 34 C48
Cole Rd LG 49 Y61
Cole Rd NR 33 E-F41
Cole Rd PB 45 A45 46 A46
Cole Rd Y 30 E32
Cole Hill Rd F 36 C56
Colebrook Rd F 36 B54
Colebrook Rd LA 36 B-C54
Coleman Dr LN 65 U59
Coleman Rd LN 65 U59
Coleman Lake Rd HL 60 T39
Coleman Mine Rd CS 100 A16
Coleraine Dr PL 30 H29
Coles Ct HT 23 L27
Coles Sdrd G 39 X-Y19
Coles Bay Rd A 87 D-E99
Coles Point Rd NR 45 B46
Colgon Rd MA 71 J4
College Av WL 23 M25
College Ln EL 15 V18-20
College Rd NI 19 T35 T36
College St T 24 K32
College St E HS 34 D-E49
College St W HS 34 E48-49
Collegeway PL 24 M30
Collegeway, The PL 24 M30
Colley Rd EL 7 X13
Collie D's Sdrd G 28 E22
Colling Rd HT 23 N28
Collingwood St G 28 D22-23
Collingwood St SM 29 C26
Collins Dr NP 95 D-E31
Collins La HS 34 D47
Collins Rd NP 96 E37
Collins Rd R 82 P55
Collins Rd SDG 67 U67
Collins Bay Rd F 36 D55
Collison Sdrd EX 4 E1-2
Collver Rd A 87 E98
Collver Rd NI 18 S-T31
Colonel Maude Tr MK 59 U-V34
Colonel Talbot Rd MD 14 T-U16
Colonel Talbot Rd NF 16 U23 V21-22 V24
Colonel William La K 32 E39
Colonial Dr HS 34 E46
Colonial Dr SDG 51 V68 52 V69
Colonial Rd OT 67 Q65-66
Colonization Rd CS 101 B-C21
Colonization Rd HS 47 B50
Colonization Rd MK 59 Q35
Colonization Rd (Blind River) A 88 F3
Colonization Rd (Spanish) A 89 F8
Colony Rd K 44 B39
Colony Rd MK 59 U34
Colpoy's Range Rd G 39 X19
Colquhoun Rd SDG 51 V67
Colterman Rd R 64 R53
Coltman Rd HS 34 E46
Colton Rd R 82 Q54
Colton St NR 33 F45
Colton Creek Rd R 98 F47
Coltsfoot Dr MD 7 W12
Columbia St WT 22 M-N23
Columbia Way PL 30 H29
Columbus Rd DH 31 G35-36
Columbus Mountain Rd MA 90 J11
Comak Cr HL 59 T36
Comb View Rd NR 33 E44
Comba La LN 65 R58
Comber Sdrd EX 5 D6 6 B-C6
Combermere Rd R 62 Q47
Comeau Rd NP 93 E26
Comerford Rd R 62 R48 63 R49
Comfort Dr HL 44 W40
Comfort Tr HD 18 T31
Comfort Rd NI 18 S31
Commanda Lake Rd PS 94 H30 H-J29
Commissioner St OX 15 R19-20
Commissioners Rd MD 14 T16 15 T17
Communication Rd C 6 A9 7 B11
Community Centre Rd NR 33 F42-43
Community Hall Rd (Shuniah) TB 103 B10
Community Hall Rd (Thunder Bay) TB 102 C-D5
Compass Lake Rd PS 77 P32
Compressor Station Rd TB 103 B6-7
Comstock Ln PB 33 C43
Conboy Rd F 48 X54
Concession Dr MD 7 W12-13 X12
Concession Rd HS 46 A48
Concession Rd LG 50 V63
Concession Rd NI 19 T-U36
Concession Rd SD 90 E12
Concession Rd WT 22 P21
Concession St DH 32 G38
Concession St F 36 D56
Concession St HM 17 Q28
Concession St OX 16 U21
Concession St PB 45 A-B45
Concession St WT 22 P24 23 P25
Concession St S LA 47 A52
Conchie Rd HS 47 B50
Condley La LG 37 A58
Conestoga Rd HL 60 V38
Confederation Ln LM 12 T8-9 13 T10-12
Confederation Rd K 32 C38
Confederation St HT 23 K27-28
Confederation St LM 12 T7
Coniston Rd CS 101 C20
Coniston Hydro Rd CS 101 C20
Conklin Rd BT 17 R-S25
Connaught Rd R 82 M-N52
Connaught Rd SDG 67 T66
Connection Rd C 6 X8
Connell Rd LG 50 W64
Connell Lake Rd G 39 B21
Conner Rd F 47 X52
Connolly Rd TB 102 E2
Connor Rd A 84 A92
Connortown Rd SDG 68 S70-71
Conroy Rd OT 66 R63
Consecon St PE 34 G49
Conservation Dr PL 24 J-K29
Conservation Dr WT 22 M22
Conservation Ln EL 9 W18-19
Conservation Rd HT 23 N27
Conservation Rd HU 20 K-L14 L15-16
Conservation Rd LM 13 U-V12
Conservation Rd MK 59 V33
Conservation Rd WL 23 L25
Conservation Drain Rd NI 18 T31
Constance Bay Rd OT 65 P60 83 P59
Constance Lake Rd OT 65 Q60
Constant Lake Rd R 82 Q52
Consumers Dr DH 31 H36
Contau Lake Rd HL 44 W39-40
Conway Cr MK 59 U34
Conway La F 36 A55
Conway Rd HL 44 W-X38
Conway Rd PR 68 P72
Cook Rd HS 46 A46
Cook Rd MD 14 U-V16
Cook Rd NR 33 D43
Cook Rd SDG 50 W65
Cook's Duck Rd MA 71 J-K5
Cooke Rd HS 46 B47-48
Cooke Armstrong Rd HS 34 D47
Cooks Dr BR 55 W-X18
Cooks Rd A 86 C95
Cooks Rd LA 35 C51
Cooks Rd LN 48 W57
Cooks Rd MD 14 U15
Cooks Rd MK 42 W33
Cooks Rd PS 58 R29
Cooks Mill Rd NP 95 D31
Cookston Rd DH 31 D36
Coolihans Sdrd PL 29 G27-28
Coon Rd EL 8 W17
Coon Lake Rd PB 45 Z42
Cooney Rd DH 32 F38
Cooney Island Rd PB 45 B42
Coons Rd LG 49 Z59
Coons Rd SDG 50 V65
Cooper Dr LN 49 Y58
Cooper Ln PB 33 C43
Cooper Rd C 6 B-C8
Cooper Rd HS 46 Z48
Cooper Rd HM 23 N25 P25-26
Cooper Rd LG 50 W63
Cooper Rd MA 72 L-M10
Cooper Rd PB 45 A42-43
Cooper Rd SDG 67 U68
Cooper Rd TB 102 G4
Cooper St WT 22 N24 23 N25
Cooper's Falls Rd MK 42 X33
Cooper's Falls Rd SM 42 X33
Cooper Hill Rd OT 66 S64 67 S65
Cooper Lake Rd MK 59 R35
Coopers Rd EX 5 H5
Coopers Rd LG 49 Z59
Coopers Rd TM 85 N27
Cootes Dr HM 17 Q27-28
Cope Rd NI 19 T34
Cope Lake Rd HL 61 U42
Copeland Rd OT 65 T60 66 T61
Copeland Lake Rd LA 63 T-U50
Copenhagen La PE 35 G50
Copenhagen Rd TB 103 C6
Copetown Rd HM 17 Q27
Copp Rd R 81 P49
Copper Bay Rd A 86 E96
Copper Cliff Rd TB 102 F4-5
Copper Kettle Dr F 36 C56
Copway Rd BR 38 A16
Cora Dr PB 32 D39
Coral Beach Rd TB 103 C8
Corbeil-Astorville Rd NP 95 F33
Corbett Ln HU 14 Q13 20 P13
Corbett's Beach Rd MA 73 L12
Corbiere Rd MA 72 K-L10
Cordova Rd HS 46 A46 Z46
Cordukes Rd F 36 C55
Corduroy Rd OT 67 R65
Corduroy Rd PS 56 Q24-25
Corduroy Tr HL 60 V40
Corey Cr BR 54 S13
Cork Ln PB 44 A39-40
Cork Rd K 44 B39
Corkery Rd NR 33 E42
Corkery Rd OT 65 S59-60
Corkoran Rd LG 49 W-X61
Corkstown Rd OT 66 R61
Corktown Ln C 6 Y7-8
Corless Rd EL 15 U19-20
Corlis Rd HM 18 S29
Cormac Rd R 81 P49
Cornell Rd OX 16 U21-22
Cornerview Rd R 82 M52
Cornish Hollow Rd NR 33 F42
Cornwall-Roxborough Boundary Rd SDG 67 T68 68 T69
Cornwall Beach Rd EX 4 E1-2 F2
Cornwall Centre Rd SDG 52 U70
Cornwell Rd BT 17 R26
Coronation Blvd LA 36 D55
Coronation Blvd WT 22 N-P24
Coronation Rd DH 31 G-H35
Coronation St BR 55 W18
Corral Post La HS 45 W45
Corrievale Rd MK 41 W29
Corrigan Rd HS 34 D46-47
Corrigan Rd R 81 P50
Coryell St DH 31 D35-36
Cosby Rd NI 18 R32
Cosby Subdivision MA 72 K10 73 K11
Cosh's Rd K 44 Z39
Cote Blvd CS 101 A20
Cotieville Rd R 82 P54
Cottage La F 36 B55
Cottage La HS 46 A49
Cottage La HS 62 U47
Cottage La LA 47 B51
Cottage La R 62 R48
Cottage Rd A 86 C95
Cottage Rd K 32 D37
Cottage Rd LN 49 W61
Cottam Sdrd EX 4 D4
Cottingham Rd K 32 C39
Cottonwood Dr LG 48 Y56
Cottonwood Dr TB 102 F4-5
Cottrell Rd PS 77 L31
Cottrelle Blvd PL 24 J29-30
Couch Rd TB 102 F3
Couch's Rd PB 45 X43
Cougar Dr HL 44 W40
Coughler Rd SDG 51 V66
Coughlin Rd SM 41 A28
Coulas Rd R 80 N46
Coulson Rd TB 102 G3
Coulter Rd EX 4 D-E3
Coulthart Rd SDG 67 T66
Coumbs Rd HL 61 U-V41
Council Ln HU 20 J13
Council Rd BR 27 F17
Country La A 84 A92
Country La DH 31 G35
Country La G 39 Z18
Country La K 43 A37
Country La WT 22 L23
Country Rd A 88 E4
Country Rd BR 39 Z18
Country St LN 65 S59
Country Bridge Rd TM 85 P28-29
Country Forest La R 80 P47
Country Lane Dr G 27 D18
Country Lane Rd CS 100 B16-17
Country Mile La Y 30 C-D32
Country Squire Rd WT 22 M23
Countryman Rd HS 46 B49
Countryside Dr CS 101 D19
Countryside Dr G 39 B20
Countryside Dr PL 24 J29
Countryview La EX 5 C5
Countryview Ln C 6 Y8-9
County Ln HD 17 T-U26
County Ln NF 17 T-U26
County Forest Rd LN 48 V56-57
County Park Rd LG 37 A60
Courchesne Rd NP 93 E25
Courchesne Rd SD 92 G22
Courneya Rd HS 47 A50
Coursey Ln MD 14 Q15
Coursol Rd NP 94 D28
Coursol Rd SD 93 E23
Courtice Rd DH 32 G-H37
Courtland Av WT 22 N23
Courtland Dr HM 17 R27
Courtland St SM 42 Z32
Courtney Lake 27 Access Rd PS 75 K25-26
Courtney Lake 32 Access Rd PS 75 K25
Courtney Lake 6 Access Rd PS 75 K25
Courtney Lake Access Rd PS 75 K24-25
Courtneypark Dr PL 24 K-L30
Courtright Ln LM 12 V7-9 13 V10-11
Courville Rd SDG 67 S-T67
Coutts Ln C 6 B-C7
Coutts Rd HS 34 C47
Coutts Bay Rd LN 49 W59
Couttsville Rd TM 85 P29
Coutu, Mtee CS 100 A18
Coutu Rd NP 93 E25
Couture Sdrd PR 68 Q69-70
Cove Rd LG 49 Y58
Cove Rd MK 58 S32
Cove Rd NF 10 X-Y23
Cove Rd PS 77 N32
Coven Rd DH 32 G39
Coveney's Rd BR 55 W18
Coventry Dr OT 66 Q63
Covert Hill Rd NR 33 E44
Coville Rd LG 50 X-Y62
Cow Path MD 15 T19
Cowal Rd EL 8 W15 14 V15
Cowan Rd HL 60 U39
Cowan Rd NR 34 E46
Cowan's Dr K 32 C39
Cowan's Sdrd MA 73 M12
Cowan Park Rd MK 58 T31
Cowbell La MK 42 X32-33
Cowdy Rd LA 47 B53
Cowell Rd OT 66 Q62-63
Cowes Rd MK 57 V28 58 V29
Cowie Rd NR 33 F44
Cowie Rd PS 77 P31
Cowling Rd NR 33 E42
Cowper Rd PS 57 S27
Cox Ln C 5 D7 6 C8
Cox Rd F 47 X52
Cox Rd LM 13 V11
Cox's La MA 72 L10
Cox Creek Rd WT 22 L-M23
Cox Mill Rd SM 30 C30
Coxfarm Rd HL 60 V38
Coxwell Av T 25 K33
Coyle Dr SDG 51 W66-67
Coyle Rd EL 9 W21 16 V21
Coyle Rd NR 33 D43
Coyne Rd EL 8 W-X14
Coyne Rd SDG 67 T66
Coyote Rd PS 77 N32
Coyote Ridge Rd NP 94 C-D28
CP Ln HU 20 J13
CPR Dr MD 7 W12 13 V12
Crab Lake Rd A 89 E-F8
Craford Rd C 7 C10
Crafts Ln C 6 Y9 7 Y10
Cragg Rd DH 31 E35
Craig Rd F 36 A54-56
Craig Rd HS 34 D49 35 D50
Craig Rd LG 50 V62-63
Craig Rd SM 41 A-B29
Craig Sdrd OT 65 R60
Craig Sdrd SM 41 Z29
Craig St LN 49 W58
Craig St PR 67 S65
Craige Lea Rd MK 58 S-T30
Craigen Rd LA 35 C52
Craigmont Rd R 62 R47
Cram Rd LN 65 T59-60
Cramahe Hill Rd NR 33 E45
Crammer Rd HM 17 Q27 23 P27
Crampton Dr MD 15 U18
Crampton Rd LN 65 U58
Cranberry Ln OX 16 U21
Cranberry Rd MK 58 U30
Cranberry Rd NP 95 F32
Cranberry Rd NR 33 G41
Cranberry Creek Rd R 80 N47
Cranberry Lake Dr HL 60 T38-39
Cranberry Lake Rd F 47 Y52
Cranberry Lake Rd K 43 Z34
Cranberry Lake Rd NR 33 F43
Cranberry Lake Rd SD 92 E21
Cranbrook Rd HU 20 J16 21 K17-18
Cranbrook Rd MD 14 T16
Crandall Rd NR 33 F45
Crane Bay Rd K 44 A38
Crane Lake Dr HL 59 S36
Crane Lake Rd BR 54 S-T16
Cranes Nest La F 36 B57 37 B58
Cransford Ln HU 26 H13
Cranston Rd HS 34 C48
Cranston Rd HD 17 U26
Cranston Rd MA 72 M9
Crathie Dr MD 14 S13-14
Crawford Dr BR 55 W18
Crawford La F 48 Y56
Crawford Rd G 28 C21 39 B21
Crawford Rd HS 62 U46
Crawford Rd K 43 Z35
Crawford Rd SD 101 C-D23
Crawford Sdrd OT 65 T60
Crawford St MK 58 S30
Crawley Rd WL 23 M25
Cream St NI 19 S-T33
Creamery Rd HU 27 H18-19
Creamery Rd MD 14 Q14
Creamery Rd PB 32 C40
Crean Hill Rd CS 100 D16
Crediton Rd HU 14 Q13 20 P13 P14-16
Creditstone Rd Y 24 J31
Creditview Rd PL 23 K28 24 K29 L29-30
Creek Ln C 6 A8
Creek Ln HU 26 G-H15
Creek Rd C 6 A9
Creek Rd EL 9 W20
Creek Rd EX 4 E1
Creek Rd PS 75 K26
Creek Rd SDG 68 Q71
Creek Rd WL 27 G19
Creek Rd (Sault Ste Marie) A 84 A91
Creek Rd (Tarbutt) A 86 D94
Creek Side Rd PS 94 H29-30
Creek Side Rd R 83 Q56
Creek View Rd K 43 A36
Creekford Rd F 36 D55
Creemore Av SM 29 C27 41 B27
Crego Lake Rd K 43 X37 44 X38
Creighton Dr HL 60 R37
Creighton Rd CS 100 B-C17
Creighton St SM 42 Z32
Crerar Rd SD 101 B23
Crescent Rd NI 19 U36
Crescent Harbour Rd SM 30 C31 42 B31
Crescentwood Rd PS 58 R29
Cress Rd MA 72 L-M9
Cresswell Rd K 31 C36
Cressy Bayside Rd PE 35 E-F53
Cressy Lakeside Rd PE 35 F53
Crest Rd HU 20 M13
Crestview Rd NR 33 D45
Crewe Rd C 5 D8 6 C8
Crewsons Ln HT 23 L26
Cricket Hollow Rd K 32 C37
Cridiford Rd MK 59 U34
Crimson Maple Rd R 81 N-P50
Crinan Ln EL 7 W-X13
Cripple Lake 15 Access Rd PS 78 N-P35
Cripple Lake 5 Access Rd PS 78 N35
Cripple Lake Access Rd PS 78 N35
Crockford Rd MK 59 T-U34
Crofton Rd PE 34 F49
Crofts Rd HS 46 Z46
Cromarty Dr MD 15 T18-19
Cromwell Rd HS 46 Z48
Cronk Rd TB 102 D2
Cronk Sdrd SM 42 X33
Cronk Woods Rd LG 37 A61 49 Z61
Crooked Rd SDG 68 Q71
Crooked Sdrd LN 65 T-U60
Crooked Tr HS 62 U47
Crooked Bay Rd MK 41 W29 58 V29
Crooked Creek La F 48 X53
Crooked Hill Rd BR 38 Z17
Crooked House Rd HL 60 U37
Crooked Lake Rd SD 92 G21
Crooked Rapids Rd R 81 N51
Crooked Toe Rd BR 55 W18
Crooks Hollow Rd HM 17 Q27
Crookston Rd HS 46 A49 B48-49
Crosby Av Y 30 H32
Crosby Rd LN 48 X57
Crosby Rd LG 49 Z58
Crosby Rd NR 33 D43
Cross Rd CS 101 D21
Cross Rd (Central Frontenac) F 48 X55
Cross Rd (Elizabethtown-Kitley) LG 49 Z61
Cross Rd (Faraday) HS 61 U44
Cross Rd (Rideau Lakes) LG 49 Y59 Z58
Cross Rd (South Frontenac) F 36 A-B54
Cross Rd (Tyendinaga) HS 34 C49 35 C50
Cross Tr HS 62 U47
Cross Cemetery Rd LG 37 C59-60

Cross Country Rd HS 62 S-T45
Cross Creek Rd K 32 C37
Cross Hill Rd MA 86 D37
Cross Lake Rd NP . . 61 Q45 80 P45
Cross Over Rd A 89 B10
Cross Over Access Rd NP. 96 F38 97 F39
Crossen Rd NR 33 F42
Crossland Rd SM . . 41 A28 Z27
Crossley Rd PS. 58 S30
Crossley Hunter Ln EL. . 15 U18-19
Crossroad Tr BR 55 Y17
Crosswind Rd K 32 C38
Crosswinds Cove Rd NR. . 59 R35
Crotch Lake Access Rd F 48 W53-54
Croton Ln C 6 X9 7 X10
Crow Rd C 6 88
Crow Lake Rd F . . 48 X56 Y55
Crowder Rd LG 50 W-X64
Crowder Rd (North Dundas) SDG. . 67 U65
Crowder Rd (South Dundas) SDG. . 51 V67
Crowe Rd HS 34 D47
Crowe River Dr HS 35 F50
Crowe River Rd NR . 34 C46 45 B46
Crowes Rd PE 35 G51
Crowes Landing Rd PB . . 45 Z43
Crowes Line Rd PB. 44 Z39
Crowland Av W 19 S-T34
Crowley Ln PB 33 D41
Crown Rd HD 18 U33
Crown Rd LM 18 S32
Crown Lake Rd HL. . 60 Q37-38
Crown Point Rd OT 83 P59
Crown Retreats Rd PS. . 76 N28
Crowsfoot Rd WT . . 22 M23-24
Crowsnest Rd R 81 L50
Crozier La DH 31 D36
Crozier Ln R 62 O54
Crozier Rd LN 48 Y56
Crozier Rd G 50 V-W63
Cruickshank St P 39 Z18
Cruise Rd F 64 U54
Cruiser Lake Dr HL . . . 60 S38
Crumby Lake Dr HL . . . 60 R37
Crumlin Rd MD. 15 S-T17
Crump Rd SDG 67 T66
Cryderman's Rd Y 30 D32
Crysler Rd R . . 19 R34-35
Crysler Rd SDG 67 S-T67
Crystal Rd LG 49 X61
Crystal Beach Rd EX . . . 4 E-F2
Crystal Beach Rd HS. . . 46 A48
Crystal Beach Rd TB . 103 B9 C8-9
Crystal Cove Rd A 86 C96
Crystal Falls Rd NP . . . 94 C28
Crystal Lake Rd PB . . . 44 X39
Crystal Springs Rd HU. . 20 M13
Crystalline Lake Access Rd NP. . . 97 F39-40
Csinos Rd EL 9 X21
Csont Ln OX 16 T22
Cuckoos Nest Rd LN . . . 65 U60
Cucman Rd LG 50 V-W64
Cuddy Dr MD. . 13 S12 14 S13
Culham Rd SM 41 B28
Culhane Rd R 82 P54
Cullimore La NF 17 V25
Cullis Rd A 87 E99
Culloden Ln OX 15 T-U20
Culloden Rd EL 15 V20
Culp Rd NI. 18 R32
Cultus Rd NF. 10 X22
Culver Rd NF. 17 U25
Cumberland Av HT 17 Q28 18 Q29
Cumberland St TB 103 D6
Cummer Av T. 24 J32
Cumming Rd SDG 68 S69
Cummings Rd F 36 C54
Cummings Lake Rd A. . . 87 C99
Cundle Ln C. 6 B9 7 B10
Cundles Rd SM. 41 B29
Cunning Rd PR 68 P72
Cunningham Dr F 36 D56
Cunningham Rd LG . . . 37 C59
Cunningham Rd PE. . . . 34 F48
Curl Rd LA. 34 C53
Curls Rd R 43 Y35
Currie Ln HU. . 20 J15 26 H16
Currie Rd EL . . 8 W14 X15
Currie Rd LN 65 T58
Curries Rd OX 16 S22
Currom Tr PS 56 Q25
Curry Rd HL 60 S40
Curry Rd CS . . 15 S20 16 S21
Curry Rd SM 41 X28
Curry Dyke Rd EX 5 H5
Curry Point Rd SD . . . 93 E24
Curtis Rd HS. 34 E47
Curtis Point Rd NR . . . 33 D-E42
Curtiss Rd R 80 P46
Curve Lake Rd PB . . 44 A40-41
Cushman Rd NI. 19 R34
Cut Line Rd HU 20 K-L13
Cuthbert Rd C 6 X9
Cuthbert Rd LM . . 6 W9 12 V9
Cuthbert Rd OX 16 S21
Cuthbert Rd (North Glengarry) SDG 68 R71
Cuthbert Rd (South Glengarry) SDG 68 S71
Cuthill La LA 35 E52
Cutler La R 98 F47
Cutler Rd LA. . 35 C53 36 C54
Cutler Rd MK 58 S-T31
Cutler Lake Rd SD . . . 90 F-G12
Cwethko Rd CS 100 D15
Cybulski Rd R 80 N-P47
Cyprus Lake Rd BR . . . 54 S14-15

D, Concession BR 27 F18
D, Mersea Rd EX 5 F6
D Ln A. 86 E94
D Ln BR. 38 Z17 55 Y17
D'Aoust Rd PR 67 S68
D'Aoust Rd SDG 68 Q71
D'Arcy St NR. 33 G42
D-E, Concession Rd SM 42 Y33 43 Y34
Dabers Rd R 81 L50
Daddy Weir Rd BR . . . 55 W16-17
Dafoe Rd R 62 R47
Dafoe Rd SDG. 51 V68
Dafoe St LA . . 35 C51 47 B51
Dagenais Rd SDG. 67 T66
Dagmar Rd DH 31 F35

Daignault Rd NR. 33 F42
Dailey Rd PS. 77 P31
Daillee Rd R 83 O56
Dainard Rd PE 35 H51
Dairy La TM 85 M-P29
Daisy Ln TM 85 P30
Daisy Lake Tr PS . . 77 L33-34
Dakers Rd LN. 65 U59
Dalby Rd EL 15 U20
Dalcourt Rd NP. 93 D25
Dale Rd (Cramahe) NR. . 33 E-F45
Dale Rd (Hamilton) NR. . 33 F41-42
Dale Rd (Port Hope) NR. . 33 G41
Dale's Rd TM 85 Q29-30
Dalewood Rd EL 15 U-V17
Daley Rd R 36 B-C55
Daley Rd HS. . 35 C51 47 B51
Daley Ditch Rd NI. 18 U32
Dalgleish Rd A 84 B91
Dalhousie Rd SDG 68 R72
Dalhousie St EX 4 N8
Dalkeith Rd SDG . 68 P-Q71 Q-R72
Dallaire St R. 67 N66
Dalle, Cote de la SM. . . 41 X27
Dalmas Rd HL 35 F50
Dalmeny Rd OT. . 66 T64 T-U63
Dalrymple Dr SM 43 Z34
Dalrymple Rd A 43 Y34
Dalton Av F. 36 D56
Dalton Rd NF. 16 V23
Dalton Rd Y. 30 O32
Dalwood Rd A 34 E-F46
Daly La PS. 77 M-N31
Daly's Rd NP 95 D32
Dam Rd HS. 61 S42
Dam Rd R 62 R48
Dam Rd SD 90 E12
Dam Rd TB 103 B6
Dan Lake Rd A 59 T36
Danceland Rd HU. . . 10 W-X24
Dancey Sdrd NF 76 P28
Dancy La PS 76 P28
Danforth Av T . . 24 K32 25 K33
Danforth Rd F . . 37 B42-43
Danforth Rd PE . . 34 G48-49
Danforth Rd T 25 K33
Daniel Dr PS 94 H29
Daniel Rd OX 15 T-U20
Daniel St R 83 Q57
Danis Rd NP 94 C28
Dankert Lake Rd BR. . . 57 2 D18
Dankey Ln A 7 X10
Daoust Access Rd NP. . . 93 F-G25
Daoust Lake Rd SD . . 92 G21-22
Darby Rd NI. 19 S34
Darby Rd SM 41 Y-Z28
Darcys Rd LN 64 T56
Dardanelles Rd HL . . . 60 T40
Dargavel Rd LG 37 A58
Dark's Sdrd LN 65 R58
Dark Bay Rd MK 58 V30
Dark Lake Rd HL 61 U41
Darkwood Rd HT 23 M27
Darling Cr PB 32 D39
Darling Rd HU. 18 T30
Darling Rd LN . 64 S56 T55-56 65 T57
Darling Rd NR 33 E45
Darling Long Lake Access Rd LN . . 64 S55-56
Darlingside Dr LG 37 O60
Darlington Blvd DH . . . 32 H37
Darlington-Clarke Townline Rd DH . 32 F-G38
Darlington-Manvers Townline Rd DH 32 F38
Darrell La C . . 6 A8-9 Y9
Darrell Lake Rd A 87 D2
Dartmoor Rd K 43 Y34-35
Dartnall Rd HM . . 17 R28 18 R29
Dashwheel Rd C 6 B-C7
Dashwood Rd HU 20 P15
Dauphin Rd C. 6 B7
Davenport Rd T. 24 K32
Daventry Rd NF . . 96 E-F36
Davern Lake La LN . . . 48 X56
Daves Rd TB 102 E2
Davey Rd R 85 Q30
Davey Rd N CS 100 B17
Davey Rd S CS 100 B17
Davey Rd PR 67 P66
David St WL 22 K23
David Fife Ln PB 102 F4
David Manchester Rd OT 65 R-S60
David Smith Rd SD . . . 90 F10
Davidson Rd C 6 C7
Davidson Rd C 36 C56
Davidson Rd HS 46 Y47
Davidson Rd K . . 31 C36 32 C37
Davidson Rd NR 33 E42
Davidson Rd OT 66 R63
Davidson Rd R. 82 M53
Davidson Sdrd MA 73 K11
Davies Rd R 62 R-S48
Davis Dr DH . . 31 E33-34
Davis Dr Y. . . 30 F31-32 31 F33
Davis Rd LM. 7 W11
Davis Rd NR 33 E43
Davis Rd PE 35 F50
Davis Rd Y. 30 F30
Davis Rd (Elizabethtown-Kitley) LG 49 Y61
Davis Rd (North Grenville) LG . . . 50 V62
Davis Sdrd LN 65 U60
Davis Lake Rd HL 43 W-X37 X37 44 X38
Davis Lock Rd LG 49 Z58
Davy Dr SM . . 42 X-Y33
Davy Rd F 36 A54
Dawes Rd T 25 K33
Dawes Lake Rd SD . . . 100 Z15
Dawn Townsite LM 6 W8
Dawn Mills Rd C 6 X9
Dawn Valley Rd C. . . . 6 X9
Dawn Valley Rd LM. . 6 W8 12 V8
Dawson Ct NF 16 V24
Dawson Rd BT 17 Q25
Dawson Rd C 36 C56
Dawson Rd DF 29 H26
Dawson Rd F . . . 48 Y53-54
Dawson Rd G 39 Y19
Dawson Rd HL 60 T38
Dawson Rd MK 58 T31
Dawson Rd TB 103 C6
Dawson Point Rd TM . . . 85 R30
Dawsons Sdrd SM . . . 41 Y-Z28

Day Dr K 43 Y34
Day Rd LN. 49 V59
Day Rd LG 49 Y-Z59
Day Rd NR 33 E-F44
Daymar Rd TM 85 M28
Days Rd F 36 D55
Dayton Rd A . . 87 E1 E99
Daytona Beach Rd K . . . 43 A37
Daytown Rd LG. 49 Z59
De la Baie Rd PR. 67 P66
De la Bergerie Rd PR. . . 68 N71
De La Tour Rd PR 67 Q-R67
De Lemieux Rd (Nation) PR. 67 R67-68
De Moyne Av A. 87 E1
Deadhorse Trail NP 77 K33-34 95 J33-34
Deadlock Bay Rd LG . 36 A57 37 A58
Deadman's Rd MD 14 U16
Dean Rd DF. 29 E26
Dean Lake Rd A. 87 E-F2
Dean Smith Rd F 36 B56
Deans Hill Rd NR 33 G42
Deans Island Rd LG . . . 37 A58
Deborah Glaister Ln WT. . 21 M20 22 M21
Debruge Rd LG 50 Z62
Decaire Rd NP. 95 F32
Decew Rd NI . . . 19 R33-34
Decewsville Rd HD . . 17 T-U28
Decker Rd MD 14 U16
Decker Rd LM . . . 13 R11-12
Declair Rd HS 46 Z49
Declerk Rd A 89 F8-9
Decosse Rd SD . . 93 E23-24
DeCosta St A . . . 83 O57-58
Decou Rd CS 100 D15
DeCou Rd NF 17 V25
Dedicke Rd NI 10 X23
Dedo La R 82 Q55
Dedrick Rd NF 10 X23
Deebank Rd MK . . . 58 S-T31
Deeks Rd NI 19 T33
Deeks Rd SDG . . 51 W66-67
Deele Rd MK 58 S-T31
Deep Bay Rd HL . . 43 W37 60 V37
Deep River Rd R. . 99 G48-49
Deer Bay Rd PB . . 44 A41 Z41
Deer Bay Reach N PB. . . 44 Z41
Deer Bay Reach S PB . . . 44 Z41
Deer Bay School Rd PB. . . 44 Z41
Deer Creek Cr G . . . 27 C-D19
Deer Fly Rd MK . . 42 W33 43 W43
Deer Lake Rd K 43 Y36
Deer Lake Rd LA . . . 61 U42-43
Deer Lake Rd OT . . 66 T64
Deer Lake Rd (Lount) PS . 76 L30
Deer Lake Rd (Perry) PS . 77 N32-33
Deer Mountain Rd A . . 84 S53
Deer Narrows Dr HL . . 59 S36
Deer Park Dr F 36 A55
Deer Park Dr Y. 30 D31
Deer Park Rd NR 32 G40
Deer Ridge Dr F 37 C58
Deer Rock Lake Rd LA. . . 47 Y50
Deer Run La R 5 E6
Deer Run Rd F 34 D47
Deer Run Rd HS. 34 D47
Deer Run Rd K 65 R57
Deer Run Rd PS. 76 M30
Deer Trail Rd R . 80 M47 81 M48
Deer Yard Tr R 81 N51
Deerbrook Dr SM 41 A27
Deerfield Dr R. 83 O56
Deerfoot Rd DH 31 E34
Deerfoot Tr MK 59 R34
Deerhead Lake Rd SD . . 90 F14
Deerhurst Dr MK. 59 R34
Deerhurst La F 47 A53
Deerwood Dr PS 58 Q32
Deewood Dr MK. . . . 58 S-T31
Degeest Rd C 6 Y9
Deguire Sdrd PR 68 P70
Degurse Rd LM 12 T-U7
Deir Rd LG 49 Y-Z60
Dejong Rd LG 50 Y63
Dejong Rd NR 33 F42
deKeer Rd BT 16 S24
Delamere Rd SD 92 G22
Delaney Rd HL 60 S40
Delaney Rd SDG. 68 T70
Delaware La R 58 Q32
Delazzer Rd TB 102 F4
Delbrook Rd MK 59 S36
Delhi St MK. 23 M25
Delia Rd MK 59 T33
Delints Rd TB 102 E1
Delion Pl WT 22 L-M22
Dell Rd, The DH 32 F39
DeLong Rd LG 49 Z58
Delores's Rd BR. . . . 55 W18
Delorme Pit Rd NP. . . . 95 D31
Deloro Rd HS 46 A47
Deloro Dam Rd HS 46 A47
Delrex Blvd HT 23 L28
Delta Rd LG 49 Z59
Delta Rd SM 42 W32
Delyea Rd A 47 X51
Delyea Rd A 47 Z51
Demara Rd DH 31 E36
Demchuck Rd TB. . . . 102 C5
Demers Rd PB 45 A42
DeMille Rd HS 47 B50
Demmys Rd MA . . 72 K10 73 K11
Demoe Rd K 43 A36-37
Demorest Rd HS 34 C47-48
Demorest East Rd A. . . . 88 D3
Demorest Lake Rd A. . 87 D2 88 D3
Demorest West Rd A . . 87 D2 88 D3
Dempsey Rd PE 34 F48
Dempster Dr A 87 E1
Den Lou Rd CS 100 D16
Denfield Rd MD . . . 14 R-S15
Dengo Rd NI 18 S31
Denison St Y. 24 J32
Denison Mine Rd A. . . . 88 C6
Denna Lake Rd HL. . . . 47 A53
Denney Dr SM 29 D28
Dennie St CS . . . 101 A20 D20
Denning Rd MD 14 U13
Dennis Rd EL 15 V19
Dennison Rd HL 60 U38
Dennison Rd NR 33 E44
Dennison Rd SM 50 V63
Denome Rd TM 85 N29
Denomme St NI 20 N13
Denridge Rd LA 35 C52
Densmore Rd NR 33 G42

Denyes Rd HS. 34 C49
Deplonty Rd A . . 86 D95-96
Depot Rd C 6 C7
Deppe La HS. 47 T50
Deramore Rd PB. 44 A41
Derby-Keppel Twnln G. . 39 Z18-19
Dereham Rd OX 15 T-U20
Derions Rd R. 81 L50
Deroche La HS 47 A51
Deroche Rd HS. 47 B50
Derouchie Rd SDG. . . . 68 S72
Derry Ln G. 39 A20
Derry Rd HT 23 M-N28
Derry Rd PL . . 24 K29-30 L-M29
Derry Sdrd LN 65 T-U60
Derven La F 48 Y53
Deryaw Rd G . . 37 B58-59
Des Cedres St PR . . . 68 N-P72
Des Chenes Dr A 84 B90
Des Eaux Paisibles Rd PR. . 68 N71
Des Epinettes Av OT . . . 66 S69
Des Pins St PR. . . . 67 R66-67
Desbarats Lake Rd A . . 101 A19
Deschene Rd CS. . . . 101 A19
Desert Lake Rd F 48 X55
Desert Point La F 36 A55
Deshane Rd HS 47 A-B51
Deshane Rd LA 47 A51
Desjardins Rd R. . . 82 L53-54
Desjardins Rd A. 98 G46
Desloges Rd CS . . . 101 C-D20
Desmarais Rd CS. . . . 101 A19
Desmond Rd C 7 A12
Desmond Rd LA 47 B53
Desmond Rd NI . . 18 U32 19 U33
Desmond Rd R 82 Q55
Desnoyer Rd PR. 67 R68
Desormeau Rd CS . . 100 D16-17
Detenbeck Rd NI 19 S35
Detlor Rd HS. 46 A48
Detlor Rd NR 33 F44
Detlor Rd LA. 47 A53
Deux Rivieres Creek Access Rd R. . 97 F40-41
Devaladares Rd MK. . 59 V33-34
Devald Rd SM. 30 F30
Development Rd NP. 95 F34 96 F35
Development Rd SDG 66 U64 67 U65
Development Rd TM . . 85 P29-30
Devenish Rd HS . . 41 T44 62 T45
Devereaux Rd OT. . . 66 T64
Deviation Rd R . . 39 A21 40 A22
Devil's Valley NR 43 X40
Devil's Elbow Rd MA. . 90 J12
Devil's Lake Rd LA . . . 43 W37
Devil Lake Rd LA 48 Z56
Devil Lake Rd LA 47 A51
Devils Door Rd LG . . . 37 A61
Devils Four Mile Rd PB. . 45 Z45
Devils Lake Access Rd R. 48 L48-49
Devine Rd OT . . . 67 R65-66
Devine Rd SD 90 F10
Devitt's Rd K 44 Z38
Devitts Rd DH. 32 E-F37
Devlin Dr R 44 W38
Devon Rd TB. 102 G1
Devonshire Av OX. . . . 16 R21
Devries Rd SDG 51 W66
Dew Drop Rd CS . . . 101 D19
Dew Drop Rd C. 7 Y10
Dew Drop Inn Rd K . . . 32 C37
Dewar Rd SDG 67 S68
Dewar Sdrd LN 65 T60
Dewey Dr C 7 B10
Dewey Rd LA . . 35 C53 47 B53
Dewitt La F 47 Y55-56
Dewitt Rd HM 18 Q29-30
DeWitt Rd SDG 52 U70
Dewley Rd PB. 46 B46
DeWolfe St OT 83 O58
Dexter Ln EL . . . 8 W19 W18
Dexter Rd HL 44 W39
Deyell Ln PB 32 E40
Deyos Rd F 36 A55
Dial Rd MA . . 72 M10 73 M11
Diamond Rd LG 50 X63
Diamond Rd WT 22 P21
Diamond Sdrd DH . . 31 F35-36
Diamond Sdrd WL 22 L23
Diamond Lake Rd A . . . 86 C95
Diamond Lake Rd R . . . 62 Q48
Diamondview Rd OT . . . 65 R59-60 83 Q59
Diana Dr Y 30 H30
Diana Rd TB 102 E3
Dicaire Rd OT . . . 67 Q-R68
Dick Rd HD 18 U30
Dick Rd PR. 68 N-P71
Dick's Rd F 82 M52
Dick Martin Rd PB . . . 45 W43
Dickenson Rd HM. . . . 17 R28
Dickey Lake Rd HS . . . 46 X46
Dickhout Rd HD 18 U31
Dickie Lake Rd MK . . . 59 T34
Dickie Settlement Rd WT. . 22 P24
Dickinson Dr SDG 51 V68
Dickinson Rd HL 61 U43
Dickinson Rd NR 33 G42
Dickinson Rd PS. 76 T28
Dickson Rd R . . . 82 Q55 83 Q56
Dickson Hill Rd Y 31 G33
Digby's Sdrd MA 72 L10
Digby-Laxton Boundary Rd K . . . 43 X35
Dignan Rd HL 44 T40
Dill Siding Rd CS . . . 101 D20
Dillabaugh Rd LG 50 V64
Dillabough Rd R 82 P53
Dillabough Rd SDG. . . 67 U67
Dillon C 47 A53
Dillon Rd LA 47 A53
Dillon Rd PB 33 C41
Dillon Rd SS 56 Q25
Diltz Rd NF. 18 T-U30
Dines Rd NR 81 P51
Dingle Ln EL 15 V19
Dingle St EL 15 V19
Dingman Dr MD. 14 U16 15 U17-18
Dingman Rd NR . . 33 E45 E-F44
Dingwall Rd A 33 E44
Dingwall Rd NR 33 G42
Dinsley St HU. 20 K15

Dionne Rd SD 92 F22
Diprose Rd HS . . . 86 D95-96
Discovery Ln LM. 12 U9
Disney Rd HL. 20 K14
Disputed Rd EX. 4 C-D3
Dissette St SM 30 E31
Distress Dam Rd MK . . 78 P34-35
Dittburner Rd R. . . 82 M54-55
Diversion Rd (North Glengarry) SDG 68 S70
Diversion Rd (South Glengarry) SDG . . 52 U72 68 T72
Division Ln (Ashfield-Colborne-Wawanosh) HU. . . 26 G-H13
Division Ln (Central Huron) HU . . . 20 K-L16
Division Ln (Huron East) HU . . . 20 L-M15
Division Rd NR 33 F42
Division Rd PB. . 33 C41 C42 45 B42
Division Rd PR . . . 67 N-P67
Division Rd R. . . 80 N47 81 N48
Division Rd (Kingsville) EX . . 4 E4
Division Rd (Tecumseh) EX. . 4 C2-3
Division Rd (Windsor) EX . . . 4 C2
Division Rd E SM . . . 42 Y31-32
Division Rd W SM . . . 42 Y-Z31
Division St F 36 D56
Division St G. . . . 39 A19-20
Division St NR 33 G42
Division St R 83 Q57
Division St (Georgian Bluffs) G . . . 39 X19
Dixie Rd DH 31 H34
Dixie Rd LG . . . 49 Y61 Z60-61
Dixie Rd NI . . . 18 U32 19 U33
Dixie Rd PL . . 24 J-K29 K-L30
Dixie Lake La R 62 Q47
Dixon Dr HS 34 E47
Dixon Dr NR 33 F44
Dixon Rd F 36 C56
Dixon Rd LG 50 Y62-63
Dixon Rd SDG . . 52 U69 67 U68
Dixon Rd T 24 K31
Doan Dr MD. 15 U19
Doane Rd Y . . 30 E31-32 31 E33
Doans Ridge Rd NI. . . . 19 T34
Dobbie Rd LN. 65 U57
Dobbie Rd SM 50 W64
Dobbie Lake Access Rd LN. 64 T54
Dobbin Rd PB . . . 32 C-D40
Dobbs Rd PS 77 M32
Dobbyn Rd LM. 7 W11
Dobie Dr MD. . . 7 W13 8 W14
Dobie Lake Rd A 88 B3
Dobrindt Rd NI 18 R31
Dobson Rd DH 31 H34
Dobson Rd OT 66 T62
Dobson Rd PS 76 N28
Dobson Rd SM 41 B29
Doc Evans Rd PB 45 W43
Dochstader Rd NI . 18 T31-32
Dock La SM 41 X26
Dock Rd NR 58 T31
Docker Rd EL 8 X15
Docking Rd C 101 D21
Doctor Johnson Rd NR . . 33 G41
Doctor Miller Dr SDG. . . 51 W66
Dodds Rd HS 33 F41
Dodge Ln OX. . . 15 S20 16 S21
Dodge Lake Access Rd F. . 64 T53
Doe Lake Rd MK . 58 V32 59 V33-34
Doe Lake Rd PS 77 N32
Doering Rd R 81 M51
Doerr Sdrd BR. 27 E17
Dog Bay Rd HS . . . 61 S-T43
Dog Lake Rd TB . . . 102 B-C5
Dogtown La HU 20 J15
Dogwood Rd MD . . . 7 W-X12
Dogwood Tr MK. . 41 W29 58 V29
Doherty Rd MK. 58 T31
Dokis Reserve Rd NP. . 93 G25
Dokis Reserve Rd SD . 93 G24-25
Dokken Rd LN 48 W56-57
Dolans La R 64 S55
Doll Sdrd BR . . . 38 A-B16
Dollar Bay Rd A 89 E8
Dolmage Rd LM 13 R10
Dolman Ridge Rd OT. . . 66 Q64
Dolson Rd EX 4 F8
Domaine Dr PR 68 N70
Domaine St PR 69 P73
Dombroskie Rd (Madawaska Valley) R . . 62 Q48 81 P48
Dombroskie Rd (Whitewater Region) R 80 N47
Dominion Blvd EX. . . 4 B-C2
Dominion Dr CS . . . 101 A19
Dominion Rd NI . 19 U35-36
Dominion Bay Rd MA . . 72 L-M8
Dominion Springs Rd OT . 65 R58
Dominion Valley Pkwy T. . 25 J-K33
Domtar Ln OX 15 S20
Domtar Rd MK. . 58 R32 59 R33
Domville St WL. . . 28 H22-23
Don's Rd MA. 72 K10
Don's Rd SDG. 67 U67
Don Anna Rd F 47 W51
Don Long Rd NR 33 G41
Don Mills Rd T 24 J32
Don Moore La F 36 B57
Don Ross Dr SM 29 C28
Don Wilson Rd PB . . . 45 Z42
Donald B Munro Dr OT. . 65 R59 R60 83 Q59
Donald Carrick La SM . . 42 Y33
Donald Cousens Pkwy Y. . 31 H33
Donaldson Rd NP . 96 E-F36
Donaldson Cr CS . . . 101 B19
Donaldson Rd (Brighton) NR 33 E45
Donaldson Rd (Hamilton) NR . . . 33 F41-42
Donavan's Rd C 63 S51
Doncaster Rd OT. . . 66 R-S64
Donegal Rd NR . . 45 B44-45
Donegal Rd R 81 P51
Donelly Rd CS. 101 D23
Donnelly Dr CS . . . 101 A19
Donnelly Dr OT. . 50 V62 66 U62
Donnelly Rd HL. 13 T12
Donnelly Rd R 98 F46
Donnybrook Dr MD. . . 15 T18
Donnybrook Ln HU 20 J14-15 26 H15
Donoghue Rd LG 50 V62

Donohue Rd LA. 47 A51
Donohue Tr R 23 Q50-51
Donovan Rd NF . . 9 W21 10 W22
Donroy Rd L. 60 V40
Dool Rd LG. 50 W63
Doolittle La PE 35 F50
Doon Dr MD . . 14 S16 15 S17
Doon South Dr WT . . 22 N-P23
Doonan Rd SDG. 68 T71
Doorley Creek Rd R . . . 63 R52
Dopson Rd LN 49 W59
Doran Rd LG . . . 48 W56-57
Doran R 81 L50
Doran Rd SM 41 B29
Doras La R 62 S48
Dorcas Bay Rd BR . . . 54 S-T14
Dorchester Rd EL . . . 15 U-V18
Dorchester Rd MD. . . 15 T-U18
Dorchester Rd NI 19 R35
Doré Rd, Ch. TM . . . 85 Q30-31
Dore Bay Rd R 81 M50
Dorion Rd SM 41 X27
Dorley Creek Access Rd R. 63 S52
Dormer Rd LG . . . 37 B58-59
Dormy Grant Rd MA . . 70 J-K3
Dornie Rd SDG. . . . 68 R70-71
Dorosz La K 43 Y36
Dorval Dr R. 24 N29-30
Dotty Lake 1 Access Rd MK 78 P35
Double Bend La WT. . . 22 M22
Double Dip Rd R 99 G48
Double Road B Rd CS. . . 91 E15
Dougall Av EX 4 C2
Douglas Av A 84 B90
Douglas Dr MA. 72 J-K8
Douglas Dr MK . 58 U32 59 U33
Douglas Dr LM . . 12 S9 13 S10
Douglas Dr A 84 X91
Douglas Rd C 7 C10
Douglas Rd HS 46 B48
Douglas Rd NR 49 V61
Douglas Rd NP 93 F25
Douglas Rd PB 45 B42
Douglas Sdrd LN . . 65 T59-60
Douglas St BT. 16 R24
Douglas St G 27 E20
Douro St OX. . . 16 Q22 22 P22
Dovehaven Rd K. 32 D37
Dovercourt Rd NP . . 94 D27-28
Dovetail Rd R 62 Q48
Dow Rd SDG. 52 U70
Dowdle Rd LA . . . 35 C52-53
Downer's Rd R 32 H37
Downey La HL 45 W42
Downey Rd HD 18 U31
Downey Rd OT 66 S63
Downey Sdrd LN 65 S63
Downie Ln EL. . . 7 X-Y13 Y12
Downie Rd SM 7 W11
Downie St PT 21 P19
Downs Rd HS. . . 34 E46-47
Dowson Rd DH 31 G36
Doxsee Rd PE. . 34 F49 35 F50
Doyle Dr R 63 T51
Doyle Ln C 6 A-B9
Doyle Rd Y 43 Y-Z36
Doyle Rd OT 66 T63
Doyle Rd (Loyalist) LA . 36 D-E54
Doyle Rd (Stone Mills) LA . 35 C53
Doyle Mountain Rd R . . 81 P48
Dozois Rd OT 66 S63
DR McLay Dr MA 73 N11
Dracup Rd K 6 B-C8
Dranoel Rd K 32 D-E39
Draper St EX 4 F2
Draper Lake Rd F . . 36 A-B56
Draycott Lake Rd MK . . 58 R30
Drevnick Rd R. 62 Q47
Drewery St NR. 34 F46
Driessens La LM 7 W10
Driftwood Dr A 86 C94
Driftwood Rd SD 92 F22
Driftwood Ln PB. 33 C41
Driftwood Rd EX 4 E2
Driftwood Rd LN 65 T59
Driftwood Beach Rd HU. . 27 G18
Driftwood Park Rd R . . . 98 F46
Driftwood Shores Rd K. . 43 A35
Driscoll Rd L . . . 37 C-D58
Driscoll Rd PB. 35 D52
Drive-In La R 85 Q30
Drive-In Rd NP 94 D27
Drive In Rd TM 27 E19
Driver Rd LG 60 Y60-61
Drizzle Lake Access Rd HS. 61 R42
Drohan Rd R 63 Q49
Drope Rd NR 33 D43
Droppo Rd SDG 67 U66
Drouin Rd R . . . 67 Q66 R67
Drum Rd K. 32 E-F38
Drumbo Rd BT . . . 16 Q23-24
Drummond Concession LN. 65 U58
Drummond Ln PB. . . . 33 C41 D42
Drummond Rd EX 4 E2
Drummond Rd LN 65 T59
Drummond Rd LG . . . 49 X-Y60
Drummond Rd MD . . . 14 R14
Drummond Rd R . . . 19 R34-35
Drummond School Rd LN . 49 V58
Drury La MK. . . 42 W32 58 V32
Drury La R 7 B10
Drury Mill Rd SM. 42 A30
Dry Lake Rd HD 17 T27-28
Dry Pine Bay Rd SD. . . 92 H22
Dry Rapids Rd SD 92 G22
Dryden Blvd OT 31 H36
Dryden Rd E CS 101 C21
Du Golf Rd PR 67 P-Q66
Du Lac Rd PR 67 P67
Du Moulin Rd PR 67 N67
Du Quai Av PR 67 N67
Du Theatre Rd PR 67 N67
Duart Rd C 7 X-Y12
Dubblestein Rd HS . . . 62 R46
Dube Rd NP 95 E33
Dubeau Rd SDG . . 58 T72 69 T73
Dublin Ln HT . . . 23 L27 M27-28
Dubois Rd PR. 67 N66-67
Duborne Rd CS 88 E4
Duborne Lake Rd A. . . . 88 E-F4
Dubroys Rd CS 101 D20
Dubuc Rd NP 94 C28
Ducharme Rd LG 48 Y54

Ducharme Beach / Faught

Ducharme Beach Rd HU 20 N12-13
Duck's Bay Rd MA 73 N11
Duck Bay Rd SM 41 X29
Duck Blairhampton Rd HL 60 U38
Duck Creek Rd NP 93 E25
Duck Lake Rd HL 60 U-V38
Duck Lake Rd (East Mills) PS 76 K27 94 J27
Duck Lake Rd (Seguin) PS 58 Q29
Duckworth St SM 42 B30
Duclos Point Rd Y 31 C33
Dudley Rd HL 60 U40
Dudley Rd MK 58 U30
Dudley Rd NR 33 F44
Duetta Rd PE 35 H51
Duff Ln EL 8 W14
Duff Rd A 86 D-E97
Duff Rd F 36 B56
Duff Rd SD 89 F9
Duffe La F 36 C57
Dufferin Av C 6 X6-7
Dufferin Av HS 34 F47
Dufferin Rd LN 49 W58
Dufferin St LN 49 W58
Dufferin St T 24 K-L32
Dufferin St Y 24 I-J31 30 F-H31
Dufferin Bridge Rd PS 76 P29-30
Duffs Rd DH 31 F-G35
Duffs Corners Rd SDG 68 T69
Duffy Ln OX 16 T21
Duffy's La MK 58 T29
Duffy's Rd SDG 51 V68
Duffys La PL 29 G28 30 H29
Dugald Rd R 64 R56
Dugald Rd R 82 P55
Dugas Rd NP 95 E32
Duhamel Rd CS 100 D18
Dukelow Rd K 43 B35
Dukelow Rd LG 50 W63-64
Dulcemaine Rd LG 37 B59-60
Dumart Rd SD 93 E24
Dumfries Rd WT 22 P24
Dummer Rd PB 45 B44
Dummer-Asphodel Rd PB 45 B42-44
Dummer Lake Rd E PB 45 A43 Z43
Dummer Lake Rd W PB 45 A42-43
Dumond Rd A 87 E99
Dumont Rd PS 75 N25
Dumont Rd SD 90 E14
Dumont 12 Access Rd PS 75 N24-25
Dumont 2 Access Rd PS 75 N25
Dumontier Rd PR 67 R68
Dumouchel Rd SD 93 D24
Dump Rd HU 20 P16
Dump Rd LA 36 E54
Dump Rd MA 70 J2-3
Dump Rd SD 101 B20
Dunbar Dr K 44 A38
Dunbar Rd NR 33 E43-44
Dunbar Rd SDG 67 U66
Dunborough Rd EL 7 W13 8 W14 X14
Dunby Rd DF 29 G26-27
Duncan Dr R 83 Q57
Duncan La HS 61 T43
Duncan's Ln PB 33 D42
Duncan's Rd LN 48 V55
Dunchurch Estate Rd PS 76 M-N28
Duncrief Rd MD 14 S15
Dundas St BT 16 R24
Dundas St DH 31 H35-36
Dundas St HS 34 E-F47
Dundas St HT 23 N-P28 24 M29-30
Dundas St LG 50 X65
Dundas St MD 15 S-T18 T17
Dundas St OX 16 R21
Dundas St PL 24 L30
Dundas St WL 23 J26
Dundas St WT 22 P24 23 P25
Dundas St E HS 34 E49
Dundas St E T 24 K32 25 K33
Dundas St W HS 34 E48-49
Dundas St W T 24 K31 K-L32
Dundela Rd SDG 51 V66
Dundonald Rd MD 7 W13 13 V12 14 V13
Dundurn St HM 17 Q28
Dunfield Rd R 82 P53
Dunford Rd (North Kawartha) PB 45 Z42
Dunford Rd (Smith-Ennismore-Lakefield) PB 32 C40
Dunford's La NR 45 B45
Dungannon Rd HU 26 H13-14
Dunham Rd LG 49 Y60
Dunham Rd NR 33 C45 45 B45
Dunks Bay Rd BR 54 S14
Dunlay Rd NR 33 C44
Dunlop Sdrd LN 48 V57 49 V58
Dunlop St E SM 42 B30
Dunlop St W SM 30 C29 41 B29
Dunlop Lake Rd A 88 C6
Dunlop Shores Rd A 88 C6
Dunmark Rd HM 17 R26
Dunmore Rd R 82 N53
Dunn Rd HL 60 S40
Dunn Rd NR 32 F-G40
Dunn St NI 19 S35
Dunn Farm Tr A 87 D99
Dunnes Rd NP 80 P43
Dunnes Rd R 82 L53
Dunnigan Rd R 81 P50
Dunning Rd OT 67 Q65 R66
Dunning Rd PR 68 N70
Dunns Ln SM 42 Y30
Dunns Lake Rd R 63 T51
Dunns Valley Rd A 86 C97 87 C98
Dunrobin Rd OT 65 Q60
Dunsdon St BT 17 R25
Dunsford Rd K 44 B38
Dunvegan Rd SDG 68 R69-70
Dunvegan Rd E SDG 68 Q70-71
Dunwoody Rd R 81 P50
Duplantie Rd PR 69 P73
Dupont Rd NP 95 E32
Dupont Sdrd PR 68 Q70
Dupont St T 24 K32
Dupuis Dr CS 101 A20
Dupuis Ln R 82 K53-54
Dupuis Rd (Espanola) SD 90 E13
Dupuis Rd (Markstay-Warren) SD 93 D24
Duquette Rd PR 67 P67
Durack Ln R 82 N53
Durand-Huronview Rd HU 20 M13
Durant Rd WT 22 M23
Durham Rd BR 27 E17
Durham Rd G 27 E20
Durham Rd NR 33 F44-45
Durham Rd NI 18 R31
Durham Rd B G 28 D22
Durham St G 28 D22
Durham St NI 19 U33-34
Durham Creek Ln LM 12 U9 13 U10
Durliat Rd NI 19 T34-35
Durward Rd DH 31 E35
Dutch La HS 34 C48
Dutch La NI 18 R32
Dutch Ln G 28 C21
Dutch Ln HU 20 K14-15
Dutch Rd PE 34 F49
Dutch Line Rd PB 44 X38
Duthill Rd LM 6 W7
Dutrisac Rd NP 94 E28
Dutton Rd TM 85 R30
Duttona Beach Rd EL 8 X15
Duval Rd PR 68 P71
Duxbury Rd HD 17 T27
Dwight Bay Rd MK 59 R35
Dwight Beach Rd MK 59 R35
Dwinnell Rd SM 41 A29
Dwyer La F 47 A53 48 Z53
Dwyer Rd F 47 A53
Dwyer Hill Rd OT 50 V61-62 65 T60 66 T-U61
Dyer Rd SDG 68 S69
Dyer Memorial Rd MK 59 Q34
Dyers Bay Rd BR 54 S16 T15-16
Dyke Rd A 88 E4
Dyke St SD 93 D24
Dymock Ln EL 7 W13
Dyno Rd HL 61 V42

E, Mersea Rd EX 5 F6
E-F, Sideroad BR 26 C14-15
E-Line Rd TB 102 D3
Eadie Rd PR 67 R-S65
Eady Rd R 81 M-N49
Eady Rd R 82 P55
Eady Station Rd SM 42 Y30
Eager Rd LG 50 V64
Eagle Av BT 17 R25
Eagle Rd BR 54 S14
Eagle Rd K 44 B39
Eagle St NI 19 T35-36
Eagle St WT 22 N24
Eagle St Y 30 F31
Eagle Lake Rd F 47 X54
Eagle Lake Rd HL 60 T38-39
Eagle Lake Rd PS 76 K30 77 K31-32
Eagle M Tr MA 73 K12
Eagle Mine Rd A 84 Y-Z92
Eagleson Ln HU 14 Q13
Eagleson Ln PB 32 E40
Eagleson Rd NR 33 E-F42
Eagleson Rd OT 66 R-S61
Eamer Rd SDG 52 U69
Eames Rd PE 35 G50
Eamon Rd SDG 51 V68 52 U69
Earl Rd LG 49 Z59
Earl Rd SDG 68 T69
Earl Rd TB 102 E2
Earl's Rd MA 72 L8
Earl Armstrong Rd OT 66 S63
Earl Dwyre Rd LG 49 Z58
Earle Rd NR 33 F42
Earles Rd HL 61 U41-42
Earls Rd MK 59 R33
Earls Rd PS 57 T28
Early Rd R 83 P56
Earth Park Rd MK 59 T34
Eashores Rd HL 60 T39
East Av NI 19 T35
East Ln MA 71 J6
East Rd BR 54 T16
East Rd HL 60 S38-39 U38
East Rd HS 46 W48
East Rd MA 73 L11
East Rd NP 93 F25
East Rd TB 102 B3
East Rd (Armour) PS 77 N31-32
East Rd (Hardy) PS 94 J27 J27-28
East St MA 72 J7-8
East St S K 44 A39 Z39
East-West Luther Townline WL 28 F23 G23-24 H24
East & West Ln NI 19 Q34-35
East Back Ln G 28 C21 C22 D23 39 B20 B21
East Bay Rd CS 101 A21
East Bay Rd F 63 V51-52
East Bay Rd HS 46 W47
East Bay Rd MK 58 U30-31
East Bay Rd PS 77 K31
East Beach Rd EX 5 E-F6
East Bear Lake Rd PS 58 Q30 76 P30
East Beehive Rd K 44 A38
East Black Lake Rd MK 58 U-V31
East Britannia Rd MK 59 R34-35
East Camp Lake Rd MK 78 P36
East Caribou Lake Rd A 87 B2
East Clear Bay Rd PB 44 X39
East Communication Rd PB 44 B40
East Cooper Lake Rd MK 59 R35
East Fox Lake Rd MK 58 Q32
East Garafraxa-West Garafraxa Townline DF 22 J24 23 J25 28 H24
East Grandview Lake Rd MK 59 S35
East Hill Ln OX 15 S20
East Hungerford Rd HS 47 A50-51
East Lake Rd HS 61 S44 62 S45
East Lake Rd PS 77 M34
East Line Rd A 86 D97 87 D98
East Linton Sdrd W G 39 Y-Z19
East Loop Rd HS 62 S46
East Luther-West Luther Townline DF 28 F-G23
East Main St LG 50 Z62
East Malden Rd EX 4 E2
East Mall, The T 24 L31
East Oliver Lake Rd TB 102 E4 F3-4
East Oxbow Lake Rd MK 59 Q35 78 P35
East Park Rd G 27 C19-20
East Pike Creek Rd EX 4 B3
East Point Rd LG 49 Z58
East Posts Rd PB 45 Z45
East Poverty Bay Rd PS 76 M29
East Puce Rd EX 4 B4
East Quarter Ln NF 17 U-V26
East Quarter Line Rd NF 10 W-X23 16 V22-23
East Quarter Townline Rd BT 16 R-S23 S-T24
East River Rd BT 16 Q24
East River Rd LM 6 W-X7
East River Rd SM 42 X33
East Ruscom River Rd EX 5 B-C5
East Shore La F 48 Z55
East Shore Rd EX 5 H5
East Shore Rd SM 42 W30
East Side Way R 64 R55
East Townline Rd DH 32 F39 F-G40
East Townline Rd LG 50 A62
East Townline Rd PS 76 M-N28
East Trout Lake Rd SD 93 F-G23
East Wanapitei Rd CS 101 Y21
East Waseosa Lake Rd MK 59 Q33
East West Rd EX 5 H4-5
Eastdale Dr SM 41 Z27
Easterbrook Rd PE 35 H50-51
Eastern Av CS 100 D18
Eastern Av T 24 K32 25 K33
Eastgate Pkwy PL 24 L30
Eastlawn Dr C 6 A9
Eastnor-Lindsay Townline BR 55 U16
Eastons Rd LN 64 U56
Eastport Dr HM 18 P-Q29
Eastshore Rd MK 58 V29
Eastside Dr PS 74 L22-23
Eastside Trout Lake La R 80 P46
Eastview La MA 73 L12
Eastview Rd HL 60 S38
Eastview Rd WL 23 L25
Easy La F 36 E56
Eaton Rd MD 15 T18
Eatonville Rd PE 34 F48
Ebbers Rd SD 93 D24
Ebbs Sdrd LN 49 V58
Ebbs Bay Dr LN 65 U58-59
Ebbs Bay Rd LN 65 U58
Ebenezer Dr MD 15 R17
Ebenezer Rd LM 13 U-V11
Ebenezer Rd OX 15 T20 16 T21
Ebenezer Rd PL 24 J30
Ebenezer Sdrd SM 41 Y28
Eberle Ln C 7 A12
Ebert Rd LN 49 V-W59
Eberts Ln C 6 Y9
Ebycrest Rd WT 22 M23
EC Row Expwy EX 4 B2-3
Ecclestone Dr MK 58 U-V32
Echo Bay Rd K 44 A38-39
Echo Bay Rd MK 59 R35
Echo Beach Rd MK 58 S31
Echo Hills Rd MK 59 R35
Echo Lake Rd A 86 B94-95
Echo Lake Rd F 36 A54 48 Z54
Echo Lake Rd HS 62 R46
Echo Lake Rd MK 59 T34-35
Echo Ridge Rd HS 45 W45
Echo Ridge Rd PS 77 N34
Eckford Rd MK 58 V31
Ed's Ln C 7 B11
Ed Briese Rd MK 58 S31
Ed Clare Rd SD 92 F22
Ed Connelly Rd SM 41 Y28
Eddison Dr R 63 T51
Eddystone Rd NR 33 F43
Eden Ln EL 15 V20 16 V21
Eden Rd K 43 B36
Eden Estates Ct HT 23 L-M26
Eden Grove Rd LG 37 B59-60
Eden Township Rd SD 91 E18 100 D18
Edenderry Ln PB 44 B39-40
Edgar Rd NR 33 C45
Edgar Sdrd EX 4 D3
Edgar Benson Rd NR 33 F42
Edge's Sdrd G 27 D20
Edgehill Dr SM 41 B29
Edgemere Rd NI 19 U36
Edgerton Rd DH 32 E37
Edges Rd LA 47 B52
Edgeware Ln EL 15 V18
Edgewater Pk PB 32 C40
Edgewater Pl HD 18 U30
Edgewater Rd CS 101 D19
Edgewood Rd HM 23 P27
Edgewood Rd K 32 E38
Edgewood Rd PS 76 M27
Edinborough Ln EL 8 W14-15
Edinburgh Rd WL 23 M25
Edison Rd CS 101 B20-21
Edith Lake Rd SD 92 F21
Edmison Rd PB 32 C40
Edmond Rd NP 95 F32-33
Edward Dr PE 34 G47
Edward St LG 50 Y64
Edward St SM 29 C26
Edward St TB 103 D6
Edward Scott Rd LG 50 V64
Edwards Av Y 30 F30
Edwards Rd CS 100 D15
Edwards Rd LG 49 Y60
Edwards Rd SDG 51 V68 67 U68
Edwin Dr PB 44 Z40
Edworthy Sdrd WT 22 P24
Edys Mills Ln LM 6 W9 7 W10
Eel Bay Rd F 36 B55-56
Eels Lake Rd PB 45 W42
Eels Lake Public Landing Rd HL 45 W42 61 V42
Effingham St NI 19 R-T33
Effingham-Grimsthorpe Hydroline Access Rd HS 46 W48-49
Effingham Lake Access Rd LA 63 U-V49
Egan La F 48 Z55
Egan Ln R 82 M52
Egan Creek Rd HS 46 W48 62 V47
Egan Creek Tr HS 62 Q47
Egan Lake Access Rd HS 62 V47
Egerton Beach Rd HU 20 M13
Eggleton Rd (Belleville) HS 34 D49
Eggleton Rd (Stirling-Rawdon) HS 34 C47-48
Eglinton Av PL 24 L-M29
Eglinton Av E T 24 K32 25 J-K33
Eglinton Av W PL 24 K-L30
Eglinton Av W T 24 K31
Eglund Dr PS 75 P25
Egremont Dr MD 13 T12 14 T13-15
Egremont Rd LM 12 S9 13 T10-11
Egret Tr HL 61 U42
Egypt Sdrd BR 26 F16
Egypt School Rd NF 16 U23
Eichstaedt Rd R 99 K50
Eigg Rd SDG 68 R71
Eight Mile Point Rd SM 42 A32
Eighteen Mile Ln HU 26 F-G13
Ekblad Rd HS 46 A49 47 A50
Elarton Rd LM 13 S-T11
Elbe Rd LG 49 Z61
Elbow Ln C 6 X7
Elbow Lake Rd SD 92 E21
Elbow Point Rd PB 44 Z40
Elbow Ridge Rd SD 92 E21
Elcho Rd NI 18 S31-32
Eldale Rd WT 22 L22
Eldanori La HL 44 W39
Elder Dr MK 59 S35
Elder La G 39 B20
Elder Rd NR 33 E43
Elderberry La F 36 A56
Elderslie-Arran Ln BR 38 B17
Eldon Av CS 100 D16
Eldon Rd K 31 C-D36 43 B36
Eldon Rd R 82 M53
Eldon Station Rd K 43 A35-36
Eldorado Rd A 88 F3
Eldorado Beach Rd TB 103 B9
Eldreds Rd LN 48 V55
Eldridge La K 43 X34
Eldridge Rd LG 49 Y61
Electric Ln C 6 Y7
Elephant Lake Rd HL 61 T42
Elevator Ln HU 20 J-K15
Elevator Rd K 32 E38
Elevator St LM 13 T10
Eley Rd A 87 E1
Elgar Rd PB 32 E40
Elgin Av HU 20 J13
Elgin Rd HS 46 X48
Elgin Rd MD 15 S-T18 U19
Elgin St EL 15 V17
Elgin St HU 14 Q15
Elgin St WT 23 P25
Elgin St (Cobourg) NR 33 G42
Elgin St (Cramahe) NR 33 F44
Elgin St (McNab-Braeside) R 83 Q57
Elgin St (Pembroke) R 81 L51
Elgin House Rd MK 58 T30
Elgin Mills Rd Y 30 H32 31 G-H33
Elgin Young Rd F 48 Y54
Elginfield Rd MD 14 R13-16
Elginfield Rd OX 15 Q18
Elginfield Rd PT 15 Q17-18
Eligh La OT 66 U63
Eligh-Beckstead Rd SDG 67 U68
Elijah Rd F 48 X54
Elim Lodge Rd PB 44 A39 A39-40
Elimville Ln HU 20 N-P15
Eliza St PR 68 N71
Elizabeth St NI 19 U33-34
Elizabeth Bay Rd MA 71 K5
Elizabeth Lake Rd SD 90 F14
Elk Dr HL 60 T39
Elk Rd PS 77 M32
Ella Rd CS 91 E15
Ella St C 6 C7
Ellen St SM 41 X29
Ellen Maloney Rd LN 66 U61
Ellerbeck Rd C 5 D-E7
Ellerbeck Rd F 36 B54
Ellery's Sdrd SM 41 Y28
Ellesmere Rd T 25 J33-34
Elliot Dr MD 13 R12 14 R13
Elliot Rd EL 16 V21
Elliot Rd LN 48 W-X57
Elliot Sdrd SM 41 Y28-29
Elliot Bay Rd LG 37 A58
Elliott Ln LM 7 W10
Elliott Rd BT 16 S24 17 S25
Elliott Rd DH 32 G39-40
Elliott Rd HL 59 Q36
Elliott Rd LM 13 Q-R11
Elliott Rd MA 72 L10
Elliott Rd SM 41 A28
Elliott Rd TM 85 M29
Elliotts Grove Sdrd HU 20 L13
Ellis Av BT 16 S24 17 S25
Ellis Rd SM 42 W-X30
Ellis Rd TB 102 B2 B3
Ellis Rd WL 23 N25
Ellis Sdrd EX 4 C-D3
Ellis Woods LN 64 R56
Ellis Lake La MK 59 T34
Ellisview Rd Y 30 C-D32
Ellisville Rd LG 37 A59
Ellwood Blvd A 86 F95
Elly Tysick Rd LN 48 X56
Elm Av TM 85 R30
Elm Ln EL 15 V18
Elm Rd BR 55 X17
Elm St BR 55 X18
Elm St CS 101 A-B19
Elm St C 7 X11
Elm St EL 15 V17
Elm St NI 19 T-U33
Elm St SDG 67 T68
Elm St E CS 101 C19
Elm St W CS 101 C19
Elm Grove Dr EX 4 B3
Elm Grove Rd LN 49 X58
Elm Tree Dr MD 13 S12 14 S13
Elm Tree Ln LM 7 W12
Elm Tree Rd F 47 Y52
Elm Tree Rd K 32 C-D37 43 A36 B36-37
Elm Tree Rd NI 18 R31
Elmac Rd R 82 M54
Elman Rd CS 91 E16
Elmar Rd HL 60 T37
Elmbrook Rd PE 35 F51
Elmdale Rd PB 32 D40
Elmhirst Rd PB 33 C42-43
Elmira Rd WL 22 M24 23 M25
Elmsley Rd LM 13 R-S10
Elmview Dr CS 101 A19
Elmwood Dr HS 34 E49
Elora St HU 27 G19
Elphin Maberly Rd LN 48 V55 W55-56
Elsie Rd NI 18 T32
Elsinore Rd BR 38 Z17
Elva La SM 42 W30
Elviage Dr MD 14 T15-16
Elwoods Rd R 63 S49
Ely Side Rd PS 77 M32
Elzevir Rd HS 47 Y-Z50
Elzner Dr MK 59 V33
Embury Rd LA 35 C53
Emerald 40 Foot Rd LA 36 E54
Emerald Isle Rd PB 44 B40
Emerson La DH 32 E37
Emerson Rd HS 34 C49
Emerson Rd HD 17 T28 18 T29
Emerson Rd MK 59 T34
Emerson Rd NI 18 T-U32
Emerson Rd PR 68 P71
Emerson Lake Rd A 86 C-D97 87 C98
Emery Rd LG 37 B59
Emery Rd MA 72 J-K8
Emile Levac Sdrd PR 68 Q69
Emily Ct A 86 E97
Emily St PT 15 Q17-18
Emily Creek Rd K 44 A38
Emily Manor Dr K 32 C40
Emily Park Rd K 32 C39
Emiry Rd SD 90 F11
Emma Rd Y 30 F31
Emma St F 37 D58
Emmett Rd OT 67 P65
Emmett Lake Rd BR 54 S15
Emon Rd R 64 S55
Empey Rd EL 15 U-V20
Empey Rd HS 46 Z47
Empey Rd LA 36 C54
Empey Rd WT 22 M22
Empire La F 48 X54
Empire Rd NI 19 U34
Emsdale Lake Rd PS 77 P33
End Side Rd A 86 B-C96
Enders Rd TB 102 C-D3
Endikai Rd A 88 B3
Endikai Strip Rd A 88 B4
Eneas Creek Rd R 63 R49
Energy Park Rd BR 26 C14
Enfield Rd DH 31 F36 32 F37
English Cl HL 44 W40
English Ln C 6 A-B9
English Ln PS 95 H32
English Ln N PB 45 A42
English Rd K 43 B35
English Rd R 64 R53
English Rd SDG 50 W-X65
English Church Rd HM 17 R28
English Line Rd PB 45 A-B42
English Settlement Rd HS 34 F46-47
Ennis Rd LN 48 V57
Ennis Rd PB 44 B40
Ennis Bay Rd MK 58 V32
Ennisclaire Dr HT 23 L-M27
Eno Rd R 81 M48
Enright Rd HS 35 C50-51
Enright Rd R 82 Q54
Enterprise Dr HL 44 W39-40
Eramosa Rd WL 23 L25
Eramosa-Erin Townline WL 23 K25-26
Eramosa-Garafraxa Townline WL 22 K24 23 K25
Erb St WT 22 N23
Erb's Rd WT 22 N21-22
Erbsville Rd WT 22 M-N22
Eric Hutcheson Rd LG 49 W60
Eric Potter Rd HL 60 U38
Erie Av BT 17 R25
Erie Av EX 4 E1
Erie Blvd NF 10 X24
Erie Rd EL 8 X15
Erie Rd EX 4 E-F2
Erie Rd NI 19 U35
Erie St C 5 E6 7 A11
Erie St EX 5 E5
Erie St HD 17 V27 V28
Erie St PT 21 P19
Erie Blue Beach La EX 4 E-F2
Erie Peat Rd NI 19 U33
Erie Shore Dr C 7 C10-11
Erieau Rd C 7 B-C10
Erin Ln EL 8 X15
Erin-East Garafraxa Townline DF 23 J25 J26 29 H26
Erin-East Garafraxa Townline WL 23 J25-26
Erin-Eramosa Town Ln WL 23 L26
Erin-Halton Hills Town Ln WL 23 K-L27
Erin Mills Pkwy PL 24 L29 M30
Erindale Station Rd PL 24 L-M30
Erlwyn Dr PB 44 B40
Ernie Rd F 36 B56-57
Errington Av CS 100 B17-18
Ervine Rd HS 47 B50
Escarpment Sdrd PL 29 H27-28
Escott-Rockport Rd LG 37 B60-61
Escott-Yonge Townline Rd LG 37 A60-61 B61
Eshkibok Rd MA 73 K-L13
Esker Rd HS 46 B49
Esker Rd K 32 C38
Esna Park Dr Y 24 I-J32 30 H32
Esquesing Ln HT 23 M28
Essa Rd SM 30 C29
Essa-Springwater Boundary Rd SM 29 C28
Essex By-Pass EX 4 D3
Essex Townline Rd EX 4 D4 5 D5
Essing Rd MA 70 J3
Esson Ln PB 33 C42
Essonville Ln HL 61 U41
Estaire Rd SD 92 E20-21 101 D20
Esten Dr N A 88 D6
Esten Dr S A 88 D6
Esterville Rd C 6 X9
Esterville Rd LM 6 W9 12 V9
Estis Rd LA 36 B54 47 B53
Estonian Camp Rd MK 59 S33
Ethel Ln HU 21 K17-18
Etienne Rd OT 67 P-Q66
Etling Rd NI 18 U32
Etonia Rd BT 16 R23
Ettyville Rd PR 67 Q67
Etwell Rd MK 58 R32 59 R33
Eugene Rd CS 100 B18
Eugene Rd NP 93 D-E26
Euphemia Ln LM 7 X11-12
Euphrasia-Holland Twnln G 28 C22 39 A-B21
Euphrasia-Saint Vincent Twnln G 40 A22
Eureka Rd HL 60 V40
Evans Av T 24 L31
Evans Rd HM 23 P28
Evans Rd NR 33 D45
Evans Point La HD 11 V29 18 U29
Evansville Dr NP 94 D28
Evanturel-Marter Rd TM 85 M28
Eveleigh Rd MK 58 T-U30
Evelyn Dr MD 15 S18
Everatt Sdrd BR 55 V17
Everett Dr PS 94 H29
Everett Dr TB 102 C4
Everett La F 36 B55
Everett Rd K 43 Y-Z37
Everetts Rd PB 45 W42-43 X42-43
Evergreen Av SM 41 Z27
Evergreen Dr K 43 A34-35
Evergreen Dr MA 72 L8
Evergreen Ln HU 20 P15
Evergreen Rd BR 55 V17
Evergreen Rd F 48 Z54-55
Evergreen Rd HS 34 C47-48
Evergreen Rd MD 14 R14
Evergreen Rd NP 95 D32 D33
Evergreen Rd NR 45 B46
Evergreen Rd TB 103 B6
Evergreen St OX 16 T21-22
Evergreen Tr MK 59 R-S33
Evergreen Beach La EX 4 F3
Evergreen Hill Rd NF 16 V24
Evergreen Line Rd C 7 Y10
Evertsen Rd NR 33 E41
Ewart St SM 30 D31
Ewing Rd SM 29 C25
Exeter Rd MD 15 U17
Exmouth St LM 12 T7
Experimental Farm Rd HS 34 F46
Expressway, The PS 77 P32

F-G, Concession Rd SM 42 Y33
F & G Ln A 86 E94
Factory Rd F 36 B-C57
Factory Rd HS 34 D48
Factory Rd R 81 N51
Fagan Lake Rd LN 48 W56
Fair Rd BT 17 R26
Fair's La LN 48 V56
Fair-lee Park Rd MK 58 S30
Fair Valley Church Rd SM 42 Y-Z30
Fairbairn Rd K 44 Z38
Fairbairn St PB 32 C40
Fairbank East Rd CS 100 C-D16
Fairbank Lake Rd CS 100 C-D15 D16
Fairbanks St LA 36 D54
Fairbrother Rd NI 18 R31
Fairfax Rd LG 37 B60
Fairfield Ln C 7 X11
Fairfield Rd BT 16 S23-24
Fairfield Rd LG 50 Y-Z62
Fairfield Bay Dr HL 60 V37
Fairground Rd NF 9 X21 10 X22
Fairgrounds Rd SM 41 A-B26
Fairgrounds Rd (Ramara) SM 42 X33
Fairgrounds Rd (Severn) SM 42 Y-Z31
Fairgrounds Rd S SM 29 C26 41 B26
Fairhurst Dr OT 66 U63
Fairmile Rd OT 66 U63
Fairport Rd DH 31 H34
Fairvalley Rd SM 42 Y-Z33
Fairview Av EL 15 V17
Fairview Av EX 4 D3
Fairview Dr BT 17 R25
Fairview Dr SDG 67 T68
Fairview La A 86 E94
Fairview Ln C 6 A9 7 A10
Fairview Rd EL 8 W17
Fairview Rd LG 49 Y-Z59
Fairview Rd MD 15 R17 S18
Fairview Rd SM 30 C29-30
Fairview Rd TM 85 Q29
Fairview St HT 18 P29
Fairway Dr PS 95 F32
Fairway Rd SM 42 B30
Fairway Rd WT 22 N23
Fairweather Rd LM 12 T-V9
Fairy Falls Rd MK 59 T34
Falconbridge Dr MD 14 U14 U13
Falconbridge Hwy CS 101 B-C20
Falkenburg Rd MK 58 T31-32
Falkirk Dr NF 16 V22
Falkland Rd BT 16 R23
Fall River Rd F 48 X55
Fallbrook Rd LN 48 V57
Fallbrook Tr HT 23 K27
Falling Snow Rd TB 102 G2
Fallis Ln PB 32 E39-40
Fallis Rd DH 32 E37
Fallon Dr MD 14 Q15-16
Fallow Field Rd SDG 68 T72
Fallowfield Rd HL 60 V39-40
Fallowfield Rd OT 66 R-S62 S-T61
Falls Rd HU 20 K13
Falls Rd PS 77 P31
Falls Bay Rd K 44 A39
Falls Lake Rd MA 70 J2
Falzetta Rd SD 100 D14
Fanning Rd NR 33 E43
Fanshawe Park Rd E MD 15 S17
Fanshawe Park Rd W MD 14 S-T16
Fansher Rd LM 7 W11 W-X10
Fansville Ln HU 20 M-N14
Faradale Dr HS 62 U45
Faraway Rd SD 90 E13
Fargey Rd HS 34 C48
Fargo Rd C 7 B10-11
Farini Rd NR 32 F40
Farlain Lake Rd E SM 41 W-X27
Farley Rd PR 67 S67
Farley's Rd PS 76 M28
Farm Rd NI 19 T-U35
Farm Rd TB 102 E-F4
Farm Lake La F 47 W52 48 W53
Farm View Rd PS 77 M32
Farmer Hays Dr HL 60 Q-R37
Farmers Ln LM 13 R11-12
Farmers Ln NP 96 F35
Farmers Rd A 87 E2
Farmers Rd K 32 E39
Farmers Way OT 66 Q-R64
Farms Rd K 43 A35 B35
Farmstead Rd K 31 C36
Farmview Rd K 32 C39
Farmview Rd OT 65 R59 83 Q58
Farnham Rd HS 34 D48-49
Farquhar Lake Dr HL 61 T42
Farr Av NI 19 U35
Farr Av Y 30 E32
Farr Rd HL 61 U41
Farr Rd HD 18 U31
Farr Rd NI 18 T32
Farr Rd NI 19 T34
Farr St NI 18 S32 T32
Farran's Point Rd SDG 51 V68
Farrell Dr BR 26 C14
Fass Rd A 86 D97
Faught Rd R 82 M53

Faulkner Av Y . . . 30 F32 31 F33
Faulkner Tr OT . . . 66 S61
Faux Rd NR. . . 33 C44
Fawcett Rd BT . . . 17 S25
Fawcett Rd SDG . . . 67 U65
Fawn Cr SM . . . 29 C27
Fawn Rd PS . . . 77 N32
Fawn Tr HL . . . 61 U42
Fawn Lake Rd MK . . . 59 T33
Feairs Dr G . . . 28 F22
Feasby Rd DH . . . 31 E33-34
Featherstone La NR . . . 32 F40
Feeder La HD . . . 18 U31
Feeder Rd NI . . . 19 T33
Feeder R E NI . . 18 U32 19 T33
Feeder Canal Rd HD. . . 18 U31
Feere Rd HD . . . 18 T30
Felbers Rd HS. . . 46 Y47
Felhaber Rd R. . . 63 O50
Felhaber Access Rd R . 63 R50
Fell Ln SM . . . 42 X30
Fellows Rd F. . . 36 C55
Fells Point Rd K . . . 43 Z37
Felsman Dr R. . . 56 O26 57 O27
Feltham Rd A . . . 87 E98
Fen Rd CS. . . 100 D16
Fenel Rd K . . . 43 A-B36
Fenmar Dr T . . . 24 J31
Fennell Av HM. . . 17 O28
Fenton Rd C . . . 7 Y12
Fenton Rd NR . . . 33 F43
Fenwick La G . . . 28 C23
Ferguslea Rd R. . . 82 Q54
Ferguson Ln EL . . 15 V17-18
Ferguson Rd A . . . 48 X-Y53
Ferguson Rd H . . . 17 R26
Ferguson Rd K . . . 43 Y36
Ferguson Rd LN . . . 65 U60
Ferguson Rd LG. . . 50 W63
Ferguson Rd PS . . . 77 N32
Ferguson Rd R . . . 82 P55
Ferguson Rd SDG. . . 51 V67
Ferguson Rd (Alnwick-Haldimand) NR . . . 38 E44
Ferguson Rd (Hamilton) NR . 33 F42
Ferguson Sdrd LG . . . 37 A-B60
Ferguson Bay La HS . . . 45 W45
Ferguson Bay Rd HL . . . 60 V40
Ferguson Hill Rd NR . . . 33 E45
Ferguson Lake Rd R . . . 64 H53
Ferguson Tatlock Rd LN. . 49 V60
Fergusons Sdrd LN. . . 48 V56
Fergusons Falls Rd LN 49 V58 65 U58
Fern Glen Rd PS. . . 77 P32
Fernbank Rd OT . . 65 S60 66 S61
Ferndale Dr SM . . 30 C29 41 B29
Ferndale Rd BR. . . 55 V17
Ferndale Rd MK . . . 58 T30
Ferne Dr MD . . . 14 U15
Fernforest Dr PL . . . 24 J29
Fernhill Dr MD . . . 14 S14
Fernlea Sdrd NF. . . 16 U-V22
Feronia Rd NP . . . 95 D32-33
Ferrar Rd MD. . . 15 T18
Ferrie Township 1 Access Rd PS . . . 76 K-L29
Ferrie Township Access Rd PS . . . 76 K28-29
Ferrier Rd LN. . . 49 W-X58
Ferrier Rd E LN . . . 49 W58
Ferris Rd A . . . 9 W-X19
Ferris Rd EX . . . 4 D3
Ferris Rd HM . . . 17 R-S28
Ferris Rd PS . . . 57 R28
Ferriss Rd EX. . . 4 E-F3
Ferry Rd OT. . . 83 P59
Ferry Tr R . . . 97 E40-41
Fertilizer Rd NF . . . 33 F44
Fesserton Sdrd SM 41 X-Y29 42 X-Y30
Festubert Blvd R. . . 99 J50
Fiat Rd C . . . 5 D7
Fices Rd DH . . . 32 G37
Fichault Rd NP. . . 95 E-F34
Fiddick Rd NI . . . 33 F45
Fiddlers Green Rd HM . 17 Q-R27
Fidlar Glen Rd HS . . . 46 A46
Fiebig Rd R. . . 82 Q52
Field Rd BR. . . 27 G18
Field Rd HM . . . 17 O26
Field's Rd MA . . . 73 K12
Fieldale Rd MA . . . 59 O35
Fielding Rd CS . . . 100 D18
Fields La MK . . . 59 S33
Fields Ln LM . . . 13 V11
Fieldside Rd BR . . 38 Z17 39 Z18
Fieldside Rd K . . . 32 C38 44 B38
Fife Rd WL . . . 22 M24 23 M25
Fife Rd WT . . . 22 M-N24
Fife's Bay Rd PB. . . 32 C40
Filion Rd NP . . . 94 C27
Filion Rd PR . . . 67 P66
Fillman Tr R . . . 83 Q51
Filton Rd HS . . . 46 Z49 47 Z50
Finch Av HM . . . 31 H34
Finch Av PL. . . 24 K30
Finch Av E T . . 24 J32 25 J33
Finch Av W T . 24 J31-32 K30-31
Finch Rd R. . . 62 Q-R48
Finch-Cambridge Boundary Rd SDG . . . 67 S67-68
Finch-Osnabruck Boundary Rd SDG . . . 67 T68 U67
Finch-Roxborough Boundary Rd SDG . . . 67 S-T68
Finch-Winchester Boundary Rd SDG . . . 67 T66-67
Finchley Rd R . . . 82 L52
Findlay Station Rd F. . 37 C58
Fingal Ln EL . . 8 W16 X15
Fingerboard Rd K . . . 31 C-D36
Finlay Ln HU . . . 27 G17
Finlay Mill Rd SM . . . 41 B29
Finlayson Rd A . . . 86 C96
Finley Rd NR . . . 33 F43
Finmark Rd TB . . . 102 B2
Finmark Rd TB . . . 102 B2
Finn La EX . . . 4 C4
Finn Ln C . . . 6 C8
Finn Rd A . . . 86 D95
Finn Rd SD . . . 90 L13
Finnegan Lake Rd HS . 45 W45
Finnerty Rd F . . . 81 P49
Finnerty Sdrd PL. . . 29 G28
Finni Rd CS . . . 101 C21
Finns Rd R . . . 63 S50
Finnwoods Rd CS. . . 100 D18
Finucan Rd LG . . . 50 X62
Fire Hall Rd SD . . . 90 E12

Firehall Rd F. . . 48 Y-Z56
Firehall Rd MA . . . 72 M9
Firehall Rd OX . . 16 S21-22
Firetower Rd R . . . 63 Q-R50
First Rd HS. . . 46 A-B46
First Rd PB. . . 46 A-B46
First School Rd LM . . . 13 S-T11
Firstbrook Line Rd TM . 85 R29
Fischer Ln HU . . . 21 K17
Fischer-Hallman Rd WT . . . 22 M-N22 N-P23
Fish Sdrd SM. . . 42 Y32
Fish & Game Ln HU . . 20 K-L14
Fish and Game Club Rd HS. . . 34 D47-48
Fish Creek Rd F . . . 48 Y-Z55
Fish Hatchery Rd MK . 58 S31
Fish Hatchery Rd NR . 33 E45
Fish Hawk Rd K . . . 43 A36
Fish Hook La MK . . . 42 W32
Fish Lake Rd PE . . 35 E51 F50
Fish Lake Rd PS . . . 77 P33
Fisher Av OT . . . 66 R62
Fisher Ln LM . . 12 S9 13 S9
Fisher Rd A . . . 86 D95
Fisher Rd CS . . . 101 B20-21
Fisher Rd TB . . . 103 C6
Fisher Rd (Alnwick-Haldimand) NR . . . 33 E-F44
Fisher Rd (Hamilton) NR . 33 F42
Fisher Rd (Port Hope) NR . 32 F-G40
Fisher St NP . . . 95 E31
Fisher Creek Rd PS . . . 58 Q32
Fisher Mills Rd WT . . . 22 N24
Fisherman's Tr HL. . . 60 S39
Fishers Sdrd G . . . 39 T30-31
Fishers Glen Rd NF. 10 W25 17 V25
Fisherside Rd SD . . . 90 E-F11
Fisherville Rd HD . . . 17 V28
Fishing Lake Rd F . . . 36 A-B57
Fishog Tr K . . . 43 X36
Fishtail Lake Rd HL. . . 61 T42
Fisk Rd LA. . . 36 C54
Fiskes Corners Rd SDG . 68 Q-R70
Fitch St G . . . 19 T33
Fitch Lane Rd PB. . . 45 W44
Fitchett Rd LA . . . 35 E52
Fitzgerald La F . . . 48 X55
Fitzgerald La K . . . 43 Z35
Fitzgerald Bay Rd PS . 56 Q-P25
Fitzpatrick Rd PR. . . 68 P-Q70
Fitzroy Rd OT . . . 83 P58-59
Fitzsimmons Rd LG . . . 37 C60
Five Points Rd MD . . . 15 T19
Flag Station Rd OT . . 66 T63
Flagg Rd SDG . . . 51 V-W66
Flagpin La F . . . 47 W51
Flamborough-Puslinch Twnln HM . . . 23 N26-27
Flanagan Rd LA . . . 47 A51
Flanagan Rd NI . . 18 T-U32
Flanagan Tr MK . . . 42 W31
Flank Rd TB . . . 102 F-G3
Flat Rd R . . . 64 R53
Flat Rapids Rd R . . . 83 Q56-57
Flat Rock Rd C . . 6 X9 7 X10
Flatrock Rd HS . . . 46 B49
Fleetwood Rd K . . . 32 D37-39
Fleming Ln EL . . . 7 X12
Fleming Rd HL. . . 60 V37
Fleming Rd LM . . . 12 S-T9
Fleming Rd TB . . . 102 D2
Fleming Bay Rd NR . . . 33 C44
Fleming Rd TM . . . 85 P29
Fletcher Dr HL. . . 60 Q37
Fletcher Rd HM . . . 18 R29
Fletcher Rd LN . . . 49 V61
Fletcher Rd MD . . . 14 S13-14
Fletcher Rd R . . . 82 M54
Fletcher Rd TB . . . 82 Q52
Flett Rd TB . . . 102 B2
Flewellyn Rd OT . . 65 S60 66 S61
Flicker Tr PS . . . 75 M24
Flindall Rd HS. . . 34 F46
Flinton Rd LA . . 47 Y50-51 Z50
Flintrock Rd R . . . 44 X38
Floating Bridge Rd LN . 66 V61
Flood Rd OT . . . 66 U61-62
Floods Rd NP . . . 96 F36
Floradale Rd WT. . . 22 L22
Floral Point Rd TB . . . 103 C7
Florapine Rd WT . . . 22 L22
Florence Rd C . . . 7 X10
Florence Rd LM . . . 7 W-X10
Florence St MD . . . 15 T17
Florida Rd F . . . 36 C54
Florida Rd LA . . . 36 C54
Flouds Bridge Rd. HS. . 34 D-E46
Flower Station Rd LN . . 64 T55
Flowers Rd CS . . . 100 D16
Floyd La F . . . 36 C55
Fly Rd NI . . . 18 R31-32
Flyboy Rd HS . . . 34 D47
Flycreek Rd HS . . . 50 Y62
Flyers Cove Rd F . . . 63 U-V51
Flying Club Rd HS . . . 34 D47
Flying Club Rd R. . . 63 S51
Flynn Rd HS . . . 47 B51
Flynn Rd MK . . . 59 S33
Flynn Rd OT . . . 66 U63-64
Flynn's Rd PB . . . 44 A40
Foerster Rd WT . . . 22 M24
Fogo St MK . . . 58 U30
Foldens Ln OX . . . 15 S20
Foley Rd PB . . . 33 D42
Foley Rd TM . . . 85 Q28
Foley Mountain Rd LG . 48 Y57
Folger Rd F . . . 64 U54
Folger Rd LN. . . 64 U54
Folkestone Rd NP. . . 95 D33
Folly Rd LG . . . 49 Z58
Footbridge Rd HL . . . 61 V43
Foote Lake Rd PS. . . 77 P33
Forbes Rd A . . . 45 A42
Forbes Ln C . . . 6 B7
Forbes Rd BR. . . 55 W16
Forbes Rd HS. . . 46 Z49
Forbes Rd LA . . . 18 V57
Forbes Rd LG. . . 50 W62
Forbes Rd MD. . . 15 T19
Forbes Rd SM. . . 41 A29
Forbes Centre Rd TB . 102 B-C3
Forbes River Rd TB . . 102 B-C3
Forced Rd OT . . . 67 R65
Forced Rd PR . . . 67 S65
Ford Cr PB . . . 32 D39
Ford Dr HT . . . 24 M30

Ford Rd EL . . . 15 V17
Ford Rd LN . . . 49 V60
Fords Rd A . . . 86 C94
Fords Rd PS . . . 76 P29
Fordwich Ln HU. . . 27 G18-19 H19
Foreman Dr BR . . . 38 Z17
Foreman Rd HM . . . 23 N-P26
Foreshew's Rd PS . 93 J26 94 J27
Forest Av SM. . . 42 Z32
Forest La F . . . 47 W51
Forest La K . . . 43 Y37
Forest La PR . . . 67 S66
Forest Ln EL . . . 7 X13
Forest Ln HU . . . 27 G-H18
Forest Rd BR . . . 54 T16
Forest Rd F . . . 36 C55
Forest Rd LM . . . 7 W10 13 S-V10
Forest Rd LN. . . 65 T58
Forest Rd OT. . . 66 T64
Forest Rd PB . . . 33 C41-42
Forest Rd PT. . . 21 F19
Forest Rd SDG . . . 51 V66
Forest Av CS . . . 100 A16
Forest Edge Dr OT . . . 65 R59
Forest Glade Dr K . . . 4 B3
Forest Glen Dr PS. . . 58 R29
Forest Harbour Pkwy SM. 41 X29
Forest Haven Rd PS. . 77 M31
Forest Hill Rd HS . 44 Z41 45 Z42
Forest Lake Rd CS . . 101 D19
Forest Lake Rd PS . 7 K33 L32-33
Forest Lawn Rd R. . 81 L50 99 K50
Forest Lea Rd R . . . 99 K51
Forest Park Rd HS . . . 46 A46
Forest Park Rd R . . . 82 L52
Forest View Rd . . . 61 T43
Forestell Rd WL . . . 23 M-N25
Foresters Rd LA . . . 43 W37
Foresters Falls Rd R . . . 82 M53-54
Foresthill Rd SD . . . 93 F24
Forestry Dr Y . . . 31 C33
Forestry Rd PS . . . 95 J32-33
Forestry Rd R . . . 99 H49
Forestry Farm Rd NF . 10 W23
Forestry Tower Rd PS 77 M34 78 M35
Forestview Dr PB . . . 44 Z40
Forfar St LG. . . 47 Y58-59
Forget Rd LG . . . 33 E44
Forget Rd PR . . . 67 R68
Forgets Rd SM . . . 41 Y28
Forgotten La K . . . 32 E38-39
Forgotten Corner Rd TM . 85 R29
Forgues Rd SDG . . . 67 T67
Forhan St C . . . 6 X7
Forks Rd HD. . . 18 T-U31
Forks Rd NI . . 18 T32 19 T33-34
Forks of the Credit Rd PL. . 23 J27
Forler St G . . . 27 F19
Forsyth Ln EL. . . 9 W18
Forsyth Rd HS . . . 34 D47
Forsythe La NR. . . 32 F39-40
Forsythe Rd LA . . . 34 D49
Forsythe Rd LG. . . 50 W-X63
Fort Rd NP . . . 94 E27
Fort Rose Rd MD . 14 R14 S13
Fort Stewart Rd HS. . . 62 T47
Fort William Rd TB . . 103 D6
Fortescue Lake Rd HL. . 44 W40
Fortune Line Rd LG . 37 A59 49 Z59
Forty Hills Rd BR . . . 55 U17
Forward Rd SDG . . . 67 U66
Foss Rd NI . . . 18 S32 19 S33
Fossil Rd MD. . . 13 S12
Fossmill Rd NP . . . 95 G34
Foster Dr DH . . . 31 D-E34
Foster La HS . . . 62 S46
Foster Rd HS . . . 65 T60
Foster Rd PE. . . 35 E51
Foster Sdrd LN . . . 49 W59
Foster Bay La LG . . . 49 Z60
Foster Hall Rd LG . . . 49 Z61
Fosters La F. . . 47 W51
Fosters Rd HS. . . 61 R43
Fothergill Rd PB . . . 44 A39
Foundry St WT . . . 22 N22
Fountain St WT . . . 22 N24
Four-O-Two Rd MA . . 72 K7-8
Four Mile Creek Rd NI 19 Q34 Q-R35
Four Mile Lake Rd NP . 95 D32
Four Points Rd K . . . 44 B38
Four Run Rd . . . 73 L11
Four Seasons Dr A . . 84 Y90 Z90
Four Seasons Park Rd . . . 62 S48 63 S49
Fourth Chute Rd R . . . 82 P52
Fowler La DH . . . 32 F37
Fowlers Rd DH . . . 31 D34
Fowlers Rd MK . . . 59 Q33
Fowlers Rd BR . . . 55 V16
Fox La EX . . . 4 E4
Fox Rd CS. . . 101 Z22-23
Fox Rd F . . . 48 Y53-54
Fox Rd K . . . 32 C39
Fox Rd NR. . . 33 G41
Fox Rd NI . . . 19 T35
Fox Rd (Madoc) HS. . . 46 Z48
Fox Rd (Quinte West) HS . 34 D-E46
Fox Run Rd . . . 73 L11
Fox St SM . . . 41 X28
Fox Back Rd PS . . . 57 T28
Fox Farm Rd PS . . . 76 P28
Fox Farm Rd SM . . . 41 A29
Fox Lake Dr HL . . . 44 W40
Fox Lake Rd SD . . 90 F-G12 G13
Fox Lake Access Rd SD. . 100 A14
Fox Point Rd (Bracebridge) . . . 59 U34
Fox Point Rd (Lake of Bays) MK . . . 59 R-S35
Fox Ridge Rd G . . . 40 B23
Fox Run Rd EX . . . 5 E6
Fox Tower Rd MA . . . 72 K8-9
Foxfire Chase DH . . . 31 F34-35
Foxmead Rd SM . . . 42 Y30-31
Foxton Rd HS . . . 34 C49
Foys Lake Rd NP . . . 80 L45
Foymount Rd R . . . 81 P50-51
Foys Lake Rd NP . . . 80 L45
Fralick Rd LA . . . 35 D53
Fralick's Beach Rd R . . . 31 D36
Frammpet Dr A . . . 88 F4
Francis Dr G . . . 39 Y19
Francis Rd HL. . . 44 W38
Francis St TB . . . 103 D6
Francoeur Rd NP . . . 95 E34
Francoeur Rd R . . . 98 G46
Frank's Rd MA . . . 73 L11

Frank Green Rd LG . . . 48 Z57
Frank Hill Rd K . . . 44 B39
Frank Kenny Rd OT . . 67 Q-R65
Frank MacDougall Pkwy NP 79 N41
Frank Ritchie Rd NR. . . 33 F41
Frankford-Stirling Rd HS . 34 D47
Frankland La SM . . . 42 W30
Franklin Blvd WT . . 22 N24 23 N-P25
Franklin Dr K . . . 32 D39
Franklin Rd Y . . 30 E32 31 E33
Franklin Lake Rd A . . . 87 C98 C99
Franks La MD . . . 14 T16
Franks Rd HS. . . 46 A48-49
Franks Rd LG . . . 49 Z58
Franktown Rd OT . . . 66 T61
Fraser Av CS . . . 100 A16
Fraser Rd C . . . 6 X-Y7 Y8
Fraser Rd EX. . . 5 E5
Fraser Rd HS . . . 34 E-F46
Fraser Rd LA . . . 47 A-B51
Fraser Rd MA . . . 72 K10 90 J10
Fraser Rd R . . . 64 R55 82 Q55
Fraser Rd TB. . . 102 D4
Fraser Rd (North Glengarry) SDG . . . 68 Q71
Fraser Rd (North Stormont) SDG . . . 68 R-S69
Fraser Rd (South Glengarry) SDG . . . 52 U72 68 T72
Fraser St SM . . . 30 F30-31 31 G30
Fraser Lake La HS . . . 62 V48
Fraser Mine Rd CS . . 100 A16
Fraserburg Rd MK . . . 59 U33-34
Frawley's La MA . . . 73 L-M11
Frayn Rd LG . . . 49 X59
Fred Brown Rd LA . 35 C53 36 C54
Fred Dubie Rd PS. . . 56 Q25
Frod Jones Rd HL . . 60 U39 U40
Frederica St TB . . . 103 E6
Frederick Rd MK . . . 42 W33
Frederick St LG. . . 50 Y64
Frederick Rd WT . . . 22 N23
Freds Dr HS . . . 34 D46
Free Rd HS . . . 34 D46
Freeborn La HS . . . 44 A48-49
Freedom La LG . . . 47 Y50
Freeland Rd LG . . . 49 Y58
Freeman Rd HM . . . 23 N27
Freelton Rd HM . . 31 E34-35
Freeman Rd F. . . 36 B-C55
Freeman Rd LA . . . 36 B-C54
Freeman Rd LG . . . 49 Z58
Freeman Rd NI . . . 19 T33
Freeman Rd SM . . . 41 A27
Freeport Rd TB . . . 102 D3
French Ln LM . . . 6 W6-7
French Ln PB . . . 44 Y39-39
French Rd HM . . . 17 R28
French Rd TM . . . 85 N-P29
French Rd TB . . . 102 C5
French Bay Rd BR. . 38 A16 Z16-17
French Hill Rd OT . . . 67 P-Q65
French Line Rd EX . . . 5 C5
French Line Rd LN . . . 64 T56
French Settlement Ct HS 46 A49
French Settlement Rd K . . 43 Y36
French Settlement Rd LN . 66 U63
French Settlement Rd SDG . . . 66 U63-64
French Settlement Rd N 46 Z49
Frenchman's Creek Rd PB 33 D-E41
Frenchman Lake Rd CS . 101 A19
Fretts La LG . . . 35 D53
Freymond La HS . . . 62 U45-46
Friendly Acres Rd NF . . 33 C44 C45 45 B45
Friendship La HL. . . 59 S36
Frizzell Rd LA . . . 47 B52
Frizzell Rd LN . . . 49 W59
Froam Rd LG. . . 50 X65
Froatburn Rd SDG . . . 51 V66
Froats Rd SDG . . . 67 U66-67
Froats Rd SDG . . . 68 T70
Frog La R . . . 99 G48
Frog Rd Y . . . 31 D33
Frog Hollow Rd SDG . . 68 S71
Front Ln C . . . 7 A11 B10-11
Front Rd EX. . . 4 C-D1
Front Rd F . . . 36 D55
Front Rd HU . . . 20 L-M15
Front Rd LA . . . 35 E53 36 E54-55
Front Rd NF. . 10 W24-25 X23-24
Front Rd PR. . . 68 N71-72 69 N73
Front Rd S EX . . . 4 C-D1
Front St BT. . . 17 R-S26
Front St K . . . 44 A39
Front St LM . . . 12 T7
Front St T . . . 24 L32
Frontenac Rd F. . . 48 Y53-54
Frontenac Rd R . . . 63 T51
Frontenac Rd OT . . . 67 R65
Frontière Rd, Ch. TM . . 85 Q31
Frost Av CS . . . 101 A19
Frost La R . . . 64 S51
Frost Rd NI . . . 18 R31-32
Fruit Ridge Ln EL . 8 W17 9 W18
Fruitland Rd HM . . . 18 Q30
Fry La HL . . . 60 T38
Fry Rd MK . . . 58 T30
Fry Rd PE . . . 35 F50-51
Fryer Rd HS. . . 36 A56
Fryer Rd SD . . . 93 G24
Fysh Ln C . . . 7 Y10

Gaebel Rd HS . . . 62 U45
Gaelic Ln EL . . . 8 W-X14
Gaffney Rd NP . . . 80 N45
Gage Av HM. . . 17 Q28 18 Q29
Gagne Rd PE . . . 35 F50-51
Gagné Rd (Clarence-Rockland) PR . . . 67 O66
Gagné Rd (Nation) PR . 67 R68
Gagner Ln C . . . 6 B9
Gagnon Rd A . . . 84 B90
Gagnon Rd MK . . . 59 V34
Gagnon Rd PR. . . 67 R66-67
Gagnon St CS . . . 100 B18
Gagnon St NP . . . 95 F34
Gaida's Rd SD. . . 90 J10
Gainer Rd HL . . . 60 V37
Gainford Rd MK . . . 59 V33
Gainsborough Rd MD. . 14 T16
Galbraith Rd LN . . . 65 T-U57
Galeairy Lake Rd NP . 79 P41
Galetta Rd OT . . . 65 P60 83 Q58
Galetta Sdrd OT . . . 83 Q58
Gallagher Lake Rd MK . 57 U28
Gallagher Rd HS . . . 46 A49
Gallagher Rd OT . . . 66 U62
Gallagher Rd R . . . 82 P53
Gallagher Rd MK . . 59 U34-35
Gallivan St MA . . . 34 C-D48
Galloway Rd K . . . 32 E38
Galloway Rd PB . . . 33 D41
Galop La SDG . . . 51 X66
Galston Rd NP . . . 96 F35
Galt St LA . . . 35 E53
Galway Rd PB . . . 44 X38-39
Galway Access Rd PB . 44 Y39
Galway Rd LA . . . 49 X59
Camble Rd BR . . . 26 D16
Gamble Rd Y. . . 30 H31
Gamble Sly Rd LG. . . 37 A58
Gambles Rd A . . . 86 B94
Gambles Sdrd LN. . . 48 W57
Gammond Rd TB . . . 102 G5
Gamsby Rd DH . . . 32 G38-39
Gananoque Lake Rd LG. 37 B59
Ganaraska Rd DH . . . 32 F39
Ganaraska Rd NR . . . 32 F40
Gander Rd AL . . . 61 U42
Gannon Ln PB . . . 44 A48-49
Gannon Rd SD . . . 90 E11-12
Gannon Rd LG . . . 48 T57
Gannon Rd SD . . . 90 E11-12
Garafraxa St G . . . 39 B20
Garafraxa St WL . . . 22 K24
Garage Rd PS . . . 77 M-N32
Garden Av BT . . . 17 R25
Garden La HM . . . 23 P27-28
Garden La TM . . . 85 N-P29
Garden St DH. . . 31 G-H36
Garden Bay Rd A . . . 84 C88
Garden of Eden Rd R. . 82 P54-55
Garden of Eden Rd SM . 29 C-D25
Garden Valley Rd HS . 102 E4
Garden Village Rd NP . 94 E28
Gardenville Rd PE . . . 34 F47
Gardiner Expwy T . . . 24 L32
Gardiner Rd LN . . . 49 V58
Gardiner Rd SD . . . 50 X62
Gardiner's Rd (Central Frontenac) F . . . 47 Y52
Gardiner's Rd (Kingston) F . 36 D55
Gardiner Access Rd R 97 F41 98 F42
Gardiners Corner Rd SM . 41 Y28
Gardner Dr K . . . 43 X34
Gardner Tr LM . . . 13 V11-12
Garland Rd NR. . . 33 F-G41
Garlandside Rd OT . . 67 R66
Garlock Rd OT . . . 66 T63
Garlough Rd SDG . . . 51 V66
Garner Rd EL . . . 9 W21
Garner Rd HM . . . 17 Q-R27
Garner Rd NI . . . 19 S34
Garnier St A . . . 89 F8
Garrard Rd DH . . . 31 F-H36
Garrett Rd F. . . 37 C58 48 Z55-56
Garrett Rd LG. . . 49 Z58
Garringer Rd NI . . 18 U32 19 U33
Garrison Lake Rd F . . . 47 Y52
Garside Rd A . . . 88 F95-96
Garson Lake Rd CS . . 101 B20
Garson-Coniston Rd CS . 101 B-C20
Garson Lake Rd CS . . 101 B20
Garter Lake La F . . 48 Z55-56
Gartersnake Lake Rd MK . 59 V33-34
Garth St HM . . . 17 Q28
Garvin Rd OT . . . 66 S-T61
Gary Rd SDG . . . 52 U66
Gary Rd SD . . . 92 G22
Gated Rd NP . . . 96 F35
Gates Blvd F . . . 38 D56-57
Gates Dr MD . . . 7 W13 14 V13
Gates Sdrd PR . . . 68 N71
Gauley's Bay Rd BR . . . 55 U15-16
Gauthier Rd NP. . . 94 D27
Gauthier Rd TM. . . 85 P28
Gauthier Rd TB. . . 102 C4
Gauthier's Rd MA . . . 73 M11
Gauy Rd NP. . . 96 F35
Gawley Rd HS . . . 46 Z47-48
Gaylord Rd F . . . 47 X52
Gazley Rd DH . . . 34 D46
Geddes La PS . . . 76 N30 77 N31
Gee Rd NI . . . 18 S32
Geen Rd HS . . . 46 B49
Geeza Rd HS . . . 44 W38
Gelert Rd HL . . . 44 W38 60 V38
Gemm La HS . . . 46 Z46
Gemmel Rd LG . . . 50 Y64
Gemmill Rd LN . . . 48 V55
Gemmill's Rd LN . . . 48 V55
Gendron Rd F . . . 47 Y52
Gendron Rd R . . . 67 O66
Gendron Rd A . . . 84 B90
General Brock Pkwy NI . 19 R34-35
Genereux, Mtée CS. . . 68 U22
Genesee Lake Rd HS . 95 G32 H33
Geneva St NI . . . 19 R33
Geneva Creek Access Rd SD . . . 100 Z13
Geneva Lake Rd SD . . 100 Z15
Genge Rd F . . . 48 Z54
Gennicks Rd R . . . 62 S48 63 S49
Gentleman Dr MD . 8 W14 14 V14
Gents Rd NI . . . 18 T32

George Pkwy SM . . . 41 B29
George Rd MK . . . 41 W29
George Rd NR. . . 33 E43
George St EL . . . 8 W-X17
George St SD . . . 33 C41
George St WT . . . 22 P24
George Rd NP. . . 95 E34
George Johnston Rd SM . 41 B28-29
George Rd LA . . . 36 B54
Georgian Dr SM . . . 42 B30
Georgian Bay Rd MK 41 W29 58 V29
Georgian Range Rd G . 39 X20
Georgina St NR. . . 34 F46
Gerber Rd WT. . . 22 M-N21
Gerhardt Rd SM . . . 41 X29
Germain Rd SD . . . 90 F10
Germain Rd LA . . . 36 B54
German School Rd BT 16 O24 17 Q25
German Rd MK. . . 59 V33
Germanicus Rd R . . . 81 N51
Germans Landing Rd HS . 34 D46
Gerow Rd LA . . . 35 D52
Gerrard St E T . . . 24 K32 25 K33
Gerrow Rd DH. . . 31 E36
Gerrie Rd WL . . . 22 K23-24
Gerrow Rd PR. . . 67 P66
German Bay Rd PS . . . 76 M28
Gervais Rd HS . . . 46 A49
Gervais Rd SD . . . 93 D24 101 D23
Gervais Rd SM . . . 41 Y29
Gervais Rd (Markstay-Warren) SD. . . 93 D24
Gesner Ln C. . . 7 Y12-13
Gesto Rd EX. . . 4 D3
Giardini Rd EX . . . 4 E3
Gibb Ln EL . . . 7 X12
Gibbon La HU . . . 26 H16
Gibbons Rd PS . . . 77 L32-33
Gibbs Rd DH . . . 32 F38
Gibbs Rd F . . . 48 X53
Gibbs Rd NR. . . 33 F41
Gibbs Rd OT . . . 68 Q72
Gibraltar Rd MA . . . 72 L10
Gibson Dr HU. . . 26 F13
Gibson Av TB . . . 103 C-D6
Gibson La OX . . . 16 Q23
Gibson Rd CS. . . 100 D18
Gibson Rd HD . . . 17 U28
Gibson Rd LA . . . 36 C54
Gibson Rd LN . . . 65 T57
Gibson Rd LG . . . 48 T57
Gibson Rd NI . . . 18 U32
Gibson Rd R . . . 82 M54
Gibson Bay Rd PS . . . 76 M28
Gibson Rd HL . . . 61 V41
Gideon Dr EL . . . 14 T-U15
Gierman Rd R . . . 65 U57
Gifford Dr PB . . . 32 C40 44 B40
Gifford Rd DH . . . 32 G39
Gifford Rd HS . . . 34 C49
Gift Rd LA . . . 36 C54
Giguere Rd A . . . 87 E99
Gil's La SD. . . 92 G22
Gil's Gully La PB . . . 52 W-X44
Gil-Mar Rd K . . . 44 A-B38
Gilbeault Rd SDG . . . 67 T66
Gilbert La MK . . . 59 V33-34
Gilbert Ln EL . . . 8 X-Y14
Gilbert Rd NF . . . 17 V25
Gilbert Rd SD . . . 92 G22
Gilbert Bay La HS . . . 45 W45
Gilbride Rd TB . . . 102 B5
Gilchrist Sdrd MA . . . 72 L8
Gilchrist Bay Rd PB . . . 45 Z42-43
Gilead Rd PE. . . 34 G49
Giles La F . . . 48 Z54
Giles Rd LN . . . 65 U58
Gilford Rd SM . . . 30 D30-31
Gill Rd SM . . . 41 A29
Gillan Rd R . . . 82 P-Q55
Gilleland Lake Rd MK . 59 T33
Gillespie Rd NR. . . 33 E45
Gillespie Rd SM . . . 27 H20
Gillespie Rd TB . . . 102 E5
Gillies Corners Sdrd LN . . . 49 V59 65 U59
Gillies Lake Rd BR. . 54 S-T16
Gillis Ln F . . . 7 Y12
Gillis Ln HU. . . 21 K17
Gilmore Rd DH . . . 32 F-G39
Gilmore Rd LA. . . 47 A52
Gilmore Rd (Fort Erie) NI . . . 19 T36 T-U35
Gilmour La PB. . . 45 W-X43
Gilmour La R. . . 77 N32
Gilmour Ln HU. . . 27 G-H17
Gilmour Rd HS . . . 46 W47
Gilmour Rd NR . . . 32 F-E40
Gilmour Rd SDG. . . 50 W65
Gilmour Rd WL . . . 23 M-N26
Gilmour Point Rd PB . . . 45 X44
Gilmours, The PB . . 45 W-X43
Gilroy Rd R . . . 50 V61
Gilroy School Rd HS. . . 62 V45
Gin Lake Rd HS . . . 31 D36
Gilsons Point Rd R . . . 31 D36
Gingerich Rd WT . . 22 N21-22
Gingras Av NP. . . 93 D26
Girard Ln C. . . 6 C8
Girl Guide Rd G . . . 39 Z19
Giroux Rd PR . . . 68 P69
Giroux Rd OT . . . 67 Q65
Given Ln C . . . 6 A-B7
Given Rd C . . . 6 A9
Given Rd WL . . . 27 G20
Glacial Hill Tr HL . . . 60 V40
Gladstone Dr MD . . . 15 U18
Gladu Rd CS . . . 101 D20
Gladys Ct BR. . . 27 F18
Glamor Lake Rd HL . . . 61 V41
Glamorgan Rd HL. . . 60 U-V40
Glamorgan Rd A. . . 32 E39
Glamorgan Rd PB . . . 32 E39
Glancaster Rd HM . 17 Q-R28 R27
Glanmire Lake La HS . . 46 X47
Glanmire Lake Rd HS . 46 X46-47
Glanville Rd HS . . . 62 T47
Glanworth Dr MD. . 15 U17-18
Glasgow Ln C . . . 6 X8-9
Glasgow St MK. . . 58 U30
Glasgow St WT . . 22 M23 N23
Glass Av NI . . . 19 R33
Glass St PT . . . 15 Q18

G Hunt Memorial Dr PS . . 56 Q26
Gabert Rd LG. . . 18 U63
Gabes Rd TB. . . 102 F2
Gabourie Rd HS. . . 34 D46

Glassford / Hargrave

Glassford Rd C ... 7 Y11-12
Glassy Lake Access Rd NP ... 95 D34
Glastonbury Rd LA ... 47 X-Y51
Glazier Rd LG ... 50 Y-Z62
Gleason La R ... 99 G-H48
Gleason Lake Rd G ... 39 X19
Gleasons Corner Rd NR ... 33 F44
Gleeson Ln C ... 6 B8 C7
Gleeson Rd LN ... 65 S58
Glen Rd MA ... 72 K7
Glen Rd NI ... 18 R32
Glen Rd R ... 82 L53
Glen Rd SDG ... 52 U71 68 T71
Glen Rd, The G ... 28 E21
Glen Rd, The K ... 43 B35-36
Glen's Hill Rd HU ... 26 H13-14
Glen Alda Rd PB ... 45 W44
Glen Allen Rd HS ... 46 A46
Glen Becker Rd SDG ... 51 V66-67
Glen Brook Rd SDG ... 52 U71 68 T71
Glen Cumming Rd BR ... 26 C16
Glen Erie Ln EL ... 9 X21
Glen Falloch Rd SDG ... 52 U70 68 T70 T71
Glen Gavel Rd NR ... 33 F41
Glen Gordon Rd MK ... 58 T-U32
Glen Haffy Rd PL ... 29 G27
Glen Isle Rd LN ... 65 T59
Glen Lawson Rd HT ... 23 L27
Glen Lynden Rd NR ... 33 E41
Glen Meyer Rd NF ... 9 W21
Glen Miller Rd HS ... 34 E47
Glen Morris Rd BT ... 16 Q24
Glen Morris Rd E BT ... 16 Q24 17 Q25
Glen Oak Rd MD ... 14 U13-14
Glen Roberts Dr PS ... 95 J32
Glen Robertson Rd SDG ... 68 R71-72
Glen Ross Rd HS ... 34 D47
Glen Sandfield Rd SDG ... 68 Q72
Glen Smail Rd LG ... 50 X64
Glen Stewart Rd SDG ... 50 W65
Glen Tay Rd LN ... 49 W58
Glen Valley Rd NR ... 32 F40
Glenannon Rd HU ... 27 G17-18
Glenarm Rd K ... 43 A35-37 B35
Glenashton Dr HT ... 24 M29-30
Glenashton Rd LN ... 65 T60
Glencairn Cr MK ... 59 Q33
Glencolin Ln EL ... 15 V18-20
Glendale Av NI ... 19 R33-34
Glendale Dr LM ... 13 R10
Glendale Rd HU ... 26 H13
Glendale Airport Rd G ... 39 B20
Glendale Heights Dr PS ... 95 G-H32
Glendon Dr MD ... 14 T15-16 U14 V13
Glenelg-Holland Twnln G ... 27 C20 28 C21
Glenfield Rd LA ... 63 T51
Glenfield Rd R ... 63 T51
Glengarry Rd K ... 32 D-E39
Glengarry Rd PL ... 24 M30
Glengarry Landing Rd N SM ... 41 A-B28
Glengarry Landing Rd S SM ... 41 B28
Glengyle Dr MD ... 14 T14
Glenhaven Beach Rd SM ... 42 B31
Glenhill Tr Y ... 31 F33
Glenmore Rd LG ... 50 Y63
Glenmorris St WT ... 22 P24
Glenmount Rd MK ... 59 S35
Glenn Ct PL ... 29 G27
Glennelm Rd LA ... 35 C51
Glenora Dr MD ... 15 S17
Glenrest Dr SM ... 42 Z33
Glenridge Av NI ... 19 R33
Glenron Rd HM ... 23 N27
Glenron Rd NR ... 33 D43
Glenroy Rd SDG ... 68 S71
Glenvale Dr NP ... 95 D33
Glenview Rd LN ... 49 V59 W60
Glenville Rd Y ... 30 F31
Glenwater Rd TB ... 102 C1
Glenwood Ln C ... 5 D8 6 C8
Glenwoods Av Y ... 30 D32
Global Tower Rd MK ... 58 V29
Glory Rd HS ... 62 T45
Glover Rd LG ... 37 A58 49 Z58
Glover Rd NR ... 33 D45
Glover Rd (Glanbrook) HM ... 17 R28 18 R29
Glover Rd (Stoney Creek) HM ... 18 Q30
Go Home Lake Rd MK ... 57 V28 58 V29
Goacher Rd NR ... 33 C-D45
Goat Hill Rd HS ... 46 A46
Gobles Rd OX ... 16 Q-R22
Godby Rd BT ... 16 S24
Godby Rd EL ... 9 X21
Goddens Rd NR ... 34 D46
Goderich St BR ... 38 B16
Goderich St HU ... 20 L-M15
Godfrey Rd F ... 36 A54-55
Godfrey Rd PB ... 33 C42-43 D43
Godfrey Rd R ... 82 N54
Godkin Rd MD ... 14 R13-14
Godolphin Rd NR ... 33 C-D45
Godreau Rd R ... 98 F47
Gogolin Rd R ... 62 R48
Gold Creek Dr MD ... 14 T15
Gold Creek Rd LN ... 65 U57-58
Gold Dust La F ... 48 Z55
Golden Beach Rd MK ... 58 U32
Golden Line Rd OT ... 65 S59
Golden Mile Way R ... 81 N50
Golden Pheasant Dr MK ... 59 R34
Golden Pond Dr BR ... 38 Z17
Goldenburgh Rd A ... 87 D1
Goldfield Rd SDG ... 67 T67
Goldfinch Dr R ... 81 N50
Goldie Rd TB ... 102 B1
Goldmine Access Rd HS ... 46 W48
Goldstein Rd SM ... 42 Y32
Golf Rd BT ... 16 R24
Golf Rd PR ... 68 N72
Golf Avenue Rd MK ... 58 S-T31
Golf Club Rd HM ... 18 R29
Golf Club Rd LG ... 49 W60
Golf Club Rd NP ... 95 E31
Golf Club Rd R ... 83 P57
Golf Club Rd SDG ... 51 W66
Golf Club Way OT ... 65 S60
Golf Course Ln C ... 7 A11-12
Golf Course Ln PS ... 95 G32
Golf Course Rd DH ... 32 G39
Golf Course Rd HS ... 34 D47
Golf Course Rd HU ... 20 J13
Golf Course Rd K ... 32 D37-38
Golf Course Rd LG ... 48 Y57
Golf Course Rd MA ... 72 J-K7
Golf Course Rd MK ... 41 X29
Golf Course Rd NP ... 94 D28 95 G33-34
Golf Course Rd NI ... 19 U33
Golf Course Rd OT ... 67 Q-R65
Golf Course Rd PB ... 45 A42 Z42
Golf Course Rd PS ... 92 H22 93 H23
Golf Course Rd SD ... 92 G22
Golf Course Rd TM ... 85 Q29
Golf Course Rd (Horton) R ... 82 P54
Golf Course Rd (Huntsville) MK ... 59 Q-R33
Golf Course Rd (Lake of Bays) MK ... 59 Q-R34
Golf Course Rd (Laurentian Valley) R ... 99 K51
Golf Course Rd (Springwater) SM ... 41 A28 B29
Golf Course Rd (Wasaga Beach) SM ... 41 A27
Golf Link Rd SM ... 41 X27-28
Golf Links Rd BT ... 16 R23
Golf Links Rd BR ... 26 D13-14
Golf Links Rd HM ... 17 Q27-28
Golf Links Rd TB ... 103 D6
Golfers La HS ... 62 Q46
Golfview Dr (Lakeshore) EX ... 5 B-C5
Golfview Dr (LaSalle) EX ... 4 C1
Goltz Rd MK ... 58 T-U32
Goltz Rd SD ... 90 F11
Gommorah Rd PE ... 35 F50
Gonder Rd NI ... 19 T34-35
Good Rd F ... 48 Y54
Goodbrand Ln C ... 7 Y12
Goodell Tr PS ... 76 N30 77 N31
Goodfellow Rd F ... 36 A55 48 Z55
Goodfellow Rd NR ... 33 D-E45
Goodhue Rd EL ... 8 W17
Goodin Rd LG ... 50 X63-64
Goodman Rd TB ... 102 B5 103 B6
Goodreau Ln C ... 5 D7
Goodrich Rd NR ... 33 E45
Goods Rd HS ... 34 C48
Goodson Rd PB ... 45 X44
Goodstown Rd OT ... 66 T62
Goodview Rd CS ... 101 D19
Goodwill Dr CS ... 101 B20
Goodwin Rd HS ... 34 E-F46
Goodwood Rd DH ... 31 F34
Goodyear Rd LA ... 35 C-D52
Goose Creek Rd NR ... 33 E42
Goose Down La HL ... 43 W37 60 V37
Goose Gap Cr MA ... 71 J5
Goose Lake Rd K ... 43 B36
Goose Lake Rd R ... 81 M49
Goosemarsh Ln LM ... 13 Q12
Gordon Rd LM ... 13 R-S12
Gordon Rd LG ... 49 Z58
Gordon Rd PS ... 76 M30
Gordon St BR ... 26 F13
Gordon St DH ... 31 H36
Gordon St WL ... 23 M25
Gordon Deans Tr PS ... 77 P32
Gordon Lake Rd A ... 86 C95 D95
Gordon Lake Rd CS ... 100 B17
Gordon Lake 3 Access Rd PS ... 75 M24-25
Gordon Lake Access Rd PS ... 75 M24
Gordon Sutherland Pkwy G ... 39 Y-Z19
Gordonier Lake Rd MK ... 59 U33
Gordons Creek Ct HT ... 23 K27
Gore Cr G ... 39 B20
Gore Ln R ... 82 L53-54
Gore Rd C ... 7 B-C10
Gore Rd EX ... 4 E2
Gore Rd F ... 36 D56
Gore Rd HM ... 23 N26
Gore Rd HU ... 26 F13
Gore Rd MD ... 15 T17-18
Gore Rd NF ... 10 X22-23
Gore Rd PE ... 34 F48
Gore Rd SM ... 42 B30
Gore Rd WL ... 23 N25
Gore Rd WT ... 23 N25
Gore Rd (Ashfield-Colborne-Wawanosh) HU ... 20 J13
Gore Rd (North Glengarry) SDG ... 68 Q72 69 Q73
Gore Rd (South Glengarry) SDG ... 52 U71 68 T72
Gore Rd (South Huron) HU ... 20 P13
Gore Rd, The PL ... 24 J29-30 29 G-H28 30 H29
Gore Sdrd NF ... 16 V21
Gore St MA ... 72 J7
Gore A Rd HD ... 18 T31
Gorevale Rd TB ... 102 C5 103 C6
Goreville Rd PS ... 77 K32 95 J32
Goreway Dr PL ... 24 J29-30
Gorham Rd NI ... 19 U35
Gorham St Y ... 30 F31-32
Gorhams Rd PS ... 76 M27
Gorman Rd R ... 81 P49
Gormanville Rd NP ... 95 E31
Gorr Rd F ... 36 C55
Gorra Hill Rd R ... 82 Q53
Gorrie Ln HU ... 27 G-H18
Gorsline Rd PE ... 35 F50
Gosford Rd LG ... 50 Y62
Goshen Ln HU ... 14 Q14 20 M-P13 P14
Goshen Rd NF ... 16 V21
Goshen Rd R ... 82 P-Q55
Gosnell Ln C ... 7 Y12
Gospel Rd HS ... 46 B46
Gossage La F ... 36 A-B55
Goudy Rd EL ... 15 V18
Gough Rd HU ... 27 H18
Gough Rd OT ... 66 S63
Goulais Av A ... 84 A-B91
Goulais Mission Rd A ... 84 Y91
Goulard Rd NP ... 94 D28
Goulbourn Forced Rd OT ... 66 R61
Gould Rd C ... 6 X9 7 X10
Gould Rd LM ... 7 W10 13 V10
Gould Crossing Rd HL ... 60 U39
Gould Lake Rd F ... 36 B55
Goulding La DF ... 29 G27
Goulet Rd C ... 6 C9
Gourley Rd PR ... 68 N72
Government Rd CS ... 101 C20
Government Rd MA ... 72 M9-10 73 M11
Government Rd R ... 82 M54
Government Rd SD ... 90 F10
Government Rd TB ... 102 C5
Government Rd (Armstrong) TM ... 85 N28
Government Rd (Huron Shores) A ... 86 D97 87 D98
Government Rd (Johnson) A ... 86 C94 D94-95 D95-96
Governor's Rd HM ... 17 Q26-27
Governors Rd BT ... 16 R22-23
Governors Rd E BT ... 17 Q-R25
Governors Rd W BT ... 16 R23-24
Gower Bay Rd PS ... 56 Q-R25
Gowing Rd MK ... 59 T34
Gowland Rd HD ... 17 T28
Goyer La PR ... 67 Q66-67 R66-67
Goyer Rd PR ... 67 R68
Grabell Rd NI ... 19 U33
Grace Rd HL ... 60 U38
Grace River Rd HL ... 61 U41
Gracey Rd NI ... 18 T32
Gracie Sdrd EX ... 5 D6 6 C6
Grady Rd LG ... 48 Y57
Grady Rd E LN ... 48 X-Y57
Graf Rd HS ... 62 U46
Graham Rd CS ... 100 D17
Graham Rd EL ... 7 W-X13 8 X14
Graham Rd F ... 36 B54-55
Graham Rd HS ... 46 Y48
Graham Rd LN ... 65 U60
Graham Rd MA ... 72 J9
Graham Rd NP ... 96 F36
Graham Rd PB ... 44 A41
Graham Rd PR ... 68 N-P71
Graham Rd SD ... 90 F10
Graham Rd SM ... 42 W30
Graham Rd (Clarington) DH ... 32 G39
Graham Rd (Georgian Bay) MK ... 57 U28
Graham Rd (Gravenhurst) MK ... 42 X32
Graham Rd (Scugog) DH ... 31 F36
Graham Sdrd EX ... 4 E4
Graham Sdrd Y ... 30 F31
Graham's Hill G ... 28 C22-23
Graham's Hill Rd G ... 39 X19
Graham Lake Rd LG ... 49 Z61
Graham Lake Rd SD ... 92 E21
Grahams Rd LG ... 37 B60
Grahamvale Rd NP ... 95 G33
Grainger Green Rd MK ... 59 R35
Grainger Park Rd OT ... 65 R58-59
Gramps La F ... 36 A55
Granary Lake Rd A ... 88 E-F4
Grand Av C ... 6 A8-9
Grand Bend Ln HU ... 14 Q13 20 P13
Grand Bend Rd MD ... 14 Q-R13
Grand Canyon Rd EL ... 8 W-X17
Grand Desert Rd NP ... 95 F34 96 F35
Grand Marais Rd EX ... 4 B-C2
Grand Ridge Dr WT ... 22 P24
Grand River St N BT ... 16 Q-R24
Grande River Ln C ... 6 B8
Grandor Rd MA ... 72 J9
Grandravine Dr T ... 24 J31
Grandview Dr MK ... 59 Q-R34
Grandview Dr NR ... 33 D42-43
Grandview Rd OT ... 66 R61
Grandview Rd PS ... 76 M30
Grandview Rd SM ... 41 X28
Grandview St N DH ... 31 F-G36 32 G37
Grandview Lake Rd MK ... 59 S35
Grandy Rd K ... 43 Y37
Grange Sdrd, The PL ... 23 J27
Granger Rd EL ... 9 W-X19
Granite Rd PS ... 74 N23 75 N24
Granite Hill Rd PS ... 95 J31
Granny's La LA ... 63 V49
Granny White Sdrd SM ... 41 X-Y29
Grant La F ... 36 A55
Grant La HS ... 62 V47
Grant Rd A ... 84 Z91
Grant Rd HS ... 61 S-T44
Grant Rd HD ... 17 T28
Grant Rd LM ... 6 W7
Grant Rd NR ... 33 E44-45
Grant Rd PR ... 67 R66
Grant Rd R ... 64 R54
Grant Rd SDG ... 67 S68 68 S69
Grant Rd TM ... 85 M27
Grant's Tr PS ... 57 T28
Grantham Av NI ... 19 Q-R34
Grantley Rd SDG ... 67 U67
Granton Ln MD ... 14 Q-R16
Grants Sdrd OT ... 65 R59
Grantsville Tr PB ... 44 A40
Graphite La HS ... 62 S45
Graphite Rd HS ... 62 S45
Graphite Rd LG ... 49 Y59
Graphite Bay Rd R ... 64 S53
Graphite Mine Access Rd R ... 98 G42
Grass Lake Ln SM ... 42 X32
Grass Lake Rd PS ... 77 M33
Grasshopper Park Rd DH ... 32 F37
Grassie Rd NI ... 18 R30
Grassmere Rd MK ... 59 Q34
Grassy Rd K ... 32 C39
Grassy Bay Rd R ... 64 R54-55
Grassy Brook Rd NI ... 19 S34
Grassy Lake Rd CS ... 91 E16
Grassy Lake Rd R ... 63 Q51
Grassy Lake Tr HS ... 62 U47
Gratrix Rd SM ... 41 X29 Y29 42 Y30
Grattan Rd R ... 82 P52
Gratton Rd SD ... 101 C23
Gratton Rd TB ... 102 C-D5
Gratton Tr R ... 82 K53
Gravel Dr CS ... 101 A19
Gravel Rd NR ... 33 D-E45
Gravel Rd TM ... 85 N29
Gravel Hill Rd SDG ... 68 S-T69
Gravel Pit La HS ... 45 W45
Gravel Pit Rd SDG ... 67 U68
Gravel S Rd G ... 27 E19
Gravelle Rd (Chisholm) NP ... 95 G34
Gravelle Rd (Papineau-Cameron) NP ... 96 E38
Gravelly Bay Rd PE ... 35 H52
Gravenhurst Pkwy MK ... 58 V32 59 V33
Graves Sdrd NF ... 10 X22
Gray Ln C ... 6 C7-8
Gray Ln EL ... 7 Y13 8 Y14
Gray Rd HS ... 34 C49
Gray Rd SDG ... 67 U66
Gray Rd TM ... 85 Q29-30
Gray Rd (Fenelon) K ... 44 A38
Gray Rd (Manvers) K ... 32 E38-39
Gray Sdrd DH ... 31 F35
Grays Rd HM ... 18 Q29
Grayshott Dr SM ... 42 Y32
Great Heron La R ... 81 N49
Great Lakes Blvd HT ... 18 P29 24 N29
Great Northern Rd A ... 84 A-B92
Green La A ... 87 E98
Green La NI ... 18 R31-32
Green La WL ... 27 H20
Green La (East Gwillimbury) Y ... 30 F31
Green La (Markham) Y ... 24 J32
Green Ln C ... 7 A11-12
Green Ln EL ... 15 V20 16 V21
Green Rd DH ... 32 G37-38
Green Rd HS ... 34 C47
Green Rd HM ... 18 Q29
Green Rd LA ... 47 A-B52
Green Rd NI ... 19 T33
Green Rd SDG ... 68 Q-R72
Green Rd (Port Colborne) NI ... 19 T34
Green Rd (West Lincoln) NI ... 18 S29
Green St BR ... 38 B16
Green's Rd OT ... 66 T61
Green Acres Rd MK ... 59 R33 S-T35
Green Acres Rd NR ... 34 C46
Green Acres Rd PS ... 94 H30 95 H31
Green Arrow Dr LN ... 49 X58
Green Bay Rd A ... 86 D-E96
Green Bay Rd F ... 48 Y-Z55
Green Bay Rd MA ... 73 K11 90 J11
Green Bay Rd SD ... 93 G23
Green Bush Rd MA ... 90 J11-12
Green Creek Access Rd HS ... 61 R-S43
Green Forest Dr K ... 32 C37
Green Forest Way F ... 48 W53 63 V53
Green Lake Rd HL ... 60 T38
Green Lake Rd (Algoma-Wilberforce) R ... 81 M51
Green Lake Rd (Greater Madawaska) R ... 64 S53
Green Lane Rd PR ... 68 N71 P71-72
Green Mountain Rd HM ... 18 R29-30
Green Point La PE ... 35 E51
Green Point Rd MK ... 59 R-S35
Green Point Rd SM ... 41 X26-27
Green Point Rd TB ... 103 C7
Green Ridge Rd R ... 81 N48
Green Spring Rd HM ... 23 N27-28
Greenbank Rd OT ... 66 R62
Greenbough Lake Rd R ... 97 F40
Greenbrooke Dr Y ... 30 H30-31
Greenbush Rd LG ... 49 Y-Z61 50 Z62
Greenery La G ... 28 C-D23
Greenfield Dr G ... 40 Z22
Greenfield La LG ... 37 A-B60
Greenfield Rd F ... 36 B56
Greenfield Rd LM ... 12 V7
Greenfield Rd SDG ... 68 R70
Greenfield Rd WT ... 22 P23-24
Greenhalgh Rd MK ... 42 W31
Greenhill Av HM ... 18 Q29
Greenhill Av NP ... 95 E31-32
Greenhouse Rd WT ... 22 M24
Greenland Rd OT ... 65 P-Q60
Greenly Rd NR ... 33 D45
Greenock-Brant Townline Rd BR ... 27 E17
Greenock-Culross Townline Rd E BR ... 26 F16 27 F17
Greenock-Culross Townline Rd W BR ... 26 F16
Greenock-Elderslie Townline BR ... 27 D17
Greenough Harbour La BR ... 55 V15
Greens Rd BT ... 16 R24
Greens Rd HD ... 17 R27 S27-28
Greens Rd R ... 81 P49
Greens Landing Rd R ... 64 S53
Greens Mountain Tr HL ... 44 W40
Greenvalley Ln C ... 6 Y8
Greenway Dr MD ... 13 Q12 14 Q13
Greenway Dr R ... 82 K54
Greenway Rd K ... 32 C38
Greenway Rd LM ... 13 Q12
Greenwich St BT ... 17 R25
Greenwood Av T ... 24 K32 25 K33
Greenwood Dr NP ... 95 F34
Greenwood Rd DH ... 31 G-H35
Greenwood Rd K ... 43 Y36
Greenwood Rd PB ... 33 D41
Greenwood Bridge Rd TM ... 85 P29-30
Greenwood Hill Rd WT ... 22 M21
Greenwood Point Rd MK ... 58 U31
Greer Rd F ... 47 W52 48 W53
Greer Rd LN ... 48 W56
Greer Rd MK ... 59 S33
Greer Rd PE ... 34 G48
Gregoire Rd PR ... 67 S-T65
Gregory Dr C ... 6 A8-9
Gregory Dr MD ... 15 R17-18
Gregory La HL ... 60 U40
Gregory Ln C ... 6 A9
Gregory Rd MK ... 58 T30
Gregory Rd NI ... 19 R33
Gregson Rd EL ... 9 W20
Greig Settlement Rd BR ... 55 X17
Grenfel Rd SM ... 41 B28-29
Grenfell Dr MD ... 15 S17
Grenn Acres Rd MK ... 59 S-T35
Grenville St LG ... 50 V62
Grey's Rd NP ... 95 D31-32
Grey's Creek Rd OT ... 66 S64
Grey-Bruce Ln G ... 27 C18 39 A-B18
Grey Duck Dr A ... 86 C95
Grey Owl Rd PS ... 76 P27-28
Grey Ox Av BR ... 26 G15
Greybow Dr PS ... 94 H29
Greystead Dr MD ... 14 S14-15
Grieves Ln HU ... 20 L16
Grieves Rd MD ... 14 R13
Griffin Dr K ... 43 Y37
Griffis Rd TB ... 102 F3
Griffith St MD ... 14 T16
Griffith Wagner Rd R ... 81 N49
Grills Rd HS ... 34 E48
Grills Rd NR ... 33 F43
Grimsby Rd NI ... 18 R30-31
Grimsthorpe Rd MA ... 72 L8
Grimsthorpe Lake Access Rd HS ... 46 W49
Grindstone Cir A ... 84 X90
Grindstone Rd PS ... 76 M30 77 L-M31
Grindstone Lake Rd F ... 63 U-V52
Grindstone Lake Rd MK ... 59 S36
Grindstone Lake Access Rd F ... 63 U52 64 U53
Grisdale's Rd PS ... 57 T27
Grise's Rd MK ... 41 W29
Grist Mill La HL ... 60 Q37
Grist Mill Rd NR ... 32 F40
Grist Mill Rd R ... 82 P52
Grosjean Rd NR ... 34 E46
Gross Rd MK ... 58 R-S31
Groth Rd A ... 84 Y-Z92
Groulx Rd LG ... 49 Y59
Groulx Rd NP ... 95 F-G33
Grouse Ct DH ... 31 F-G35
Grouse La F ... 48 Z56
Grouse Rd R ... 62 Q48
Grove Rd C ... 5 D7 6 C7
Grove St SM ... 42 B30
Grove Mills Ln C ... 7 X10
Groves Rd PR ... 67 S66
Groves Rd SDG ... 51 V67-68
Groveton Rd LG ... 50 W64
Grozell Rd K ... 43 X35
Grubb Rd BR ... 27 F17
Gryffin Lodge Rd MK ... 59 R-S33
Guelph Av WT ... 22 N24
Guelph Ln HT ... 18 P29 23 L-M26 M27 N28
Guelph St HT ... 23 L26-27
Guelph St WL ... 22 K24
Guelph-Nicol Townline WL ... 22 L24 23 L25
Guelph-Pilkington Townline WL ... 22 L-M24
Guenette Dr CS ... 101 A20
Guenette Rd NP ... 94 D27
Guerin Rd PR ... 67 S67
Guerin Rd, Mtée SD ... 93 G24
Guertin Rd NR ... 33 E45
Guest Av BR ... 26 F15
Guest Rd SM ... 42 A31
Guigue Rd F ... 48 X55
Guild Rd LG ... 37 B61
Guildwood Pkwy T ... 25 J34
Guillemette Rd (East Ferris) NP ... 95 F33
Guilmette Lake Access Rd NP ... 96 G35
Guindon Rd PR ... 67 Q66
Guiney Rd R ... 62 Q48
Gulf Rd HS ... 46 A46 Z46
Gull Lake La F ... 47 X52
Gull Lake Rd F ... 47 X51-52
Gull Lake Estates La F ... 47 W52
Gull Wing Lake Rd MK ... 58 V31
Gulley Ln HU ... 20 M14
Gulley Rd F ... 48 V55
Gully Rd NR ... 33 G43
Gully Mor Rd LM ... 13 U-V12
Gum Bed Ln LM ... 12 V9
Gummow Rd NR ... 33 D44
Gun Club Rd CS ... 100 D15
Gun Club Rd MK ... 59 R33
Gunn Rd SDG ... 67 T68 68 T69
Gunn's Hill Rd OX ... 16 S21-22
Gunns Rd R ... 80 M47
Gunsmith Rd R ... 83 Q56
Gunter Lake Rd HS ... 46 W48
Gunter Settlement Rd HS ... 34 D47 E46
Gurlitz Rd R ... 82 P52
Gus Wouri Rd TB ... 102 C5
Gustavus St BR ... 38 B16
Guswood Rd TB ... 102 B-C5
Gut Tr, The HS ... 45 X45
Gutheinz La F ... 47 W52
Guthrie Rd LN ... 49 V-W61
Gutzman Rd (Laurentian Hills) R ... 99 H48
Gutzman Rd (Petawawa) R ... 99 K50-51
Guy Rd LG ... 50 V63
Guy Rd SDG ... 67 U65
Guyatt Rd HM ... 18 R29
Gypsie Flats Rd LM ... 12 U-V9
Gypsy Rd OT ... 83 Q58

H-I, Concession Rd SM ... 42 X-Y33
Hacienda Rd EL ... 9 W19 15 V19
Hackbart Rd WT ... 22 M21
Hackmatack Rd HS ... 62 V45
Hacquoil Rd TB ... 102 E5
Hadden Rd Y ... 31 C33
Haddington St HD ... 17 S27-28
Haddo Rd SDG ... 50 W65
Hadlington Rd HL ... 61 V41
Hagan Rd BT ... 17 S25
Hagen Rd HL ... 61 U43
Hagerman La HS ... 34 C49
Hagerman Rd HS ... 34 C48 46 B48
Hagerty Rd MD ... 7 W12
Haggart Lake Rd MK ... 58 T29
Haggarts Side Rd LG ... 50 Z62
Haggerty Rd LA ... 47 B52
Haggerty Rd LM ... 7 W11-12
Haggerty's Sdrd F ... 37 B58
Hagmier Rd MD ... 13 Q12
Haig Ln LM ... 13 Q12
Haig Rd LG ... 37 C59
Haig's Reach Rd NR ... 33 C-D45
Haines Rd PS ... 57 Q27
Hainesville Rd SDG ... 50 W65
Hairpin Rd LG ... 36 A57
Haist St NI ... 19 S33
Hald-Dunn Townline Rd HD ... 18 T-U30
Haldibrook Rd HM ... 17 R27-28
Haldimand Tr HD ... 18 U30
Haldimand Tract Rd HD ... 18 U30
Hale St MD ... 15 T17
Hale School Rd C ... 7 X10
Hale School Rd LM ... 7 W10 13 V10
Haleway Dr MK ... 42 W31
Haley Rd R ... 83 P57
Haley Lake Rd LN ... 65 U58
Haleys Bay Tr R ... 81 P51
Half Moon Rd EL ... 9 W-X19
Halfway Dump Rd BR ... 54 S15
Haliburton Lake Rd HL ... 60 S-U39
Hall Dr PB ... 44 Z40
Hall Rd HM ... 17 S28 18 S29
Hall Rd MD ... 13 R12
Hall Rd NR ... 33 D-E43
Hall Rd OT ... 66 R64
Hall Rd (Augusta) LG ... 50 X63
Hall Rd (Elizabethtown-Kitley) LG ... 49 Z61
Hall Rd (Leeds and the Thousand Islands) LG ... 37 A59
Hall's Rd K ... 43 B37
Hall's Rd PS ... 77 P33
Hall's Hill Ln HU ... 26 G-H14
Hall Shore La LN ... 48 V56
Hallecks Rd LG ... 50 A62
Hallecks Rd E LG ... 50 A62
Hallecks Rd W LG ... 50 A62
Hallett Cr K ... 31 D36
Hallett Rd MK ... 58 T29
Halliday Rd PB ... 45 W42
Halliday Creek Rd R ... 64 R55
Hallman Rd WT ... 22 P22
Halls Rd DH ... 31 G-H35
Halls Rd PB ... 45 X44
Halls Rd PS ... 76 L30 77 L31
Halls Rd (Gravenhurst) MK ... 42 W33
Halls Rd (Muskoka Lakes) MK ... 58 T30
Halls Lake Rd HL ... 60 T37
Halls Lake Sdrd PL ... 30 G29
Halm Rd WT ... 22 L-M23
Halstead Rd A ... 86 D97
Halstead Rd NR ... 33 D43
Halstead Beach Rd NR ... 33 E-F41
Halter Rd K ... 32 C38
Ham Rd LA ... 36 D54
Ham Lake Rd SD ... 92 H22
Hambly Rd DH ... 31 F36
Hambly Rd LA ... 35 D-E52
Hamburgh Rd, The LA ... 35 D52-53
Hamer Bay Rd PS ... 58 S29
Hamers Rd DH ... 31 G36
Hamersveld Rd CS ... 100 D16
Hamill Rd G ... 39 A21
Hamills Point Rd A ... 88 E3
Hamilton Dr A ... 86 E96
Hamilton Dr PB ... 45 A42 Z42
Hamilton La G ... 28 C-D22
Hamilton Rd BT ... 17 S26
Hamilton Rd G ... 39 B21
Hamilton Rd HL ... 44 W38 60 V38
Hamilton Rd HS ... 34 E47 E47-48
Hamilton Rd LN ... 65 S59
Hamilton Rd MD ... 15 T17-19
Hamilton Rd NR ... 33 F-G41
Hamilton Rd OX ... 15 S-T19
Hamilton Rd PR ... 67 R-S65
Hamilton Rd WT ... 22 N-P21
Hamilton St A ... 89 F8
Hamilton St HM ... 23 P28
Hamilton Bay Rd A ... 86 E95-96
Hamilton Bay Tr HS ... 61 S-T43
Hamilton Farm Rd PS ... 95 G-H31
Hamilton Island Rd SDG ... 52 U72
Hamilton Lake Rd PS ... 77 K31-32
Hamilton Plank Rd NF ... 17 V26
Hammel Av PS ... 56 Q26
Hammersley Rd WL ... 23 M-N26
Hammil's Point Rd MK ... 58 T29
Hammill Rd NR ... 32 F40
Hammond Rd BT ... 17 R26
Hammond Rd MK ... 59 S-T35
Hammond Rd SD ... 90 F11
Hammond Rd (Hastings Highlands) HS ... 61 R42
Hammond Rd (Tudor and Cashel) HS ... 46 W48
Hampshire Mills Ln SM ... 42 Y31-32
Hampson Rd SDG ... 68 Q71-72
Hanbidge Rd PB ... 32 D40 33 D41
Hanbury Rd TM ... 85 Q29-30
Hancock Rd DH ... 32 G-H37
Hand Dr HL ... 44 W39
Hand's Rd LN ... 49 V58
Handford La R ... 63 R51
Hands Rd LG ... 50 X64
Handy Spot Rd A ... 89 F7
Hanes Rd MK ... 59 R33
Hanes Rd SDG ... 51 W66
Hanlon Pkwy WL ... 23 M25 N26
Hanlon Rd WL ... 23 M25
Hanlon Bay Rd LG ... 37 A58
Hanmer Ln OX ... 16 T22
Hanmer Lake Rd CS ... 101 A19 Z19
Hanna Rd F ... 48 Y56
Hanna Rd LN ... 48 X56
Hanna Rd TB ... 102 E4
Hannah Ln HU ... 20 M15
Hannah Rd HS ... 34 D47
Hannah Rd LG ... 49 Y60
Hannah Rd PB ... 33 E41
Hannah Rd SD ... 90 F11
Hannah Lake Rd SD ... 90 F14
Hanselman Dr PS ... 95 H32-33
Hansen Blvd DF ... 29 G26
Hansen Rd NR ... 34 E46
Hansen Rd TB ... 103 B-C10
Hansford Rd MD ... 14 S-T14
Hansler Rd NI ... 19 S33
Hanson Sdrd OT ... 65 R58
Happy Days Tr K ... 43 Y35
Happy Hollow Rd PR ... 68 P71
Happy Landing Rd SD ... 93 F-G23
Happy Valley Rd CS ... 101 B21
Harbard Rd PE ... 34 F47
Harbinson La HL ... 44 W39
Harbison Rd OT ... 66 T62
Harbour Dr G ... 39 Y21
Harbour Expwy TB ... 103 D6
Harbour St NR ... 34 F46
Harbour St OT ... 83 P-Q58
Harbour St SM ... 30 D31
Harbour Beach Dr G ... 40 Z22
Harbour Vue Rd MA ... 90 J12
Harbourview Rd NI ... 19 U33
Harburn Rd HL ... 60 T40 U39
Harcourt Rd HL ... 61 T-U42
Harcourt Rd HS ... 34 E47
Hard Island Rd LG ... 49 Z60-61
Hard Scrabble Rd PS ... 76 K29
Hard Wood La HL ... 61 U41
Hardies Rd PS ... 57 Q28 76 P28
Harding La F ... 48 X55
Harding Rd LN ... 65 T57
Harding Smith Ln EL ... 9 X18
Hardman's La BR ... 55 W17
Hardwick Cove Rd BR ... 55 V16
Hardwood Dr A ... 86 D94
Hardwood La F ... 48 Z57
Hardwood Rd SD ... 90 D-E13
Hardwood St K ... 43 Z36
Hardwood Ridge Rd LN ... 64 U56
Hardy Rd BT ... 16 R24 17 R25
Hardy Creek Rd LM ... 13 U12
Hardy Creek Access Rd NP ... 94 G27
Hardy Lake Rd MK ... 58 U31
Hare's Hill Rd LG ... 50 W62
Hares Rd MK ... 59 R33
Hargrave Rd K ... 43 Z36

Harju Rd *TB*. 102 E2
Harlem Rd *LG* 49 Y59
Harlequin La *R* 62 U48
Harley Rd *BT* 16 S22-23
Harlock Ln *HU* 20 K15-16
Harlowe Rd *LA* 47 X51
Harmans Rd *TM* 85 M-M28
Harmer Rd *HS* 34 E46
Harmer's Beach Scdrd *H* . 31 G36 32 G37
Harmony Rd *DH* . . . 31 G36 32 G37
Harmony Rd *HS* . 34 D48-49 35 C50
Harmony Rd *MD* 14 Q-R13
Harmony Rd *SDG* . . 66 T64 67 T65
Harmony Rd N *DH* 31 F-G36
Harmony Acres La *EL* . . . 15 V20
Harmony Bay La *R* 82 M54
Harmony Beach Rd *A* . . . 84 X92
Harmony Point Rd *SD* . . . 93 F24
Harnett Rd *OT* 66 U62
Harold Rd *F* 48 X53-54
Harold Rd *HL* 61 T43
Harold Rd *HS* 46 B46-47
Harp Ena Dr *MK* 59 Q34
Harp Lake Rd *MK* 59 Q34
Harpenden Rd *CS* . . . 100 D15-16
Harper Ln *HU* 26 G14-15
Harper Rd *DH* 31 E35-36
Harper Rd *EL* 48 W57
Harper Hill Rd *MA* . . 71 K6 72 K7
Harpers Point Rd *NR* . . . 45 B45
Harpurhey Rd *HU* 20 L-M15
Harrietsville Rd *MD* . . 15 U18-19
Harrington Ln *PB* 44 B40
Harris Cr *A*. 87 E99
Harris Ln *OX* 15 T20
Harris Rd *BT* 17 R26
Harris Rd *DH* 32 F38
Harris Rd *F*. 36 A-B57
Harris Rd *HL* 59 Q36
Harris Rd *NR* 33 F-G41
Harris Rd *PR*. 68 R69
Harris Rd (Middlesex Centre) *R* .
. . . . 14 U15
Harris Rd (Thames Centre) *R* . . .
. . . . 15 T18
Harris St *OX* 15 S20
Harris Boatworks Rd *R* . . 59 U34
Harrisburg Rd *BT* 17 Q25
Harnsburg Rd *HM*. 17 Q25
Harrison Rd *HM* . 17 S28 18 S29
Harrison Rd *MK* 59 U34
Harrison Rd *PB* 44 Z39
Harrison Tr *MK* 57 T-U27
Harrison Tr *R* 63 S50
Harrison Lake Rd *PS* . . . 77 P31
Harrison Landing Rd *PS*. . 56 Q26
Harriston Rd *HU*. 27 H17-19
Harrowsmith Rd *F* 36 B55
Harry Dick Rd *R*. 82 Q52-53
Harry Quirk Access Rd *HS* . . . .
. . . . 62 V47-48
Harry Thede Scdrd *BR* . . 38 B58
Harry White Dr *MD* 15 U17
Harstone Dr *TB* 102 D-E4
Harstone Rd *TB* 102 E3
Hart Rd *HD* 18 T30
Hart Rd *LG* 50 X62
Hart Rd *SDG*. 67 U67-68
Hart Rd (Callander) *PS* . . 95 F32 G31
Hart Rd (Seguin) *PS* . . 58 U-P29
Hartin Rd *LA* 47 Y51
Hartley Rd *K*. 43 A-B36
Hartley Bay Rd *SD*. . . 92 H21-22
Harts Rd *HS* 46 A48 Z48
Harts Gravel Rd *LG* . . 49 Z58-59
Hartsmere Rd *HS*. . . . 62 T-U48
Hartsmere Link Access Rd *LA* . . .
. . . . 63 T-U49
Hartt Rd *A* 87 E-F2
Hartzel Rd *NI*. 19 R34
Harvest Rd *K* 44 B38
Harvey Av *HL* 59 S36
Harvey Rd *LG* 50 X62-63
Harvey Creek Rd *F* 98 F46
Harvey Lake Dr *HL* 59 R36
Harvie Settlement Rd *MA* . 42 Z31
Harwich Rd *C* . . 6 A9 7 A10 B10-11
Harwick Ranch Rd *R*. . . . 63 Q49
Harwood Av *DH* . 25 I-J35 31 H35
Harwood Rd *NR* 33 E-F42
Haryett Rd *HS* 62 S47
Haskell Rd *C* 5 D8 6 C8
Haskett's Dr *MK* 41 W29
Haskill Rd *NR*. . . . 32 G40 33 G41
Haskin Point Rd *LG* 37 A58
Haskins Rd *LG* 50 V62
Haskins Landing Rd *A* . . . 87 C98
Hass Rd (Admaston-Bromley) *R* . .
. . . . 82 Q53
Hass Rd (Brudenell, Lyndoch and
Raglan) *R* 62 S47
Hass Rd (Carlow Mayo) *HS*. 62 S47
Hass Rd (Hastings Highlands) *HS*.
. . . . 61 R44 62 R45
Hass Rd (Madoc) *HS* . . . 46 Z48
Hastings Dr *HL*. 10 X23
Hastings Ln *C* 7 Y12
Hatchery Rd *CS* 101 Y19
Hatchley Rd *BT* 18 T22-23
Hatt St *BR* 54 S14
Hatten Dr *G* 39 B20
Haultain Rd *PB* 45 Z42
Haute-Rive St *PR* 68 N70
Havelock St *BR* 26 G14-15
Haven Av *G* 27 E20
Haven Rd *MK* 59 V33
Haven Rd *NP* 93 D25
Havens Lake Rd *EL* . . 7 Y13 8 Y14
Havensford Dr *HL*. 61 U42
Havergal Rd *F* 62 S47
Havilland Causeway Rd *A*. 84 X-Y92
Havilland Shores Rd *A* . 84 X-Y91
Hawdon Dr *A*. 86 F94
Hawk Rd *MA*. 72 K9
Hawk Cliff Rd *EL* 8 W-X17
Hawk Hill Way *PL* 29 H28
Hawk Lake Access Rd *HS* 62 U-V45
Hawke Dr *K*. 32 C39
Hawkesbury Access Rd *NP*. . . . .
. . . . . . 96 G38 97 F39 G39
Hawkesville Rd *WT* 22 M22
Hawkins Rd *HS* 62 U46
Hawkins Rd *HU* . . 20 J14 26 H13
Hawkins Rd *NR*. 33 G41

Hawkins Rd *OX* 15 U-V20
Hawkins Bay Rd *HS* 46 A49
Hawley Rd *LG* 49 W60-61
Hawley Rd *NF*. 16 V21
Hawn Rd *MK*. 59 V33
Haws Rd *LG* 37 B61
Hawthorn Dr *C* 4 C4
Hawthorne Dr (Machar) *PS* . 77 K31
Hawthorne Dr (Patterson) *PS* 94 H29
Hawthorne Rd *OT*. 66 R64
Hawthorne Rd *R* 82 L54
Hawtrey Rd *NF* 16 V23
Hay Rd *SDG* 52 U71-72
Hay Bay Rd *BR* 54 S13-14
Hay Bay Tr *HS* 61 T43
Hay Creek Rd *NP* 79 P41
Hay Creek Access Rd *NP* 61 Q41
Hayden Rd *NR* 33 F43
Haydon Rd *SDG* 68 Q72
Hayes Ln *PB* . . 32 C39-40 D39
Hayes Rd *F* 47 Y52
Hayes Lake Av *BR* 26 F15
Haynes Rd *NR* 33 E-F44
Haystack Logging Rd *MA*. 96 G-H13
Haystead Rd *SD* 51 V67
Haysville Rd *WT* 22 P21
Hayward Rd *PS* 75 M26
Hazard Hill Rd *PS* 77 M33
Hazel Glen Rd *PS* . . 95 G31-32
Hazeldean Rd *OT*. 66 S61
Hazelwood Dr N *TB*. . . . 103 B6
Hazelwood Rd *NP*. . . . 96 E37-38
Hazen Rd *NF*. . . 10 W22 X23 16 V22
Hazley Bay Rd *R*. 82 L52
Hazzard's Rd *HS*. 46 Z48
Hea Rd *BR*. 55 X17
Head Rd *DH* 31 E36
Head Rd *F* 47 W51
Head St *BR* 54 S14
Head St *MD* 14 T13-14
Head Pond Rd N *LN* . . . 65 Q57
Head Pond Rd S *LN* . . . 65 Q57
Headline Rd *SDG* 52 U70
Headon Rd *HT* . . 18 P29 24 N29
Healey Rd *LG* 49 Y60
Healey Rd *PL* 30 F29
Healey Lake Rd *MK* . . 59 U33-34
Healey Lake Rd *PS* 57 T27-28 58 T29
Healey Lake Lodge Rd *PS* . 57 T28
Healy Rd *LN* 49 V59
Heaphy Rd *OT* 90 V61-62
Heards Hill Rd *TM*. 85 R30
Hearns Rd *HS* 34 D47
Heart Lake Rd *PL* . . . .
. . . . 23 J28 24 J29 K29 29 H27
Heaslip Rd *NI* 18 S32
Heasman Rd *HS*. . . . 34 C47-48
Heath Dr *NR*. 33 C-D44
Heath Lake Access Rd *LA* . 63 U49
Heather Dr *HL* 61 V43
Heather St *PL* 29 H27
Heatly Dr *MD*. 14 U15
Hebron La *OT* 50 V62
Hedge Rd *Y*. 30 C32
Hedley Dr *MD*. 14 S-T14
Heeney Lake Rd *MK*. . . . 59 T34
Heffernan Rd *LG* 49 Z60
Hegadorn Rd *LA* 36 C-D54
Heideman La *R* 63 T51
Heideman Rd *R*. 82 P52
Heights Rd *K* . . 32 C38 44 B38
Heino Rd *CS* 101 B20
Heins Rd *R* 63 R49
Hekkla Rd *MK* 58 R30-31
Helder Rd *MD*. 15 U19
Helen St *K* 43 A37
Helena St *NI* 19 U36
Helens Rd *F* 37 D58
Helferty Ln *R* 82 N-P53
Helkaa Ln *EL* 15 V18
Hellyer Rd *BR* 54 S14
Helmar Lake Access Rd *NP*. 61 Q45
Helmer Rd *F*. 35 H51-52
Helmer Rd (North Dundas) *SDG* . .
. . . . 67 U66
Helmer Rd (South Stormont) *SDG*.
. . . . 67 T-U68
Helyer Rd *HS* 34 E46-47
Hemitite Rd *HS* 46 Z48
Hemling La *LA* 35 C52
Hemlock Dr *K* 43 Y37
Hemlock Rd *PS*. 95 H32
Hemlock Hill Dr *WT* 22 M22
Hemlock Point Rd *MK* . . 58 T30
Hemlock Point Scdrd *MK*. . 58 T30
Henan Rd *R* 81 L51
Henders Rd *HM* 18 T-U31
Hendershot Rd *NI*. 18 T-U31
Henderson Av *Y* 24 J32
Henderson Dr *Y* 30 G31
Henderson Ln *C* 7 Y11
Henderson Ln *PB* 33 C42
Henderson Rd *BT*. 16 R24
Henderson Rd *EX*. 5 H5
Henderson Rd *HS* . . . 46 W-X46
Henderson Rd *LA* 47 B51
Henderson Rd *NI* 18 T32
Henderson Rd *PB* 45 A42
Henderson Rd *SDG* . 50 V65 51 V66
Henderson Rd (Central Frontenac)
F. 47 X51-52
Henderson Rd (South Frontenac) *F*
. . . . 36 C54-55
Hendrick Rd *HU*. 20 P13
Hendricks Rd *HS* 34 F47
Hendrie Rd *SM*. 41 A-B29
Hendrie Township Rd *SD* 92 E21-22
Hendry Side Rd *LG*. 49 Z61
Henfryn Ln *HU* 21 K18
Hennessey Rd *HS* . . . 34 F46-47
Hennessy Rd *CS* 91 E16
Hennessy St *PE* 34 E49
Hennig Rd *HS* 84 T44
Henniger Rd *LA* 47 W50
Henri St *CS*. 101 D19
Henrie Rd *PR* 67 P67
Henry La *HS* 46 Y48
Henry Rd *HU* 32 F-G39
Henry Rd *EL* 7 X13
Henry St *HS*. 34 C47
Henry St *DH* 31 H36
Henry St *WT*. 22 M22
Henry Rd *K* 44 A38
Henry Coghlan Rd *NP* . . 61 Q43
Hensall Rd *HU* . . . 20 L16 M-N15
Henshaw Lake Rd *MK*. . 58 T-U30

Henshel Rd *CS* 101 D21
Herald Rd *Y* . . 30 E32 F32 31 E33
Herb's Rd *HL* 73 L13
Herb Lake Dr *HL* 60 S37
Herbert Corners Rd *OT* 66 S64 S-T63
Herbs Rd *HS*. 62 S47
Herchmer Av *HS*. 34 E49
Herd's Scdrd *BR*. . . . 26 F15-16
Heritage Dr *LN*. 49 V-W61
Heritage Dr *SM* 41 Y28
Heritage Ln *C* 6 X-Y7
Heritage Ln *EL*. . . 9 W20 15 U20
Heritage Ln *PB* 33 C-D42
Heritage Rd *EX* 4 E4 F3
Heritage Rd *MD*. 15 R-S18
Heritage Rd *NR*. 33 G43
Heritage Rd *PL* 23 K28
Heritage Rd *R* 81 N49
Heritage Rd *SDG* 51 V66
Heritage River Rd *SD* . . 92 G22
Herkimer St *A*. 84 B91
Herley Rd *NR*. 33 F44
Herlihey Rd *HL* 61 U42
Herman Rd *MK* 59 R35
Herman Tibbel Rd *MK*. . 58 S31
Hermanns Rd *F* 59 R35
Hermiston Rd *NR* 33 D44
Hern Ln *HU* 20 P16
Heron La *F*. 48 Z54
Heron Ln *C* 6 A7-8
Heron Ln *HU* 20 J14
Heron Rd *DH* 31 F-G35
Heron Rd *HS* 46 Z49
Heron Rd *OT*. 66 R63
Heron Rd *SDG*. 68 T71
Heron Rd *WA* 73 L12
Herrgott Rd *WT* 22 L-M22
Herrington La *LA* 35 D52
Herron Rd *NR* 33 F44
Herron Mills Rd *LN* 65 U57
Herschel Forest Tr *HS* . . 61 S43
Herzberg Rd *OT*. 66 R61
Hespeler Rd *WT*. 22 N24
Hess Rd *HL* 50 V64
Hessen Strasse *WT* 22 M21
Hetherington Rd *C* 7 Y12
Heuvelmans Rd *OT*. . . . 67 Q65
Hewitt Rd *HL* 60 U37
Hewitt Rd *NI*. 19 T33
Hewitt St *MK* . . 42 W32 58 V32
Hewitt's Corner Rd *R* 81 M51 82 M52
Hewlett Packard Rd *F* . 36 B56-57
Heyden Lake Rd *A* 84 Z92
Hiawatha La *F*. 36 B57
Hiawatha Ln *PB*. 45 A42
Hiawatha Rd *PB*. 33 D42
Hiawatha Rd *HS* 58 V29
Hickerson Pioneer Rd *NR*. . 33 F42
Hickey Rd *C* 6 C8
Hickey Rd *F* 48 Z55
Hickey Rd *HS*. 62 S-T45
Hickey Rd *PB* 44 B41
Hickey Tr *HS* . . . 61 T44 62 T45
Hickey Hill Rd *HS*. . . . 62 T45
Hickman Rd *SD*. 93 E24
Hickory Dr *MD*. 14 T14
Hickory La *F*. 37 D58-59
Hickory La *LA* 35 E51
Hickory Ln *LG*. 37 A59
Hickory Acres Dr *EX*. 4 E3
Hickory Beach La *HD* . . . 17 V17
Hickory Beach Rd *K* . . . 44 A38
Hickory Creek Ln *LM* . 13 S10-11
Hicks Rd *HS* 62 Q46
Hicks Rd *LA*. 47 B53
Hickson Rd *EX* 5 E6
Hickson Rd *HS* 32 D38
Hickson Rd *PB*. 45 A43
Hicock Rd *LG* 49 Z59
Hidden Acres La *WT* . . . 22 L23
Hidden Bay Access Rd *SD*. 100 Y15
Hidden Forest Dr *Y* 30 F32
Hidden Glen Rd *MK*. . . 41 W29
Hidden River Rd *R* 83 Q56
Hidden Trail Rd *F* . . . 81 N-P48
Hidden Valley Rd *BR*. . . . 54 T15
Hidden Valley Rd *F* 36 A56
Hidden Valley Rd *K* 32 C39
Hideaway La *F* 36 B57
Hideaway Rd *MA* 72 J9
Hietanen Rd *CS* 100 D18
Higgins La *DH* . . . 31 F34-35
Higgins Ln *HU*. 20 J16
Higgins Rd *PS* 77 M33
Higgins Rd *SD* . . . 90 L13-14 S18
High La *R* 82 Q55
High Rd *A*. 88 F4
High Rd *NI*. 18 R32
High Rd *OT*. 66 R63
High St *BR*. 38 A16
High St *LN*. 65 T59
High St *MK*. 58 T29
High St *PR*. 68 P71
High St *T* 77 L32
High St *SM* 40 A25
High St *Y* 30 C32
High Country Rd *R* 81 P48
High Falls Rd *CS* 100 D15
High Falls Rd *LN*. 48 V55
High Falls Rd *MA*. . . . 73 K-L12
High Falls Rd *MK* . 58 U32 59 T33
High Falls Tr *HS* 62 T45
High Hill Rd *BR*. 38 T17
High Park Rd *K* 31 D36
High Point Rd *DH* 31 F33
High Rock Rd *PS* . . . 77 L-M32
High Shore Rd *HS*. 46 A46
Highbanks Rd *C* 7 C10
Highbury Av *EL* 15 U-V17
Highbury Av N *MD* 14 R16 15 S-T17
Highbury Av S *MD* . . . 15 T-U17
Highgate Rd *A* . 43 A36 Z36
Highland Dr *BT* 16 R24
Highland Dr *G* 28 D22
Highland Dr *MK* 59 R34
Highland Dr (Essa) *SM*. . . 30 C29
Highland Dr (Oro-Medonte) *SM*. . .
. . . . 42 A30
Highland Ln *LN*. 18 V56
Highland Rd *EL*. 8 W14
Highland Rd *F*. 36 E56-57
Highland Rd *HM*. . . . 18 R29-30
Highland Rd *NR* 33 F41
Highland Rd *R*. . . . 64 R56 65 R57
Highland Rd *SDG*. . 68 S69-70
Highland Rd *TM*. 85 Q28
Highland Rd *WL* 27 G19
Highland Rd *W* 22 N22-23

Highland Park Rd *MK*. . . . 59 S36
Highland View Dr *NR* . . . 33 F44
Highpoint Scdrd *PL*. . . . 29 H26
Highview Cr *PB* 32 D-E39
Hila Rd *F*. 82 L53
Hilker Rd *PB* . . 45 W44 61 V44
Hill Ct *HT*. 23 K27
Hill Dr *PB*. 44 Z41
Hill Rd *A* 84 A90
Hill Rd *C* 7 A11-12
Hill Rd *F*. 36 A55
Hill Rd *MA* 72 L10
Hill Rd *TB*. 102 B-C3
Hill St *CS* 101 C21
Hill St *HS*. 34 C48
Hill St *LM* 12 U7
Hill St *MA* 72 K10
Hill St *WT*. 22 L23
Hill & Gully Rd *PS*. 77 L33
Hill 60 *NR* 33 G42-43
Hill and Dale La *F* 48 Z56
Hill Brook Rd *LG* . . . 50 Y63-64
Hill Fourteen Rd *PS* . . . 77 L33
Hill Top Rd *PE*. 35 H51
Hill Valley Rd *PS*. . . . 77 L31-32
Hillcrest Av *R* 81 P48
Hillcrest Dr *CS*. 100 D18
Hillcrest La *F* 48 Y55
Hillcrest Rd *NP*. . . . 95 F-G33
Hillcrest Rd *PB* 32 F40
Hillcrest Rd *PB* . . 45 Z42-43
Hillcrest Rd *SM*. 41 X26
Hilldale Rd *TB* 103 C6
Hillen Rd *DH*. 32 F39
Hillhead Rd *F* 32 C38
Hilliard-Ingram Township Rd *TM*. .
. . . . 85 N29-30
Hillardton Rd *TM*. . . . 85 N28-29
Hills Rd *PB*. 32 C40
Hillman Rd *NP*. 93 E26
Hillman Sdrd *EX* 5 E6
Hills Rd *HU* 20 J14
Hills Rd *K*. 43 Y34
Hills Lake Rd *F* 63 V52
Hills of Peace Rd *LN*. . . . 64 T55
Hills Siding Rd *NP* . . . 95 G32-33
Hills Siding Rd *PS*. 58 U32
Hillsboro Rd *LM*. 13 S-T10
Hillsdale Dr *Y* 31 F33
Hillsdale Rd *MK* 42 X33
Hillside Dr *A* 90 J10
Hillside Dr *K* . . . 43 Y37 44 Y38
Hillside Dr *NI* 18 R31-32
Hillside Dr *PS*. 56 Q25-26
Hillside Rd *HS* 62 T45
Hillside Rd *TM* 85 Q30
Hillsview Rd *HS* 62 S45
Hilltop Rd *HL*. 60 U39
Hillview Ck *SM* 41 A29
Hillview Dr *NR* 33 E42
Hillview Dr *PB* 32 D39
Hillview Rd *TM*. 85 Q-R29
Hilly Rd *LN* 18 U11
Hilly Grove Tr *MA* 73 M12
Hilton Rd *A*. 86 E94-95
Hilton's Point Rd *K* 43 X36
Hilton's Point Rd N *K* . . . 43 X36
Hilton's Point Rd W *K* . . . 43 X36
Himbury La *PS* 77 N33
Hinch Rd *LA* 35 C52
Hinchey Rd *PS* 35 D50
Hinchinbrooke Rd *F*. . . 36 A54-55
Hinoha Bay Rd *MA* 90 J10
Hindman Sdrd *G* 39 Y19
Hindman Tr *MA*. 72 J8
Hindon-Anson Access Rd *HL*. . . . .
. . . . 59 U36
Hindon Forest Access Rd *HL* 59 T35
Hinds St *CS* 101 C22
Hines Rd *HD* 18 T31
Hinkiss Dr *HL* 60 S40
Hinkson Rd *HU* 20 P16
Hinton St *NI* 18 R31-32
Hooper Rd *TM* 85 R28
Hoards Rd *NR* 34 C46
Hoards Church Rd *NR*. . . 34 C46
Hoares Rd *HS* 62 Q46
Hobbs Rd *NR* 33 E45
Hobson Rd *EL*. . 9 W18 15 V18
Hobson Rd *PB* 85 W43
Hobson's Harbour Dr *BR*. 55 V-W16
Hochreiter Rd *Y*. 30 E31
Hockley Rd *DF*. . . 29 F-G27 G26
Hoddinott La *LN* 48 V57
Hoddys Side Rd *PS* 57 Q27
Hodgins Rd *MD* 14 S13
Hodgins Rd *SM* . 41 X29 42 X30
Hodgins Sdrd *OT* 65 R59
Hodgkins Rd *NI*. 18 S32
Hodgson Rd *HL* 60 S40
Hodvick Rd *C* 5 D-E7
Hofstetter Rd *OX*. 22 P22
Hogaboam Rd *SDG* 67 U65-66
Hogan Rd *HS* 33 E44
Hogan Rd (Frontenac Islands) *F* . .
. . . . 36 D-D57
Hogan Rd (South Frontenac) *F* . . .
. . . . 36 B55-56
Hogan Lake Rd *PB* 45 W44
Hogback Rd *SM*. 29 C27
Hogg Valley Rd *SM* 41 Y29
Hogs Back Rd *HS*. 47 B50
Hogsback Rd *PB* 32 D39
Hogsback Rd *SM* 41 Y28
Holancin Rd *Y* 30 F30
Holborn Rd *Y* 30 E31-32
Holbrook Rd *LN* 49 V60
Holdaway Ln *C* 7 A-B11
Holdcroft Rd *PB* 45 Y-Z44
Holden Rd *EX* 4 C-D2
Holden Rd *LA* 47 B52
Holden Rd *PS* 44 B40
Holderney Rd *PS* 58 Q31
Holditch School Rd *HL*. . . 17 P26
Hollandsworth Dr *HL*. . . . 60 U40
Hole In Wall Rd *PS* . 75 K25 93 J25
Holiday La *F* 48 W54
Holiday La *R* 81 N51
Holiday Rd *MK*. . 41 W29 58 V29
Holiday Beach Dr *A* 84 W91

Holiday Beach Rd *EX*. . . 4 E1-2
Holiday Bluff Dr *EX* 4 F3
Holiday Haven Rd *MA*. . 73 L12
Holiday Highpoint Dr *WT* . . 22 N24
Holiday Park Dr *MK*. . . . 59 T33
Holland Rd *LG* 37 B60
Holland Rd *NI*. 18 S33
Holland Rd *TB*. 102 D3
Holland-Sydenham Twnln *G* . . . . .
. . . . 39 A20-21
Holland Lake Rd *HS*. . . . 62 T46
Holland Landing Rd *Y* . . 30 E-F31
Holland Mills Rd *WT*. . . 22 P21
Holleford Rd *F* 36 A-B55
Hollen Rd *WL* 32 K21
Hollen Rd *SM*. 18 S33
Holliday Creek-Moosehead Lake
Access Rd *F* . 64 S53-54 T54
Holliday Point Rd *F* . 36 D57 37 D58
Hollister Rd *HS* 46 A49
Hollister Rd *SDG*. 67 U66
Hollow Rd *NI*. 19 S33
Hollow Rd *PE* 34 G47-48
Holloway Rd *HS* 34 C48
Holloway Bay Rd *NI* . . . 19 U35
Hollowtree Rd *K* 43 A36-37
Hollowview Rd *HS*. 34 C47-48 46 A48
Holly La *R* 63 Q49
Holly Rd *HS* 82 N52
Holly's La *PS* 56 Q25-26
Holly's Rd *PS* 76 P28
Holly Hill Rd *SDG* 68 T71
Hollywood La *MA*. 73 M12
Holman Rd *HS*. 34 D48
Homeland Dr *PS* 77 P33
Homer Watson Blvd *WT* . 22 N23-24
Homestead Dr *HM* 17 R28
Homestead Dr *NR* 33 D44
Homestead Rd *A* . 84 Z92-93
Homestead Rd *EL* 8 W15
Homestead Rd *HL* 61 V42
Homestead Rd *HU* 20 M13
Homestead Rd *LA* . . 47 B51-52
Homestead Rd *MA* 72 L10
Homestead Rd *NP*. 96 F36
Homestead Rd *R* 63 R49
Homestead Rd *SD* . . . 101 C23
Homesteaders Rd *OT* . 83 Q58-59
Homewood Rd *EX* . . . 5 H4-5
Homewood La *MD* . . 14 T-U16
Honey Ln *MD*. 33 D44
Honey Rd (Cramahe) *NR* . 33 F45
Honey Rd (Port Hope) *NR* . 33 E-F41
Honey Harbour Rd *MK*. . 41 W-X29
Honeysuckle Rd *K* . . 43 Y35-36
Honeywell Hill Rd *NR* . . . 33 F42
Honora Bay Rd *MA*. 90 J10
Honora Lakeshore Rd *MA* . . . . . .
. . . . 72 K10 90 J10
Hood Dr *DH*. 31 D36
Hood Rd *HM*. 23 N26
Hood Rd *NR* 59 R-S33
Hood Rd *SD*. 101 B-C22
Hoodstown Rd *MK* . . 50 Q-R32
Hoodstown Shores Dr *MK* . . . . . .
. . . . 58 Q-R32
Hoogeveen Rd *SD* 90 F12
Hook Lake Access Rd *HL* 61 V41-42
Hoover La *F* 48 Z55
Hoover Rd *HU* 20 J15
Hoover Rd *LN* 64 U55
Hoover Point Rd *HD* . . . 17 V28
Hope La *EX*. 5 E5
Hope Scdrd *OT* 66 S61
Hope-Ouimet Rd *SDG*. . 68 Q-R72
Hope Bay Rd *BR* . . . 55 V-W18
Hope Mill Rd *PB* 33 D-E40
Hopefield Rd *A*. . . 62 U48 81 P48
Hopeness Rd *BR* . . . 55 V17-18
Hopewell Creek Rd *WT*. . 22 N23-24
Hopkins Ln *K* 44 Y-Z38
Hopkins Rd *MK* . 43 W34 59 V34
Hopkins St *DH* 31 H36
Hopkins Bay Rd *A*. 87 E1
Hopkins Hill Rd *SD* 90 F13
Hopper Rd *A* 86 D-E97
Horan Rd *A* 86 C97
Horizon Rd *PS* 77 N32
Horizon View Rd *HU*. . . . 26 G13
Horn Rd *EX*. 16 S21
Hornby Rd *HT* 23 L28
Horncastle Rd *K*. 43 Y-Z35
Horne St *SM*. 41 Z29
Horne Lake Rd *LN* 64 U55
Horner Rd *PS* 76 M30
Hornes Rd *Y* 30 E32
Hornibrook Rd *PS* 77 L31
Hornick Ln *C* 6 X9
Horning Rd *F* 36 C55-56
Hornsberger Av *NI* . 18 R32 19 R33
Horrigan Rd *HS*. . . 47 B50-51
Horse Creek Rd, Concession *PS*. .
. . . . 68 P69-70
Horse Shoe Rd *PS* . 80 N47 81 N48
Horseshoe La *A* 84 X91
Horseshoe Bay Rd *A* . . . 84 X91
Horseshoe Hill Rd *PL* . . 29 G-H27
Horseshoe Lake Rd *CS* . 101 D-E20
Horseshoe Lake Rd *MK* . 60 V37-38
Horseshoe Valley Rd E *SM*. 41 A29
Horseshoe Valley Rd *SM* 42 Z30-31

Horseshoe Valley Rd W *SM*. . . . . .
. . . . 41 A28-29
Horton Av *NI* 19 R33
Horton Ln *C*. 6 B9 7 B10
Horton St *MD* 15 T17
Hoskin Rd *NR* 33 F43
Hoskins La *C* 7 Y12-13
Hospitality Rd *HL* 60 V37-38
Hossack La *LG* 49 Y59
Hoto Ln *HD* 18 U31
Hough Lake Rd *TM* . . . 85 L26-27
Houghton Rd *EL* 8 W15-16
Houghton Lake Access Rd *NP*. . . .
. . . . 97 F39-40
Houle Av *CS* 100 B16-17
Houle Rd *SD* 93 G24
Hound Lake Tr *HS*. 61 T44
House Ln *EL* 8 X16
House Rd *NI*. 19 T-U35
House Rd *PE* 35 H50-51
House Lake Rd *SD*. 90 G13
Houseys Rapids Rd *MK* . 42 W33
Houston Av *SM*. 30 C31
Houston Rd *DH* 31 F34
Houston Rd *HL*. 61 V43
Houston Rd *LN*. 49 V58
Houston Rd *MK*. 58 U32
How's Rd *K*. 44 A38-39
Howard Av *EX*. 4 B-E2
Howard Ln *TM*. 85 Q29
Howard Rd *A*. 81 P51
Howard Rd (Chatham-
Kent[Chatham]) *C*. 6 B9
Howard Rd (Chatham-
Kent[Howard]) *C* . . . 7 A10-11
Howard Thompson Rd *HL*. . 60 T38
Howards Rd *NF* . . . 9 W21 16 V21
Howards Sdrd *F* 48 X54
Howden Rd *DH* 31 F-G36
Howden Quarter Ln *PB* . . 32 D40
Howdenvale Rd *BR*. . . . 55 W16-17
Howe Lake Rd *LG* . . . 50 A62 Z62
Howe Island Dr *F* . . 36 D57 37 D58
Howe Island Ferry Rd *F* . . 36 D57
Howe Island Ferry Rd *LG* . 37 C58
Howell Rd *BT* 17 Q25
Howes Rd *F* 36 C54-55
Howes Rd *HS* 34 D47
Howes Rd (Loyalist) *LN* . . 36 C-D54
Howes Rd (Stone Mills) *LA* . 47 B52
Howes Lake La *F* 36 A54-55
Howey Dr *CS* 101 C19
Howey Ln *EL*. 16 V21
Howick-Minto Ln *WL* . . . 27 G-H19
Howick-Turnberry Rd *HU*. . . . .
. . . . 27 G18-19 G-H17
Howie Rd *OT*. 65 S60
Howland Junction Rd *HL*. 44 W-X38
Hoxton St *DH* 31 G34
Hoy Ln *C*. 6 C8
Hoyer Rd *DH* 32 E37
Hubb's Rd *PE* 34 F48-49
Hubbard Ln *LM*. 13 S10
Hubbard Rd *OX*. 16 Q22
Hubbard & Montgomery La *HL* . . .
. . . . 60 U40
Hubble Rd *PB* 45 Z44
Hubbs Creek Rd *PE* . . . 34 G48
Hubers Rd *F* 81 P49
Hudson Rd *A* *TM*. 85 Q28
Hudson Rd A3A *TM* . . 85 Q-R28
Hudson Rd C *TM* 85 R28
Hudson Rd C2 (Pike Lake Rd) *TM*
. . . . 85 R28
Hudson Rd C3 *TM*. 85 R28
Hudson Lake Dr *HL* 61 U42
Hueston Sdrd *LN* 49 V58
Huey Lake Rd *R* 98 F47
Huff Rd *HS* 46 B46-47
Huff Rd *NR* 33 F45
Huffman La *F* 7 A-B10
Huffman Rd *EX*. 4 E3
Huffman Rd *HS*. 34 D47
Huffman Rd *LA*. . . . 36 B54 47 B53
Huffman Rd *R*. 81 N50
Huff's Island Rd *PE* . . . 34 E-F49
Hugel Av *SM* 41 X28
Hugh Kennedy Rd *SDG*. . 68 R71
Hughes Dr *HL* 60 Q-R37
Hughes Rd *C* 6 X9
Hughes Rd *K* 43 Z37 44 Z38
Hughes Rd *LN*. 49 W-X59
Hughes Rd *MK* 43 X59-60
Hughes Rd (Central Frontenac) *F*. .
. . . . 48 X53
Hughes Rd (Kingston) *F*. . 36 C57
Hughes Lake Rd *PS*. . . . 76 M30
Hughes Landing Rd *LA*. . 47 W-X50
Hugill Rd *K* 43 Y37
Humans Rd *OT*. 67 Q65
Hulbert Rd *SDG* 50 V65
Hull La *HL* 43 W37
Hull's Rd *PB* 45 Z43
Hullett-McKillop Rd *HU* . . . .
. . . 20 J14 K15 L16 21 L17
Hult Rd *A* 84 Y94
Humber Station Rd *PL* . . . .
. . . . . . 29 G-H28 30 H29
Humbercrest Pkwy *PL* . 24 J29-30
Hume Ct *HT* 23 L27-28
Hume Rd *TB* 102 D3
Hume Rd *WL* 23 M26
Hume St *SM* 41 X28
Humes Rd *A*. 86 D93-94
Hummel Ln *PS* 95 H-J32
Hummingbird La *A* 84 X91
Hummingbird Rd *SDG* . . 67 U66-67
Hummingbird Hill Rd *SM* . 41 Z29
Humphrey Cir *A* 84 X91
Humphrey Rd *HL* 43 W37
Humphries Ln *PB* 33 C43
Humphries Rd *R* . 82 P55 83 P56
Hunata Rd *TB* 102 F1
Hungarian Rd *CS* 101 D21
Hungry Bay La *A*. . . . 47 X52 48 X53
Hungry Bay Rd *MK* . . . 58 V29

Hunsberger / Kent Bridge

Hunsberger Rd WT ... 22 M23
Hunsden Sdrd PL ... 29 G28 30 G29
Hunt Ln PS ... 95 H33
Hunt Rd HS ... 46 B49
Hunt Rd MD ... 15 S-T19
Hunt Rd MK ... 58 T29
Hunt Rd NR ... 33 F45
Hunt Rd SD ... 90 F12
Hunt Rd TB ... 102 D2-3
Hunt Rd (Addington Highlands) LA ... 47 X50
Hunt Rd (Stone Mills) LA ... 35 C53 47 B53
Hunt's Line Rd PB ... 44 A40
Hunt Club Rd HS ... 46 A48-49 Z48
Hunt Club Rd MK ... 59 V34
Hunt Club Rd OT ... 66 R63
Hunt Line Rd OT ... 83 Q58
Hunter Dr NF ... 10 X23
Hunter Dr PS ... 57 R27
Hunter La TB ... 102 E3
Hunter Ln (Dutton-Dunwich) EL ... 14 V14
Hunter Ln (Southwold) EL ... 8 W16
Hunter Pkwy DF ... 29 E25
Hunter Rd HM ... 17 Q25-26
Hunter Rd PR ... 68 P-Q70
Hunter Rd SD ... 101 B23
Hunter Rd (Grimsby) NI ... 18 Q-R30
Hunter Rd (Niagara-on-the-Lake) NI ... 19 Q34-35
Hunter Sdrd LN ... 48 V57
Hunter's Rd LG ... 49 W-X60
Hunter Creek Rd HL ... 43 W37
Hunters La PS ... 77 P31-32
Hunters Rd SDG ... 67 U67
Huntington Rd Y ... 24 J30
Huntingwood Dr HS ... 34 D48
Huntley Rd OT ... 66 S61
Huntmar Dr OT ... 65 R60 66 R61
Hunts Rd F ... 48 Z56-57
Hunts Rd MK ... 59 Q33
Hunts Rd R ... 81 L51 99 H49 K51
Hurd Rd LG ... 50 V63
Hurdville Rd PS ... 57 Q27 Q28 76 P27
Hurley Rd LG ... 50 X63
Hurley St A ... 86 B94
Hurling Point Rd MK ... 58 U30
Huron Av TB ... 103 C-D6
Huron Ln A ... 86 F94
Huron Rd HU ... 20 K13 L14-15
Huron Rd PT ... 21 M17
Huron Rd WT ... 22 N23 P21-23
Huron Rd (Huron-Kinloss) BR ... 26 F13
Huron Rd (South Bruce Peninsula) BR ... 55 W-X17
Huron St BR ... 38 A16
Huron St MD ... 15 S-T17
Huron St PT ... 21 P19
Huron St SDG ... 52 U71
Huron St SM ... 40 A25
Huron St WT ... 22 N22-23 P21
Huron St (Central Huron) HU 20 L14
Huron St (South Huron) HU ... 20 P13-16
Huron Ter BR ... 26 E13-14
Huron Tr MK ... 41 W29
Huron-Bruce Rd BR ... 27 G17-18
Huron-Kincardine Townline Rd E BR ... 26 E14-15
Huron-Kincardine Townline Rd W BR ... 26 E14
Huron-Kinloss Townline Rd BR ... 26 F14-15
Huron Church Rd EX ... 4 B-C1 C2
Huron Park Rd HU ... 14 Q15 20 P15
Huron Sands Rd HU ... 26 G13
Huron Shores Rd HU ... 26 G13
Hurondale Rd HU ... 20 N14-15
Huronia Rd (Innisfil) SM ... 30 C-D30
Huronia Rd (Severn) SM ... 42 Y32
Hurontario St DF ... 29 F-G26
Hurontario St PL ... 23 J28 24 L30 29 H26-27
Hurontario St SM ... 40 A25
Hurricane Rd NI ... 19 S33 S34
Hurst Dr SM ... 30 C30
Hurtubise Rd NP ... 95 F33
Husky Trail Rd SD ... 101 C23
Hussey Rd R ... 82 P-Q52
Hutcheson Rd MK ... 59 Q34-35
Hutcheson Beach Rd MK ... 59 R33
Hutchings Rd HL ... 60 U39
Hutchings Rd LG ... 48 Z57
Hutchinson Dr PB ... 32 D-E40
Hutchinson Rd HD ... 18 T-U31 U31-32
Hutchinson Rd MA ... 73 M11
Hutchinson Rd MD ... 13 Q12 14 Q13
Hutchinson Rd NR ... 33 D-E45
Hutchison Rd LG ... 37 B61
Hutchison Rd WT ... 22 M21
Hutsell Rd NR ... 33 F42
Hutson Rd R ... 83 Q56
Hutson Lake Rd R ... 63 T51
Hutt Rd SDG ... 51 W66
Hutton Rd LN ... 49 W60
Hutton Rd LG ... 49 W60
Hutton Access Rd CS ... 100 Z18
Hutton Hill Rd G ... 27 E20
Huyck St LA ... 35 E53
Huycke Rd NR ... 33 E45
Huycks Bay Rd PE ... 34 G48
Hybla Rd HS ... 62 S45-46 T45
Hyde Park Rd MD ... 14 R-S15 S-T16
Hydro La F ... 64 U53
Hydro Rd SD ... 101 A20
Hydro Bay Rd R ... 82 M53
Hydro Dam Rd NP ... 94 C28
Hydro Dam Rd R ... 64 S53
Hydro Line Rd HU ... 20 L15 M16
Hydro Line Rd TM ... 85 P-Q29
Hydroline Rd A ... 88 C3 C5
Hyland Rd EX ... 4 D3
Hyland Creek Rd R ... 63 S50-51
Hyler Ln K ... 44 Z38
Hymers Fair Dr TB ... 102 E2
Hyndford Rd R ... 82 P52-53
Hyndman Dr MD 7 W13 8 W14 14 V14
Hyndman Rd LG ... 50 V-W64
Hyndman Rd SDG ... 66 U64
Hysert Rd HS ... 62 U46
Hysert Rd NI ... 18 R30
Hyslop Ln LM ... 12 S8-9

I Ln A ... 86 E94 E95
Iawah Rd F ... 48 Y-Z56
Iber Rd OT ... 66 S61
Ice Lake Dr MA ... 72 J-K8
Ida St G ... 28 E24
Ida's Rd MA ... 72 K7
Ida Hill Rd F ... 36 B-C57
Iekel Rd HS ... 62 U45
Iikka Dr TB ... 102 C3
Ilderton Rd MD ... 14 S15-16 T14-15
Iler Rd EX ... 4 E-F3
Illman Rd HL ... 60 U39
Imperial Rd EL ... 9 W19 15 U19
Imperial Rd WL ... 23 M25
Imperial St SD ... 90 F10-11
Inadale Dr MD ... 14 T-U14 U-V13
Indian La LM ... 13 R10
Indian Ln BT ... 17 S25 T26
Indian Ln HD ... 17 U28 18 U29
Indian Rd LM ... 12 T7
Indian Rd PL ... 24 M30
Indian Rd R ... 82 L52-53
Indian Tr BR ... 55 Y17
Indian Tr HM ... 17 Q-R26
Indian Tr WL ... 23 L26
Indian Acres Rd W G ... 39 Z19
Indian Bay Rd TM ... 85 P-Q27
Indian Creek Ln C ... 6 A9
Indian Creek Rd C ... 6 A-B9
Indian Creek Rd LM ... 6 W7 12 V7
Indian Creek Rd OT ... 67 R66
Indian Creek Rd PR ... 67 Q-R66
Indian Harbour Rd BR ... 54 S14
Indian Hill Rd LN ... 65 R58
Indian Lake Rd LG ... 48 Z57
Indian Mountain Rd MA ... 73 K11-12
Indian Point La MA ... 73 N11-12
Indian Point Rd HL ... 60 T-U40
Indian Point Rd K ... 43 Z36
Indian Point Rd MA ... 72 K7
Indian Portage Rd A ... 88 F3
Indian Reserve Rd SD ... 90 F10-11
Indian River Ln PB ... 33 C42 45 B42
Indiana Rd E HD ... 17 T28 18 T29
Indiana Rd W HD ... 17 T28
Industrial Av OT ... 66 Q63
Industrial Blvd LA ... 35 D52
Industrial Pkwy SM ... 29 E28
Industrial Pkwy Y ... 30 G31-32
Industrial Rd C ... 7 Y10
Industrial Rd WT ... 22 P23
Industrial Rd S CS ... 100 C18 101 C19
Industrial Park Rd C ... 6 C7
Industrial Park Rd HL ... 60 U39
Industrial Park Rd NI ... 18 R-S31
Industrial Park Rd SM ... 30 C30
Ingersoll Rd OX ... 16 R-S21
Ingersoll St OX ... 15 S-T20
Inglehart Rd NI ... 18 R30-31
Inglesby Rd LA ... 47 B51-52
Inglis Cr BR ... 27 G18
Inglis Rd NR ... 33 F44
Inglis Rd R ... 82 Q54
Inglis Falls Rd G ... 39 A19
Ingoldsby Rd HL ... 60 V38
Ingram Rd A ... 87 E98-99
Ingram Rd HS ... 61 V44 62 V45
Ingram Rd SM ... 41 Z29 42 Z30
Ininatig Inamo R ... 81 N50
Inkerman Rd SDG ... 67 U65
Inkinen Tr HL ... 60 U40
Inksetter Rd HM ... 17 Q27
Inlet Bay Rd HL ... 61 U43
Inlet Creek Rd PS ... 77 L32
Inman Rd HD ... 18 U31
Inman Sdrd EX ... 4 D-E4
Inn Rd, The PS ... 76 P28
Innes Rd OT ... 66 Q64
Inneswood Tr PS ... 76 M-N30
Innis Lake Rd PL ... 24 I-J29 29 H28 30 H29
Inniscara Rd PB ... 44 B39
Innisfil Beach Rd SM ... 30 C30 C-D29
Innisfree Rd MK ... 58 U30
Inter-Provincial St PR ... 69 P73
Internal Ln C ... 7 C11
Intersection Rd EX ... 4 B3
Intola Rd TB ... 102 C4
Inukshuk Rd R ... 81 P48
Invader La HL ... 60 S38-39
Inverlochy Rd PS ... 56 Q25
Inverness Rd MK ... 58 S-T31
Inwood Rd LM ... 7 W10 13 U-V10
Iona Rd EL ... 8 W15 W-X16
Ipperwash Rd LM ... 13 Q-R11
Ira Lake Rd BR ... 55 U16
Ira Needles Blvd WT ... 22 N22
Irace Cr LG ... 50 Z63
Ireland Rd LG ... 49 X61
Ireland Rd NF ... 17 U-V25
Irena Rd SDG ... 50 W65 51 W66
Iris Dr K ... 43 A36
Irish Dr MD ... 14 U14-15 V13-14
Irish Ln HD ... 17 U28
Irish Ln MA ... 73 K11
Irish Ln PB ... 44 B40
Irish Ln SM ... 42 X30
Irish Rd LA ... 36 D54
Irish Block Rd G ... 39 Z20-21
Irish Headline Rd SDG ... 50 V65
Irish Lake Rd G ... 28 D22
Irish Lake Rd LG ... 49 Y60
Irish Line Rd HL ... 60 T38
Irish School Rd C ... 6 X9
Irishtown Rd LG ... 50 V63
Iron Bridge La HS ... 62 U46-47
Iron Bridge Tr HS ... 46 Z46
Iron Bridge Airport Rd A ... 87 E2
Iron City Rd LN ... 64 U54
Iron Mine Rd HL ... 43 W37 44 W38 X38
Iron Mine Rd LN ... 48 V56-57
Iron River Rd A ... 86 B94-95
Iron Springs Rd HU ... 20 L13
Irondale Rd HL ... 44 W39
Ironside Lake Rd CS ... 101 Y19
Ironside Lake Rd E CS ... 101 Y19
Ironside Lake Rd N CS ... 101 Y19
Iroquois Rd MK ... 58 V29
Iroquois Bay Rd SD ... 90 G13
Irvine Rd HD ... 18 S29
Irvine Rd NI ... 19 Q34
Irvine Rd (North Glengarry) SDG ... 68 Q72
Irvine Rd (South Dundas) SDG ... 50 W65
Irvine St WL ... 22 K23
Irving Dr Y ... 31 C33-34
Irving Goheen Rd NR ... 33 F41
Irwin Rd A ... 84 X92
Irwin Rd C ... 6 C8
Irwin Rd MD ... 15 T19
Irwin's Rd K ... 44 Z38-39
Irwin's Rd PS ... 76 N28
Isaac Lake Rd BR ... 55 X17
Isabella Lake Rd PS ... 57 Q28 58 Q29
Isaiah Hicks Rd HL ... 60 V38-39
Isbister Rd A ... 86 C94
Isku Park Rd TB ... 103 C6-7
Island Av TB ... 102 G5 103 G6
Island Rd A ... 84 Z91
Island Rd CS ... 100 D16-17
Island Rd DH ... 31 E36
Island Rd HS ... 46 Y48
Island Rd MD ... 14 S13
Island Rd PE ... 34 G49 35 G50
Island Rd SDG ... 68 T70
Island Rd SD ... 93 F24
Island Rd SM ... 42 X30
Island Rd (Elizabethtown-Kitley) LG ... 49 X-Y61
Island Drive La F ... 48 Y55
Island Lake Rd PS ... 77 M33
Island Park Rd MK ... 58 T30-31
Island View Dr A ... 86 E97
Island View Dr EX ... 4 F2
Island View Dr PS ... 56 Q26
Island View Rd R ... 81 N50
Island View Rd NR ... 33 D43
Islander Av MK ... 58 S30
Islandview Dr PB ... 33 E41
Islay Rd K ... 43 A36
Isle of Man Rd F ... 36 C57
Islington Av T ... 24 J-K31
Islington Av Y ... 24 J30
Issac Rd NR ... 33 E42
Issacson Rd CS ... 91 E15
Isthmus Rd LG ... 49 Z58
Isthmus Bay Rd BR ... 55 U17
Ivan Dr MD ... 14 T14
Ivans Rd R ... 82 P53
Ivy La HL ... 59 R36
Ivy La MA ... 73 L12
Ivy Acres Rd OT ... 65 R58 83 Q58
Ivy Ridge Rd PE ... 34 F49
Ixl Rd NR ... 33 C45
Izatt Lake Rd LN ... 48 V55

J-1, Sideroad BR ... 26 C14-15
Jack La PB ... 32 D39
Jack's Lake Rd PS ... 94 J28
Jack Chute Rd R ... 80 M47 81 M48
Jack Gordon Rd NR ... 33 F42
Jack Hills Rd PB ... 44 Z41
Jack Lake Rd PB ... 45 X-Y43
Jack Pine Tr K ... 43 X36
Jackies La HS ... 45 X45
Jacklin Cr PS ... 57 R28
Jacklin Rd SD ... 90 E13
Jacknife Rd PS ... 56 Q-R25
Jacks La HS ... 61 T44
Jackson Dr LN ... 64 T55
Jackson Dr NR ... 33 F45
Jackson Ln EL ... 9 W20-21
Jackson Rd G ... 39 Z18
Jackson Rd LA ... 47 B53
Jackson Rd LM ... 12 T8
Jackson Rd MD ... 15 T17
Jackson Rd MK ... 59 S33
Jackson Sdrd NF ... 16 U22
Jackson Mills Rd F ... 36 C-D55
Jacksons Rd PS ... 76 M30
Jacksons Falls Rd PE ... 35 G51
Jacksonville Rd MA ... 72 J9
Jacob Rd C ... 6 A-B7
Jacob St G ... 27 F19
Jacques Bay Rd LA ... 47 W50
Jadovin Rd NP ... 96 E37
Jakobi Rd NR ... 33 E44
Jakobsen Rd TB ... 103 C10
Jalna Blvd MD ... 15 T-U17
Jalonen Rd CS ... 91 E15
James Ln EL ... 9 W20
James Rd F ... 63 V52-53
James Rd HS ... 62 Q46
James Rd HD ... 18 T30
James Rd NR ... 33 D45
James Rd PB ... 45 A43
James Rd TM ... 85 M-N28
James St A ... 87 E2
James St HS ... 46 A46
James St HM ... 17 Q28
James St NF ... 16 U-V23
James St PT ... 15 Q18
James St TB ... 103 D6
James Bay Junction Rd PS ... 57 R27
James Camp Rd PS ... 77 N31-32
James Naismith Way LN ... 65 S58
James Rider Rd PS ... 75 P25
James Snow Ln HT ... 23 M28 24 M29
James Snow Pkwy HT ... 23 M28 24 M29
James Wilson Rd F ... 36 A55 48 Z55
Jamestown Ln EL ... 9 W18-19
Jamestown Rd HU ... 21 J18 26 H16 27 H17
Jamieson La HS ... 62 U46-47
Jamieson Pkwy WT ... 22 N24 23 N25
Jamieson Rd F ... 36 B55
Jamieson Rd HS ... 34 E46
Jamieson Rd NR ... 34 E46
Jamieson Rd (Hamilton) NR ... 33 F41
Jamieson Rd (Port Hope) NR ... 33 F41
Jane Rd C ... 7 X11
Jane St C ... 7 Y10-11
Jane St T ... 24 J-K31
Jane St Y ... 24 I-J31 30 F30 G-H31
Janes La SM ... 42 X30
Janet Dr LN ... 65 T57
Janet Bay Lighthouse Rd MA ... 72 J7
Janetville Rd K ... 32 D37-38
Janti Rd CS ... 91 E15
Janveau Rd NP ... 96 E38
Jarden Rd HD ... 18 T30
Jardun Mine Rd A ... 84 A93 86 B93
Jarrett Dr A ... 86 E97
Jarvi Rd CS ... 101 D19
Jarvies Rd MK ... 58 R32
Jarvis Rd NR ... 33 G42
Jarvis Rd (Madoc) HS ... 46 A47
Jarvis Rd (Quinte West) HS ... 34 E46
Jarvis St T ... 24 K-L32
Jarvis Bay Rd TB ... 102 G4-5
Jasper Av LN ... 49 W60
Jasper Dr K ... 43 A36
Jasper Rd LG ... 49 W60
Jasper Martin Rd NR ... 33 E42
Jay Bryant Sdrd MA ... 73 L12
Jaynes Rd DH ... 32 G-H39
Jean Rd SD ... 101 B22-23
Jean St SD ... 92 G22
Jean Marie Rd PS ... 58 S29
Jeanne d'Arc Rd OT ... 66 P-Q64
Jeannette's Creek Rd C ... 6 B-C7
Jeff Rd PB ... 45 W42-43
Jefferies Rd MD ... 14 T15
Jefferson Blvd EX ... 4 B2
Jefferson Sdrd Y ... 30 H31
Jeffery Dr HS ... 34 E48
Jeffray Ln HU ... 27 G17
Jeffrey Rd A ... 86 D96-97
Jeffrey Rd HL ... 61 U41
Jeffrey's Rd PS ... 77 M-N31
Jeffrey Lake Rd HS ... 62 U45
Jelly Rd TB ... 102 D4
Jelly Rd N TM ... 85 Q30
Jellyby Rd LG ... 49 Y61 50 X62 Y62
Jenkins Rd HU ... 20 K-L14
Jenkins Rd K ... 43 Z37
Jenkins Rd LG ... 37 A61
Jenkins Rd NF ... 16 T24 17 S25
Jenkins Townline NF ... 16 T24
Jenna Rd LM ... 13 Q12
Jenner Ln C ... 7 A10
Jennings Rd R ... 98 F46
Jennings Rd SDG ... 67 U65
Jennison Rd HS ... 46 X46
Jenny Jump Rd HD ... 18 T-U31
Jenson Rd LG ... 37 B58
Jericho Rd LM ... 13 R11
Jericho Rd LN ... 65 U59
Jericho Rd PE ... 34 F49
Jermey Rd SM ... 42 X31
Jermyn Ln PB ... 33 E41
Jerome St LN ... 65 U58
Jeromes Rd R ... 62 R48 63 R49
Jerseyville Rd BT ... 17 R26
Jerseyville Rd HM ... 17 Q27 R26
Jerusalem Rd PS ... 76 K30 77 K31
Jerusalem Hill Rd MA ... 72 K9
Jesse Pl WT ... 22 L22
Jesse Thomson Rd Y ... 30 F32 31 F33
Jessie Rd R ... 83 Q56
Jessup La MK ... 59 Q33
Jessup Rd HS ... 62 R45
Jessup Rd (Brudenell, Lyndoch and Raglan) R ... 63 R49
Jessup Rd (North Algona Wilberforce) R ... 82 N52
Jessups Falls Rd PR ... 67 P68
Jewel Rd DH ... 32 F-G39
Jewel Bridge Rd BR ... 55 Y17
Jewell Rd NR ... 33 E43
Jewellville Rd R ... 62 R48
Jibb Rd NR ... 33 F41-42
Jig St LG ... 50 W62-63
Jigs Hollow Rd WT ... 22 L-M23
Jill La PB ... 32 D39
Jim Barr Rd R ... 82 P55
Jim Kimmett Rd LA ... 35 D52
Jim Snow Dr LA ... 36 D-E54
Jim Wood La MK ... 42 W31
Jim Young Rd PS ... 77 K31
Jingo Lake Rd MK ... 59 Q33
Jinkinson Rd OT ... 65 S60
Joanette Rd CS ... 100 B17
Joanisse Rd PR ... 67 P-Q66
Jobb Rd DH ... 32 E37
Jobidon Rd R ... 98 F46
Jocelyn St NR ... 33 G41
Jochem Rd LG ... 50 W63-64
Jock Tr OT ... 66 T61
Jocko Point Rd NP ... 94 D-E29
Jockvale Rd OT ... 66 S62
Jocques Bay Rd A ... 86 F96
Joe's Lake Rd LN ... 64 T55
Joe Baye Tr LN ... 65 T57-58
Joe King Rd MK ... 41 W29
Joe Koran Rd PS ... 77 L31
Joe Lake Rd CS ... 101 A19 Z19
Joe Oliver Rd NR ... 33 G42-43
Joe River Rd MK ... 58 T30
Jogi Rd HS ... 61 T43
John St A ... 89 F8-9
John St DF ... 29 H26
John St EL ... 15 V19
John St G ... 40 Z22
John St K ... 32 E38
John St MA ... 72 L9
John St NI ... 18 R32
John St TB ... 103 D6
John St Y ... 24 J32
John St (Champlain) PR ... 68 N71
John St (Hawkesbury) PR ... 68 N71
John's Rd DH ... 32 E37
John Aselford Dr OT ... 65 Q-R60
John Buchler Rd MK ... 41 W29
John Counter Blvd F ... 36 D56
John Creek Rd SD ... 100 C-D14
John F Scott Rd F ... 36 C57
John Kennedy Way OT ... 65 S59
John Lake La HS ... 62 V46
John Markell Rd SDG ... 51 V66
John Martin Cr HM ... 23 P28
John Martin Rd F ... 36 A55
John McInroy Rd HS ... 34 C48
John Meyers Rd HS ... 34 D47-48
John Park Ln C ... 6 X7-8
John Pound Rd OX ... 16 U21
John Quinn Rd OT ... 66 S64
John Shaw Rd OT ... 83 Q59
John Stone Rd PB ... 45 Z42
John Street Rd TB ... 102 D4-5
John Watson Rd R ... 62 Q48
John Wise Ln EL ... 8 W17 9 W18-20 14 V16
Johnnie Lake Rd MA ... 91 H17
Johnny Lake Access Rd R ... 81 L49
Johnnys La F ... 63 V53
Johnson Rd BT ... 17 R25
Johnson Rd EX ... 4 E3
Johnson Rd HD ... 18 U30
Johnson Rd NP ... 95 E33
Johnson Rd NI ... 18 T32 U32
Johnson Rd (Lorne Twp) CS ... 91 E15 100 D15
Johnson Rd (Scadding Bay) CS ... 101 A22
Johnson Rd (Wahnapitae) CS ... 101 C21
Johnson St F ... 36 D56
Johnson St PE ... 35 F-G50
Johnson Tr R ... 82 Q52
Johnson's Sdrd LA ... 35 D51
Johnson's Beach Sdrd HU ... 20 K13
Johnson Bay Rd HL ... 60 S40
Johnsons Rd PS ... 76 N30
Johnsons Ferry Rd PR ... 67 Q68
Johnsons Harbour Rd BR ... 54 T15
Johnston Dr PB ... 33 D41
Johnston Ln EL ... 7 X12-13
Johnston Ln HU ... 21 J17
Johnston Rd F ... 48 X-Y53
Johnston Rd K ... 43 A37
Johnston Rd LM ... 7 W-X11
Johnston Rd LG ... 37 A61 50 A62
Johnston Rd MA ... 73 L11
Johnston Rd NR ... 33 E44
Johnston Rd OT ... 66 R63
Johnston Rd PE ... 35 G51
Johnston Rd PR ... 67 Q67
Johnston Rd R ... 82 P55
Johnston Rd (Athens) LG ... 49 Y61
Johnston Rd (Augusta) LG 50 X-Y63
Johnston Rd (Centre Hastings) HS ... 46 B49
Johnston Rd (Madoc) HS ... 46 A48
Johnston Rd (North Grenville) LG ... 50 V63
Johnston's Sdrd G ... 28 C22
Johnstone Rd NR ... 33 E-F42
Johnstown Rd HS ... 34 E47
Johny's Park Dr MA ... 72 L10
Joice Rd NR ... 33 F43
Jolee Dr HL ... 60 R37
Jolliffe La PS ... 56 Q24
Jonas St LG ... 37 A59
Jones Baseline WL ... 22 J23-24 K24 23 L25
Jones Dr MD ... 14 U15-16
Jones Rd HL ... 60 U37
Jones Rd HM ... 18 Q30
Jones Rd MK ... 58 V32
Jones Rd PE ... 35 F50
Jones Rd PS ... 57 Q28 76 P28
Jones Rd (Centre Hastings) HS ... 46 A49
Jones Rd (Cramahe) NR ... 33 E44
Jones Rd (Malahide) EL ... 9 W-X19
Jones Rd (Marmora) HS ... 46 A46-47
Jones Rd (Port Port Hope) NR ... 32 G40
Jones Rd (Southwold) EL ... 8 W-X16
Jones Falls Rd LG ... 37 A58
Jones Quarter Ln PB ... 32 D39
Jopling Rd HL ... 44 W-X38
Jopling Rd PB ... 44 A41
Jordan Ln OX ... 15 S-T20
Jordan Rd LG ... 50 X65
Jordan Rd NI ... 18 R32
Jordon La F ... 47 Y52
Joseph St PS ... 57 Q-R27
Josephine St HU ... 26 H16
Josie La R ... 99 G48
Joslin Rd NI ... 18 S31
Joslin's La F ... 37 D58
Joudrey Rd CS ... 101 C21
Journey's End Tr HL ... 60 V40
Joy Rd F ... 36 D-E57
Joy Rd MK ... 42 W32
Joy's Rd OT ... 66 S-T61
Joy Bible Camp Rd HS ... 61 U44 62 U45
Joyce Rd HS ... 46 B48
Joyce Rd LA ... 35 C52
Joyce Rd MA ... 70 J2
Joyceville Rd F ... 36 C57
Joywind Rd HS ... 46 B46
Jubilee Dr MD ... 14 V14-15
Juddhaven Rd MK ... 58 S-T30
Judge Jordan Rd HL ... 60 V37
Jules La MA ... 72 K10
Jules Leger, Rue SM ... 41 X26
Julia's Creek Rd PB ... 45 Z43
Julian Dr BR ... 55 W16
Julian Lake Rd PB ... 45 Z42
Juliana Rd Y ... 30 F31
Jumbo Rd CS ... 101 C-D21
Junction Rd HD ... 18 T29
Junction Rd LM ... 13 V12
Junetown Rd LG ... 37 A61
Juniper Dr MK ... 42 W31 58 V31
Juniper Rd R ... 63 T51
Juniper Tr K ... 43 Z35
Juniper Isle Rd K ... 43 Z37
Juniper Point Rd PB ... 45 Z42
Junot Av TB ... 103 D6
Jura Ln LM ... 13 S11-12
Jury Rd BT ... 17 R26
Jury Rd MD ... 14 T15

K Ln A ... 86 E95 E-F94
Kaboni Rd MA ... 73 L13
Kagawong Rd K ... 43 A37 Z37
Kahles Rd A ... 88 F3-4
Kaihla Rd A ... 84 W90-91
Kain Rd LG ... 50 X65
Kains Rd MD ... 14 T16
Kairshea Av BR ... 26 F-G15
Kaiser Crossroad PE ... 35 F52-53
Kakapshe Rd A ... 84 W90
Kaladar Gun Club Rd LA ... 47 Y51
Kalar Rd NI ... 19 R-S34
Kale's Spur Rd PS ... 77 K31
Kalio Rd CS ... 100 D18
Kallio Rd PS ... 77 N34
Kallio Rd SD ... 101 C22-23
Kalman Dr PB ... 32 E40
Kalmo Rd CS ... 101 A-B19
Kamaniskeg Lake Rd HS ... 62 Q46
Kamp Kagawong Rd MA ... 72 K8
Kanata Av OT ... 66 R61
Kantola Rd CS ... 100 D18
Kantor Ln C ... 6 B7
Kapikog Dam Rd PS ... 57 T28
Kapikog North Rd PS ... 57 T28
Kapikog South Rd PS ... 57 T28
Kapkigwan Rd TM ... 85 M28
Karalash Rd A ... 84 Y92
Karek Rd BT ... 17 R25
Kargus Rd R ... 63 R50
Kari Rd CS ... 101 C21
Karn Rd OX ... 15 S20
Kartuzy Rd R ... 80 P46-47
Kasaboski Rd R ... 82 P54-55
Kashagawigmog Lake Rd HL ... 60 U39 V38
Kashwakamak Lake Rd F ... 47 W-X51
Katesville Dr MD ... 13 T12 14 T13
Katherine St WT ... 22 L-M23
Kathleen Rd CS ... 101 Z22
Kathleen Rd R ... 64 S53
Katimavik Rd OT ... 66 R61
Katona Rd R ... 63 R49
Katrine Rd PS ... 77 N32
Kauffeldt Rd R ... 63 Q49
Kavanaugh Rd LG ... 50 Z62
Kawagama Lake Rd HL ... 59 S36 60 S37
Kawagama Lake Rd MK ... 59 R-S36
Kawartha Hideaway Rd PB ... 44 A40
Kawartha Park Rd PB ... 45 A42 Z42
Kay La FO ... 47 Y52
Kay Rd W MK ... 59 S33
Kean Rd R ... 99 H48
Kearnan Rd SM ... 29 C28
Kearney Rd PS ... 77 N-P33
Kearney Lake Access Rd NP 96 E36
Keating Rd HS ... 34 D47
Keating Rd PB ... 45 A44-45
Keays Rd LN ... 48 V-W57
Kecil Rd A ... 89 E8-9
Kedroski Rd R ... 80 N46
Keech Rd LA ... 47 B53
Keegan's Rd LA ... 47 A51
Keele St T ... 24 J-K31
Keele St Y ... 24 I-J31 30 F-H31
Keeler Rd MK ... 58 U-V30
Keeley Rd F ... 36 B55-56
Keenansville Rd SM ... 29 F28
Keene Rd HS ... 46 Z48
Keene Rd PB ... 33 C-D41
Keewaydin Rd BR ... 38 A16-17
Keewaydin Rd HL ... 60 V38
Keezel Rd R ... 80 P47
Keg La BT ... 16 R23-24
Keil Dr C ... 6 A8-9
Keir La F ... 36 B56
Keith Rd R ... 82 P55 83 P56
Keith Richardson Pkwy HD ... 17 U26
Kellam Rd MD ... 14 U13
Kellar Rd LA ... 47 Y51
Kellars Crossroad PE ... 35 F-G52
Kelleher Rd NR ... 33 D45 34 D46
Keller Rd R ... 63 Q51
Kellers Bridge Rd HS ... 46 Z47-48
Kellett Rd OX ... 16 U21
Kellogg Rd NR ... 32 F-G40
Kells Rd NP ... 95 G33
Kelly Dr NR ... 33 E44
Kelly Rd EX ... 4 C1-2
Kelly Rd HS ... 34 C48
Kelly Rd LM ... 12 V9
Kelly Rd NR ... 33 E41-42
Kelly Rd PE ... 35 H50-51
Kelly Rd (Elizabethtown-Kitley) LG ... 50 Z63
Kelly Rd (North Dundas) SDG ... 67 T66
Kelly Rd (Rideau Lakes) LG ... 48 Y57
Kelly Rd (South Dundas) SDG ... 50 W65
Kelly Rd, The HL ... 60 R-S38
Kelly St LM ... 13 T11
Kelly's Rd LG ... 49 X60
Kelly's Bay Rd K ... 44 A38
Kelly Creek Rd A ... 84 Z91
Kelly Jordan Rd LN ... 49 V60
Kelly Lake Rd CS ... 101 C19
Kelly Lake Rd R ... 81 L-M50
Kellys Rd R ... 64 R53
Kellyville Rd LA ... 47 A53
Kelson Av NI ... 18 Q-R30
Kelvin Rd NF ... 16 T23
Kelvin Rock Rd K ... 43 Y37
Kemble By-Pass G ... 39 Y19-20
Kemble Rock Rd G ... 39 X19
Kemp Ln C ... 5 D7 6 C7
Kemp Rd MK ... 58 U30
Kemp Rd NI ... 18 R30-31
Kemp Lake Rd MA ... 71 J4
Ken Av R ... 81 L51
Ken Dr R ... 81 L51
Ken's Rd PB ... 44 Z39
Ken Dick Rd R ... 82 Q52-53
Kendal Rd NF ... 10 W24
Kendall Rd C ... 6 C9
Kendall Rd LA ... 47 B51
Kendon Rd MK ... 58 T29
Kendrick Creek La HL 44 W38 60 V38
Kendricks La LG ... 49 Z59
Kenedon Dr K ... 32 C39 44 B39
Kenelly Rd R ... 82 P53
Kenesserie Rd C ... 7 A12 Y11
Kenilworth Av HM ... 18 Q29
Kennaway Rd HL ... 60 U40
Kennebec Rd F ... 47 X51
Kennebec Rd LA ... 47 X51
Kennedy Dr PB ... 44 Z40
Kennedy La LG ... 37 A59 49 Z59
Kennedy Ln LM ... 13 R11-12
Kennedy Rd C ... 6 Y7
Kennedy Rd HS ... 62 S47
Kennedy Rd LG ... 50 V63 66 U63
Kennedy Rd NR ... 33 F41
Kennedy Rd OT ... 67 T65
Kennedy Rd PL ... 23 J28 24 K29 L30 29 H27
Kennedy Rd R ... 64 R-S54
Kennedy Rd SDG ... 68 S71
Kennedy Rd T ... 25 J33
Kennedy Rd Y ... 25 I-J33 30 C-G32 31 G-H33
Kennedy Bay Rd K ... 44 B38
Kennelly Rd HS ... 35 D51
Kennelly Mountain Rd R ... 64 R-S53
Kennesis Lake Rd HL ... 60 S38
Kenneth Av NF ... 17 V26
Kenneth Dr CS ... 101 A19
Kenney's Rd LG ... 37 A58
Kenning Pl WT ... 22 L22-23
Kennisis Lake Rd HL ... 60 T38-39
Kenny Rd R ... 98 F46
Kenrei Rd K ... 43 B37
Kens Rd PB ... 44 Z39
Kenshore La EX ... 4 F3
Kensington Rd A ... 86 D95
Kensington Rd HL ... 61 U41
Kenstone Beach Rd K ... 44 A39
Kent Line HU ... 21 K17
Kent Ln LM ... 6 X8-9 7 X10
Kent Rd PS ... 77 M32-33
Kent St K ... 32 C37
Kent Bridge Rd C ... 6 X9 7 A-B11 X10

Kent Mill Access Rd PS 77 L34
Kents Bay Rd PB . . . 33 D41-42
Kents Mill Rd PS 77 L33-34
Kentucky Hill Rd HD. . . . 18 T30
Kenwood Dr G 40 Z23
Kenyon Rd R 49 W58
Kenyon-Roxborough Boundary Rd
SDG. 68 N-S69
Kenyon Dam Rd SDG . 68 R-S71
Kenyon Point Dr EX. . . . 5 E-F5
Kepler Rd F 36 C55
Kerby Rd HS 46 B48
Kerford Rd LG 50 W-X62
Kerns Rd HT 23 P28
Kernsghan Rd NR . . 33 F-G44
Kerr Ln LM. 6 W8
Kerr Ln R 82 N54-55
Kerr Rd EL . . . 7 X13 8 Y14
Kerr Rd F 36 B54
Kerr St HT 24 N30
Kerr Point Rd LA. 36 E54
Kerrie Glen Rd MK . . . 58 U32
Kerrigan Rd LM. 12 T9
Kerrs Rd TM. 85 M28
Kerrs Ridge Rd SDG . 66 U64 67 U65
Kerry Ln PB 44 B39-40
Kerry Rd LM. 7 W11
Kerry's Ln HU. 26 G13-14
Kerry Point Rd LG. . . . 37 B61
Kerwin Rd OT 66 R61
Kerwood Rd MD . 13 S-U12 14 R-S13
Keswick Rd OX . . . 15 U20 16 U21
Ketchanookeem Tr MA . 72 L9-10
Ketcheson Rd HS 46 Z48
Ketchesons Rd HS . . . 34 D48
Kett Rd K 43 X34
Kettle La LM 12 U9
Kettle's Beach Rd SM . 41 W27
Kettleby Rd Y. 30 F-G31
Kettles Rd OT 66 T61
Ketto Rd CS 100 D15
Keyhole Rd PS 56 R25
Kidd Ln C 6 C8
Kidd Rd LA. 4 B51-52
Kidd Rd LN. 65 T-U60
Kidd Rd N LG. 37 B60
Kidd Rd S LG 37 B-C60
Kieffer Ln HU 27 H17
Kilally Rd MD. 15 S17
Kilbourne Rd MD 14 U16
Kilbride St HT . . . 73 N27-28
Kildeer Rd E 5 F6
Killmanjaro La G. . . 39 Y20-21
Kilkenny Rd LG 50 Z62
Kilkenny Tr SM 30 E30
Killaly St NI. 19 U33-34
Killarney Bay Rd K . . 43 A36-37 B37
Killarney Beach Rd SM . 30 D30-31
Killpecker Creek Access Rd LA. .
. . . . 63 U50
Kilmarnock Rd LG 49 W61
Kilmartin Rd HS 62 S47
Kilmaurs Sdrd OT . . 83 P-Q59
Kilts Rd NI 18 T32
Kilworthy Rd MK 42 W32
Kimball Rd C 6 X7
Kimball Rd LM. 12 U-V7
Kimberly Dr HU 26 G13
Kimberly Rd PB. 44 B40
Kimmerly Rd HS. 35 D51
Kimmett's Sdrd LA . . . 35 D52
Kinburn Ln HU. 20 L15
Kinburn Sdrd LN. . . . 65 R58
Kinburn Sdrd OT. . . . 83 Q59
Kincardine Av BR . . 26 E13-14
Kincardine-Kinloss Townline Rd
BR 26 E-F15
Kinch Rd LG 50 X62
Kinch St LG 49 X60-61
Kinch's Sdrd G. . . . 39 X-Y19
Kinders La R. 63 U49
King Rd HS 46 A49
King Rd HD 18 U31
King Rd HT . . 18 P29 23 P28
King Rd NI. 19 T35
King Rd OX 16 Q22
King Rd PR 67 R66
King Rd TB 102 E5
King Rd Y 30 G31 H30
King Rd (Alnwick-Haldimand) NR . .
. . . . 33 F42
King Rd (Hamilton) NR . . 33 E41
King Rd BT 16 S24
King St BR 26 C-D14
King St C. 6 X7
King St F. 36 D56
King St HD 17 T27
King St HU 20 N14-15
King St MD 14 R15
King St NF 16 U23
King St NR 33 G42
King St OX 15 S20
King St PL . . . 23 J28 30 H29
King St PT 21 M-N20
King St SD 93 D24
King St SM 29 E28
King St TM 85 M30
King St WT 22 N23-24
King St Y 30 F31
King St (Brock) DH . . 31 D34
King St (Clarington) DH . 32 G38-39
King St (Essa) SM . . 30 D-E29
King St (Flamborough) HM. 17 Q27
King St (Hamilton) HM 17 Q28 18 Q29
King St (Kawartha
Lakes[Omemee]) K . . 32 C39
King St (Kawartha
Lakes[Woodville]) K. . 43 B35
King St (Lansdowne) LG. . 37 B60
King St (Lincoln) NI. . . 18 R31
King St (Midland) SM . 41 X28
King St (Niagara-on-the-Lake) NI . .
. . . . 19 Q35
King St (Oshawa) DH. 31 H36 32 H37
King St (Port Colborne) NI . 19 U33
King St (Scugog) DH . 31 F35-36
King St (Welland) NI . . 19 T33
King St N 22 M22
King's Row 18 U30
King's Creek Rd LN . . 65 U60
King's Farm Rd MK . . 41 W29
King's Wharf Rd K . . 44 B38-39
King-Vaughan Rd Y . . 30 G31
King & Whittle Rd C . 5 D7 6 C7
King Edward St BT . . . 16 R24
King George Rd BT . . 17 R25

King George Rd MK. . . . 41 W29
King Lake Rd PS . . . 77 K31 95 J31
Kingfisher La K 43 Z36
Kingma Cr BR 55 W17
Kings Cr BR 55 W17
Kings Dr PS. 77 P31
Kings Ln K 43 B36-37
Kings Rd BR 26 G16
Kings Rd PB. 44 Y40-41
Kings Rd PE 35 H50
Kings Rd PS 95 H31
Kings Rd R 99 H49
Kings Rd SDG . 68 S72 T70-71 69 S73
Kings Rd WT. 22 P23
Kings Ferry Rd C 6 X8
Kings Grant Rd NR . . 45 B46
Kings River Rd SM . . 42 X33
Kingsbridge Ln HU . . 26 G13
Kingscote Lake Rd HL . 61 S41-42
Kingscourt Rd Y 30 G31
Kingscross Dr Y 30 G31
Kingsett Rd MK 58 T30
Kingsford Lake Dam Rd F . 48 B58
Kingsland Av DF. . . 29 E26-27
Kingsley Rd PE 35 G51
Kingston Dr G. 27 D19
Kingston Ln LN 48 W55
Kingston Rd DH . . 31 H34-35
Kingston Rd T . . . 25 J34 K33
Kingston Mills Rd F . . 36 C-D56
Kingsway CS . . . 101 C19-20
Kingsway NI 19 T33
Kinhuron Rd BR 26 D14
Kinlin Rd HS 35 D51
Kinloch Rd SDG . 52 U71 68 T70-71
Kinloss-Culross Townline Rd BR. .
. . . . 26 F-G16
Kinnaird Rd LM . . . 13 R-S11
Kinnear Sdrd SM. . . . 42 X30
Kinnos Rd CS. . . 91 E15 100 D15
Kinogama Av F. 36 D57
Kinsale Rd DH. 31 G35
Kinsale Rd PB. 44 A40
Kinsmen Rd NI . . . 18 R31-32
Kintail Ln HU . . . 26 F-G13
Kintyre La R 7 X-Y12
Kintyre Tr R 81 P50
Kipling Av R . . . 24 J30 K-L31
Kipling Av Y . . . 24 J30 30 H30
Kippen Rd HU . . 20 M15 N13-14
Kippen Rd R . . . 64 R56 83 Q56
Kippen Rd SDG. 68 R69
Kirby Rd A 84 Z92
Kirby Rd Y. 97 9 H30-31
Kirbyson Rd TM . . . 85 N28-29
Kirk Ln M. 59 U33
Kirk Ln W MK. 59 U33
Kirk Rd LM. 18 S29
Kirk Rd LA 47 A53
Kirk Kove Rd F 47 X52
Kirker Rd SDG. 50 V65
Kirkfield Rd (Kawartha
Lakes[Carden Dalton]) K 43 Z34-35
Kirkfield Rd (Kawartha
Lakes[Eldon]) K. . . 43 A35-36
Kirkham Rd LN 48 W56
Kirkpatrick La HS . . 46 A48 Z48
Kirkpatrick Rd PS. . . . 56 R26
Kirkton Rd HU . . . 20 P13-16
Kirkwood Rd HM. . . . 23 P26
Kirkwood Rd SDG. . . . 50 V65
Kirkwood Mine Rd SD . 101 B20
Kirwin Rd SD . . . 101 C22-23
Kister Rd NI. 19 T33
Kit Pak Rd MK 59 S-T34
Kitchen Rd R . . . 10 W25 17 V25
Kitchen Sdrd SM . . . 42 X30-31
Kitchen School Rd BT. . 16 Q-R24
Kitchens Rd HM 17 Q26
Kitchigami Rd A 84 Z90
Kitley-Bastard and South Burgess
Townline Rd LG. . . 49 Y59-60
Kitley-Elizabethtown Townline Rd
LG. 49 Y59-60
Kitley-South Elmsley Townline Rd
LG. 49 X59-60
Kittle Rd SDG. 67 T-U66
Kitty Murray La HM . . 17 Q27-28
Kivela Rd TB 102 F1 F-G2
Kivi Rd CS 101 D21
Kivikoski Rd TB. . . . 102 C5
Kivinen Rd TB 102 B5
Kivipelto Rd TB 102 C3
Klages Rd TB . . . 102 E-F4
Kleiner Rd NI. 19 T33
Kleinsteuber Parks Rd PE . 35 G50
Klima La F. 63 V52
Klitbo Rd LG 60 R37
Klock's Rd NP 97 E-F39
Klock's Access Rd NP. .
. . . . 96 E38 F38 97 F39
Kloepfer Rd BT 16 S23
Klondike Rd HL 60 T39
Klondike Rd LN. . . . 65 S57
Klondike Rd OT. . . . 66 R61
Klondike Rd R 63 Q51
Klondike Rd E OT . . . 66 T62
Klondike Rd W OT . . . 66 U62
Klondike Bay Rd CS. . 101 A22
Klondike Park Rd SM . 41 A-B27
Klondyke Ln C 7 A12
Klondyke Rd C 5 E-67
Klondyke Rd LM. . . . 13 Q12
Knapdale Dr MD . 7 W12 13 V12
Knapps Island Rd EX. . . 4 E1
Knappville Rd G . . . 27 E19
Knight La F 47 Y52
Knight La NI 13 Q12
Knight Rd TM 85 M27
Knights Ln C . . . 36 C55-56
Knights La C 7 A10
Knox Rd C 7 Y11
Knox Rd NP 95 D33
Knox Rd S DH. . . . 23 C42
Knox Rd W SM . . 41 A26-27
Knox St NP 95 D33
Knox Point Rd PB . . 45 W43
Knoxville Rd NR. . . 33 F-G41
KOA Campground Rd HS. 46 A47
Koabel Rd (Niagara Falls) NI . .
. . . . 19 T34-35
Koabel Rd (Port Colborne) NI . .
. . . . 19 T34
Kodiac Rd PS . . . 76 N-P28

Kodiak Rd K 43 A36
Kodiak Rd NI 22 N21
Kohl Rd WT. 22 N21
Kohler Rd HD 17 U28
Kohlsmith Rd R. . . 82 M-N54
Koivu Rd TB 102 C5
Kokamis Inamo Rd R . 81 N50
Kokomo Tr MA 73 M12
Kollsneke Rd PS. . . . 56 R25
Komoka Rd MD 14 T15
Kontola Rd CS . . . 101 D21
Kopernik Rd R . . . 62 Q47-48
Koshlong Lake Rd HL. . 60 V39
Kossuth Rd R 22 N24
Kotala Rd TB 102 G2
Kottmeier Rd NI . . . 19 S34
Kowal Rd R 62 R47
Kozy Kove Rd K . . . 43 Y37
Kraft Rd WT 22 M23
Kraft Rd NI 19 U36
Kraft Rd R 81 M50
Kraft Rd SDG 68 T72
Kramp Rd WT. 22 M24
Kranz Rd R 81 N49
Kratz Rd EX 4 E4
Krauter Ln HU 21 K18
Kress Rd C 7 A12
Kressler Rd WT . . . 22 M22
Kribs Rd BR 55 X18
Kring's Rd SD. 89 F9
Krings La F 63 V52
Krista La MD . . . 14 U-V14
Kubesheski Rd R . . . 62 Q46
Kuglin Rd HL 34 D48
Kuiack Rd R 81 P48
Kuiack Lake Rd R. . . 62 Q48
Kukagami Rd CS . 101 A22 Z22
Kukagami Lake Rd SD 101 A-B22 Z22
Kully Tr HL 61 U42
Kuno Rd (Carlow Mayo) HS. 62 S47
Kuno Rd (Hastings Highlands) HS. .
. . . . 62 T45
Kunopaski Rd K . . . 43 Q57
Kushog Lake Rd HL . 60 T-U37
Kuskita Rd CS. 91 E16
Kutschke Rd R 81 N51
Kuusisto Rd TB . . . 102 C4
Kydd La DH. 31 D34
Kydd Rd DH 31 D34
Kyes Rd LG 37 B-C59
Kyle Rd F. 36 C55
Kyle Rd LG 50 X62-63
Kyle Rd (North Dundas) SDG 67 T66
Kyle Rd (North Stormont) SDG . .
. . . . 67 T68

L St MA 70 J1
L&J La MA 73 L-M12
L'Amable Creek North Access Rd
NP. 80 P42
L'Amable Creek South Access Rd
NP. 61 Q42 80 P42
La Grande Montée Rd PR. 69 P-Q73
La Passe Rd R . . . 82 L53-54
La Salette Rd NF . . . 16 Q23
La Source Rd PR . . . 67 N68
Labarge Rd HS . . 46 A49 47 A51
Labelle Rd NP 94 D28
Labelle Rd PR. 67 N68
Labelle Rd (French River) SD93 G24
Labine Rd SD 93 D24
Labine St CS 100 B18
Labombard Rd R . . 82 P-Q53
Labonte Rd PR . . . 67 P66-67
Laborosse St PR . . . 68 P72
Lac, Av du NP. 93 E26
Lac Clair Rd NP . . . 94 D27
Lac Claire Rd SD . . . 93 G23
Lac George Rd PR . . 67 N68
Lacasse Rd PR . . . 67 N68
Lacelle Rd PR . . . 68 N70-71
Lacey La MD 15 T19
Lachance Dr SD . . . 90 F13
Lacharity Rd R . . . 62 R48
Lackey La F. 48 Y56
Lackner Blvd WT . . 22 N23-24
Laclie St SM 42 Z32
LaCloche Lake Rd SD . 90 F11
Lacoste Rd SD . . . 101 B23
Lacourse La LN. . . . 64 S56
Lacroix Rd PR. . . . 67 R67
Lacroix Rd (Hammond) PR . .
. . . . 67 Q66-67
Lacroix St C. . . . 6 A-B9
Lacroix Bay Rd R . . 82 K54
Lacy Bay La HL . . 60 U39-40
Ladd's Rd PS . . . 76 M28
Ladybug Tr HL . . . 60 R37
Ladysmith Rd LM . . 12 U-V7
Lafaivre Rd PR . . . 67 P68
Lafleche Rd PR. . . 67 S67
Lafleche Rd SDG . . 67 S66
Lafleur Rd OT . . . 67 Q65-66
Lafleur Rd (North Dundas) SDG . .
. . . . 67 T66
Lafleur Rd (North Stormont) SDG . .
. . . . 68 T70
Lafond Rd NP 94 D27
Lafontaine Rd PR . . 67 R67
Lafontaine Rd SM . . 41 X26-27
Laforest Rd TM. . . 85 Q29
Laframboise Rd NP . 94 C28
Lafrance Rd (East Hawkesbury)
PR. 69 P73
Lafrance Rd (Nation) PR . 67 S67
Lafreniere Rd NP. . . 95 E25
Lafreniere Rd SDG . 67 S67-68
Lafreniere Rd SD . . 93 F23-24
Laggan Rd SDG . . . 68 Q72
Laggan-Glenelg Rd SDG . 68 Q71
Lagoon Dr PS. . . . 75 P24
Lagoon Rd C . . . 6 B9 7 B10
Lagoon Rd LM . . . 13 Q12
Lahey Rd HS . . . 46 A47-48
Laidlaw Av K 42 X33
Laidlaw Dr K 43 X37
Laidlaw St DH. . . . 31 C35
Laidman Rd HM . . 18 S29
Laidlaw Dr H 15 S19
Laidlaw Rd (Strong) NP . 77 L32
Laidlaw Rd (Tehkummah) MA . .
. . . . 73 N11
Lakeshore Rd (Wainfleet) NI . .
. . . . . 18 U32 19 U33 U34
Laird Nelson Rd NI . . 34 T46
Laird Dr K 43 Y37
Laird Dr T 24 K32
Laird Rd W WL . . . 23 M25
Lajeunesse Rd, Ch PR . 68 N-P69
Lajoie Rd HS 46 A49

Lajoie St PR 68 N69
Lajoule Creek Rd A . 87 C2 88 C3
Lake Av HM. 18 Q29
Lake Av HU 20 J13
Lake Av LN 65 T59
Lake Dr G 40 Z23
Lake Dr K 43 Y37
Lake Dr N Y 30 D31
Lake Dr S Y . . . 30 C31 D31
Lake Drwy DH. . 25 I-J35 31 H35
Lake Rd A 88 E4
Lake Rd EL 8 X15
Lake Rd F 36 B56
Lake Rd K . . . 63 V53 64 U53
Lake Rd LA 47 B53
Lake Rd MK 41 W29
Lake Rd PB 44 W40
Lake Rd SD 93 E24
Lake Rd (Cambellford-Seymour)
NR 45 B45
Lake Rd (Cramahe) NR. . 33 F45
Lake Rd (Hastings Highlands) HS. .
. . . . 62 T45
Lake Rd (Kettle and Stony Point
IR) LM 13 Q10
Lake Rd (Stirling-Rawdon) HS . .
. . . . 34 C47
Lake St A. 86 B94
Lake St LG . . . 37 A61 49 Z61
Lake St NI 19 Q-R33
Lake Clear Rd R . . 63 Q50
Lake Dalrymple Rd K . 43 Y34
Lake Dore Rd R . . 81 N50-51
Lake Eloida Rd LG . . 49 Y-Z60
Lake Erie La HD . . . 17 U28
Lake Forest Dr PS . . 57 Q27
Lake George Rd A . . 86 C94
Lake Hope Rd A . . . 88 E3
Lake Huron Dr A . 86 U95
Lake Huron Dr MA . 72 L-M8
Lake Huron Rd A . 87 E-F1
Lake Lapinskie La R . 62 Q48
Lake Lorraine Rd HL . 61 V41
Lake Nipissing Rd PS. . 95 G31
Lake Nosbonsing Rd NP 95 F32-33
Lake of Islands Rd HS. . 46 X46
Lake Park Rd LN . . 65 T-U59
Lake Range Dr BR . . 26 E13
Lake Range Rd BR . . R-S52
Lake Ridge Rd DH . 31 C-E34 F-H35
Lake Saint Peter Rd HS . 61 R43
Lake Shore Blvd E T. . 25 K34
Lake Shore Blvd W T . 24 L31-32
Lake Shore Dr A . . 86 D94
Lake Shore Rd HD. 17 V27 18 U29-30
Lake Shore Rd (Sucker Creek) MA
. . . . 90 J11
Lake Shore Rd (Wikwemikong) MA
. . . . 73 L13
Lake Sun La F . . 36 A56-57
Lake Travers Rd NP. . 98 J42-43
Lake View Ln EL . . 8 X14-15
Lake View Haven Dr LM. 13 R10
Lake Wolsey Rd MA . 72 K-L7
Lake Woods Dr Y . . 31 F33
Lakebreeze Rd K . . 43 Z37
Lakefield Dr F . . . 36 C56
Lakefield Rd PB . . 44 B41
Lakefront Rd TB . . 102 G5
Lakehurst Rd PB. . 44 A40 Z40
Lakehurst Circle Rd PB . 44 A40
Lakeland Rd K . . . 44 A39
Lakeland Estates Rd HU . 26 H13
Lakeland Lodge Rd CS. . 101 Z22
Lakelet Rd HU . . . 27 G18
Lakeport Rd NR . . 33 G44
Lakeport Rd NI . . . 19 Q-R33
Lakerange Rd BR . 26 C15 38 B15
Lakeshore Blvd BR . 55 Y17
Lakeshore Blvd G. . 28 C23
Lakeshore Dr CS . . 101 B19
Lakeshore Dr EX. . . 5 E6
Lakeshore Dr K . . 44 A-B39
Lakeshore Dr MK . 58 V31-32
Lakeshore Dr NP . 95 E31 F32
Lakeshore Dr SDG . 51 W66-67
Lakeshore Dr SD . . 103 C7 C8
Lakeshore Dr (Oro-Medonte) SM . .
. . . . 42 B30
Lakeshore Dr (Ramara) SM . .
. . 42 A33 43 A34
Lakeshore Dr N MK . 59 U34
Lakeshore Dr S MK . 59 U34
Lakeshore Ln EL. . . 9 X21
Lakeshore Rd C . . 7 B-C12
Lakeshore Rd DH . 32 G-H39
Lakeshore Rd F . . 47 X52 48 X53
Lakeshore Rd HT . 18 P29 24 M-N30
Lakeshore Rd K . . 44 A38-39
Lakeshore Rd LM. . .
. . . 12 S8-9 S-T7 13 Q12 R10-11
Lakeshore Rd LN . . 64 S56
Lakeshore Rd MA . 72 L9
Lakeshore Rd NF . .
. . 9 X21 10 W24 X22-24
Lakeshore Rd PL. . 24 L31 M30
Lakeshore Rd SDG. . 68 S71
Lakeshore Rd TM. . 85 P29-30
Lakeshore Rd Y . . 31 F33
Lakeshore Rd (Alnwick-
Haldimand) NR . . . 33 G43
Lakeshore Rd (Armour) PS . .
. . . . 77 M32-33
Lakeshore Rd (Billings) MA . 72 K9
Lakeshore Rd (Brighton) NR . .
. . 33 F45 34 F46
Lakeshore Rd (Cockburn Island)
MA 70 H1
Lakeshore Rd (Lincoln) NI . 18 Q32
Lakeshore Rd (McKellar) PS 77 L33
Lakeshore Rd (Niagara-on-the-
Lake) NI 19 Q34-35
Lakeshore Rd (Port Hope) NR . .
. . . . 33 G43
Lakeshore Rd (St Catharines) NI .
. . . 19 Q33-34 R33
Lakeshore Rd E SM . 42 A31-32
Lakeshore Rd S G . . 40 Y22
Lakeshore Rd W SM . 42 B31

Lakeshore Lodge Rd PE . .
. . . . 34 H49 35 H50
Lakeside Av A . . . 88 F3-4
Lakeside Dr A . . . 87 E98
Lakeside Dr HD. . . 17 V27
Lakeside Dr K . . . 43 Y37
Lakeside Dr MD. . 15 S17
Lakeside Dr NP. . . 95 E32
Lakeside Dr PE . . 34 F-G48
Lakeside Dr PS. . . 76 P28
Lakeside Rd SM. . 42 Y32
Lakeside Rd F . . . 36 B56
Lakeside Rd LN. . 48 V56
Lakeside Rd PB . . 33 D42
Lakeview Cr PS . . 77 M32
Lakeview Dr C . . 7 A10
Lakeview Dr MA . 72 K-L10
Lakeview Dr NR . . 45 B45
Lakeview Dr PS . . 77 P33
Lakeview Rd EL . . 9 W-X20
Lakeview Rd G. . 28 C24 29 C25
Lakeview Rd HS. . 62 U45-46
Lakeview Rd NI . . 33 E41
Lakeview Rd PS . . 94 H29
Lakeview Rd (Edwardsburgh-
Cardinal) LG. . . . 50 V64
Lakeview Rd (Elizabethtown-Kitley)
LG. 50 Z62
Latour Cr PS 95 G32
Latourell Rd LG . . . 50 V64
Latreille Rd PR . . . 67 R67
Latalippe Rd SDG. . 68 Q72
Lau-Ren Rd R . . 98 G47 99 G48
Lau Camp Rd A . . 88 F4-5
Laughlin Falls Rd SM. . 42 X30-31
Laughrin Rd NP . . 95 D32-33
Laura La MA . . . 72 K7-8
Laurel Dr A 86 C93
Laurel Rd HL . . . 60 Q37
Laurel St A 24 J32
Laurelwood Dr WT . 22 M-N22
Laurentian Dr R. . 99 K50
Lauretta La HS . . 62 U46
Laurier Av OT . . 66 Q63
Laurier Dr EX . . . 4 C1
Laurier La R . . . 26 F13
Laurier St (Clarence-Rockland) PR
. . . . 67 P66
Laurier St (Nation) PR . 67 R67-68
Laurila Rd TM. . . 85 M27
Lautsch Rd TB . . 102 G3
Lauzon Pkwy EX . . 4 B-C2
Lauzon Rd EX . . . 4 B2
Lauzon Village Rd A . 88 F5
Laval St PR 67 Q67
Lavallee Pl HS . . 62 S-T46
Lavallee Rd CS. . . 100 B17-18
Lavallee Rd R . . . 83 P56
Lavalley Way MK. . 41 W28-29
Lavant-Darling Rd LN . . 64 T55
Lavender Hill Rd SM . 29 C-D26
Laventure Rd R . . 83 Q56
Lavery Rd WT . . 22 L21
Lavigne Rd A . . . 87 E-F2
Lavigne Rd NP . . 95 F33
Lavigne Rd PR . . 67 Q66-67
Lavis La SM . . . 42 W30
Lavola Rd G. . . . 101 D20
Law Rd LG. . . . 50 V63
Law Rd R . . . 99 H48-49
Law Rd TB. . . . 102 C5
Lawes Rd TB . . . 102 B5
Lawfords La LN . . 49 V59
Lawhead La EX . . 4 C3
Lawland Heights Rd MK . 58 S32
Lawrence Av E T . . 25 J34
Lawrence Av W T . 24 K31-32
Lawrence Dr MK . 42 X33
Lawrence Ln C . . 7 X11-12
Lawrence Rd A . . 86 C96
Lawrence Rd BT . 16 R-S23
Lawrence Rd BR . 36 C30
Lawrence Rd EL . 8 W15 14 V15
Lawrence Rd HM . 18 Q29
Lawrence Rd TB . 102 C-D5
Lawrence Rd R . 10 W25 17 V25
Lawrence Rd SDG . 67 U65
Lawrence Pit Rd MK . 58 S31-32
Lawrie St R . . . 27 H17-18
Lawson Ln SM. . . 42 X-Y30
Lawson Rd C. . . . 22 L21-22
Lawson Rd HL . . 7 W-X10
Lawson Rd MK . . 58 T34-35
Lawson Rd NR . . 34 F46
Lawson Rd PS . . 77 N-P33
Lawson Rd SDG . . 52 U69
Lawson Rd SM . . 41 Z27
Lawson Rd TB . . 25 J34
Laxton-Lutterworth Ln HL . 43 X37
Laxton South Quarter Ln K . .
. . . . 43 Y36-37
Lazier Rd HS. . . . 35 D50
Lazy La LM 13 Q12
Le Baron Dr PR. . 67 N68
Leach La F . . . 36 B55-56
Leach Rd TM . . . 85 Q29
Leach Rd (Alnwick-Haldimand) NR
. . . . 33 E43
Leach Rd (Hamilton) NR . 33 F42
Leach's Rd LN . . 49 V58
Leachmen Rd A . . 82 M52
Leacock Rd LG. . . 49 X61
Leader Rd A . . . 99 H48
Lean Dr PB . . . 45 X42
Leander Rd MK . 58 R31-32 S31-32
Learmont Rd MA. . .
Learn Rd NI . . 19 U34-35
Leask La MA. . . 73 M12
Leask Rd DH. . . 32 G37
Leaskdale Rd DH. . 31 D34
Leason Bay Tr MA . 73 N11
Leavoy La R . . . 72 J9
LeBar Rd MA. . . .
Leblanc Rd NP. . 94 C27
Leblond Rd NP . 94 C27
Lebrun Rd PR . . 67 R-S67
Leclair Rd NP . . 93 D26
Leclair Rd SD . . . 90 E13
Leclaire La R . . . 63 S52
Leclerc Rd MK . . .
Leclerc Rd PR . . 67 S65

Ledge / Main

Ledge Rd HS ... 46 Z46
Ledge Rd PB ... 44 Z39
Ledge Hill Rd K ... 44 Y-Z38
Ledgerock Rd G ... 39 Z18-19
Leduc La MK ... 41 X29
Leduc Sdrd PR ... 68 P70
Ledyit Rd A ... 86 D97
Lee La F ... 48 Y56
Lee La F ... 48 Z55
Lee Rd F ... 48 Y-Z56
Lee Rd HS ... 46 A48
Lee's Rd HL ... 61 V41
Lee's Rd K ... 43 A37
Lee's Rd PS ... 76 P28
Lee Bay La F ... 48 Y56
Lee Valley Rd SD ... 90 F11-12
Leech Rd R ... 82 N53
Leeder Cottage Rd LG ... 49 Y60
Leeftink Rd SD ... 101 C23
Leeland Dr LG ... 49 W60
Leeman Rd F ... 36 C56
Leeming Rd HM ... 17 R28
Leeper Rd TB ... 102 E-F2
Lees Ln C ... 7 Y12
Lees Rd NP ... 95 E32
Lees Rd SD ... 89 F9
Lefebvre Rd PR ... 68 Q69
Legacy Rd HL ... 61 U-V42
Legault Rd PR ... 67 Q66-67
Legere Dr R ... 99 G-H49
Leggat Lake Rd F ... 48 Y54
Leggetts Rd PS ... 77 N32
Legion Rd BR ... 39 Z18 55 Y18
Legrous Lake Rd PS ... 76 K28 94 J28
Lehman Dam Sdrd NF ... 16 U-V23
Lehovitch Rd R ... 80 P47
Leighs Bay Rd A ... 84 B91
Leighton Rd PS ... 77 K32
Leinster Access Rd SD ... 100 Y16
Leisure Point La LG ... 48 Z57
Leitch Rd DH ... 31 D33
Leitch Rd SDG ... 68 T71
Leitrim Rd OT ... 66 R63-64
Lekx Rd LG ... 37 C59
Leland Rd F ... 36 B56
Lele La F ... 36 A56
Lemieux Rd NP ... 93 F25
Lemieux Rd (East Hawkesbury) PR ... 68 Q72 69 Q73
Lemke Rd R ... 81 M51
Lemko Rd G ... 27 D19
Lemon Rd NI ... 19 T34-35
Lemonville Rd HT ... 23 P28
Lennon Rd HM ... 23 N26
Lennon Rd LG ... 48 X-Y57
Lennox Rd HS ... 46 Y48
Lennox Rd NP ... 95 D33
Lenny Rd R ... 81 P48
Lenser Rd R ... 81 P51
Leo Jay La LN ... 48 V56
Leo Lake Rd F ... 37 B58
Leonard Rd SM ... 30 F30
Leonard Sdrd LN ... 48 W57
Leonard St SM ... 30 C31
Leonard Lake Rd 1 MK ... 58 U31
Leonard Lake Rd 2 MK ... 58 U31-32
Leone's Cove Rd F ... 37 D58
Lerch Rd WT ... 22 M24
Leroux Rd PR ... 67 R68
Les Davey Rd NR ... 33 F42-43
Les Jackson Rd PB ... 45 X44
Leskard Rd DH ... 32 F38
Leslie La WL ... 22 K21
Leslie Rd HS ... 34 C49
Leslie Rd WL ... 23 N26
Leslie St T ... 24 J32 25 K-L33
Leslie St Y ... 30 E31 F-H32
Leslie Hill Rd HT ... 23 K27-28
Lesnick Rd TB ... 102 F5
Lesperance Rd EX ... 4 B3
Lester Dr EX ... 4 C4
Lester Rd HS ... 34 E47
Lester Rd OT ... 66 R63
Lesters La F ... 48 Z55
Letang Rd NP ... 94 D28
Lethbridge Rd MD ... 7 W13 8 W14
Letson Dr WT ... 22 L23
Lett's Cemetery Rd R ... 81 N51
Letter Breen Rd G ... 27 F20
Letterkenny Rd R ... 63 Q-R49
Lettner Rd DH ... 32 F-G37
Levac Rd NP ... 94 D27
Leveque Rd F ... 36 A54
Lever Rd NI ... 19 T34
Levere Rd F ... 47 W51
Levere Rd (North Dundas) SDG ... 67 U65
Levere Rd (South Dundas) SDG ... 50 W65
Levergood Dr EX ... 4 E-F2
Levergood La EX ... 4 E-F2
Leveridge Rd HS ... 62 V45
Levert Dr NP ... 94 D28
Levis St PR ... 67 Q67
Lew Harris Rd NR ... 33 E42
Lewis Ln HU ... 27 G17
Lewis Rd F ... 48 X54
Lewis Rd HL ... 61 V43
Lewis Rd HM ... 16 Q30
Lewis Rd LN ... 65 U59
Lewis Rd MD ... 15 T-U19
Lewis Bay La F ... 37 D-E58
Lewisham La K ... 43 X34
Lewisham Rd MK ... 43 W34 59 V34
Lex Rd TB ... 102 G3
Lexington Rd WT ... 22 M23
Libbys Rd R ... 83 Q56
Liberty St DH ... 32 G38
Liberty St N DH ... 32 F37-38
Lichty Rd WT ... 21 M20 22 L21
Lidderdale St HU ... 20 L-M13
Liddicoat Rd TB ... 102 E-F3
Liedtke Rd R ... 62 S48 63 S49
Lieury Rd MD ... 14 Q14
Liezert Rd LG ... 50 W65
Lifford Rd K ... 32 D38
Lift Lock Rd K ... 43 Z35
Light Ln EL ... 9 W21
Lighthall Rd PE ... 35 H51
Lighthouse Dr EX ... 5 H5
Lighthouse Dr HD ... 18 U30-31
Lighthouse La F ... 36 D57
Lighthouse La NR ... 34 G46
Lighthouse Rd MA ... 91 J15
Lighthouse Rd PS ... 95 F31-32
Lighthouse Sdrd EX ... 6 B-C6
Lightning St SDG ... 51 V66
Lightning Point Rd K ... 43 Z37
Lilac La BR ... 38 Z17
Lilac Rd K ... 32 C38 44 B38
Lilac Valley Rd NR ... 33 E42
Lillico Rd SDG ... 66 U64
Lillie Sdrd OT ... 83 Q58-59
Lilly Cr MA ... 72 J9
Lillydale Av EX ... 4 B4
Lily Bay Rd N LG ... 50 A62
Lily Lake Rd MA ... 70 J2-3
Lily Lake Rd PB ... 32 C40
Lily Pad Rd R ... 63 R49-50
Limberlost Rd BR ... 55 W17
Limberlost Rd MK ... 59 Q34-35
Limberlost Point Rd PS ... 94 H29
Limberts Rd PS ... 57 Q27
Lime Kiln Rd G ... 27 C20
Lime Kiln Rd R ... 82 Q55
Lime Lake Rd HS ... 47 B51
Lime Lake Rd LA ... 47 B51
Limebank Rd OT ... 66 R-S63
Limekiln Ln HU ... 20 J15 K14
Limekiln Rd MA ... 73 K11
Limerick Rd C ... 7 W-X12
Limerick Rd SDG ... 67 U66-67
Limerick Forest Rd LG ... 50 W63
Limerick Lake Rd HS ... 46 W46-47
Limerick Lodge Rd HS ... 46 W47
Limeridge Rd HM ... 17 Q28 18 Q29
Limestone La HL ... 60 V40
Limestone Rd HT ... 23 M27-28 N27
Limestone Rd OT ... 83 Q59
Limestone Rd R ... 81 M-N51
Limestone Lake La HS ... 62 T-U47
Limoges Rd PR ... 67 R66
Lincoln Av (Lincoln) NI ... 18 R31
Lincoln Av (Niagara-on-the-Lake) NI ... 19 R34
Lincoln St (Niagara Falls) NI ... 19 T34
Lincoln St (Welland) NI ... 19 T33
Lincoln M Alexander Pkwy HM ... 17 Q28
Linda La PS ... 56 R25
Lindala Rd CS ... 100 D16
Linden Dr CS ... 101 A20
Linden Rd EL ... 7 W-X13
Linden Valley Rd K ... 43 B35-36
Lindenwood Rd G ... 39 Y19
Lindey La F ... 47 W-X52
Lindgren Rd MK ... 59 R33
Lindquist Ln PS ... 95 G32
Lindsay Hwy K ... 32 C39
Lindsay Rd BR ... 54 T15 55 U15
Lindsay Rd C ... 6 Y9
Lindsay Rd LG ... 50 V63
Lindsay Rd PB ... 32 C40
Lindsay St (Kawartha Lakes[Fenelon Falls]) K ... 43 A37
Lindsay St (Kawartha Lakes[Lindsay]) K ... 32 C37
Lindsay's Hill Rd PS ... 95 J32
Line Hill Rd MK ... 59 Q-R33
Lingenfelters Rd PS ... 95 J31
Lingham Lake Rd HS ... 46 Y48-49
Lingham Lake Access Rd HS ... 46 W48 Y48-49
Link Rd HD ... 17 U28
Link Rd LA ... 36 D54
Link Rd R ... 82 N-P52
Link Rd SDG ... 67 U66
Links Sdrd BR ... 38 A16
Linktert Rd HL ... 61 U41
Linquist Rd A ... 86 D96
Linton Rd MK ... 41 W29
Linton Rd (Hamilton) NR ... 33 E42
Linton Rd (Trent Hills) NR ... 33 D44
Linwell Rd NI ... 19 Q33-34
Lioness Rd PS ... 57 R28
Lions Club Rd EX ... 4 C4
Lippert La HS ... 61 U44 62 U45
Lisbon Rd WT ... 21 N20 22 N21
Liscumb Rd SDG ... 67 U65
Lisgar St R ... 82 P54-55
Lisk Rd R ... 81 N-P49
Lisk Sdrd G ... 39 Y18
Listowel Ln PB ... 44 B40
Listowel Rd WT ... 22 L22
Liswood Rd HL ... 60 T39
Little Av SM ... 30 C30
Little Rd HD ... 17 U28
Little Rd NR ... 33 F41
Little Base Line Rd EX ... 4 B3
Little Bob Lake Rd HL ... 43 W37
Little Britain Rd K ... 31 C36 D35-36 32 C37
Little Brule Rd SD ... 93 D24
Little Burnt Lake Access Rd HS ... 46 X-Y46
Little Cedar Bridge Rd LG ... 48 X57
Little Church Dr MD ... 14 V16
Little Cove Rd BR ... 54 S14
Little Creek Rd LA ... 35 D52-53
Little Creek Rd PE ... 34 G48
Little Crosby Lake Rd LG ... 48 X-Y57
Little Duck Pond Rd PB ... 45 Z42-43
Little Falls Rd PS ... 77 P31
Little Finch Lake Rd LA ... 63 U51
Little Green Rd LN ... 64 S55
Little Green Lake Access Rd F ... 63 T52 64 T53
Little Hawk Lake Rd HL ... 60 T37
Little Ireland Rd LM ... 13 U-V11
Little Ireland Rd R ... 62 S-T48
Little John Rd EL ... 8 X15
Little Kapikog Lake Rd PS ... 57 T28
Little Lake Rd LG ... 49 Z58
Little Lake Rd NF ... 16 T23
Little Lake Rd NR ... 33 F45
Little Lake Huron Rd MA ... 71 K5
Little Lakes Rd HU ... 20 K14
Little Long Lake Rd F ... 36 B55-56
Little Long Lake Rd PS ... 75 K26 93 J26
Little Norway Rd TB ... 102 E5
Little Panache Rd CS ... 91 E16
Little Papineau Lake Rd HS ... 62 R45
Little Pautois Lake Accecs Rd NP ... 96 F37
Little Pickerel Lake Rd A ... 87 B-C1
Little Pike Bay Rd BR ... 55 V16-17
Little Pine Dr BR ... 55 U15
Little Pond Rd F ... 47 X50-51
Little Rapids Rd A ... 87 D-E98
Little Rideau Lake Rd LG ... 48 Y57 49 Y58
Little River Blvd EX ... 4 B3
Little River Rd EX ... 4 B3
Little River Rd PS ... 94 J29
Little Russia Rd SDG ... 68 R72
Little Serpent River North Rd SD ... 89 E9
Little Silver Lake Rd LN ... 48 X56
Little Sturgeon Rd NP ... 94 D29
Little Timber Tr R ... 63 S50
Little Trout Bay Rd TB ... 102 G4
Little Trout Lake Rd A ... 89 E9-10
Little Twin Lakes Access Rd NP ... 95 G34
Littlejohn Rd C ... 7 X-Y12
Littlewood Dr MD ... 14 U-V16
Liverpool Rd DH ... 25 J35 31 H34
Livingston La MK ... 59 R35
Livingstone Ln HU ... 21 K17-18
Livingstone St SM ... 41 B29
Livingstone Lake Rd HL ... 59 R36 60 R37
Lizzie's La PS ... 76 P28
Lloyd Sdrd DH ... 31 C34
Lloyd Francis Blvd OT ... 66 R61
Lloyds Rd LA ... 47 Y51
Lloydtown-Aurora Rd Y ... 30 G30-31
Loach's Rd CS ... 101 C19
Loback Rd R ... 81 M51
Lobb Rd HU ... 20 K14
Lobelia Dr MD ... 13 V12
Lobsinger Ln WT ... 22 M21-22
Loch Erne Rd PS ... 76 P27
Loch Garry Rd SDG ... 68 S70
Loch Lomond Rd TB ... 102 E5
Lochiel Rd SDG ... 68 R71
Lochinvar Rd SDG ... 68 Q71
Lochlin Rd HL ... 60 V38
Lochwinnoch Rd R ... 83 P56
Lock Rd LG ... 37 A58
Lockart St BR ... 26 G15
Locke Rd HS ... 34 E47
Locke Rd NR ... 33 F43
Locke Rd PS ... 77 P33
Lockerby Mine Access Rd CS ... 100 C16-17
Lockhart Dr NI ... 19 R33
Lockhart Rd DH ... 32 G38
Lockhart Rd NR ... 33 D-E43
Lockhart Rd SM ... 30 C30-31
Lockhead Rd E OT ... 66 T63
Lockhead Rd W OT ... 66 T62-63
Lockie Rd WT ... 23 P25
Lockie Sdrd Y ... 30 C-D32
Lockridge Rd LA ... 35 C52 47 B52
Locks Rd BT ... 17 R25
Locksley Rd R ... 81 L-M51
Lockwood La LG ... 49 Z58
Lockwood Rd LG ... 49 X60
Locust La NI ... 18 R31
Lodge La LG ... 37 A59
Lodge Rd K ... 44 A38
Lodge Rd MK ... 41 W-X29
Lodi Rd SDG ... 67 S68
Lodore Rd LN ... 64 U56
Log House Rd K ... 44 B38
Logan Rd HD ... 18 U30-31
Logan Rd NI ... 19 S35
Logan Rd TB ... 102 E1-2
Loggers Way OT ... 83 Q58
Loghrin Rd TB ... 102 D3
Lois La MA ... 72 L9
Lombard Av EX ... 4 E3
Lombard St LN ... 49 W60
Londesboro Rd HU ... 20 K14-15
London Ln LM ... 12 T8-9 13 T10
London Rd G ... 28 G21
London Rd HU ... 20 J16 J-K15 M14-15 N15 26 H16
London Rd (Ashfield-Colborne-Wawanosh) HU ... 26 H13
London Rd (Kettle and Stony Point IR) LM ... 13 Q10
London Rd (Sarnia) LM ... 12 T7
Lone Pine Dr MK ... 58 S-T32
Lone Pine Rd MK ... 41 W-X29
Lonely Lake Rd A ... 86 C95
Lonesome Pine Tr MA ... 73 M12
Lonestar Rd TB ... 102 F4
Loney La CS ... 101 Z22-23
Long Rd SD ... 101 C23
Long St A ... 88 F5
Long Bay Rd PS ... 56 Q24
Long Bay Tr MA ... 72 K8
Long Beach Rd K ... 43 A37
Long Lake Rd CS ... 101 C-D19
Long Lake Rd F ... 48 Y53-54
Long Lake Rd LN ... 49 X58
Long Lake Rd PB ... 45 Y42
Long Lake Rd (East Mills) PS ... 76 K28 94 J28
Long Lake Rd (Huntsville) MK ... 58 S32
Long Lake Rd (Laurentian Valley) R ... 81 L50
Long Lake Rd (Madawaska Valley) R ... 62 Q47
Long Lake Rd (Muskoka Lakes) MK ... 58 V30
Long Lake Rd (Perry) PS ... 77 P32-33
Long Lake Estates Rd PS ... 57 Q27 76 P27
Long Meadows Rd R ... 81 N49
Long Point Rd G ... 40 A25
Long Point Rd LA ... 36 E54
Long Point Rd LG ... 37 A-B59
Long Point Rd MK ... 58 R31-32 U31
Long Point Rd NF ... 10 X23
Long Point Rd PE ... 35 G52-53
Long Point Rd PS ... 95 F31
Long Point Way R ... 82 Q55
Long Reach Rd NR ... 34 E-F46
Long Sault Pkwy SDG ... 51 V68 52 V69
Long Swamp Rd F ... 36 B54
Longbay Lake Access Rd F ... 64 T53
Longfields Dr OT ... 66 S62
Longford Mills Rd SM ... 42 Y32
Longhurst Ln EL ... 14 V16
Longhurst Rd MK ... 58 T31
Longlee La EX ... 5 E5
Longline Lake Rd MK ... 59 S35
Longsault Rd DH ... 32 F37-38
Longtin Rd PR ... 67 S67
Longueuil Sdrd PR ... 68 P70
Longueuil St PR ... 68 N71
Longwood Rd SM ... 30 C30 42 B30
Longwoods Rd C ... 6 A9 7 X11 Y10
Longwoods Rd MD ... 7 W13 14 U16 U-V14 V13-14
Longyear Dr CS ... 101 B20-21
Longyear La NR ... 32 F40
Lonsberry Dr EX ... 4 F3
Lonsdale Rd WT ... 22 N24
Lookout Rd R ... 82 L53
Lookout St NI ... 19 S33
Loomis Rd NR ... 33 E45
Loon La F ... 48 Z56
Loon St K ... 32 D37
Loon Lake Rd HL ... 60 U40
Loon Lake Rd MK ... 58 V31-32
Loon Lake Rd (Kearney) PS ... 77 M33
Loon Lake Rd (Magnetawan) PS ... 77 M31
Loop Ln K ... 32 C39
Loop Rd HL ... 61 T42 U41 U42-43
Lorain La EX ... 5 H5
Lorbetskie Rd R ... 62 Q47
Lord Rd NR ... 34 E46
Lord Mills Rd LG ... 50 Y63
Lori Lea Tr PS ... 76 P27
Lorimer Lake Rd PS ... 76 N27-28 P27
Lorne Av PT ... 21 P19
Lorne La HL ... 60 U39
Lorne Rd MK ... 59 U34
Lorne St CS ... 101 C19
Lorne St LN ... 49 W60
Lorne Beach Rd BR ... 26 D14
Lorne Falls Rd CS ... 91 E15
Lorne Park Rd PL ... 24 M30
Lorne School Rd SDG ... 68 Q-R71
Lorneville Rd K ... 43 B35-36
Lorraine Av WT ... 22 N23
Lorraine Rd NI ... 19 U34
Losey Rd SDG ... 52 U69
Lost Channel Rd HS ... 46 B49 47 B50
Lost Channel Rd PS ... 75 K24 93 J24
Lost Mile Rd BT ... 17 R26-27
Lothlorien Rd F ... 63 V53
Lotus Rd K ... 32 E38
Lou-ren Rd R ... 98 G47 99 G48
Loucks La HL ... 60 V38
Loucks Rd NR ... 33 C45 34 C46
Loucks Rd PB ... 33 D42
Loucks Rd PS ... 57 R-S28
Loucks Rd SDG ... 67 T66-67
Lough Rd SDG ... 50 V64-65
Loughborough Rd F ... 36 B55
Loughborough View Rd F ... 36 B57
Loughlin Ridge Rd SDG ... 66 U64
Louis La SM ... 42 Z33
Louis Ernest Rd PR ... 67 R-S67
Louis St-Laurent Av HT ... 23 M28 24 M29
Louisa St K ... 43 A37 Z37
Louisa St PS ... 57 R27
Louise La HL ... 60 V38
Louiseize Rd OT ... 66 R64
Loukala Rd TB ... 102 G2
Lount Township Access Rd PS ... 76 K30
Louth St NI ... 19 R33
Love Rd LA ... 35 C53 36 C54
Love's Rd HL ... 61 V41
Love Rock Rd LG ... 37 A59
Lover's La PS ... 94 J27
Lover's La R ... 82 L53
Lover's Ln R ... 81 N50
Lovering Ln SM ... 42 X30
Lovering Lake Rd SD ... 92 F21
Lovers La HM ... 17 Q27
Lovers La WL ... 28 G21
Loves La LN ... 64 T55
Loves Rd LN ... 64 T55
Lovshin Rd NR ... 33 G42
Lowbank Dr HL ... 61 V41-42
Lowe Rd OT ... 65 S59-60
Lowell Lake Dr R ... 63 Q49
Lower Sdrd NF ... 9 X21 10 X22
Lower Side Rd F ... 37 D58
Lower 40 Foot Rd LA ... 36 E55
Lower Base Ln HT ... 24 M-N29
Lower Beverley 1 Rd LG ... 49 Z59
Lower Big Chute Rd SM ... 42 Y30
Lower Cow Path MD ... 15 T19
Lower Craigmount Rd R ... 62 R47
Lower Faraday Rd HS ... 45 W45 61 U-V44 62 V45
Lower Frys Lake Rd PS ... 58 Q30
Lower Island Lake Rd A ... 84 Z92
Lower Monmouth Lake Rd HL ... 44 W41 61 V41
Lower Oak Leaf Rd LG ... 49 Z59-60
Lower Rosenthal Rd R ... 62 R48
Lower Round Lake Rd F ... 36 B56-57
Lower Slash Rd HS ... 35 D51
Lower Slash Rd MA ... 73 M-N11
Lower Spruce Hedge Rd R ... 64 R55 82 Q55 83 Q56
Lower Turriff La HS ... 62 V46
Lower Turriff Rd HS ... 62 U-V46
Lower Valley Rd G ... 28 C23
Lowery La HS ... 47 Y-Z50
Lowery Rd HS ... 46 A47
Lowes Rd PS ... 58 Q30
Lowes Sdrd EX ... 4 E1
Lowney Lake Rd LN ... 64 S56
Lowrie Ln OX ... 16 U21
Lowrie Lake Access Rd HL ... 61 V43-44
Loxton Ln PS ... 95 H32
Loyal Ln HU ... 20 J13
Loyalist Pkwy HS ... 34 F47
Loyalist Pkwy LA ... 35 F52 36 D-E54
Loyalist Pkwy PE ... 34 G48-49 35 F-G51 G50
Loyalist Rd NR ... 32 F40
Loyalist Rd SDG ... 68 T72
Loyer Ln C ... 6 B7
Lubitz Rd R ... 81 L50
Lucan Point Rd MA ... 72 K-L10
Lucas Rd LA ... 36 D54
Luckens Rd TB ... 102 D3
Luckey Rd MK ... 58 S32
Lucknow Ln HU ... 20 J14 26 G-H14
Luckovitch Rd R ... 80 P47
Lucks Crossroad PE ... 35 G51
Lucky La R ... 64 S53
Lucy Rd OX ... 16 V21
Ludgate Tr PS ... 74 K23 93 J23
Luffman Dr NI ... 19 S33
Luffman Rd HS ... 47 B51
Luger's Rd HL ... 60 V37-38
Luigi Rd MK ... 42 W32-33
Luiting Rd SD ... 101 C23
Luker Rd LN ... 64 S55
Luloff La R ... 63 Q49
Lumber La A ... 84 Z92
Lumsden Rd (Chelmsford) CS ... 100 A17-18
Lumsden Rd (Val Thérèse) CS ... 100 A18
Lundstrom Rd TB ... 102 C3
Lundy Rd G ... 39 Y19
Lundy Rd WT ... 22 M23
Lundy's La NI ... 19 S34-35
Lunney Rd OT ... 83 Q58
Lunny La NR ... 32 E-F40
Lutesville Rd NF ... 17 T25
Lyle Rd EL ... 14 V16 15 V17
Lyle St NR ... 33 F-G43
Lyle's Ln K ... 44 Z38
Lyman Rd HS ... 61 U44
Lymburner Rd NI ... 18 S30
Lyn Rd LG ... 50 Z62
Lyn Valley Rd LG ... 50 A62
Lynch Rd HS ... 46 A49
Lynch Rd R ... 82 P54 Q53
Lynch's Rock Rd PB ... 44 B41 45 B42
Lynch Lake Rd PS ... 77 K-L33
Lyndebrook Rd DH ... 31 G35
Lynden Rd BT ... 17 R25-26
Lynden Rd HM ... 17 Q26 23 P26
Lyndhurst Rd LG ... 37 A59 49 Z59
Lyndoch Lake Rd R ... 63 R49
Lynedoch Rd NF ... 16 V23
Lynn Rd TB ... 102 C3
Lynn Valley Rd NF ... 17 V25
Lynx Dr PS ... 77 N33-34
Lynx Hollow Rd LN ... 65 R58
Lynx Lake Rd MK ... 59 S33
Lyon's La MA ... 73 L11
Lyons Av A ... 84 B92
Lyons Ln EL ... 15 U-V19
Lyons Rd BT ... 17 Q25
Lyons Rd LG ... 49 X60
Lyons Creek Rd NI ... 19 S35 T34
Lypps Beach Rd EX ... 4 F2

M, Fire Rte CS ... 100 C18
M-N, Concession Rd SM ... 42 X33
M & N Ln A ... 86 E95 F94
Ma Brown's Rd DH ... 31 E36
Maas Park Dr WL ... 28 G21
Mabees Sdrd NF ... 16 V21
Mabels Rd DH ... 32 D-E37
Mabels Rd R ... 83 Q57
Maberly Station Rd LN ... 48 X56
MacAvalley Rd SM ... 41 X27
MacCormish La F ... 48 Z57
MacCuaig Rd SDG ... 68 Q71
MacDonald Dr MD ... 13 R12
MacDonald Dr NI ... 19 U36
Macdonald La HS ... 62 V48
Macdonald Rd F ... 64 U54
MacDonald Rd HU ... 20 N-P15 P14
MacDonald Rd (East Hawkesbury) PR ... 68 Q72
MacDonald Rd (Nation) PR ... 68 Q70
MacDonald Rd (Russell) PR ... 67 S65
MacDonald's Grove Rd SDG ... 68 R-S69
Macdonald-Cartier Frwy DH ... 31 H35-36 32 G39-40 H37-38
Macdonald-Cartier Frwy EL ... 7 X-Y13
Macdonald-Cartier Frwy EX ... 4 C3-4 5 C5
Macdonald-Cartier Frwy HS ... 35 D50-51
Macdonald-Cartier Frwy HT ... 23 M28
Macdonald-Cartier Frwy LA ... 36 D54-55
Macdonald-Cartier Frwy LG ... 37 B61 C58-59 50 Y-Z63
Macdonald-Cartier Frwy NR ... 33 F45
Macdonald-Cartier Frwy OX ... 16 Q-R22
Macdonald-Cartier Frwy SDG ... 51 V68 68 T72 69 T73
Macdonald-Cartier Frwy T ... 24 J32 K30-31 25 J33
MacDonalds Rd G ... 28 C23
MacDonell Rd SDG ... 68 R71
MacDonnell Rd F ... 48 W55
MacDuff Rd HL ... 61 V41
MacEwan Rd C ... 7 X12
Macey Bay Rd MK ... 41 W29
MacFarlane Rd LM ... 12 S-T9
MacFarlane Rd OT ... 66 R62-63
Machar Strong Boundary Rd PS ... 77 K32 L31
Machardy Rd OT ... 83 Q58
Machesney Lake Rd LA ... 63 V50
Machesney Lake Access Rd LA ... 63 U-V49
MacHill's Rd PE ... 35 E-F51
MacIntyre Rd A ... 84 A92
MacIntyre Rd K ... 43 A35 Z35
MacIver Dr A ... 88 F3
Mack Tr NR ... 45 B45-46
Mack's Corners Rd SDG ... 68 Q71-72
MacKannas Rd SD ... 93 D24-25
Mackay Dr A ... 87 E99
MacKay Rd A ... 86 C97
MacKay Line Rd LN ... 48 V57
MacKelcan Rd SD ... 101 Y22
Mackenzie La HS ... 62 V46-47
MacKenzie Rd A ... 86 C-D96
MacKenzie Rd HS ... 34 D-E48
MacKenzie Rd K ... 43 X35 Y34-35
MacKenzie Rd SDG ... 67 U67
Mackenzie Beach Rd TB ... 103 C8
Mackenzie Camp Rd HU ... 26 G13
Mackenzie Heights Rd TB ... 103 B8
Mackenzie Pioneer Rd SM ... 29 E28 30 E29
Mackenzie Station Rd TB ... 103 B-C8
Mackey Rd OT ... 66 Q62
Mackey Creek Rd R ... 98 G46
MacKillican Rd SDG ... 67 S68 68 S69
Mackler Sdrd LN ... 49 W-X58
Macklin Rd NR ... 33 E43
Macks Rd MK ... 59 S33
Macks Rd R ... 82 Q53
MacLachlan La LN ... 64 R-S56
Maclarens Sdrd OT ... 83 P59
MacLean Rd A ... 87 D-E98
MacLean Rd SD ... 101 C22
MacLean Lake North Shore Rd SM ... 42 W-X30
MacLean Point Rd F ... 48 X54
MacLeish Dr K ... 43 Y34
MacLennan Dr CS ... 101 A21
MacLennan Rd A ... 86 D94
MacLennan Mine Rd CS ... 101 A21
MacLeod Dr BR ... 26 D14
MacLeod Rd (North Glengarry) SDG ... 68 Q71
MacLeod Rd (North Stormont) SDG ... 68 S69
MacLeod Rd (South Stormont) SDG ... 51 V68
MacLeod Sdrd PR ... 68 Q70
MacMaster Rd SDG ... 68 Q-R70
MacMillan Rd BT ... 17 R25
MacMillan Rd LG ... 49 Y61
MacMillan Rd SDG ... 67 T68
MacPhail Rd A ... 86 D96-97
MacPhail's Rd LN ... 49 V59
MacPhee Rd SDG ... 68 R71
MacPherson Dr NP ... 95 E32-33
MacPherson Rd C ... 7 Y12-13
MacPherson Rd F ... 48 W-X55
MacPherson St LN ... 49 V60
MacPherson's La WL ... 23 N26
MacRae Rd SDG ... 52 U69 67 U68
Madawaska Blvd R ... 83 Q57-58
Madawaska Rd HS ... 62 Q-R45
Madawaska St NP ... 79 P41
Madawaska Mine Loop HS ... 61 U44 62 U45
Maddaugh Rd HM ... 23 N26
Madden Rd BT ... 17 R26
Madigan Rd R ... 63 R49
Madill Dr DF ... 29 G26
Madill Rd HL ... 60 V40 61 V41
Madill Rd PS ... 77 N32
Madill Church Rd MK ... 59 R33
Madoc St HS ... 46 A46
Maebar Rd HL ... 60 U37-38
Mag View Rd PS ... 77 N32
Magdala Rd EL ... 14 V15-16
Magee Rd LG ... 50 V64
Maggies Sdrd MA ... 70 J2
Magill St CS ... 100 C-D18
Magladry Rd OT ... 67 Q65-66
Magnavilla Ln C ... 7 Y10
Magnesium Rd R ... 82 N54
Magnetawan River Rd PS ... 74 L23
Magnificent Rd HL ... 61 U42
Maguire Rd MD ... 14 Q-R15
Maguire Rd PB ... 33 C43
Mahoney Blvd EX ... 5 J5
Mahoney Rd NR ... 33 C-D45
Mahoney Bay Rd LG ... 36 A57 37 A58
Mahons Rd LG ... 49 X58-59
Mahood Rd PB ... 33 D41
Mahood's Rd DH ... 32 E37
Maiangowi Rd MA ... 73 L13
Maidstone Av EX ... 4 D3
Mail Rd NR ... 32 G40
Mailloux Rd SD ... 89 F9
Main Ln C ... 7 X11
Main Rd MA ... 73 K-L13
Main Rd PS ... 76 M30
Main St A ... 87 E98
Main St CS ... 100 B18 C18 101 B19
Main St DH ... 32 G38
Main St DF ... 29 E25
Main St EX ... 4 E4
Main St G ... 28 E24
Main St LA ... 35 C53
Main St MA ... 72 J7
Main St MD ... 7 W13 14 V13
Main St NF ... 17 T-U25
Main St NP ... 95 E31
Main St OT ... 66 Q63
Main St PR ... 68 N-P71
Main St PS ... 77 N33
Main St R ... 99 H49
Main St SM ... 30 F29
Main St TB ... 103 D6
Main St T ... 25 K33
Main St WL ... 23 J26-27
Main St WT ... 23 P25
Main St (Billings) MA ... 72 J9
Main St (Bishops Mills) LG ... 50 W62-63
Main St (Brampton) PL ... 24 K29
Main St (Brock) DH ... 43 B34
Main St (Burgessville) OX ... 16 S-T22
Main St (Caledon) PL ... 29 H26-27
Main St (Callander) PS ... 95 F32
Main St (Casey) TM ... 85 P30
Main St (Dunnville) HD ... 18 U30-31
Main St (Flamborough) HM ... 23 P28
Main St (Fort Erie) NI ... 19 T35
Main St (Garnet) HD ... 17 T27 U26
Main St (Grand Valley) DF ... 28 H24
Main St (Grey Highlands) G ... 28 C22
Main St (Grimsby) NI ... 18 R30-31
Main St (Haileybury) TM ... 85 R30
Main St (Halton Hills) HT ... 23 K28 L28
Main St (Hamilton) HM ... 17 Q28
Main St (Huntsville) MK ... 59 R33
Main St (Huron East) HU ... 20 M15
Main St (Innerkip) OX ... 16 R21
Main St (King) Y ... 30 G30
Main St (Lake of Bays) MK ... 59 S36
Main St (Lambton Shores [Thedford]) LM ... 13 R12
Main St (Lucan-Biddulph) MD ... 14 R15
Main St (Markham) Y ... 31 H33
Main St (Markstay-Warren[Hagar]) SD ... 101 C23
Main St (Markstay-Warren[Ratter & Dunnett]) SD ... 93 D24
Main St (Milton) HT ... 23 M28
Main St (Mitchell's Bay) C ... 6 A9 Y9
Main St (Newmarket) Y ... 30 F31
Main St (Niagara Falls) NI ... 19 S35
Main St (North Grenville) LG ... 50 V62
Main St (North Middlesex) MD ... 14 R13
Main St (Northern Bruce Peninsula) BR ... 55 V17
Main St (Norwich) OX ... 16 T22
Main St (Otterville) OX ... 16 U22
Main St (Port Colborne) NI ... 19 U34
Main St (Powassan) PS ... 95 G-J32
Main St (Princeton) OX ... 16 R23
Main St (Rideau Lakes) LG ... 49 Z58
Main St (Ridgetown) C ... 7 A11
Main St (Sables-Spanish Rivers) SD ... 90 E12
Main St (South Bruce Peninsula) BR ... 38 Z17
Main St (South Huron) HU ... 20 P15

Main / McMillan

Main St (St Catharines) NI. 19 Q-R33
Main St (Thornloe) TM 85 P29
Main St (Uxbridge) DH 31 E34
Main St (Welland) NI 19 T33-34
Main St (West Grey) G 27 D18
Main St (Whitchurch-Stouffville) Y. 31 G33
Main St Lisle SM 29 D27
Main St Rockford HD 17 U26
Main St Unionville Y 31 H33
Maines Rd HS 46 B49
Mainhood Rd MK 58 S32
Mainsville Rd LG 50 X65
Mainville Rd PR 68 R69
Mainway HT 18 P29
Mair Ln HU 21 J17
Maisonneuve Rd PR 67 P67
Maitland Av HU 20 K13
Maitland Av OT 66 R62
Maitland Dr HS 34 D48
Maitland Dr MD 14 U15
Maitland Ln HU 20 K14
Maitland Rd HD 18 U31
Maitland Rd LG 49 X61
Maitland Block Rd HU 20 J14
Major Ln EL 15 V17
Major Rd CS 101 C-D21
Major St K 44 A38
Major Lake Rd NP 80 N42 N-P43
Major Mackenzie Dr Y 24 I-J30 30 H30 H31-32 31 H33
Makada Dr CS 100 D18
Makala Rd CS 91 E16
Maki Rd A 84 A91
Maki Rd CS 101 B20
Maki Rd PS 77 P31
Maki Rd (Gorham) TB 102 B5 103 B6
Maki Rd (Lybster) TB 102 F2
Maki Rd (Oliver Paipoonge) TB 102 C-D4
Maki Lake Rd A 84 A92
Maki Lake Rd TB 103 B6
Makynen Rd SD 101 D21
Malakoff Rd OT 66 T-U62
Malbeuf Dr SD 90 E12
Malcolm Ln HU 27 G-H19
Malcolm Rd DH 32 E37
Malcolm Rd NR 33 C45 45 B45
Malcolm C Rd C 6 Y7
Malcom Rd HL 61 V43
Malden Rd (Essex) EX 4 D2-3
Malden Rd (Kingsville) EX . . . 4 D3-4
Malden Rd (LaSalle) EX 4 C-D1
Malden Rd (Tecumseh) EX . . . 4 C-D3
Malden Rd (Windsor) EX 4 C1
Maley Dr CS 101 B-C20
Mall Rd OX 16 U22
Mallard Ln C 6 A7
Mallard Rd MD 14 T-U14
Mallard Bay Rd K 44 B39
Mallard Haven Rd NP 95 G33
Mallard Lake Rd HS 62 T47
Mallens Rd LG 49 Z58
Malloch La OT 65 T60
Mallory Rd PE 35 G50
Mallory Beach Rd BR 55 X18
Mallory Lake South Access Rd LA 63 V51
Mallorytown Rd LG 37 A-B61
Mallott Rd WT 22 L22
Malloy Rd HS 62 V46
Malloy Rd R 82 K54
Malone Rd HS 46 Z47
Malone Quarry Rd HS 46 Z47
Maloney Rd HS 46 A46
Maloney Rd SDG 52 U69
Maloney Mountain Rd R 64 R53
Malotte Creek Access Rd R. 63 R52
Malowany Rd NI 19 U33
Maltby Rd WL 23 M26
Manchoff Rd NR 32 F-G40
Mandalane Dr SM 30 F30
Mandaumin Rd C 6 X8
Mandaumin Rd LM 12 S-V8
Mandawoub Rd BR 38 A16
Manery Sdrd EX 5 E6
Manes Rd PS 56 Q25
Manhire Dr HL 61 U42
Manion Rd LA 35 C52
Manion Rd OT 65 S60
Manitoba St MK 58 U32
Manitou Dr PS 76 P28
Manitou Dr WT 22 N23
Manitou La MA 73 L-M11
Manitou Rd MA 72 L8
Manitou St PR 67 R-S67
Manitou Birches Tr MA 73 K11
Manitouwabing Estates Rd PS 57 Q28 76 P28
Manitowaning Rd MA 90 J12
Manley Ln HU 20 L16 21 L17
Manley Rd SDG 67 T67
Mannheim Rd WT 22 N23
Mannie's Tr HL 60 Q37-38
Manninen Rd CS . . . 91 E15 100 D15
Manning Dr MD 15 U17-18
Manning Rd DH 31 H36
Manning Rd EX 4 B-C3
Manning Rd R 81 P51
Manning Rd SDG 52 U-V69
Manor La F 48 W53
Manor Ridge Tr Y 30 D32
Manotick Main St OT 66 S63
Manotick Station Rd OT . . 66 S-T63
Mansel Hill Rd R 82 N53-54
Mansell Rd MK 59 Q35
Manser Rd WT . . 21 M20 22 L21 M21
Mansfield Dr HL 60 T38-39
Mansfield Rd OT 66 S-T61
Mantha Rd NP 95 D31
Mantil Sdrd OT 65 R59
Manvers Station Rd K 32 E39
Maple Av LG 50 Y64
Maple Av NI 18 Q-R31
Maple Av (Burlington) HT . . . 18 P29
Maple Av (Halton Hills) HT . . 23 L28
Maple Av N BT 16 R23
Maple Av S BT 16 S24
Maple Dr MA 72 J9
Maple Dr MD 7 X13
Maple Dr PS 75 K26
Maple Dr SD 90 F-G13
Maple Dr (Northern Bruce Peninsula) BR 54 T16 55 U16
Maple Dr (South Bruce Peninsula) BR 38 Z17
Maple La HS 62 V48
Maple La MA 73 L11
Maple Ln C 6 B7
Maple Ln HU 20 L-M16
Maple Rd HS 34 C46-47
Maple Rd LA 36 C-D54
Maple Rd SDG 68 S72 T71
Maple Rd SM 30 C-D31
Maple Rd (Bonfield) NP 95 E-F33 F34
Maple Rd (Chisholm) NP . . 95 G-H33
Maple St NI 18 S32
Maple St SDG 67 T68 68 T69
Maple Avenue Rd LA 47 B53
Maple Beach Rd DH 43 B34
Maple Bend Rd R 83 Q56
Maple Bend Rd WT 22 M23
Maple Crest La LN 49 X58-59
Maple Dell Rd OX 16 T21-22
Maple Grove La F 48 Y55
Maple Grove La R 81 N51
Maple Grove Ln EL . . . 15 V20 16 V21
Maple Grove Rd BT 16 S24
Maple Grove Rd DH . . . 32 G37 H38
Maple Grove Rd LG 37 C58
Maple Grove Rd NR 33 F44
Maple Grove Rd NI 18 R32
Maple Grove Rd OT 66 R-S61
Maple Grove Rd SM 42 B31
Maple Grove Rd WT 22 N24
Maple Grove St PR 67 R-S66
Maple Hill Rd BR 27 E18
Maple Hill Rd LG 50 W63
Maple Hill Rd PS 95 G-H32
Maple Island Rd PS 76 L-M28
Maple Keys Ln HU 21 J-K18
Maple Lake Estates Rd PS 58 Q-R29
Maple Landing La HS 46 W-X48
Maple Lane Dr K 43 B37
Maple Lane Rd LN 49 V58
Maple Leaf Dr EX 4 F3
Maple Leaf Dr T 24 K31
Maple Leaf Rd A 86 C94
Maple Leaf Rd F 36 A56-57
Maple Lodge Dr MD 14 R15
Maple Manor Rd WT 23 P25
Maple Point Rd MA 72 J9
Maple Ridge Dr HL . . 59 R36 60 R37
Maple Ridge Dr K 32 C40
Maple Ridge La LG . . 37 A59 49 Z59
Maple Ridge Ln LM 13 V12
Maple Ridge Rd LN 65 R-S58
Maple Ridge Rd SDG 67 U66
Maple Ridge Rd (Blind River) A 88 F3
Maple Ridge Rd (Maple Ridge) A 87 E99
Maple Ridge Tr PS 77 L33
Maple Row Rd PR 68 P72
Maple Sugar Rd HS 35 C50
Maple Valley Rd PS 77 L32
Maple Valley Rd SM 42 X-Y31
Maple View Rd HS 34 D46
Maplehurst Dr MK 59 R34
Maplehurst Rd PS 58 S30
Mapleton Av SM 30 C29
Mapleton Ln EL 15 V18-19
Mapleview Dr SM 30 C30
Mapleview Dr E SM 30 C30-31
Mapleview Dr W SM 30 C29-30
Mapleward Rd TB 102 B-D5
Maplewood Dr LG 50 A62
Maplewood Dr PR 68 N71
Maplewood Pkwy SM 42 A32
Maplewood Rd G 27 E20
Maplewood Rd HS 62 Q47
Maplewood Rd WT 22 M21-22
Maplewood Sdrd OX . 15 Q20 21 P20
Mar Sdrd BR 55 W17-18
Mara Rd DH 43 B34
Mara-Carden Boundary Rd K43 Z34
Mara-Eldon Boundary Rd K. 43 A34
Mara-Eldon Boundary Rd SM 43 A34
Mara-Rama Boundary Rd SM 42 Y32-33
Marble Lake Rd F 47 W51
Marble Point Rd HS 46 A46
Marble Rock Rd LG 37 C58-59
Marburg Rd NF 17 V26
Marcellus Rd SDG . . . 51 V66 67 U66
March Rd LN 65 S59
March Rd OT 65 R60 66 R61
March Valley Rd OT 66 R61
Marchand-Kearns Rd R 82 Q52
Marchmount Rd SM 42 Z31
Marchurst Rd OT 65 Q-R60
Marcil Rd PR 67 Q67
Marcoux Rd SDG 68 S71
Marden Rd WL 23 L25
Marentette Beach Rd EX 5 F7
Margaret Av C 6 X7
Margaret Dr NP 94 D-E30
Margaret St TB 103 F6
Margaret Lake Rd MK 59 T36
Margarete La LN 65 T57
Marie Louise Dr TB 103 D9
Marier St CS 100 B18
Marina Dr OT 66 T63
Marina Rd A 84 A92
Marina Rd CS 100 B16
Marina Rd LG 48 Z57
Marina Rd MK 58 U31
Marine Dr NR 33 C44
Marine Station Rd SDG 50 X65
Mariner's Rd EX 6 B6-7
Mariners Cove Rd A 86 E93-94
Marion Dr PS 95 F31
Marion St MD 15 T18-19
Marion Lake 1 Access Rd MK 78 P36
Marionville Rd OT 67 T65
Marionville Rd PR 67 S-T66
Marisett Rd PE 35 G50
Maritime Rd K 43 Y-Z36
Marjorie Rd R 82 N53-54
Marjory Dr C 6 B7
Mark Rd K 43 A37
Mark Settlement Dr MD 13 Q12 14 Q13
Mark Twain Rd HL 44 W-X38
Markart Rd G 28 C22-23
Markell Rd SDG 51 V-W66
Markham Rd T 25 H-J33
Markham Rd Y 31 G-H33
Markham-Pickering Ln Y . . . 31 G33
Markham-Pickering Townline Y 31 H34
Markinspa La F 47 W52
Markles Rd MK 59 R33
Marks Rd HS 46 B46-47
Marks Rd TB 102 E2
Marl Lakes Rd BR 27 E18
Marlbank Rd HS 47 B50-51
Marleau Av SDG 52 U70-71
Marleau Rd NP 94 E27-28
Marlette Dr A 84 X90
Marlin Rd LA 47 B52
Marlin Rd LG 50 V63
Marmora Mine Rd HS . . . 46 A46-47
Marni La SM 41 A28-29
Marnoch Ln HU 20 J15
Marquardt Rd LA 63 T50
Marr Dr BT 16 S24
Marr Rd MD 15 U19
Marr Rd NI 18 T32
Marriott Rd NR 33 E42
Marrisett Rd HS 46 B49
Marsh Dr NP 95 D31
Marsh Ln C 6 A7
Marsh Ln EL 7 Y13 8 X14
Marsh Rd LG 37 A61
Marsh Rd MK 59 R33
Marsh Rd NR 32 G40 33 G41
Marsh Rd PE 34 E-F49
Marsh Rd R 81 M51
Marsh Rd SM 41 A28
Marsh Rd TM 85 Q30-31
Marsh Rd (Essex) EX 4 E2-3
Marsh Rd (Kingsville) EX 4 D4
Marsh Hill Rd DH 31 E35
Marsh Hill Rd HS 34 D48
Marsh Point Rd HS 34 D47
Marshagen Rd HD 18 T31
Marshall Av NP 95 E31-32
Marshall Dr A 84 B90
Marshall Rd HD 18 U30
Marshall Rd LM 12 T-U8
Marshall Rd NI 19 S35
Marshall Rd SM 41 Y28
Marshall 40 Foot Rd LA 36 E55
Marshall Cota Rd F 48 Y54
Marshall Lake Rd LN 65 S57
Marshland Lake Rd A 88 E6
Marshwood Rd OT 65 R59
Marston Sdrd PR 68 N70
Martel Rd PR 67 R67
Marthas Rd R 81 N49
Marthaville Rd LM 6 W9 12 U-V9
Martin Dr LA 35 C53
Martin La EX 4 C1
Martin La PS 77 M33
Martin Ln HU 20 J-K16
Martin Rd A 88 F6 89 F7
Martin Rd CS 101 A-B19
Martin Rd F 47 W52
Martin Rd HS 46 Z49
Martin Rd MA 73 M11
Martin Rd NI 18 R32
Martin St HT 23 M28
Martin St N LN 65 S58-59
Martin's Rd K 44 Z38
Martin's Tr HL 43 W-X37
Martin Creek Rd WT 22 M22
Martin Grove Rd T 24 K30
Martin Grove Rd WT 22 M23
Martin Grove Rd Y 24 J30
Martin Recoskie Rd R 62 Q48
Martin Siding Rd R 80 P46-47
Martindale Rd (Lincoln) NI . . 18 R32
Martindale Rd (St Catharines) NI 19 R33
Martinelli Rd SM 42 X33
Martyn Ln EL 9 W18
Marvelville Rd OT 66 T64 67 T65
Mary St HS 46 A46
Mary St NI 19 Q35
Mary's Rd SDG 51 V67 67 U67
Mary Joanne Dr R 64 S54
Mary Moore Rd F 47 A53
Marydale Park Rd NR 32 G40
Maryhill Rd WT 22 L23-24
Marysville Rd HS 35 C50-51 D51
Maryville Lake Rd BR 38 Z17
Mask Rd R 81 N48-49
Mason La HL 60 U37
Mason Ln C 6 Y9 Y10
Mason Ln MA 71 J4-5
Mason Rd CS 100 C16
Mason's Rd PS 77 P32
Mason Lake La PS 77 M33
Massassauga La F 36 A57
Massassauga Rd F . . . 36 A57 48 Z57
Massassauga Rd PE 34 E-F49
Massecar La NF 16 V23
Massey La NR 33 E45
Massey Rd (Alnwick-Haldimand) NR 33 F43
Massey Rd (Port Hope) NR 33 F-G41
Massey Tote Rd A 89 B10
Massicotte Rd SD 90 F10
Massie Rd G 39 A20-21
Massiedale Rd SDG 68 R71-72
Mast Rd DH 31 F35
Mast Rd R 83 P56-57
Masters Rd NR 33 D-E43 D-E44
Masterson Rd SDG 68 S70-71
Mastwoods Rd NR 32 G40
Matagamasi Lake Rd CS 101 A22 Z22
Mataseje Rd NI 18 S31
Matawanooka La R 63 T51
Matawatchan Rd LA 63 T-U51
Matawatchan Rd R 63 S-T51
Matcheski Rd R 80 P46
Matchett Ln PB 33 D41
Matchette Rd EX 4 C1
Mates Rd TB 102 F4
Mather Rd HS 62 U47
Matheson Blvd PL 24 L30
Matheson Dr LN 49 V61 W60
Matheson Rd A 86 D96
Matheson Rd K 43 A34-35
Matheson Rd SM 41 A29
Mathews Rd NI 19 S-T34
Matson Rd TB 102 G3
Matthews Rd NI 19 U35
Matthiasville Rd MK 59 V33
Matthie Rd PE 34 G49 35 G50
Matts Rd MK 58 V32
Matures La PS 58 T29
Maunula Rd TB 103 B9
Maurys Run PS 56 Q26
Maves Rd R 81 L50
Mavis Rd PL 24 L30
Mavrinac Blvd Y 30 G32
Mawlam Rd LM 7 W-X10
Maws Rd MK 59 Q33 77 P33
Maws Rd PS 77 P33
Maws Hill Rd MK 59 Q33 77 P33
Max Wilson Rd PB 45 X42-43
Maxfield Blvd HS 34 E48
Maxwell Rd TB 102 C-D3
Maxwell Tr HL 60 V40
Maxwell Settlement Rd HS . 62 T45
May Rd PE 35 F-G50
May Rd SDG 67 U67-68
May St TB 103 D6
May Bay Rd PB 44 Z40
Maybee Rd HS 34 D-E47
Maybrook Rd TM 85 P28-30
Mayer Rd SD 93 G23
Mayer Rd SM 41 B28-29
Mayer Rd SW 41 B28-29
Mayfair Dr DH 31 D34
Mayfair Rd MD 14 V13-14
Mayfield Rd PL 23 K28 24 J29
Mayhew Rd HS 62 R-S46
Maynard Ln C 7 A10
Maynard Rd DH 32 F39
Mayo Lake Rd HS . . . 62 T47-48 V48
Mayor Rd TM 85 M28
Maypul Layn Rd PE 35 G-H51
Mazan Ln C 7 Y12
Mazinaw Heights North Rd F 47 W50 63 V50
MBC Service Rd MK 59 R-S33
McAdoo's La F 36 D56
McAllister Rd MA 72 L9-10
McAlpine Rd F 37 C58
McAndrews La F 48 Z56
McAndrews Rd F 48 Z56-57
McAndrews Rd LG 48 Z57
McAnulty Rd R 99 G48
McArthur Av OT 66 Q63
McArthur Dr SM 41 X28
McArthur Rd BR 54 S14
McArthur Rd MD 14 V13
McArthur Sdrd SM 42 X33
McArthur Tr MA 72 K8
McArthur Point Rd MK 59 T35
McArton Rd OT 65 S-T60
McAulay Rd MK 42 W33
McAuley La PE 35 G52
McAuley Rd PB 44 B40
McAuslan Rd LM 7 W10 13 V10
McAvoy Rd LG 49 Z60-61
McBain Rd A 86 D97
McBay Rd BT 17 R26
McBean St OT 66 T61-62
McBeth Rd OX 15 T20 16 T21
McBrian Access Rd NP 96 F36
McBride Rd R 83 P57
McBride Rd (Alnwick-Haldimand) NR 33 E-F43
McBride Rd (Hamilton) NR . . 33 F42
McBrides Rd TM 85 N28
McCaffrey Tr OT 65 T60
McCain Sdrd EX 4 D-E4
McCall Ln HU 20 K16
McCallum Dr R 83 Q56
McCallum Ln LM 6 W8
McCallum Bay Rd A 87 D99
McCallums La PR 68 P71
McCamus Dr PB 32 E40
McCann Rd LN 65 T59
McCann Rd LG 49 Y58
McCann Rd NR 33 D45
McCanns Rd PS 58 S29-30
McCarey Rd F 36 C57
McCarrel Lake Rd A 86 C95
McCarthy Dr SM 29 C28
McCarthy Rd EX 4 F2
McCarthy Rd OT 66 R63
McCarthy Lake Rd A 89 E7
McCaslin Rd SDG 50 W65
McCauley Rd HS 34 E47
McCauley Rd PS 58 R29-30
McCauley's Rd PB 45 X44
McCauley's Sdrd MA 73 L12
McCauley Lake Rd NP 80 N42
McCauley Mountain Rd R 63 Q50 81 P50
McCauley North Access Rd NP 80 N42
McCauley South Access Rd NP 80 N-P42
McCaw Rd HS 62 T-U47
McCaw Rd LG 49 W60
McCharles Av SD 90 E14
McCharles Ln PS 95 G32
McCharles Rd F 48 X54
McCharles Lake Rd CS 100 D17
McClarty Rd LG 50 Z62
McCleary Rd HS 46 A-B46
McClelland Rd NR 33 F-G41
McClelland Sdrd A 86 C95
McClements Rd F . . . 36 C57 37 C58
McClinchey Rd HU 20 J15
McClintock Rd HL 59 R36
McClung Rd HD 17 S28
McCluskey Dr TB 102 E4
McCluskie Rd A 86 D94-95
McColl Rd EL 7 Y13
McColl Rd HS 34 D46
McColl Rd PB 45 X44
McColls Rd HL 60 V40
McCollum Rd NI 18 S31
McComb Point Rd HL 60 R-S37
McConnell Av SDG 52 U70
McConnell Dr BR 26 D13-14
McConnell Rd F 36 C54
McConnell Rd HS 46 B47
McConnell Rd LN 49 V-W61
McConnell Rd R 63 Q51
McCool Rd TM 85 P28-29
McCordick Rd OT . . . 66 T62 U62-63
McCormick Rd HS 62 T46
McCormick Rd MK 42 W-X32
McCormick Rd SDG 68 R71-72
McCormick Rd (Essex) EX 4 E3
McCormick Rd (Pelee) EX 5 H4
McCormick's Sdrd G . 27 D20 28 D21
McCormick Beach Rd EX . . . 4 F2-3
McCowan Rd T 25 J33
McCowan Rd Y . . 30 D-E32 31 F-H33
McCoy Rd HS 46 Z48
McCoy Rd PB 45 X44
McCracken's La HL 60 U-V38
McCrackens Landing Rd PB 45 A42 Z42
McCrackin Av K 43 Y34
McCrea Rd HL 61 V41
McCrea Rd LN 49 W61
McCrea Rd LG 50 X63
McCrea Station Rd WL 23 N27
McCready Ln OX 16 S-T22
McCready Rd LM 7 W-X11
McCreary Ln C 6 X8-9
McCreights Rd A 87 D98
McCrimmon Rd F 48 Y53
McCrimmon Rd PR 68 Q70
McCubbin Rd MD 14 S13-14
McCullough Rd DH 32 G40
McCullough Rd HS 35 C51
McCullough Rd LN 48 V56
McCullough Lake Rd G . . 27 C19-20
McCully Rd LG 50 X63-64
McCumber Rd HS 46 B48
McCutcheon Rd LA 47 B52
McCutcheon Rd LM 7 W-X10
Mcdermid Rd SDG 67 S-T67
McDermid Rd SDG 68 S70
McDiarmid Ln EL 8 W16
McDiarmid Rd OT 66 T64
McDiarmid Sdrd LN 65 T59
McDimond Rd NP 96 E-F37
Mcdonald La F 37 D58
McDonald La F 48 Y53
McDonald Ln C 7 A12 Y12-13
McDonald Ln HU 21 J-K17
McDonald Rd LG 50 W63
McDonald Rd MK 42 W32
McDonald Rd NP 93 D25
McDonald Rd NR 33 E43
McDonald Rd PS 95 F-G31
McDonald Rd SDG 68 T69
McDonald Rd SM 41 Z29
McDonald Rd WL 28 H21-22
McDonald Lake Access Rd HL 59 T-U36
McDonald Mine Rd HS 62 T46
McDonalds Corners Rd LN . . 48 V57
McDonell's Sdrd SDG 68 R70
McDonough La BR 55 V15
McDougal Rd BT 16 T23
McDougall Dr MD 13 V12
McDougall Ln C 6 B7-8
McDougall Ln EL 7 X-Y12
McDougall Rd PS 57 Q27
McDougall's Tr MA 73 K11
McDowell Rd NF 10 W22-23 16 V23-24
McEachern Ln R 82 P53
McElhaney Rd A 88 E4
McEvoy Rd MD 14 T-U14
McEwen Dr MD 14 S14-15
McEwen La F 48 Y55
McEwen Rd NR 33 G43
McFadden Dr G 28 C21
McFadden Ln PS 95 J32
McFadden Rd F 36 B56
McFadden Rd OT 67 Q65
McFaddens Rd PB 45 X42-43
McFarlane Rd F 36 C57
McFarlane Rd HS 35 D50
McFarlane Rd HD 18 T29
McFarlane Rd LG 50 W62
McFarlane Rd R 82 M53
McFarlane Rd TB 102 D4
McFarlane St LA 35 E53
McFarlane Lake Rd CS 101 D19
McFarlin Dr G 28 G21
McFaul Rd PE 34 F49
McGaghran Rd R 82 N52-53
McGarry Rd HS 61 S-T44
McGarvey Rd F 36 C56
McGaugh Rd A 84 Y92
McGaw Rd HU 20 J13
McGee Rd HS 34 C47-48
McGee Sdrd OT 65 R-S60
McGibbon Lake Rd HS 62 U46
McGill Dr K 32 D37
McGill Rd BT 17 S25
McGill Rd LA 47 B52-53
McGill St PR 68 N71
McGillis Rd SDG 52 U69 68 T69
McGillivary Rd LM 7 W10
McGillivray Dr MD 14 Q13-15
McGillivray Rd F 36 A56-57
McGillivray Rd SDG 68 T71
McGillivray Rd Y 24 J30
McGillvray Rd HL 61 V43
McGinnis Rd K 44 B38
McGinnis Rd PB 44 X41
McGivney Lake Rd A 89 E8
McGlashan St NI 18 S32
McGonegal Rd R 82 L53
McGovern Rd LG 50 V63
McGovern Rd E LG 50 V63
McGowan Rd HD 17 S27
McGrath Rd HS 47 B51
McGrath Rd R 63 Q51 81 P51
McGrath's Rd LA 47 A51
McGregor Dr K 44 A39
McGregor La HS 46 Z46
McGregor La NR 33 F44
McGregor Ln C 6 X7-8
McGregor Rd HS 62 R46
McGregor Rd SDG 68 T71
McGregor Sdrd LM 12 T-U7
McGregor Bay Rd MA 90 H13
McGregor Bay Rd PB 33 D42
McGruthers Rd NP 95 D32
McGuey Rd NP 80 P42
McGuffin Hills Dr MD 14 R13-14
McGuinty Rd R 82 N53
McGuire Rd LA 47 A51
McGuire Rd LN 49 V59-60
McGuire Rd OT 66 T63
McGuire Beach Rd K 43 Z35
McGuire Settlement Rd LA 47 A51 Z51
McHugh Rd R 64 R55
McIlquham Blair Rd LN 49 V58
McIndoo Falls Tr PS 77 N31
McIndoos Cemetery Rd K 31 C35 43 B35
McInnes Rd R 83 P56
McInnis Rd MD 14 Q-R13
McInnis Rd SDG 51 W66
McIntee Rd SDG 68 R72 69 R73
McIntosh Ln HU . . 21 J18 27 G-H18
McIntosh Rd LG 50 Y64
McIntosh Rd (North Stormont) SDG 68 S-T70
McIntosh Rd (South Dundas) SDG 51 V-W66
McIntosh Inkerman Rd SDG 67 U65
McIntosh Lake Access Rd LN 64 T54
McIntyre Rd LA 35 D53 36 D54
McIntyre Rd MD 14 R13
McIntyre Rd PE 34 F48
McIntyre Rd SDG 50 V64
McIsaac Dr R 98 F42-43
McIver Rd BR 55 W18
McIvor Dr BR 55 U15
McIvor Rd F 36 D55
McKague Rd BR 55 V17
McKay Rd LG 50 Y62
McKay's Ln C 7 Y11
McKay Creek Access Rd R 81 L49 99 K49
McKay Farm Rd LN 49 W-X58
McKay Lake Rd PB 45 X42
McKechnie Rd TB 102 E2-3
McKechnie Sdrd BR 38 B16
McKechnie's Sdrd MA 73 M11
McKee Rd DH 32 E37
McKellar Lake Rd PS . . . 76 P27-28
McKelvey Rd K 43 A35 Z35
McKendry Rd F 36 C56
McKenna Rd OT 66 U61
McKenna Casey Dr OT 66 S62
McKenny Rd NI 19 S34
McKenzie Ln EL 7 W13 8 W14
McKenzie Rd CS 100 B17
McKenzie Rd HD 17 S28 T27
McKenzie Rd MK 58 U-V31
McKenzie Rd SD 101 C23
McKenzie Rd TB 102 C4
McKenzie Lake Rd NP 61 Q43
McKenzie Lake Rd N NP . . . 61 Q43
McKeown Av NP 95 F31
McKeown Farm Rd OT 67 S65
McKerral Rd SD 101 C23
McKibbon Rd LN 49 V61
McKibbons Way R 82 N52
McKillop Rd EL 8 X-Y14
McKinlay Rd NR 33 E42
McKinlay Rd (Morpeth) C . . 7 A-B11
McKinlay Rd (Tilbury) C 6 C7
McKinley Crossroad PE 35 G51
McKinley Dr R 99 G48
McKinley Rd MA 71 K6
McKinley Rd PR 68 Q69
McKinnon Rd SM 29 C28
McKinnon Sdrd A 86 C95
McKinnon Creek Rd SD 90 G12
McKinstry Rd SM 30 E30
McKnight Rd A 86 D94
McKnight's Sdrd LA 35 C-D51
McLachlan Rd R 64 R56 83 Q56
McLachlin Rd LN 49 V59
McLaren La PR 67 S66
McLaren Pt LN 49 X58
McLaren Rd LN 49 W-X58
McLaren Rd PL 23 J27 29 H27
McLaren Rd R 82 P-Q54
McLaren's Creek Rd K 43 B37
McLarens Ln PS 77 L32
McLarty Ln C 7 A11 Y11
McLarty Rd R 82 P52
McLary Rd SD 90 E12
McLaughlan Rd LN 65 R57
McLaughlin Rd DH 32 E37
McLaughlin Rd HD 18 T30-31
McLaughlin Rd LA 47 B52
McLaughlin Rd PL 23 J-K28 24 K29 L29-30
McLaughlin Rd R 82 L-M53
McLaughlin Rd SDG 67 T66
McLauglin Rd NP 96 F35
McLean Dr (Arnprior) R . . 83 Q57-58
McLean Dr (McNab Braeside) R 83 P-Q56
McLean Ln C 7 Y12
McLean Ln EL 7 X12-13
McLean Ln HU 26 H16
McLean Rd BR 26 C16
McLean Rd C 5 E6
McLean Rd EX 4 E3
McLean Rd HS 62 S45-46
McLean Rd HM 23 P25
McLean Rd LN 49 V59
McLean Rd MD 14 R14
McLean Rd SDG 67 S68 68 S69
McLean Rd TM 85 Q29
McLean Rd WL 23 N26
McLean Rd (Alnwick-Haldimand) NR 33 F43
McLean Rd (Brighton) NR . . 34 F46
McLean Rd (Central Frontenac) F 48 Y53 Z54
McLean Rd (South Frontenac) F 36 B54
McLean's Rd MA 73 M11-12
McLean's Mountain Rd MA 90 J11-12
McLean School Rd BT 16 Q24 17 Q25
McLeansville Rd LG 50 X63
McLellan Rd BT 17 S26
McLellan Rd LN 49 V59 65 U59
McLennan Dr MK 59 S36
McLennan Rd PR 68 P71-72
McLennan's Creek La MA . . 73 M12
McLeod Av EX 4 E1
McLeod Rd A 86 C96
McLeod Rd MK 58 T30
McLeod Rd NI 19 S34-35
McLeod Rd R 83 Q56
McLeod Rd SDG 68 S-T71
McLeod St NI 18 R31
McLeod Creek Rd C 6 Y7
McLiesh Rd MD 14 S13
McLinton Rd OT 65 T60
McMahon Rd R 82 Q54
McMann Rd NR 33 F42-43
McMann Sdrd SM 41 Y28-29
McManus Rd LG 49 Y61
McManus Sdrd LN 65 R57
McManus Lake Rd NP 81 J48
McMartin Rd NP 96 E38
McMaster Rd R 82 P52-53
McMaster Rd (Quinte West) HS 34 F47
McMaster Rd (Stirling-Rawdon) HS 46 B47
McMaster Lake La R 80 P46
McMichael Rd NF 17 T25
McMillan Ln EL 7 Y13
McMillan Rd DH 32 F39
McMillan Rd R 81 N50

McMillan / Mulberry

McMillan Rd (North Dundas) SDG. 67 U66
McMillan Rd (North Glengarry) SDG 68 R71
McMillan Sdrd SM 42 Y33
McMillans Corners Rd SDG. 68 T69-70
McMullen Rd HS 34 D-E47
McMullen Rd OT 66 U62-63
McMullen's Sdrd MA. 73 L12
McMurchy Av PL 24 K29
McMurchy Ln EL 7 W-X13
McMurray La NR 32 F40
McMurray Rd HS 34 F46
McNab La G 28 D-E21
McNab Rd NI 19 Q34
McNab St G 39 B20
McNabb Ln HU 14 Q13 21 K17
McNabb Ln MD 14 Q13
McNabb Rd K 43 Y34
McNabb Rd SD 101 B22-23
McNabb Rd SM 41 B26-28
McNabb St A 84 B92
McNair Rd BR 54 T16
McNally Rd TB 102 D4
McNallys La LG 48 Y-Z57
McNamee Rd K 43 Z35
McNaught Ln HU 21 K-L17
McNaughton Av C 6 A8-9
McNaughton Ln C 6 A9
McNaughton Rd LN 48 W56
McNaughton Rd SDG 68 P71-72
McNaughts Rd PS 57 R28
McNeely Av LN 65 T59
McNeely Rd OT 67 Q-R65
McNeil Rd F 48 Y56
McNeil Rd SDG 67 S68 68 S69
McNeilly Rd HM 18 Q30
McNeilly Rd LG 50 X64
McNichols La F 48 Z55
McNicoll Av T 24 J32 25 J33
McNiece Farm Rd PS 57 R27
McNiven Rd HM 17 Q27
McNiven Rd HT 23 N27
McNutt Rd NP 96 E-F35
McNutty Rd R 82 P-Q53
McParland Rd LN 48 X57
McPeak Ln R 82 N53
McPhail Rd HL 60 T37-38
McPhail Rd SDG 68 T70
McPhail Sdrd LN 65 S58-59
McPhee Rd PR 68 P71
McPhee Bay Rd R 62 R48
McPherson Rd TM 85 M27-28
McPherson School Rd BT 16 Q24
McQuaid Rd F 48 X55
McQuay Blvd DH 31 H35-36
McQuay Rd LA 36 B54
McQuiggan Ln EL 9 W20
McRae Rd BR 38 A17
McRae-Hay Lake Rd NP 61 Q42
McRae-Mink Lake Access Rd HS 61 Q-R42
McRae-Mink Lake Access Rd NP 61 Q-R42
McRae-Otter Creek Access Rd NP 61 Q41-45
McRae Park Rd SM 42 Z32-33
McRea Side Rd LG 37 A61
McSourley Lake Tr R 98 F45
McTaggart Ln HU 20 N-P15
McTeer Rd PR 67 P66
McVagh Rd OT 67 R65
McVean Dr PL 24 J29-30
McVeety Rd LN 49 W-X59
McVeigh La F 48 W-X55
McVeigh Rd LN 48 W57
McVitties Rd SD 92 E20
McWatty Rd LN 65 R58
MD 0 Access Rd PS 77 K34
MD 13 Access Rd PS 77 K34
Meach Rd LA 35 C51
Meach Lake Access Rd HS 61 R42
Mead Blvd SD 90 E-F13
Meadow La LG 49 Z58
Meadow La PS 77 L31-32
Meadow La (Central Frontenac) F 48 Y54
Meadow Lane Ct LN 48 W56
Meadow Lark Pl MA 72 K8
Meadow Wood Rd R 81 N51
Meadowland Rd BR 55 Y17-18
Meadowlands Dr OT 66 R62-63
Meadows Rd EX 4 E2
Meadows Rd HD 18 U29
Meadowvale Blvd PL 24 L29
Meadowvale Ln C 6 Y7
Meadowvale Rd PB 33 D41
Meadowvale Rd T 25 H-J34
Meadowview Rd K 32 C39
Mearns Av DH 32 G38
Meath Hill Rd R 82 L52
Mechanic St NF 17 T25
Medd Rd DH 31 F35
Medland La PB 44 A41 45 A42
Medora Lake Rd MK 58 U30
Medway Rd MD 14 S16 15 S17
Meeks La F 36 A54
Meeks Rd HS 47 B50-51
Meeting Tr HL 60 S37
Meilleur Rd SD 93 G23
Meilleurs Rd R 98 F-G47
Meitz Rd R 81 L51
Mel's La SDG 51 V67-68
Mel Lake Rd A 88 F4-5
Melancthon-Artemesia Townline DF 28 D23-24
Melancthon-Mulmur Townline DF 29 D-E25 E-F26
Melancthon-Osprey Townline DF 28 D24 29 D25
Melancthon-Southgate Townline DF 28 E-F24
Melbourne Rd MD 14 T-U13 U-V14
Melbourne Rd TB 102 C5 103 C6
Melena Beach Sdrd HU 20 L13
Melick Rd HD 18 T30
Melin's Rd CS 100 D18 101 D19
Melissa La SM 41 X26
Mellor Rd EL 8 W17
Meloche Rd EX 4 D-E1
Melody Dr A 86 C94
Melody Dr EX 6 B6
Melody La WL 28 H23
Melody Bay Rd PB 44 Z40
Melody Lodge La F 36 B57
Melon Rd EL 9 W19
Melrose Dr MD 14 T15
Melrose Rd HS 35 D50-51
Melville Ct SM 42 A30
Melville Rd PE 34 F48-49
Melwel Rd A 87 D99 D-E1
Melwood Dr MD 13 U12 14 U13
Memorial Av SM 42 Z32
Memorial Av TB 103 D6
Memorial Dr NI 18 S32 19 S33
Memorial Park Dr NP 95 G33-34
Memorial Park Dr NI 19 T34
Memorial Park Dr PS 95 G32-33
Memory La NP 95 G33
Memory La PS 77 M34
Memquisit Rd NP 93 F25
Menard Cr SD 89 F9
Menard Rd A 86 C96
Menard Rd SDG 68 Q-R72
Menet Lake Rd R 98 F45
Menet Lake Access Rd R 98 F43-45
Menie Rd NR 34 C46
Menin Rd R 99 J50
Menno St WT 22 M-N24
Menoke Beach Rd SM 42 Y32
Menzies Rd PB 45 A-B45
Menzies Munro Sdrd LN 48 W-X57
Mephisto Lake Ldg HS 62 V47
Mer Bleue Rd OT 66 Q64
Mercer Rd DH 32 F39
Mercer Rd SD 93 F-G24
Mercer Lake Rd NP 93 G25
Merchand-Kearns Rd R 82 Q52
Meredith La F 36 A55
Meredith St MA 90 H-J12
Merganser Tr HL 60 S39
Merivale Rd OT 66 Q-R62
Merkley Rd LN 48 Y57 49 Y58
Merkley Rd MK 43 W34 59 V34
Merkley Rd SDG 67 T65
Merlin Rd C 6 B8 C8-9
Merrick Dr MK 59 U34
Merrick Rd HS 34 C47
Merrickpark Dr PS 77 K31
Merritt Ln C 6 Y9 7 Y10
Merritt Rd (Lincoln) NI 18 R32
Merritt Rd (Thorold) NI 19 S33
Merritt St NI 19 R34
Merrittville Rd NI 19 S33
Mertz Rd HS 62 V45
Mertz Corner Rd SM 41 Y28
Mervin Ln PB 32 D40 33 D41
Mervyn Beatty La HL 60 T40
Merwin La LG 50 Y64
Metcalfe St MD 14 T13-14
Meteorite Lake Rd HL 61 U42
Methodist Point Rd SM 41 W-X27
Methot Sdrd PR 68 Q70
Metler Rd (Pelham) NI 18 S32 19 S33
Metler Rd (Wainfleet) NI 18 T32
Metro Rd Y 30 C32 C-D31
Mewburn Rd NI 19 R34
Meyer Rd R 83 Q57
Meyer Rd SD 93 E24
Meyers Rd DH 31 D-E33
Meyers Rd NR 33 F42-43
Meyers Creek Rd HS 34 E47-48
Meyers Island Rd NR 33 D45
Mhusk Rd R 82 P-Q53
Mica Point La F 48 Y55
Michael Rd NI 19 U34
Michael's Bay Rd MA 72 M-N10
Michaud Rd NP 94 D28
Michel Rd NP 93 E25
Michener Rd NI 19 U35
Michigan Av LM 12 T7
Michigan Ln LM 12 T8-9 13 T10
Michon Rd W SD 90 E13
Mickelson Dr TB 103 C8
Micksburg Rd R 82 M52 N52-53
Mid-Huron Beach Rd HU 26 H13
Middaugh Rd MK 58 T32
Middle Ln C 6 C7-8 7 B10
Middle Rd DH 32 F-G37 G38
Middle Rd EX 4 C3-4 5 C5 6 C6
Middle Rd PS 58 Q30-31
Middle Rd (Central Frontenac) F 48 Y54
Middle Rd (Kingston) F 36 D57
Middle Sdrd EX 4 D1-2
Middle Sdrd LM 13 R10
Middle Block Rd WT 22 N24
Middle Lake Rd CS 101 C-D19
Middle March Rd DH 31 F35
Middle Ridge Rd NR 34 F46
Middle River Rd EL 8 W17 15 V17
Middle Townline Rd BT 16 R-S23
Middlebrook Rd WL 22 K-L23
Middlebrook Rd WT 22 L23
Middlemiss Dr MD 14 V15
Middleport Rd BT 17 R27 S26
Middleton Ln C 5 E6
Middleton-North Walsingham Townline Rd NF 16 V22
Middleton Church Rd NF 16 U22
Middletown Ln OX 16 S21-22 T-U22
Middletown Rd HM 17 Q27 23 N26 P27
Midland Av F 36 D55
Midland Av T 25 J33
Midland Point Rd SM 41 X28
Midlothian Rd PS 76 N30 77 N31
Mighton Rd TB 102 F3
Mikkola Rd CS 100 D18
Milberta Rd TM 85 P28-29 Q28-29
Milburn Rd F 36 B57
Milburn Rd HL 44 W38-39
Mile 38 Rd A 84 W91-92
Mile Hill Rd BT 16 R24
Mile of Memories Rd PB 45 A45
Mile Point La HS 46 A48
Mile Point Rd LN 49 W58
Miles Rd HM 17 R28
Miles Rd PB 45 Z43
Miles Rd Y 30 D32
Miles Shore Rd PB 45 Z43
Milford Bay Rd MK 58 U31
Milford Haven Rd A 86 F95-96
Military Rd SM 41 X27
Military Tr A 86 D94
Milk Run Rd HS 46 A46-47
Mill La MD 14 R15
Mill La PL 29 H28
Mill Ln OX 15 S20
Mill Rd BR 39 B18
Mill Rd CS 101 C21
Mill Rd EL 8 W16 14 V16
Mill Rd F 48 X53
Mill Rd G 39 B21
Mill Rd HS 46 A48
Mill Rd HD 17 V26
Mill Rd HU 20 M15
Mill Rd MA 73 L11
Mill Rd T 24 L30
Mill Rd WL 23 L25
Mill Rd Y 30 H30
Mill Rd (Norfolk) NF 17 V25
Mill Rd (Port Dover) NF 17 V26
Mill Rd (Strathroy-Caradoc) MD 14 U15
Mill Rd (Thames Centre) MD 15 T18
Mill St BT 16 R-S24
Mill St BR 27 G19
Mill St DH 32 G-H39
Mill St G 28 E24
Mill St HM 23 P28
Mill St HT 23 L27
Mill St LM 7 W10
Mill St MA 90 J12
Mill St NR 32 F40 33 G41
Mill St OX 16 R-S21
Mill St PB 45 B44
Mill St PL 23 J-K28
Mill St PR 67 P68
Mill St PT 21 L19 M20
Mill St SM 29 C28
Mill St SM 42 A31
Mill St (Greater Madawaska) R 64 R54
Mill St (Killaloe, Hagarty, & Richards) R 81 N49
Mill St E SM 41 Z29
Mill St W SM 41 Z29
Mill Bay Rd PB 44 X39
Mill Lake Rd PB 45 X42-43
Mill Line Rd (Douro-Dummer) PB 45 B44
Mill Line Rd (Galway-Cavendish & Harvey) PB 44 Z39
Mill Pond Rd NF 17 V25
Mill Pond Sdrd SM 42 Z30
Mill Ridge Rd R 83 Q56
Mill Run Gt DH 31 F33
Millage Rd PB 44 A41
Millaire PR 67 R67
Millar Rd LG 50 W64
Millar Brooke Way LN 49 W58-59
Millar Heights Dr TB 102 C3-4
Millar Hill Rd MK 59 Q35
Millard Dr MK 41 W29 42 W30
Millburough Ln HT 23 N27 N28
Milldale Rd OX 16 T22 T-U21
Millen Av HM 18 Q29
Miller Av NI 19 T36
Miller Dr LN 49 V58
Miller Dr PS 76 P27
Miller Dr SM 30 C29 41 B29
Miller La F 37 D-E58
Miller La HS 62 R47
Miller La LN 49 W58
Miller Rd A 86 C96 D97
Miller Rd EL 8 W14
Miller Rd F 36 A54
Miller Rd K 43 Z34
Miller Rd LA 47 B52
Miller Rd LN 65 T58
Miller Rd LG 49 Y61
Miller Rd MD 14 U15
Miller Rd PB 44 A41
Miller Rd PE 35 G51
Miller Rd SD 90 E-F12
Miller Rd TM 85 P29
Miller Rd (Bonnechere Valley) R 81 P51
Miller Rd (McNab Braeside) R 83 P-Q56 99 H49
Miller Rd (Niagara Falls) NI 19 S35
Miller Rd (Port Colborne) NI 19 T-U34
Miller's Sdrd Y 30 F31
Miller Lake Rd BR 54 T15-16
Millers La NR 33 C44 45 B44
Millers Rd PS 76 L-M30
Millers Rd TB 103 B6
Millgrove Sdrd HM 23 P27-28
Millhaven Rd LA 36 D54
Milliken Mine Rd A 88 D6
Millrace Rd NI 18 T32 19 T33
Millrand Rd NP 93 D25
Mills Cir SM 41 A-B29
Mills La F 47 W51
Mills Rd A 86 C97
Mills Rd LG 49 Y61
Mills Lake Rd TM 85 N27
Milltown Rd SM 29 C25
Milne Rd MK 59 U34
Milne Rd TB 102 G4
Milnet Rd CS 101 Y19
Milo Rd EX 5 E6
Milsap Rd LA 47 B53
Milton Rd OT 67 Q65
Milton Heights Cr HT 23 M28
Milton Stewart Av R 83 P-Q56
Miltons Rd LN 48 V56
Milty Lake Rd R 63 S51
Mindle Rd PB 45 W44 61 V44
Miner's Point Rd LN 49 X-Y58
Miner Lake La F 48 Z55
Mineral Springs Rd HM 17 Q27
Mineral Springs Rd MK 59 Q33
Miners Bay Rd HL 43 W37
Miners Cliff Dr HL 44 W39
Mines Rd HD 17 R-S27
Mineview Rd R 82 N54
Mini Farm Rd TM 85 N28-29
Minielly Rd LM 12 T9 13 T10
Minifie Rd NR 33 F42
Mining Rd TB 102 D4
Minister's La PS 56 Q24
Mink Ln C 7 B10-11
Mink Rd HL 60 U40
Mink Lake Rd HS 61 R42-43 Q45
Mink Lake Rd R 81 N51 82 N52
Mink Mountain Dr TB 102 G5
Mink Point Rd A 86 D95
Minnetonka Rd NR 33 D43
Minnicock Lake Rd HL 60 U40
Minnie Rd R 82 P52
Minor Rd HD 18 U32
Minor Rd (Port Colborne) NI 18 U32 19 U33
Minor Rd (West Lincoln) NI 18 S31
Mint Ln C 6 B-C7
Minto Rd HS 34 C47 46 B47
Minto St SD 90 E14
Minto-Normanby Twnln G 27 G19-20
Minto Pines Rd WL 27 G20
Mira St MA 72 M9
Miramichi Bay Rd BR 38 A16
Miramishi Rd NP 95 E32
Miriam Dr K 59 V35
Miriam Dr MK 59 V35
Miron Rd HS 34 E47
Mirwin Rd C 6 X7
Misener Rd HM 17 Q-R26
Misener Rd (Niagara Falls) NI 19 S-T34
Misener Rd (Wainfleet) NI 18 T32
Misery Bay Park Rd MA 71 K5
Mishomis Inamo R 81 N50
Miskwabi Lake Rd HL 60 U40
Mission Rd A 84 Y90-91 Z90
Mission Rd G 40 A24
Mission Rd TB 103 E6
Mississaga St HT 24 N29
Mississaga St SM 42 Z32
Mississagagon Lake Rd F 47 W51
Mississagi Bay Rd A 87 F2
Mississagi Lighthouse Rd MA 70 J2
Mississagua Dam Rd PB 44 Y40-41
Mississagua Gold Lake Rd PB 44 Y40-41
Mississagua Lake Rd PB 44 X-Y41 Y40
Mississauga Av A 88 D6
Mississauga Rd BT 17 T26
Mississauga Rd PL 23 K28 24 L29-30 M30 29 H26-27
Mississaugas Tr DH 31 E36
Mississippi Dr OT 83 Q58
Mississippi Rd LA 62 U48
Mississippi Rd LN 65 T59
Mistele Sdrd EL 8 Y14
Mitch Owens Rd OT 66 R64 S63-64
Mitchell Ln MD 14 Q16
Mitchell Rd EL 9 W20
Mitchell Rd EX 5 C5
Mitchell Rd HS 34 D-E49
Mitchell Rd LN 65 U57
Mitchell Rd MK 42 X32-33
Mitchell Rd NR 33 E44
Mitchell Rd R 80 P46
Mitchell Rd TB 103 C7
Mitchell Sdrd LN 48 W56
Mitchell's Rd K 43 Z37 44 Z38
Mitchell Lake Access Rd F 63 V51
Mitchells Crossroad PE 35 G51
Mitchellview Rd K 43 Z35
Mitton Ln C 7 A11
Moccasin Tr MK 41 W29
Moccasin Lake Rd R 62 S48
Mockingbird La K 43 Y36
Mockingbird Rd R 80 M47
Modeland Rd LM 12 T7
Modler Rd LG 37 C59
Moffat Rd DH 32 G39
Moffat Rd HM 23 P27
Moffat Rd PB 45 W44
Moggy Pkwy MA 73 K12
Mohawk Rd BT 17 S25-26
Mohawk Rd HM 17 Q28
Mohawk Rd WT 22 N24
Mohawk St BT 17 R25
Mohawk Tr R 82 Q52
Mohawk Point Rd HD 18 U31-32
Mohrs Rd OT 83 Q58-59
Moira Rd HS 34 C48-49
Moira St E HS 34 E49
Moira St W HS 34 E48
Mokomon Rd TB 102 C3
Mole Rd EX 4 D3
Mole Sdrd NF 10 W24
Moles Sdrd G 39 Y19
Molesworth Ln HU 21 J-K18
Mollard Ln HU 13 Q12 20 P12
Moloney Ln PB 44 B40
Molson Rd BT 17 R26
Mon-O-Kel Rd LG 48 Z57
Mona Dr HL 59 S36
Monaghan Rd HS 34 D46
Monaghan Rd PB 33 C41
Monarch Rd K 32 C37 43 B37
Monck Dr MK 58 U32
Monck Rd HS 61 U43-44 62 U45
Monck Rd K 43 X37 X-Y35 Y34
Monck Rd PB 44 X38
Monck Rd SM 42 Y33 Z32 43 Y34
Monck St HS 62 U45
Monck Lake Rd HL 61 U42
Moncrief Ln PB 32 D40
Moncrief Rd PB 32 C40
Moncrieff Rd HU 20 J15 K16 21 K17
Monette Rd A 84 Z92-93
Monetville Rd SD 93 F-G24
Moneymore Rd HS 46 B49 47 B50-51
Monkhouse Rd MA 73 L12
Monkman Rd LG 50 V62
Mono-Adjala Townline SM 29 E-G27
Mono-Amaranth Townline DF 29 F-G26
Mono Centre Rd DF 29 F-G26
Monrock Lake Rd HL 61 V42
Monsell Rd MK 59 U33-34
Montague Boundary Rd OT 66 U61
Monteith Rd TB 102 E4
Monterra Rd G 40 A24-25
Montgomery Rd LN 48 V57 65 U57
Montgomery Rd MK 58 T31
Montgomery Rd NR 33 E43
Montgomery Rd (Athens) LG 49 Z60
Montgomery Rd (Elizabethtown-Kitley) LG 49 Y60
Montpelier Rd CS 100 A-B17
Montpetit Rd C 6 B-C7
Montreal Rd SDG 52 U-V71
Montreal St F 36 D56
Montreal St TB 103 E6
Montréal Rd OT 66 Q63
Montrose Rd HS 34 E48
Montrose Rd NI 19 R-T34
Monument Rd MA 72 L-M9
Moodie Dr OT 66 R-S62
Moody's La MA 72 L10 73 L11
Moon Ln N PB 44 Z39
Moon Rd F 36 A54-55
Moon Line Rd PB 44 Z39
Moon Point Dr SM 42 Z32
Moon River Rd MK 58 U29-30
Mooney Rd CS 100 B17
Mooney Rd HS 62 S45
Mooney Rd SD 90 F11
Moonlight Av CS 101 C20
Moonlight Bay Rd LN 65 U59
Moonlight Bay Rd NP 80 N45
Moonlight Bay Rd SD 92 G22 93 G23
Moonlight Beach Rd CS 101 C20
Moonshadow La LG 49 Z60
Moonstone Rd OT 65 S60
Moonstone Rd W SM 41 Z29 42 Y30
Moor Rd K 43 A35 B36
Moorcroft Rd HS 46 Z48
Moore Ct HU 20 N13
Moore Dr PB 32 D40
Moore Dr PS 76 M28
Moore La F 48 W53
Moore Ln LM 12 U7-8
Moore Rd C 7 A11-12
Moore Rd EL 8 W16
Moore Rd F 36 A54 48 Z54
Moore Rd MK 58 T32
Moore Rd NR 33 E44
Moore Rd NI 19 U33
Moore Rd PR 69 P73
Moore Rd SDG 50 V65
Moore Rd TB 102 F2
Moore St BR 55 V17
Moore's Rd R 99 G48
Moore's Service Rd NR 33 G41
Moore Farm La F 36 B54-55
Moore Lake Rd R 98 G47
Moore Orchard Rd NR 33 G43
Moore Point Rd MK 41 X29
Moorehead La LG 37 A-B60
Moores Rd HS 47 Z50
Moores Rd HD 17 S28
Moores Rd LN 49 W58-59
Mooresville Dr MD 14 Q13-16
Moorings Dr K 43 Z37
Moose St A 86 C97
Moose Creek Rd TM 85 P30
Moose Head Rd NP 96 E37
Moose Lake Rd CS 100 A16-17
Moose Lake Rd HL 60 T39-40
Moose Lake Rd TM 85 R29
Moose Lake Access Rd PS 75 N24
Moose Lodge Rd TB 102 G3-4
Moose Mountain Mine Rd CS 101 Y-Z20
Moose Point Rd NP 94 C28
Moot La MK 59 T34
Moot Lake Rd MK 59 T34
Moote Rd HD 18 T30
Moote Rd NI 18 S32
Mooze Miikun Rd NP 94 D29
Moraine Dr HL 61 U42
Moran Rd HS 34 D46
Moran Rd LG 49 X59
Morden Noaks Rd MA 71 K5-6
Moreau Rd NP 96 E-F35
Moreau Rd R 83 Q57
Moreland Dixon Rd F 36 C56-57
Moreland Lake La HS 46 B48
Morest Rd A 87 E1
Morewood Rd SDG 67 T65-66
Morey La F 36 A55
Morgan Rd CS 100 A-B17
Morgan Rd HS 34 C48
Morgan Rd PE 34 G49
Morgan Rd SDG 51 V68 67 U68
Morgan Tr HL 43 X37 44 X38
Morgan's Point Rd NI 19 U33
Morgan Bay Rd PS 58 S30
Morgans Rd DH 32 G39
Morganston Rd NR 33 E44
Morglans Tr R 82 K54
Morinus Rd MK 58 T30
Morley Dr NP 93 F-G25
Morning Sdrd Y 30 F31
Morning Glory Dr HL 44 W40 60 V40
Morning Glory Rd Y 31 C33
Morning Star Dr PL 24 K30
Morning Star Rd HS 34 E-F47
Morningside Av T 25 J34
Morningside Dr NR 45 B45
Morningside Rd LG 49 W-X60
Morningstar Rd NI 19 T35
Morningstar St PT 21 N-P19
Morog Rd NI 19 T33
Morphets Sdrd MA 90 J11-12
Morris La PS 77 L31
Morris Ln C 6 B-C8
Morris Rd HU 20 M12
Morris Rd NI 19 S-T34
Morris-Turnberry Rd HU 21 J17 27 H17
Morris Island Dr OT 83 P-Q58
Morris Tract Ln HU 20 J13
Morrish Church Rd NR 32 G40
Morrison La LN 64 U55
Morrison La PS 56 Q26
Morrison Ln HU 20 M-P15
Morrison Rd C 7 A12-13
Morrison Rd EL 7 X13
Morrison Rd F 36 B55-56
Morrison Rd LG 49 X-Y61
Morrison Rd SDG 51 V68
Morrison Rd WT 23 P25
Morrison Rd (Madoc) HS 46 Z47
Morrison Rd (Stirling-Rawdon) HS 46 B46-47
Morrison St NI 19 R35
Morrison Point Rd PE 35 G51-52
Morrow Rd EL 14 V16
Morrow Rd F 48 V54
Morrow Rd LG 37 B-C60
Morrow Rd NR 33 D44
Morrow Rd TB 102 C4
Morrow Rd TM 85 Q28-29
Morrow Lake Rd R 63 S-T52
Morse Av EX 5 E5
Morse Rd MD 14 S-T13
Mortensen Rd EL 15 U-V18
Mortimers Point Rd MK 58 U30-31
Morton Av Y 30 D31
Morton Dr EX 4 C1
Morton La K 43 X34
Morton Ln PB 32 D39-40
Morton Rd DH 32 F-G39
Morton Rd HS 46 B49
Morton Rd NR 33 F41
Moscow Rd LA 47 B53
Moscow Sdrd BR 26 E-F16
Moser-Young Rd WT 22 L-M21
Mosher Rd A 87 E1
Moskal Rd A 84 Y92
Mosley St SM 41 A27
Mosport Rd DH 32 F38
Mosque Lake Rd F 63 V53
Mosquito Tr R 97 E41
Mosquito Lake Pkwy F 48 W53
Moss Rd A 84 A-B92
Mosside Ln LM 7 W11
Mossley Dr MD 15 T19
Mother Barnes Rd LG 49 Y-Z60
Motheral Rd OX 16 Q23
Moto Park Rd G 27 C20
Motts Mills Rd LG 49 X60
Moulinette Rd SDG 52 U-V69
Moulinette Island Causeway SDG 52 V69
Moulton Rd LN 49 V59
Moulton-Aiken Rd HD 18 U31
Moulton-Sherbrooke Townline Rd HD 18 U31-32
Mount Albert Rd Y 30 E32 E-F31 31 E33
Mount Albion Rd HM 18 Q29
Mount Baldy Rd TB 103 C7
Mount Carmel Dr MD 14 Q15
Mount Carmel Rd HU 14 Q13-14
Mount Carmel Rd PE 35 E51
Mount Chesney Rd F 36 C56-57
Mount Elgin Rd OX 15 T20 16 T21
Mount Everest Access Rd R 97 F41
Mount Healy Rd HD 17 T28
Mount Hope Rd PL 29 G28 30 G29
Mount Horeb Rd K 32 D38
Mount Julian Viamede Rd PB 45 Z42
Mount Nebo Rd K 32 C-D39
Mount Nemo Cr HT 23 N28
Mount Olivet Rd HD 18 U29
Mount Pleasant Ln HU 21 J18
Mount Pleasant Rd BT 16 S24 17 S25
Mount Pleasant Rd HS 34 C47
Mount Pleasant Rd NP 96 F35
Mount Pleasant Rd NR 33 E44
Mount Pleasant Rd PB 32 C40 D39-40
Mount Pleasant Rd PL 29 G28 30 G29
Mount Pleasant Rd T 24 K32
Mount Pleasant St BT 17 R25
Mount Pleasant Tr Y 30 D32
Mount Saint Louis Rd E SM 42 Y-Z30
Mount Saint Louis Rd W SM 41 Z29 42 Z30
Mount Saint Patrick Rd R 64 R53
Mount Stephen Rd SM 42 X30-31
Mount Wolfe Rd PL 30 G29
Mount Zion Rd A 86 C96-97
Mountain Rd F 63 V52
Mountain Rd LA 47 A52 Z52-53
Mountain Rd LG 48 Y57
Mountain Rd NI 18 R-S31
Mountain Rd R 82 M52
Mountain Rd SDG 50 V64 66 U64
Mountain Rd SM 40 A25
Mountain Rd TB 102 E5
Mountain Rd (Armour) PS 77 N32
Mountain Rd (East Ferris) PS 95 F32
Mountain Rd (Grimsby) NI 18 R31
Mountain Rd (Lincoln) NI 18 R31
Mountain Rd (Niagara Falls) NI 19 R34
Mountain St HL 60 U39
Mountain St LG 37 A60
Mountain Brow Blvd HM 18 Q29
Mountain Brow Rd HM 23 P28
Mountain Chute Rd F 64 T53
Mountain Grove Rd F 48 X-Y53
Mountain Lake Dr G 39 Y19
Mountain Lake Rd G 39 Y19
Mountain View Rd HL 60 V37
Mountain View Rd LN 65 R-S58
Mountain View Rd NP 95 D33
Mountain View Rd R 65 R57 81 P48 83 Q57
Mountain View Estates La F 48 Y54
Mountainash Rd PL 24 J29
Mountainview Rd A 88 E4
Mountainview Rd HT 23 L28
Mountainview Rd NI 18 R31
Mountainview Rd PL 29 G-H27
Mountjoy Rd DH 32 F37-38
Mountney Rd HS 62 T46
Mountsberg Rd HM 23 N27
Mouse Lake Access Rd LA 63 U50
Moustik Rd NP 93 D25
Mowat St SM 41 B26
Mowat Landing Rd TM 85 R29
Mowat Township Access Rd PS 74 K23 75 K24
Mowbray Rd HS 35 D51
Mowbray Rd PE 35 G50-51
Mowhawk Rd MK 58 V29
Moxam Ldg CS 100 D18
Moxam Rd HS 62 S45
Moxam Rd R 82 M54
Moxley Rd HM 23 P27
Moyer Rd (Lincoln) NI 18 R32
Moyer Rd (Welland) NI 19 S34
Moyer Sdrd HD 18 T31
Moyer St NI 19 R-S33
Moyes Tr HL 59 T36
MTO Rd HU 20 J13
Muchmore Rd LG 37 A58
Mud St HM 18 Q-R29 R30
Mud St NI 18 R30-31
Mud Bay Rd A 88 F5
Mud Creek Ln C 6 Y7
Mud Creek Rd MA 72 K9
Mud Lake Ln N HU 27 G19
Mud Lake Ln S HU 27 H19
Mud Lake Rd DH 31 F35
Mud Lake Rd LA 36 C-D54
Mud Lake Rd TB 102 C4 D4
Mud Lake Rd (Bonnechere Valley) R 81 N51
Mud Lake Rd (Laurentian Valley) R 81 L51 82 L52
Mud Lake Access Rd PS 75 L24-25
Mudcat Rd (Belleville) HS 34 D48-49
Mudcat Rd (Hastings Highlands) HS 62 R45
Mudcreek Rd LG 50 Y62
Mufferaw Pl R 83 Q56
Muir Ln OX 16 R-S22
Muir Rd N OX 16 R22
Muir Rd S OX 16 S22
Muir St G 40 Z22
Muirkirk Ln C 7 Y12
Mulberry La DH 31 H34

Old Hamburg Rd LA . . . 35 D52-53
Old Hastings Rd HS
. . . 46 W46 X-Y47 62 S45 U-V46
Old Herman Rd N 62 T47
Old Highway Rd (East Mills) PS. .
. . . . . 94 J28
Old Highway Rd (Magnetawan)
. . . . . 76 M29
Old Hines Rd HD 18 U30
Old Homestead Rd Y . . . . .
. . . 30 D31-32 31 C33
Old Hungerford Rd HS46 B49 47 B50
Old Hwy 17 Rd NP . . . . .
. . . 93 D25-26 96 E36-37
Old Hydro La HS 46 W48
Old Hydro Rd A. 88 F6
Old Kingston Rd LG . . . 49 W-Y59
Old Lake Shore Rd NF . . 17 V26
Old Lakeshore Rd LM . . . 12 S8
Old Madawaska Rd HS. . 61 R-S44
Old Madoc Rd HS. 34 C-D48
Old Mail Rd G. 40 A23
Old Malden Rd EX. 4 D2-3
Old Marmora Rd HS . . 46 A47-48
Old Milford Rd PE. 35 G51
Old Military Rd SDG . . . 68 Q-R71
Old Mill Rd BT. 16 R23
Old Mill Rd G. 39 X18
Old Mill Rd H. 60 T37
Old Mill Rd K. 32 C-D38
Old Mill Rd MA 72 L8
Old Mill Rd MK. 41 W29
Old Mill Rd NP 95 D33-34
Old Mill Rd TB 102 E-F2
Old Mill Rd (Aweres) A. . 84 Z92-93
Old Mill Rd (Billings) MA. . . 72 J9
Old Mill Rd (Clear Creek) NF . . .
. . . . . 10 X-Y22
Old Mill Rd (Delhi) NF . . 16 U-V23
Old Mill Rd (Johnson) A . 86 C-D95
Old Mill Access Rd NP. . . 95 D34
Old Mill Beach Rd R. . . 88 C96-97
Old Mill Bridge Rd R. . . 82 L53
Old Mine La F 36 A55
Old Mine Rd A 87 E2
Old Mine Rd LN 48 W57
Old Mine Rd R 82 N52
Old Montreal Rd OT . . . 67 P65
Old Moore Lake Rd A . . 98 F-G47
Old Morris Rd LN 48 V-W57
Old Muskoka Rd MK . . . . .
. . . 58 S-T32 59 R-S33
Old Muskoka Rd SD . . . 90 E14
Old Nairn Rd SD 77 K-L31
Old Nicholas Rd A 88 B4
Old Nipissing Rd (Lount) PS. 76 L30
Old Nipissing Rd (Pringle) PS94 J30
Old North Rd MK 59 Q33
Old North Rd NF . . 9 W21 16 V21
Old Norwood Rd HS. . . . 46 A46
Old Norwood Rd (Havelock-
Belmont-Methuen) PB . . 45 B44-45
Old Norwood Rd (Otonabee-South
Monaghan) PB 33 C41-42
Old Novar Rd PS 58 Q32
Old Oliphant Rd BR. . . 55 X-Y18
Old Onondaga Rd BT. . . 17 R26
Old Orchard Rd PB. . . . 33 C44
Old Orchard Rd PE. . . . 34 F47
Old Orchard Rd SM . . . 41 B28-29
Old Parry Sound Rd MK. . 58 S31
Old Penetanguishene Rd SM . . . .
. . . . 41 Y28 Z29
Old Perth Rd LN 65 S-U58
Old Pine Tree Rd BR. . . 55 U15
Old Portage Rd HS 34 F47
Old Poupore Mine Rd SD . . . .
. . . . 101 A20-21
Old Prescott Rd OT . . . 66 S64
Old Railroad Rd G. 28 E21
Old Rainy Lake Rd PS . . 77 P31
Old Ranch Rd PS 77 L32
Old Red Rd LG 50 Z62
Old Red Bay Rd BR . . . 55 X17
Old River Rd HU 20 L13
Old River Rd LG 37 B61
Old River Rd MD 14 T15-16
Old River Rd NI. 18 T32
Old Sawmill Rd BT 16 S24
Old School Ln OX. 16 T19
Old School Rd PL. 23 J28 K28 24 J29
Old School Rd T 102 F3
Old School House Rd MK . 59 Q33
Old School House Rd SM 41 Y27-28
Old Scugog Rd DH. 32 E-F37 G37-38
Old Shelter Valley Rd NR . . 33 F44
Old Shiloh Rd Y 31 D33
Old Silver Mountain Rd TB 102 E-F2
Old Simcoe Rd DH . . 31 D-E35 E-F36
Old Sinclair Rd MK 59 Q35
Old Skead Rd CS 101 B20
Old Snow Rd HS. 62 U47
Old Soo Rd A 86 C95-96
Old Soo Rd CS 100 D18
Old Stage Rd OX . . . 16 S21-22
Old Station Rd CS 101 A-B21
Old Steel Rd A 88 E4
Old Still River Rd PS . . 74 K-L23
Old Stone Rd E MK. . 58 V31-32
Old Stone Rd W MK . . . 58 V31
Old Stouffville Rd DH . . 31 F34
Old Street Ln C 7 B-C10
Old Surrey La A. 44 A39
Old Tower Rd MK 58 V-W29
Old Trestle Rd R. 81 N48-49
Old Troy Rd HS. 46 A49
Old Udney Sdrd SM . . . 42 Y33
Old Union Hall Rd LN . . 65 S-T58
Old Victoria Rd MD . . . 15 T-U18
Old Victoria Rd MK. . . . 59 V35
Old Village Rd N MA . . . 90 H13
Old Village Rd S MA . . . 90 H13
Old Wagon Rd MK . . . 59 T-U35
Old Walnut Rd LA 13 U-V11
Old Wanup Rd CS. 101 D20
Old Webbwood Rd SD . . 90 E13
Old Welsh Rd HS 62 S46
Old Weston Rd T 24 K31
Old Wilton Rd LA. 36 C-D54
Old Wooler Rd NR . . 33 E45 34 E46
Old York Rd HT. 23 P28
Oldcastle Rd EX. 4 C2
Olde Dr MD 14 U14 U-V13
Olde Hwy MA 72 K7

Olde Baseline Rd PL . . . . .
. . . 23 J27 J28 29 H28
Olde Wagon Rd MK . . . 59 T35
Oldfield Ln C 6 X-Y8
Oldfield Rd NI 19 S35
Oleksuk Rd TB 102 G4
Olinda Sdrd EX 5 D-E5
Oliphant Way BR 55 W-Y17
Olive Av DH 31 H36 32 H37
Oliver Dr MD. 15 R17-18
Oliver Rd LA 47 Y51
Oliver Rd TB . 102 D3-4 D5 103 D6
Oliver Sdrd LA. 35 D52
Oliver's Rd K 44 Z39
Oliver Creek Rd TB . . . 102 E4
Olivers Rd PS 94 J29
Olives La R 62 R48
Olivier Rd NP 93 D26
Olivier St U 19 R33
Olmstead-Jeffrey Lake Rd R 82 N54
Olrig Access Rd NP 95 D34
Olsen Rd TB. 102 F-G3
Olsheski Rd R. . . . 62 Q47 80 P47
Olson Rd TB 102 D2
Olympic Dr HM 17 Q28
Omagaki Tr K 81 M50
Omega Rd K 43 A36 Z36
Omer St TM. 85 P30
Omila Rd TB 103 B6
Otty Lake Rd K 49 X58
Onaping Lake Rd SD . . 100 V14-15
Onaping Dr CS 100 A16
One Mile Rd DL. 59 U36
Oneida La EL 8 W16 14 V16
Oneida Rd HD 17 S-T27
Oneill Rd TB 102 F2
Onex Shaft Rd CS. . . 100 A16-17
Onion Lake Rd TB 103 B-C6
Onja-Gah-Bo Rd BR . . . 38 A17
Onoko Ln C 7 A-B12
Onondaga Rd BT 17 S-T26
Onondaga Townline Rd BT 17 R-S27
Ontario Rd NI 19 T33-34
Ontario St HT 23 M28
Ontario St HU 20 L14
Ontario St MA 91 J15
Ontario St PS 77 M-N32
Ontario St PT. 21 P19
Ontario St (Brighton) NR . . 34 E47
Ontario St (Cobourg) NR . . 33 G42
Ontario St (Lincoln) NI. . 18 R31-32
Ontario St (Port Hope) NR . 33 G41
Ontario St (St Catharines) NI 19 R33
Onwatin Lake Rd CS . . . 83 P59
Opeongo Rd OT 67 P61
Opeongo Rd (Admaston Bromley)
R 82 Q54-55
Opeongo Rd (Bonnechere Valley)
R 63 Q50 82 Q52
Opeongo Rd (Madawaska Valley)
R. 80 P46 P47
Opeongo Access Rd NP. . 80 N-P45
Opeongo Lake Rd NP. . 79 M-N40
Opeongo Point La F . . . 48 Y54
Opinicon Rd F 36 A56-57
Opiongo Tr PS. 77 K33
Opmar Rd K 32 C37 43 B37
Oram Rd HS. 62 O-R47
Oram Rd PE 34 F49
Orange Corners Rd K . . 32 C39-40
Orange Hall Rd NF 16 V21
Orange Hill Rd HU 27 H17-19
Orange Valley Rd PS . . . 76 P29
Orangeville-Fergus Rd DF 29 H25-26
Orchard Ct Y 31 E33
Orchard Dr G 39 V-Y29
Orchard La HU. 21 J17
Orchard La EL. 9 X20
Orchard La HU. 20 K-L13
Orchard Rd SDG. 52 U71
Orchard Hill Rd NI. 19 S33
Ordnance Av NF . . . 10 W-X24
Orenda Rd PL. 24 K29
Orford Rd C. 7 Y12
Oriel Ln OX 16 S22
Orimat Rd SM. 42 W32
Oriole Dr MD 14 T-U15
Oriole Dr Y. 30 E31
Oriole Beach Rd NR . . . 33 E41
Oriole Park Dr EX 4 C4
Oriole Park Rd MA 72 K8
Orkney Beach Rd SM. . . 42 Z32
Orleans Blvd OT 66 Q64
Ormiston Rd DH 32 F37
Ormond Rd SDG . . . 67 T65-66
Ormond St LG 50 Z63
Ormond Rd OT. 65 T60
Ormsbee Rd F. 36 B57
Orr Dr MD 14 V16 15 V17
Orr Rd NI 24 M30
Orr's Sdrd MA 90 J12
Orrell Callahan Dr A . . . 86 G95
Orser Rd F 48 Y55
Ort Rd NI 19 S-T35
Orth Dr BT. 16 S22
Ortt Rd HD. 18 T30
Osawamick Rd MA . . 73 M13-14
Osborne La F 36 B57
Osborne Rd LG. 49 Z61
Osborne St DH 43 B34
Osborne St R 83 Q57
Osborne St SM 41 X29
Osborne Point Rd MK . . 59 R34-35
Osbourne Rd DH 32 H37
Oscar Boehme Rd R. . . 82 R48
Osgoode Main St OT . . . 66 T63
Osler Bluff Rd SM. 40 A25
Osnabruck Centre Rd SDG 67 T-U68
Osoyoos Rd F 48 W-X54
Osprey Rd HS 60 U38
Osprey Rd LN. 48 W56
Osprey Rd PS. 93 J25
Osprey-Artemesia Twnln G . 28 C23
Osprey-Clearview Ln SM . . . .
. . . . 29 C25 40 B25
Osprey-Clearview Ln TwnLn
G 40 B24-25
Ossie Traynor Rd PB . . . 44 Y40
Ostick Rd PS 77 N33-34
Ostrander Rd OX 15 U20

Ostrander Point Rd PE. . . 35 H52
Ottawa Av PS 77 K32
Ottawa St HM 18 Q29
Ottawa St PB. 66 T61-62
Ottawa St PS 45 B44-45
Ottawa St WT. 22 N23
Ottawa River Pkwy OT . . 66 Q-R62
Otte Rd TB 103 B8
Otter La K 43 Y37
Otter Ln C. 6 X7
Otter Rd K. 43 Z36
Otter View MK. 59 R34
Otter Creek Rd HS 47 A50
Otter Creek Rd LA . . 47 A51 Z51
Otter Lake La R. 80 P46
Otter Lake Rd BR. 54 T16
Otter Lake Rd HS. 62 U45
Otter Lake Rd LA 63 U50
Otter Lake Rd LG 49 X59
Otter Lake Rd MA . . . 72 K-L10
Otter Lake Rd MK 59 R34
Otter Lake Rd PS. . . 57 R-S27
Otter Lake Tr HL. 43 W37
Ottergate Ln EL. 15 V20
Otterville Rd OX . . . 16 U21-22
Otto La F 47 W51-52
Otto Rd SDG. 67 U68
Otty Lake Sdrd LN 49 W58
Otty Lake South West Shore LN . .
. . . . . 49 X58
Oudaze Lake Rd MK . 77 P33 78 P34
Ouderkirk Rd SDG. . . 67 S-T67
Ouellette Av EX. 4 B1-2
Ouellette Rd C 6 A7
Ouellette Rd NP 95 F33
Ouellette Rd PR 68 N69
Ouellette Rd SDG 68 R71
Ough's Rd NR 33 F-G41
Ouimet Rd PR. 67 S67
Outaouais, Mtée PR . . . 67 P66
Outer Dr EX. 4 C2
Outer Dr LM 13 Q11
Outlet Rd LG 37 B60
Outlook Loop HS 61 T43
Outram Rd HL. 61 U41
Outred Rd NI 19 T-U33
Over the Hills Rd F. . . . 48 W54
Overhead Bridge Rd SM . 41 X27
Overholt Rd NI 19 S33 T33
Overlea Blvd T 24 K32
Overpass Rd OT 65 T60
Overton Rd F. 63 U51
Owen Rd C. 6 Y7
Owen Rd DH 31 F34
Owl Dr SD 92 F22
Owl's Nest Rd SD 92 F22
Owl Bay Tr HL 60 U40
Owl Cage Rd EL 9 W21
Owl Lake Rd PS 77 N32
Oxbow Dr MD 14 T15
Oxbow Rd BT. 17 R-S25
Oxbow Lake 1 Access Rd MK. . . .
. . . . . 59 Q35
Oxby La K 43 X34
Oxford Av LG. 50 Z63
Oxford Av OX 16 R21
Oxford St E MD. 15 T17
Oxford St W MD 14 T16
Oxford-Waterloo Rd WT . 22 P21-23
Oxford Centre Rd LG. . 16 S21-22
Oxford Station Rd LG. . 50 V-W63
Oxtongue Lake Rd MK . . 59 Q36
Oxtongue Rapids Rd MK . 59 R35

P Ln A 86 E-F95
Paauw Rd OT 66 T62
Pacaud-Catherine Rd TM. . 85 L28
Pacific Av TB 103 D6
Pacific Rd LG 37 B60
Pack Rd MD 61 T42
Packard Rd HL 61 T42
Packer Rd NR. . . . 33 E42-43
Packers Bay Rd MK . . . 58 U31
Paddock Rd DH . . . 31 G34-35
Paddy Rd HS 46 A49
Paddy's Lake Access Rd LN 64 U55
Paddy Greene Rd HM . . 17 Q27
Paddy Lake Rd SD 92 E20
Paden Rd OT 50 V62 66 U62
Padres Rd TB 102 F3
Page Rd OT 66 Q64
Page's Corners Rd SDG . 51 V66-67
Pago Dr PR 67 P66
Paige La PB 44 A41 Z41
Pain Court Ln C. 6 B7-8
Paington House Rd MK . . 58 T30
Paint Box Dr HL 60 S39
Paint Lake Rd MK . . . 59 S35-36
Painter Rd BT 17 R26
Paisley Dr PS 77 K-L33
Paisley Rd WL 23 M25
Pajamaki Rd TB 102 C3
Pakeshkag Lake Access Rd PS . .
. . . . . 93 J23
Pakkard Rd TB. 102 E1
Palangio Rd NP. 95 F33
Palestine Rd K 43 A35-36
Pallisades Rd TB. 102 F2
Palmateer Rd HS 46 A49
Palmateer Rd TM. 85 M27
Palmer Rd HS 46 A49
Palmer Rd LN 48 X57
Palmer Rd R 62 R48 63 R49
Palmer Rd (Belleville) HS . . 34 E48
Palmer Rd (Madoc) HS. . . 46 Z47
Palmer Rd (Quinte West) HS 34 E46
Palmer-Burris Rd PE. . . 34 G48
Palmers Rd C 56 Q24
Palmyra Rd C 7 A12
Panache Lake Rd CS . . . 91 E16
Panache Rd SD 66 S64 67 S65
Panache North Shore Rd CS 91 E16
Panazzola La CT. 66 U63
Pancake La N 19 S33
Panel Mine Rd A . . . 88 B6 89 B7
Pangborn La MA. 72 L10
Panmure Rd LN 65 R-S58
Panmure Rd OT 65 R59
Pannell La MD. 14 T13
Pantry School Rd C 6 X9

Pantry School Rd LM . . 6 W9 12 V9
Pants Lake Rd A. 84 Z93
Pape Av T 24 K32
Papineau Rd NP . . 96 E37-38 E-F36
Papineau Access Rd NP. 96 F37-38
Papineau Lake Rd R . . . 62 R45
Papineau West Access Rd HS . . .
. . . . . 62 Q-R45
Paplinskie Rd NP 82 Q42-43
Pappin Rd R. 82 M53
Papple Rd BT 17 R25-26
Paquette Rd R. 82 M53
Paquette Rd TB . . 102 C5 103 C6
Paradis Rd SD 90 F12-13
Paradise La R 82 P52
Paradise Rd NP. 79 P41
Paradise Cove Rd HL . . 60 U40
Paradise Lake St BR . . . 26 G15
Paradise Landing HS . . . 61 T44
Paragon Rd SDG 52 U71
Paramount Dr HM . . 18 Q-R29
Parchers Rd HS 62 Q47
Pardee Rd TB 102 G3
Parent St PR 68 R69
Paris Plains BT. . . . 16 Q23-24
Paris Rd BT 16 R24
Paris St CS 101 C19
Paris Links Rd BT 16 Q24
Parish Rd LG 48 Y57
Parish Line Rd HL 60 U39
Parisien Rd HS 62 Q46
Park Av C. 6 A-B9
Park Ln PS 95 H32
Park Rd A 88 F3
Park Rd BT 17 R25
Park Rd BR 39 A18
Park Rd CS 100 C15-16
Park Rd DH 31 H36
Park Rd HS. 62 S47
Park Rd HU. 20 P15-16
Park Rd NF 16 U24
Park Rd NI 18 R31
Park Rd PS 77 K31
Park Rd SM. 41 Z27
Park Rd Y . . 30 C32 31 C33 D33
Park St BR. 27 G19
Park St C 6 X9
Park St EX 4 E4
Park St NF 10 W-X24
Park St PB. 33 C41
Park St SM 41 X29
Park Head Rd BT . . 38 Z17 39 Z18
Park Lawn Rd T 24 L31
Park Valley Rd F . . . 36 B-C56
Parkdale Av NF 18 Q29
Parkdale Av E LG. . . . 50 Z63
Parkdale Av W LG. . . 50 Z62-63
Parker Rd PR 68 Q69
Parker Rd TB. 102 E3
Parker Bay Rd PS 76 M27
Parker Point La F 48 Z57
Parkers Point Rd MK . . 58 V32
Parkes La F. 77 L31
Parkewood Dr A . . . 84 B90-91
Parkhill Dr MD . . . 13 R12 14 R13
Parkhill Rd PB . . 32 C40 33 C41
Parkhouse Rd MD. . 14 U14 V13-14
Parkhurst Lake Access Rd LA . . .
. . . . . 62 T48
Parkinson Rd (Blandford-
Blenheim) OX. 16 Q23
Parkinson Rd (Woodstock) OX . .
. . . . . 16 R21
Parks Rd F. 47 Y52
Parks Rd HS 34 E47
Parkside Av BR 55 X17-18
Parkside Dr HM. 23 P28
Parkside Dr PB. . . . 44 Y38-39
Parkside Dr T . . . 24 K-L31 K-L32
Parkside Rd K 43 Z36
Parkview Cr LM 13 Q12
Parkview Dr HL. 17 T27
Parkway, The PB . . 32 C40 33 C41
Parkway Dr LM 13 Q11
Parkway Dr PS 56 Q26
Parkway Rd OT 66 R-S64
Parkwood Rd BR 26 D14
Parliament Rd NR 33 F45
Parliament St T 24 K-L32
Parlow Rd SDG 51 W66
Parolins Rd PS 94 J27
Parr Ln HU. 20 L13 L-N14 P14
Parrot Rd C 7 A10
Parry Dr HS. 34 D47
Parry Sound Dr PS . . . 57 Q-R27
Parslow Rd LG 7 A10
Parson Rd C 14 V16
Parson Rd EL 17 R26
Parsonage Rd HM 17 R26
Parsons La F. 64 U54
Parsons La MK 59 Q33
Parsons Rd EX. 5 H5
Parsons Rd HL. 60 T39
Parsons Rd (Cramahe) NR. . 33 E44
Parsons Rd (Port Hope) NR. 32 F40
Parsons Way LN 48 V56
Parton Rd PS 57 Q27
Partridge Rd SM 58 U32
Partridge Rd NR. 42 B30
Partridge La MK 42 X46
Partridge Tr A 87 D99
Partridge Bay Dr PS . . . 56 Q25
Partridge Hollow Rd PE. 34 G47-48
Partridge Lake Rd HS . . . 60 T37
Partridge Lake Tr HS . . . 62 V48
Partridge Lake Access Rd HS . . .
. . . 46 W48 62 V48
Pascal Lake Access Rd R . . . . .
. . 95 F34 G34 96 F35 G35
Pashwood Dr BR 38 Z16
Pass Lake Rd TB 103 B10
Passage Lake Crsrd TB . 103 C10
Passaw Rd R 81 N51
Pasture Rd K. 44 B38
Pasture Point Rd A. . . . 86 D94
Pastway Rd R 82 P55
Pataud Rd NP. 94 C27
Pathfinder Tr R 98 F46
Patillo Rd EX 4 B-C3
Patricia Dr PS 58 U32
Patrick Rd HM 17 Q25
Patte Rd PR. 28 N-P72
Patterson Rd MD 14 U13
Patterson Rd OT 65 R59
Patterson Rd PE 34 G49
Patterson Rd C 7 A12
Patterson Rd HM 23 P28

Patterson Rd K 44 A38
Patterson Rd LN. 48 X56
Patterson Rd LG. 50 X64
Patterson Rd MK . . . 58 S-T32
Patterson Rd NI 18 S31
Patterson Rd R. 82 N53
Patterson Rd SM 30 C29
Patterson Sdrd PL. . . 29 G-H28
Patterson St SM. . . . 30 E-F29
Pattersons Corners Rd LG 50 V-W63
Pattullo Av OT 16 R21-22
Paudash St PB 33 E42
Paugh Lake Rd R. 80 M47
Paugh Lake North Shore Access
Rd R 80 M46 N46-47
Paul's Rd LN 65 U58
Paul's Point La MA 73 L11
Paul Foster Rd LG . . 49 Y61 50 Y61
Paul Metivier Dr OT . . . 66 S62
Pauley Rd HS 62 U45
Pauline's Rd CS 100 B15-16
Pauline Johnson Rd BT . . 17 R-S26
Pautois Rd NP. 96 E36
Pavdash School Rd HS . . 15 S11
Pavey Ln C 6 X-Y9
Pavillion Rd HU 20 M13-14
Paxton Dr NR 34 G46
Payn Rd NR 33 F42-43
Payne La R 82 N-P54
Payne Rd C. 7 A10
Payne Rd SDG 51 V66
Payne's Rd PS 75 N24
Payne Line Rd PB 45 B42
Paynes La F 64 U54
Paynes Rd HL . . . 60 U40 61 U41
Paynes Mills Rd EL. . . . 14 V16
Peace Rd K 32 C38-39
Peace Valley Dr PS 77 P33
Peace Valley Rd MK. . . 59 T33
Peacefull La NP 96 F35-36
Peachey Rd R. 81 P50-51
Peacock Rd HS. 62 T47
Peacock Rd PB. 44 B41
Peacock Rd PS. 77 K32
Peacock Bay Rd MK . . 58 Q-R32
Peak Lake Rd A 88 D4
Peak of Mosa Rd LM. . 13 U-V12
Pearce Rd K 43 Y36
Pearceley Rd PS. . 76 L30 77 L31
Pearl Rd PR. 68 P71
Pearl Carrick Rd SM. . . 42 Y33
Pearn's Rd K 43 A37
Pearson Dr A 88 D6
Pearson La PB 44 A41
Pearson Rd NI. 19 T34
Pearson Rd TB. 102 F3
Peat's Point La F 34 E49
Peat Moss Rd PR 68 P69
Peavinery Rd BT. 16 S24
Pebble Rd MA. 71 K5
Pebblestone Rd DH . . . 32 G37
Pebblestone Rd TB . . . 102 D4
Pecarski Rd F 80 P47
Pecors Lake Rd A 89 D7
Pecoskie Dr R 80 M47
Pedden Rd MD 14 S14
Peddleboat Bay La HL . . 44 W40
Peddlers Dr NP . . 96 E-F36 F35
Pede Rd EL 9 W19
Pedwell Point Dr BR. . . 54 T14
Peebles Ln OX 16 T21
Peebles Rd PB. 45 W43
Peek-a-Boo Rd SM . . . 41 X27-28
Peel Rd HL 61 T42
Peel St BR 38 A16
Peel St G 40 Z23
Peel St (Wilmot) WT . . . 22 P21
Peel St (Woolwich) WT . . 22 L-M23
Peelow Rd HS. 62 S45
Peepy Horn Rd HS . . . 46 A46
Peever Ln PS 95 G32
Pefferlaw Rd Y 31 C33-34
Pegg Rd LG. 49 X59
Peggs Mountain Rd PS . 77 N31-32
Peladeau Rd PR. . . 68 N69-70
Pelaw Tr HL. 60 S39
Pelham Rd NI 19 R33
Pelham St NI 19 R33
Pellerin Rd NP. 93 E26
Pellinen Rd CS 101 D21
Pelow Rd LG 37 B-C58
Pelton Rd LG 50 V63-64
Pemberton Rd SDG . . . 67 U65
Pembroke St R. 99 K51-52
Pencil Lake Rd PB. . . . 44 W40
Peneshula Rd LN. . . 64 R-S56
Penetangor Row BR . . . 26 E13
Penetanguishene Rd (Oro-
Medonte) SM . . 41 Z29 42 A30 B30
Penetanguishene Rd
(Penetanguishene) SM . . . . . .
. . . 41 X27-28 Y28
Penfold Lake Rd NP. . . . 59 S33
Penfound Rd HU. 20 K14
Pengelley Dr PB 33 E41
Pengelly Rd PS 56 R25
Penhale Rd EL. 15 V18
Peniel Rd K . . . 31 C36 43 B36 B37
Peninsula Dr LN 49 X58
Peninsula Dr PB 44 Z40
Peninsula Rd HL. 60 U39
Peninsula Rd HS. 46 X46
Peninsula Rd NP . . . 95 E32-33
Peninsula Rd PB. 45 Y44
Peninsula Rd (Gravenhurst) MK . .
. . . 42 W3 31-32
Peninsula Rd (Muskoka Lakes) MK
. . . . . 58 S-T30
Peninsula Point Rd SM. . 42 X32
Peninsula Rd SM 42 Y32
Penman Av CS 101 B20
Penna Shaft Rd TM. . 85 Q30-31
Penny Av MA 72 N10
Penny La C. 101 C21
Penny Rd TB 102 E1
Penryn Rd NR. 33 E-F45
Pentecostal Rd NR. . . . 33 G43
Pentney Rd CS 91 E16
Penzance Tr HL 61 V41
Peoples Rd A 84 A-B92
Pepler Lake Rd A. 84 A90
Peplinski Homestead Rd R . 80 N47
Peplinskie Rd R 62 R47
Pepper Rd HU 20 N-P13
Pepperville Rd SDG . . . 50 V64
Perault La F. 36 A54
Perch Rd K 43 A37
Perch Bay Rd A 86 E97
Perch Bay La F 36 A55
Percy Rd LN . . . . 35 C-
Percy Sy St NR 33 D44
Percy Boom Rd NR . . . 33 D45
Percy Lake Rd HL 60 S40
Percy Rose Rd NR 33 F41
Perdue Rd G. 39 B20
Perdue Rd PB. . . . 32 C40 44 B40
Peregrine Rd PR 68 R69
Perivale Rd E MA 72 K-L8
Perivale Rd W MA 72 K-L8
Periwinkle La HL 43 W37
Perjen Rd A. 87 D99
Perkins Rd LN 48 W57
Pero La F. 36 A55
Perrault Dr CS 100 B-C18
Perrault Rd OT. 67 Q-R65
Perrault Rd R 82 Q52
Perrier Rd R 62 Q-R47
Perrin Point Rd PB 33 E41
Perry Av MA 91 H15
Perry La HS 34 E46
Perry La K 43 X36
Perry Rd F 47 W51
Perry Rd NI 18 T32
Perry's Rd PS 77 M34
Perrytown Rd NR 32 F40
Perth Ln WT 21 M20
Perth Rd LG 48 Z57
Perth Rd (Kingston) F . . 36 C-D56
Perth Rd (South Frontenac) F . . .
. . . 36 A-C56 48 Z56
Perth St N LG 48 Y57
Perth St OT 66 S62 T61
Perth St (Brockville) LG . 50 Z62-63
Perth St (Elizabethtown-Kitley) L
. . . . . 50 Z62
Perth-Oxford Rd PT . . . . . .
. . . 15 Q19 21 P20 22 P21
Pertula Rd CS 101 D20
Peskett Rd OT 65 S60
Pete's La Y 31 C34
Pete's Rd NR. 33 F43
Pete's Dam Rd TM 85 Q29
Pete Sebe Rd MD 13 R12
Peter La HS 46 W46
Peter Rd C 7 X12
Peter Rd F. 48 X55
Peter Rd MK 59 U34
Peter St NR 33 G41
Peter St SM 41 Y29 42 Y30
Peter's Rd TM. 85 P28
Peter Robinson Rd OT . . 65 R-S59
Peterborough St PB . . . 45 B44
Petermann Rd R 82 L-M52
Peters Cr G 28 C23
Peters La F 64 U54
Peters Rd LA 36 C54
Peters Rd NR 33 F45
Peterson Rd EX 4 E4
Peterson Rd K 60 U37
Peterson Rd LA. 47 X51
Peterson Rd LG. . . . 49 Y-Z61
Peterson Rd MK 59 V33
Peterson Rd NI. 18 U32
Peterson Rd (Hastings Highlands)
HS 61 S42-44
Peterson Rd (Tweed) HS . 46 A49
Peterson's Rd LN 64 U54
Petes Hill Rd PS 77 N31
Pethericks Rd NR. 34 C46
Petite Quatorze Rd PR. . . . .
. . . 68 Q72 69 Q73
Petrel Point Rd BR 58 W-X16
Petrie Rd LN 65 U59
Petrolia Ln LM . . 12 U7-9 13 U10-12
Pettem Rd LG 50 Z62
Petticoat La LM 13 S11
Petticoat Point Rd PE. . . 35 H52
Pettit Rd NI. 18 T-U32
Petty St MD 14 R-S14
Petworth Rd F 36 B54-55
Petworth Rd LA 36 B54
Petznicks Lake Rd R. . . 81 M50-51
Pevensey Rd PS 77 L-M32
Pheasant Run R 64 S54
Pheasant Farm Rd LA . . 47 Y50
Phelan Dr WL 23 M25
Phelan Rd E 66 T63
Phelan Rd W OT 66 T62-63
Phelans Rd LN 65 U57-58
Phelps Rd BT 17 S25
Phelpston Rd SM 41 A28
Philburn Rd HS 34 D-E48
Phillip Murray Av DH . . . 31 H36
Phillips La F. 48 Z54
Phillips Rd HS 46 W47
Phillips Rd LG. 49 X61
Phillips Rd NI. 19 T33
Phillips Rd TM. . . . 85 Q28-29 R28-29
Phillips Rd (Limerick) HS. . 46 W47
Phillips Rd (Tyendinaga) HS. 35 C50
Phillips Sdrd A 86 D95
Phillips Bay Rd A 87 D99
Phillipston Rd HS 34 C49
Philp Rd NI 18 R31
Philrick Dr PB 44 Z40
Phipps St NI 19 T36
Picadilly Bay La HL 60 S39
Piche Rd PR 67 Q68
Pick Ln OX. 16 T22
Pickard Rd A 84 Y92
Pickens Rd NR. 33 C44-45
Pickerel Bay Rd LN . . . 64 S56
Pickerel Point Rd A 43 B37
Pickerel Point Rd MK. . . 41 W29
Pickerel River Rd PS . 92 J22 93 J23
Pickering Beach Rd DH . . 31 H35
Pier Rd C 5 E6
Pierce Rd PE 66 U62
Pierce Rd PE 34 G49 35 G50
Pierre Ln HU 21 K17
Pietz Rd NI 18 T33
Pifer Rd TB 102 D3
Pigden Rd HS 46 A48
Pigeon Dr A. 88 F3
Pigeon Beach Rd K. . . . 4 F2
Pigeon Creek Rd K . . . 32 D38
Pigeon Hill Rd SDG . . . 66 S70
Pigeon Island Rd F 36 C56
Pigeon Lake Rd K 32 C38 44 A39 B38
Pigeon Trail Rd TB 102 E5
Pigram Rd EL 16 U20
Pigram Rd MD. 15 T19
Pihach St NI 19 T33
Pike Rd EX. 4 E1-2
Pike Rd MD 14 T13

Pike St BR 55 V16
Pike Tr R 63 Q50
Pike Bay Rd BR 55 W16-17
Pike Lake Rd MA 73 K11
Pike Lake Rd NP 94 C27
Pike Lake Rd TB 103 B6
Pike Lake Rd WL 27 G9-H20
Pike Lake Rd (Hudson Rd C2) TM
. . . . 85 R28
Pikes Peak Rd HS . . 61 U44 62 U45
Pilger's Rd PS 94 H-J30
Pilgrim Rd R 63 R49
Pillette Rd EX 4 B2
Pilon Cr CS 100 B17
Pilon Rd PR 67 P67
Pilon Rd, Mtée SD . . . 93 G23
Pilon Point Rd SDG . . 52 U72
Pilons Creek Access Rd LN . 64 T55
. . . . 84 B92
Pim St A 84 B92
Pine Av HL 60 U39
Pine Av PL 29 G28
Pine Av SM 30 D31
Pine Dr PS 77 P31
Pine La LN 48 W56
Pine La LS 77 L31-32
Pine Ln C 6 A8
Pine Rd MD 7 W12
Pine Rd NP 95 D33
Pine Rd SD 100 D14
Pine St A 84 B92
Pine St NI 19 R34
Pine St SM 41 X29
Pine Beach Rd SD . . . 93 G23
Pine Cliff Rd F 62 Q47
Pine Creek Rd WT . . . 22 M24
Pine Gate Rd DH 31 F35
Pine Glen Rd LG 49 Z58
Pine Grove La NR . . . 32 F40
Pine Grove Rd A 84 W91
Pine Grove Rd F 27 B58
Pine Grove Rd LA . 35 C51 47 B51
Pine Grove Rd LN . . 65 U57-58
Pine Grove Rd NR . . . 33 E45
Pine Grove Rd PS . . 77 N-P33
Pine Grove Rd R 83 Q57
Pine Hill Cr HS 34 C48
Pine Hill Rd A 86 D94
Pine Island Rd A 86 D94
Pine Lake Rd HL 60 T30
Pine Lake Rd MA 73 L12
Pine Lake Rd MK . . . .
. . . . . 58 V31-32 59 U33-34
Pine Lake Rd NP 95 E34
Pine Lake Hydro Access Rd CS
. . . . 101 Y20
Pine Needle Point Rd MK . 58 U29-30
Pine Plains Rd SM . . . 29 D27
Pine Point La R 81 N48
Pine Point Rd DH 31 E36
Pine Point Rd F 60 S38
Pine Point Rd HS 46 A48
Pine Ridge Dr MK . . 59 R34-35
Pine Ridge Dr SD . . . 92 H22
Pine Ridge La HS 62 Q-R46
Pine Ridge Rd A 87 E98
Pine Ridge Rd (Gravenhurst) MK
. . . . 43 W34
Pine Ridge Rd (Huntsville) MK
. . . . 59 R33
Pine River Access Rd R . 80 L-M47
Pine Shore Rd A 84 Z91-92
Pine Springs Rd HL . . 59 T36
Pine Tree Rd LG 37 A-B59
Pine Tree Way PS . . . 77 P33
Pine Valley Dr Y . . 24 I-J30 30 H30
Pine Valley Rd R 82 N52
Pine View Rd TB 102 D3
Pine View Ridge Rd HS . 46 W-X47
Pinebush Rd WT . . 22 N24 23 N25
Pinecone Rd CS 101 A21
Pinecreek Rd PS 95 F32
Pinecrest Rd HS 62 S47
Pinecrest Rd LA 35 C53
Pinecrest Point Rd NI . 19 U34
Pinedale Dr PS 77 P33
Pinedale Rd MK 59 T33
Pinegrove Rd R 43 Z36
Pinegrove Rd NF 16 V23
Pinegrove Rd PS 75 K26
Pinegrove Rd R . . . . .
. . . . 29 C28 30 C29 41 B28
Pinehill Rd PB 44 B40
Pinehill Rd WT 22 P22
Pinehurst Av PB 44 A-B40
Pinehurst Ln C 6 A9 7 A10
Pinehurst Rd BT 16 U24
Pineland Dr NP 95 E34
Pineridge Dr PS . 56 Q26 57 Q27
Pineridge La HS 62 S45
Pineridge Rd SDG . . . 68 T70
Pinery Ln HU 20 J14
Pinery Rd K X-Y38
Pinery Rd LN . . . 49 V60 65 U60
Pines, The DH 31 D35
Pineshores La F 48 Y55
Pinetree Dr LM 13 Q12
Pinetree Rd MK 58 V32
Pinetree Tr MA 72 L8
Pinetree Harbour Rd BR
. . . . 54 T15 55 U15
Pineview Tr HT 23 M27
Pineview Tr SM 30 C29
Pinewood Dr G 28 D22
Pinewood Dr PS 57 Q27
Pinewood Rd SD 93 F24
Pinewood Park Dr NP . 95 E34
Pinewood Park Rd R . 82 N54
Pinewood School Rd HS . 33 E44-45
Pinhey Point Rd OT . 65 Q60 66 Q61
Pinkerton Rd EX 4 D3
Pinnacle Rd HS 62 U46
Pinnacle Rd R 82 P54
Pioneer Dr G 39 B20-21
Pioneer Ln C 6 A8-9
Pioneer Ln EL . . 7 Y13 8 W15 X14
Pioneer Rd CS 101 D19-20
Pioneer Rd LG 50 W62
Pioneer Rd NP 95 G33-34
Pioneer Rd NR 33 F42
Pioneer Rd PB 32 F53
Pioneer Rd R 80 P46-47
Pioneer Rd (Echo Bay) A . 86 B-C94
Pioneer Rd (Huron Shores) A . 82 L-M7
Pioneer St SD 101 C22-23
Pioneer Tr WL 23 M25
Pioneer Tower Rd WT . 23 N25
Pioneer Village La SM 42 Y33 43 Y34
Pipe Lake Dr HS 62 U45

Pipe Lake Rd A 87 B98-99
Pipedream La R 80 P46
Pipeline Rd A . . . 88 D4 D4-5 D5
Pipeline Rd CS 101 A21
Pipeline Rd NI 33 F43-44
Pipeline Rd TM 85 P-R29
Piper Dr TB 102 E4-5
Piper St WT 16 Q23
Piquette Rd NP 93 D25-26
Pirates Glen Dr PB . . 44 Z39-40
Pit Rd A 86 D94
Pit Rd BR 55 W18
Pit Rd F 47 Y-Z52
Pit Rd K 32 E38
Pit Rd MK 58 U29
Pit Rd NR 32 G40
Pit Rd R 82 N53
Pit Rd TB 102 G4
Pit Bray Rd PR 67 R67
Pitch Off Rd PS . . 67 P68 68 P69
Pitchers Rd HS 34 D47
Pitman Bay Rd MK . . 59 S33
Pitre Rd A 87 Q68
Pitre Rd SD 93 G24
Pitt Rd C 7 X-Y11
Pitt Rd LG 50 W64-65
Pitt St SDG 52 U70
Pittdale Rd LG 50 V-W64
Pitter Rd F 99 K50
Pivot Lake La HL . . . 60 T39
Plain Rd EL 14 V15
Plains Rd HT 23 P28
Plains Rd WT 22 P23
Plane Tree Dr MD . . 14 S16
Plank La OX . . . 15 S-T20 16 U21
Plank Rd EL 9 W21 16 V21
Plank Rd HD 17 S-T27
Plank Rd LM . . . . . 12 T U8
Plank Rd NF 16 V22
Plant Rd R 99 H49
Plantation Rd HL . . 60 V37
Plantation Way R . . 48 W46
Plante Rd NP 93 E25
Plantes Rd A 89 B8 B9
Platt Rd HS 34 D-E47
Platt Rd NI 33 D-E45
Plaunt Rd R 82 P53-54
Pleasant Dr LA . . . 35 C52
Pleasant La LG . . . 50 Z62
Pleasant Bay Rd PE . 34 G48
Pleasant Beach Rd NI . 19 U34-35
Pleasant Corner Rd PE 68 P71-72
Pleasant Park Sdrd EX . 4 C3
Pleasant Point Rd D . 33 D-E41
Pleasant Point Rd (Kawartha Lakes[Fenelon]) K . . 44 B38
Pleasant Point Rd (Kawartha Lakes[Mariposa]) K . . 44 A39
Pleasant Ridge Rd BT . 16 R-S24
Pleasant Valley Rd EL . 9 W18
Pleasant Valley Rd MA . 72 J-K8
Pleasant Valley Rd OX . 16 T21-22
Pleasant Valley Rd R . 82 L53-54
Pleasant Valley Rd SD . 90 F12
Pleasant Valley Rd (South Dundas) SDG 50 V64-65
Pleasant Valley Rd (South Stormont) SDG . 51 V68 67 U68
Pleasant View Point Rd MK . 58 U31
Pleasantview Rd BR . . 38 A11
Pleasure Bay Rd HS . 46 W47
Pleasure Point La F . 36 E57 37 E58
Pleasure Point Rd LG . 60 U37
Plenty La LN 48 W56
Pletsch Ct BR 27 E17
Plouffe Rd SD 92 G23
Plover Mills Rd MD 14 R16 15 R17-18
Plowing Match Rd LM . 12 T-V9
Plowmans Ln NF . . 16 U-V21
Plug Hat Rd T 25 H34
Plugtown Ln HU . . . 20 P16
Plum Hollow Rd LG . 49 Y-Z60
Plum Point Rd EL . . 8 X15
Plum Point Rd SM . 44 Z32-33
Plumb Rd HS 35 D51
Plummer Rd A 85 B8-9
Plumpton Rd HS . . 34 D48-49
Plunkett Rd PB . . . 33 D42
Pluto Tr HL 60 T40
Plymouth Rd LN . . 48 W-X58
Poechman La BR . . 27 E18
Poff Rd R 82 M53
Pogue Rd DH 31 D-E36
Pogue Rd NR 33 E-F45
Point Rd G 28 C23
Point Rd MD 14 V14
Point Rd PB 44 A-B41
Point Rd R 64 R56
Point Tr R 82 K53
Point Abino Rd NI . 19 T-U35
Point Church Dr R . 81 N51
Point Ideal Rd MK . 59 S35
Point Petre Rd PE . 35 H50
Point Simcoe Rd MA . 72 M9
Pointe C Rd A 6 X-6
Pointe Rd C 6 A7
Pointe Anne Rd HS . 34 E49
Pointe aux Pins Dr A . 84 B91
Pointe de Meuron Rd TB . 102 D4
Poirier Rd NP 93 E26
Pokki Rd TB 102 C2-3
Pole Line Rd TB . . 102 D4
Poli La F 48 Z55
Polk Rd LG 49 X60
Pollard Dr A 86 D95
Pollard Ln C 6 C7-8
Pollard Rd DH . . . 32 G38
Pollard Rd LG . . . 48 Y56
Pollard Rd NR . . . 33 F42
Pollock Rd OT . . . 66 T62
Pollock Rd Y 30 D32
Poly-Ure Rd TM . . 85 P28-29
Polymoore Dr LM . 12 U7
Pomeroy Rd PS . . 58 U32
Pommainville Rd PR . 67 R66-67
Ponacka Rd HS . . 61 T43
Pond Rd C 6 X8
Pond Rd LN 48 X56
Pond Rd LG 37 A61
Pond Rd PS 76 L30
Pond Meadows Rd MK . 59 R34
Pond Mills Rd MD . 15 T-U17
Ponderosa Rd PS . 95 H-J31
Pondview Rd HU . 32 C38
Pondview St K . . . 32 C38
Pontypool Rd K . . 32 E38-39

Pook Rd C 7 B10
Pool Rd TB 102 D2
Pooles Rd SM . . . 41 B29 42 B30
Poonamalie Rd LG . 49 W60
Poonamalie Sdrd LN . 49 W59-60
Popkie Rd (Greater Madawaska) R 63 S52
Popkie Rd (Laurentian Valley) R 81 L50
Poplar Dr HD 17 V28
Poplar Rd MA 72 K-L7
Poplar Sdrd SM . . 40 A25
Poplar Beach Rd HU . 20 P13
Poplar Bluff Dr EX . 4 F3
Poplar Dale Rd A . 86 B97 B-C97
Poplar Heights Dr HL . 59 T36
Poplar Hill Rd MD . 14 S14
Poplarvale Rd NP . 95 G-H34
Poppe Rd C 6 C8
Porchuck Rd A . . 86 C93-94
Porcupine La HS . 61 V44 62 V45
Porcupine Way LN . 48 V56
Porky's Rd HL . . . 60 V38
Port Rd C 5 D8 6 C8
Port Britain Rd NF . 32 G40
Port Cunnington Rd MK . 59 R-S35
Port Davidson Rd NI . 18 S31
Port Elgin Rd BR . 55 W18
Port Elmsley Rd LN . 49 W59
Port Findlay Rd A . 86 D94
Port Franks Rd LM . 13 Q11
Port Hoover Rd K . 31 D36
Port Ideal Rd MK . 59 S35
Port Maitland Rd HD . 18 U30-31
Port of Newcastle Dr DH . 32 H39
Port Robinson Rd NI . 19 S33-34
Port Ryerse Rd NF . 17 V25
Port Severn Rd MK . 41 X29
Port Sydney Rd MK . 59 S33
Port Union Rd T . . 25 J34
Portage Dr TB . . . 103 C10
Portage Rd HL . . . 60 U40
Portage Rd MK . . 41 W29
Portage Rd NI . . . 19 R35 S35
Portage Rd R . . . 99 K50
Portage Rd SD . . 90 D-E13
Portage Tr SM . . 41 B28
Portage Lake Rd CS . 101 Z22
Portage Lake Rd PS . 57 S28 58 S29
Portage Point Rd MA . 71 J5
Portelance Rd CS . 101 Y20 Z20
Porter Rd K 32 D38-39 E39
Porter Rd LN . . . 49 V-W59
Porter Rd NR . . . 33 E44
Porter Rd (North Grenville) R 50 V64
Porter Rd (Rideau Lakes) LG 48 Y56-57
Porter's Hill Ln HU . 20 K13
Porter Lake Rd SD . 90 D13
Porterfield Rd PL . 29 H26-27
Porters Landing Rd PS . 94 H29
Portland Rd LG . . 49 Y-Z59
Portland St G . . . 39 Z18
Portsmouth Av F . 36 D56
Portview Rd DH . . 31 E36
Posey Ln WT . . . 22 L21-22
Post Rd HS 34 D46
Post Rd R 32 C38 44 B38
Post Rd SDG . . . 52 U69-70
Post Office Rd A . 84 Y92
Post Office Gate La F . 36 E57
Posters Rd TB . . . 102 B4
Potato Island Rd R . 41 X29
Potchett Rd LA . . 47 A52
Poth Rd HD 18 U31-32
Potlake Rd R . . . 19 T33
Pother Rd SDG . . 93 D24 101 D23
Potlake Rd EX . . 4 E-F2
Potspoon La F . . 48 Z55
Potter Rd HS . . . 34 E46
Potter Rd LG . . . 60 U38
Potter Rd PE . . . 35 E-F50
Potter Settlement Rd HS 47 A50 Z50
Potters Rd A . . . 43 Z37
Potters Rd OX . . 16 U22-23
Pottruff Rd BT . . 16 R24
Potts Rd HS . . . 34 C47
Poulsom Rd K . . 43 Z37
Poupart Rd PR . . 67 P66
Poupore Rd CS . 101 A21
Poupore Rd TM . 85 N-P28
Poverty La F . . . 87 C99
Poverty La NR . . 59 R35
Powell Dr SD . . . 90 D-E12
Powell La K . . . 43 Y36
Powell Ln HU . . 27 H17
Powell Rd MA . . 72 L22
Powell St LN . . . 65 U60
Powell Lake Tr R . 98 F44-45
Power Rd HS . . 35 C50
Power Rd LM . . 13 T12
Power Rd OT . . 66 R64
Power St CS . . 100 C18 101 C19
Power Dam Rd SDG . 52 U-V70
Power House Rd A . 89 F8
Power Line Rd BT . 16 R24 17 R25
Power Line Rd HM . 18 R29-30
Power Line Rd NR . 32 E40
Power Plant Rd PS . 95 G31
Powerdam Rd SDG . 68 R71
Powerhouse La PE . 34 D46
Pumphouse Rd Y . 30 E-F31
Pumpkin St LA . 43 T50
Pumpkin Point Rd A . 86 C93-94
Purbrook Rd MK . 59 U34
Raby's Rd PS . . 74 M23 75 N24
Raby's Shore Dr K . 43 A37

Presqu'ile Pkwy NR . 34 G46
Presqu'ile Rd G . . 39 Y19-20
Presqu'ile Rd PR . 68 N69
Presqu'ile Rd SD . 92 G22
Pressey Ln EL . . 14 V15
Prest Rd HS . . . 46 B47
Prest Rd HS . . . 46 B48
Preston Rd SM . . 41 Y28
Preston Rd (Cavan-Millbrook-North Monaghan) PB . 32 C-D40
Preston Rd (Havelock-Belmont-Methuen) PB . . 45 A45
Preston Rd (Smith-Ennismore-Lakefield) PB . . 44 A41
Preston Hill Rd HS . 34 D46
Prestonvale Rd DH . 32 H37
Prestonvale Rd LN . 49 V58 65 U58
Prestwick Tr HL . 61 U42
Pretty Dr LN . . . 65 U57
Pretty River Pkwy SM . 40 A25
Pretty River Rd G . 40 B24-25
Prevost Rd HS . . 47 A50
Prevost Rd SD . . 93 G24
Price Rd F 48 X-Y53
Price Rd R 82 P54-55
Prices Point Rd MK . 59 S34
Priebe Rd R . . . 99 K50
Priest Camp Ln R . 82 N52
Priestman Rd NI . 18 T32
Priest Rd SDG . . 52 U69
Prince Rd A . . . 84 A-B90
Prince Rd EX . . 4 B-C1
Prince Rd R . . . 62 Q48
Prince St HT . . . 23 K28
Prince St LM . . . 12 U9
Prince Albert Rd R . 6 A9 X-Y8
Prince Edward Dr T . 24 K-L31
Prince of Wales Dr NI . 19 T33
Prince of Wales Dr OT . 66 R-T62
Prince of Wales Rd DF . 29 D-E26
Prince William St MI . 14 R15
Prince William Way SM . 30 C30
Princess Blvd F . 36 D55-56
Princess Rd F . . 36 C56-57
Princess St F . . 36 D55
Princess St G . . 39 Z18
Principale, Mtée G . 24 J5
Principale Rd (Casselman) PR 67 R67-68
Principale St (Wendover) PR 67 R67-68
Pringle Rd HL . . 60 V39
Pringle's Sdrd J La CS . 35 C-D52
Prinyers Cove Cr PE . 35 F53
Prisque Rd MK . . 41 W29
Pritchard Rd HS . 62 R46
Pritchard Rd HM . 18 R29
Proctor Av PL . . 29 H28 30 H29
Progressive Av NI . 19 Q-R35
Progress Rd HM . 23 N-P27
Promenade Rd TM . 85 P30
Promontory Rd LN . 48 V55
Pronto Rd A . . . 88 F5
Proof Ln LM . . . 13 R10
Prospect Rd A . . 43 A-B35
Prospect Hill Rd MD . 15 R-S18
Prospect Lake Rd MK . 59 U-V34
Prosperity Ln HU . 20 J14
Proudfoot Rd MK . 59 R33
Proudfoot Rd PR . 68 Q69
Proudfoot Rd (Joly) PS . 77 M33
Proudfoot Rd (Powassan) PS 95 H32
Proulx La LN . . . 65 U57
Prouse Rd DH . . 31 F33
Prouse Rd OX . . 15 U20
Prout Rd Y 31 D33
Proutt Rd DH . 31 E36 32 E37
Proven Ln R . . . 66 T-U62
Proven Line Rd OT . 66 T-U62
Providence Ln PB . 33 C41-42
Providence Rd DH . 32 G38
Providence Rd K . 44 A38
Provincial Rd A . . 4 C2
Provost La HL . . 60 T40
Pruce Rd A 84 Z92
Prunneville La PS . 62 V48
Quesnel Rd NP . 94 E27-28
Quiet Rd CS . . . 6 C7
Quiet Valley Rd G . 40 B22-23
Quigley Hill Rd OT . 67 P65
Quilty Rd F . . . 82 Q54
Quin-Mo-Lac Rd HS . 46 A48-49
Quince Rd EX . . 4 C4
Pucker St R . . . 82 O54-55
Puckering La PL . 23 J27
Puddicombe La G . 39 B20
Puddicombe Rd WT . 22 P22
Puddingstone Rd A . 86 C-D95
Puffers Rd PB . . 45 Z43
Pulham Rd MD . . 14 T16
Pulley Rd EL . . . 9 W18
Pulley Rd EX . . . 5 E6
Pulver Rd PE . . 34 E-F48
Pump Rd C . . . 6 B7
Pumphouse La PE . 34 D46
Pumphouse Rd Y . 30 E-F31

Q & R Ln A . . . 86 E-F95
Quabbin Rd F . . 36 C54-55
Quabbin Rd LG . 37 A-B61
Quabbin Hill Rd LG . 37 B60-61
Quackenbush Rd F . 63 T-U51
Quadeville Rd F . 63 Q50
Quae Quae Rd NP . 95 F33
Quail Rd SDG . . 68 T69
Quaker Ln EL . . 13 S-T12
Quaker Rd K . . 31 C35-36
Quaker Rd NI . . 19 U33
Quaker Rd PE . 35 F-G50
Quarry Ln HU . . 21 J18 27 H18
Quarry Rd BR . . 55 X17
Quarry Rd F . . . 36 B54
Quarry Rd HS . . 62 U45-46
Quarry Rd LN . . 65 T58-59
Quarry Rd NI . . 18 R32
Quarry Rd SM . 41 X29 42 X30
Quarry Rd TM . . 85 R30
Quarry Point Rd R . 82 N52
Quartz La HL . . 60 V40
Quebec St MD . 15 T17
Queen St C . . . 5 A9 C7
Queen St DH . . 31 G36
Queen St EX . . 4 E2-3
Queen St G . . . 27 D18 F19
Queen St HS . . 47 B51
Queen St HU . . 17 Q28
Queen St K . . . 20 J-K15
Queen St LM . . 12 S9
Queen St MA . . 73 L12-13
Queen St OT . . 66 P64 67 P65
Queen St OX . . 15 R19
Queen St PB . . 44 B41
Queen St PT . . 15 U17-18
Queen St R . . . 81 N49
Queen St T . . . 25 H34
Queens Blvd F . 36 S55-56
Queen St (Brampton) PL . 24 K-L29
Queen St (Brockton) R . 27 D18
Queen St (Caledon[Alton]) PL 29 H26
Queen St (Caledon[Bolton]) PL 30 H29
Queen St (Cambridge) WT 22 N24 23 N25
Queen St (Essa) SM . 30 E29
Queen St (Kincardine) R . 26 D-E14
Queen St (New Tecumseth) SM 30 F-G29
Queen St (Norfolk[Delhi]) NF 10 W24
Queen St (Norfolk[Nanticoke]) NF 11 U-V24
Queen St (Springwater) SM . 41 Z28
Queen St (Wilmot) WT . 22 P22
Queen St A . . . 84 B92
Queen St E T . 24 K32 25 K33
Queen St W LM . 13 S10
Queen St W T . 24 K-L32
Queen's La MA . 73 L11
Queen's Ln C . . 6 B8 B-C7
Queen's Bush Rd WT 20 M20 22 M21
Queen's University LG 36 A57 48 Z57
Queen St SDG . 68 S-T72
Queen St (Springwater) SM . 41 Z28
Queen St (Wilmot) WT . 22 P22
Queensborough Rd HS . 46 Z48-49
Queenston Rd HM . 18 Q29
Queenston St NI . 19 R34
Queensville Sdrd Y . 17 U25
Queensway OT . 63 063 R62
Queensway Y . . 30 D31
Queensway, The T . 24 L31
Queensway, The Y . 30 D31
Queensville La HS . 62 V48
Radley's Hill Rd TM . 85 R29-30
Radmore Rd C . . 6 C8
Radtke Rd R . . 99 K50-51
Rae Rd A . . . 65 S59 T58
Rae Rd (North Dundas) SDG 67 U66
Rae Rd (South Glengarry) SDG 52 U71

Rae's La WL . . 27 G19-20
Raft Lake Rd CS . 101 D19
Raged Rapids Rd MK . 58 U29-30
Ragged Chutes Rd F . 4 M48
Ragged Falls Park Rd HL . 59 Q36
Ragged Lake Rd HS . 62 V45
Raglan Rd C . . 7 B11
Raglan Rd DH . 31 F36
Raglan St A . . 85 P-055
Raglan St SM . 40 A25
Raglan St R . . 62 R48
Rahmel Rd PB . 33 D41
Rahn's Rd F . . 81 L50
Railroad Rd LM . 13 V11
Railroad St NI . 19 Q-R35
Railton La F . . 36 C55-56
Railton Rd F . . 36 B-C55
Railway St A . . 38 A16
Railway St NP . 94 D27
Railway St (Leeds and the Thousand Islands) LG . 37 B60
Railway St (Rideau Lakes) LG 49 Z59
Rain Lake Rd PS . 77 N33-34 78 N35
Rainbow Dr PB . 33 E41
Rainbow La F . . 48 Z55
Rainbow La LN . 48 X56
Rainbow La SM . 59 U34
Rainbow Ridge Rd K . 32 D37
Rainbow Valley Rd SD . 90 H13
Rainbow Valley Rd E SM . 41 A29
Rainbow Valley Rd W SM . 41 A29
Raindrop Lake Access Rd F 64 U53
Rainham Rd D . .
. . . . 17 V26-27 V27-28 18 U30
Rainie Rd HS . . 34 C47
Rainville Rd PR . 67 R67
Rainville Rd SD . 101 D23
Rainville Rd (Bonfield) NP . 95 F33
Rainville Rd (West Nipissing) NP 93 D-E26
Raison Rd LG . . 49 Z59-60
Ralston Rd HL . 43 W37
Ralston Rd MK . 78 P35-36
Rama Rd SM . . 42 X-Z32
Rama-Dalton Boundary Rd SM 42 X33 43 X-Y34
Ramage La G . . 39 A21
Ramage Rd PR . 67 N-P66
Rambling Rose La LG . 37 B58
Ramparts La F . 36 B57
Ramparts Rd F . 36 B57
Ramsay La HU . 21 J17 27 H17
Ramsay Rd HS . 46 Z48-49
Ramsay Rd TM . 85 R29-30
Ramsay St TB . 102 B4
Ramsayville Rd OT . 66 R64
Ramsbottom Rd HS . 62 T47
Ramsey Rd R . . 18 U30
Ramsey Rd K . . 31 D36 32 D37
Ramsey-Johnston Rd PS 57 S27-28
Ramsey Lake Rd CS . 101 C19
Ranch Rd BT . . 17 R26
Ranch Rd PB . . 44 Z39
Ranch Rd (Kawartha Lakes[Bobcaygeon Verulam]) K . . 44 A39
Ranch Rd (Kawartha Lakes[Mariposa]) K . 31 C-D36
Rancher's Rd F . 43 A37
Randolph Rd CS . 100 D16
Randy's Rd F . . 81 P51
Raney Clark Rd F . 36 B56-57
Raney Rd E LN . 77 L31
Raney Rd E PS . 77 L31
Raney Rd W PS . 77 L31
Range Rd G . . 39 Z19
Range Rd MA . . 73 M11
Range Rd SA . . 42 B30
Range St MA . . 72 J7
Range A Sdrd MA . 72 J9
Range Lights Rd A . 86 D94-95
Rangelight Rd SM . 41 X28
Ranger Dr MD . 14 U16
Ranger Rd PR . 68 P72
Ranger Bridge Rd SDG . 68 O72
Ranger Camp Rd LN . 64 U55
Ranger Lake Rd A . 84 Y94
Rankin Rd PE . . 35 H50
Rankin Bridge Rd BR . 55 Y17
Rankin Lake Rd PS . 57 S27-28
Rankin Rink Rd F . 81 M51
Ransley Rd HL . 60 V37
Ranta Rd CS . . 91 E15
Rantz Rd R . . . 99 K50
Ranwood Rd MK . 58 T31
Rapid Rd R . . . 82 K53
Rapids Rd HS . 46 A-B49
Rapids Rd HS . 59 R35
Rapids Run La HL . 60 U37
Rapier Resource Rd A . 99 D8-9
Rat Bay Rd MK . 59 R34-35
Rat Lake Rd PS . 77 N32-33
Rathburn Rd T . 24 K31
Rathfon Rd F . . 36 B-C55
Rathwell Rd LN . 49 W58-59
Rattler Lake Rd SD . 101 C22-23
Rattie Rd LA . . 35 C52
Rattlebear Dr PS . 74 N23
Rattler Rd NI . . 19 U33
Rattlesnake Rd HD . 18 T-U31
Rattlesnake Rd MK . 42 W31
Rattray's Rd PS . 77 P33
Raven La HL . . 59 S36
Raven La R . . . 63 R51
Raven Rd K . . 43 Z36
Ravencrest Rd Y . 30 D32
Ravenscliffe Rd MK 58 Q32 59 Q-R32
Ravenscroft Rd DH . 31 H35
Ravenshoe Rd Y .
. . . . 30 D32 D-E31 31 D33-34
Ravenswood Ln LM . 13 R11-12
Ravine Rd HL . . 43 W37
Rawlings Rd LM . 13 Q-R11 R10
Ray Rd (Centre Hastings) HS 46 B48
Ray Rd (Hastings Highlands) HS 62 T45
Ray Lawson Blvd PL . 24 K-L29
Ray Wilson Rd OT . 57 S65
Raymo Rd F . . 48 Z54
Raymond Rd F . 36 C55
Raymond Rd MK . 58 T32

Raymond / St. David

Raymond Rd SDG 67 U68
RCAF Rd HS 34 E47
Reach St DH 31 E34-35
Read Rd HS 35 C-D50
Read Rd NI 19 Q34
Reader Rd DH 31 E36
Reagan Bourne EL 15 U-V17
Reaume Rd EX 4 C1
Reavie Rd LA 47 Y50
Reay Rd MK 59 V33
Rebecca Rd MD 15 S17
Rebecca St HT 24 N29-30
Recoskie La R 80 M47 81 M48
Recoskie Rd R 80 M47 81 M48
Red Bay Rd BR 55 X17
Red Cedar Point Rd LA 47 B53
Red Chalk Lake Rd MK 59 S36
Red Cloud School Rd NR 33 E44
Red Deer Lake Rd N CS 101 C21
Red Deer Lake Rd S CS 101 C-D21
Red Fox Rd K 43 Y36
Red Fox Tr R 98 F45
Red Horse Lake Rd LG 37 A59
Red Lodge Rd MA 73 K11
Red Oak Rd PS 56 Q25-26
Red Pine Rd LN 48 X56
Red Pine Rd R 82 N54
Red Pine St BR 26 C14
Red River Rd TB 103 D6
Red Rock Rd K 44 A38
Red Rock Rd LN 65 U59
Red Rock Rd R 81 M48
Red Rock Rd (Huron Shores) A 87 E1
Red Rock Rd (Sault Ste Marie) A 84 A91
Red Town Rd SDG 68 T69
Redan Rd LG 49 Y61
Reddick La OT 50 V62
Reddy's Creek Access Rd F 64 S54 T53-54
Redford Dr LA 63 U50
Redford Rd LG 49 Z61
Redhawk Rd MK 58 V29
Redhorse Lake Rd F 64 U53-54
Redkenn Rd HL 60 S38-39
Redmond Rd F 36 B55
Redmond Rd PB 33 C-D41
Redner Rd HL 60 U38
Rednersville Rd PE 34 E-F48
Redpath Rd LN 65 U58
Redstone Rd Y 30 H32
Redstone Lake Rd HL 60 T39
Redwing Dr MK 42 W32 58 V32
Redwood Rd MK 58 T30
Reed's Bay Rd F 36 E56-57
Reeders Ln C 7 A11-12
Reeds Rd HD 17 T28
Rees Rd LA 36 D54
Reesor Rd Y 31 G33 H34
Reevecraig Rd OT 66 U63
Reeves Rd HS 62 U47
Reeves Rd SM 41 Y29
Reg Schell Rd MK 42 W32
Regal Rd NP 95 E32
Regan Rd HS 34 D46
Regan Rd R 82 R47
Regent Dr SDG 68 T71
Regent St CS 101 C-D19
Regent St SM 41 A26
Regimbald Rd OT 67 Q65
Rego Rd NR 45 B46
Regs Tr HL 60 U40
Reiche Rd R 81 M51
Reicheld Rd HD 11 V29 18 U29
Reichert Dr WT 22 P24
Reid Rd A 86 E95
Reid Rd HU 26 H16
Reid Rd LG 37 B-C60
Reid Rd PB 44 X39
Reid Rd R 82 P54
Reid Rd (Bancroft) HS 62 U45
Reid Rd (Clarington) DH 32 G39
Reid Rd (Quinte West) HS 34 D46
Reid Rd (Uxbridge) DH 31 F34-35
Reid Sdrd HT 23 M27
Reid St LG 49 W61
Reid St PB 44 X38
Reid's Rd LN 64 U55
Reid's Rd PB 45 Z42
Reid Settlement Rd HS 46 B48
Reid Woods Dr WL 22 L22
Reid Woods Dr WT 22 L22-23
Reidel Dr WT 22 P23
Reids Hill G 40 B24
Reids La HS 62 V48
Reids Rd A 86 C-D94
Reids Mills Rd SDG 66 U64
Reidsville Rd WT 22 P23
Reiger Rd EL 8 W17 15 V17
Reilly La HS 46 Y47
Reily Dr MD 14 U15
Reily Rd A 86 C94
Reinhart Rd NI 19 T34-35
Reinink Rd LA 47 B53
Reive Blvd SM 30 D30
Reixinger Rd NI 19 S35
Rejean Levac Sdrd PR 68 Q69
Relative Rd PS 77 M-N32
Remy Bay Rd PS 56 Q24-25
Renaud Rd OT 66 Q64
Renaud Rd PR 68 R69
Renaud Line Rd EX 4 B-C4
Renault Creek Rd A 89 D9
Render Rd LG 50 W63
Renwick Dr HU 27 G17
Renwick Rd PB 45 X44
Reserve Rd SD 91 E17 100 D17
Resort Rd F 37 C58
Rest Acres Rd BT 16 R24
Reuter Rd NI 19 U34
Reveler Rd SDG 67 S-T66
Revere Dr MD 14 Q16 15 Q17
Rexdale Blvd T 24 K30-31
Reynolds La F 36 A54
Reynolds Rd HL 60 U38
Reynolds Rd HS 46 A47-48
Reynolds Rd R 99 H48
Reynolds Rd (Elizabethtown-Kitley) LG 49 Y61
Reynolds Rd (Leeds and the Thousand Islands) LG 37 B-C60
Reyns Rd NR 33 E42
Rhapsody La HL 59 Q36
Rhineland Rd NF 16 V22-23
Rhodes Dr EX 4 C2
Rhodes La HS 62 Q-R46
Rice Ln R 82 N52-53
Rice Rd HL 43 W37 60 V37
Rice Rd LN 49 V60
Rice Rd LG 49 W-X60
Rice Rd NI 19 S33
Rice Lake Dr NR 33 F41
Rice Lake Scenic Dr NR 33 E42
Richard St CS 100 D16
Richard's Rd NP 96 E37-38
Richard Lake Rd CS 101 C-D20
Richard Lake Access Rd NP 96 F37
Richards Dr BR 26 C14
Richards Rd HS 34 D46
Richards Lake Rd PS 56 Q-R25
Richardson Dr A 86 C-D95
Richardson Rd C 6 X8
Richardson Rd F 47 X52
Richardson Rd LN 49 V-W61
Richardson Rd NR 33 C-D44
Richardson Rd PE 35 E51
Richardson Rd PS 77 P31-32
Richardson Rd SM 41 B28
Richardson Rd (Northern Bruce Peninsula) BR 55 V18
Richardson Rd (Saugeen Shores) BR 38 B15
Richardson Sdrd EX 5 D6 6 C6
Richardson Sdrd LN 49 V59
Richardson Sdrd OT 65 R60 66 R61
Richardson's Rd NR 32 F40
Richer Rd NP 94 C28
Richer Rd SDG 68 T70
Richer Rd SD 93 D24
Richert Rd HD 17 U28 18 U29
Richie Sdrd OT 65 R58
Richmire Rd SDG 51 V67
Richmond Dr SDG 52 U69-70
Richmond Rd EL 9 W20
Richmond Rd F 48 Y53-54
Richmond Rd LN 65 U60
Richmond Rd OT 66 Q62 S61-62
Richmond Rd PS 56 Q25
Richmond Rd SDG 52 U72
Richmond St C 6 A-B9
Richmond St NR 33 E45
Richmond St NI 19 R34
Richmond St (Lucan Biddulph, Middlesex Centre London) MD 14 Q15 R-T16
Richmond St (Thames Centre) MD 15 S-T18
Richmond Bay Rd A 86 F96
Richmonds Rd LN 49 V58
Richvale Dr PL 24 K29
Richwood Dr PS 75 N24
Rickard Rd DH 32 H38
Rickards La F 36 B56
Ricker Rd HD 18 T30
Riddell Dr OT 66 Q-R61
Riddell Rd DF 29 H26
Riddell Rd R 82 P-Q54
Riddell Rd SDG 67 U65
Riddledale Rd OT 83 Q58
Rideau Rd F 37 B58
Rideau Rd OT 66 S63
Rideau St LN 49 W59
Rideau St OT 66 Q63
Rideau Ferry Rd LN 49 W58-59
Rideau Ferry Rd LG 49 X59
Rideau Forest Rd OT 66 S63
Rideau Glen La LG 66 U63
Rideau Lake Rd LN 49 X58
Rideau River Rd LN 49 W61
Rideau Valley Dr OT 66 T63
Rideau Valley Dr S OT 66 T63
Rider La F 48 Z55
Rider Rd WT 22 M24
Ridge Dr K 43 Z36
Ridge Ln C 7 A-B11
Ridge Rd DH 31 C35
Ridge Rd EL 16 V21
Ridge Rd EX 4 E-F3
Ridge Rd F 36 E57
Ridge Rd HM 18 Q29-30
Ridge Rd LA 35 E53
Ridge Rd LM 13 R11
Ridge Rd LN 65 S58
Ridge Rd MK 58 V30-31
Ridge Rd OT 66 Q64
Ridge Rd PE 34 F48
Ridge Rd PR 68 P70-71 Q69
Ridge Rd SDG 51 W66
Ridge Rd SM 42 A-B31 B30
Ridge Rd (Fort Erie) NI 19 U35
Ridge Rd (Grimsby) NI 18 R31
Ridge Rd (Rawdon) HS 34 C47-48
Ridge Rd (Tyendinaga) HS 35 E50-51
Ridge Rd, The HS 45 W-X45
Ridge St HM 18 R29
Ridgeland Rd F 48 X-Y53
Ridgemount Rd NI 19 T35
Ridgetop Rd OT 65 Q60
Ridgeview Rd NR 32 F40
Ridgeway Dr PL 24 M29-30
Ridgeway Dr PS 56 Q25
Ridgeway Rd NI 19 U35
Ridgewood Rd K 32 C37
Riding Ranch Rd PS 77 K31 95 J31
Riding Stable Rd NP 94 C-D29
Ridler Dr TB 102 D-E4
Ridout St MD 15 T17
Riels Rd LG 49 Y59-60
Rifle Rd OT 66 R61
Riga Rd SM 30 D29
Riggs Rd HS 46 A48
Rignalls Rd MK 59 U34-35
Rigsby La HL 43 X37 44 X38
Ril Lake Rd MK 59 T35
Ril Lake 10 Access Rd MK 59 T35
Riley La K 43 A36
Riley Rd DH 32 G-H39
Riley Rd LG 49 Y60
Riley Rd NR 33 E44
Riley Lake Rd MK 42 W33 43 W34
Rimington Rd HS 46 Z48
Rintala Rd SD 92 E20
Riopelle Rd R 82 Q55
Ripley's Way K 43 X35-36
Ripple La MK 59 Q33
Ripple Rock Dr HL 60 V39
Risto Rd (Bonnechere Valley) R 81 P50-51
Risto Rd (Petawawa) R 99 K51
Rit Lake Access Rd R 97 F40
Ritchance Rd PR 68 N70 P69-70
Ritchie Dr PS 75 P25
Ritchie Rd F 36 B56
Ritchie Sdrd LN 48 Y56
Ritchie Falls Rd HL 60 V38-39
Ritson Rd DH 31 F-H36
Ritter Rd WT 22 K22
Ritz Rd HS 34 D49
Ritz Rd LG 37 A58
Rivard Ln C 6 A7-8
River Cr A 84 A92
River Dr HT 23 K28
River Dr R 99 K51
River Dr (North Middlesex) MD 13 S12 14 S13
River Dr (Southwest Middlesex) MD 7 W13
River La MK 42 X32
River Ln C 6 A9 7 X-Y11 Y10
River Ln HU 20 J-K14
River Rd BT 17 R25 S25
River Rd DF 29 D-E26 E25
River Rd G 28 C24
River Rd HS 62 T45
River Rd HD 17 S27 S-T28 18 U29-30
River Rd HU 26 H14
River Rd K 32 C38 C-D37
River Rd LA 35 D52
River Rd LN 65 T59
River Rd LG 50 V62 66 U63
River Rd MA 72 M9
River Rd MD 15 T17-18
River Rd NP 95 F-G33
River Rd OX 22 P22
River Rd PS 77 N32
River Rd R 81 P48
River Rd SD 89 F9 90 F10
River Rd SM 30 F30
River Rd TB 102 E4
River Rd TM 85 Q29
River Rd WT 22 N23 N24 23 N25
River Rd (Asphodel-Norwood) PB 33 C43-44
River Rd (Belleville) HS 34 D48
River Rd (Blind River) A 88 F3
River Rd (Central Frontenac) F 63 V53
River Rd (Douro-Dummer) PB 44 B41
River Rd (Hastings Highlands) HS 62 Q46
River Rd (Horton) R 82 P55
River Rd (Joly) PS 77 K32-33
River Rd (Magnetawan) PS 76 M30
River Rd (McNab Braeside) R 83 P56 Q57
River Rd (Niagara Falls) NI 19 R-S35
River Rd (North Dundas) SDG 67 U66
River Rd (North Glengarry) SDG 68 R71
River Rd (North Lambton) LM 13 Q12
River Rd (Otonabee-South Monaghan) PB 33 C42
River Rd (Ottawa[Gloucester]) OT 66 S63
River Rd (Ottawa[Osgoode]) OT 66 T63
River Rd (Powassan) PS 95 J32
River Rd (South Frontenac) F 36 B54
River Rd (Thessalon) A 87 E98
River Rd (Valley East) CS 101 A-B19
River Rd (Walden) CS 100 D16
River Rd (Walpole Island IR) LM 6 X-Y6
River Rd (Welland) NI 19 T33
River Rd (West Grey) G 27 D19
River Rd E SM 41 A27 Z27
River Rd W SM 41 A27
River Rd, The BR 38 B16
River St A 87 E98
River St LM 13 U-V11
River St SM 42 Y30
River St (Brock) DH 31 D34-35
River St (Scugog) DH 31 D36
River Tr C 7 X11
River Bend Dr R 62 R48
River Farm La LN 64 T56
River Garden Rd HS 46 A46
River Glen Blvd HT 24 M-N29
River Heights Rd HS 46 A46
River Mill Ln HU 26 H13-14
River Valley Dr MK 59 T33
River Valley Rd HS 34 C-D47
River Valley Rd SD 90 F12
River View Ln C 6 A-B8
Riverbank Dr WT 22 N24
Riverbank Rd PR 67 Q68
Riverbend Rd NP 95 F32
Riverdale Dr SM 42 X33
Riverlea Rd MK 59 R33
Rivers Rd OX 15 S20 16 S21
Rivers Rd E PS 95 F-G32
Rivers Rd W PS 95 F32
Riverside Dr CS 100 B16
Riverside Dr DH 31 H35
Riverside Dr EX 4 B2-3
Riverside Dr HD 17 V26-27
Riverside Dr LM 13 Q11
Riverside Dr NI 19 T33
Riverside Dr OT 66 Q-R63
Riverside Dr PB 44 Z39
Riverside Dr PS 74 L22
Riverside Dr R 62 R47-48
Riverside Dr SDG 51 V-W67
Riverside Dr SM 29 C26
Riverside Dr (Middlesex Centre) MD 14 T16
Riverside Dr (Southwest Middlesex) MD 8 W14 14 V14
Riverview Cr HS 46 A46
Riverview Dr SM 42 W32
Riverview Dr (French River) SD 92 G22
Riverview Dr (Markstay-Warren) SD 101 C21-22
Riverview Dr, South EX 4 D1
Riverview Rd A 89 F7
Riverview Beach Rd Y 31 C33
Riverwood Dr OT 83 P59
Rivière Veuve Rd NP 93 D26 94 D27
Rizzo Nicola Dr EX 4 E2
Road of Memories HS 46 A46 Z46
Robb Rd A 88 F4
Robb Rd F 36 B57
Robbins Dr BR 54 T15 55 U15
Roberge Rd NP 93 D26
Robert La LN 48 W57
Robert St SM 41 X27-28
Robert Allen Dr BR 54 T14
Robert Johnston Rd MK 58 T30
Robert Murray Rd LN 64 S56 65 S57
Roberts La MA 72 M10 73 M11
Roberts Ln EL 8 W17 9 W18
Roberts Rd LN 48 V57 65 U57
Roberts Access Rd SD 100 Y18
Roberts Bay Rd MK 58 T29-30
Roberts Lake Rd W PS 57 S28
Robertson Dr LN 65 U57
Robertson Ln LN 65 R57
Robertson Ln R 83 Q56-57
Robertson Rd A 87 E1
Robertson Rd HL 60 V38
Robertson Rd MA 72 J-K8
Robertson Rd NI 18 T32
Robertson Rd (South Dundas) SDG 51 V-W67
Robertson Rd (South Glengarry) SDG 68 T70
Robertson Lake Rd A 84 Y92
Robertsville Rd F 48 W55
Robillard Rd PR 67 Q67
Robin La MA 73 M12
Robin Ln C 6 Y7
Robin Rd K 43 B37
Robin Rd MK 59 R33
Robins Rd NR 33 D43
Robins Rd PS 77 M31-32
Robins Hill Rd MD 15 S17-18
Robins Point Rd SM 41 X29
Robinson Av K 43 Z36
Robinson Rd BT 16 R24
Robinson Rd C 6 X9
Robinson Rd HD 18 T30
Robinson Rd LA 35 C53
Robinson Rd LM 6 W9 12 V9
Robinson Rd MD 15 T19
Robinson Rd NF 16 T24 17 T25
Robinson Rd OX 15 T19-20
Robinson Rd PB 44 B40
Robinson Rd PE 35 E51
Robinson Rd R 82 L52
Robinson Rd (Centre Hastings) HS 46 B49
Robinson Rd (Hastings Highlands) HS 62 S45
Robinson Rd (Madoc) HS 46 Z47-48
Robinson Rd N HS 46 Z49 47 Z50
Robinson Rd S HS 62 S45
Robinson's Corners Rd SDG 68 S69
Robinson Lake La HS 46 Y48
Robinson Lake Rd HS 62 V46
Robitaille Rd NP 94 C28
Roblin Rd HS 34 D-E48
Roblin Rd LA 35 C51-52
Robotham Rd MD 14 S-T13
Robson Rd G 39 B21
Robson Rd HM 23 P28
Robson Rd NR 33 E42
Robson St EX 5 F5
Rochefort Rd R 81 P49
Rochester Lake Rd PS 77 P33
Rochester Townline Rd EX 5 C5
Rochon Rd SD 92 G22
Rock Crossroad PE 35 F52-53
Rock Rd F 36 C55
Rock Rd LG 50 V63
Rock Rd PB 45 A-B42
Rock St LG 50 W64
Rock's Mill Ln OX 16 U22
Rock Chapel Rd HM 17 Q28 23 P28
Rock Cliff La F 36 B57
Rock Coady Tr OT 65 R58
Rock Forest Rd OT 65 P60
Rock Glen Rd LM 13 S12
Rock Hill Rd PS 76 P30
Rock Island Lake Rd PS 75 N25
Rock Lake La F 36 A57
Rock Lake La PS 77 N33
Rock Lake Rd A 86 C96-97
Rock Lake Rd F 48 X55
Rock Lake Rd MK 59 Q33
Rock Lake Rd NP 79 N40
Rock Lake 1 Rd SD 92 F21
Rock Lake 2 Rd SD 92 F21
Rock Lake 3 Rd SD 92 F21
Rock Point Rd PS 77 N34
Rockcliff Dr HL 60 V39
Rockcliffe Dr PS 56 Q26
Rockcliffe La PS 77 P33
Rockcliffe Pkwy OT 66 Q63-64
Rockdale Rd OT 67 Q-R65
Rockfield Rd LG 37 B60
Rockhaven Rd MK 59 Q33
Rockies Rd HS 46 Y-Z49
Rockingham Rd R 62 Q47-48
Rockley Rd TM 85 R29
Rocksborough Rd MK 59 U33
Rockside Rd PL 23 J27
Rocksprings Rd LG 49 Y61 50 X62
Rockton Rd HM 23 P26
Rockview Rd K 43 A35
Rockville Rd MA 72 K10
Rockville Rd (Central Manitoulin) MA 72 L10
Rockwood Dr MK 59 S36
Rocky Rd A 88 F4
Rocky Rd LG 50 Y63
Rocky Rd PS 76 L-M30
Rocky Acres La HS 61 U44
Rocky Church Rd G 27 D20
Rocky Narrows Rd MK 59 U34
Rocky Ridge Rd R 62 Q47-48
Rocky Saugeen Rd G 27 D20
Rodden Rd R 63 Q50 81 P50
Roddick La LG 37 A59
Roddick Rd MD 13 R-S12
Rodeo Dr HL 59 R36
Rodeo Rd PS 77 L-M31
Rodger Rd LN 65 U57
Rodger's Creek Rd MA 73 M-N11
Rodgerville Rd HU 20 N14-15
Rodick Rd Y 30 H32
Rodney La SDG 67 T65
Roe Dr LN 65 U60
Roesler Rd R 82 N55
Roger Lake Access Rd HL 60 Q37
Roger Lalonde Sdrd PR 68 Q70
Roger Stevens Dr OT 66 T62-63 U61-62
Roger Stevens Rd LN 49 V61 V-W60
Rogers Rd EL 9 W19 15 V19
Rogers Rd EX 4 C4 5 C5
Rogers Rd LA 47 A52-53
Rogers Rd TM 85 M-N29
Rogers Sdrd F 36 D57
Rogers St C 6 C7
Rogge Lake Access Rd E NP 61 Q44-45 80 P44-45
Rogge Lake Access Rd W NP 61 Q44 80 P44
Rohallion Rd K 43 Z34-35
Rokeby Ln LM 12 U7-9 13 U10-12
Rokeby Sdrd NF 16 U-V21
Rokeby Orchard Rd OX 16 U-V21
Roland Rd NI 19 S33
Rolland Massie Rd SDG 68 R72
Rollin Rd PR 67 P-Q67
Rollinbank Rd LG 37 A60 49 Z60
Rolling Hills La HL 43 W37
Roman Ln MD 14 Q15-16
Roman Rd HU 20 M14-15
Romany Ranch Rd K 43 A36
Rombough Rd (North Stormont) SDG 68 T69
Rombough Rd (South Stormont) SDG 67 U68
Romeo St PT 21 N-P19
Rommel Rd EL 9 W19
Ron Rd HL 44 X38
Ron Jones Rd SM 41 Y28-29
Ron McNeil Ln EL 15 V18-20
Ronald Rd BT 17 R26
Ronald Rd SM 41 B28
Ronald St PS 77 L32
Rondeau Rd C 7 B-C12
Rondeau Rd PR 67 Q67
Rondeau Estates Ln C 7 B11
Ronka Rd CS 91 E15
Ronson Rd SDG 50 V64 66 U64
Ronville Rd MK 59 R35
Rooney Rd LG 50 X64-65
Root Rd SD 90 F11-12
Rorke Av TM 85 R30
Rosa Landing Rd PB 33 D41
Rose La F 36 A55
Rose Rd A 84 Y92
Rose Rd HS 34 D47
Rose Rd LA 36 D54
Rose Rd NR 33 F42
Rose St DH 31 F35
Rose Beach Ln C 7 B12
Rose Hill Rd LA 63 T50
Rose Hill Rd NI 19 U36
Rose Island Rd HS 45 W45
Rose Island Rd PB 45 X46
Rose Lake Rd A 86 D97
Rose Lake Rd MK 58 S32
Rose Point Rd PS 57 R27
Rose Ridge La DF 29 G27
Rosebank Rd DH 31 H34
Roseberry Hill Rd NR 32 G40
Roseborough Rd EX 4 E2
Rosebrugh Rd R 82 Q55
Rosebush Rd HS 34 C-D47
Rosedale Ln C 6 C7
Rosedale Rd F 36 B55
Rosedale Rd LN 49 W60
Rosedale Rd N LN 49 V60
Rosedale Rd S LN 49 V-W60 W61
Rosedene Rd NI 18 S32
Rosemarie Blvd NF 16 V22-23
Rosemount Rd SM 41 Y29
Rosenblath Rd LA 36 D53
Roseneath Landing Rd NR 33 D-E43
Rosengren Rd TB 102 E2
Roses Crossroad PE 35 F52
Roses Bridge Rd LG 49 W-X61
Rosetta Rd LN 65 T-U57
Roseville Rd WT 22 P23-24
Rosewarne Dr MK 59 U33
Rosewood La MA 73 K11
Rosien Rd R 63 Q50
Ross La C 7 C11
Ross Rd HS 34 E46
Ross Rd MD 14 S14
Ross Rd NR 33 D45
Ross Rd R 82 M52
Ross Rd SDG 68 T71
Ross Rd SM 42 A31
Ross St SM 41 B29 42 B30
Ross Lake Rd HL 60 S40
Rossclair Rd MK 58 U30-31
Rosseau Crossroad PE 35 F-G51
Rosskopf Rd PS 76 M-N30
Rossland Rd DH 31 G-H36 H35
Rosslyn Dr Y 31 C34
Rosslyn Rd TB 102 E5
Rossmere Lake Rd A 88 D5
Rossmere West Rd A 88 D5-6
Rossmoyne Rd PS 58 S30
Rostrevor Rd MK 58 S-T31
Roswell Rd BT 16 S23
Roszell Rd WL 23 N25
Rothbourne Rd OT 65 S60 66 S61
Rothwell Park Rd LN 65 U58
Rougemont Dr DH 25 J34
Roughan Rd MD 14 U14-15
Rouleau, Mtée CS 100 B18
Round Barn Rd A 87 E99
Round Lake Rd A 86 C-D96
Round Lake Rd F 36 B56
Round Lake Rd PB 45 A45
Round Lake Rd R 81 L50 M-N48
Round Lake Access Rd PS 75 P26
Roundtree Rd K 32 C37
Rourke Line Rd EX 4 B-C4
Rouse Rd BR 55 X18
Rousseaux St HM 17 Q27
Router Rd LG 37 A60
Routh Rd EL 14 V15
Rowan Rd R 82 P53
Rowanwood Rd MK 59 S33
Rowbotham La HL 61 U41
Rowe Rd NR 33 F41
Rowena Rd SDG 51 W66
Rowland Rd HU 21 K18
Rowley Rd HL 61 U42-43
Rox Siding Rd R 82 N53
Roxboro Ln HU 20 K-L16
Roy Dr NP 95 D31
Roy Rd SDG 67 U67
Roy Benn La F 48 Y54
Royal Rd PE 35 H51
Royal Oak Rd K 31 D35-36
Royal Orchard Blvd Y 24 J32
Royal Pines Rd R 81 N51
Royal Windsor Dr HT 24 M30
Royal York Rd T 24 K-L31
Royer Rd A 88 F3-4
Roys Rd SDG 69 T73
Royston Rd PS 77 N31
Rozek Rd R 81 N48
Rozel Rd TM 85 M29
Ruby Rd R 81 N-P49 N-P50
Ruby Mine Rd R 63 S49
Rubyville Rd R 80 P47
Ruddy La HS 62 S46
Rudell Rd DH 32 G38-39
Rudl Rd LG 49 Y61
Ruggles Rd WT 22 L22
Ruggles Run EX 5 H5
Rumleski Rd R 80 P47
Rumley Rd MA 71 J-K4
Rumney Rd SM 41 Y29
Run Rd HS 46 Z47
Rundle Rd DH 32 G37 G38
Runnall's La HS 62 Q47
Runnalls Rd NR 32 G40
Running Creek Rd C 6 X7
Rupert Acres Dr A 84 Z92
Ruperts Rd HS 46 Z48
Rupke Rd SM 30 F30
Rupnow La HS 62 U46-47
Rusaw La PB 45 A43
Rusaw Rd PB 45 W44
Rush Rd NR 34 E46
Rush City Rd SDG 67 T68 68 T69
Rush Cove Rd BR 55 V17-18
Rush Creek Ln EL 9 W18-19
Rushmore Rd OT 66 S61-62
Rusholme Rd NI 19 T34
Russ Rd NI 18 R31
Russ Brown Rd F 63 U51
Russ Hammell Rd MK 58 S31-32
Russell Dr PB 44 W39
Russell Rd DH 31 F36
Russell Rd LG 37 B59
Russell Rd OT 66 R64 67 R65
Russell Rd PR 67 Q66-67
Russell Rd R 81 P49
Russell Rd SM 41 A29
Russell Landing Rd HL 59 R36 60 R37
Russellet Rd OT 67 Q66
Russett Dr R 83 Q56-57
Russett Rd HS 34 E47
Russett Rd K 43 A37
Russham Rd R 99 K51
Russland Rd OT 67 R66
Rustic Tr K 43 Y37
Rusty Rock Rd MK 58 V32
Rutherford Rd PL 24 K29
Rutherford Rd Y 24 J30-31 30 H31
Rutherford Sdrd LN 48 W57
Rutherglen Ln NP 96 E-F35
Rutledge Rd F 36 B55-56
Ruttan Rd R 82 P55
Ruttan's Rd E MK 59 V33
Ruttan's Rd W MK 42 W33 59 V33
Ruuth's La LA 35 F51
Ryan Rd HS 34 C48
Ryan Rd PR 68 Q69
Ryan Duncan Sdrd LN 65 Q57-58
Ryans La HL 61 T42
Ryans Rd TB 102 B5
Rydall Mill Rd A 86 D94
Rydholm Rd TB 102 D3
Rye Rd (Lount) PS 76 K30
Rye Rd (Nipissing) PS 94 J30 95 J31
Ryerse Rd NF 17 V25
Rykert St NI 19 R33
Rylstone Rd NR 45 B46
Rymal Rd HM 17 Q-R28 18 R29
Rymer Rd HD 18 U31
Ryther Rd SM 41 A27

Saari Rd TB 102 C3
Saars La R 81 L51
Sabourin Rd CS 101 D21
Sabourin Rd NP 94 D27-28
Sabourin Rd OT 67 R65
Sabourin Rd SDG 68 P71-72
Sack Rd R 99 K50-51
Sacred Heart Rd R 63 R50
Saddlemire Rd SDG 51 V66
Sadowa Rd K 43 X-Y34
Safari Rd HM 23 P26-27
Safford Rd LG 50 W-X65
Sagamo Blvd MK 58 S30
Sager Rd HM 17 Q25 23 P25
Sailing Club Rd WL 22 K21
St-Albert Rd (Casselman) PR 67 R-S68
St-Albert Rd (Embrun) PR 67 S66
St-Andre Rd PR 67 S66
St-Augustin Rd PR 67 R-S66
St-Edouard Rd PR 67 S66
St-Georges Rd SD 93 E23
St-Guillaume Rd PR 67 R65-66 S66
St-Isidore Rd PR 68 Q69
St-Jacques Rd PR 67 S66
St-Jean Rd NP 93 E26
St-Joseph Rd PR 67 S66
St-Laurent Blvd OT 66 Q63
St-Pascal Rd PR 67 P67
St-Philippe St PR 68 N-P69
St-Pierre St PR 67 R-S66
St-Thomas Rd (East Hawkesbury) PR 69 P73
St-Thomas Rd (Russell) PR 67 R-S66
St. Agnes St CS 100 B18
St. Alban Rd K 32 D-E37
St. Alban's Rd K 44 Z38
St. Amant Rd SM 41 X29 42 X30
St. Andrew St EX 12 T7
St. Andrew's Ln C 6 A8
St. Andrew's Rd PL 29 G-H27
St. Andrews Rd SDG 52 U70
St. Andrews St WT 22 P24
St. Andrews Lake La F 48 Z55
St. Anne Ln C 6 Y7
St. Augustine Ln HU 20 J14 26 H15
St. Bernadin Rd PR 68 Q70
St. Charles St MA 91 H-J15
St. Charles St WT 22 M23-24
St. Christopher's Beach Rd DH 32 D37
St. Clair Av E T 25 K33
St. Clair Av W T 24 K32
St. Clair Pkwy C 6 X6
St. Clair Pkwy LM 6 W6 12 U6-7
St. Clair Rd C 6 A8 Y7-8
St. Clair Rd EX 5 B5 6 B6
St. Cloud Rd CS 101 C-D21
St. David St SD 93 G24

St. David's Rd NI . . . 19 R33-34
St. Edwards Rd HS . . . 47 B50
St. Elmo Dr MK . . . 58 S31
St. Felix Rd PR . . . 67 Q66-67
St. Fillians Rd LN . . . 65 T59-60
St. George Rd BT . . . 17 Q25
St. George St LI . . . 15 V17
St. George Lake Rd F . . . 48 Y54-55
St. Germain Rd SD . . . 101 B23
St. Helen's Ln HU . . . 26 G-H15
_ SM . . . 41 X28
St. Hilaire Rd PR . . . 68 P69
St. Jean Rd PR . . . 68 P69
St. Jean St PR . . . 67 P66
St. John's Rd SM . . . 30 C31
St. John's Rd E NF . . . 17 V25-26
St. John's Rd W NF . . . 16 V24
St. John's Sdrd Y . . . 30 F31-32 31 F33
St. Joseph Blvd OT . . . 66 P-Q64
St. Laurent St CS . . . 100 B18 101 B19
St. Lawrence Rd HS . . . 46 A48
St. Luke's Rd K . . . 44 B38-39
St. Luke's Rd SDG . . . 67 T68
St. Mary's Rd K . . . 32 D38
St. Mary's Rd SDG . . . 67 U67
St. Michael's Rd . . . 20 J-K16 21 K17-18
St. Ola Rd HS . . . 46 W47
St. Paul Av BT . . . 17 R25
St. Paul Av NI . . . 19 R35
St. Paul St NI . . . 19 R33
St. Paul St PR . . . 67 S67
St. Peter St EX . . . 6 B6
St. Peters Rd L . . . 60 T-U38
St. Philippes Ln C . . . 6 A7-8
St. Pierre Rd PR . . . 67 N67-68
St. Pierre Lake La R . . . 64 S54
St. Pierres Rd F . . . 48 V54-55
St. Pothier Rd CS . . . 100 D16
St. Vincent St SM . . . 41 B29 42 B30
St. Vincent-Sydenham Twnln G . . .
. . . 39 A21 Y21
Ste-Anne Rd PR . . . 68 N71
Ste-Catherine St PR . . . 68 Q69
Ste-Marie Rd PR . . . 67 S66
Ste-Rose Rd PR . . . 67 R68
Ste. Anne Rd SDG . . . 68 Q72
Saintfield Rd DH . . . 31 D35
Saintsbury Ln MD . . . 14 Q15
Salacoa Rd PB . . . 44 W40
Sale Barn Rd OT . . . 66 S64
Sale Barn Rd TM . . . 85 P-Q30
Salem Rd BR . . . 39 Z18
Salem Rd DH . . . 31 G-H35
Salem Rd HS . . . 34 C47 45 W45 46 B47
Salem Rd MU . . . 27 G18-19 H17
Salem Rd K . . . 31 C36
Salem Rd LM . . . 13 U12
Salem Rd LS . . . 48 Y57
Salem Rd MD . . . 14 Q13
Salem Rd PE . . . 34 F48
Salem Rd SM . . . 30 C29
Salerno Lake Rd HL . . . 44 W39
Salford Rd OX . . . 15 T20 16 T21
Salisbury Rd PE . . . 34 E49
Sally St WL . . . 28 G21
Salmon Rd SDG . . . 67 U67
Salmon Sdrd BR . . . 38 B16
Salmon Lake Rd F . . . 36 A55-56
Salmon Lake Rd PB . . . 44 W40
Salmon Lake Rd PS . . . 57 S27
Salmon Point Rd PE . . . 35 H50
Salmon River Rd LA . . . 35 C52
Salmon Side Rd LG . . . 49 W60
Salmon Trout Lake Rd HS . . . 44 W39
Salmonberry La R . . . 47 W51
Salo Rd TB . . . 102 F-G3
Salo Rd (St Cloud) CS . . . 101 D20-21
Salo Rd (Worthington) . . .
. . . 91 E15 100 D15
Salt Rd LM . . . 13 T11
Salt Springs Church Rd BT . . . 17 S26
Salter Backline SD . . . 90 F10
Salter La LN . . . 49 W60
Salter Rd LN . . . 49 W60
Saltford Rd HU . . . 20 J13
Salter St NP . . . 94 D28
Sam Cook Rd MK . . . 42 W33
Sam English Rd MK . . . 59 R33
Sammon Rd R . . . 82 Q53
Sanatorium Rd MU . . . 14 T16
Sanctuary Ln HU . . . 20 L15
Sand Cr PS . . . 95 H32
Sand Rd OT . . . 67 R65
Sand Rd PB . . . 33 C43 45 B43
Sand Rd R . . . 81 P51
Sand Rd SDG . . . 68 S69
Sand Rd Y . . . 30 E31
Sand Rd, The MA . . . 72 L8 M9
Sand Bar Rd A . . . 84 Z91
Sand Bar Rd K . . . 32 D37
Sand Bay La LG . . . 37 B59
Sand Bay Rd A . . . 84 Y90
Sand Bay Rd LG . . . 37 B59
Sand Bay Rd PS . . . 56 Q24
Sand Bay Rd SD . . . 90 E14
Sand Gulley Rd . . . 37 C-C58
Sand Hill Rd F . . . 36 C57 37 C58
Sand Hill Rd PS . . . 77 K-L32
Sand Hill Rd TB . . . 102 G4
Sand Lake Rd F . . . 63 V52
Sand Lake Rd LG . . . 37 A58 49 Z58
Sand Lake Rd PS . . . 94 H29
Sand Lake Access Rd NP . . . 94 G29
Sand Lake Access Rd R . . . 99 K48
Sand Point Rd A . . . 84 W91
Sand Point Rd HL . . . 60 T-U40
Sand Point Rd R . . . 82 L53
Sandalwood Pkwy PL . . . 24 K29
Sandaraska Rd K . . . 32 E39
Sandcock Rd HS . . . 34 E47
Sandcock Rd NR . . . 33 D43
Sanderson Rd LG . . . 50 V-V62
Sandford Rd DH . . . 31 E33-34
Sandford St MD . . . 15 S-T17
Sandhill Ln HU . . . 20 J14
Sandhill Rd C . . . 6 X8
Sandhill Rd SM . . . 41 X-Y29
Sandhills Rd K . . . 43 A-B36
Sandhills Rd WT . . . 22 N21-22 P22
Sandown Sdrd PR . . . 68 Q69
Sandpit La F . . . 48 Y55
Sandringham Rd K . . . 43 A35 B35-36
Sandringham Rd SDG . . . 68 K-S69
Sands Rd F . . . 36 B57
Sands Rd MK . . . 58 S-T30
Sandusk Rd HD . . . 17 U-V27
Sandwich St EX . . . 4 B-C1

Sandwood Dr PS . . . 77 N31
Sandwood Rd MK . . . 58 S-T31
Sandy Rd DH . . . 31 F36
Sandy Rd PS . . . 75 N25
Sandy Row SDG . . . 50 V65
Sandy Bay Rd HC . . . 43 W37
Sandy Bay Rd HD . . . 18 U30
Sandy Bay Rd NR . . . 33 D43
Sandy Bay Rd (Penetanguishene) . . .
. . . 41 X28
Sandy Bay Rd (Tiny) SM . . . 41 X26
Sandy Bay Point Rd A . . . 89 C7
Sandy Beach La F . . . 37 C-D58
Sandy Beach Rd CS . . . 101 B19
Sandy Beach Rd DH 25 I-J35 31 H35
Sandy Beach Rd K . . . 43 Z37
Sandy Beach Rd R . . . 81 Q50-51
Sandy Beach Rd TB . . . 103 E6
Sandy Cove Dr PS . . . 34 E49
Sandy Cove Dr PS . . . 77 N32
Sandy Cove Rd CS . . . 101 D19
Sandy Creek Rd SDG . . . 50 W65
Sandy Falls Rd NP . . . 94 D28
Sandy Flats Rd NR . . . 33 D44
Sandy Hill Rd PR . . . 68 N71
Sandy Hills Dr WT . . . 22 L22-23
Sandy Hook Rd K . . . 32 E39 E-F38
Sandy Lake Rd PB . . . 45 Y44-45
Sandy Plains Rd PS . . . 57 R-S28
Sandy Point Rd K . . . 44 A38
Sandy Point Rd NP . . . 94 C28
Sandy Point Rd (Galway-
Cavendish & Harvey) PB . . . 44 A39
Sandy Point Rd (Smith-
Ennismore-Lakefield) PB . . . 45 A42
Sandytown Rd EL . . . 16 V21
Sanitary Landfill Rd CS . . . 101 A19
Sann Rd NI . . . 18 R32
Santala Rd CS . . . 100 D18
Santas Village Rd MK . . . 58 U32
Sapling Rd K . . . 60 V37
Sapphire Dr HL . . . 90 V39-40
Sarah's Sdrd MA . . . 90 J11
Sarah-Prissila Dr R . . . 82 N54
Sararas La HS . . . 61 T44 62 T45
Sararas Rd HS . . . 62 T45
Sararas Rd HU . . . 20 N13
Saratoga Ln NU . . . 20 J14 26 H14
Saratoga Rd BR . . . 26 E13-14
Sarawak-Keppel Twnln G . . . 39 Y19
Sarles Rd HS . . . 46 B47-48
Sarnia Rd MD . . . 14 T16
Sarsfield Rd OT . . . 67 O65
Saskatchewan Lake Rd HL . . . 60 T37
Sassafras Rd MD . . . 7 X12
Sauble Falls Pkwy BR 38 Z17 55 Y17
Sauble Falls Rd BR . . . 55 Y17
Sauer Rd NI . . . 19 T35
Saugeen Beach Rd BR . . . 38 B15
Saugeen Bluffs Rd BR . . . 38 A15
Saumure Rd OT . . . 67 Q-R66
Saunders Rd HL . . . 61 U41
Saunders Rd LN . . . 65 T-U60
Saunders Lake Spur PS . . . 78 N29
Sauve Rd SD . . . 101 B23
Sauve Sdrd PR . . . 68 P70
Sauve St CS . . . 100 B16-17
Savage St PR . . . 67 R66
Savage Settlement Rd PS . . . 77 P33
Savard-Robillard Township Rd TM . . .
. . . 85 M26-27
Savers La R . . . 26 H14
Savignac Rd NP . . . 93 D-E26
Saving St (South Dundas) SDG . . .
. . . 51 V66
Savoie Rd TB . . . 102 G4
Savor Rd SDG . . . 51 W66
Savory Rd NR . . . 33 E42
Sawdust Bay Rd PS . . . 56 O26
Sawmill Rd EL . . . 8 W19-20
Sawmill Rd HM . . . 17 R27
Sawmill Rd LN . . . 20 L16 L16 21 L17
Sawmill Rd MA . . . 70 J1
Sawmill Rd NR . . . 32 G40
Sawmill Rd NI . . . 18 R31 S32 19 S33
Sawmill Rd PB . . . 45 A42
Sawmill Rd TM . . . 85 Q28
Sawmill Rd WT . . . 22 M23
Sawmill Rd (Laurentian Valley) R . . .
. . . 81 L51
Sawmill Rd (Mississippi Mills) . . .
. . . 65 R57
Sawmill Bay Rd PB . . . 45 A45
Saxton Rd EL . . . 9 W-X20
Saxton Rd MD . . . 14 T14
Scane Rd C . . . 7 A11 Y10
Scanlon Rd C . . . 36 B-C55
Scarcliffe Rd MK . . . 58 T-U31
Scarlett Ln SM . . . 41 Y-Z29
Scarlett Rd PS . . . 77 K31
Scarlett Rd R . . . 24 K31
Scenic Dr BT . . . 16 Q24 17 Q25
Scenic Dr HM . . . 17 Q28
Scenic Rd R . . . 81 N-P48
Scenic Caves Rd BR . . . 59 V17-18
Scenic Caves Rd G . . . 40 A24-25
Schadeview Rd HU . . . 20 P13
Schaefer Rd A . . . 27 F17-18
Schaefer's Rd HL . . . 43 W37
Schafer Rd EL . . . 16 V21
Scharf Sdrd NF . . . 16 U22-23
Scharf La LN . . . 43 X37
Schaubel Rd NI . . . 19 T35
Schavens Lake Rd R . . . 63 Q51
Scheel Dr R . . . 83 P-Q56
Schell La R . . . 44 Y-Z38
Schell Rd HL . . . 44 Y-Z38
Scheuermann Hwy A . . . 86 D-E97
Schiestel Ln HU . . . 27 G17
Schill Rd NI . . . 19 T34-35
Schimmen's Rd R . . . 63 R49
Schisler Rd NI . . . 19 S-T35 T34
Schlosser Ln PS . . . 95 H31-32
Schmeler Rd PS . . . 76 L30
Schmidt Rd BR . . . 27 E-F17
Schmidt's Rd R . . . 77 L-M33
Schmidt Lake Rd BR . . . 26 E16
Schneider Rd NI . . . 19 T34-35
Schnupp Rd PR . . . 67 Q67
Schofield Rd HL . . . 61 U41
Schonauer Rd F . . . 63 V53
School Ln C . . . 7 B11
School Rd HU . . . 20 J14

School Rd K . . . 43 A36
School Rd LA . . . 47 A-B53
School Rd MD . . . 14 S-T13
School Rd R . . . 81 N51
School House La PS . . . 77 M31-32
School House Ln C . . . 7 X-Y11
School House Rd F . . . 36 E56
School House Rd HS . . . 34 C48
School House Rd K . . . 43 Y34
School House Rd PE . . . 35 H50-51
School House Rd SDG . . . 68 T12
School House Rd SM . . . 42 A31
Schooley Rd NI . . . 19 U35
Schooner Rd F . . . 63 U52
Schram Rd NI . . . 18 S32
Schriver Rd HS . . . 34 E46
Schroder Rd R . . . 62 R48
Schufelt Rd MK . . . 59 S-T34
Schultz Sdrd A . . . 84 A92
Schultzs La R . . . 81 L51
Schummer Ln WT . . . 21 L20 22 L21
Schutt Rd R . . . 62 S48
Schwan Rd R . . . 81 L51
Schwartz Rd R . . . 81 L50
Schweig Rd HS . . . 62 Q47
Schweig Rd R . . . 62 Q47
Schweitzer Ln C . . . 7 Y12-13
Scobie Rd R . . . 8 W16-17
Scotch Ln HD . . . 17 U26
Scotch Ln LM . . . 48 X57 49 W58
Scotch Ln MA . . . 73 K11
Scotch Ln SM . . . 29 D-E28
Scotch Bush Rd HS . . . 61 S44
Scotch Bush Rd R . . . 82 P-Q52
Scotch Corners Rd LN . . . 65 T58 U59
Scotch Line Rd K . . . 60 V37
Scotch Line Rd K . . . 44 A38
Scotch Line Rd WT . . . 22 L22-23
Scotch Line Rd E LG . . . 50 V62
Scotch Line Rd W LG . . . 50 V62
Scotch Mountain Rd G . . . 40 A22
Scotch River Rd PR . . . 67 Q68 68 Q69
Scotch Settlement Rd BR . . .
. . . 38 A16-17 Z16-17
Scotch Settlement Rd HS 46 Z47-48
Scotchmere Dr MD . . . 14 T-U14 U-V13
Scotia Rd PS . . . 77 P32-33
Scotland Dr MD . . . 15 U17-18
Scotland Rd LA . . . 36 C-D54
Scotland Rd MA . . . 72 J7-8
Scots Ln, The NR . . . 33 F43
Scott Av R . . . 16 Q24
Scott Ct BR . . . 26 F16
Scott Ct LN . . . 48 W56
Scott Dr PS . . . 76 N30
Scott Dr TB . . . 103 B9
Scott La MK . . . 59 Q35
Scott Ln C . . . 7 Y12
Scott Ln HU . . . 20 J15 26 H16
Scott Rd F . . . 47 Y52
Scott Rd HS . . . 34 E46
Scott Rd LM . . . 12 T-U7
Scott Rd MA . . . 72 L7-8
Scott Rd MK . . . 59 T33
Scott Rd NI . . . 18 S31
Scott Rd PR . . . 67 Q68 68 Q69
Scott Rd (Athens) LG . . . 49 Y60-61
Scott Rd (Edwardsburgh Cardinal
Cardinal) LG . . . 50 X65
Scott Rd (North Grenville) LG50 V62
Scott Sdrd EX . . . 4 C3
Scott St NF . . . 19 Q34 R33
Scott St NI . . . 19 Q34 R33
Scott's Hill Rd PS . . . 45 X43
Scott Island Rd LG . . . 48 Z57 49 Z58
Scott Line Rd HS . . . 61 S44 62 S45
Scott Settlement Rd PB . . . 45 W43
Scotts Rd K . . . 43 A36
Scotts Rd PB . . . 44 X40-41
Scotts Church Rd HS . . . 34 D47
Scotts Mill Rd PE . . . 35 G51
Scout Rd MD . . . 13 R12
Scriven Rd PB . . . 33 E41
Scrivens Dr OT . . . 66 S64
Scriver Rd NR . . . 34 F46
Scugog Rd DH . . . 32 E37
Scugog-Manvers Townline DH . . .
. . . 32 E-F38
Scugog Point Rd DH . . . 32 D-E37
Scugog Lake Rd R . . . 64 S53
Scuttlehole Rd HS . . . 34 C49
Sea Breeze Rd MK . . . 59 R35
Seabrooke Rd F . . . 37 B58
Seacliff Dr EX . . . 4 E4 5 E5
Seadon Rd SM . . . 41 B29
Seagull Lake Rd PS 76 K27-28 94 J28
Seal Lake Rd CS . . . 100 A16
Seapoint La F . . . 36 A57
Sears Rd HS . . . 62 T45
Searson Rd R . . . 82 P52
Seaton Rd HM . . . 23 P25
Seaway Haulage Rd NI . . . 19 Q-R34
Seburn Rd NI . . . 19 S33
Secord Rd DH . . . 31 F33-34
Secord Rd SD . . . 92 E20 E21 101 D20
Secord Access Rd SD . . . 92 E20
Sedgwick Rd HL . . . 44 W38 60 V38
Sedore Rd MK . . . 42 W32
Seed Rd MD . . . 14 S-T13
Seed's Rd TM . . . 85 R29
Seehaver Rd MK . . . 59 V34
Seeker Rd LG . . . 50 Y62
Seeley Rd LG . . . 49 Z61 50 Z62
Seeley Rd R . . . 62 R45
Seeley Rd SDG . . . 51 W66
Seeney Rd NR . . . 32 E40 33 E41
Seguin Rd PR . . . 67 Q68
Seguin Rd PS . . . 76 M-N30
Seguin Rd SDG . . . 68 S69
Seguin Rd SD . . . 93 G24
Seguin St CS . . . 100 B18
Seguin St PS . . . 57 R27
Seguin Trail Rd PS . . . 57 R28
Seguinbourg St PR . . . 67 R67
Seibert Rd SDG . . . 50 V65
Seip La WL . . . 27 G19
Seip Rd WL . . . 27 G19
Seldom Seen Rd SD . . . 90 F10
Selena Dr PS . . . 77 M31-32
Selinger Rd WL . . . 22 K21
Sell Rd R . . . 81 M51 82 M52
Sellwood Av CS . . . 101 Z20

Selton Ln C . . . 7 Y11
Selton Rd E LG . . . 37 C60
Selton Rd NI . . . 56 Q25 75 P25
Selwyn Bay La PB . . . 44 A41
Selwyn Shores Dr PB . . . 44 A40-41
Seneca Rd BT . . . 17 S26
Senlac Rd C . . . 7 X10
Seouls Corners La F . . . 48 X53-54
Serendipity La MA . . . 73 J9
Serenity Bay Rd SD . . . 93 F-G24
Serpent Mounds Rd PB . . . 33 D42
Serran Rd R . . . 62 R47
Service Rd SDG . . . 52 U70-71
Service Rd BR . . . 27 D17
Settlement Rd K . . . 44 B39
Settlement Rd LG . . . 49 Y59 Z58
Settlement Rd WT . . . 22 N21
Settlers La MK . . . 59 T-U33
Settlers Ln PB . . . 33 C-D42
Settlers Rd MK . . . 58 T31
Settlers Rd K . . . 32 C38 44 B38
Settlers Rd PS . . . 94 H30
Settlers Way R . . . 63 Q51 81 P51
Seven Hill Rd SDG . . . 68 P71
Seven Oaks Dr PS . . . 33 D41
Seven Lakes Spa LG . . . 49 Z60
Seventeenth Rd, The SDG . . . 68 Q71
Sewells Rd T . . . 25 H-J34
Sextant Point Dr MA . . . 72 J9
Sexton Rd MA . . . 13 S-U12
Sexton Sdrd EX . . . 4 C2
Seymour St NP . . . 95 E31-32
Seymour St R . . . 83 Q57
Seys Ln C . . . 6 X7
Shabaqua Hwy TB . . . 102 D5 103 D6
Shabaqua Rd TB . . . 102 B1
Shabaqua Corners Rd TB . . . 102 B1
Shabomeka Lake Rd F . . . 47 W51
Shackleton Ln EL . . . 8 W15 X14
Shad Hill Rd R . . . 81 M49
Shadow Cr MA . . . 72 K10
Shady La F . . . 48 W53
Shady La NI . . . 58 V31
Shady La PB . . . 45 X43
Shady Glen La DF . . . 29 F27
Shady Maple La HS . . . 62 T45
Shafley Rd NI . . . 18 T31
Shaftsbury Av Y . . . 30 H31-32
Shagbark Rd MD . . . 15 U18
Shakell Rd PS . . . 76 N27-28
Shakey Rd F . . . 36 A56
Shamess Rd R . . . 99 K49-50
Shamrock Rd K . . . 32 C38-39
Shamrock Rd MK . . . 58 T30
Shamrock Beach Rd HU . . . 26 G13
Shanahan Tr (Blairhampton) HL . . .
. . . 60 U38
Shanahan Tr (Minden) HL . . . 60 V38
Shane Rd PR . . . 67 Q68
Shane Rd SDG . . . 68 T67
Shane St LA . . . 36 D54
Shangri-La Rd HL . . . 60 T37
Shangrila Rd HU . . . 20 M-N13
Shanick Rd HS . . . 46 Z46
Shank Rd SD . . . 93 E24
Shanks Rd LN . . . 48 W56
Shanly Rd LG . . . 50 W64 X65
Shanly Rd NR . . . 33 E-F45
Shanna Rd OT . . . 66 S65
Shannette Rd SDG . . . 51 V-W66
Shannick Rd HS . . . 62 T45
Shannon Rd HS . . . 34 C49 35 C50-51
Shannon Rd MK . . . 58 T29
Shannon Rd PE . . . 35 G50
Shannon Hall Rd MK . . . 58 R31
Shannonville Rd HS . . .
. . . 34 C49 35 C-D50
Shanty La BR . . . 55 W16-17
Shanty Bay Rd SD . . . 93 F-G24
Shantz Station Rd WT . . . 23 M-N24
Sharon Dr MD . . . 14 U16
Sharon Dr NI . . . 59 Q34
Sharp Rd C . . . 7 Y10
Sharpe La PB . . . 32 D39-40
Sharpe La R . . . 34 D53
Sharpe's La LG . . . 50 Z63
Sharpes Corners Rd LA . . . 35 C52
Sharpes Creek Ln HU . . . 20 J-K14
Sharrow Rd C . . . 7 X10
Shatruck Dr A . . . 84 B90
Shattuck Dr A . . . 17 R27
Shaver Rd (South Dundas) SDG . . .
. . . 51 W66
Shaver Rd (South Stormont) SDG . . .
. . . 51 V68 52 V69
Shaw Rd A . . . 87 B-C98 D98
Shaw Rd BR . . . 55 V16
Shaw Rd HS . . . 34 D49
Shaw Rd K . . . 65 R57-58
Shaw Rd LG . . . 49 Z61
Shaw Rd NI . . . 18 S31
Shaw Rd (French River) SD . . .
. . . 92 F22 93 F23
Shaw Rd (Sables-Spanish Rivers) . . .
. . . 90 F12
Shaw's Rd F . . . 44 Z40
Shaw Dam Rd A . . . 87 D98
Shaw Woods Rd R . . . 82 N52
Shawanaga rd N PS . . . 75 P24-25
Shawanaga Lake Rd R S PS . . . 56 Q25 75 P25
Shawanaga Lake Rd PS . . . 76 N27
Shawanaga Landing Rd PS . . . 75 P24
Shawanaga Tr HS . . . 46 X46
Shawmorr La LN . . . 60 V38
Shaws La HL . . . 60 V38
Shaws Creek Rd PL . . .
. . . 23 J26 J27 29 H26
Shay Rd SDG . . . 67 U66
Shea Rd MK . . . 58 T31
Shea Rd OT . . . 66 S61
Shearer Point Rd NR . . . 33 D-E42
Sharpin Bay Tr MA . . . 73 K-L11
Sheatown Rd LG . . . 37 A60 49 Z60
Shebeshong Rd PS . . .
. . . 56 Q25 Q26 75 P25
Shebeshong Estate Rd PS . . .
. . . 56 Q25 75 P25
Shebeshong Estate Rd N PS . . .
. . . 75 P25

Shebeshong Estate Rd S PS . . . 56 Q25 75 P25
Shedden Back Line Ln A . . . 89 F8-9
Shedden Rd NI . . . 18 S-T32
Sheehan La PB . . . 45 B42
Sheffield Rd HM . . . 17 Q25 23 P25
Sheffield Boundary Rd LA . . 47 A-B51
Sheffield Bridge Rd LA . . . 47 B52
Sheila La F . . . 36 B55
Shelby La LN . . . 48 V56
Sheldon La HS . . . 62 S46
Sheldon La R . . . 49 Y58
Sheldrake Lake Rd LA . . . 47 W-X50
Shellard La BT . . . 16 R-S24 17 R25
Shellard Sdrd WT . . . 23 P25
Shellrock Loop Rd A . . . 87 Q98
Shelly Rd HS . . . 35 D51
Shelter Valley Rd NR . . . 33 F44
Shelton La HM . . . 23 P27
Shennamere Rd MK . . . 58 T31
Shepard Lake Rd G . . . 39 Y18
Shepherdson Rd TM . . . 85 R29
Shepley Rd LM . . . 6 W7
Sheppard Av DH . . . 25 J34
Sheppard Av E T . . . 24 J32 25 J33-34
Sheppard Av W T . . . 24 J31-32
Sheppard Lake Rd TM . . . 85 M29-30
Sheppards La A . . . 88 F6
Sherborne Lake Access Rd HL . . .
. . . 59 S36 60 S37
Sherbrooke Dr LN . . . 48 X-Y56
Sherbrooke St PB . . . 32 C40
Sherbrooke Rd R . . . 81 P49
Sheridan Point Rd EX . . . 5 H4-5
Sheridan Rapids Rd LN . . 48 V56-57
Sherk Rd (Fort Erie) NI . . . 19 T35
Sherk Rd (Niagara Falls) NI . 19 I35
Sherk Rd (Port Colborne) NI . . .
. . . 19 T34 U34
Sherkston Rd NI . . . 19 U35
Sherman Access HM. 17 Q28 18 Q29
Sherman La HM . . . 17 Q28
Sherman's Point Rd LA . . . 35 E-F51
Sherry Rd HS . . . 46 B49
Sherwin Rd K . . . 44 B38
Sherwood Dr TB . . . 103 D6
Sherwood Dr WL . . . 23 L25
Sherwood Rd A . . . 87 E98
Sherwood Rd LG . . . 49 Y58
Sherwood Rd MK . . . 58 T30
Sherwood Bay Rd LG . . . 50 A62-63
Sherwood Forest La SM . . . 42 W31
Sherwood Forest Rd MK . . . 59 U34
Sherwood Springs Rd LG . . . 50 A62
Sheshegwaning Rd MA . . . 71 J4
Shetland Rd LM . . . 7 W10-11
Shewbury Rd C . . . 7 Y11
Shibagua Rd LA . . . 47 A-B52
Shibley Rd F . . . 48 X-Y55
Shibley Rd LA . . . 35 D53 36 D54
Shield's Point Rd NP . . . 95 E34 96 E35
Shields Dr PB . . . 32 D39
Shields Siding Dr MD . . . 13 V12
Shiloh Ln LM . . . 12 U-V9 13 V11
Shiloh Rd DH . . . 32 F39
Shiloh Rd NR . . . 33 E-F45
Shiloh Church Rd LG . . . 50 X-Y62
Shiner Rd F . . . 48 W55
Shipka La HU . . . 14 Q13 20 N-P13 P13
Shipton La F . . . 48 Z56
Shirley Dr TB . . . 31 F36
Shirley La F . . . 49 V59
Shirley Rd TB . . . 102 C5
Shoak Rd A . . . 88 E4
Shoal Point Rd DH . . . 31 H35
Shoal Point Rd NR . . . 34 F46
Shoal Lake Rd MK . . . 59 S36
Shoebottom Rd PS . . . 57 R27-28
Shootabuck Rd R . . . 82 Q53-54
Shore Rd A . . . 86 D94
Shore Rd F . . . 36 C57 37 C58
Shore Rd HS . . . 34 F46-47
Shore Rd K . . . 44 T16
Shore Acres Dr SM . . . 30 D30-31
Shore Line Rd DH . . . 43 A34
Shorelea Rd EL . . . 15 V17
Shoreline Av BR . . . 55 X17
Shoreline Rd HL . . . 46 A48
Shoreline Rd HU . . . 26 H13
Shoreline Rd NP . . . 94 C28
Shoreline Tr HU . . . 18 U30
Shoreview Rd K . . . 44 B39
Shorewood Rd NP . . . 95 E33
Shorey Rd LA . . . 35 D53
Short Ln C . . . 6 X8
Short Ln HU . . . 20 J14
Short Ln HU . . . 21 J19 27 H19
Short Ln WL . . . 27 H19
Short Rd F . . . 36 E57
Short Rd LM . . . 13 T12
Short Rd NI . . . 18 S29
Short Rd NI . . . 18 S30
Short Rd SD . . . 90 E13
Short Cut Rd A . . . 87 D98
Short Horn Rd HL . . . 60 U38
Short Point Rd LG . . . 37 A59 49 Z59
Shorties Sdrd NF . . . 16 V22
Shortill Rd HT . . . 23 K27
Shorts Rd F . . . 47 X51-52
Shouldice Sdrd WT . . . 22 P24
Shouldice Block Rd G . . . 39 Z18
Shouldice Lake Rd BR . . . 54 T16
Shrike Rd K . . . 43 Y35-36
Shrine Hill Dr R . . . 81 P48
Shuniah St TB . . . 103 C-D6
Shurie Rd NI . . . 18 S31
Shuswap Rd NP . . . 93 F25-26
Shuttleworth Rd K . . . 43 Y37
Shuyler's Island Rd HL . . . 60 U-V38
Siberia Rd K . . . 62 Q46
Siberia Rd R . . . 62 Q46 80 P46
Sibley Av K . . . 32 C39
Siddall Rd MD . . . 14 R15
Siddon Lake Rd PS . . . 76 L29
Sideen Dr TB . . . 102 E3
Sider Rd (Fort Erie) NI . . . 18 T35
Sider Rd (Wainfleet) NI . . . 18 T-U32
Sidney St CS . . . 34 D-E48
Sieber Rd PS . . . 77 N31
Siegner Ln WT . . . 21 M20 22 M21

Silas La R . . . 62 Q48
Silem Rd TB . . . 102 B3
Silk La HL . . . 43 W37
Silk Ln SM . . . 42 X30
Sills Rd (Belleville) HS . . . 34 D49
Sills Rd (Hastings) HS 34 C48 46 B48
Sills Bay Rd F . . . 36 B55
Silo Rd K . . . 32 E38
Silv'ry Moon Rd SD . . . 93 F23
Silvaggio Rd TB . . . 102 E2
Silver St BT . . . 16 Q24
Silver St NI . . . 18 S30-31
Silver Bay Rd MA . . . 73 L11
Silver Bay Rd NI . . . 19 U34
Silver Beach Dr TB . . . 103 C8
Silver Birch Dr SM . . . 41 X26-27
Silver Clay Ln EL 7 Y13 8 W15 X14-15
Silver Creek Dr HT . . . 23 K27
Silver Falls Rd TB . . . 102 B3
Silver Harbour Rd TB . . . 103 C8
Silver Heights Rd NR . . . 33 C-D44
Silver Hill Sdrd NF . . . 10 W23
Silver Lake Rd MK . . .
. . . 42 W33 58 V32 59 V33
Silver Lake Rd R . . . 81 P51
Silver Lake Rd (Huron-Kinloss) BR 26 F15
Silver Lake Rd (South Bruce
Peninsula) BR . . . 38 Z17
Silver Maple Rd NR . . . 33 E43
Silver Mine La F . . . 47 W51
Silver Sands Rd NI . . . 58 T-U29
Silver Springs Cr DH . . . 31 F34
Silver Springs Rd TB . . . 103 C6
Silvercreek Pkwy WL . . . 22 L-M24
Silverdale Rd NI . . . 59 R33
Silverdale Rd NI . . . 18 S32
Silverwood Dr F . . . 36 C56
Silverwood Rd HL . . . 60 V38
Silvery Rd A . . . 48 X56
Sim La TB . . . 102 C-D4
Simcoe Rd (Bradford West
Gwillimbury) SM . . . 30 E31 E-F30
Simcoe Rd (Ramara) . . .
. . . 42 A33 43 A34
Simcoe St BT . . . 16 S-T24
Simcoe St EX . . . 4 E1
Simcoe St K . . 31 C35 D36 43 A-B35
Simcoe St OX . . . 16 U21
Simcoe St (Brock) DH 31 C35 43 B34
Simcoe St (Scugog, Oshawa) DH . . .
. . . 31 E-H36
Simko Dr TB . . . 102 C4-5
Simmons La F . . . 48 Z54
Simmons La CS . . . 100 B16-17
Simmons La A . . . 35 D53 36 D54
Simon Lake Dr CS . . . 100 D17-18
Simoor Cr SM . . . 42 A-B30
Simpresca Rd SM . . . 41 X28
Simpson Av BR . . . 54 S13
Simpson La F . . . 37 A58
Simpson Ln C . . . 5 D8
Simpson Ln C . . . 6 X8
Simpson La F . . . 37 A58
Simpson HS . . . 46 Y-Z47
Simpson Rd MD . . . 7 W13
Simpson Rd NR . . . 33 F-G45
Simpson Rd PB . . . 45 S44
Simpson Rd PE . . . 35 H50-51
Simpson Sdrd EX . . . 5 D-E6
Simpson St TB . . . 103 D6
Simpson's Hill Rd PS . . . 77 K31-32
Simpson Hill Rd NR . . . 33 E43
Simpson Hill Rd PS . . . 95 H31
Simpson Pit Rd R . . . 81 N48
Simpson Side Rd LG . . . 37 A58
Sims Rd MA . . . 73 M12
Simzer Rd SDG . . . 67 U65
Sinclair Dr MD . . . 14 T14-15
Sinclair Ln C . . . 7 B11
Sinclair Rd C . . . 6 B7
Sinclair Rd NI . . . 59 Q-R33
Sinclair Rd TB . . . 102 D3
Sinclairville Rd HM . . . 18 S29
Sinden Sdrd NF . . . 16 V23
Sine Rd HS . . . 34 C47
Singer Rd HD . . . 18 S-T29
Sipolins Rd F . . . 63 T52
Sir Frederick Banting Rd SM 29 E28
Sir John A Macdonald Blvd F . . .
. . . 36 D56
Sir S Fleming Dr PB . . 32 D40 33 D41
Sir Sam's Rd HL . . . 60 T39
Sir Sam's Rd HL . . . 60 U40
Sitch Rd TB . . . 102 E2
Site 9 Rd PS . . . 75 N24
Sitter Rd LM . . . 13 R11-12
Six Foot Bay Rd PB . . . 44 A40
Skakum Rd LG . . . 50 X63-64
Skead Rd CS . . . 101 A21 B20
Skeeds Rd R . . . 80 P46
Skelding Rd DH . . . 31 E33
Skeleton Lake Rd 1 MK . . . 58 S32
Skeleton Lake Rd 2 MK . . . 58 S31
Skeleton Lake Rd 3 MK . . . 58 S31
Skeleton Lake Rd 4 MK . . . 58 S31
Skeleton Lake Rd 5 MK . . . 58 S31
Skelly Rd R . . . 81 N49
Skene Rd HS . . . 46 X46
Skerryvore Community Rd PS . . .
. . . 75 P24-25
Ski Rd WL . . . 27 G20
Ski Hill Rd K . . . 32 C-D39
Ski Hill Rd LN . . . 65 R57-58
Ski Hill Rd PS . . . 95 H31-32
Ski Trails Rd SM . . . 42 A-B30
Skidder Trail Rd F . . . 62 Q48
Skinkle Rd MK . . . 59 R33
Skinner Dr MD . . . 14 T14
Skinner Rd MK . . . 59 R33
Skipness Rd BR . . . 38 Z17
Skiview Dr PB . . . 32 D40
Skookum Lake Rd A . . . 86 B97
Skootamatta-Grimsthorpe Access
Rd HS . . . 46 W48
Skootamatta-Grimsthorpe Access
Rd LA . . . 47 W50
Skootamatta Lake Rd LA . . 55 W-X17
Sky View Dr PR . . . 67 Q70
Skye Rd PR . . .
Skyhills Rd MK . . . 59 R33
Skylark Rd SM . . . 41 Y-Z27
Skyline Dr MK . . . 59 Q-R34

Skyline Dr PS 77 N32-33
Skyline Rd K 31 C36
Skyline Rd PB 44 B40
Skyline Park La HL 60 U39
Slab St HS 46 B48
Slabtown Rd G 40 A23
Slack Rd LG 49 Z60
Slack Rd OT 66 R62
Slack Rd SD 89 F9
Slade Rd LG 37 A60-61
Slant Rd OX 16 S-T22
Slanted Rd K 32 C38
Slash Rd MA 73 M11-12
Slate Falls Rd LA 63 S-T50
Slate Falls-Madawaska South
Access Rd LA 63 S50
Slater Rd LG 50 V64
Slaters Rd Y 30 F-G32
Slaven Rd PE 34 G49
Sleapview La F 36 A55
Sleeper Green Access Rd HS
. . . . . 62 U-V48
Sleepy Haven La F 36 A57
Sleepy Hollow La NR 32 F40
Sleepy Hollow Rd CS 100 D16
Sleepy Hollow Rd G 40 A24
Sleepy Hollow Rd LN 48 X56
Sleepy Hollow Rd R . 64 R56 83 Q56
Sligo Rd G 28 G21
Sloan Rd C 6 C7-8
Sloat Rd HS 46 B48
Sloman La WT 22 L21-22
Slote Rd HM 17 Q27
Slow La HL 60 U-V40
Smaglinski-Stoppa Pkwy R
. . . . . 80 P47 81 P48
Smail Rd LG 50 X64
Smail Rd SDG . . 50 V65 51 V66
Small Cr SM 42 A31
Smart Rd TB 102 D3
Smeltzers Rd MA 73 M11
Smirle Rd SDG 67 T66
Smirnoff Ln HU 20 M14
Smith Blvd Y 30 D32
Smith La HL 60 U39-40
Smith Ln LM 6 W6-8
Smith Rd A 88 E-F4
Smith Rd C 6 X9
Smith Rd EL 8 W17
Smith Rd EX 4 E2
Smith Rd HM . . 17 Q-R28 18 R30
Smith Rd MK . . 42 W31 58 U31
Smith Rd NP 95 D-32
Smith Rd NR 33 C44-45
Smith Rd NI 18 T32
Smith Rd OT 67 Q65
Smith Rd PS 77 K31
Smith Rd SM 29 C28
Smith Rd TB 102 E3
Smith Rd (Kingston) K . . 36 C-D55
Smith Rd (North Dundas) SDG . . . .
. . . . . 67 U66
Smith Rd (North Frontenac) F . . . .
. . 48 W53 63 V53
Smith Rd (North Grenville) LG . . . .
. . . . . 50 W63
Smith Rd (Plummer Additional) A . . . .
. . . . . 86 C97
Smith Rd (Quinte West) HS 34 C-D48
Smith Rd (Rideau Lakes) LG . . . .
. . . . . 49 Z58-59
Smith Rd (South Stormont) . . . .
. . . . . 67 T-U68
Smith Rd (Tarbutt) A . 86 D94-95
Smith Rd (Tyendinaga) HS . . . .
. . . . 34 C49 35 C50
Smith Sdrd DH 31 F35
Smith Sdrd SM 42 Y33
Smith St NR 34 F46
Smith St SD 90 E14
Smith's Rd PS 57 Q28
Smith's Bay Rd R 81 N51
Smith Bay Rd PS 93 J24
Smith Bay Rd E MA 72 J7
Smith Bay Rd W MA 72 J7
Smith Falls Rd LM 7 W11
Smith Industrial Dr EX 4 D2
Smith Settlement Rd NR . . 33 F42
Smiths Rd SDG 51 V-W67
Smiths Falls Rd OT 66 T62-63 U61-62
Smiths Ferry Rd PR 67 Q68
Smiths Mill Rd NF 17 S-T25
Smithson La R 64 R54
Smithson Rd PB 33 D-E41
Smithville Rd HD 18 T30
Smithville Rd NI 18 S30 S31
Smoke Ln C 7 Y10
Smokes Point Rd PE 34 F47
Smylie Rd NR 33 F42
Smyth Rd OT 66 Q63
Smythe Rd SD 92 G22
Snake La EX 4 C-D2 E2-3
Snake Rd HT 23 P28
Snake Island Rd OT . . 66 S-T64
Snake Rapids Rd LA 63 S50
Snake River Ln R 82 M53
Snedden Dr LN 65 S58
Snider Rd LA . . 63 T50-51
Snider Rd NI 19 T-U34
Snider Rd PE 34 F48
Snider Rd TM 85 Q30
Snider Rd (North Frontenac) F . . . .
. . . . . 47 W51
Snider Rd (South Frontenac) F . . . .
. . . . . 36 A54
Sniders La R 63 T51
Sniders Bay Rd MK . 58 V31-32
Snively La NF 17 T25
Snobelen Rd C 7 A10
Snodden Rd SD 101 C-D23
Snoddon Rd DH 31 D33
Snow Rd HS 62 U45
Snow Valley Rd SM . . 41 B29
Snowbird Rd SDG 50 V65
Snowcrest Tr MK 59 V34
Snowden Rd LG 50 W62
Snowdon Dr HL 44 W38
Snowdon Rd HL 50 W62
Snowdon Rd PS . . 76 P27-28
Snowdons Corners Rd LG . . 50 W62
Snowdrifters Rd R 82 N52
Snowshoe Cr A 87 B99
Snowshoe La PS 77 N32
Snug Harbour Rd K . . 43 B37 44 B38

Snug Harbour Rd PS 56 Q25
Snyder Rd NI 18 S31-32
Snyder Rd WT 22 N21-22
Snyders Flats Rd WT 22 M23
Snye Rd LN 64 S56
So Ho Mish Rd PS 77 N-P32
Soaking Branch Access Rd HS . . . .
. . . . . 61 R42
Soaking Lake Access Rd HS . . . .
. . . . . 61 R42-43
Sobie Rd NI 18 R31
Sobie Lake Access Rd NP . . 95 G34
Sodom Rd HM . . 17 Q27 23 P27
Sodom Rd NI 19 T35
Sokay's Rd NI 32 F40
Solanum Way K . . 32 E38-39
Soldier's Ln OT 19 U35
Solina Rd DH 32 G-H37
Somers Rd EL 15 V20
Somers St G 39 Z19
Somerville Rd LG 50 V63
Somerville Rd NI 19 T35
Songbird La R 82 P52
Songis Rd NP 95 D33-34
Songsparrow La PB . . 45 X43
Sonneveld Rd F . . 36 B-C57
Soo Line Rd A 86 C96
Soper Rd DH 32 F39
Soper Rd SD 49 X-Y61
Sophers Landing Rd MK . 42 W32
Soudant La R 48 Z54
Soul Rd PS 95 F32
Soules Av SM 42 Y32
Soup Harbour Rd PE . . 35 H50
Sour Springs Rd BT 17 S25
Source Lake Rd NP 78 N38
South Baseline Rd R 26 F13
South Diagonal Rd 55 Y17
South Dr MK 58 R32
South La HS 62 U47
South Ln BR 26 E14
South Ln MA 71 J6
South Ln A G 28 D-E22
South Ln B G . . 28 D23-24
South Ln C G . . 28 D24 29 D25
South Rd F 47 W52
South Rd HS 61 R43
South Rd HU 14 Q13-14
South Rd MK . . 45 W-X45
South Sdrd EX 4 E1-2
South St BR 38 A16
South St EX 4 C4
South St HU 26 H13
South St LN 49 W58
South Arm Rd A 87 B98-99
South Arterial Rd PL 29 H26
South Baptiste Lake Rd HL . . . .
. . . . . 61 T43 U42
South Baptiste Lake Rd HS . . . .
. . . 61 T43-44 62 T45
South Bass Lake Rd G 39 Y19
South Bay Dr MA 73 M13
South Bay La MK 78 P34
South Bay Rd CS 101 C19
South Bay Rd EX 5 J5
South Bay Rd MA 73 M13
South Bay Rd MK 41 W29
South Bay Rd PB 45 Z43
South Bay Rd TB 102 F3
South Bayshore Rd PB 45 Z43
South Beach Rd PB 44 A41
South Beaver Lake La HL . 43 X37
South Big Island Rd PE . . . . . .
. . . . . 34 F49 35 E50
South Blair St 31 H36
South Boulter Access Rd NP 95 H34
South Boundary Rd PT . . 20 N15-16
South Branch Rd LG . . 50 X62-63
South Branch Rd (South Dundas)
SDG 50 W65
South Branch Rd (South Stormont)
SDG 52 V70
South Brookfield Rd NI 19 T34
South Burns Rd NR 33 F43
South Bush Rd F . . 48 V54 63 V53
South Camp Lake Rd MK . 59 Q36
South Camp Lake Access Rd MK .
. . . . . 59 Q36
South Campbell Rd LG 50 Y64
South Canal Bank Rd Y 30 F30
South Cayuga Rd HD . . 18 U29
South Chippawa Rd NI . . . .
. . . . 18 S30 T30-31
South Coast Dr HD 17 V27
South Connors Rd PB . . 45 Y44-45
South Crane Lake Rd PS . 57 S27-28
South Dwight Beach Rd MK . 59 R35
South Edgeware Rd EL . . 15 V17-18
South Fork Rd PS . . 57 S27-28
South Gibson Lake Rd MK . 58 V29
South Gower Dr LG . . 50 V64 66 U63
South Horn Lake Rd PS . 77 M31-32
South Kahshe Lake Rd MK . 42 W33
South Kash Lake La F . . 47 W52
South Kingsway T 24 L31
South Kinloss Av BR . . 26 G14-15
South Lake Rd LB 37 B58
South Lake Rd PB 45 A44
South Lake Bernard Rd PS . . . .
. . . . . 77 L-M32
South Lancelot Rd MK . . 58 R32
South Lane Rd CS . . 101 D19-20
South Lavant Rd F 64 U54
South Lavant Rd LN . . 64 U55-56
South Limberlost Rd MK . . 59 S33
South Malden Rd EX . 4 D3 D-E2
South Mary Lake Rd MK . 59 S33
South Mazinaw Heights Rd F . . . .
. . . . . 47 W50
South McKenzie Lake Rd NP 61 Q43
South McNaughton Rd R 82 P53-54
South Menominee Lake Rd MK . . .
. . . . . 59 S34
South Middle Rd EX . . . . . .
. . 4 C3 5 C6 6 C7
South Mine Rd SD 100 D14
South Monck Dr MK 58 U32
South Moot Lake Rd MK . . 59 T34
South Morrison Lake Rd MK . . . .
. . . . 42 W31-32
South Mountain Rd K . . 43 Z36

South Muldrew Lake Rd MK 42 W32
South Oliphant Rd BR . . 55 Y17
South Orr Lake Rd SM . . 41 Z28-29
South Parry Rd PS 57 R27
South Pelham Rd NI 19 T33
South Pine View Ridge La HS . . . .
. . . . . 46 X47
South Pinnacle Point La F . 47 X52
South Plympton Rd LM . . 13 T10
South Portage Rd MK 59 R34-35 S34
South Ril Lake Rd MK 59 T35
South River Rd HS 35 D51
South River Rd WL 22 K24
South River Access Rd NP . . . .
. . . . 94 G30 95 G31
South Russell Rd PR . . 67 S65-66
South Salmon Lake Rd PB . . . .
. . . . . 44 X39-40
South Seguin Estates Rd PS . . . .
. . . . . 58 Q29-30
South Service Rd DH . . 32 H37
South Service Rd HM . . 18 Q30
South Service Rd NI 33 G41
South Service Rd NI . . 18 Q-R31 R32
South Service Rd PS 77 M32
South Service Rd SDG . . 69 T73
South Shore Dr F 48 W53
South Shore La F 48 Y54
South Shore Rd CS 100 D18 101 D19
South Shore Rd F . . 36 D-E57
South Shore Rd PS 75 N24
South Shore Rd (Greater Napanee)
LA 35 E-F52
South Shore Rd (Loyalist) LN . . . .
. . . . . 36 E54-55
South Side Way R 64 R54
South Slope Dr NR 33 F41
South Sparrow Lake Rd SM . . . .
. . . . . 42 X-Y32
South Talbot Rd EX . 4 C2-3 D-E4
South Toad Lake Rd MK . 59 Q35-36
South Tooke Lake Rd MK . 59 S-T34
South View La G 28 D24
South Waseosa Lake Rd MK 59 Q33
South Wing Rd SDG . . 67 T65-66
South Wood Dr 47 Y52
Southbrook Dr HM . . 18 R-S29
Southcote Rd HM 17 Q-R27
Southdale Ln EL . . 8 W17 9 W18
Southdel Bourne MD . . 14 V16
Southdown Rd PL 24 M30
Southeast Bypass CS . . 101 C19-20
Southfield Dr WT . . 22 L22-23
Southgate-Glenelg Twnln G . . . .
. . . . . 27 E20 28 E21
Southgate-Melancthon Twnln G . . .
. . . . . 28 E-F24
Southline G 28 D-E22 E21
Southline Av BR . . 26 E-F15
Southminster Bourne MD . . . .
. . . . 14 V16 15 V17
Southorn Rd SM 42 Y30
Southshore Rd NP. . 94 C27 95 F33-34
Southview Dr CS 101 C-D19
Southview Dr PB. 33 E41
Southwest Bypass CS . . . .
. . . . 100 D18 101 D18-19
Southwinds Dr HT 23 K27
Southwood Rd MK . . . . . .
. . . . 42 W31 W-X32 58 V31
Southwood Beach Blvd SM . . . .
. . . . . 42 Y32-33
Sovereign Rd NI 19 T34
Sovereign Rd TB 102 D2-3
Sowerby Rd A 87 E99
Soyers Lake Rd HL 60 U38
Spadina Av T 24 K32
Spadina Rd T 24 K32
Spadina Rd Y 30 H32
Spadina Sdrd DH 31 E35
Spanish River Rd CS 91 E15 100 D15
Spar Lake Rd HL 43 X37
Sparrow Lake Rd MK . . 42 W-X32
Sparta Ln LN . 8 W19 9 W18-19
Spectacle Lake Rd NP . . 80 N-P45
Speechley Rd NI 33 F43
Speedsville Rd WT . . 22 N24
Speedvale Av WL . . 22 L-M24
Speedway Rd OT 65 S60
Speers Rd HT 24 N29-30
Spen Haven Rd K 44 B39
Spence Av PR 68 N71
Spence Ln C 7 Y11-12
Spence Rd HS 62 S47
Spence Rd LN 49 W58
Spence Rd R 82 N-P53
Spence Rd TB 102 D3
Spence Lake Rd E PS. . . 76 P30
Spence Lake Rd W PS. . 76 P29-30
Spencer Av LA 47 X50
Spencer La NR 34 E46
Spencer Rd HS 47 W-X51
Spencer Rd HS 34 C47
Spencer Rd PE 34 E-F48
Spencers Tr PB 44 X39
Spencertown Rd HU . 27 H18-19
Sperberg La F 81 N50
Sperling La F 48 Z55
Spicer Rd LG . . 50 Y63 Z62
Spiece Rd NI 18 R32
Spilek Rd HS 62 S45
Spine Rd A 88 D6
Spithead Rd R 36 D57
Spitzig Rd WT 22 M23-24
Splake Lake Rd A . . 89 C9-10
Splinter Ln C 7 Y10
Split Rail La F 36 A57
Spooks Bay La HL. . 45 W42 61 V42
Spooky Hollow Rd NF 10 W24 16 V24
Sport La F 48 X54
Sportsman La F . . 45 W45 62 V45
Sportsmen Ln C 6 X-Y9
Sportsworld Dr WT 22 N24
Sprague Rd PE 35 E50
Spragues Rd WT 22 L-M23
Spratt Rd OT 66 S63
Spring Rd MK 59 T34
Spring Rd NR 33 F41
Spring Access Rd NP 95 D34

Spring Bay St MA 72 K9-10
Spring Creek Rd BR. . 55 Y17-18
Spring Creek Rd NI . . 18 R-S32 S31
Spring Creek Rd R . . 87 E98
Spring Creek Rd SDG 52 U71 68 I/I
Spring Flowers La F 47 X51
Spring Gardens Rd HT 17 Q28 23 P28
Spring Hill Rd (McKellar) PS . . . .
. . . . 76 P27-28
Spring Hill Rd (Ryerson) PS 77 N31
Spring Lake Rd (Bracebridge) MK.
. . . . . 59 U34
Spring Lake Rd (Lake of Bays) MK
. . . . . 59 R35
Spring Mill La F 36 B56
Spring Valley Rd NI 60 V37
Spring Valley Rd NR 34 E46
Springbank Av OX 16 R21
Springbank Dr MD 14 T16
Springdale Park Rd MK . . 59 T33
Springer Rd MD 14 U15
Springer Rd R 81 N50
Springer Brook Tr MA . . 73 L12
Springer Hill Rd EL 15 V20
Springfield Rd EL . 9 W19 15 V19
Springfield Rd MD . . 14 U13 V14
Springfield Rd MK 59 R34
Springtown Bridge Rd R . 64 R55
Springwater Rd EL 15 V18
Springwater Rd MD . . 14 T-U15
Sproats Dr HL 60 U40
Spruce Av A 88 D6
Spruce Dr LN 65 T58
Spruce Dr SDG 67 T65
Spruce Dr TB . . 102 E-F4
Spruce Rd A 86 C97
Spruce Rd MA 72 K10
Spruce St CS. 101 B20
Spruce St MA 72 K10
Spruce Grove Rd NR . . 32 F39
Spruce Grove Rd TM . 85 M28
Spruce Lake La HL 60 U39
Spruce Lake Tr HS 62 U47
Spruce Ridge Rd OT . . 65 S60
Spruce River Rd TB . . 103 C7
Sprucedale Rd PS . 95 J31-32
Sprucewood Av EX 4 C1
Spruit Rd SDG 67 U65
Spry Rd BR 55 V16
Spry Rd HS 46 B47
Spry Lake Rd BR 55 X17
Spry Shore Rd BR. 55 V16
Spur La PS 77 P31
Spur Rd PS 94 J27-28
Spur 7 Rd PB 44 Y41
Spurr Lake Dr HS 62 U45
Spurway Dr A 86 D95
Squair Rd DH 32 G38
Square Bay Rd MA . . 72 L-M8
Square Pt LG 37 B59
Squaw Bay Rd (Neebing) TB 103 E6
Squaw Bay Rd (Sibley) R . 103 C10
Squaw Lake Rd PS . . 76 P28
Squaw Point Rd LN . . 65 U59
Squire Rd HS 46 B47
Squire Rd SDG. 68 U67
Squire Beach Rd DH 25 I-J35 31 H35
Squireson Lake Rd R . . 80 M47
Squirrel Rd HU 14 Q16
Squirrel Rd PS 57 Q27
Squirrel Town Rd MA . . 73 M12
Stacey Rd NR 34 E46
Stack Rd R 81 P49
Staffa Rd HU 20 M14-15
Stafford La F 37 A-B58
Stafford Rd EL 14 V16
Stafford Rd NI 9 X21
Stage Rd BT 16 S22
Stage Rd T 7 Y10-11
Stage Coach Rd F . . 36 B-C55
Stage Coach Rd SB . 58 U-V32
Stagecoach Rd OT . 66 S63-64 T64
Stahls Rd MK 59 Q33
Stajkowski Rd TB 102 G3
Stalker Ln EL 7 X13
Stamp Sdrd SM 42 Y31
Stampeville Rd SDG. 50 W65 51 W66
Standard Rd SM 29 D28
Standish La PB 45 X44
Standish La HS 62 V46
Stanhope Airport Rd HL . . 60 T38
Stanley Av SM 42 A31
Stanley Ln LM 12 V-8
Stanley Rd LN 49 X58
Stanley Rd NI 19 T35
Stanley's Rd NP 95 D32
Stanley Hall Rd LG 49 Y61
Stanley Olsheski Rd R . . 62 Q48
Stanleyville Rd LN . . 48 X57 49 X58
Stanrock Rd A . . 88 C6 89 C7
Stans Rd OT 83 Q58
Stanyers Rd PS 76 M29
Stanton Rd NR 33 G42
Stanton Rd PS 76 M29
Staples La LA 35 F51
Stapleton Rd DH 32 G39
Stapleton Rd MA 73 L11
Stirling St HD 17 S27
Star Hill Rd K 32 C-D38
Star Hill Rd LN 49 X58
Star Lake Rd (Perry) PS . . 77 P32
Star Lake Rd (Seguin) PS . 58 Q-R29
Stardale Rd E PR 68 P72
Stardale Rd W PR 68 P72
Starkweather Ln C 6 X8
Starr Blvd K . . 31 D36 32 D37
Starratt Rd PS . 76 N30 77 N31
Stata Rd SDG 92 G22
Station Rd E 7 Y10
Station Rd F 27 F19
Station Rd G 31 C35
Station Rd LA 47 X51
Station Rd LN 49 W59
Station Rd NI 33 G43
Station Rd NI 18 U32
Station Rd PE 34 G48
Station Rd PR 68 P69
Station Rd PS 77 P33
Station Rd PT. . 21 N-P18
Station Rd SD 92 G22
Station Rd Y 31 C33
Station Rd (Dayton) A . . 87 E99
Station Rd (Leeds and the
Thousand Islands) LG. . 37 C59
Station Rd (Marmora) HS 46 A46-47

Station Rd (Rideau Lakes) LG . . . .
. . . . 49 X59 Y59
Station Rd (Thessalon) A . . 87 E98
Station Rd (Tweed) HS . . 47 A50
Station Rd (Wabos) A . . 84 Y94
Station St DF 32 G38
Station St HS 34 E49
Station St NI. 18 R-S31
Station Hill Rd R 26 F15
Statters Lake Av BR . . 22 P23
Staunton Rd MK 59 U34
Staunton Rd NI 19 T34
Stauffer Dr WT 22 P23
Steel St SM 42 B30
Steele Rd F 48 Y55
Steele Rd SDG 67 T68
Steele St SM 19 U33
Steeles Av HT . . 23 M28 N27
Steeles Av PL 24 K-L29
Steeles Av T 24 J30
Steeles Av E Y . . . . .
. . 24 J32 25 J33 31 H33-34
Steeles Av W Y . . 24 J31-32
Steeles Ln A 44 A39
Steeles Ln SM 42 Y30
Steeles Rd HS 62 R45
Steeles Rd PS 58 T31
Steen Rd C 7 A11 Y11
Steenburg Rd R 81 L50
Steenburg Lake North Rd HS . . . .
. . . . . 46 W46
Steenburg Lake South Rd HS . . . .
. . . . . 46 W47
Steeple Hill Cr OT . . 66 S62
Steeplechase Dr HL . . 60 T38
Steffan Rd R 64 R55
Steffler Rd WT . . 22 L-M22
Stefina Ln C 7 B11
Stegman's Mill Rd Y . . 30 H30
Steiger Rd F 47 X52
Stein Rd LA 63 T50
Steiner Rd NF 16 T23
Steinke Rd SD 90 F11
Stella 40 Foot Rd LA . . 36 E54
Stencell's Rd R 81 L50
Stephanie Blvd Y 30 H30
Stephen Rd MK . . 58 T30-31
Stephen Rd NR 33 F43
Stephens Bay Rd MK . 58 U-V32
Stephens Rd PR 68 P71
Stephens Mill Rd MK . . 52 G38
Stephenson Rd DH . . 32 G-H39
Stephenson Point Rd DH . . 31 H36
Sterling La HL 60 V38
Sterling Bay Rd A 86 D95
Stetterington La EX 5 E5
Steve Babcock La F . . 48 Z55
Steven St MA 72 K8
Stevens Rd (North Dundas) SDG . .
. . . . . 67 S-T66
Stevens Rd (South Dundas) SDG . .
. . . . . 51 V67
Stevenson Dr R 83 P56
Stevenson La F . . 36 E-F57
Stevenson Rd DH 31 H36
Stevenson Rd LG 5 D8
Stevenson Rd N DH . 31 F36 G36
Stevenson Lake La R . . 80 M47
Stevensville Rd NI 19 T35
Steward Dr SDG. 51 W67
Stewardson Rd LM 13 T10
Stewart Blvd LG . 50 Z62-63
Stewart Ln C 6 X6-7
Stewart Ln PB . . 32 D39-40
Stewart Rd DH 32 G39
Stewart Rd EL 15 V20
Stewart Rd EX 5 H-J5
Stewart Rd LN . 64 R56 65 R57
Stewart Rd NP 94 D27
Stewart Rd NR 33 F43
Stewart Rd SD 19 Q-R34
Stewart Rd TB 102 G3
Stewart Rd (Bancroft) HL. . 61 V40
Stewart Rd (Carlow-Mayo) HS . . . .
. . . . . 62 S47
Stewart St R 82 P54-55
Stewart's Rd MA . . 72 L10 73 L11
Stewart-Long Lake Access Rd LA . .
. . . . . 63 U49
Stewart Gibson Rd LN . . 64 U56
Stewart King Rd PS . . 57 T27
Stewart Lake Rd MK . . 58 T29
Stewarts Rd NP 96 F36
Stewartville Rd R 83 O56
Stickles Rd HS 34 E47
Stickney Rd TM 85 N26
Sticky La K 43 Y37
Stillar Side Rd PS 95 H31
Stillaway Ln PS . . 95 G31-32
Stills Side Rd A . . 86 E-F95
Stillwater Dr K. 32 D38
Stinchcombe Rd F . . 48 Y54
Stinson's Bay Rd K . . 44 A38
Stinson Block Rd PE . . 34 G47
Stinson Hydro Rd CS. . 101 C21-22
Stirling St HD 17 S27
Stirling's Ln HU 20 L14
Stirling-Marmora Rd HS . . 46 B47
Stirling Falls Rd PS . 77 M31-32
Stisted Rd N PS. 77 N-P31
Stisted Rd S PS. . 58 Q32 77 P31-32
Stisted Landfill Rd PS 58 R31-32
Stobie Dam Rd CS. 100 B17
Stockdale Rd HS . . 34 D-E47
Stockdale Rd PB 32 C40
Stockdale Rd SM. . 42 Y31-32
Stoco Rd HS 47 A50
Stoegers Rd PS 77 N34
Stokes Bay Rd BR. . 55 U-V16
Stokes River Rd BR. . 55 U16
Stone La NI . . 33 E45 34 E46
Stone Rd A 88 C6
Stone Rd HU . . 20 M-N15
Stone Rd LN 49 W59
Stone Rd NR 33 D44
Stone Rd R 82 P53
Stone Rd WL 23 M25
Stone Rd (North Grenville) LG . . . .
. . . . . 50 V62-63
Stone Rd (Rideau Lakes) LG 49 Z58
Stone Church Rd EL 8 W17

Stone Church Rd HM . . . 17 Q28
Stone Church Rd R. . 81 P48-49
Stone Cutter's Rd CS. . 95 G31
Stone Gate La MK 59 V34
Stone Hedge Rd LA . . 47 B51-52
Stone Hill Rd G 28 E21
Stone House Rd F . 47 X52 48 Y54
Stone House Rd NR 34 E46
Stone Quarry Rd ND . . 17 U26
Stone School Ln HU . . 20 K-L14
Stone School Rd G . . 39 Y-Z18
Stone School Rd HU . . 26 H16
Stone School Rd OT . . 66 S64
Stonecrest Rd OT . . 83 P-Q59
Stonecrop La Z . . 63 R52 64 R53
Stonegate Dr K 43 Z36
Stonehaven Dr OT. . 66 R-S61
Stonehaven Dr Y 30 F32
Stonehaven Rd HD . . 18 U30
Stonehaven Rd NI 33 E44
Stonehouse Ln MD . . 14 Q-R16
Stoneleigh Rd MK 59 T33
Stoneman Rd HD 17 S28
Stonemill Rd NI . . 19 U35-36
Stoneridge La F 48 Y56
Stoneridge Rd F 65 Q60
Stones Rd R 82 M52
Stones Lake Rd R 64 R-S55
Stoneway Rd PS . . 77 N33-34
Stoney Rd PB 58 V31
Stoney Rd PS 77 M31
Stoney Bay Rd BR . . 55 W18
Stoney Bay Rd CS 91 E16
Stoney Creek Rd HD . . 17 S28
Stoney Creek Rd R . . 32 C-D38
Stoney Lonesome Rd R. 64 T54
Stoney Lonesome Rd NR 33 E44-45
Stoney Point Rd HS 34 F46
Stoney Point Rd S NR. . 34 F46
Stoney Settlement Rd HS . . 46 Y47
Stony Lake Rd R 45 A42
Stony Point Rd PB 45 Z44
Stoppa Rd R 82 N54
Stoqua Creek Rd R 82 M52
Storell Rd PB 33 D41
Storey Rd HS 61 T43
Storey St LA 35 D-E53
Storie Rd LN 48 V57 65 U57
Storie Rd R 83 P56
Stories Rd PS 95 H31
Storms La F 36 A54-55
Storms Rd A 87 C-D99
Storms Rd R 46 A-B47
Story Dr MD 15 R17
Story Book Park Rd G . . 39 A20
Storyland Dr R 82 N55
Storyland Rd R 82 P55
Stouffville Rd DH . . 31 H33
Stouffville Rd Y . . 30 G32 31 G33
Stoughton Sdrd R 64 S54
Stover St OX 16 T22
Strachan Point Rd MK . . 58 U30
Strader Rd SDG 51 V66
Strader Hill Rd SDG . . 51 V66
Strandherd Rd OT 66 S62
Strasburg Rd WT 22 N23
Strathaven Rd Z 39 A-B21
Strathcona Av PS 103 C6-7
Strathdee Rd MK 58 T31
Strathmore Rd SDG . . 68 T70
Stratton Lake Rd SD . . 90 F14
Strattonville Cr DH . . 31 F35
Strawberry Dr HL 60 V38
Strawberry La Y 30 F30
Strawberry Hill Rd A . . 53 A37
Strawberry Point Rd MA . . 72 K8
Strawn Rd NI 19 T34
Street La LG 49 X60
Street Rd SDG 52 U71
Streicher Ln WT . . 21 M20 22 M21
Streit Quarry Rd LN . . 66 U61
Strickland Rd LG . . 49 X59-60
Strickland Rd R 44 B41
Strickland St PB 44 B41
Stride Rd E 8 W15
Stringer Dr HS 62 U-V45
Stringer Rd HD 18 T30
Stringer Lake Rd A . . 87 B-C2
Stroms Rd TB 102 D2
Strong Rd EX 5 B-C5
Strong Sdrd LN 48 W56
Strong Joly Rd PS. . 77 K-L32
Strongville Rd SM . . 41 B27-28
Stroud Beach Rd MK . . 58 R-S31
Strouds La DH 31 H34
Struthadam Rd R . 63 V52-53
Struthers Rd F . 36 A54 48 Z54
Stu Black Rd NR . . 33 F41-42
Stuart Blvd EX 4 C1
Stuart Rd F 82 P52
Stuart's Spur Rd NF . . 98 J43
Stub Rd K 31 D36
Stub Creek La F 48 Y53
Studiman Rd WT 23 P25
Studio La HL 60 T42
Stufko Rd R 82 Q53-54
Stumpy Bay Rd PS. . 75 K24 93 J24
Sturgeon Bay Rd K . 32 C39 44 B38
Sturgeon Bay Rd TB. . 102 F-G5 G4-5
Sturgeon Glen Rd K . 43 A37 44 A38
Sturgeon Lake Rd NP 96 E37-38 F38
Sturgeon Mountain Rd R . . 82 M53
Sturgeon Point Rd K . . 44 A38
Sturgess Rd LN 48 W56
Sturgess Rd LG . . 49 W60-61
Styles Sdrd OT 16 S21
Substation Rd OX . . 16 S21-22
Subway Ln OX 16 R22
Subway Rd SM 41 Y28
Sucie Rd HL 61 T42
Sucker Creek Rd SD. . 93 F24
Sucker Lake Rd MA . . 73 L12
Sucrerie Rd NP 94 C27
Suddaby Park Rd A . 86 D95-96
Suez Dr CS 101 A20
Suffolk Rd OX 4 E3
Sugar Beet Ln C 6 X8-9
Sugar Bush La F . . 48 V55-56
Sugar Bush Rd F 48 Y54
Sugar Bush Rd LN 65 S58
Sugar Bush Rd PS . . 76 L30 77 L31
Sugar Bush Rd (Kawartha
Lakes [Carden Dalton]) K. . 43 Y34

Sugar Bush Rd (Kawartha Lakes[Laxton Digby & Longford]) K 43 X36
Sugar Bush Rd (Kawartha Lakes[Manvers]) K . . 32 E37-38
Sugar Bush Hill Rd LG . . 49 X59
Sugar Forest Pl WT. . . . 22 L23
Sugar Lake Rd PS 58 O29
Sugar Lake Rd G 58 O29
Sugarbush Blvd PB . . 44 A39-40
Sugarbush Cr PB . . 44 A39 Z39
Sugarbush La LG . . 37 A60 49 Z60
Sugarbush Rd HU 20 M13
Sugarbush Rd PB 45 A45
Sugarbush Way LN 64 U56
Suggitt Rd K 43 Z37
Suikhola St CS 91 E16
Sullivan Rd HL 60 T40
Sullivan Rd MD 13 T12
Sullivan Rd R. 81 P49
Sullivan Rd SDG 92 T52
Sullivan Lake Access Rd R . 98 G47
Sullivan Point Rd R. . . . 82 L52
Sully Rd R 33 E42
Sulphide Rd HS . . . 47 A50 Z50
Sulphide Rd LA 47 Z51
Sulphide Varty Rd HS. . . 47 A50
Sulphur Spring Rd NI . . . 19 S33
Sulphur Springs Rd HM . . 17 O27
Sumac Rd F 36 C55
Sumach La M 33 E45
Sumbler Rd NI. 19 T33
Sumcot Dr PB 44 A40
Summer Av BR. 55 W17
Summer Leigh Tr MK . . 58 S32
Summerhaven Sdrd HU . 20 L12-13
Summerhill Rd K . . 20 K-L15 L16
Summers Rd LG . . 37 A59 49 Z58-59
Summers Rd R. 99 K50
Summers Rd SDG. . . . 67 U66
Summers Lake Rd A. . . 88 C5-6
Summerstown Rd SDG . 52 U71-72
Summerville La OX. . . . 16 U22
Summit Dr DH. . . 31 E36 32 E37
Summit Rd MK 58 V31
Summit Rd PS 77 K32 95 J32
Summit View Ct G 40 A24
Sun Valley Rd K 31 D36
Sunbury Rd F 36 B-C57
Sunday Lake Dr F. . . . 64 U54
Sunderland Rd CS . . . 101 B20
Sunderland Rd DH 31 D34
Sunnidale Rd SM . . . 41 A26-27
Sunnidale Rd (Clearview) SM 41 B27
Sunnidale Rd (Springwater) SM 30 C29 41 B29
Sunningdale Dr HS . . . 34 D48
Sunningdale Rd E MD. . 15 S17
Sunningdale Rd W MD. . 14 S-T16
Sunny Hill Rd R. 80 P46
Sunny Lake Rd MK . . 42 W33 93 V33
Sunny Ridge Rd HM. . . 17 R26
Sunny Ridge Rd PS . . . 77 L32
Sunny Valley Rd G . . . 39 A19-20
Sunny Valley Rd S G. . . 39 A19-20
Sunnybrae Rd NR. . . . 33 C44
Sunnylea Av PS 77 N32
Sunnyridge Rd HU . . . 20 N-P16
Sunnyshore Estates Rd PS . 58 R29
Sunnyside Dr MD. . . 14 S16 15 S17
Sunnyside Rd CS . . . 101 D19
Sunnyside Rd F. 36 D56
Sunnyside Rd LG . . . 48 Y-Z57
Sunnyside Rd NP 95 F33-34
Sunnyside Rd R 81 L-M50
Sunnyside Beach Rd A . 84 B90
Sunnywood Rd R 44 B39
Sunova Cr OX 15 R18-19
Sunrich La R 98 E42
Sunrise Dr PE 34 E49
Sunrise La F 48 Z55
Sunrise Rd K . 32 C39 C40 44 B39 B40
Sunrise Rd R 81 N48
Sunrise Tr MK 41 W29
Sunrise Bay Dr PS . . . 95 F31
Sunrise Beach La F . . . 47 W51
Sunrise Shores Rd SD . 90 D13
Sunset Blvd G 40 Z23
Sunset Blvd LN 49 W58
Sunset Cv HU 20 N13
Sunset Dr EL 15 V17
Sunset Dr LN. 49 W-X58
Sunset Dr NI. 19 T-U36
Sunset Dr PB. 32 E39
Sunset Dr (Saugeen Shores) BR 38 B14-15
Sunset Dr (South Bruce Peninsula) BR 55 W16
Sunset La SM 41 B28
Sunset Rd EL 15 V17
Sunset Rd SD 101 C22
Sunset Bay Dr SD . . . 89 E-F9
Sunset Bay Rd LN . . . 64 S55
Sunset Bay Rd (Gravenhurst) 58 V32
Sunset Bay Rd (Muskoka Lakes) MK 58 U30
Sunset Beach Rd A . . . 87 E1
Sunset Beach Rd HU . . 20 J13
Sunset Beach Rd K . . 43 X-Y36
Sunset Beach Rd (Georgina) Y 31 C33
Sunset Beach Rd (Richmond Hill) Y. 30 G32
Sunset Cottage Dr HL . 61 U41
Sunset Cove Rd CS . . 101 A22 Z22
Sunset Cove Rd PS . . 95 F-G31
Sunset Lake Rd PB . . 102 F1
Sunset Pass Dr PS . . . 77 N32
Sunset Point Rd PS . . . 57 T27
Sunset Shores La F . . 48 Y-Z55
Sunset Strip La F . . 63 V53 64 V53
Sunshine La HU. . . . 20 N-P16
Sunshine Loop TB 102 C3
Sunshine Alley Rd MA . 90 H13
Sunshine Creek Rd TB . 102 B3
Sunshine Cross Rd TB . 102 B3
Sunset Estates Rd MA . 73 K12
Suomi Rd PS. 77 N31
Superior Rd PS. 77 N31
Superior St G 39 Z19-20
Supersign Rd PS. 77 P33
Surprise Rd E TB 102 B5
Sussex Dr OT 66 O63
Sutcliffe Rd HS 46 Z48
Sutcliffe Rd SD 93 D24
Sutherland Rd HS . . . 46 A48

Sutherland Rd MD 14 U14
Sutherland Rd (Bonnechere Valley) R. 82 Q52
Sutherland Rd (Whitewater Region) R 82 N52
Sutor Rd HD 18 U29
Sutorville Rd LM . . . 13 U-V11
Suttaby Rd MK 58 V30
Sutter Rd BR 55 W16
Sutter Creek Dr NR . . . 33 E42
Sutton D HT. 24 N29
Sutton La PB 44 A41
Sutton Rd HS 46 W47
Sutton Rd TM 85 M28
Sutton St BR 26 D14
Suurdt Rd H 34 D46
Suzannes Rd NR 96 E36
Swallow Rd PS 57 Q27
Swallowdale Rd MK . . 59 R34
Swamp Rd F 48 X53
Swamp Rd R 82 O54-55
Swamp Rd TB 102 B2
Swamp Rd TM 85 M29
Swamp College Rd PE . 34 G49
Swan Ln C. 6 X-Y7
Swan Rd HL 60 U37
Swanton Ln C. 6 C8
Swartze Rd PS 94 H27
Swauger Lake Rd F. . 47 W52 63 V52
Swayze Rd HD 18 T30
Sweaburg Rd OX . . 15 S20 16 S21
Sweeney Ln PB. . . . 33 C41-42
Sweeney Rd A 88 F4
Sweet Rd HS. 46 B46
Sweet's Portage Rd MK . 41 W29
Sweets La R 63 T51-52
Sweets Corners Rd HD . 18 U30
Sweets Corners Rd LG . 37 A58-59
Sweets Lake La S HS. . 46 W46
Swift Rapids Rd SM . . . 42 X31
Swimming Pool Rd MK . 16 U21
Swinburne Rd HS 46 B46
Swinson Rd HL 44 X38
Swisha Rd R 98 F47
Swiss Meadows Blvd G . 40 A22
Switch Rd NL 19 T35
Switch Rd SM. 42 Y32-33
Switchback Dr HL 60 U37
Switzer Dr MD 8 W14 14 V14
Switzer La LA 47 B53
Switzer St SM 29 C27
Switzerville Rd LA . . . 35 C-D53
Swordfingal Lake Rd HS . 62 U47
Swords Rd MK 58 R29
Swords Rd PS 76 N27-28
Sydenham Ln C. 6 X9
Sydenham Ln LM . . . 13 V11-12
Sydenham Rd F. . . 36 B-C55 C-D56
Sydenham Rd HM . . 17 Q27 23 P27
Sydenham St G. 28 D22
Sydenham Tr SM 40 B25
Sydenham-Lakeshore Dr G 39 Y-Z20
Sydenham-Walker Rd F 36 A54 B55 47 A54
Sydney St SDG 52 U-V70
Syer Ln PB. 32 D40 D-E39
Sykes La 7 C11
Sykes St G. 40 Z22
Sylvan Rd MD 13 R12
Sylvan Glen Rd NR. . . 33 G41
Sylvan Valley Rd S G. . 39 A20
Symons Rd NR 32 G40
Syndicate Av TB . . . 103 D-E6
Syne Rd C 6 X7
Syvret Rd MK 59 V33
Szalawiga Rd H 32 G40
Szucs Rd KF 10 W24 16 V24

T
T-Way Dr PB 32 E40
Tabasaga St MA 72 K10
Tabernacle Rd HS. . . . 34 D46
Table Rock Dr A 88 F4-5
Tack Rd BR 27 G18
Tackaberry La MK . . . 59 T34
Tackaberry Rd MK . . . 59 T34
Taft Rd PE 34 F47
Taggart La F 48 Z57
Taggart Lake Rd NP. . 96 E36-37
Tahinca Rd PS 76 M28
Tailfeather Rd HL 61 U41
Taillefer Rd NP 95 E33
Taillon Rd SD 93 G23
Tait Rd A 87 E1-2
Tait Rd NR 33 E44
Tait's Island Rd PS . . . 57 R27
Taits Rd MD 7 W13 14 V13
Talbot La EL . . 7 Y13 8 W15-16 X14-15 . . . . . . 14 V16 15 V17-20
Talbot Rd EX 15 V19
Talbot Rd EX. . 4 C2 C-D3 D4 5-6 R4
Talbot Rd HD 17 U27 18 T29
Talbot Rd IS 43 Y36
Talbot St EL 15 V17
Talbot St PE 35 G50-51
Talbot St SM. 41 X28-29
Talbot Tr C. 5 D-E7 6 C9 7 A12 B11 B-C10
Talbot River Rd K . . . 43 Z35-36
Talbotville Gore Rd EL . 15 V17
Tall Timbers Sdrd HU . . 20 L13
Tallan Lake Rd PB . . . 45 W43
Tally-Ho Winter Park Rd MK 59 Q-R34
Tally Ho-Swords Rd PS . 58 Q-R29
Talon Lake Rd NP . . 95 E34 96 E35
Tama Kwa Rd PS . . . 95 F31-32
Tamarack Dr PS 75 N24
Tamarack La HS 46 W47
Tamarack La MA 90 J10
Tamarack Ln LM . . . 13 S11-12
Tamarack Rd LN . . . 48 W-X56
Tamarack Rd F 45 X51
Tamarack Tr F. 48 X54
Tamarack Lake Rd HL . 44 W40
Tamdragee Rd SM . . . 29 F27
Tammy's Cove Rd BR . 54 T16
Tamworth Rd LA 47 A52
Tanbark Rd NI 19 R34-35
Tangamong La HS . . . 45 Y45
Tangamong Lake Rd PB. . 45 Y45
Tank St LM 12 U9
Tank Farm Rd HS 34 D49
Tanner Rd BT. 17 P-Q25
Tannery Rd HS 46 A48
Tannery Rd SDG 68 Q71
Taot Tr HL 60 U38
Tapley Quarter Ln PB . 32 D-E39
Tapleytown Rd HM . . 18 Q-R29
Tara Rd PB 44 B40

Taricani Rd SD 90 F13-14
Tashmoo Av LM . . . 12 T-U7
Tasker Rd C 6 C8
Tasko Rd MD 14 Q15
Tate Rd HS 34 E-F47
Tate's Rd PB 44 Z39
Tates Rd PB 44 Y40
Tatlock Rd LN 65 T57-58
Tattersal Rd LN 65 S59
Tatty Hill Rd HS 64 S54
Taunton Rd H. 31 G35-36 H34-35 32 G37-38
Taverner's Rd PS 77 M33
Tay Point Rd SM 41 X28
Taylor Dr G 39 B21
Taylor La PB 44 A41
Taylor Ln EL 15 U18
Taylor Rd C 7 A12
Taylor Rd BR 27 C17
Taylor Rd HD 18 U30-31
Taylor Rd LS 43 Y34
Taylor Rd LG 50 V63-64
Taylor Rd MK 59 U33
Taylor Rd NR 33 E43
Taylor Rd NI 19 R34
Taylor Rd PS. 58 U30
Taylor Rd SDG 50 V-W65
Taylor Rd E LG 37 B58-59
Taylor Rd W LG 37 B58
Taylor Sdrd G 39 X-Y19
Taylor St A 86 D-E96
Taylor's Rd C 31 C36
Taylor Kidd Blvd F . . . 36 D55
Taylor Kidd Blvd LA . . 36 D54-55
Teal Rd HS. 34 E46
Teal Tr PS 75 M24
Teal Nevill Rd EL. . . 9 W-X20 W-X21
Tecumseh Ln C 6 B7
Tecumseh Rd (Saint Clair) LM 12 U-V7
Tecumseh Rd (Walpole Island IR) LM. 6 X6
Ted's La PB 44 Z39
Tedford Dr PB 45 Z42
Tee Lake Rd R. 98 G47
Teeple-Haley Rd R . . . 63 R51
Teeter St NF 17 T28
Teeterville Rd NF . . 16 T23 U24
Teetzel Ln C 7 A12 Y12
Teitto Rd TB 102 C3
Telecom Rd K 32 E38
Telephone Rd HS . . 34 E46-47
Telephone Rd HL . . . 20 L13
Telephone Rd (Alnwick-Haldimand) NR. . . 33 F43 F44
Telephone Rd (Hamilton) NR 33 G41-42
Telephone Rd E NR . . 33 F43 F44
Telephone Rd W NR . . 33 F43
Telephone Bay Rd HL . 60 V40
Television Rd PB. 33 C41
Telfer Rd LM 12 T-V8
Telford Ln SM 42 Y31-32
Tellier Rd NF 93 D26
Temperance Rd WT . . 22 L22
Temperance Lake Rd LG . 49 Z61
Temperance Valley Rd SD . 90 F11
Ten Mile Bay Rd MK . . 59 R35
Tenkulard Rd TB 102 F2
Tennant Rd R 63 O49
Tennyson Ln LM 12 V8
Tennyson Rd HL . . 43 W37 60 V37
Tennyson Rd LN . . . 49 V58-59
Tenth MA 72 J8
Tenth, The MA 72 J8
Teresa La F 48 Z55
Teron Rd OT 66 R61
Terrace Rd HS 46 A46
Terrace Rd PB 46 A46
Terrace Rd PS 95 F32
Terry St PL. 29 H27
Terry's La LA 63 V49
Terry Fox Dr OT. 66 P61
Teskey Rd L 47 B52
Teston Rd Y 30 H30-31
Tett Cr F 48 Z57
Tex's Rd SD 101 B-C23
Texas Rd EX 4 D1-2
Thackery Rd SD 93 G24
Thames Rd HD 20 P16
Thames Rd MD. 14 V13
Thamesview Ln EL. . . . 8 W14
Thanet Lake Rd HS. . . 46 X46
Thaxter Rd SD. 90 F11
The Scots Ln NR. 33 F43
Theatre Rd NR 33 F-G41
Thebury Rd BR . . . 55 V16-17 V17-20
Ther-Tell Rd DH 32 F39
Theriault Rd HS 101 A19
Therrien Rd SD . . . 93 E23-24
Thibadeau Rd HS . . . 62 U46
Thibault Ct SDG 67 T66
Thibeault Rd NP 94 D27
Thickson Rd DH . . . 31 G-H36
Thielman Rd A. 84 D91
Thistle Tr K 43 Y36
Thistledown La MA. . . . 72 L9
Thistlewood Rd G . . 28 C21-22
Thomas Dr Y. 30 D32
Thomas La EL 8 X16
Thomas Rd A. 86 C-D96
Thomas Rd R 8 W17
Thomas Rd EX 4 D2
Thomas Rd LG 37 A58
Thomas Rd NR 33 F-G44
Thomas Rd OX 15 T19-20
Thomas St A 87 E98
Thomas St PL 24 L-M29
Thomas A Dolan Pkwy OT. 65 O60 83 Q59
Thomas Argue Rd OT. . 65 R60
Thomas Elliot Rd R. . . 83 O58
Thompson Dr MD 15 T18
Thompson La HS 46 X46
Thompson Rd BT. . . . 17 R26-27
Thompson Rd DH 32 F39
Thompson Rd HS 34 D46
Thompson Rd HT. . . . 25 M28
Thompson Rd HU. . . . 20 K14
Thompson Rd LN. . . . 65 N65
Thompson Rd MD. . . . 15 T17
Thompson Rd MK . . 15 U24 17 U25
Thompson Rd NF. . 16 U24 17 U25
Thompson Rd NR . . . 32 G40
Thompson Rd NI 19 T36
Thompson Rd PE . . 35 G50-51
Thompson Rd R 76 M30
Thompson Rd SDG . . 67 T65-66
Thompson Rd TB. . . 102 C-D5

Thompson Rd (Central Frontenac) F. 43 Y54
Thompson Rd (Centre Hastings) HS. 46 A-B48
Thompson Rd (North Frontenac) F 47 X51
Thompson Rd (Quine West) HS 34 D-E47
Thompson's Sdrd G . . 39 X-Y18
Thompson Hill Rd LA . . 47 A52
Thompson Lake La HS . 46 Z46
Thompson Lake Access Rd NP. 96 E37
Thompson Point Rd LA . 35 F51
Thoms Bay Rd MK . . . 59 S33
Thomson Ln C 7 Y12-13
Thomson Ln LM . . . 13 R11-12
Thomson Ln (Central Elgin) EL 15 U18
Thomson Ln (West Elgin, Dutton-Dunwich) EL . . . 7 Y13 8 W15 X14-15
Thomson Rd NR. 34 C46
Thomson Rd R . . . 82 P55 83 P56
Thomson Sdrd LN . . . 49 V58
Thorah Sdrd LN . . . 43 A34 B35
Thorah Park Blvd DH . 31 C34 43 B34
Thorburn Rd MD 42 Y31
Thorburn St HD. 17 T28
Thorn Dr MD 14 T15
Thorn Rd PB 33 D41
Thorndale Rd MD. . . 15 S17-18
Thorne Dr PB 32 E40
Thornridge La G 39 Y20
Thornton Rd DH . . . 31 G-H36
Thorold Rd NI 19 T33
Thorold Townline NI. . . 19 R-S34
Thorold Stone Hd NI . 19 R34-35
Thorpe Rd LA 36 C54
Thousand Islands Pkwy LG. 37 A61 C59-60 50 A62
Thrasher Rd HS. . . . 34 C-D49
Three Bridges Rd WT . 22 L-M22
Three Brothers Dr HL . 61 U43
Three Camp Rd SD . . 92 F22 93 F23
Three Legged Lake Rd PS 57 R-S27
Three Mile Bay Rd LN . 64 S56
Three Mile Lake Rd 1 MK 58 S31-32
Three Mountain Rd R . . 63 R-S50
Thunder Rd SDG. . . . 51 V66
Thunder Bay Expwy TB . 103 D6
Thunder Bay Rd NI. . . 19 U35
Thunder Beach Rd SM . 41 X26-27
Thunder Bridge Rd K . . 43 B37
Thunder Bridge Rd PS . 77 K32
Thunderbird Dr HL . . 61 U-V43
Tice Rd NI. 18 S32 19 S33
Tickle Lake Access Rd HS. 46 X46
Tie Rd BR 26 C14
Tie's Mountain Rd PB . 44 Z39-40
Tienhaara Rd TB . . . 102 C2-3
Tiffen Rd HS. 46 A-B46
Tiffin St SM 30 C29 41 B29
Tilbury West & Romney Rd EX 5 D6
Tile Rd HU 20 M15
Tile Yard Rd LM 12 U-V9
Till Sdrd DH 31 E35
Tillicum Bay Rd PS . . . 95 F31
Tillson Ox 16 U21
Tilman Rd WT 22 L22-23
Tilt Dr WT 22 N-P23
Tilton Lake Rd CS . . . 101 D19
Tim Lake 9 Access Rd PS . 77 L34
Tim Lake Access Rd PS 77 L34 78 L35
Timber Rd R 8 X15-16
Timber Bay Rd MK . . 72 M9-10
Timber Bay Rd MK. . . 59 R34
Timber Ridge Rd LN . 64 T55
Timm Dr OT 66 R61
Timm Rd R 82 K53
Timmins Rd OT 65 R58
Timmins Rd SDG . . 50 V65 67 U65
Timms La F 48 Z55
Timos Rd TB 102 B3
Tindle Bay Rd PB 32 C40
Tingey Rd MK. 59 U34-35
Tinkerville Rd NR 32 F40
Tinney Dr SM 41 B28
Tinney Rd F 7 W10
Tinney Rd MK 59 R34
Tinsmoor Rd R 82 P55
Tintern Rd HD. 18 R32
Tiny Beaches Rd N SM. 41 X26 X-Y27
Tiny Beaches Rd S SM. . 41 Y-Z27
Tiny Springwater Townline SM 41 Z27-28
Tipperary Ln HU 20 L14
Tipperary Rd PB 44 B40
Tipperary Camp Rd R. . 63 S52
Tisdale Rd EL 15 V18
Tisdale Rd HS 17 R-S28
Tisdale Rd NF 17 V25
Tisdale Sdrd NF 16 V23
Tisdelle Dr EX 6 B6
Tittley Rd PE 68 Q72
Tobacco Rd NR. 33 E45
Tobacco Lake Rd MA . 72 K7-8
Tobacco Lake Rd N MA. . 72 K7-8
Tober Rd NI 18 S31
Tobin Rd F 48 Z56
Tobler's Rd TM 85 L30
Toby's Rd MK 41 W29
Tock La NI 59 R36
Todd La EX 4 C1-2
Todd Lakes Access Rd LA. 63 V49
Todd School Rd LG . . . 50 V62
Toledo Rd LG 49 Y-Z59
Toll Rd Y 30 E31
Toll Gate Ln HU 27 G-H18
Toll Gate Rd BT. 17 R25
Toll Gate Rd EL . . . 9 W21 16 V21
Toll Gate Rd SDG . . . 52 U70
Tollandal Mill Rd SM . . . 41 B29
Tollgate Rd SDG 51 V66
Tolmies Corners Rd SDG . 68 S59
Tolpts Rd PS 57 S28
Tom Bolton Rd NI. . . 60 U39 V38-39
Tom Greer Rd MK . . . 59 U36
Tom Parris Rd HL . . . 59 U36
Tom Thomson La G . . 39 Z20
Tomahawk Tr MK 41 X-Y46
Tomek Rd C 7 A10

Tomingas Rd MK. 59 V33
Tomken Rd PL 24 K-L30
Tompkins Rd LG. . . . 50 V63-64
Toms Rd TB 102 D5 103 D6
Tondern Island Rd MK . 58 U31
Toner Rd R 83 P57
Tooley Rd DH 32 G37
Toonders Rd SDG . . . 51 V67
Topaz La R 63 R52 64 R53
Topping Rd MD 14 U14
Topps Dr HU 61 U42
Tor Pitt Rd SM 42 X32
Torbolton Ridge Rd OT . 83 P-Q59
Torbram Rd PL 23 J28 24 J-29 29 H28
Tornado Dr SM 30 F30-31
Tornados Rd PS . . . 75 K26 93 J26
Torono Sydenham St G . 39 A-B20
Toronto Rd G 28 D22-23
Toronto Rd NR 33 G41
Toronto St G 28 C22
Toronto St (Clarington) DH. 32 H38-39
Toronto St (Uxbridge) DH . 31 E-F34
Torrance Rd ME 58 V30-31
Torrance St BR 26 G15
Torrie Rd TB 102 D3
Torwood Dr OT 65 O60
Tote Rd SD 90 E-F10
Totem Ranch Rd E LG. 50 V63-64
Totem Ranch Rd W LG. 50 X63
Tottenham Rd SM . . . 29 E-F28
Touchwood Tr HL . . . 60 V38
Tousseants Lake Access Rd R. 81 L-M49
Tout's Grove Hill BR . . 26 E13
Touzin Rd TM. 85 P-Q31
Towbridge Rd MK . . 42 W-X33
Tow Rd MD 13 Q-R12
Tower Cr MK 42 W32
Tower Dr NP 95 E32
Tower La F 47 W51
Tower Ln C 7 A12
Tower Ln (Ashfield-Colborne-Wawanosh) HU . . . 26 G-H14
Tower Ln (Bluewater) HU 20 M13-14
Tower Ln (Central Huron) HU 20 L13
Tower Rd A 87 D98
Tower Rd CS 91 E16
Tower Rd C 7 A12
Tower Rd EL 15 V18
Tower Rd HS 62 T-U47
Tower Rd K 32 C-D38
Tower Rd MA. 72 K10
Tower Rd TB. 102 F4
Tower Rd (Addington Highlands) LA 63 U50
Tower Rd (Armour) PS . 77 N32
Tower Rd (Georgian Bay) MK 58 T29
Tower Rd (Huntsville) MK. 58 T32
Tower Rd (Leeds and the Thousand Islands) LG . . 37 B60
Tower Rd (Northern Bruce Peninsula) BR 55 V18
Tower Rd (Rideau Valley) LG. 49 W-X59
Tower Rd (South Bruce) BR . 27 F17
Tower Rd (Stone Mills) LA . 47 B53
Tower Rd (Strong) PS . 77 K-L32
Tower Bay Rd SD . . . 100 B15
Tower Hill Rd R 63 T51
Tower Lake Rd A . . . 86 B-C95
Tower Lake 13 Access Rd PS 77 K33
Tower Lake Access Rd PS. 77 K33 95 J33
Tower Line Rd NR . . . 33 E45
Tower Line Rd SM . . 42 W-X30
Tower Manor Rd NR . . 33 E-F41
Towerhill Rd PB . 32 C40 33 C41
Towerline Rd OX 16 R22
Town Ln NI 19 O34
Town Ln SM 42 Y30-31
Town Line Ln C 6 A-B7
Town Line Rd DH 31 G-H36
Town Line Rd F 36 A56
Town Line Rd LG . . 50 V63-64
Town Line Rd MK . . . 59 R35
Town Line Rd NR . . . 33 F-G44
Town Lot Rd HL 60 U37
Townline EX 5 D6-7
Townline Rd A. 86 D94
Townline Rd BT. . . . 16 R23 T23
Townline Rd DH. . 31 F-G36 32 G-H37
Townline Rd EX 4 D2
Townline Rd LA . . . 35 D-E53
Townline Rd LN . . . 65 T59
Townline Rd MA. . . . 90 J11
Townline Rd TB . . . 102 C5 D5
Townline Rd WT 23 N25
Townline Rd (Fort Erie) NI 19 T35-36
Townline Rd (Jarvis) HL. . 17 U26
Townline Rd (Lowbanks) NI 18 U31-32
Townline Rd (Niagara Falls) NI. 19 R35
Townline Rd (Welland, Wainfleet) NI 18 T29
Townline Rd E (Tehkummah) MA 73 M11
Townline Rd W HD . 17 T27-28
Townline Rd W (Tehkummah) MA. 73 M11
Townline St NF . . . 10 W24 24 N28
Townsend Ln LM 13 S11
Townsend Ln MD. . 13 S12 14 S13
Townsend Pkwy HD . . 17 U26
Townsend Rd HS 34 C48
Townsend Lake Rd G. . 28 C21
Township Ln A 87 E99
Township Boundary Rd LN . 48 V57
Toye Hill Rd SDG . . 50 V65 51 V66
TR 10 Access Rd PS . . 78 M35
TR 11 Access Rd PS 77 M34 78 M35
TR 4 Access Rd PS . . 77 M34
TR 5 Access Rd PS . 77 M34 78 M35
Tracey Rd HS 34 C49
Tracey Rd SD 90 E11
Tracey's Hill Rd K . . 32 C38 44 B39

Tracy Rd MA 72 L9
Tracy's Point Rd LN . . 49 Y58
Trader Cowan Rd SM . . 42 X30
Tradewind Dr HM 17 R27
Tradvista Rd HT. . 23 L28 24 M28
Trafalgar Rd WL . . 23 K26-27
Trafalgar St MD . . 15 S-T18 T17
Trafalgar Bay Rd MK . . 58 U30
Trail Rd OT 66 S62
Trail Blazers Rd R . 81 M-N50 N51
Trail End's Rd NP 93 G25
Trailaine Rd PS 94 J27
Traill Rd NR 33 E42
Traill Rd PS 76 P27
Trainors Side Rd A . . 86 F95-96
Tramore Rd A 81 M-N49
Tramway Rd C 6 X9
Tramway Rd LT 16 W9 12 V9
Tramway Access Rd HS . 46 W48
Tranberg Rd A 86 Q95
Trapper's Trail Rd HL . . 60 U40
Trapper Lake Access Rd F . 63 T52
Trappers Rd NP 95 G32-33
Traquility La F 47 X51
Travellers Rd G 39 B21
Traver Rd NI 18 T32
Traverse Lake La F . . . 37 A58
Traverston Rd G 28 C21
Traynor Rd PB. 44 Y40
Treadwell Rd PR . . . 67 N-P68
Trebbien Rd A 63 Q51
Trebinski Rd R 80 P46
Tree Haven Rd SDG . 52 U72 68 T72
Treeview Ln K 44 Z38-39
Treleaven La F 48 Z55
Trella Rd LM. 6 W7
Trellis Tr HL 60 V37
Tremaine Rd HT . . . 23 M-N28
Trembley Rd EX. 4 D-E2
Trendiak Rd TB 102 E5
Trenear Rd NR. 33 F45
Trent Dr HL 61 V42
Trent Canal Rd K . . . 43 Z37
Trent River Rd PB. . . . 45 B45
Trent Valley Rd PS . . . 33 F45
Trenton-Frankford Rd HS . 34 E47
Trentwood Estates Rd NR . 33 C44
Trepanier Rd EX 4 C3
Trepanier Rd C 5 C5
Triangle Tr HL 43 X37
Tribag Mine Rd A 84 W91
Tribble Rd MK 58 R-S31
Tribble Rd WT. 22 L23
Trillium Dr LN 49 W58
Trillium Dr MD . . . 7 W12-13 X12
Trillium Dr R 45 B45
Trillium La MK 41 W29
Trillium Ln OX 16 S21
Trillium Ln SM. 41 X-Y26
Trillium Rd HS. 34 D48
Trillium Rd MK 58 U31
Trillium Rd SDG 67 U67
Trillium Tar HT 23 L27
Trillium Tr HL 60 U40
Trillium Tr L 47 B53
Trillium Way LN . . . 49 V59-60
Trillium Point Rd MK. . 59 R33
Trim Rd OT 67 Q65
Trimble Rd HM 18 S29
Trinity Dr K 44 A38
Trinity Rd HL. 61 U42-43
Trinity Rd R 17 R27
Trinity Church Rd HM 17 R28 18 R29
Triple Bay Rd SM 41 X-Y28
Triple D Tr MA 73 L12
Triple Tower Rd LN. . . 64 T-U55
Trip Rd PE 35 F-G50
Tripps Rd HS 46 W47
Troders Rd R 80 P46
Trolley Rd HS 62 S47
Troops Rd MD. 14 U15
Trotter Rd F 36 A56
Trotter's Hill Rd MA . . 90 J12
Trottier Rd PB 45 W42
Trottiers Rd PB 45 W42
Trottier Rd F 93 E26
Trottman Rd NR 33 F45
Troup Rd NI. 19 T34 U34
Trousdale Rd F 36 B55
Trout La F 48 Z56
Trout Lake Rd A 84 A92
Trout Lake Rd HS 62 U45
Trout Lake Rd NP . . . 95 E32
Trout Lake Rd PS . . . 57 Q27
Trout Lake Rd R . . . 52 S-T48
Trout Pond Rd NP . . 95 F-G34
Troutling Bay Access Rd HS 45 Y45
Troutspawn Lake Rd HL. 59 Q36 60 T39
Trowbridge Rd TB . . 103 C6-7
Troy Rd HM 17 Q25-26
Troy Lake Rd LG 37 A58
Truck Terminal Rd A . . 88 C6
Trudgeons Rd PS. . . 77 L32-33
Trudyville Rd CS . . . 101 C21
True North Rd HL 60 T40
Truelove Rd LN. 48 W57
Trulls Rd DH. 32 H37
Truman Ln F. 15 U17-18
Truman Rd MD 14 T13
Trumble Rd HS 46 W47
Trumble Rd PE 35 F50
Trumpour Rd PE 34 G48
Trunk Rd NP 95 E32
Trunk Rd (Bruce Mines) A . 86 D-E96
Trunk Rd (Nestorville) A. 86 E97 87 E98
Trunk Rd (Sault Ste Marie) A 84 B92 86 B93
Trunk Rd (Spanish) A . . 89 F92
Truscott Dr TB 24 M30
Trussler Rd OX . . 16 Q23 Q22
Trussler Rd WT 22 N-P23
Tryon Rd F 48 Y54
Tryon Rd MK 42 W33
Tubbs Rd PE 35 F50
Tucker Rd HS 35 D51

Tucker / West Ruscom River

Tucker Rd NR 33 E43
Tucker Rd PR 67 P66
Tucker's Rd MA . . . 72 K8
Tucker Lake Rd MK . . 59 S34
Tuckers Rd PB 45 X42
Tudhope Blvd SM . . . 42 A31
Tudor-Hydroline Access Rd HS . . .
. . . 46 X47-48
Tufford Rd NI 18 R32
Tuftsville Rd HS . . . 34 C47-48
Tulip Rd HL 60 U38
Tulloch Ln LM 6 W8
Tully's Rd PB 44 Z39
Tumbledown Rd LG . . 37 C60
Tumbleweed Rd K . . . 43 Y36
Tunacliffe Rd NI . . . 19 T33
Tundra Rd C 6 Y7
Tundra Tr R 43 X37
Tunnel Ln EL 9 W-X21
Tupper Rd A 84 X92-93
Tupper St PR 68 N71-72
Tupperville Rd C . . . 6 K8
Turcot Rd SD . . . 93 O24 101 D23
Turcotte Rd HS. . . . 47 A50-51
Turcotte Rd LA 47 A51
Turcotte Rd R 82 M53
Turenne Rd SD 92 G22
Turfyn La HL 60 V40
Turin Ln C 7 Y11-12
Turk Rd TB. 102 F2
Turk Rd (Alnwick-Haldimand) NR . .
. . . 33 F44
Turk Rd (Hamilton) NR . . 33 F42
Turk Rock Rd LG . . . 37 A59
Turkey Trail Rd TB. . . 102 F3
Turnberry St HU . . . 21 J-K17
Turnberry-Culross Rd W HU 26 G16
Turnbull Ln HL 21 K17
Turnbull Rd HS. . . . 46 W47
Turnbull Rd HD. . . . 18 S-T29
Turnbull's Rd HU. . . 20 P13
Turner Rd EL 14 V15
Turner Rd K 43 X35
Turner Rd NI 19 S33-34
Turners Rd LN 65 S-T59
Turners Rd R 80 M47
Turnstone La R 62 O47
Turtle Creek Rd R . . . 62 O48
Turtle Lake Dr HT . . . 23 L26-27
Turtle Lake La K . . 47 W52 63 V63
Turtle Lake Rd MK . . 58 R29 V31
Turtle Lake Rd PS. . . 58 R29
Turtle Rock La HL . . . 60 V39
Tuscarora Rd BT . . . 17 S26
Tusk Tr HL 61 T42
Tutecky Rd LG 50 X64
Tutela Heights Rd BT . . 17 S25
Tuyll St HU. 20 L13
TV Tower Rd R . . . 99 K51
Tweed Rd LA. . . . 47 A51
Tweedle Lake Rd A . . 89 E8
Twelve Mile Bay Rd MK . 57 U27
Twenty Rd NI 18 R-S30
Twenty Mile Creek Rd NI. 18 S31-32
Twiddy Rd HS 46 B48
Twigg Rd K 32 E38
Twilight La F 36 A56
Twilight Rd K. . . . 32 D37
Twin City Crsrd TB . . 102 D5
Twin Elm Rd OT . . . 66 S-T62
Twin Gables Dr EX . . 4 F3
Twin Harbours Rd MA . 72 K-L8
Twin Lakes Rd TM . . 85 Q28-29
Twin Oaks Rd F . . . 47 W52
Twin Ponds Access Rd NP 97 F-G39
Twin Rocks La HL . . 60 U37
Twin Sister Lakes Rd HS . 46 Z46
Twiss Rd HT 23 N27-28
Twist La HL 44 W39
Two Horse Lake Forest Access Rd
A 86 B95-96
Two Island Lake Rd R . 63 R52
Two Island Lake Access Rd R . .
. . . 63 R50-51
Twyn Rivers Dr T . . . 25 J34
Tyandaga Park Rd HT. . 23 P28
Tye Rd WT 22 P22
Tymnchuk Rd CS . . . 100 B16
Tyne Lake Rd PS . . . 95 J33-34
Tyner Rd HS 47 B50-51
Tyneside Rd HM . . . 17 R-S28
Tyotown Rd SDG . . . 52 U71
Tyrone Access Rd SD. . 100 Y17-18
Tysick Rd LN 48 W-X57
Tyson Access Rd R . .
. . . 91 G18 92 F19 G19

U Ln A 86 F95
Ubdegrove Rd LG . . . 37 B58-59
Uens Rd HS 46 B49
Uffington Rd MK . . . 59 V34
Umfraville Rd HL . . . 62 V45
Umpherson Rd LN . . 64 T55-56
Uncle Tom's Rd C . . . 6 X9
Under Way WL 27 G19
Underpass Rd HL . . . 13 T11
Unger Island Rd LA . . 35 D-E52
Unicorn Rd HL 60 U39
Unimin Rd PB 45 Y44
Union Av DH 31 F36
Union Av EX 5 E5
Union Dr MD 14 T14
Union Ln C 6 Y8
Union Ln HU 20 P16
Union Ln OX 16 U21
Union Rd EL . . . 8 W16-17 14 V15-16
Union Rd HS 46 Z47
Union Rd HU. . . . 20 K13
Union Rd LG 37 B60
Union Rd MA . . . 71 K6 L6 72 L7-8
Union Rd NR 33 F45
Union Rd OX 15 T20
Union St F 36 D56
Union St PS. 77 L32
Union St (Arran-Elderslie) BR 39 A18
Union St (South Bruce) BR. . 26 F16
Union Creek Rd C . . . 44 Y38
Union School Rd DH. . . 32 F37
Union School Rd TB . . 102 F3
United Church Rd NF . . 36 C54-56
Unity Rd HL 36 D54
Unity Rd HD 17 R-S28
Universal Rd HL . . . 60 V39

University Av T. . . . 24 K-L32
University Av WT. . . 22 M23 N22-23
University Rd PB. . . . 33 C41
University Rd LN . . . 64 U55-56
Unpherson's Mill Rd LN. . 64 U55-56
Upcott Sdrd EX 4 E4
Uplands Dr OT 66 R63
Upper Beverley 1 Rd LG. . 49 Z59
Upper Beverley 2 Rd LG. . 49 Z59
Upper Big Chute Rd SM. . 42 W-Y30
Upper Canada Rd SDG . . 51 V-W67
Upper Centennial Pkwy HM. 18 R29
Upper Dutch Line Rd HL. . 44 W38
Upper Dwyer Hill Rd OT . .
. . . 65 R58-59 S59-60 83 Q58
Upper Flinton Rd HS . . 47 Z50
Upper Island Lake Rd A . 84 Z93
Upper James St HM . . 17 Q-R28
Upper Lorne Beach Rd BR . 26 D14
Upper Middle Rd HT . .
. . . 18 P29 24 M29-30 N29
Upper Mount Albion Rd HM
. . . 18 Q-29
Upper Oak Leaf Rd LG. . 49 Z60
Upper Ottawa St HM. . 17 Q-R28
Upper Paradise Rd HM. . 17 O28
Upper Paudash Rd HL . . 61 V43
Upper Perth Rd LN . . 65 T-U58
Upper Rideau Dr L . . . 48 Y57
Upper Rosenthal Rd L. . 62 O48
Upper Scotch Ln LN . . 48 X57 49 W58
Upper Sherman Av HM . . 17 Q-R28
Upper Slash Rd HS . . . 35 D50-51
Upper Spruce Hedge Rd R. 64 R55
Upper Turriff Rd HL . . 62 U46
Upper Walker Lake Dr MK . 59 U34
Upper Wellington St HM . . 17 Q28
Upper Wentworth St HM. . 17 Q-R28
Upper Woolwich Pl WT . . 22 K22
Upton Rd TB 102 C5
Ursa Rd HL 60 V40
Ushers Rd SM 41 Z28
Utility Ln OX 16 T22
Utronki Rd R 82 N54
Uttoxeter Rd LM . . . 13 S-T10
Uxbridge-Pickering Townline DH.
. . . 31 G34-35
Uxbridge Heights Rd DH . . 31 D34

V, Fire Rte CS 100 B18
V Ln A 86 E95
V Lake Tr HL 62 U47
Vachon Rd NP. . . . 94 D27
Vachon St CS 100 A17
Vaile Rd R 82 O55
Valade Rd SDG . . . 52 U70 68 T70
Valens Rd HM 23 P26
Valentia Rd K 32 C-D37
Valetta St C 6 C7-8
Valhalla Rd MA 71 K4
Vallance Rd SDG. . . 68 S70
Vallance St PR 68 O69
Valley Cr G 28 C22
Valley Dr NR 33 F45
Valley La F 36 B57
Valley Rd A 86 B-C94
Valley Rd HM . . . 17 O28 23 P28
Valley Rd PE 34 F48-49
Valley St SDG 67 S68
Valley St TB. 103 D6
Valley Farm Rd DH. . . 31 H34-35
Valley Ridge Rd G. . . 28 C23
Valley View Dr Y. . . 30 C-D32
Valley View Rd SDG . . 77 L31-32
Valley View Rd SDG . . 68 S71
Valleymede Dr Y . . . 30 H32
Valleyview Rd BR . . . 38 Z17
Valleyview Rd CS . . 100 B18 101 D19
Valleyview Rd MD . . . 15 R-S17
Valleyview Rd R . . . 82 L53
Vamplew Rd LG . . . 50 Y63
Van Exen Rd LN . . . 49 V61
Van Park Rd TM . . . 85 Q28-30
Van Patter Ln EL . . . 9 W19
Vance Dr LM 13 R10
Vance La HL 47 Y50
Vance Rd WT 22 M24
Vance's Sdrd OT . . . 65 Q60
Vandecar Ln OX . . . 16 S22
Vanderhoeven Sdrd NF. . 16 V17
Vanderwater Rd HS. . 46 B49 47 B50
Vandorf Rd Y 30 F-G32
Vandorf Sdrd Y 30 G31-32
Vanedie Rd C 6 C7-8
Vanessa Rd BT 16 T24
Vankoughnet Rd HL . . 59 U36
Vankoughnet Rd MK . . 59 V35-36
Vanluven Rd F 36 B55
Vanluven Rd LA . . . 35 D52
VanLuven Rd NR . . . 33 F42
Vanneck Rd MD . . . 14 R-T15
Vannest Rd DH 32 G37
VanOrder Rd F 36 C55
Vansickle Rd BT . . . 17 S26
Vansintart Av OX . . . 16 R21
Varley Rd A 87 B2 C1-2
Varney Rd C 27 E20
Varney Rd Y. . . . 30 C-D31
Varty Lake Rd LA . . . 47 B53
Vasey Rd SM 41 Y29
Vaughan Rd NP. . . . 96 E37
Vaughan Rd HL. . . . 18 S31-32
Vaughan Sdrd OT. . . 65 R-S59
Vault Works Rd G . . . 39 Z19
Veley La TB 102 D4
Veley Rd PR 47 X52
Vent Rd LA 35 D53
Ventnor Rd LG 50 W64
Ventress Rd PR . . . 33 F45
Verch Rd R 81 P50
Vermeulen Rd NF . . . 10 W24
Vermilion Lake Rd CS . 100 B16-17
Vermilyea Rd HS. . . 34 D48
Vern Dr CS 101 A19
Vernonville Rd NR . . . 33 F44

Verona Sand Rd F. . . 36 A54
Verulam Rd K 32 C37-38
Vespra Valley Rd SM. . 41 A-B28
Veterans Dr SM. . . . 30 C-D30
Veterans Rd SM. . . . 30 C-D30
Veterans Rd N G. . . . 39 A-B20
Veterans Rd S G . . . 28 C21
Veterans Memorial Pkwy
. . . 15 T17-18
Viamede Rd PB. . . . 45 Z42
Viau Rd SD 93 G24
Vic Lightle Rd NR . . . 33 F41
Viceroy Rd NP. . . . 95 E32
Vick La HL 44 W38
Vickers Rd BR 55 U16-17
Vickers Rd DH. . . . 32 G39
Victor Mines Rd CS. . 101 A21
Victoria Av HS 34 E49
Victoria Av HM 17 Q28
Victoria Av (Lincoln) NI . 18 R-T32
Victoria Av (Niagara Falls) NI. .
. . . 19 R-S35
Victoria Backline SD. . 89 F9
Victoria Dr HU. . . . 14 Q15
Victoria Rd BR. . . . 26 F13
Victoria Rd C. . . . 7 A11 Y11
Victoria Rd EL 15 U18
Victoria Rd EX 5 H4-5
Victoria Rd K . . . 43 X-Y35 Z36
Victoria Rd LG. . . . 50 Z62
Victoria Rd OT. . . . 66 S65
Victoria Rd PE 34 F47-48
Victoria Rd SD. . . . 93 E24
Victoria Rd SM 41 Z28
Victoria Rd WL . . . 23 L-M25 M-N26
Victoria Rd Y. . . . 31 D34
Victoria St BR 26 C-D14
Victoria St DH. . . . 31 H35-36
Victoria St EX 4 F13
Victoria St G 39 A21
Victoria St MD. . . . 14 T13
Victoria St NF 17 V25
Victoria St OX. . . . 15 S19-20
Victoria St PB 45 W44
Victoria St R 99 J-K50
Victoria St (Central Huron) HU. .
. . . 20 L14
Victoria St (Hastings) NR . 33 C44
Victoria St (Innisfil) SM. . 30 C30
Victoria St (Kitchener) WT . 22 N23
Victoria St (New Tecumseth) SM. .
. . . 29 E28
Victoria St (Port Hope) NR . 33 G41
Victoria St (Wawanosh) HU . 20 J13
Victoria St (Woolwich) WT. 22 M24
Victoria Beach Rd NR. . 33 G41
Victoria Corners Rd DH . 31 E34-35
Victoria Lake Rd NP. . 80 M48
Victoria Park Av T . 24 J32 25 J33
Victoria Varty Rd HS . 47 Z50
Victory St LM 12 T7
Vienna Ln EL 9 W19-20
Vienna Rd OX. . . . 16 U-V21
Vienna Rd PE 34 F47
Viewbank Rd OT . . . 66 S62
Viewpoint Tr MK . . . 58 S32
Vigo Rd SM 41 A27-28
Villa Nova Rd NF . . . 17 S-U25
Village Rd NP. . . . 95 F-G33
Village Rd SM 23 P25
Village Rd (Blind River) A . 88 F3
Village Rd (Cutler) A . 89 F7-8
Village View Rd WT. . 22 M24
Villa Rd HD. . . . 18 U31
Villeneuve Rd NP . . . 96 E38
Villeneuve Rd (East Hawkesbury)
PR . . . 69 P-Q73
Villeneuve Rd (Nation) PR . .
. . . 67 O68 68 O69
Villiers Ln PB. . . . 33 C42
Vimy Rd NI 19 U34
Vimy-Ridge Rd NR . . 33 F41
Vincent Ln EL 16 V21
Vincent Massey Dr SDG . 52 U69-70
Vinden St SM 41 X28
Vine La HS 62 R46
Vine La MA 73 M12
Vine St NI 19 Q-R33
Vine Ln PB. . . . 45 B40
Vinette Rd PR 67 P66
Vinkle Rd F 48 Y55
Violet Dr MK 41 X29
Violet Rd LA 35 D53
Virginia Blvd Y . . . 31 C33
Viscount Rd MD . . . 14 T16
Visiting Rd LG. . . . 66 U63
Visser Rd LG 49 X-Y59
Vista Rd HL 60 S37
Vista Beach Rd HU . . 20 N12-13
Vistula Rd R 62 O47
Vittoria Rd NF . 10 W24 16 V24 17 V25
Vivian Rd Y . . . 30 F32 31 F33
Voicey Rd HL 60 U38
Voyer Rd NP 95 E32
Vsetula Rd C . . . .

W, Fire Rte CS 100 A-B18
Waba Ln NI 65 R57-58
Wabagishik Rd CS . . 91 E15
Wabalac Rd LN . . . 64 S55-56
Wabalac Sdrd LN . . . 64 S55
Wabash Ln C 6 X-Y9
Wabewawa Rd TM . . 85 L-M28
Wabit Pit Ln TM. . . . 85 P-Q28
Wabkamigad Rd MA . . 73 L13-14
Wabun Lake Rd R. . . 64 S53
Waddell Rd LA 47 A51
Waddell Rd SDG . . . 51 W66
Waddingham Rd HS. . 35 D51
Waddle Creek Rd LN. . 64 T-U56
Wade Rd PR 67 S65-66
Wagar Rd F 43 A37
Wagarville Rd F . . .
Wagg Rd LA . . . 36 B54 47 B53
Wagg Rd NI. . . . 19 U34
Wagner Rd F. . . . 48 X55
Wagner Rd R 82 L52

Wagon Tr PS. . . . 75 M26
Wahamaa Rd CS . . . 101 D20-21
Wahta Rd MK 58 U29
Wahta Rd 2 MK . . . 58 V29
Wahwashkesh Rd PS. . 76 M27
Wainfleet-Dunnville Townline Rd
NI. . . 18 T31 U31-32
Wainman Ln SM . . . 42 Y30-31
Waite Rd K 32 E38
Waite's Rd NR. . . . 33 F45
Wakelin Way K 43 Y36-37
Wakomata Access Point Rd A. .
. . . 87 B99
Wakomata Dam Rd A. . 87 B99
Wakomata Shores Rd A . 87 B99
Waldenwood Rd CS . . 100 C16
Walder Creek Access Rd NP. .
. . . 95 D-E33
Waldo's Way La F . . 36 D-E57
Waldroff Rd SDG. . . 67 T68
Wales Dr R . . . 62 O47 80 P47
Wales Rd SDG 52 U-V69
Walford Rd R 81 L51
Walford Rd SD 89 F9
Walker La A 87 E98
Walker La R 87 E98
Walker Rd A 87 E98
Walker Rd EL . . . 9 W20 15 V20
Walker Rd EX 8 B-E2
Walker Rd K 43 Q12
Walker Rd MA 86 E95
Walker Rd MK . . . 42 W33 43 W34
Walker Rd NI. . . . 18 R31
Walker Rd OT . . . 66 S64 67 S65
Walker Rd PL 29 H28
Walker Rd R 82 P53
Walker Rd TB 102 F-G5
Walker Rd WT 22 P21
Walker Rd (Cramahe) NR. 33 F44-45
Walker Rd (Port Hope) NR . 32 F40
Walker Sdrd EX 4 D2
Walker Sdrd G 39 B20
Walker's Ln BR 26 F15
Walker's Rd A 44 Z38
Walker's Rd F 43 Y35
Walker Dam Rd SD. . . 91 F15
Walker Lake Dr MK. . . 59 U34
Walker Lake Access Rd R . 80 M47
Walker Line Rd HL . . . 60 U37
Walkers Dr MD. . . . 14 U-V13
Walkers Ln HT . 18 P29 23 N28 24 N29
Walkers Glenn Cr MK . 59 Q34-35
Walkers Point Rd MK . 58 U31
Walkes Rd PB 45 W44
Walkhouse Rd MA . . 71 K4
Walkinshaw Rd TB . . 103 B8
Walkley Rd OT. . . . 66 Q-R63
Wall Rd OT . . . 66 Q64 67 Q65
Wallace Ln OX 15 T19-20
Wallace Rd CS 100 B17
Wallace Rd F. . . . 36 B54
Wallace Rd NP 95 E32
Wallace Rd SD 90 E14
Wallace Sdrd BR. . . . 38 B16
Wallace St C 6 X-Y9
Wallace Terr A 84 B91-92
Wallace Jibb Rd NI . . 33 F42
Wallace Line Rd EX. . . 4 B-C3
Wallace Point Rd PB . .
. . . 32 E40 33 D41 E41
Wallace Wood Rd NR. . 32 G40
Wallbridge Rd HS . . . 34 D48
Wallbridge-Loyalist Rd HS 34 D-E48
Wallis Dr PB 32 C40
Wallis Rd A 84 B90
Walls Rd EX 4 C3-4
Walmac Shore's Rd K . 44 A39
Walmsley Rd PE . . . 35 H51
Walnut Dr MD 7 X12
Walnut La R 8 W-X15
Walnut Rd R 20 N14
Walnut St A 86 E95
Walpole-Rainham Rd HD. 17 U27-28
Walsh La F 36 B56
Walsh Rd K 32 G39
Walsh Rd MK. . . . 59 T34
Walsh's Rd R 82 M52
Walt Rd HS. . . . 34 D-E46
Walt St HS 34 F46
Walter's Rd R 81 L51
Walter Bradley Rd OT. . 65 R58
Walters La R 46 W47
Walters La PS 58 R29
Walton Dr MK 58 T29
Walton Rd HU . . 20 K16 21 K-L17
Waltonen Rd A 86 E96
Waltonian Dr PS . . . 95 F31
Waltons Pool Rd PS . . 56 Q-R25
Wanakita Rd HL . . . 60 V39
Wanamaker La HS. . . 42 U47-48
Wanapitei River Rd CS . 101 Y20 Z21
Wanda St SM 30 F30
Wanless Dr PL. . . . 29 C27
Wannamaker Rd HS. . 34 C48 D47
Wannamaker Rd A . . 62 T48
Wanstead Rd LM . . . 13 T-V10
War Rd BT 17 S25
Warburton Rd LG . . . 37 B60
Warcoe Rd DH. . . . 32 G-H37
Ward Ln LM 6 W6-7
Ward Rd DH 31 E-F35
Ward Rd NR 33 D44
Ward St NR 33 G41
Ward St PB 44 B40
Wardell Dr MD 14 S13-14
Warden Av T 25 J33
Warden Av Y 30 D-H32
Warden Rd SDG . . . 52 U71
Wardens Rd LN . . . 64 T56
Warder Rd HL 60 V38-39
Wardrope Av TB . . . 103 C6
Warina Rd SDG . . . 68 S69
Wark's Rd LN . . . 64 T56 65 T57
Warminster Rd SM. . . 42 Y31
Warminster Sdrd SM. . 42 Z30
Warner Rd LN. . . . 48 A57-58
Warner Rd NI 19 R34
Warner Bay Rd BR . . 54 U14
Warner's Rd PB. . . . 45 W43
Warnica Rd K 43 Y37
Warren Av SD 93 D25
Warren Rd F 36 B54
Warrington La F . . . 48 X55

Warrington Rd SM . . 41 B26
Warsaw Rd PB 45 B42
Wartman Rd LA. . . . 35 C52
Wartman Rd NR . . . 33 D44
Warwick Ln F. . . . 36 C57
Warwick Village Rd LM . 13 S-T11
Waseosa Lake Rd MK . 59 U33
Washburn Rd F 36 C57
Washburn Rd LG. . . 49 Z60
Washburn Island Rd LG. 32 D37
Washington Rd DH. . . 32 G37
Washington Rd OX . . 22 P22
Wasing Rd NP . 95 G33-34 H33-34
Wasmund Rd HS . . . 62 T46-47
Wasmund Rd R . . . 62 R48
Wasmund Meadow Access Rd R . .
. . . 62 R48
Wasnage Rd MA . . . 70 J2
Water Cr A 84 Z91
Water Rd PE 35 E50-51
Water St DF 28 H24
Water St HL 60 V37
Water St MA 70 J2
Water St NF . . . 16 V24 17 V25
Water St SDG 52 V70
Water St WT 22 P24
Water St (Bonnechere Valley) R. .
. . . 81 N-P51
Water St (Bruce Mines) A . 86 E96
Water St (Chatham-Kent/Raleigh)
C . . . 7 C10
Water St (Chatham-
Kent/Wallaceburg) C . 6 X7
Water St (Killaloe, Hagarty, &
Richards) . 81 N49
Water St (Thessalon) A . 87 E98
Water Tower Ln EL . . 15 V17
Waterdown Rd HT. . . 23 P28
Waterfalls Rd SD. . . . 89 F9
Waterloo St TB 103 D6
Waterloo St WT. . . . 22 N21
Waterloo Lake Access Rd R 98 F42
Waters Rd MK. . . . 59 V33
Watersedge La MA . . 73 L13
Waterview Rd R . . . 82 M53
Waterworks Rd LM . . 12 T-V8
Watkins La F 48 W53
Watra Rd G 28 E21
Watson La MK . . . 58 S32 59 S33
Watson Pkwy WL . . . 23 L25
Watson Rd F 36 B54
Watson Rd MD 13 S12
Watson Rd NP 95 F33-34
Watson Rd PS. . . . 95 G32
Watson Rd R 82 Q53
Watson Rd SD 90 F11-12
Watson Rd SM 41 X28
Watson Rd WL 23 M-N26
Watson Rd (MacDonald, Meredith,
& Aberdeen) . 86 B-C94 C94-95
Watson Rd (Sunset Beach) A. 87 E1
Watson Bay Rd MA . . 73 M11
Watson Mill Rd NF . . 16 V21
Watsons Corners Rd LN. .
. . . 48 V56 64 V56 65 V56
Watt La K 43 Y34
Watt's Rd HL 60 S38
Watt's Pond Rd BT . . 16 Q23-24
Watters Rd OT 67 O68
Watterworth Rd LM. . 7 W12 13 V12
Watties Hill Rd R. . . . 82 P53
Watts Ln F 83 Q56
Watts Rd F. . . . 53 S-T49
Waubuno Rd LM . . 6 W8 12 U-V8
Waugh's Rd F 55 W18
Waugush Lake Rd A. . 88 F6
Waupoos Island La PE. . 35 G52
Wavell St MD. . . . 15 T17
Waverly Rd DH 32 G-H38
Wawanaisa Rd PS . . 56 Q24-25
Way St DH 31 G35-36
Waynco Rd WT . . 22 P24 23 P25
Wayne Gretzky Pkwy BT . 17 S25
Wayside Dr LN 49 V58
Wayside Tr K 44 X38
Weatherhead Rd PE . . 34 E49
Weaver Rd (Niagara Falls) NI. 19 S35
Weaver Rd (Port Colborne) NI. .
. . . 19 U34
Webb Rd HS 31 G34
Webb Rd HU 20 M13
Webb Rd R 33 D43
Webb Rd (North Dundas) SDG . .
. . . 67 U66
Webb Rd (South Dundas) SDG. .
. . . 50 W65
Webber Bourne EL . . 15 U17
Webber Rd NI . . . 18 T32 19 T33
Webber St SM 30 F30
Webbs Rd NP. . . . 95 F33-34
Weber Sdrd BR . . . 17 S26
Weber St WT 22 M-N23
Webster Rd LG 37 A59
Webster Rd PB. . . . 45 B42-44
Webster Dr SM 29 C27
Webster's La MK. . . 57 U28
Weeby Pl WT . . . 22 M23 N22
Weeden Rd TB 102 C4
Weedmark Rd LN . . 64 V61
Weedmark Rd LG . . . 49 X61
Weedmark Rd OT. . 50 V62 66 O62
Weegar Rd SDG . . . 67 U66-67
Weeks Rd SD 93 F24
Wees Rd DH 31 F33
Weese Rd HS 35 C-D50
Weese Rd PE 34 F48
Weidman Ln LM . . . 13 S13-14
Weiler Ln PS 95 H32
Weimar Ln WT 22 M22
Weinbrenner Rd NI . . 19 S35
Weir Rd HM 17 Q27
Weir Rd LG 50 X64
Weir's Sdrd Y 31 C-D33
Weirs La HM 17 Q27
Weirs Rd A 88 C95
Weirs Rd R 88 X17
Weisenberg Rd WT . . 22 L23
Welbeck Rd G 28 H24
Welch Dr MD 8 W14
Welch Ln C 7 A-B10
Weldon Dr K 43 Y37
Weldon Way HD . . . 17 R-S28
Weldrick Rd Y 30 H31-32
Welks Rd R 63 R49
Welland Av NI 19 R33-34

Welland Rd NI. . . . 19 S33
Welland St NI 19 S33
Welland Canal Pkwy NI . 19 R34
Wellandport Sdrd NI. . 18 T31
Wellbanks Rd PE . . . 35 H50
Wellburn Rd MD . . . 15 Q17 R18
Weller Av F 36 D56
Weller Rd PB. . . . 45 B42
Weller Rd PS. . . . 94 H30
Welling La F 47 Y53
Wellington Rd EL . . . 15 U-V17
Wellington Rd LG . . . 37 B56
Wellington Rd MD . . . 15 T-U17
Wellington Rd S A . . . 84 B92
Wellington Rd S MD . . 15 U17
Wellington St A 87 B57
Wellington St HM . . . 17 Q28
Wellington St LM . . . 12 T7
Wellington St MK . . . 58 U32
Wellington St NI . . . 19 T34
Wellington St WL . . . 23 M25
Wellington St E Y . . . 30 G31-32
Wellington St W Y . . . 30 G31
Wellmans Rd HS. . . . 34 C47
Wells Rd A 87 C-D99
Wells Rd SDG 51 W67
Wells St WL 28 H22-23
Wellwood Rd C 6 C8
Welly Smith Rd F . . . 48 Y-Z53
Wembley Dr K 43 Y37
Wemp Rd F 48 Y55
Wendigo Lake Rd R. . 97 G40
Wendigo Lake Rd TM . 85 G40
Wendy's La PS 76 P28
Wendy's Rd OX. . . . 16 U23
Wenigo Rd TM 85 M28-29
Wenona Rd, E HL . . . 60 U40
Wenona Lake Rd HL. . 60 U40
Wenona Lodge Rd MK . 42 X32
Wentland Rd F 82 P52
Wentworth Rd SDG . . 68 T72
Wentworth St DH . . . 31 H36
Wentworth Rd HM . . . 17 Q28
Werry Rd DH. . . . 32 G37
Wes Clarke Tr HL . . 59 R36 60 R37
Weslemkoon Lake Rd HS . .
. . . 46 W48 W-X47
Wesley Acres Rd PE . 34 G49 35 G50
Wesleyville Rd NR . . . 32 G40
Wessel Dr NI 19 R-S33
Wessell Rd A 43 X37
Wesson Rd SM 30 E29
Wesson Dr PL 29 C27
West Ln A 86 E-F96
West Rd A 86 C-D96
West Rd BL 55 V16
West Rd HL 60 U37-38
West Rd MK 46 H47
West Rd NR 33 E-F41
West Rd PS 76 P27-28
West Rd TM 85 B29
West St BT 17 R25
West St G 39 Z19
West St K 43 X37
West St NF 42 Z32
West Aux Sables River Rd A. 89 C94
West Back Ln (Chatsworth) G . .
. . . 28 C21 39 B20
West Back Ln (West Grey, Grey
Highlands) G. . 28 C22 D22-23
West Bay Blvd K . . . 43 Z36
West Bay La NI 61 V43
West Bay Rd CS . . . 101 A21 Z20
West Bay Rd NP . . . 93 F26
West Bay Rd PB 44 Y40-41 45 W-X43
West Bay Rd PS . . . 77 N33-34
West Bear Lake Rd PS. . 58 Q30
West Belle River Rd EX . 4 B-C4
West Bothwell Rd C . . 7 X11
West Branch Rd A . . 89 B11
West Branch Rd SD . . 90 F12
West Browns Rd MK . 59 R33-34
West Buck Lake Rd R . 59 U34
West Camp Lake Rd MK. .
. . . 59 O36 78 P36
West Clear Bay Pt PB. . 44 X39
West Clear Bay Rd PB. . 44 X38
West Corner Dr MD. . 14 Q-R13 R14
West Devil Lake La F . 48 Z56
West Diamond Lake Rd HL 61 T-U43
West Dotty Lake Rd MK. .
. . . 59 O35 78 P35
West Dumfries Rd BT . 16 Q23-24
West Eels Lake Rd HL . 61 V42
West Eels Lake Rd PB. .
. . . 45 W42 W42 61 U43
West End La F 48 X54
West End Way OT . . . 58 O32
West Fox Lake Rd MK . 58 O32
West Gate Rd F . . . 47 Y52
West Heritage Dr WL . 27 G19
West Hill Dr WT. . . . 30 N22
West Hill Ln OX. . . . 15 S20
West Hunt Club Rd OT . 66 R62
West Ipperwash Rd LM. . 13 S-T11
West Kosh Rd PB . . . 45 Y-Z44
West Kosh Rd PB. . . 45 Y-Z44
West Lake Rd PE . . . 35 G50
West Lake Rd SD. . . . 90 E10-11
West Lewis Ln C . . . 6 Y7
West Lionshead Rd MK . 42 W31-32
West Loon Rd TB . . . 103 B10
West Main St LG. . . 50 A62 Z62
West Mall, The T . . . 24 L31
West McGregor Rd A . 86 D96
West Mullet Lake Dr HS. . 48 Z56
West Oxbow Lake Rd MK . 59 O35
West Palmerston Dr F . 63 V53
West Peninsula Rd PB . 95 E32
West Peters Island Rd PB . 44 X39
West Point Sands HS. . 59 S33
West Poverty Bay Rd PS. . 76 P29
West Puce Rd EX . . . 4 B-C4
West Pump Rd EX. . . 5 H4-5
West Quarter Line Rd NF . .
. . . 10 W22 X22-23 16 V22
West Quarter Townline Rd BT . .
. . . 16 R22 S-T23
West Ridge Blvd SM. . 42 Z30
West Ridge Dr OT . . . 66 S61
West River Rd BT. . . . 16 Q24
West River Rd LM . . . 6 X7
West River Rd WT . 16 Q24 22 P24
West River Rd S BT. . 16 Q24
West River St A 87 E98
West Ross Rd R . . . 82 M53
West Ruscom River Rd EX . 5 B-C5